Monetary Macroeconomics

MONETARY MACRO-ECONOMICS

THOMAS M. HAVRILESKY
DUKE UNIVERSITY

JOHN T. BOORMAN
INTERNATIONAL MONETARY FUND

AHM Publishing Corporation
Arlington Heights, Illinois 60004

Copyright © 1978

AHM PUBLISHING CORPORATION

All rights reserved

ISBN: 0-88295-401-6

Library of Congress Card Number: 77-85996

PRINTED IN THE UNITED STATES OF AMERICA
738

Contents

Preface

In the last decade and a half one of the most fertile areas of economic controversy has been monetary theory. Relegated to a relatively obscure niche in the mosaic of Keynesian developments of the 1940s and early 1950s, monetary theory surged into prominence in the 1960s. Spurred by the failures of stabilization policy (in particular the persistence of inflation in the face of historically high levels of unemployment) the controversies of monetary theory came into greater prominence during the 1970s.

Skirmishes in the continuing struggle between Keynesians and Monetarists are increasingly in the public eye. The issues are numerous and complex: Can the money supply be readily controlled by the Federal Reserve System? Is either the money stock or some other monetary aggregate superior to "the" interest rate as a target for monetary policy? Is fiscal stabilization policy effective? What is the relation between current and expected rates of inflation and interest rates and the level of employment? These are only a sampling of the questions facing the policy maker and his constituency. At the core of much of the controversy there lies a fundamental disagreement among economists about monetary theory.

How can the undergraduate economics student taking a course in money and banking or macroeconomic theory or a beginning graduate student be given a grounding in monetary theory sufficient to understand this disagreement? Aside from his own teaching skills, the economist educator has only three tools in his arsenal: the book on money and banking, the book on macroeconomic theory, and the book of readings on monetary economics. When it comes to this task, all these tools have evident shortcomings.

Macroeconomics textbooks are dominated by a model of the expenditures sector that assumes fixed prices and interest rates. Standard textbooks use this model as the basic engine of analysis. Conventional topics such as national income accounting, the demand for money, and the theory of consumption are often presented in a manner consistent only with this model. Much that is obsolete and irrelevant must be unlearned before the student can reach the frontiers of modern monetary theory.

Money and banking textbooks are often simply watered down versions of macroeconomics texts with added descriptive chapters on banking operations and monetary history and policy. The basic behavior of individuals and banks is usually treated at a fairly superficial level.

Good, up-to-date books of readings in monetary theory are becoming difficult to find. Moreover, a book of excellent contemporary readings can only supplement the textbook, it cannot replace it.

This book is tendered as a conceptually integrated approach to monetary theory. It strives to present in as simple a manner as possible the essentials of money supply, money demand, and aggregate economic theory necessary to carry the student to the threshold of recent developments. It can be used in intermediate macroeconomic theory, money and banking, and monetary theory courses for undergraduates. It is well suited for first-year graduate courses in monetary and macroeconomic theory and for specialized study and review by advanced undergraduates and graduates.

An attempt has been made to develop theory from first principles and to elaborate and expound on developments that are relevant to contemporary problems. In order to sustain this integrated approach and keep the book within manageable proportions, we avoid elaborate mathematical derivation, and relegate our inquiry to closed, static models. We feel no compunction to imitate convention when that convention would tend to lead the student far afield. For example, we do not believe it necessary to indulge in exercises such as *ad hoc* reconciliation of Keynes' consumption function to statistical evidence or identifying the 57 varieties of "cost push" inflation.

In contrast, our integrated approach requires a thorough discussion of national income accounting, not as an exercise in measuring expenditures, but as a way of showing the relationship between income, wealth, and financing constraints that is generally overlooked in modern textbooks even though it is absolutely fundamental to understanding modern monetary theory. Our perspective requires careful attention to the labor market and to the aggregate supply sector, not as a way of celebrating the differences between Keynesian and neoclassical views, but as a means of indicating their similarity and reconcilability. Money supply theory is handled not as a separate advanced topic but as an elemental building block of the aggregate model. The theory of money demand is presented not as the invention of Keynes or Milton Friedman but as a corpus of evolving knowledge to which hundreds of economists have made important contributions. With the essential theory in hand policy issues are addressed toward the end of the book, not as concessions to "relevance" completely unrelated to economic theory, but as problems that can be analyzed with the basic analytical framework developed by this book.

In order to benefit from this book, the reader needs only some training in algebra and a one-year course in economics principles; differential calculus would be helpful, but is by no means necessary. Since the book's main audience consists of students, sets of class-tested questions are appended to each chapter in order to allow the student to check his understanding of the material. For further reading and for research purposes, a selected bibliography follows each chapter.

The book is not specifically addressed to monetary policy issues which lie outside the realm of monetary theory. Many of these topics, such as Federal Reserve independence, receive treatment in books of readings on monetary economics.

Likewise, it is not intended as a comprehensive study of all monetary theory; rather it is concerned with money supply, money demand, and closed static monetary (macroeconomic) models. Such important matters as the theory of the term structure of interest rates, the monetary theory of an open economy, and monetary growth theories fall outside its domain.

We are grateful for the suggestions of Lloyd Atkinson, Edward Kane, Raymond Lombra, Dwight Jaffee, William Yohe, Maurice Weinrobe, James Dean, Jeremy Siegel, Michael McElroy, Richard Froyen, Arthur Benavie, Martin Bronfenbrenner, Neil Murphy, E. Roy Weintraub, Robert Schweitzer, Bruce Bolnick, Pieter Korteweg, James Johnson, Michael Thomson, Marjorie Williams, John Dutton, Debbi Allen, Susan Kramer, Harlan Davidson, and the late Harry Metzger, as well as for the reactions of numerous undergraduate and graduate students at Duke University.

We are indebted to Susan Havrilesky for her patience and her helpful comments in proofreading, typing, and retyping the manuscript; to Ziska Lalamentik and Annie Sarino for their typing assistance; and to Paul Funk for editorial assistance.

Thomas M. Havrilesky
John T. Boorman

Introduction

A major concern of modern man is his "standard of living." Although there are several measures of the level of prosperity man enjoys, the most common is the level of per capita income in an economy. The level and growth of an economy's per capita income are closely related to the degree to which that economy utilizes its productive resources and thereby eliminates underemployment. Measurement of income requires the use of a monetary unit in terms of which the value of newly produced goods and services may be gauged. The real value of a dollar of income changes over time, however, because it depends on the general level of prices for goods and services that income can buy. If the general price level rises more quickly than nominal income, the real value of that income declines. Consequently, modern man is concerned with the general level of prices, as well as with the level of his nominal income.

Modern economists are often called upon by business and government to evaluate alternative means of maintaining and increasing man's prosperity. To do this, they develop models to explain and predict the level of income, employment, and prices in the economy as a whole. These models generally focus on the aggregate behavior of economic entities: households, government, and business firms.

Practically all theories about the level of aggregate income, employment, and prices assign an important role to the supply of and the demand for money. This book proposes to examine theoretical issues regarding the supply of and the demand for money because they are so intimately related to overall prosperity and well-being in society.

The term "money" appears regularly when economists theorize about how aggregate household, business, and government behavior affects the level of aggregate income, employment, and prices. Why do economists believe that the supply of and demand for money have a more prominent effect on the level of economic activity than the supply of and demand for, say, used cars?

The answer is that economists believe that money, among all goods, performs unique functions, and because of these functions it affects and is affected by the level of income and prices in a unique manner. First, money functions as a *universally acceptable medium of exchange*. As there is usually a time lag between the receipt and disbursement of income, money might be held to facilitate transactions. Economists long have maintained that since money is held between its receipt as income and its disbursement in exchange for goods and services, it can affect the volume of goods and services produced, or their price level, or both. For instance, an elemental theory in economics states that, as the quantity of money supplied increases, proportionately more money is exchanged for goods and services, and the prices of these goods and services invariably are bid upward. One inference from this theory is that price inflation can be prevented simply if the money supply is allowed to grow at a slower rate relative to the growth of output of goods and services.

Another function of money is that it may serve as a *store of value*. Some economists have emphasized the advantages of holding money because it can easily be converted to other asset forms with little cost or inconvenience, that is, you do not have to "cash it in" in order to acquire another asset—it requires no intermediate transaction. Other economists have emphasized the advantages of holding money because its nominal market value is usually more predictable than that of other assets; by holding money, individuals avoid the risk of a decline in the market value of their wealth.

Both of these approaches view holding money as an alternative to holding other assets. Therefore, the demand for money as a store of value depends on the benefits from holding other assets (for example, their yields). Since a change in the quantity of money can induce individuals to change their demand for these alternative assets, it thereby affects the prices and yields of other assets. Elementary economic theory teaches that a change in the yields of financial assets (the level of interest rates) affects the level of investment spending and, thereafter, the level of income, employment, and prices in the economy.

Other less important functions or characteristics of money have been adduced, but these two reflect its most relevant aspects in modern monetary macroeconomic theory.

Economists differ in the emphasis they place upon the medium-of-exchange and store-of-value characteristics of money. Some eschew these *a priori* distinctions altogether, believing them to be misleading. As we shall see in Chapters 1 and 2, relating to the supply of money, and in Chapters 4 through 8 relating to the demand for money, these differences in emphasis lead to dissimilar theoretical explanations of the public's desire to hold money, explanations which, as we discover in Chapters 9 through 15, lead to distinct theories about the manner in which money affects the level of income, employment, and prices.

The aggregate money supply is believed to be important in a modern economy because of its influence on the level of economic activity. Chapters 1 and 2 examine the theory of the supply of money. They develop a series of simplified models of the real-world behavior of banks and individuals as it affects the quantity of money supplied. These chapters carry the reader to the threshold of modern money-supply theory.

Practically all the money that people receive and spend reaches them through banks—because it is either borrowed from a bank or held by them in a checking account at a bank. Because bank activities are of paramount influence in the determination of the money supply, Chapter 3 deals with the behavior of modern commercial banks.

In elementary microeconomic theory it is learned that supply and demand determine equilibrium prices and quantities in the market. So it is with money: an hypothesis about the determination of the money supply discussed in Chapters 1 and 2 must be combined with an hypothesis about the determination of the demand for money in order to understand how certain market variables (for example, the interest rate and the level of income) are affected. Different hypotheses about the demand for money are presented in Chapters 4 through 8.

When a specific hypothesis about the determination of the demand for money is combined in a more extensive macroeconomic model with specific hypotheses about the determination of (1) the supply of money, (2) the level of aggregate expenditures, (3) the supply of and demand for labor, and (4) an assumption about the technical conditions of production, differing policy prescriptions emerge. In Chapters 9 through 15 a series of macroeconomic models is developed, showing how different policy implications follow from different hypotheses.

We began this Introduction by saying that money is believed to be an important device because it has characteristics that relate it more closely than other specific goods to theories about the determination of the level of aggregate income, employment, and prices. It is primarily with basic theories of the supply of and demand for money and their impact on aggregate economic models that we are concerned in the fifteen chapters of this text.

1

A Framework for the Determination of Money Supply

Introduction

While it has frequently been assumed in both theoretical and empirical analyses that the money stock (demand deposits plus currency in circulation) is determined unequivocally by the monetary authority, this tradition is being superseded by an alternative approach that views the money supply as an endogenously determined variable. It is now customary to present the determination of the money stock as a process which results from the complex interaction of the behavior of various economic agents rather than as a process dominated solely by an external authority.

To understand the work being done in this field, it is necessary to examine both the behavior of the various groups that influence the money supply and the institutional framework within which this behavior occurs. In this chapter we shall describe this framework and the role of these behavioral patterns. The analysis begins with the derivation of the bank reserve equation from the Federal Reserve balance sheet and the monetary accounts of the Treasury.

Monetary Accounts

The monetary system of the United States is made up of the nation's 14,400 commercial banks, the twelve Federal Reserve district banks, the Board of Governors of the Federal Reserve System, and the United States Treasury. The primary business of commercial banks in this system is to issue deposit liabilities (demand deposits and time and savings deposits) to the public and to acquire income-earning financial assets with the funds created through these deposits. The characteristic that best distinguishes commercial banks from the other (nonmonetary) institutions in our financial system is their ability to issue deposit liabilities that are due on demand, that is, deposit liabilities that may be converted into currency or legal tender money immediately upon request of the depositor or transferred to another person simply by writing a check. No other institution in our system may issue liabilities with this characteristic.[1] Essentially it is the acceptance by the public of these liabilities as "money" which explains the preeminent role of commercial banks in our economy. In July 1977, for example, the average total money supply in the United States was approximately 327 billion dollars. Slightly under 75 percent of this amount, 242 billion dollars, consisted of demand deposit liabilities of the nation's commercial banks.

As money-creating institutions, commercial banks are subject to special regulation and supervision. For example, they are required to hold some of their assets in a legally approved form specified by the Federal Reserve System or by state banking authorities. Specifically, for every dollar of deposit liabilities outstanding, commercial banks must hold some fraction (also set by the monetary authority) in one of the approved asset forms. For example, commercial banks that are members of the Federal Reserve System are currently permitted to hold their legally required reserves either in the form of deposit balances at a district Federal Reserve bank or as cash in their own vaults. As a result of these requirements, the most important restrictions on the volume of member bank deposit liabilities outstanding at any

Consolidated Balance Sheet of the 12 Federal Reserve Banks

Assets	Liabilities and Net Worth
Gold certificates	Federal Reserve notes outstanding
Special drawing rights certificates	Member bank reserve deposits
Cash	Deposits due to
Federal Reserve credit	The U.S. Treasury
U.S. government securities	Foreign Depositors
Acceptances	Other
Discounts and advances	Other (capital and minor items)
Float	
Other	

[1] Money which has been declared "legal tender" by the government must be accepted as payment for all debts, public and private. In the United States, Treasury issues and Federal Reserve notes, which form the bulk of our "paper money," have been declared "legal tender." In some states thrift institutions, such as savings and loan associations, may issue liabilities which approximate this characteristic. The existence of such instruments, called negotiable order of withdrawal (NOW) accounts, blurs the traditional distinction between commercial banks and other financial institutions.

time are the fractional reserve requirements set by the monetary authority and the stock of legal reserves that are available for these banks to hold.

In this section we shall examine the accounts of the Federal Reserve banks and the United States Treasury to determine how the stock of these reserve funds is created. We begin with a consolidated balance sheet of the twelve Federal Reserve banks.

The twelve Federal Reserve district banks, like commercial banks, issue deposit liabilities (claims against themselves held primarily by member commercial banks, the United States Treasury, and foreign central banks and institutions) and purchase income-earning assets (primarily United States government securities and loans to commercial banks).[2] In addition, these banks issue Federal Reserve notes (claims against the district banks which serve as the primary form of paper money used in the United States) and hold gold certificates (claims against the gold stock owned by the Treasury) as well as special drawing rights certificates.[3]

A glance at the consolidated balance sheet above shows that if the entire currency stock consisted of Federal Reserve notes, the total amount of funds available to be held as reserves by commercial banks would depend upon the willingness of the Federal Reserve to issue certain liabilities (Federal Reserve notes outstanding and reserve deposits of member banks) and on the distribution of the Federal Reserve notes between the banks and the public. However, the United States Treasury also has the power to issue currency, and these coins and notes perform the same functions as Federal Reserve notes. Therefore, if the Treasury increased the volume of its outstanding currency (by making expenditures with newly printed bills, for example) there would be more funds available to be held by the public or by the commercial banks as vault cash. Since vault cash can be counted as reserves by member banks, the issuance of Treasury currency could increase total bank reserves.

We may account for the influence of Treasury currency on bank reserves by means of the *bank reserve equation*. Basically, the bank reserve equation is an accounting statement that lists sources and uses of funds which are potentially available as bank reserves. This statement is derived by modifying the consolidated balance sheet of the Federal Reserve banks to take account of Treasury influences on the monetary system. The bank reserve equation is as follows:

---

[2] Loans to banks based on their own promissory notes and a corresponding pledge of collateral are called "advances." Either United States government securities or eligible paper may be required as collateral. Eligible paper consists of evidences of debt which have been acquired by banks from their customers for short-term operating loans. Loans to banks based on eligible paper that is "sold" directly to the Federal Reserve bank (rediscounted) are called "discounts." Of the two forms, advances are the more popular because of the difficulty a bank may have in finding the exact desired quantity of eligible paper for discounting.

[3] Special drawing rights certificates are instruments allocated by the International Monetary Fund to participants in the special drawing account of the Fund. Special drawing rights are generally counted as part of a country's international reserves and may be transferred between central banks in exchange for foreign currencies.

The Bank Reserve Equation

Sources	Uses
Federal Reserve credit	Currency in circulation outside the Federal
U.S. government securities	Reserve, the Treasury, and commercial
Acceptances	banks (i.e., currency in circulation with
Discounts and advances	the nonbank public) (a)
Float	Treasury cash holdings (a) and (b)
Gold stock (b)	Deposit liabilities of the Federal
Treasury currency outstanding (a)	Reserve due to:
Special drawing rights	The Treasury
	Foreign depositors
	Others
	Other accounts (net)
	Bank reserves:
	Member bank reserve deposits plus
	commercial bank vault cash

A reconciliation between this statement and the consolidated Federal Reserve bank balance sheet is fairly easy to establish. All the accounts listed under "Federal Reserve credit" and "deposit liabilities of the Federal Reserve" appear in the bank reserve equation exactly as in the Federal Reserve balance sheet. The modifications made in the other accounts are as follows.

(*a*) Treasury Currency Outstanding.   This account includes all current *monetary* liabilities of the United States Treasury. It appears as a source of bank reserve funds since any currency issued by the Treasury could find its way into the commercial banking system and, as vault cash in that system, could serve as bank reserves. For example, if an employee of the Federal government were to be paid in newly printed paper money issued by the Treasury, he would be perfectly free to take this currency to a commercial bank and deposit it in his account with that bank. In either case it would increase both bank deposit liabilities and bank reserves (in the form of vault cash). When the Treasury first pays out the newly issued currency, according to the bank reserve equation, a source of funds, namely, Treasury currency outstanding, and a use of funds, namely, currency in circulation with the nonbank public, would both increase. When this currency is deposited with a commercial bank, an alternative use of funds, currency in circulation with the nonbank public, would decrease, and bank reserves (vault cash) would increase. Hence the net effect of these transactions would be to increase commercial bank reserves.

There are two other differences between the Federal Reserve balance sheet and the bank reserve equation that involve Treasury currency. One difference is that *cash* in the Federal Reserve balance sheet refers simply to Treasury currency in the vaults of the Federal Reserve banks. In the bank reserve equation, this item is included under "Treasury currency outstanding." Thus Treasury currency outstanding in the bank reserve equation refers to the total stock of outstanding currency issued by the Treasury, whether held by the nonbank public, commercial banks, or the Federal Reserve. A second difference is that Federal Reserve notes outstanding appear as a single, explicit item in the Federal Reserve balance sheet, but in the bank reserve equation these central bank liabilities are divided among several different accounts. Federal Reserve notes held by the nonbank public are combined with Treasury currency held by the nonbank public under "total currency in circulation." Federal Reserve notes held by the Treasury are included under "Treasury cash holdings." And Federal Reserve notes held by commercial banks appear together with bank holdings of outstanding Treasury currency as "vault cash" under bank reserves. As a result, the difference between Federal Reserve notes outstanding in the Federal Reserve balance sheet and Federal Reserve notes in circulation with the nonbank public, listed under "currency in circulation" in the bank reserve equation, is that the latter account excludes notes held by the Treasury and notes held by commercial banks. These modifications provide some insight into currency flows between the public, the banks, and the Treasury, and their effects on commercial bank reserves.

(*b*) Gold Stock. A further modification made in deriving the bank reserve equation involves the treatment of the gold stock. Gold certificates, claims against the gold stock that is held by the Treasury, are issued by the Treasury and held by the Federal Reserve banks. The difference between the volume of gold certificates outstanding (all of which are held by Federal Reserve banks) and the total Treasury gold stock is obviously that value of gold against which no certificates have been issued. This is gold held by the Treasury for backing of certain outstanding Treasury currencies and other minor uses. It generally represents a very small portion of the total gold stock and is included within the category of "Treasury cash holdings." Hence the bank reserve equation includes the entire Treasury gold stock as a source of bank reserves, and counts under the category of "Treasury cash holdings" (as an alternative use of those funds) that value of the Treasury gold stock which does not have gold certificate claims outstanding against it.

Hence the differences between the Federal Reserve balance sheet and the bank reserve equation involve only the issuance and holding of currency within the monetary system (specifically, the role of the United States Treasury in this process) and the treatment of the Treasury gold stock and of special drawing rights.

The bank reserve equation is written to focus attention on total commercial bank reserves (either reserve deposits held at Federal Reserve banks or commercial bank vault cash). A more useful concept that will find frequent application in the following discussion involves the combined measure of total bank reserves and currency in circulation. This quantity, referred to as the *monetary base* (or high-powered money, or reserve money), can easily be derived from the bank reserve equation.[4] This derivation is as follows:

[4] For an interesting perspective on this equation, see Leonall C. Andersen, "Three Approaches to Money Stock Determination," *Federal Reserve Bank of St. Louis Review* (October, 1967), 6–13. See also Jerry L. Jordan, "Elements of Money Stock Determination," *Review*, Federal Reserve Bank of St. Louis, vol. 51 (October 1969), 10–19; reprinted in Thomas M. Havrilesky and John T. Boorman, *Current Issues in Monetary Theory and Policy* (Arlington Heights, IL: AHM Publishing Corporation, 1976).

{Sources}	−	{Alternative uses}	=	{Monetary base}
Federal Reserve credit		Treasury cash holdings		
U.S. govt. securities		Deposits of the Federal		Member bank
Acceptances		Reserve due to		reserves
Discounts and advances	−	Treasury	=	+
Float		Foreigners		Currency in
Gold stock		Other		circulation
Treasury currency outstanding		Other accounts (net)		
Special drawing rights				

A comparison of the figures in this monetary base equation at two different points in time will illustrate the process by which bank reserves and currency are supplied to the economy. In Table 1.1, approximate figures are presented for end-December 1974 and end-December 1975.

Table 1.1.   Factors Supplying and Absorbing Reserve Money
(millions of dollars)

	Dec. 1974	Dec. 1975	Change
Sources	115,176	121,956	6,780
Federal Reserve credit			
U.S. government securities	86,679	92,108	5,429
Member bank borrowing	299	229	−70
Acceptances	1,126	753	−373
Float	2,734	3,142	408
Gold stock	11,630	11,599	−31
Special drawing rights	400	500	100
Treasury currency outstanding	9,179	10,091	912
Other Federal Reserve assets	3,129	3,534	405
Alternative uses	6,458	8,807	2,349
Treasury cash holdings	220	440	220
Deposits of the Federal Reserve due to			
U.S. Treasury	1,741	3,955	2,214
Foreigners	357	259	−98
Other	874	906	32
Other Federal Reserve liabilities and capital	3,266	3,247	−19
Monetary base	108,718	113,149	4,431
Member bank reserves			
Deposits with Federal Reserve banks	29,767	27,330	−2,437
Currency and coin	7,174	7,771	597
Currency in circulation*	71,777	78,048	6,271

* Currency held by the nonbank public and by nonmember banks.
Source: Federal Reserve Bulletin (January 1976).

During 1975 the monetary base increased by almost four and one half billion dollars. This was comprised of an *increase* of almost six billion three hundred million dollars in currency in circulation outside of member banks, that is, currency held by the nonbank public and by nonmember banks, an *increase* in vault cash of member banks of almost six hundred million dollars, and a *decrease* of almost two and one half billion dollars in member bank reserve deposits with Federal Reserve banks. At the same time, the United States Treasury deposits at Federal Reserve banks and Treasury cash holdings (alternative uses that absorb reserve funds) increased by almost two and one half billion dollars. To provide for these changes, factors supplying reserve funds must have increased on balance by almost seven billion dollars.

Examination of Table 1.1 indicates that the bulk of these funds were supplied through net purchases of government securities by the Federal Reserve. The monetary authority increased its portfolio of these securities by almost five and one half billion dollars. Thus, net open market purchase of securities was the primary means used by the Federal Reserve to bring about the increase that occurred in the monetary base during 1975. Other accounts in the table indicate that another one billion three hundred million dollars was supplied through increases in Treasury currency issues and Federal Reserve float. Another four hundred million dollars became available through an increase in other Federal Reserve assets listed as an alternative source of reserve funds in the monetary base equation. Decreases in member bank borrowing from the Federal Reserve and in Reserve banks' holdings of acceptances partially offset the increase in other sources of Reserve funds. All the other accounts show relatively small changes.

A sense of the pivotal role of the Federal Reserve in the monetary system can be gained from Table 1.1. Although the Federal Reserve cannot control all accounts in the monetary base equation, its absolute control over one account, the volume of United States government securities that it chooses to hold in its portfolio, gives the Federal Reserve an adequate means to offset or to supplement changes that occur in any of the other accounts in the statement. Therefore, control over its own holdings of government securities provides the Federal Reserve with the necessary power to determine the size of the monetary base. During the period represented by the data in Table 1.1, for example, the Federal Reserve used open market operations not only to offset a decrease in reserve money caused by a small gold outflow and by an increase in Treasury deposits, but also to bring about a substantial net increase in the total monetary base.

In the next section we will analyze the link between the monetary base and the nation's money supply, defined as currency plus demand deposits at commercial banks. We then will examine the means by which control over the monetary base allows the Federal Reserve to determine the size of the money stock. In Chapter 13 of this book we will see how various assumptions about the determination of the money stock may be incorporated into aggregate models of the determination of income, employment, and price level.

The Mechanism of Money Supply Expansion

Introduction

The derivation of the monetary base equation represents the first step in the analysis of the monetary system of the United States. The money stock is customarily defined as *currency in circulation* (that is, currency outside banks, the Federal Reserve, and the Treasury) and *demand deposits adjusted*. Certain minor difficulties are introduced into the analysis by the fact that demand deposits adjusted and total demand deposits at commercial banks are not the same. The differences are caused by the special treatment of the demand deposits of the United States government (the tax and loan accounts), interbank deposits, and other minor items such as deposits "in the process of clearing." These differences are relatively minor, will not affect our results in any substantive manner, and therefore will be ignored in the remainder of this chapter.

A more important consideration which makes this presentation somewhat unrealistic is the fact that not all commercial banks belong to the Federal Reserve System and that, of those banks that do belong to the System, not all are bound by the same legal reserve requirements. Currently the Federal Reserve System sets different legal reserve requirements for different classes of member banks.[5]

In the presentation which follows we shall abstract from these complications. It will be assumed that the reserve requirement ratios on demand and time deposits employed refer to weighted average requirements which take account of these special institutional arrangements.

This part of the chapter will indicate the way in which the total money supply depends on the size of the monetary base and the allocation of that base between member bank reserves and nonbank currency holdings. The discussion proceeds on the basis of extremely restrictive simplifying assumptions concerning commercial bank operations and the public's asset preferences. These assumptions will be successively relaxed in order to produce more realistic models.

---

[5] The Federal Reserve distinguishes between two classes of commercial banks, "reserve city banks" and "other banks." The reserve requirement limits established by Congress and the actual requirements set within those limits by the Board of Governors of the Federal Reserve as of May 1977 are shown below. The actual figure shown for the "other" category is for banks with net demand deposits in the $100–400 million range. For banks in the $10–100 million range, the requirement is 11¾%. For banks in the $2–10 million range it is 9½%; for banks with less than $2 million, it is only 7%.

| | Net Demand Deposits | | Time and Savings Deposits | |
	Reserve City	Other	Under $5 Million	Over $5 Million
Maximum	22%	14%	10%	10%
Minimum	10%	7%	3%	3%
Actual	16¼%	12¾%	3%	6%

Throughout this chapter, static equilibrium models shall be employed to analyze and describe the mechanism of money supply expansion (and contraction). The models will consist of systems of equations embodying interdependencies among the relevant variables. In the initial formulations of these models, all the equations will be linear in form and will embody either a simplified description of the behavior of some agent important in the determination of the money stock, or an institutional, legal, or definitional relation required to characterize our monetary system. In the next chapter certain nonlinear forms will be introduced. The solution of these systems of equations will yield equilibrium values for the dependent variables. These are values which could be maintained indefinitely in the absence of changes in the behavioral, institutional, or legal characteristics (parameters) of the model. Through the use of these models, the following types of questions shall be addressed: by what amount will the money supply change if legal reserve requirements are raised by one percent? Or, by what amount will the volume of demand deposit liabilities change if the monetary authority allows the monetary base to increase by one billion dollars?

Model 1. A Monetary System with Only Demand Deposits

The analysis begins with a set of very restrictive assumptions. First, we assume that commercial banks issue only demand deposit liabilities (no time or savings deposits) and that these deposits comprise the total money supply (the nonbank public holds no currency). Second, we assume that banks automatically create as great a volume of demand deposits liabilities as is legally possible with the reserves at their disposal. In short, commercial banks desire no reserves in excess of legal requirements.

The symbols which shall be employed in our analysis are defined as follows:

Variables

RT Total commercial bank reserves

RR Commercial bank reserves legally required against deposit liabilities; $RR_D + RR_T = RR$

RR_D Reserves legally required against demand deposit liabilities; $RR_D = r \cdot DD$

RR_T Reserves legally required against time deposit liabilities; $RR_T = b \cdot TD$

RE Excess reserve holdings of commercial banks; $RE = RT - RR$

RB Borrowed reserves

RU Unborrowed reserves; $RU = RT - RB$

C Currency holdings of the nonbank public

DD Demand deposit liabilities of commercial banks

TD Time deposit liabilities of commercial banks

B Monetary base; $B = RT + C$

i_T Interest rate on commercial bank time deposits
i_D Federal Reserve discount rate
i_m A rate of interest on some class of marketable securities
M Money stock; $M = DD + C$
L Loans outstanding at commercial banks

Parameters

r Average legal reserve requirement on commercial bank demand deposit liabilities
b Average legal reserve requirement on commercial bank time deposit liabilities

Abstracting from all but the most relevant accounts and assuming the net worth is zero, the balance sheet of an individual bank in this system appears as follows:

A Single Commercial Bank in a Multibank System
(millions of dollars)

Assets		Liabilities and Net Worth	
Reserves (reserve deposits with the Federal Reserve plus vault cash)	20	Demand deposits	100
Loans and securities	80		

Under the assumption that the legal reserve requirement on demand deposits is 20% ($r = .20$), this bank would be required to hold 20 cents in reserves for each dollar of deposit liabilities. Therefore, it is exactly meeting its legal reserve requirements by holding 20 million dollars in reserves against total deposit liabilities of 100 million dollars.

Assume that, by means of a sale of securities which it currently holds in its asset portfolio, this bank increases its reserves by 10 million dollars to 30 million dollars. For example, the bank may sell these securities to the Federal Reserve in return for an increase in the bank's reserve deposit account of $10 million. In the bank reserve equation a source of bank reserves, United States government security holdings of the Federal Reserve, has increased by $10 million. Since there is no corresponding decrease in any other source of funds and no increase in any alternative use of funds, this transaction increases total bank reserves by $10 million, the amount of the security purchase by the Federal Reserve.[6]

Bank A—Balance Sheet
(millions of dollars)

Assets		Liabilities	
Reserves	30	Demand deposits	100
Loans and securities	70		

[6] This transaction is assumed simply as a starting point for our analysis. It should be noted that such a transaction could generally occur only at the initiative of the Federal Reserve with

Bank A is now holding $10 million in reserves *in excess* of the amount required against its deposit liabilities.

By what amount can this bank expand its loan and security holdings and its demand deposit liabilities on the basis of these new reserves (that is, what volume of loans and securities can this bank purchase through the creation of demand deposit liabilities)? Let us assume that we are dealing with a small commercial bank in a large multibank system and that the demand deposit created in the process of making the loan will be spent by the borrower. Unless the bank is geographically isolated and has some degree of regional monopoly, it must consider the possibility that the person receiving the check will deposit it at a different bank (call it Bank B). When the check is deposited in the recipient's account at Bank B and cleared against the borrower's account at the lending bank (Bank A), the lending bank will lose reserves to Bank B in an amount equal to the value of the check. Since people usually borrow to facilitate expenditures, it is quite reasonable to assume that checks equal to the total value of the loan will soon be drawn against the new account in the lending bank, therefore causing that bank to lose reserves in the amount of the newly created deposits.[7]

Under these circumstances, the lending bank (Bank A) is in a position to lend only an amount equal to the reserves that it can afford to lose without impairing its legal responsibility to maintain 20% of the value of its original deposit liabilities in the form of reserves. In other words, given some original level of deposits, it may lend and hence create new demand deposits in an amount equal to the difference between total reserve holdings RT and reserves required against those original deposits RR, an amount equal to excess reserves RE, that is, $RE = RT - RR$.

The above process is depicted in the following balance sheets:

Bank A—Balance Sheet
Before Extension of New Loans
(millions of dollars)

Assets		Liabilities	
Reserves	30	Demand deposits	100
Loans and securities	70		

Addendum: $RT = 30$
$RR = 20[(.20)(100)]$
$RE = 10$

the cooperation of the bank. In usual circumstances, the Fed buys from government securities dealers. The dealer may or may not be acting as a broker for a commercial bank.

[7] This statement would have to be modified in a situation in which the lending bank requires the borrower to maintain a "compensating balance," that is, a balance equal to some percentage of the loan, on deposit at the lending bank for the duration of the loan contract. This, in effect, lowers the usable value of the loan to the borrower and raises the effective rate of interest. This modification could affect our analysis of the operation of an individual bank, but it would not change our conclusions about the operation of the commercial banking system as a whole in any substantial way. See Joseph E. Burns, "Compensating Balance Requirements: Integral to Bank Lending," *Business Review*, Federal Reserve Bank of Dallas (July 1972), 1–8.

Bank A—Balance Sheet
After Extension of $10 Million in Loans through
the Creation of Demand Deposits
(millions of dollars)

Assets		Liabilities	
Reserves	30	Demand deposits	110
Loans and securities	80		

Now if, as assumed, the borrower spends the amount of the loan and this check is deposited in another bank (Bank B), when the check clears, the lending bank (Bank A) will lose deposits and reserves equal to the amount of the new deposit created by the loan:

Bank A—Balance Sheet[8]
(millions of dollars)

Assets		Liabilities	
Reserves	20	Demand deposits	100
Loans and securities	80		

For Bank B, the recipient bank, deposit liabilities and reserves will increase by an equal amount.

Bank B—Changes in Balance Sheet
(millions of dollars)

Assets		Liabilities	
Reserves	+10	Demand deposits	+10

Note: Only the *changes* in Bank B's balance sheet are shown as it is assumed that prior to this transaction Bank B was exactly meeting its legal reserve requirements.

There are many mechanisms through which the transfer of the demand deposit assumed in this example may be facilitated. For simplicity, assume that both banks maintain their reserves in the form of deposit balances with their district Federal Reserve bank. In this case the check can clear through the Federal Reserve System. The clearance will take place when the Federal Reserve bank decreases Bank A's reserve balances by $10 million, the amount of the check, and increases Bank B's (the recipient bank's) reserve deposit account by an equal amount. There is no

---

[8] Although this balance sheet appears to be exactly the same as the initial balance sheet assumed for Bank A, one important change must be noted. In moving from the initial position to this final equilibrium the bank sold government securities for reserves and then lost the reserves after the expenditure of the deposit which was created in the loan transaction. In effect, government securities have been exchanged for an I.O.U. from a private party, say a corporation. This changes the characteristics of the asset portfolio of Bank A and may have further repercussions on its behavior. These questions will be examined in detail in Chapter 3.

change in total reserves in the system, but the check clearing process has lowered the reserves of the lending bank and increased the reserves of the bank of deposit (the recipient bank).

After this transaction is completed, Bank A again has $20 million in reserves and $100 million in demand deposit liabilities. With a reserve requirement of 20%, it is exactly meeting its legal reserve requirements. If it had loaned out more than $10 million, the amount of its excess reserves, the expenditure of that amount by the borrower would have reduced its reserves below $20 million, resulting in a deficiency of legal reserves. Likewise, if it had loaned less than $10 million, it would have something over $20 million in reserves against its $100 million deposit liabilities, and would still have excess reserves that it did not desire (by assumption) and that could facilitate further expansion. Thus we may conclude that, in a large multibank system, in which individual banks are small relative to the system and in which banks do not desire to hold reserves in excess of the legal minimum, *a single bank will lend an amount exactly equal to its excess reserves and no more.*

But what about Bank B? It was assumed that this bank was exactly meeting its reserve requirements before the inflow of reserves took place. After the $10 million increase in both its demand deposit liabilities and its reserve balances (assuming a required reserve ratio of .20 on demand deposits) it must hold an additional $2 million in reserves against these newly acquired deposit liabilities. But since its total reserves have increased by $10 million, it now has $8 millon in excess reserves ($RT - RR = RE$; $10 million − $2 million = $8 million). Bank B will expand its loans by creating $8 million in new demand deposit liabilities. When the borrower spends his newly created demand deposit, in accordance with our previous assumption, these funds will be deposited in another bank, Bank C. The lending bank (Bank B) will lose both reserves and deposit liabilities equal to the amount of the expenditure, $8 million.

Bank B—Changes in Balance Sheet
After Loan Expansion and Check Clearing Process
(millions of dollars)

Assets		Liabilities	
Reserves	+2	Demand deposits	+10
Loans and securities	+8		

Bank C will gain an equal volume of both reserves and deposit liabilities.

Bank C—Changes in Balance Sheet
(millions of dollars)

Assets		Liabilities	
Reserves	+8	Demand deposits	+8

Bank C now has 6.4 million dollars that it can lend out. Its reserves required against newly created deposit liabilities are $1.6 million ($8 million × .20 = $1.6

million). It has excess reserves of $6.4 million ($8 million − $1.6 million = $6.4 million). This process will continue until all these reserve funds have been absorbed into required reserves at various banks.

The amounts loaned and the deposits created at each stage in this process may be summed to calculate the total loan and deposit expansion for the banking system as a whole. Bank A loaned out an amount x, equal to its excess reserves (in this example, x = $10 million). This amount cleared against Bank A and became the reserves of Bank B. But Bank B's demand deposit *liabilities* increased by the same amount x. Consequently, Bank B could loan out only an amount equal to $(x − rx)$, that is, the amount of its new total reserves x in excess of its new requirements rx. This amount cleared against Bank B and became the reserves of Bank C. Bank C, therefore, can loan out an amount equal to its new reserves $(x − rx)$ in excess of new requirements, that is, an amount $(x − rx) − r(x − rx)$. By a continuous process one may add the amounts loaned out at each stage in the expansion process and derive the total expansion of loans, deposits, and the money supply. This process is demonstrated in Table 1.2.

Table 1.2.   Banking System Expansion on the Basis of New Reserves
(millions of dollars)

	Deposits Received in Check Clearing Process		Reserves Required against Received Deposits	Reserves in Excess of Legal Requirements	Demand Deposits Created in the Loan Process		Reserves and Deposits Lost in Check Clearing Process
Bank A	—		—	10		10	10
Bank B	10	= x	2	8	$x − rx$ =	8	8
Bank C	8	= $x − rx$	1.6	6.4	$x(1 − r)^2$ =	6.4	6.4
Bank D	6.4	= $x(1 − r)^2$	1.28	5.12	$x(1 − r)^3$ =	5.12	5.12
Bank E	5.12	= $x(1 − r)^3$	1.024	4.096	$x(1 − r)^4$ =	4.096	4.096
Bank F	4.096	= $x(1 − r)^4$	.819	3.277	$x(1 − r)^5$ =	3.277	3.277
Bank G	3.277	= $x(1 − r)^5$	.655	2.622	$x(1 − r)^6$ =	2.622	2.622
Bank H	2.622	= $x(1 − r)^6$	.			.	
	.		.			.	
	.		.			.	
Total	50.0		10.0			50.0	

Since the expansion at each step in this sequence may be represented as the expansion in the previous step times some constant factor $(1 − r)$, the process may be represented by a geometric series; the total expansion of demand deposits and loans may be expressed as follows:

$$\Delta DD = x + (x − rx) + [(x − rx) − r(x − rx)] + \cdots$$
$$= x + x(1 − r) + x(1 − r)^2 + \cdots + x(1 − r)^n.$$

Thus, as the sum of a geometric progression, total expansion is equal to

$$\Delta DD = \frac{x - x(1 - r)^{n+1}}{1 - (1 - r)}.^{9} \tag{1.1}$$

But as *n*, the number of stages in the expansion process, becomes large, this expression simplifies greatly; for if $r < 1$, which it always will be,

$$\lim_{n\to\infty} \frac{x - x(1 - r)^{n+1}}{1 - (1 - r)} = \frac{1}{r} x = \frac{1}{r} \Delta B \tag{1.2}$$

where *r* is the reserve requirement on demand deposits and *x* is the initial injection of excess reserves (the change in the monetary base, ΔB). Thus the total expansion of loans and deposits in the entire multibank system in our example will be $(1/.20)(\$10 \text{ million}) = (5)(\$10 \text{ million}) = \$50 \text{ million}$.

AN ALTERNATIVE APPROACH

The multiple expansion of bank loans and demand deposit liabilities may be demonstrated much more succinctly with the aid of a model that assumes a few simple relationships between the monetary base, bank reserves, and demand deposits. By the assumption of no currency in circulation, the first of these basic relations is

$$B = RT. \tag{1.3}$$

That is, in the absence of currency holdings by the nonbank public, the entire monetary base would consist of bank reserves. Furthermore, by assuming that banks wish to hold no reserves in excess of the legal requirements, total reserves would be employed solely as reserves required against demand deposit liabilities. This relationship would be implied by a model that assumed that profit maximization was the goal of bank management, and that bank portfolio managers had perfect knowledge (certainty) about the safety, risk, and liquidity characteristics of both their assets and their liabilities.[10] Under these conditions bankers would always prefer

---

[9] Let $k = x + x(1 - r) + x(1 - r)^2 + \cdots + x(1 - r)^n$.

Then

$$(1 - r)k = x(1 - r) + x(1 - r)^2 + \cdots + x(1 - r)^n + x(1 - r)^{n+1}.$$

Subtracting,

$$k - (1 - r)k = x - x(1 - r)^{n+1}.$$

Factoring the left-hand side and dividing,

$$k = \frac{x - x(1 - r)^{n+1}}{1 - (1 - r)}.$$

[10] The influence of these factors in the allocation of bank portfolios is discussed in Chapter 3.

interest yielding loans and securities to noninterest yielding reserve balances, and the presence of excess reserves would immediately generate an expansion of deposits as banks attempted to replace reserve balances with earning assets.

Therefore, equilibrium—the absence of any current forces for change—would prevail only when, for each individual bank and for the banking system as a whole, total reserves were employed solely as required reserves against demand deposit liabilities:

$$RT = RR_D \tag{1.4}$$

$$RR_D = r \cdot DD = RT. \tag{1.5}$$

Substitution of Equation (1.5) into (1.3) yields

$$B = r \cdot DD$$

$$DD = (1/r)B \tag{1.6}$$

or, in terms of changes in the levels of the variables,

$$\Delta DD = (1/r)(\Delta B). \tag{1.7}$$

The term $1/r$ is referred to as the demand deposit expansion coefficient since it defines the relation between a given change in the size of the monetary base and the expansion of demand deposits which that change will bring about. This expression is identical to Equation (1.2) derived above. The emphasis in that derivation, however, was on the logic of $1/r$ as the outcome of an explicit behavioral process.

The assumptions required to derive the conclusion stated in Equation (1.7) include the following:

(1) Banks issue only demand deposit liabilities.

(2) There is no currency in the system.

(3) Banks desire to hold no reserves in excess of legal requirements, that is, banks are assumed to be profit maximizers in a regime of perfect knowledge.

(4) Individual banks suffer a loss of reserves in the expenditure and check clearing process equal to the amount of loans they extend.

Note: the fourth assumption was made for convenience and is not necessary for the result presented above.

In the discussion which follows we relax some of these simplifying assumptions. We examine more realistic models of loan and deposit expansion by successively adding currency and time deposit holdings of the public and desired holdings of excess legal reserves and borrowings of commercial banks. In this process only the monetary base equation is considered. We leave it to the reader to derive the manner in which the geometric expansion of demand deposits takes place under these new assumptions through the flow of reserve funds among individual banks.

Model 2. A Monetary System that Includes Both Currency Holdings and Demand Deposits

Let us now introduce currency holdings into the system. We continue to assume that there are no time deposits and that banks wish to hold no excess legal reserves. Under these assumptions the monetary base is defined as the sum of total bank reserves plus currency in circulation:

$$B = RT + C. \tag{1.8}$$

So long as we continue to assume that banks issue no time deposits and that desired reserves in excess of legal requirements are zero, banks will be in equilibrium (in the sense of desiring no expansion or contraction of loans and deposits) only when all reserves are required against their demand deposit liabilities. Thus,

$$RR_D = r \cdot DD \tag{1.9}$$

$$RT = RR_D = r \cdot DD \tag{1.10}$$

Substitution of Equations (1.9) and (1.10) into (1.8) yields

$$B = r \cdot DD + C. \tag{1.11}$$

Within this model the nonbank public determines the *relative* amounts of currency and demand deposits it holds. Although the size of the total money stock (or the monetary base) may actively be controlled by the monetary authorities, the composition of that stock is determined by the public's own preferences. However, from Equation (1.8) it can be seen that the greater the public's currency holdings, the smaller the stock of funds available out of a given monetary base to serve as reserves against demand deposit liabilities. Therefore, the total level of deposit liabilities and loans outstanding at commercial banks will depend on the public's relative preferences for the different forms in which they may hold their monetary assets.

Rewriting Equation (1.11), we derive the following basic relation:

$$DD = (1/r)(B - C). \tag{1.12}$$

Writing this relation in a form that expresses the *change in the stock of deposits* with respect to a *change in the base,*

$$\Delta DD = (1/r)(\Delta B - \Delta C). \tag{1.13}$$

If the monetary base changes, but currency holdings of the public remain constant ($\Delta C = 0$), then $\Delta DD = (1/r)(\Delta B)$, which is identical to Equation (1.2). Thus if we include currency holdings within our model but assume that those holdings remain constant, the expansion mechanism of the commercial banking system is seen to operate exactly as in a model that assumes that no currency is held by the public. However, rather than assuming that currency holdings remain constant, it may be more realistic to assume that the public desires to hold the components of its total monetary wealth ($DD + C$) in fixed proportions.

Assume, for example, that the public wishes to maintain a 4:1 ratio between its holdings of demand deposits and currency, that is, for each dollar held in checking accounts, individuals wish to hold twenty-five cents in currency. This may be expressed as follows:

$$C = s \cdot DD = .25 \cdot DD \qquad (1.14)$$

and for changes in the levels of these variables,

$$\Delta C = s \cdot \Delta DD = .25 \cdot \Delta DD. \qquad (1.15)$$

Substitute this expression into the bank reserve Equation (1.11) as follows:

$$\Delta B = r \cdot \Delta DD + \Delta C$$
$$= r \cdot \Delta DD + s \cdot \Delta DD$$
$$= \Delta DD(r + s)$$
$$\Delta DD = \frac{1}{r + s}(\Delta B). \qquad (1.16)$$

Assume, as before, that $r = .20$, $s = .25$, and bank reserves increase by $10 million, $\Delta B = \$10$ million,

$$\Delta DD = \frac{1}{r + s}(\Delta B) = \frac{1}{.20 + .25}(\$10 \text{ million}) = \frac{1}{.45}(\$10 \text{ million})$$
$$= (2.22)(\$10 \text{ million}) = \$22.22 \text{ million.}$$

Thus an increase in the monetary base of $10 million (which supplies undesired excess reserves to the banking system and thereby disrupts the initial equilibrium and stimulates expansion) will bring about an increase in demand deposits outstanding of $22.22 million.

When we assumed that there were no currency holdings, an increase in the monetary base of $10 million increased demand deposit liabilities by $50 million; but with currency holdings introduced, the same expansion in the base increases deposit liabilities by only $22.22 million. In the first model, every new dollar of funds supplied by the increase in the monetary base was available to serve as reserve backing for newly created demand deposits. In the second model, *for every dollar of demand deposits created, an additional twenty-five cents is withdrawn from the banking system by the public to be held in the form of currency.* Currency drains represent a decrease in the amount of funds remaining within the banking system available to be held as reserves against deposit liabilities. Therefore, with an assumed currency drain, the given increase in the base supports a smaller increase in the volume of deposit liabilities than would occur in the absence of such a drain.

By how much will currency holdings increase in this process? This figure may be derived from the actual change that occurred in demand deposits:

$$\Delta C = s \cdot \Delta DD$$
$$= (.25)(\$22.22 \text{ million}) = \$5.56 \text{ million}$$

or by substitution,

$$\Delta C = s \cdot \Delta DD = s[1/(r + s)](\Delta B) = [s/(r + s)]\Delta B \qquad (1.17)$$
$$= \frac{.25}{.20 + .25} (\$10 \text{ million}) = (5/9)(\$10 \text{ million}) =$$
$$\$5.56 \text{ million}$$

where $s/(r + s)$ is referred to as the currency expansion coefficient. To double check our computations we can calculate the total amount of funds that flow out of the banks in the form of currency plus the amount which remains in the banks to support the newly created demand deposit liabilities. This total must exhaust the increase in the monetary base:

$$\Delta B = \Delta RT + \Delta C = \Delta RR_D + \Delta C$$
$$= (.20)(\$22.22 \text{ million}) + (\$5.56 \text{ million})$$
$$= (\$4.44 \text{ million}) + (\$5.56 \text{ million})$$
$$= \$10 \text{ million.}$$

Remember our assumption of an initial increase in excess reserves with no initial change in deposits (the result of an open market purchase). For the banking system as a whole, loans outstanding, not including securities given up in the open market purchase, have increased by an amount equal to the total expansion of currency *and* demand deposits. For example, given an injection of $10 million in excess reserves, a single bank will create new deposits and expand its loans by exactly that amount. As the $10 million in newly created demand deposits is spent and the checks which transfer these deposits clear, an amount of currency equal to $2 million will be withdrawn from the banking system and only $8 million will be redeposited. The joint expansion of demand deposits and currency by $8 million and $2 million, respectively, maintains the 4:1 ratio between these two forms of monetary wealth that the nonbank public is assumed to want to maintain. In addition, we see that the sum of the new currency holdings of the public and the new deposit liabilities at the second bank is equal to the volume of loans created at the first bank.

The second bank in this process will expand its loans by an amount equal to its inflow of *excess* reserves [$8 million − (.2)($8 million) = $6.4 million]. Of this amount, $1.28 million will be withdrawn as currency and $5.12 million will be redeposited in the third bank. At each stage of the expansion, the outflow of currency from the system enables the nonbank public to maintain the desired ratio between the components of its monetary wealth, but at the same time reduces the volume of reserves that flow to the next bank in the expansion process. Loans created at each stage of the process equal the outflow of currency at that stage plus the value of demand deposits which flow to the bank at the next stage of the expansion process. The process continues in this fashion throughout the banking system.

Therefore we may calculate the total volume of loan expansion (not including the reduction in securities caused by the initial open market purchase) as follows:

$$\Delta L = \Delta DD + \Delta C = \$22.22 \text{ million} + 5.56 \text{ million}$$

$$= \$27.78 \text{ million}. \tag{1.18}$$

The measure ΔL represents the *total* change in loans that occurs as a result of the existence of excess reserves in the banking system. By our assumption this process began with an open market sale of securities to the Federal Reserve by a bank. Consequently, those excess reserves were a concomitant of the equivalent decrease in that bank's holdings of securities. To reflect this, one may wish to define the *net* increase in loans *and* securities which takes place as a result of the entire chain of events (open market sale to the Federal Reserve *and* bank loan expansion). In this case, that *net* increase would be

$$\Delta L_{net} = \Delta L - \Delta B$$

where ΔB represents the initial sale of securities to the Federal Reserve and the initial generation of excess reserves in the commercial bank's portfolio. Since it is assumed that banks desire no excess reserves, the change in the base must ultimately be absorbed as required reserves or currency:

$$\Delta B = r \cdot \Delta DD + \Delta C.$$

Therefore,

$$\Delta L_{net} = \Delta L - \Delta B = \Delta DD + \Delta C - (r \cdot \Delta DD + \Delta C)$$
$$(1 - r)\Delta DD = \$22.22 \text{ million} - (.2)(\$22.22 \text{ million})$$
$$= \$17.78 \text{ million}$$

which agrees with the balance sheet identity,

$$\Delta loans + \Delta securities + \Delta reserves = \Delta deposits$$
$$= \$27.78 \text{ million} - \$10.0 \text{ million} + \$4.44 \text{ million} = \$22.22 \text{ million.}^{11}$$

Using the definition of the money supply, we can show that the money stock expansion coefficient equals $(1 + s)/(r + s)$:

$$M = DD + C$$
$$\Delta M = \Delta DD + \Delta C. \tag{1.19}$$

Substituting Equation (1.16) for ΔDD and Equation (1.17) for ΔC into Equation (1.19),

$$\Delta M = \left(\frac{1}{r + s}\right)\Delta B + \left(\frac{s}{r + s}\right)\Delta B = \left(\frac{1 + s}{r + s}\right)\Delta B. \tag{1.20}$$

In the present example,

$$\Delta M = \frac{1 + .25}{.20 + .25} (\$10 \text{ million}) = (2.778)(\$10 \text{ million}) = \$27.78 \text{ million,}$$

by coincidence equal to the gross expansion of loans.[12]

Model 3. A Monetary System that Includes Time Deposit Liabilities

We continue to assume that banks want no excess legal reserves and therefore will expand or contract their outstanding loans and securities any time total reserves differ from required reserves. In addition, we assume that banks may now issue time and savings deposits as well as demand deposits. Reserve requirements against the time and savings deposit accounts will now absorb some bank reserves. To take account of this, we formulate a third model as follows:

$$B = RT + C$$
$$RT = RR_D + RR_T = r \cdot DD + b \cdot TD \tag{1.21}$$

where $b = .10$ is assumed to be the reserve requirement ratio on time and savings deposits. Substituting Equation (1.21) into the monetary base equation yields

---

[11] Note that the change in reserves in the final balance sheet is not equal to the initial change in the monetary base because of the leakage of currency into circulation.

[12] As seen subsequently, the equality between the expansion of the money supply and the expansion of loans outstanding is *not* a necessary result.

$$B = r \cdot DD + b \cdot TD + C \tag{1.22}$$

or in terms of changes in the levels of the variables,

$$\Delta B = r \cdot \Delta DD + b \cdot \Delta TD + \Delta C. \tag{1.23}$$

By what amount will demand deposits (and currency, time deposits, loans, and the money supply) expand in response to a given increase in the monetary base? As in the case of currency holdings, rather than assume a constant stock of any monetary asset, we assume that the public maintains fixed proportions between time deposits and demand deposits, that is, $TD = n \cdot DD$. Specifically, we assume that for every dollar of demand deposits the public wishes to hold fifty cents in time deposits.

$$TD = n \cdot DD = .50 \cdot DD. \tag{1.24}$$

We continue to assume the desired 4:1 ratio between currency holdings and demand deposits and substitute Equations (1.14) and (1.24) into Equation (1.22); expressing the result in terms of changes in the levels of the variables,

$$\Delta B = r \cdot \Delta DD + b \cdot \Delta TD + \Delta C$$
$$= r \cdot \Delta DD + b \cdot n \cdot \Delta DD + s \cdot \Delta DD$$
$$= \Delta DD \cdot (r + bn + s)$$
$$\Delta DD = \left(\frac{1}{r + bn + s}\right) \cdot \Delta B. \tag{1.25}$$

Returning to our example, if the base is increased by $10 million, demand deposits will increase by $20 million:

$$\Delta DD = \frac{1}{.20 + (.10)(.50) + .25} (\$10 \text{ million}) = \frac{1}{.50}(\$10 \text{ million})$$
$$= (2)(\$10 \text{ million}) = \$20 \text{ million}.$$

In this case the expansion of demand deposits on the basis of the $10 million increase in the monetary base is smaller than in either of the two previous models. The reason for this should be obvious. In the first model, the entire increase in the monetary base was available to serve as reserves required against newly created demand deposits. In the second model the increase in the monetary base ultimately served two functions, increased currency holdings by the public and increased required reserves against demand deposits issued by commercial banks. In the third model, however, in addition to the drain into currency holdings, there is a further drain into reserves required against newly created time deposits. Notice again that it makes no difference how the initial increase in the base comes about nor in what form the banks prefer to expand their liabilities. The final result will be the same since the public, through its asset preferences, decides how the new funds shall be allocated.

In this model, time deposits will expand by

$$\Delta TD = n \cdot \Delta DD = n \frac{1}{r + bn + s} \cdot \Delta B = \frac{n}{r + bn + s} \cdot \Delta B$$

$$= (.50/.50)(\$10 \text{ million}) = \$10 \text{ million}$$

where $n/(r + bn + s)$ is the time deposit expansion coefficient. Currency holdings will increase by

$$\Delta C = s \cdot \Delta DD = s \frac{1}{r + bn + s} \cdot \Delta B = \frac{s}{r + bn + s} \cdot \Delta B$$

$$= (.25/.50)(\$10 \text{ million}) = \$5 \text{ million}$$

where $s/(r + bn + s)$ is the currency expansion coefficient.

These increases exhaust the increase in the monetary base:

$$\Delta B = r \cdot \Delta DD + b \cdot \Delta TD + \Delta C$$

$$= (.20)(\$20 \text{ million}) + (.10)(\$10 \text{ million}) + \$5 \text{ million}$$

$$= \$10 \text{ million}.$$

The money supply expansion in this case is

$$\Delta M = \Delta DD + \Delta C$$

$$= \frac{1}{r + bn + s} \Delta B + \frac{s}{r + bn + s} \Delta B = \frac{1 + s}{r + bn + s} \Delta B = \$25 \text{ million}.$$

Finally, total loans outstanding increase by the sum of the expansion of currency, demand deposits and time deposits:

$$\Delta L = \Delta DD + \Delta TD + \Delta C = (\$20 \text{ million}) + (\$10 \text{ million}) + (\$5 \text{ million})$$

$$= \$35 \text{ million}$$

but loans *net* of the initial decrease in securities brought about by the open market sale of securities to the Federal Reserve will have expanded by only $25 million:

$$\Delta L_{net} = \Delta L - \Delta B$$

$$= \Delta DD + \Delta TD + \Delta C - (r \cdot \Delta DD + b \cdot \Delta TD + \Delta C)$$

$$= \Delta DD + \Delta TD - r \cdot \Delta DD - b \cdot \Delta TD = (1 - r)\Delta DD + (1 - b)\Delta TD$$

$$= \$20 \text{ million} + \$10 \text{ million} - (.2)\$20 \text{ million} - (.1)(\$10 \text{ million})$$

$$= \$25 \text{ million}$$

which agrees with the balance sheet identity,

$$\Delta loans + \Delta securities + \Delta reserves = \Delta deposits,$$

$$\$35 \text{ million} - \$10 \text{ million} + \$5 \text{ million} = \$30 \text{ million}.$$

Note that in this case total loan expansion is *greater than* the expansion in the money stock. If the reader investigates what would have happened had we defined "money" to include time deposits, he will see why this is so.

Model 4. A Model with Desired Excess Legal Reserves

It is quite reasonable (and historically accurate) to assume that commercial banks may not act like the "automatic dispensers of credit" pictured above. On the contrary, they may quite possibly wish to hold reserves in excess of legal requirements, even though these reserves yield no explicit monetary income. That is, commercial banks may choose not to expand loans and deposit liabilities to the full extent permitted by law. For various reasons they may wish to maintain a positive level of excess reserves as a contingency against unusually large adverse clearing balances, unusually large withdrawals of currency, or as a speculative balance. This assumption is completely consistent with our assumed goal of profit maximization by the bank management. In the face of uncertainty, an individual bank must weigh the cost of holding reserves in excess of legal requirements with the cost of falling below the required reserve minimum if unexpected cash withdrawals or adverse clearing balances occur at a time when the bank is just meeting its reserve requirements. The former cost may be represented by the income foregone on earning assets which could have been acquired with excess reserves. The latter cost may be represented by the cost of borrowing from the Federal Reserve or in the Federal funds market to correct a reserve deficient position. When the cost of a reserve deficiency is greater than zero and there is some finite probability attached to the risk of such a deficiency, it is perfectly reasonable for a profit maximizing bank to hold reserves in excess of those required by law.

This extra complication is easily integrated into the analysis. We may assume that banks wish to maintain a fixed proportional relation between their holdings of excess reserves and their demand deposit liabilities, that is,

$$RE = w \cdot DD \tag{1.26}$$

The rationale for this assumption is that the larger the demand deposit liabilities, the greater is the risk of a deposit loss of a given size and the greater the demand for excess reserves to protect the bank from this risk. We must modify the monetary base equation to allow for these holdings of excess legal reserves:

$$B = RT + C \tag{1.8}$$

but

$$RT = RR_D + RR_T + RE$$
$$= r \cdot DD + b \cdot TD + RE.$$

Thus,

$$B = r \cdot DD + b \cdot TD + RE + C.$$

Employing the proportionality relations assumed before,

$$C = s \cdot DD \tag{1.14}$$
$$TD = n \cdot DD \tag{1.24}$$
$$RE = w \cdot DD \tag{1.26}$$

and making the appropriate substitutions,

$$B = r \cdot DD + b(n \cdot DD) + w \cdot DD + s \cdot DD$$
$$= DD(r + bn + s + w)$$
$$DD = \frac{1}{r + bn + s + w} \cdot B \tag{1.27}$$

or in terms of changes in the levels of the variables,

$$\Delta DD = \frac{1}{r + bn + s + w} \cdot \Delta B. \tag{1.28}$$

Substituting back into Equations (1.14), (1.24), and (1.26) and employing changes in the levels of the variables,

$$\Delta C = s \cdot \Delta DD = \frac{s}{r + bn + s + w} \cdot \Delta B \tag{1.29}$$

$$\Delta TD = n \cdot \Delta DD = \frac{n}{r + bn + s + w} \cdot \Delta B \tag{1.30}$$

$$\Delta RE = w \cdot \Delta DD = \frac{w}{r + bn + s + w} \cdot \Delta B. \tag{1.31}$$

Likewise, since $\Delta M = \Delta DD + \Delta C$,

$$\Delta M = \frac{1 + s}{r + bn + s + w} \cdot \Delta B. \tag{1.32}$$

Equations (1.28) through (1.32) represent a rather general model for bank expansion and contraction caused by increases or decreases in the monetary base.[13] The multiplicative terms in these equations are asset expansion coefficients.

Continuing with our example (assuming all parameter values as before, $r = .20$, $b = .10$, $n = .50$, $\Delta B = \$10$ million, and assuming further that $w = .10$),

$$\Delta DD = \frac{1}{(.20)+(.10)(.50)+(.25)+(.10)} \, (\$10 \text{ million}) = \frac{1}{(.6)} \, (\$10 \text{ million})$$

$$= (1.677)(\$10 \text{ million}) = \$16.67 \text{ million}$$

$$\Delta C = s \cdot \Delta DD = (.25)(\$16.67 \text{ million}) = \$4.17 \text{ million}$$

$$\Delta TD = n \cdot \Delta DD = (.50)(\$16.67 \text{ million}) = \$8.34 \text{ million}$$

$$\Delta RE = w \cdot \Delta DD = (.10)(\$16.67 \text{ million}) = \$1.67 \text{ million}$$

$$\Delta M = \Delta DD + \Delta C = \$4.17 \text{ million} + \$16.67 \text{ million} = \$20.84 \text{ million}$$

$$\Delta L = \Delta C + \Delta DD + \Delta TD = \$4.17 \text{ million} + \$16.67 \text{ million} + \$8.34 \text{ million}$$

$$= \$29.18 \text{ million}.$$

Check:

$$\Delta B = r \cdot \Delta DD + b \cdot \Delta TD + \Delta RE + \Delta C$$

$$= (.20)(\$16.67 \text{ million}) + (.10)(\$8.34 \text{ million}) + (\$1.67 \text{ million}) +$$
$$(\$4.17 \text{ million}) = \$10 \text{ million}$$

In accord with the balance sheet identity

$$\Delta \text{loans} + \Delta \text{securities} + \Delta \text{reserves} = \Delta \text{deposits}$$

$$\$29.18 \text{ million} - \$10.0 \text{ million} + \$5.83 \text{ million} = \$25.01 \text{ million}.$$

Summary

In the section of this chapter entitled "Monetary Accounts" we examined various accounts of the Federal Reserve banks and the United States Treasury and presented statements specifying all the major factors affecting the generation or absorption of the monetary base (total commercial bank reserves plus currency in circulation). The section entitled "The Mechanism of Money Supply Expansion" demonstrated how the total money supply (demand deposits plus currency in circulation) and other commercial bank deposit liabilities against which reserves

[13] For further discussion of models of money supply determination based on proportionality relations see Jerry L. Jordan, *op. cit.*, and Jane Anderson and Thomas Humphrey, "Determinants of Change in the Money Stock, 1960–1970," *Monthly Review*, Federal Reserve Bank of Richmond (March 1972), 2–6.

are required may be supported by this monetary base. That section began with a highly abstract model which assumed that demand deposits were the only liabilities issued by commercial banks and that there was no currency in the system. We then developed progressively more realistic models, concluding with one in which the asset preferences of the public for currency and time deposits and of the banks for excess reserves influence the money supply process.

QUESTIONS FOR CHAPTER 1

1. Assume that the public and commercial banks are in "equilibrium," that is, that the public is holding its preferred relative amounts of currency, demand deposits, and time deposits and banks are holding their desired level of excess reserves. Given the data below, use the kind of proportionality relations we employed in the early models of this chapter to answer the following questions.

   Current required reserve ratio on demand deposits = .15
   Current required reserve ratio on time deposits = .10
   Currency outstanding = $50 billion
   DD liabilities of commercial banks = $200 billion
   TD liabilities of commercial banks = $100 billion
   Total reserves held by banks = $50 billion

   a. What is the value of the demand deposit expansion coefficient?
   b. By how much will demand deposits increase if the Fed increases bank reserves by $5 billion (by a direct purchase of government securities from banks, for example)?
   c. By how much will the injection of reserves in (b) increase the money supply?
   d. What volume of excess reserves will the banks hold *after* the above deposit expansion has been completed?
   e. What volume of new loans will be generaterd by the banking system through this process.

2. The currency needs of the public are strongly influenced by "seasonal" factors. For example, the traveling, shopping, and gift giving traditions associated with Christmas greatly increase the public's need for cash. Describe the problems which this seasonal variation in currency demand might cause for the monetary authorities. How would such variations affect their ability to control the money stock?

BIBLIOGRAPHY FOR CHAPTER 1

ANDERSEN, LEONALL, C., "Federal Reserve Open Market Transactions and the Money Supply," *Review,* Federal Reserve Bank of St. Louis, vol. 47 (April 1965), 10–16.
———, "Three Approaches to Money Stock Determination," *Review,* Federal Reserve Bank of St. Louis, vol. 49 (October 1967), 6–13.

ANDERSEN, L. C., and J. JORDAN, "The Monetary Base: Explanation and Analytical Use," *Review,* Federal Reserve Bank of St. Louis, vol. 49 (August 1967), 7–11.

ANDERSON, JANE, and THOMAS HUMPHREY, "Determinants of Change in the Money Stock, 1960–1970," *Monthly Review,* Federal Reserve Bank of Richmond (March 1972), 2–6.*

ARGY, V., "Money Supply Theory and the Money Multiplier," *Australian Economic Papers,* vol. 4 (June/December 1965), 27–36.

BRUNNER, KARL, "A Schema for the Supply Theory of Money," *International Economic Review,* vol. 11 (January 1961), 79–109.

BRUNNER, KARL, and ALLAN H. MELTZER, "Some Further Investigations of Demand and Supply Functions for Money," *Journal of Finance,* vol. 19 (May 1964), 240–283.

BURGER, ALBERT E., *The Money Supply Process.* (Belmont, CA: Wadsworth, 1972).

BURNS, JOSEPH E., "Compensating Balance Requirements: Integral to Bank Lending," *Business Review,* Federal Reserve Bank of Dallas (July 1972), 1–8.*

GOLDFELD, STEPHEN, *Commercial Bank Behavior and Economic Activity* (Amsterdam: North Holland, 1966).

JORDAN, JERRY L., "Elements of Money Stock Determination," *Review,* Federal Reserve Bank of St. Louis, vol. 51 (October 1969), 10–19.†

* Reprinted in THOMAS M. HAVRILESKY and JOHN T. BOORMAN, *Current Perspectives in Banking* (Arlington Heights, IL: AHM Publishing Corporation, 1976).
† Reprinted in THOMAS M. HAVRILESKY and JOHN T. BOORMAN, *Current Issues in Monetary Theory and Policy* (Arlington Heights, IL: AHM Publishing Corporation, 1976).

2

Generalized Models of Monetary Expansion

Introduction

The models of money supply determination developed in the preceding chapter depended on a set of fairly simplistic assumptions about the asset holding behavior of the banks and the public. This chapter examines the changes that occur when alternative assumptions are specified to describe these asset preferences.

We continue to assume that the monetary base is determined outside the commercial banking system by the monetary authority, and that commercial banks can regard its size as given. In the most "general" case (model 4 of the preceding chapter) in equilibrium, the monetary base would be divided among the following uses:

(1) Currency in circulation C

(2) Reserves required against demand deposits RR_D

(3) Reserves required against time deposits RR_T

(4) Excess legal reserves held by commercial banks RE.

These alternative uses of the monetary base are shown in Equation (2.1).

$$B = r \cdot DD + b \cdot TD + RE + C. \qquad (2.1)$$

Assuming that the size of the base B and the reserve requirement ratios r and b are determined by the authorities, we have one equation in four unknowns. In deriving a solution for these quantities, simple behavioral equations were specified to represent the asset holding behavior of banks and the public. These were formulated as proportionality relations within our model:

$$C = s \cdot DD \tag{2.2}$$

$$TD = n \cdot DD \tag{2.3}$$

$$RE = w \cdot DD \tag{2.4}$$

where *s, n,* and *w* are the factors of proportionality.[1]

Assuming that the values of these parameters *s, n,* and *w* are known from past experience and that the ratios they represent remain stable over time,[2] the system now contains *four* equations in *four* unknowns. Substitution of Equations (2.2), (2.3) and (2.4) into Equation (2.1) yields

$$B = r \cdot DD + bn \cdot DD + s \cdot DD + w \cdot DD$$

$$DD = \frac{1}{r + bn + s + w} \cdot B. \tag{2.5}$$

Thus the demand deposit expansion coefficient is derived. Equation (2.5) is identical to Equation (1.27) in Chapter 1. As shown in Chapter 1, all other expansion coefficients can be derived from Equation (2.5) taken together with Equations (2.2)–(2.4) and the definition of money, $M = DD + C$. Note, however, that the results rely heavily on the forms assumed for the asset holding relations. These very special (and not very realistic) assumptions greatly limit the general applicability and empirical value of the results.

Consider what would happen if one of these relations had a different form. A way is needed to describe the holdings of time deposits and currency desired by the public and the holdings of excess legal reserves desired by commercial banks which will allow solution of the monetary base equation (2.1). This was done by assuming one of the simplest possible relations (proportionality) between these holdings and the level of demand deposits. Let us suppose that empirical tests indicate that the assumption of proportionality does not accurately describe asset holding behavior in one of these cases. In particular, let us assume that proportionality is found to be a good description of banks' holdings of excess legal reserves and the public's holdings of time deposits, but that currency holdings do not conform to this pattern. It will then be necessary to try a different functional form to describe the relationship between the public's holdings of demand deposits and currency.

---

[1] If we assume that *DD* may be taken as a proxy variable for nonhuman wealth, the interpretation given to these relations within the model may be broadened substantially. The importance of wealth in the money (and deposit) demand function is pointed out in Chapters 4 and 8. Nonhuman wealth may also be an important variable in the consumption function. This is discussed in Chapters 10 and 12.

[2] In fact, these ratios have not remained constant over time and can be highly volatile even over a short period of time. We shall see below how we may incorporate more complicated behavioral forms into our model.

Relaxing the Proportionality Assumption

Suppose that we chose a *linear but nonproportional* form to explain currency holdings,

$$C = a + d \cdot DD. \tag{2.6}$$

Our model would now appear as follows:

$$B = r \cdot DD + b \cdot TD + RE + C \tag{2.1}$$
$$TD = n \cdot DD \tag{2.3}$$
$$RE = w \cdot DD \tag{2.4}$$
$$C = a + d \cdot DD \tag{2.6}$$

This change would modify the expansion coefficients derived in Chapter 1. To derive the demand deposit expansion coefficient substitute the asset holding relations (2.3), (2.4), and (2.6) into the monetary base equation (2.1),

$$B = r \cdot DD + b \cdot n \cdot DD + w \cdot DD + a + d \cdot DD$$
$$= DD(r + bn + w + d) + a$$
$$DD = (B - a)/(r + bn + w + d).$$

To derive the currency expansion coefficient, we substitute this result into Equation (2.6):

$$C = a + d \cdot DD = a + \frac{d(B - a)}{r + bn + w + d}.$$

The slight complication in the currency demand function adds a complicating factor to all the results.

This example shows that although the money supply mechanism described above is not completely "general" as it stands, it provides a flexible framework within which an analyst may experiment with various functional forms.

Models with Interest Rates and Other Variables in the Behavioral Relations

In reality, perhaps only quite complicated functions may accurately describe the true relationships that determine the public's asset holdings.[3] This may involve the

---

[3] See Frank de Leeuw and Edward Gramlich, "The Channels of Monetary Policy: A Further Report on the Federal Reserve MIT Model," *Journal of Finance*, vol. 24, no. 2 (May 1969), 265–290. Reprinted in Havrilesky and Boorman, *Current Issues in Monetary Theory and Policy, op. cit.*

introduction of new variables into our model. Let us suppose, for example, that we found a linear currency demand function to be a satisfactory explanation of the "true" relationship between the public's holdings of demand deposits and currency, and we found, too, a proportional relationship to be a sufficient explanation of actual bank holdings of excess legal reserves. However, what if neither of these functional forms satisfactorily explains the time deposit holdings of the public? We must search for an explanation through other functional forms which might include new variables.

The fact that time deposit balances yield an interest return to their holders while demand balances do not ought to influence the public's decisions as to how to allocate their monetary assets. For example, the higher the rate of interest on time deposits, *ceteris paribus,* the more costly it would be in terms of foregone income to hold a dollar in the form of demand deposits or currency. Therefore, the level of the interest rate on time deposit balances as well as the size of demand deposit balances (as a proxy for wealth) may influence desired time deposit holdings. One might postulate, for example, that time deposit holdings are a linear function of both the stock of demand deposit balances and the rate of interest on time deposits, that is,

$$TD = e + f \cdot DD + j \cdot i_T. \tag{2.7}$$

These modifications in the time deposit demand equation would affect all the expansion coefficients derived in Chapter 1. Replacing Equation (2.3) in the previous model with Equation (2.7),

$$B = r \cdot DD + b \cdot TD + RE + C \tag{2.1}$$

$$RE = w \cdot DD \tag{2.4}$$

$$C = a + d \cdot DD \tag{2.6}$$

$$TD = e + f \cdot DD + j \cdot i_T. \tag{2.7}$$

Substituting,

$$B = r \cdot DD + b[e + f \cdot DD + j \cdot i_T] + w \cdot DD + a + d \cdot DD$$

$$= DD(r + bf + w + d) + b[e + j \cdot i_T] + a$$

$$DD = \frac{B - a - be - bj \cdot i_T}{r + bf + w + d}.$$

By substituting the behavioral relations representing the public's and the banks' asset holding behavior into the definition of the monetary base, we have derived a "reduced form" equation[4] that specifies the equilibrium volume of demand deposits

---

[4] A reduced form equation specifies the equilibrium value of an endogenous variable—a variable whose value is determined within the framework of the model, such as demand deposits—as a function of the parameters and exogenous variables that appear in the structural equations (asset preference equations and definitions) of our model.

consistent with given values of the monetary base B, the interest rate on time deposits i_T, and the legal (r and b) and behavioral (w, a, c, d, f, j) parameters of the monetary system. Since the legal parameters and the monetary base are under the control of the monetary authority, if we could estimate the behavioral parameters of the system (say, by regression techniques) a knowledge of the current level of the interest rate on time deposits would enable us to predict the equilibrium level of demand deposit balances.

As one further example, let us suppose that the preferred asset holdings of the banks and the public are dependent on some market interest rates.[5] For example, the public may consider very-short-term United States government securities as an alternative to their holdings of currency and time deposits.[6] The greater the rate on these securities with all other interest rates unchanged, the greater the opportunity cost of holding currency or time deposits. Likewise, commercial banks may be influenced by the rate on these securities when determining their desired level of excess legal reserves.[7] The greater the market rate, the more costly it is to hold non-earning excess reserves. In this instance the asset demand functions may be written as linear equations:

$$TD = e + f \cdot DD + g \cdot i_m \qquad (2.7)$$

$$C = a + d \cdot DD + c \cdot i_m \qquad (2.8)$$

$$RE = v + w \cdot DD + h \cdot i_m. \qquad (2.9)$$

In each case desired asset holdings depend upon both the volume of bank demand deposit liabilities and the market rate of interest i_m. We assume that when the rate of interest on marketable securities changes, all other rates, including the rate paid on time deposits i_T, are unchanged. The relation between these asset holdings and the market rate will be inverse, that is, the signs attached to g, c, and h will be negative. Therefore, when the interest rate on short-term securities or some other market instrument rises, the public will desire a smaller volume of currency and time deposits and the banks will desire fewer excess legal reserves.

Incorporating these relations into our basic framework,

$$B = r \cdot DD + b \cdot TD + C + RE \qquad (2.1)$$

$$B = r \cdot DD + b[e + f \cdot DD + g \cdot i_m] + a + d \cdot DD + c \cdot i_m + v$$
$$+ w \cdot DD + h \cdot i_m$$

---

[5] Though very many individual interest rates exist on the market at any one moment, let us assume that one of those rates or some composite of those rates is the most important rate in determining the asset preferences specified in the model. This would represent a formidable problem if we were to try to estimate the model empirically.

[6] The empirical importance of the role of the interest rate in the determination of the demand for money (whether or not we consider time deposits in our definition of the money stock) is discussed in Chapters 7 and 8.

[7] For example, the rate on these securities may influence the tradeoff between the income foregone and the risk averted when commercial banks hold excess legal reserves. This is discussed in detail in Chapter 3.

$$= r \cdot DD + bf \cdot DD + d \cdot DD + w \cdot DD + be + a + v + bg \cdot i_m$$
$$+ c \cdot i_m + h \cdot i_m$$

$$= DD[r + bf + d + w] + [be + a + v] + [bg + c + h]i_m$$

$$DD = \frac{B - [be + a + v] - [bg + c + h]i_m}{[r + bf + d + w]}.$$

Let

$$\zeta = [be + a + v]$$
$$\gamma = [bg + c + h].$$

Then

$$DD = \frac{B - \zeta - \gamma \cdot i_m}{r + bf + d + w} = \frac{1}{r + bf + d + w} \cdot (B - \zeta - \gamma \cdot i_m). \quad (2.10)$$

Equation (2.10) is a "reduced form" equation. In this expression, $\gamma \cdot i_m$ represents the total influence of the short-term market interest rate on the volume of demand deposit liabilities through its effects on the preferred asset holdings of the public and the banks. Since the parameters $g, c,$ and h above are negative and b is positive, γ is also negative. Since (negative) γ is preceded by a minus sign in Equation (2.10), as the market rate increases, the equilibrium quantity of demand deposits increases. This relation is depicted graphically in Figure 2.1.

As the market rate of interest increases, less currency is demanded, which increases the level of total reserves; fewer time deposits are demanded, which increases reserves available to support demand deposits and fewer excess reserves are desired, which also increases reserves required to support demand deposits. Therefore, for a given base $B,$ the higher the market rate $i_m,$ the more demand deposits can be supported by that base. The numerator of Equation (2.10) varies directly with the market rate $i_m.$

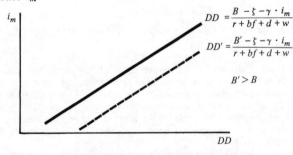

$$DD = \frac{B - \zeta - \gamma \cdot i_m}{r + bf + d + w}$$

$$DD' = \frac{B' - \zeta - \gamma \cdot i_m}{r + bf + d + w}$$

$$B' > B$$

FIGURE 2.1. Reduced form DD relation.

An examination of the intercept term

$$\frac{B - \zeta}{r + bf + d + w}$$

reveals that an increase in the monetary base B will cause the curve to shift to the right, increasing the quantity of demand deposits supplied at all levels of the interest rate as shown in Figure 2.1. Similarly, the curve will shift out to the right if any one of the parameters in the denominator of the intercept term is decreased. For example, a reduction in the reserve requirement ratio on bank demand deposits will increase the supply of deposits at all interest rates. A function similar to this one will be employed in Chapter 13 when the money supply relationship is included as one of the behavioral equations in a model of the determination of aggregate income.

This discussion shows that there could be numerous money multipliers or expansion coefficients, and that the money supply could be influenced by several different interest rates. The form of the expansion coefficients and the choice of interest rate variables that affect the money supply, as demonstrated, depend directly on the form of behavioral relations employed to explain the asset holdings of the banks and the public. These equations could be expanded to include additional variables such as income, wealth, expectations, and the many other factors that may be important in the determination of the public's and the banks' asset preferences. The "best" money supply model will be the one that explains the actual data (actual past values of these variables) and predicts future values better than any of the other models tested.[8]

A Nonlinear Model of the Money Supply Relation[9]

In previous models, desired holdings of currency, time deposits, and excess reserves were treated in a very simple fashion. We assumed in Chapter 1 that the demand for each of these assets was proportional to the level of demand deposits. Earlier in this chapter this strict proportionality assumption was relaxed, but it was still assumed that the size of these desired holdings would vary in a linear fashion with the level of demand deposits. Finally, in the preceding section we introduced the market rate of interest into the demand relations. Nevertheless, strict linearity was still assumed.

A more general, somewhat more sophisticated and realistic approach is to express the desired ratios of currency, time deposits, and excess reserves to demand deposits, not as constants as in Equations (2.2), (2.3), and (2.4), but as functions of other

[8] For a survey of empirical estimation of money supply models, see Robert H. Rasche, "A Review of Empirical Studies of the Money Supply Mechanism," *Review*, Federal Reserve Bank of St. Louis (July 1972), 11–19. Reprinted in Havrilesky and Boorman, *Current Issues in Monetary Theory and Policy, op. cit.*

[9] Much of the material in this section is derived from Albert E. Burger, *The Money Supply Process* (Belmont, CA: Wadsworth, 1972).

variables.[10] As in Equations (2.7), (2.8), and (2.9) of the previous model, the market rate of interest will have an influence on asset-holding behavior. In this case, however, the interest rate together with the level of income shall determine these desired ratios.[11] Thus the proportions of currency, time deposits, and excess reserves to demand deposits will vary with the market rate of interest i_m and the level of aggregate income Y as follows:[12]

$$\frac{C}{DD} = F(i_m, Y), \qquad F_{i_m} > 0, \quad F_Y < 0 \qquad\qquad (2.11)$$

$$\frac{TD}{DD} = G(i_m, Y), \qquad G_{i_m} < 0, \quad G_Y > 0 \qquad\qquad (2.12)$$

$$\frac{RE}{DD} = H(i_m), \qquad H_{i_m} < 0. \qquad\qquad (2.13)$$

Equation (2.11) indicates that the desired ratio of currency to demand deposits is assumed to vary directly with the market rate of interest, that is, $F_{i_m} > 0$. The reason for this is that, while both the demand for currency and the demand for demand deposits vary inversely with the market rate, demand deposits may reasonably be assumed to be closer substitutes for interest bearing securities. Hence the demand for demand deposits is assumed to be more sensitive to changes in the market rate of interest than is the demand for currency.

Equation (2.12) indicates that the desired ratio of time deposits to demand deposits is assumed to vary inversely with the market rate of interest, that is, $G_{i_m} < 0$. The reason for this is that, while both the demand for time deposits and the demand for demand deposits vary inversely with the market rate of interest, time deposits may reasonably be assumed to be better substitutes for interest bearing securities. Hence the numerator in this ratio is assumed to be more sensitive to changes in the

[10] For example, studies by George Kaufman and Phillip Cagan have suggested that the desired currency ratio varies *inversely* with the level of income, because as income increases, proportionately more transactions are handled by check. In addition, the desired time deposit ratio may vary *directly* with income, if time deposits are a luxury good. See Phillip Cagan, *Determinants and Effects of Changes in the Stock of Money 1875–1960* (New York: Columbia University Press, 1965), and George G. Kaufman, "The Demand for Currency," Staff Economic Study, Board of Governors of the Federal Reserve System (1967).

[11] In Chapters 6–8 the demand for currency *plus* demand deposits is expressed as being dependent on the level of permanent income, wealth, expected price level increases, and other variables. These other variables could enter the relations below but would clutter the analysis without adding much to our understanding at this point. Many of the relationships postulated in the present chapter to exist between interest rates and income as explanatory variables and the demand for currency, demand deposits, and time deposits as dependent variables have been empirically estimated. Chapters 7 and 8 survey many of these studies.

[12] The notation F_i, F_Y, etc., means $\partial(C/DD)/\partial i$, $\partial(C/DD)/\partial Y$, etc. In other words, F_i, F_Y, etc., are *partial* derivatives of the desired ratios on the left-hand side of Equations (2.11), (2.12), and (2.13) with respect to the rate of interest and the level of income. In short, this notation signifies the expected magnitude (less than or greater than zero) of the change in the desired ratios when either the market rate of interest or the level of income change by a small amount while all other variables are assumed to remain constant.

yield on these securities than the denominator. (We assume that the interest rate paid on time deposits i_T remains unchanged as the market rate fluctuates.)

By similar reasoning, the bankers' desired ratio of excess reserves to demand deposits in Equation (2.13) is assumed to vary inversely with the market rate of interest. That is, $H_{im} < 0$. This occurs because the interest rate is the opportunity cost to the banker of holding excess reserves. As a result, a higher market rate of interest causes banks to reduce excess reserves relative to demand deposits.[13]

Equation (2.11) indicates that the desired ratio of currency to demand deposits varies inversely with the level of income, that is, $F_Y < 0$. While both the demand for currency and the demand for demand deposits vary directly with the level of income, demand deposits may reasonably be assumed to be superior goods relative to currency. Moreover, there are likely to be greater economies of scale in the demand for currency than in the demand for demand deposits.[14] As the level of an individual's income rises, he generally makes more use of checking account services, and therefore carries, on average, a larger checking account balance. In turn, time deposits are assumed to be superior goods relative to demand deposits. As income rises individuals may reasonably be assumed to add proportionately more to their savings accounts and hold more certificates of deposit than they add to their checking accounts. Therefore, in Equation (2.12) the desired ratio of time deposits to demand deposits varies directly with the level of income, $G_Y > 0$.

In the linear money supply relation of earlier models a money supply expansion factor or "multiplier" was explicitly derived that was a constant regardless of the level of income or the interest rate. In the models where currency, time deposit, and excess reserve demands were strictly proportional to demand deposits, the money stock varied in direct proportion to the monetary base, and changes in the interest rate or level of income had no effect. In models where these demands varied inversely with the market rate of interest, increases in currency, time deposit, and excess reserve holdings brought about by decreases in the market rate were viewed as causing a reduction in the level of reserves available for money supply expansion, but as having no effect on the expansion coefficient itself. For example, in Equation (2.10), with the level of income and interest rates paid on time deposits assumed unchanged, as the market rate of interest declined: the desired level of currency holdings rose and the level of total reserves decreased; the desired level of time

---

[13] The behavior of banks has considerable influence on the determination of the money supply. Here we focus on only one aspect of bank behavior. In the next section of this chapter bank borrowing (of reserves) is introduced. In the next chapter more sophisticated representations of bank behavior are developed, including the consideration of additional variables.

[14] See Cagan, *op. cit.,* and Kaufman, *op. cit.* Stephen Goldfeld and William Hosek indicate, in contrast, that the desired currency ratio may vary *directly* with the level of income. See Stephen M. Goldfeld, *Commercial Bank Behavior and Economic Activity* (Amsterdam: North Holland, 1966); William Hosek, "Determinants of the Money Multiplier," *Quarterly Review of Economics and Business* (Summer 1970), 37–46. Alan Hess contends that the desired currency ratio may vary either inversely or directly with income, depending on the stage of the business cycle. See Alan C. Hess, "An Explanation of Short-Run Fluctuations in the Ratio of Currency to Demand Deposits," *Journal of Money, Credit and Banking* (August 1971).

deposits increased and reserves available to support demand deposit expansion fell; and the desired level of excess reserve holdings rose and reserves available to support demand deposits declined. Consequently, as the market rate declined, the level of demand deposits fell, even though the expansion coefficient itself, $1/(r + bf + d + w)$, was unaffected.

In the present model changes in the market rate of interest and the level of income are viewed as actually affecting the money multiplier itself. Thus we express the money supply relation in general form as

$$M = \phi \left(\frac{RR}{DD}, \frac{RR}{TD}, \frac{C}{DD}, \frac{TD}{DD}, \frac{RE}{DD} \right) \cdot B \qquad (2.14)$$

where $\phi(\ )$ is the expansion factor by which the monetary base is multiplied to determine the equilibrium stock of money. Unlike all previous models this multiplier is no longer a constant. Instead it depends upon five basic ratios: the ratio of required reserves to demand deposits RR/DD, the ratio of required reserves to time deposits RR/TD, the desired ratio (by the public) of currency to demand deposits C/DD, the desired ratio (by the public) of time deposits to demand deposits TD/DD, and the desired ratio (by banks) of excess reserves to demand deposits RE/DD.

The first two of these ratios are our old friends, the legal reserve requirements against demand and time deposits and may be treated as constant terms r and b, respectively. We have already seen that the multiplier varies inversely with each of these legal reserve requirement ratios, that is, $\phi_r < 0$ and $\phi_b < 0$.[15]

The latter three ratios also affect the multiplier. As we have seen from our earlier, linear models, an increase in any of the three ratios will cause the multiplier to decrease, that is, $\phi_{C/DD}, \phi_{TD/DD}, \phi_{RE/DD} < 0$.

These three desired ratios are also the dependent variables in Equations (2.11), (2.12), and (2.13); as such, each ratio is now viewed as a function of the market rate of interest and the level of income. This allows us to rewrite the money supply relation as

$$M = \phi[r, b, F\ (i_m, Y), G(i_m, Y), H(i_m)] \cdot B \qquad (2.15)$$

where $\phi_r, \phi_b, \phi_F, \phi_G, \phi_H < 0$ and from Equations (2.11)–(2.13) $F_{i_m}, G_Y > 0$ and $F_Y, G_{i_m}, H_{i_m} < 0$.

The multiplier $\phi[\ \ ]$ is now a function of the variables i_m and Y. Because we are multiplying variables (i_m and Y) by a variable (B, the monetary base) to determine the money stock, the expression is *nonlinear*.

Therefore we can simplify the previous relation as follows:

$$M = \eta(\ r, b, i_m, Y) \cdot B \qquad (2.16)$$

where $\eta_r, \eta_b, < 0$ but η_{i_m} and η_y are ambiguous.

---

[15] This subscript notation is explained in footnote 12 on page 36.

The word ambiguous means that without further information we cannot deduce the effect of a change in income or the interest rate on the magnitude of the money multiplier. An increase in either of the legal reserve requirement ratios will always cause the money multiplier to decrease, that is, η_r and $\eta_b < 0$, but the effect of an increase in the market rate of interest and the level of income is not so clear. For example, if the market rate of interest rises, the desired ratio of currency to demand deposits will rise ($F_{i_m} > 0$). This will *reduce* the money multiplier ($\phi_{C/DD} < 0$). However, the desired ratio of time deposits to demand deposits and the desired ratio of excess reserves to demand deposits will *fall* if the interest rate rises ($G_{i_m} < 0$, $H_{i_m} < 0$). These changes will *increase* the money multiplier ($\phi_{TD/DD} < 0$, $\phi_{RR/DD} < 0$). This is what is meant when we say η_{i_m} is *ambiguous*. The final effect depends on the relative sizes of these partial influences. However, empirical observation may help to resolve the ambiguity.

Time deposit (including certificates of deposit) movements are quantitatively an important element in our financial system. In recent years they have become quite interest sensitive. It is likely therefore that the effect of a change in the market interest rate on the money multiplier (working through the desired time deposit ratio and the desired excess reserves ratio) outweighs the effect of change in the market interest rate on the money multiplier (working through the desired currency ratio). Consequently, the "net" effect of an increase in the market rate of interest on the multiplier for the narrowly defined money stock may be reasonably assumed to be positive, that is, $\eta_{im} > 0$.

The effect of an increase in the level of income on the money multiplier is also ambiguous. For example, if the level of income rises, the desired ratio of currency to demand deposits will *fall* ($F_Y < 0$). This will increase the money multiplier ($\phi_{C/DD} < 0$). However, the desired ratio of time deposits to demand deposits will *rise* ($G_Y > 0$). This will *reduce* the money multiplier ($\phi_{TD/DD}, < 0$).

Once again, because time deposits are quantitatively such an important element in our financial system, it is likely that the effect of changes in the level of income, working through the desired ratio of time deposits to demand deposits, outweighs the effect of changes in the level of income working through the desired currency ratio. Consequently, the net effect of an increase in the level of income on the money multiplier is likely to be negative ($\eta_Y < 0$).

Several economists have empirically estimated the effect of interest rates on the money supply relation. Generally, empirical work does show that there is, indeed, a positive relationship between various market rates of interest and the money multiplier. The effect of income on the money multiplier has not been extensively estimated.[16]

So far this chapter has revealed the sensitivity of the form of the money supply

---

[16] For a survey of empirical estimates of the money supply relation, see Robert H. Rasche "A Review of Empirical Studies of the Money Supply Mechanism," *Review*, Federal Reserve Bank of St. Louis (July 1972), 11–19 reprinted in Thomas Havrilesky and John Boorman, *Current Issues in Monetary Theory and Policy, op. cit.*

mechanism to the specific behavioral assumptions that underlie the model. Modifications in the behavioral relations have considerable effect on the reduced form equations for demand deposits and the money supply. It has also been shown that, given the monetary base, the currency and deposit demands of the public and the demand for excess legal reserves by banks could reasonably be assumed to respond to changes in various interest rates and the level of income. Therefore, the equilibrium quantities of demand deposits and money may also be so regarded.

The Monetary Base and Member-Bank Borrowed Reserves

Quite often it is assumed that the monetary base B is exogenously determined by the monetary authority. Let us investigate this assumption and its implications more closely. All factors which either supply or divert to alternative uses funds that are potentially available to serve as currency or bank reserves are listed in the monetary base equation. Therefore, to determine which factors influence the size of the monetary base B, we must examine the determinants of the items in that statement.[17]

The only item in the statement of the sources and uses of bank reserves over which the monetary authority, the Federal Reserve, has absolute control, is "United States government securities" held by the Federal Reserve, listed under "Federal Reserve credit." This account represents the largest single source of funds in the monetary base equation. Other items listed as sources and all alternative uses of funds are not under the control of the Federal Reserve. For example, variations in the level of the gold stock are determined primarily by the decisions of the U.S. Treasury and of official international organizations. Foreign deposits at the Federal Reserve and deposits other than those of member banks are varied at the discretion of the holder. "Float,"[18] a technical item that arises in the check clearing process, can be affected by strikes, by the weather, and by any other factors than can delay the delivery of checks.

From the point of view of the monetary authority, however, control over just one item in the source of the monetary base equation, particularly an item as important and flexible as government security holdings, may be as good as control over all accounts. If the Federal Reserve can predict the changes that will occur in the items which it does not directly control, it can take appropriate measures to offset the effects of these changes by adjusting its holdings of United States government

[17] A fairly complete exposition of the monetary base equation appears on pages 5–7 of Chapter 1.

[18] Federal Reserve "float" is the difference between "cash items in process of collection" and "deferred availability cash items" in the consolidated balance sheet of the Federal Reserve banks. Float results from the practice of crediting a member bank's reserve account for checks deposited in Federal Reserve banks before the checks are actually collected from another commercial bank. Consequently, strikes and bad weather that interfere with the check collection process can cause an increase in float and, thereby, an increase in the monetary base.

securities through open market operations.[19] Even if the monetary authority cannot predict these changes before they occur, the director of the System's Open Market Account can move fairly rapidly to take corrective measures to offset the effects of any change that comes to his attention. For example, suppose there is a decrease in Treasury deposits at the Federal Reserve. As an alternative use of funds in the monetary base equation, this would lead to an increase in bank reserves (assuming other accounts remain constant). However, if the Treasury notifies the Federal Reserve of impending changes in the level of its deposits, the Federal Reserve can sell securities on the open market, thereby decreasing the size of their security portfolio and offsetting the effects of the Treasury action on bank reserves. As another example, suppose there is an outflow of Treasury gold to a foreign country. By itself, this movement would decrease the Treasury's gold stock, a source of the monetary base. However, this result could be negated by a purchase of securities by the Federal Reserve. Thus it would appear that through defensive (offsetting) open market operations, the monetary authorities can control the level of the monetary base.

However, there is an item in the source base that is varied primarily at the discretion of commercial banks. This is member bank borrowing from the Federal Reserve, included under "discounts and advances" in the monetary base equation. When a commercial bank finds itself temporarily short of reserves for whatever reason, it has the privilege of borrowing reserves from its district Federal Reserve bank. These funds are borrowed on a very short term basis (under conditions set by the Federal Reserve Board) to restore its reserves to the level required by law.

By itself, an increase in member bank borrowing from the Federal Reserve increases the total member bank reserves. If there is no change in the other accounts in the monetary base equation, this borrowing causes an increase in the monetary base and will support a multiple expansion of loans and deposits just as an increase in reserves from any other source would; yet many observers believe that the Federal Reserve generally (though perhaps only partially) offsets changes in commercial bank borrowing through open market operations. For example, when commercial banks borrow, the monetary authority could sell an equal volume of securities on the open market. The net effect of these two actions would be to maintain the monetary base at a constant level determined by the monetary authority.

Whether the Federal Reserve actually offsets every change in the level of member bank borrowing or simply lets such borrowing change the monetary base is an empirical question (with very important policy implications).[20] Regardless of its

---

[19] For a related discussion of aspects of trying to achieve control of the money supply, see Alan R. Holmes, "Operational Constraints on the Stabilization of Money Supply Growth," *Controlling Monetary Aggregates* (Boston: Federal Reserve Bank of Boston, 1969), 65–78, reprinted in Havrilesky and Boorman, *Current Issues in Monetary Theory and Policy.*

[20] For example, the impact of monetary policy on income is estimated to be relatively weak if the unborrowed base is used as an exogenous measure of monetary policy. See Michael J. Hamburger, "The Lag in the Effect of Monetary Policy: A Survey of Recent Literature,"

actual policy, we may assume that the monetary authority finds it useful to be able to predict member bank borrowing. Let us view the role of these borrowed reserves within the linear money supply framework. This modification in our linear model may be demonstrated rather simply.

We may view the total reserve stock available to commercial banks as composed of two separate elements:

(1) All reserve funds supplied to the commercial banks by the Federal Reserve other than through the borrowing mechanism. This component is called unborrowed reserves, RU.

(2) Those reserves created through commercial bank borrowing from the Federal Reserve, RB.

Therefore, we write the following definition:

$$RT = RU + RB. \tag{2.17}$$

If the Federal Reserve does not offset every movement in reserve borrowing by changes in the level of unborrowed reserves (RU) supplied to commercial banks, bank borrowing will affect the total stock of reserves in the system.

How will this new element introduced into the analysis modify the money multipliers and expansion coefficients derived in the previous chapter? Let us assume that the sum of the unborrowed reserve and currency components of the monetary base are determined by the Federal Reserve. This does not deny the possibility that the monetary authority could in fact offset member bank borrowing through variations in RU, but it does provide a convenient framework to relate borrowed reserves to our money expansion model.

Recall the two definitions of aggregate bank reserves:

$$RT = RR + RE$$

$$RT = RU + RB.$$

Monetary Aggregates and Monetary Policy (New York: Federal Reserve Bank of New York, 1974), 104–111.

The procyclical variation of elements of the source base, such as borrowing, is the foundation of the "reverse causation" controversy. If the base varies procyclically, then estimates of a strong positive relationship between it, as a purported explanatory variable, and income, as a dependent variable, do not reflect one-way causality. Raymond Lombra and Raymond Torto have suggested a resolution of this problem in "Measuring the Impact of Monetary and Fiscal Actions: A New Look at the Specification Problem," *Review of Economics and Statistics*, vol. 56, no. 1 (February 1974), 23–27. Both articles mentioned in this footnote are reprinted in Havrilesky and Boorman, *Current Issues in Monetary Theory and Policy, op. cit.*

By substitution,

$$RU = RR + RE - RB.^{21} \qquad (2.18)$$

Define a new measure, the unborrowed monetary base $\bar{B}$:

$$\bar{B} = B - RB$$

$$\bar{B} = RT - RB + C = RU + C. \qquad (2.19)$$

Therefore, by substituting Equation (2.18) into (2.19), we get

$$\bar{B} = RR + RE - RB + C.$$

Using the definition of required reserves given in Equation (2.1) yields

$$\bar{B} = r \cdot DD + b \cdot TD + RE - RB + C.$$

To derive the money multipliers and expansion coefficients we need only to specify behavioral relations for each of the variables in the equation and to substitute these relations in the equation for the unborrowed monetary base and solve. For example, we may once again assume the familiar proportionality relations for time deposits and currency:

$$C = s \cdot DD \qquad (2.2)$$

$$TD = n \cdot DD. \qquad (2.3)$$

What can we assume about the demand for excess reserves and the demand for borrowed reserves by commercial banks? This question will be taken up in detail in Chapter 3. At the present, in anticipation of the results of that discussion, assume that the demand for excess reserves of commercial banks is a linear function of some market interest rates and the volume of demand deposit liabilities,

$$RE = v + w \cdot DD + h \cdot i_m. \qquad (2.9)$$

[21] We may define another measure called "free reserves," equal to excess reserves less commercial bank borrowing, $RF = RE - RB$. Some analysts have chosen to focus on this measure as the behavioral variable in studying commercial bank behavior and in relating that behavior to the money supply process. For several very good reasons presented elsewhere, we choose not to focus our attention on this combined measure, but rather to investigate each of the components separately. See A. J. Meigs, *Free Reserves and the Money Supply* (Chicago: University of Chicago Press, 1962), and Karl Brunner and Allan H. Meltzer, "The Federal Reserve's Attachment to Free Reserves," Testimony before the Subcommittee on Domestic Finance of the House Committee on Banking and Currency, 88th Congress, 2nd Session (May 7, 1964), 1–27.

The discount rate is the explicit cost of borrowed reserves. Assume that bank borrowing depends on the relationship between this rate and a market interest rate (the return to be earned from acquiring earning assets with the borrowed funds). Assume also that the instability or volatility of commercial bank deposits will influence borrowing behavior. Let this latter factor remain unspecified but be represented by the symbol λ. Then postulate that the level of commercial bank borrowing is a linear function of the stability factor λ and the algebraic difference between the market interest rate i_m and the discount rate i_D:

$$RB = a + d(i_m - i_D) + z(\lambda). \tag{2.20}$$

Substituting these behavioral relations into the basic relation (2.1) yields the reduced form equation for demand deposits:

$$\bar{B} = r \cdot DD + bn \cdot DD + s \cdot DD + v + w \cdot DD + h \cdot i_m - a$$
$$- d(i_m - i_D) - z(\lambda)$$
$$= DD[r + bn + s + w] + [v - a] + h \cdot i_m - d(i_m - i_D) - z(\lambda)$$
$$DD = \frac{\bar{B} - h \cdot i_m + d(i_m - i_D) + z(\lambda) - (v - a)}{r + bn + s + w}. \tag{2.21}$$

Since the money supply has been defined as demand deposits plus currency in circulation, we may write

$$M = DD + C = DD + s \cdot DD = (1 + s)DD$$

$$M = \frac{1 + s}{r + bn + s + w}[\bar{B} - h \cdot i_m + d(i_m - i_D) + z(\lambda) - (v - a)]. \tag{2.22}$$

This result represents a reduced form equation relating equilibrium values of the money stock to the legal and behavioral parameters and exogenous variables of our model. Suppose, for example, that the reserve requirement ratios b and r, the parameters of the behavioral equations (n, s, v, w, h, a, d, z), λ, and the market interest rate all remain constant, but that the Federal Reserve increases the discount rate. What effect will this action have on the money supply? Since all factors but i_D remain constant and the coefficient d is likely to be positive, an increase in i_D will lower $(i_m - i_D)$ and thereby lower the money supply.

Estimates of the parameters of the behavioral equations and information on the usefulness of our assumed functional forms can be derived through the use of statistical methods—primarily regression analysis. Work has been done on this problem over the past several years.[22] Some of this work has been inspired by the

[22] For a review of theoretical money supply models which incorporate assumptions regarding portfolio adjustments differing from those presented here, see David I. Fand, "Some Issues in Monetary Economics: Can the Federal Reserve Control the Money Stock," *Review,* Federal

"new view" that the behavior of the public and the commercial banks (as influenced by factors such as the rate of interest, the level of income, and other economic conditions) so dominates the money supply determination process that there is no close predictable relationship between the money supply and the variables controlled by the monetary authority.[23] Although only limited confidence can be attached to the estimates derived through econometric analysis, they can provide some guidance to the monetary authority on problems such as this.

Summary and Conclusion

In Chapters 1 and 2 we have attempted to describe a framework within which to analyze the process through which the money stock is determined. This task has included the derivation of the bank reserve equation from the Federal Reserve banks' consolidated balance sheet and certain United States Treasury accounts, the demonstration of the role and operation of individual banks within a multibank system and the influence of the behavior of the banks and the public on the equilibrium money stock. Our objective has not been to present the money supply process in a completely precise and empirically relevant manner. We have indicated, however, the outlines of several models of money supply determination and the role of assumed behavioral relations in such models. In later chapters some of the forms derived from these models will be used in the development of macroeconomic models.

QUESTIONS FOR CHAPTER 2

1. What relationship is generally hypothesized between the market rate of interest and

   a. The demand for currency as a percentage of demand deposits
   b. The demand for time deposits as a percentage of demand deposits
   c. The demand for excess reserves
   d. The quantity of money supplied (Be sure you can explain this one by using a, b, and c above).

Reserve Bank of St. Louis, vol. 52 (January 1970), 12–16. For a survey of an empirical estimation of money supply relations, see Robert H. Rasche, *op. cit.*

[23] For stimulating debate regarding this controversy, compare Alan R. Holmes, *op. cit.*, to Thomas Mayer's "Statement in Monetary Policy Oversight," Hearings, Committee on Banking, Housing and Urban Affairs, U.S. Senate, 94th Congress, 1st Session (1975), 179–186. See also Arthur Burns, "The Role of the Money Supply on the Conduct of Monetary Policy," *Monthly Review,* Federal Reserve Bank of Richmond (December 1973), 2–8; Milton Friedman, "Letter on Monetary Policy," *Monthly Review,* Federal Reserve Bank of Richmond (May–June 1974), 20–23; Paul Samuelson and Milton Friedman, "Statement on the Conduct of Monetary Policy," Hearings, Committee on Banking, Housing and Urban Affairs, 94th Congress, 1st Session, (November 1975). All of these are reprinted in Havrilesky and Boorman, *Current Issues in Monetary Theory and Policy, op. cit.*

2. In the linear money supply model the rate of interest did not influence the expansion coefficient but it did influence the quantity of money supplied. Explain.

3. In the nonlinear model the rate of interest influenced the expansion coefficient. Explain.

4. What is the unborrowed base? How would one reasonably assume borrowed reserves would vary with the discount rate? with the market rate of interest?

5. Why is the relationship between the level of income and the expansion coefficient in the nonlinear model regarded as "ambiguous"?

6. What relationship is generally postulated between a change in the interest rate on time deposits and the quantity of time deposits demanded as a percentage of demand deposits? How does this relationship affect the quantity of money supplied?

BIBLIOGRAPHY FOR CHAPTER 2

ASCHEIM, JOSEPH, "Commercial Banks and Financial Intermediaries: Fallacies and Policy Implications," *Journal of Political Economy,* vol. 67 (February 1959), 59–71.

BLACK, ROBERT P., "The Impact of Member Bank Reserves upon the Money Supply," *Southern Economic Journal,* vol. 29 (January 1963), 199–210.

BRUNNER, KARL, and ALLAN H. MELTZER, "The Federal Reserve's Attachment to Free Reserves," Testimony before the Subcommittee on Domestic Finance of the House Committee on Banking and Currency, 88th Congress, 2nd Session (May 7, 1964), 1–27.

BURGER, ALBERT E., *The Money Supply Process* (Belmont, CA: Wadsworth, 1972).

BURNS, ARTHUR, "The Role of the Money Supply in the Conduct of Monetary Policy," *Monthly Review,* Federal Reserve Bank of Richmond (December 1973), 2–8.*

CAGAN, PHILLIP, *Determinants and Effects of Changes in the Stock of Money 1875–1960* (New York: Columbia University Press, 1965).

DE LEEUW, FRANK, and EDWARD GRAMLICH, "The Channels of Monetary Policy: A Further Report on the Federal Reserve MIT Model," *Journal of Finance,* vol. 24, no. 2 (May 1969), 265–290.*

FAND, DAVID I., "Some Implications of Money Supply Analysis," *The American Economic Review,* vol. 57 (May 1967), 380–400.

——, "Some Issues in Monetary Economics: Can the Federal Reserve Control the Money Stock," *Review,* Federal Reserve Bank of St. Louis, vol. 52 (January 1970), 10–27.

FRIEDMAN, MILTON, and ANNA SCHWARTZ, *A Monetary History of the U.S. 1867–1960* (Princeton, NJ: Princeton University Press, 1963), app. B.

FRIEDMAN, MILTON, "Letter on Monetary Policy," *Monthly Review,* Federal Reserve Bank of Richmond (May–June 1974), 20–23.*

GOLDFELD, STEPHEN M., *Commercial Bank Behavior and Economic Activity* (Amsterdam: North Holland, 1966).

* Reprinted in THOMAS M. HAVRILESKY and JOHN T. BOORMAN, *Current Issues in Monetary Theory and Policy* (Arlington Heights, IL: AHM Publishing Corporation, 1976).

GURLEY, JOHN G., and EDWARD S. SHAW, *Money in a Theory of Finance* (Washington: The Brookings Institution, 1960).

GUTTENTAG, JACK M., and ROBERT LINDSAY, "The Uniqueness of Commercial Banks," *Journal of Political Economy,* vol. 67 (October 1968), 991–1014.

HAMBURGER, MICHAEL J., "The Lag in the Effect of Monetary Policy: A Survey of Recent Literature," in *Monetary Aggregates and Monetary Policy* (New York: Federal Reserve Bank of New York, 1974), 104–111.*

HESS, ALAN C., "An Explanation of Short-Run Fluctuations in the Ratio of Currency to Demand Deposits," *Journal of Money, Credit and Banking* (August 1971).

HOLMES, ALAN R., "Operational Constraints on the Stabilization of Money Supply Growth," in *Controlling Monetary Aggregates* (Boston: Federal Reserve Bank of Boston, 1969), 65–78.*

HOSEK, WILLIAM, "Determinants of the Money Multiplier," *Quarterly Review of Economics and Business* (Summer 1970), 37–46.

KAUFMAN, GEORGE, "The Demand for Currency," Staff Economic Study, Board of Governors of the Federal Reserve System.

LOMBRA, RAYMOND, and RAYMOND TORTO, "Measuring the Impact of Monetary and Fiscal Actions: A New Look at the Specification Problem," *Review of Economics and Statistics,* vol. 56, no. 1 (February 1974), 23–27.*

MAYER, THOMAS, "Statement in Monetary Policy Oversight," Hearings, Committee on Banking, Housing and Urban Affairs, U.S. Senate, 94th Congress, 1st Session (1975), 179–186.*

MEIGS, A. J., *Free Reserves and the Money Supply* (Chicago: University of Chicago Press, 1962).

NEWLYN, W. T., "The Supply of Money and Its Control," *Economic Journal,* vol. 74 (June 1964), 327–346.

ORR, DANIEL, and W. G. MELLON, "Stochastic Reserve Losses and Expansion of Bank Credit," *American Economic Review,* vol. 51, no. 4 (September 1961), 614–623.

PHILLIPS, C. A., *Bank Credit* (New York: Macmillan, 1926).

RASCHE, ROBERT H., "A Review of Empirical Studies of the Money Supply Mechanism," *Review,* Federal Reserve Bank of St. Louis (July 1972), 11–19.*

SAMUELSON, PAUL, and MILTON FRIEDMAN, "Statement on the Conduct of Monetary Policy," Hearings, Committee on Banking, Housing and Urban Affairs, 94th Congress, 1st Session (November 1975).*

SMITH, PAUL F., "Concepts of Money and Commercial Banks," *Journal of Finance,* vol. 21 (December 1966), 635–648.

SMITH, WARREN, "Financial Intermediaries and the Effectiveness of Monetary Controls," *Quarterly Journal of Economics,* vol. 73 (November 1959), 533–553.

TEIGEN, RONALD, "Demand and Supply Functions for Money in the United States: Some Structural Estimates," *Econometrica,* vol. 32, no. 4 (October 1964), 476–509.

TOBIN, JAMES, "Commercial Banks as Creators of 'Money'," in *Banking and Monetary Studies,* Deane Carson, ed. (Homewood, IL: Richard D. Irwin, 1963), 408–419.

3

Bank Reserves and Balance Sheet Management

Introduction

The previous chapters present a framework for analyzing the determinants of the money stock. The models developed in those discussions demonstrate how the public's demand for currency and time deposits, as well as the commercial banks' demand for excess reserves and borrowings, may be incorporated into an analysis of the money supply determination process. The influence of the demand functions in those models was explicitly summarized in the money supply expansion coefficient in the reduced form money supply equation.

To understand the money supply determination process more completely, we must examine the behavior of the public and of the banks as it influences the values of the parameters in the models of Chapters 1 and 2. In this chapter, one objective is to analyze the commercial banks' demand for excess reserves and borrowings from the Federal Reserve. This task necessitates an extensive study of bank operations.[1] The analysis, therefore, begins with an examination of the major accounts in a commercial bank's balance sheet and the relation between these accounts and a bank's liquidity. The major constraints and priorities of bank asset management will be studied in order to isolate some of the primary factors that determine the total

[1] As in the previous chapters, we ignore the difficulties posed by the existence of member and nonmember banks and the distinctions made among the various "classes" of member banks.

liquidity needs of a commercial bank. In recent years banks have managed their liquidity needs by adjusting their liabilities as well as their assets. As a result a complete conceptual model of the banking firm requires that we consider both sides of the bank balance sheet. Within this framework we can then develop a better understanding of the role of excess reserves and borrowings in providing the desired level of bank liquidity.

The Commercial Bank Balance Sheet

The analysis begins with an examination of the major accounts in the commercial bank balance sheet. A summary balance sheet for all member banks of the Federal Reserve System is displayed in Table 3.1.

All commercial banks that belong to the Federal Reserve System[2] are required by law to hold reserve balances equal to some minimum percentage of their demand and time deposit liabilities. Prior to 1959 these banks could count as legal reserves only balances held on deposit with Federal Reserve district banks. Since that time, however, member banks have been permitted to count their vault cash as reserves as well. In the consolidated balance sheet of Table 3.1 total member bank reserves are $37.2 billion.

If the total volume of reserves held by banks is greater than the amount that they are required to hold against deposit liabilities, these banks are said to be holding *excess reserves* (excess reserves = total reserves − required reserves). Total reserve balances serve two primary purposes: they satisfy legal requirements on deposit liabilities (required reserves) and they provide the ultimate in liquidity to the banks (excess reserves). In Table 3.1, for example, if the reserve requirement ratio on demand deposits were 10 percent and the ratio on time and savings deposits were 3 percent, required reserves against demand deposits would be 24.2 billion dollars ($242 billion × .10 = $24.2 billion) and required reserves against time deposits would be 10.5 billion dollars ($350 billion × .03 = $10.5 billion). Total required reserves would be 34.7 billion dollars. With total reserves of 37.2 billion dollars excess reserves would be 2.5 billion dollars. Since these reserves are in excess of the amount which the banks are required to hold against their current deposit liabilities, they are immediately available to the banks for a variety of purposes: to meet currency withdrawals, to cover reserve losses which occur in the check clearing process, or to serve as loan funds in the case of increased customer loan demand.

[2] As of 1976, though less than forty percent of all commercial banks belonged to the Federal Reserve System, member banks accounted for over 75% of all commercial bank deposit liabilities, and an even higher percentage of total bank transactions (check clearings, etc.). Over the last several years there has been a significant decline in the number of member banks as many banks have come to judge the cost of Federal Reserve membership excessive in terms of the benefits it provides.

Table 3.1. Summary Balance Sheet of Member Banks of the Federal Reserve System*
(billions of dollars)

Assets			Liabilities and Net Worth	
Total bank reserves		37.2	Deposits	
Vault cash	9.0		Demand deposits	242.0
Reserve deposit balances	28.2		Savings deposits	132.0
			Other time deposits	218.0
Other deposit balances and				
cash items		68.7	Federal funds purchased and	
Investments		191.9	securities repurchase agreements	56.0
U.S. Treasury and				
Agency securities	86.7		Borrowed reserves	0.4
Securities of states and				
political subdivisions	74.5		Other liabilities	25.6
Federal funds sold and				
securities resale			Reserves on loans and securities	2.0
agreements	26.8			
Other investments	3.9		Capital accounts	52.0
Loans		388.0	Total liabilities, reserves, and capital	728.0
Real estate loans	100.5			
Commercial and industrial	140.1			
Installment loans	61.2			
Other	86.2			
Other assets		42.2		
Total assets		728.0		

* Amounts presented approximate actual data for June 30, 1976.
Source: Federal Reserve Bulletin (April 1977).

In the summary commercial bank balance sheet, earning assets are separated into two classes, (1) loans and (2) investments. A loan is generally an individual credit transaction personally negotiated between the borrower and his bank. Loans are frequently of relatively short maturity. Most often there exists no broadly based, well-organized market for the resale of such assets. Included in the loan account are short-term (one year or less) commercial loans, bankers' acceptances, brokers' loans, mortgages on residential and business property, consumer installment loans, personal and automobile loans, and loans to other financial businesses.

An investment, on the other hand, generally represents the purchase of an open market instrument, a security for which there exists some organized trading market.[3]

[3] The existence of a "trading market" does not necessarily imply a specific geographical location, such as the New York Stock Exchange. It denotes only the ability to resell an asset to another party before maturity. Consequently, "marketability" cannot be represented by any

Investments are usually of longer maturity than are loans. The investment portfolios of commercial banks include, among other things, holdings of United States government securities, the securities of federal agencies and state and local governments, certain loans to individuals which are guaranteed by federal agencies, and the securities of corporations.[4]

This distinction between loans and investments in terms of their marketability is somewhat arbitrary, however, and by no means represents a clearcut delineation of all bank lending activity. For example, a well-organized secondary market exists for trading in F.H.A. and V.A. guaranteed mortgages. These assets may be converted to cash at very low transactions cost with little loss in present market value. Yet these are classed as "loans." Likewise, although there often exists little market for the resale of the securities of some small municipalities, these assets are classed as "investments." Listed in Table 3.2 are the more important components of loans and investments and their relative sizes in December 1945, December 1962, and June 1976.

The other accounts in the member bank balance sheet (Table 3.1) should be self-explanatory. "Borrowed reserves" are the reserves borrowed from the Federal Reserve district banks. This account does not include interbank borrowing in the Federal funds market.[5] Such operations involve very short-term borrowing by reserve deficient banks from banks holding excess legal reserves or from dealers specializing in these transactions. Federal funds borrowing among banks does not alter the total stock of bank reserves in the system but merely shifts reserves between banks. Although the availability of interbank borrowing surely affects the behavior of banks, reserves borrowed from the Federal Reserve System through the discount mechanism are the sole means by which banks may independently increase the total stock of bank reserves.

---

unique measure. Clearly, the better organized the market is for a security, the larger the daily volume of trade in that security; and the more broadly based the holdings of that security are, the easier it will be to resell one's holding of such a security. This, of course, influences the price at which the security can be sold and the cost of facilitating that sale. Thus, the "marketability" of an asset has been said to refer to ". . . the proportion of its present market value that can be realized in cash at different time intervals after the decision to sell." Basil J. Moore, *An Introduction to the Theory of Finance* (New York: The Free Press, 1968), 13.

[4] The term "investments," as employed in this chapter, refers solely to financial assets or transactions in financial assets. This should not be confused with "investment" employed in later chapters of this book to refer to purchases of newly produced capital goods—the produced means of production.

[5] Federal (Reserve) funds are deposits in Federal Reserve banks. As we have seen in Chapter 1, the largest of these deposits are those of member commercial banks. Although large non-financial corporations, government securities dealers, and foreign banks all trade in the Federal funds market at times, most activity in this market (approximately 80 percent of the total dollar volume of transactions reported) involves transactions between commercial banks. The typical transaction in this market involves an unsecured overnight loan from one commercial bank with excess legal reserves on deposit with the Federal Reserve to a reserve deficient bank. Frequently the lending bank in these transactions is a relatively small suburban or rural bank supplying funds to a larger money market or urban bank.

Table 3.2.   Loans and Investments of Member Banks of the Federal Reserve System

	Percent of Total Loans and Investments*		
	Dec. 31, 1945	Dec. 28, 1962	June 30, 1976
Loans	21.3%	60.6%	66.7%
Commercial and industrial	8.0	22.4	24.3
Agricultural	0.9	2.2	2.1
To brokers and others for purchasing or carrying securities	6.2	3.4	1.2
To financial institutions	N.A.†	5.3	6.1
Real estate	3.2	13.8	17.5
To consumers and individuals	1.8	12.6	13.4
Other‡	1.1	1.9	2.1
Investments	78.7%	39.4%	33.3%
U.S. government securities (including agencies)			
Bills (initial maturity less than 1 year)	18.0	6.2 ⎫	
Notes (initial maturity 1 to 5 years)	13.3	10.0 ⎬	14.9
Bonds (initial maturity more than 5 years)	41.8	10.9 ⎭	
State and local government securities	3.0	10.6	12.9
Other (including Federal funds and securities under resale agreements)	2.6	1.6	5.5

* Figures may not add to totals because of rounding.
† N.A.—Not available.
‡ Loans to financial institutions are included under "Other loans" for Dec. 31, 1945.
Source: Federal Reserve Bulletins, October 1965, November 1969, and December 1976.

Constraints on Bank Portfolio Management: Commercial Bank Liquidity

One of the major problems facing bank management is the maintenance at minimum cost of an adequate level of liquidity. Liquidity is a concept that applies both to individual classes of assets as well as to the entire balance sheet. In neither sense is liquidity an operationally measurable magnitude. Rather, it depends on certain generally nonquantifiable characteristics either of assets or of the collection of assets and liabilities in a balance sheet.

Most simply, the liquidity of an *asset* reflects the ease, convenience, and cost (in terms of time, specific fees, and lost principal value) of converting an asset into money. For an asset held by a bank, the definition may be extended to consider the exchange of that asset for legal reserves.

The liquidity of a *balance sheet* may be defined as a measure of the ability of the individual or firm represented in that statement to meet claims presented to it for payment. For individual commercial banks, the importance of the liquidity of the balance sheet arises primarily from adverse *net* claims against a bank's cash or reserves that result from the check clearing (and currency withdrawal) process.

Since a large proportion of a commercial bank's liabilities are payable on demand, balance sheet liquidity is of paramount concern.[6]

The ability of a bank to provide for its liquidity needs depends on various characteristics of its asset and liability portfolios, and other factors such as its loan commitments, guaranteed lines of credit, and so forth. Before examining some of the ways in which banks may manage their asset and liability portfolios to satisfy their liquidity needs, we first examine the sources of these needs and describe the major constraints that impinge upon commercial bank operations. These constraints originate from two primary sources, (1) the legal statutes that restrict the freedom of banks in acquiring assets and (2) the nature of the commercial banking industry.

Legally Required Reserves—The Basic
Constraint on Commercial Bank Earnings

We shall assume that commercial banks are fundamentally profit-making organizations. Their primary business is to create claims against themselves in exchange for claims against others. They attempt to profit from the differential between the rate of return on the claims they hold and the rate they must pay on the claims they issue against themselves (after covering operating expenses).

As indicated in Table 3.1, demand and time deposits comprise the bulk of claims issued by commercial banks. These deposit liabilities may originate in several different ways and may be characterzed as either *primary* or *derivative* deposits. The important distinction between these types of deposits lies in their relation to reserve generation and reserve use for individual banks. For example, through the acceptance of a primary deposit, a deposit of coin or currency, a bank (Bank A) acquires a claim against the government or the Federal Reserve in return for an increase in its deposit liabilities. The depositor exchanges high powered money (the Treasury currency or Federal Reserve notes) for a deposit claim against the commercial bank. The effect of this transaction may be shown in terms of a T-account.[7]

Commercial Bank A

Assets	Liabilities
Reserves:	
Vault cash +$100	Deposit liabilities + $100

A primary deposit then involves a transaction such as an inflow of coin or paper money which increases *both* bank deposit liabilities *and* bank reserves.

A derivative deposit, on the other hand, has the effect of increasing deposit lia-

---

[6] The forces that give rise to these adverse clearings and other sources of liquidity needs will be examined in detail in the next section of this chapter.

[7] A T-account reflects the change in a bank's balance sheet that results from a single transaction.

bilities but not *aggregate* bank reserves. For example, if a bank (Bank B) purchases a nonmonetary earning asset through the creation of a new deposit liability, this represents an exchange of a nonmonetary claim against another (a security or an I.O.U.) for a claim against itself. The T-account representing the effect of a purchase of an I.O.U. from a customer in return for a demand deposit liability is shown below:

Commercial Bank B

Assets		Liabilities	
Loans	+$100	Demand deposits	+ $100

The difference between this transaction and the one in the preceding example is that it results in an increase in the bank's earning assets rather than an increase in its reserves. However, since banks are required to hold fractional reserves against *all* deposits, the deposit liability created in this transaction increases the total amount of legal reserves that this bank must hold.

Thus since primary deposits increase bank reserves, banks are restricted in the expansion of their liabilities only by their ability to attract such deposits.[8] But since derivative deposits do not increase reserves, banks are seriously restricted in the purchase of earning assets through this mechanism. Deposits may be created to purchase earning assets only as long as the bank possesses adequate reserves, since reserves will be lost when these deposits are spent and redeposited in other banks.[9] As a result, the total volume of deposits that may be created depends upon (1) the ability of a bank to attract reserves through primary deposits, and (2) the legal reserve requirements against deposit liabilities.

As discussed in previous chapters for the banking system as a whole, the volume of claims that it may issue against itself will be limited by the current stock of bank reserves available and the size of the fractional reserve requirements. Thus the legal reserve requirement may be veiwed as the primary constraint on bank management.

Constraints Imposed by the Nature of Commercial Bank Deposit Liabilities

In many of their operations commercial banks may be viewed as engaging in *financial intermediation,* defined as the process of accepting claims from borrowers in direct negotiations and directly issuing specialized claims to lenders. Financial intermediation is not unique to commercial banks. A sizable number of institutions (such as commercial banks, savings and loan associations, mortgage banks, insurance com-

---

[8] When a depositor deposits a check drawn on a second bank in his account, this may be viewed as a primary deposit *for his bank* since both deposit liabilities and his bank's total reserves increase. However, this is not a primary deposit for the banking system. Aggregate bank reserves are simply redistributed; they do not increase.

[9] As demonstrated in Chapter 1, a single bank in a multibank system can only create derivative deposits equal to the value of its excess reserves (assuming the total deposit is lost by the lending bank when the borrowed funds are spent).

panies, consumer finance companies, etc.) acquire debt claims in direct negotiations with borrowers. But not all these institutions directly issue to lenders specialized debt claims against themselves. Some, for example, consumer finance companies, simply issue claims in the capital markets and have no direct contact with lenders. Nevertheless, in the issuance of *time* and *savings* deposit claims (which are not due on demand and generally yield an interest return), the commercial bank is much like several other institutions.

The issuance of demand deposit claims, however, has traditionally separated the commercial bank from other financial institutions. Specifically, demand deposit claims may be readily transferred from person to person by means of checks.[10] Consequently, these deposits serve as a medium of exchange and have come to constitute the major part of our money supply.

Special problems in commercial bank management derive, in part, from the banks' issuance of these deposit liabilities. Since these *monetary* deposits are due on demand (immediately convertible into legal tender currency or bank reserves), each bank in the system must be prepared to honor requests by depositors for either the withdrawal of currency or the shift of funds to another bank (via the check clearing process). As a result, the issuance of monetary claims creates serious liquidity problems for the commercial bank. These deposit shifts and currency withdrawals are potentially highly volatile and may lead to a net loss of reserves that the bank must be able to cover.

Among the factors influencing the stock of liquid assets that a bank will hold to protect itself against net reserve losses, will be the expected size and variability of cash and reserve drains. Any factor that increases deposit volatility may increase bank liquidity needs. Thus fluctuations in the public's relative demand for demand deposits, currency, and other assets, as well as its expenditure and saving patterns, will influence the volume of liquid assets desired by commercial banks.

Since commercial banks issue various types of deposit liabilities, each with its own very distinctive characteristics, an individual bank's liquidity needs will be influenced by the relative proportions of these deposits in its portfolio. The larger the proportion of highly active and/or erratic deposit accounts among total bank liabilities, the larger will be these desired holdings.[11] Inasmuch as demand deposits may be withdrawn at any time without notice, relatively large amounts of these deposits

[10] The development of electronic funds transfer systems in recent years has reduced the role of the check as a vehicle of transferring funds. For an excellent survey of recent developments in this area, see Robert E. Knight, "The Changing Payments Mechanism: Electronic Funds Transfer," *Monthly Review,* Federal Reserve Bank of Kansas City (July–August 1974), 10–20. Reprinted in Havrilesky and Boorman, *Current Perspectives in Banking* (Arlington Heights, IL: AHM Publishing Corporation, 1976).

[11] This will depend in part on the number and average size of individual accounts as well as the distribution of deposit accounts among personal, corporate and government holders. See, for example, Neil Murphy and Paul S. Anderson, "Running the Bank's Money Position: A Study in Demand Deposit Fluctuation," *New England Economic Review,* Federal Reserve Bank of Boston (November 1967). Reprinted in Havrilesky and Boorman, *Current Perspectives in Banking, op. cit.*

outstanding may induce commercial banks to hold a larger stock of liquid assets to ensure their ability to meet potential drains. Time deposits, on the other hand, generally represent a more secure and stable source of funds to the bank, both because of the purposes for which they are employed by depositors and because, legally, the depositor can be required to present 30 days notice of his intention to withdraw funds from passbook savings accounts. Furthermore, some types of time deposits commit funds to the bank for a specified period of time, 30 days or 90 days, for example. Consequently, as a rule, *a bank's desired liquidity increases as the proportion of demand deposits in total liabilities increases.*

There are several considerations that may qualify this rule. First, since the legal reserve requirements on time and savings deposits are significantly lower than the requirements on demand deposits, a one dollar withdrawal of funds from a time or savings account lowers total required reserve balances by less than a similar withdrawal from a demand deposit account. This may induce banks to hold a greater amount of liquidity (other than legally required reserves) against time and savings deposit withdrawals than they would if equal requirements were applied to all accounts. Second, in practice, banks do not require time and savings depositors to give prior notice of withdrawal. They usually honor such withdrawal requests on demand. Hence a greater volume of liquid assets are held against savings deposits than would be maintained if the 30-day notice requirement were enforced. Finally, the issuance of certain types of instruments by commercial banks, such as negotiable certificates of deposit (CDs), has changed the traditional character of time deposit accounts. A large percentage of funds in these accounts are not held by the small saver, who rarely moves his funds in response to interest rate movements. Rather, the new claims have attracted large blocks of corporate funds that are highly sensitive to market interest rate variations and continually seek the highest rate of return available. As a result, a change in the open market rate (say, on Treasury bills or commercial paper) may cause a massive movement of funds out of commercial bank and other depository-type time deposits into open market instruments. Therefore, the stability once attributed to time deposits is not characteristic of these new accounts.[12]

In summary, the exact influence of a bank's liability configuration on desired liquidity is very difficult to predict on *a priori* grounds alone; but generally our expectation would be that the greater the proportion of time deposit liabilities other than large denomination negotiable CDs, the lower the liquidity needs of the commercial banks.[13]

---

[12] For an analysis of the relative volatility of private demand deposits, savings deposits, CDs, and other time deposits, see George R. Morrison and Richard D. Shelden, *Time Deposit Growth and the Employment of Bank Funds.* Chicago: Association of Reserve City Bankers, 1965.

[13] Non-deposit sources of bank funds may be more easily controlled by the bank than deposit sources and may permit a less liquid (and possibly higher earning) configuration of bank assets. The issuance of long-term capital notes and debentures on the national credit market by large banks has provided a stable source of long-term funds and allowed a lengthening of the maturity structure of assets. This development is discussed later in this chapter.

Regardless of the deposit mix of a commercial bank, the liquidity needs of that bank will be strongly influenced by its growth pattern. In general, *the greater the overall growth (decline) of a bank's total deposit liabilities, ceteris paribus, the less (greater) need there will be to provide liquidity through asset allocation.* For example, if a bank is expanding, either because of success in competition with other banks or because all banks in its area are expanding, it will experience a net inflow of deposits, currency, and reserves. If the bank expects this trend to continue, it will come to rely on this continuous, predictable net inflow as a source of liquidity. This will reduce its need for liquidity from other sources. Conversely, if a bank is located in an area of deposit decline and continually suffers adverse clearing balances (a net loss of reserves in the check clearing process), it must prepare to meet this decline by replenishing its holdings of liquid assets through the sale of earning assets such as loans and investments. These reserve movements throughout the banking system have important implications for both seasonal and secular aspects of liquidity and asset management.

Therefore, the unique character of commercial bank deposit liabilities imposes special liquidity requirements on these institutions. The extent of these liquidity requirements for any one bank will be determined by the particular configuration of its deposit liabilities and by its rate of growth or decline.

Constraints Imposed by the Nature of Commercial Bank Earning Assets

The nature, size, and stability of bank *liabilities* and the pattern of "net" deposit flows are not the only constraints on commercial bank portfolio management. Further restrictions result from the nature of the *assets* in which these banks tend to specialize. Traditionally, commercial banks have emphasized that their role as lending institutions primarily involves the direct extension of credit to local borrowers who do not have the alternative of direct and/or easy access to national credit markets. Most often, these borrowers are also the regular customers of the bank's nonlending services. These borrowers may represent the younger, growing, predominantly local business firms. The need for bank funds may even arise from a firm's inability to generate sufficient capital expansion funds internally because of a lower than average level of profitability.[14]

The concentration of commercial bank assets in this type of loan was temporarily reduced during World War II when the banks were called upon to supply a large share of the wartime credit needs of the Federal government. However, in the postwar era, direct loans to local businesses (and consumers) have again come to dominate bank asset portfolios. This is evidenced by the (almost) continual increase in the (loan)/(loan plus investment) ratio since 1945 (see Table 3.2). In 1945, when the extraordinarily large government financing operations ended, the average

[14] See Roland I. Robinson, *The Management of Bank Funds* (New York: McGraw-Hill, 1962), Ch. 8.

ratio for all banks was .213. By 1962, because of the trend away from market instruments to direct loans, the ratio was .606. In 1976 it was .667.

This specialization has provided the commercial banks with a competitive advantage in the business of direct customer loans. Furthermore, a bank's borrowing customers are most often also depositors of the bank. Current legal ceilings on interest payable on demand deposits and time deposits make it difficult for banks to compete for deposit funds when market rates exceed the legal ceilings. As a consequence, among other means of attracting deposits (low service charges on checking accounts, promotional activities, etc.) the cultivation of a good loan relationship promises a source of deposits and a regular inflow of funds for the bank. In order to protect this relationship and, in part, to compensate its customers for holding large demand deposit balances which yield no interest income, banks provide many technical and advisory services to their regular borrowers. They may also provide a line of credit to a customer with a sizable average deposit balance at a rate somewhat below the rate the customer would otherwise have to pay. Donald Hodgman has emphasized this aspect of the customer relationship. As he notes:

> The customer relationship into which a bank enters with a typical *demand deposit holder* (original italics), especially a business firm, has many aspects. Foremost among these are (1) the deposit itself with attendant costs and benefits to the bank, (2) an implied and often explicit obligation by the bank to make loans to the customer on terms and in amounts which vary with particular circumstances, and (3) the provision by the bank of various other financial services such as registrarships and trusteeships, specialized payroll and account collection services, and others.[15]

Consequently, as the bank nurtures local lending business, a fairly intimate relationship develops between the banker and his loan customer. The customer eventually comes to expect the banker to supply readily all his legitimate needs for credit. Therefore, if a bank desires to maintain a business firm as a "regular

---

[15] Donald R. Hodgman, *Commercial Bank Loans and Investment Policy* (Champaign: IL: Bureau of Economic and Business Research, 1963), 99. The larger the average deposit balance of a good customer, the greater the line of credit the bank will be willing to extend at a rate below the rate the customer would otherwise have to pay. The bank may either extend the low-cost line of credit based on the borrower's deposit record or require a "compensating balance" as a condition for making a loan. These are deposits held at a lending bank by a borrower from that bank. See Joseph E. Burns, "Compensating Balance Requirements: Integral to Bank Lending," *Business Review*, Federal Reserve Bank of Dallas (July 1972), 1–8.

In addition, the bank can extend other low-cost services to the large depositor. In general, the larger the average deposit and the greater the market rate of interest, the greater the differential between what the bank actually charges for a service and what the customer would otherwise have to pay. Bank management, therefore, has an incentive to monitor the accounts of major customers. See Robert E. Knight, "Customer Profitability Analysis," *Monthly Review*, Federal Reserve Bank of Kansas City (April 1975), 11–20. Both of these articles are reprinted in Havrilesky and Boorman, *Current Perspectives in Banking, op. cit.*

customer," it must generally satisfy that firm's credit requests.[16] This entails serious liquidity problems for the bank, however.[17]

Since the type of business to which the commercial bank makes the bulk of its loans is usually sensitive to changes in the general level of economic activity (both nationally and locally), the total demand for credit by these bank customers is highly volatile and involves wide cyclical and seasonal variations. While in recent years in order to meet this demand some banks have attempted to issue more liability claims against themselves by borrowing or issuing large-denomination, negotiable CDs, volatile customers' credit demands have traditionally forced the bank to maintain assets in some highly liquid form (a form that can easily be converted into reserves) to permit the extension of credit whenever customer loan demand increases.

Banks are further constrained in their operations by the necessity of taking special precautions to maintain the principal value of earning assets. This involves reducing the probability of default and capital loss in order to ensure the value of its liabilities. Thus while the goal of bank operation is the maximization of long-run earnings, commercial banks are constrained in achieving this goal by the need to guarantee the continuous *safety* (as well as the *liquidity*) of their asset portfolio. This places severe restrictions on the asset mix that banks may acquire. For example, the need for continuous safety to maintain a relatively constant value of the asset portfolio limits the possibilities for commercial banks to hold highly speculative but sometimes high-yielding market instruments.

One of the main concerns in selecting an earning asset portfolio is *diversification*. We shall see in the Appendix to Chapter 5 a critical consideration in determining the contribution of an asset to the overall risk of a portfolio is the expected comovement between its return and the return of other assets. For example, a bank in rural Kansas makes a large proportion of its loans to local farmers. There will be a high degree of comovement between the returns on individual loans in its portfolio. Its overall portfolio risk will be large. If a drought would strike, many of these loans would simultaneously be in danger of default. In contrast, in a more diversified earning asset portfolio consisting of loans to firms in a variety of industries, there will be considerably less danger of a sizable number of borrowers defaulting simultaneously.

[16] Often the bank will extend a "line" of credit or make an advanced lending commitment, whereby a customer (to smooth out his cash needs or to finance the acquisition of inventory) can have an unsecured, short-term (30- to 90-day) loan over a certain period of time up to a certain specified maximum amount.

[17] For discussions of recent developments in this area see Paul Homan, "Asset Growth— New Techniques, Diversification, Less Regulation, Poorer Quality and Less Liquidity," *Compendium of Major Issues in Bank Regulation,* Committee on Banking, Housing and Urban Affairs, U.S. Senate, 94th Congress, 1st Session (May 1975), 251–257. See also Edward J. Kane, "All for the Best: The Federal Reserve Board's 60th Annual Report," *American Economic Review,* vol. 64, no. 6 (December 1974), 842–850. Both of these are reprinted in Havrilesky and Boorman, *Current Perspectives in Banking, op. cit.*

In summary, then, a commercial bank is not completely free to allocate its asset portfolio so as to maximize its profits in some absolute sense. A commercial bank is subject to various restrictions in this aim. It must first satisfy legal requirements, and then provide, in part, for the unique liquidity needs dictated by the characteristics of its asset and liability accounts, as well as take due regard of the need to assure continuous safety of its earning assets.

Priorities in Commercial Bank Asset Management[18]

The constraints on bank balance sheet management outlined above suggest that commercial banks allocate their asset portfolio according to the following set of priorities: legal reserves, operating cash balances and "protective" liquid assets, customer loans, and open market instruments. Let us examine the implications of this set of priorities in more detail.

Legal Reserves

The first priority in bank asset management is the provision of a sufficient level of reserves to satisfy the legal requirements against its outstanding deposit liabilities. The volume of reserves required is determined by the *level* of bank time and demand deposit liabilities outstanding and the size of the fractional reserve requirements set by the monetary authorities.

Operating Cash Balances and "Protective" Liquid Assets

The requirement that commercial banks hold a portion of their assets in a legally approved form of reserves is of little help in satisfying their liquidity needs. Inasmuch as required reserve balances are reduced by only a small fraction of any deposit withdrawal, banks must rely on other (liquid) assets and the issue of new liabilities to meet the major part of these cash drains. (It is commonly held that legal reserve requirements were instituted to provide governmental *control* over deposit volume and the money supply rather than to provide *liquidity* to the banks.) Consequently, after the provision of *legal* reserve balances, banks still face the task of providing for their basic liquidity needs. As indicated above, these liquidity needs may be satisfied in a variety of ways. We are presently interested only in the contribution of bank asset management to that solution.

---

[18] This discussion draws on material presented by Roland Robinson in *The Management of Bank Funds, op. cit.*

A bank may hold specific assets strictly for their liquidity characteristics, or it may attempt to arrange the maturity distribution of the total asset portfolio in order to ensure a steady inflow of funds from repayment. We shall examine each of these alternatives in turn.

Three rough measures may be used in judging the liquidity characteristics of a particular credit instrument: (1) marketability, (2) capital certainty, and (3) date of maturity. *Marketability* refers to the existence and breadth of a regular transactions market for a particular type of investment. This clearly influences the immediate cash value that can be expected from the sale of an asset before maturity. The *capital certainty* of an asset refers to the predictability with which its expected (future) market value is anticipated. Therefore, the more easily marketable the assets held by a commercial bank and the more certain their capital value, the more liquid the loan and investment account of that bank.

The provision of liquidity through manipulation of the maturity spectrum of the asset portfolio is a more difficult task. In general, the greater the average period to maturity of the earning assets held by a bank, the more remote the cash inflow from repayments and the less reliable this source of liquid funds. (This generalization strictly holds only in the case of nonmarketable loans held by the bank.) On the other hand, if the maturity dates of the asset (particularly the loan) account are rather well distributed relative to the cash needs of the bank, there will be a stream of assets "coming due," providing cash to meet the bank's needs and allowing potentially attractive reinvestment as interest rates change. The funds realized from payments on these instruments may provide a reliable cash flow to the bank and will reduce the desired size of the liquid asset portfolio. Although liquidity generated in this fashion is significant, the cash flow will be reliable only to the extent that the economic climate and deposit flows are relatively stable.

Banks have come to favor various specific assets to satisfy the bulk of their liquidity needs. The safest and most "liquid" of all bank assets are the reserves that it holds in excess of its legal requirements. Deposit balances at other commercial banks are another possibility for the individual bank. (These cancel out in the consolidated balance sheet.) Holding excess reserves or bank balances, however, is also the most costly way of satisfying liquidity needs, for these balances yield no interest return. As a result, we find that banks actually hold a large proportion of their funds for "protective" purposes in the form of very short-term, highly liquid, income earning assets such as short-term United States Treasury bills and callable brokers' loans. (These types of assets are generally referred to as secondary reserves.) Treasury bills, for example, yield an interest return, yet are easily salable at a relatively stable principal value. These securities have further advantages. Under law all government deposits at commercial banks have to be backed by government securities held by the bank. Thus these assets are the basis for government deposit balances and provide earnings for the bank. In addition, these securities can serve as collateral for borrowing from the Federal Reserve.

Customer Loans

In terms of priorities, once the commercial bank has satisfied its legal reserve requirements, it provides for its liquidity and safety through the allocation of sufficient funds to various liquid asset accounts. The extent of its liquidity and safety will also depend to a great degree on the character of its direct loan operations. These loans represent the most risky and least liquid part of the bank's asset portfolio, yet over the long run, they are also the most profitable, in part because of the deposit balances which the loan relationship attracts.[19]

Earlier we mentioned the role of *diversification* in assuring the safety of the loan portfolio. Bank management must also be able to assess the degree of default risk associated with each individual potential borrower. For large borrowers, for example, national firms whose stocks and bonds regularly trade on an organized market, a loan officer can obtain at low cost a good deal of information on the credit worthiness of the firm by examining the level and volatility of the firm's stock price, its earnings and other financial data. As this information is available to banks throughout the nation, borrowers in this category are part of a national loan market.

The information for smaller firms and for households is costlier to obtain. Consequently, local banks have a comparative advantage in compiling such information. Commercial banks are most favorably equipped for direct lending to smaller customers in a relatively narrow geographic market. Within the economy's credit structure, banks have developed a distinct comparative advantage in extending, servicing, and collecting this type of loan. They have never been well disposed to compete with insurance companies and other institutions much better suited to operate in the national market. Consequently, except in special circumstances generally dictated by the characteristics of the community in which the bank is located, the legitimate needs of the bank's customers are met before the bank resorts to the investment markets to find an outlet for its funds.

Upon ascertaining the riskiness of a loan request and the profitability of other relationships with the customer, the bank will determine the *risk premium* it will add to the *prime rate of interest,* the interest rate paid ordinarily on the least risky loans. If for regulatory or competitive reasons there is a maximum rate it can charge high-risk borrowers and if certain customer's credit demands are sizable enough, the bank may have to *ration credit* to some borrowers.[20]

Overall, because of the ability to diversify more broadly, larger banks may have some advantage at making larger and riskier loans and may not have to engage in as costly a credit information search procedure as smaller banks. On the other hand, smaller banks may have a comparative advantage in acquiring detailed information

---

[19] See footnote 15, page 58.

[20] For further discussion of the prime rate, see Randall C. Merris, "The Prime Rate," *Business Conditions,* Federal Reserve Bank of Chicago (April 1975), 2–12. Reprinted in Havrilesky and Boorman, *Current Perspectives in Banking, op. cit.*

Credit rationing is discussed in greater detail in the Appendix to this chapter. Banks that are part of a bank holding company will often direct high-risk borrowers to nonbank subsidiaries, such as consumer finance companies, that specialize in riskier loans.

about each local borrower and can ask a larger, correspondent bank to participate in larger loan requests from good customers. Similarly smaller banks may participate in syndicates organized by large banks to provide funds for large national or international customers. These options will enable banks to reduce their risk without necessarily reducing their expected return.[21]

Open Market Instruments

Although high rates of interest on open market instruments relative to the rates on direct customer loans may at times tempt commercial banks to forego direct loans in favor of investments, the long-run profitability of the bank will depend on its continuous service to its borrowing customers. The bank that puts too large a stake in open market investments will not only lose its traditional local markets and fail to develop new ones, but it also may suffer a highly variable income over the long run as returns to a less diversified earning asset portfolio rise and fall with the market.[22]

These arguments suggest that commercial banks should invest in open market instruments only as a means of meeting their current and future liquidity needs under the second priority, "operating cash balances," or as an outlet for funds seeking employment after all reasonable customer demands have been met. This prescription, however, must be modified in light of the tax advantages available to banks that invest in open market instruments. "Tax swapping," for example, arises from the fact that banks may write off net capital losses against current income. This makes it profitable for banks to sell securities to establish a capital loss as a writeoff against current income and then repurchase similar securities to recover the loss which will be taxed (at a lower rate) as a capital gain in the future.

As another example, the combination of the tax-exempt status of state and local securities and the increased banking needs of the municipalities issuing these securities, provide interesting opportunities for profitable operations with these customers (especially in attracting their deposits). The attractiveness of these opportunities is

[21] The gains from diversification are discussed in greater detail in the Appendix to Chapter 5. Correspondent banking is a relationship whereby a *respondent* bank will keep deposits in another, *correspondent,* bank, in return for which the larger bank will process its checks and provide many other services. The main service is the participation of one bank in the loans of another. Other services include the correspondent bank providing the respondent bank with financial advice and assistance in foreign exchange and Federal funds transactions as well as many other areas. Like any customer relationship, charges for these services vary inversely with the average size of the respondent bank's deposit balance and directly with the level of interest rates (see footnote 15). For an excellent survey article, see Stuart Greenbaum, "Correspondent Banking," *Monthly Review,* Federal Reserve Bank of Kansas City (March–April 1965), 9–16. Reprinted in Havrilesky and Boorman, *Current Perspectives in Banking, op. cit.*

[22] For an interesting discussion of some methods of managing the bond portfolio, see Ronald D. Watson, "Bank Bond Management: The Maturity Dilemma," *Business Review,* Federal Reserve Bank of Philadelphia (March 1972). Reprinted in Havrilesky and Boorman, *Current Perspectives in Banking, op. cit.*

evidenced by the rapid increase in bank holdings of state and local debt in recent years (see Table 3.2).[23]

The existence of state and local securities and of tax swapping opportunities does not invalidate our basic list of priorities, for the degree to which a bank can take advantage of the possibilities suggested above depends to some extent upon its size, location, and sophistication. The largest banks in the financial centers perhaps conform least to our scheme. However, these institutions represent a small percentage of all banks in the system and might better be described as "financial department stores" rather than strictly "commercial banks."

This list of priorities derives primarily from the special constraints placed on banking operations. But commercial banking is a rapidly changing industry, and exceptions to the statements above will be easy to find. We have given a general description of the operating characteristics of an industry in which over one half of the members have less than 5 *million* dollars in deposits while a few of the largest members have deposits in excess of 10 *billion* dollars. Generalizations regarding the nature of such a heterogeneous industry hardly can be considered absolute rules.

Innovations in Liability Management

Asset management is the practice of adjusting the cost and availability of bank loans as well as bank investments in response to changes in deposits, reserves, and economic conditions. Until the depression of the 1930s, the bank's continual need to find the desired balance between earnings and liquidity was satisfied primarily by adjustments in its holdings of self-liquidating assets. Short-term loans made to business firms were considered liquid if they could be secured by the physical output or inventory of the borrower. When the borrowing firm's output was sold, the proceeds of the sale were used to repay the loan. In this sense, such loans were self-liquidating. This "philosophy" of banking, the real-bills doctrine or commercial loan theory of bank lending, derived from the traditional principle that the maturity structure of a firm's assets should match the maturity structure of its liabilities. For the banking firm with a high proportion of current liabilities, a high proportion of current (liquid) assets was deemed necessary. During the Depression, because of declining business activity, many of these "self-liquidating" loans proved illiquid, and banks had a difficult time meeting deposit withdrawals.

As a consequence of this experience, banks began seeking alternative ways of meeting their liquidity needs. The large stock of short-term government securities generated by the federal deficits of the World War II years were the answer to banking's quest for a safe, liquid asset. As seen in Table 3.2, by the end of World War II banks held a considerable stock of these liquid assets. At the same time their

[23] An excellent survey of this and other tax shelters for commercial banks is Margaret E. Bedford, "Income Taxation of Commercial Banks," *Monthly Review,* Federal Reserve Bank of Kansas City (July/August, 1975), 3–11. Reprinted in Havrilesky and Boorman, *Current Perspectives in Banking, op. cit.*

deposit base was quite stable. From this balance sheet position commercial banks were able to accommodate the business loan demands of the 1940s and 1950s, even though many of these loans could not have qualified under the traditional tenet that they be "self-liquidating."

During the late 1950s deposit growth began to lag. As market rates of interest rose, bank depositors increasingly channeled their idle demand deposits into marketable securities. In addition, intensive competition from nonbank financial intermediaries, especially the thrift institutions, diverted a considerable share of local and regional time deposit flows away from commercial banks.

As discussed earlier, customer lending is generally viewed as the *raison d'être* of the commercial bank. The availability of low-cost credit to "good" customers is the source of a sizable and fairly stable share of a bank's deposits. Consequently, with lagging deposit growth, the necessity of maintaining good customer relations increased and banks had to sell off a vast portion of their United States government securities holdings in the 1950s in order to finance loan expansion. This is reflected in Table 3.2. In 1945 the ratio of bank investment assets to investments plus loans was .787; by 1962 this ratio had fallen to .394.[24] One might say that the banks "traded off" liquidity for earnings.

In the early 1960s, in order to continue to finance accelerating loan demand in an expanding economy, commercial banks were forced to become more competitive with thrift institutions, such as savings and loan associations. The "thrifts" were becoming increasingly competitive bidders for deposit funds. Although retained earnings and the issuance of new equity claims played some role in bank loan expansion during this period, there was little doubt that growth in bank liabilities would have to be the main source of loanable funds. At the same time, many felt that continued reliance on local and regional deposit growth would severely constrict the growth of commercial banking.

As discussed earlier in this chapter, the degree of liquidity maintained on the asset side of the bank's balance sheet depends on the composition, stability, and growth rate of its deposits, the composition and stability of the bank's loans, and the bank's ability to engage in borrowing. In the 1960s it was argued that superfluous liquid assets were being held by banks because they were either unable or unwilling to influence significantly the liability side of their balance sheets. But how were these liabilities to be influenced? Access to the Federal Reserve's discount window was generally expected to be temporary. Federal funds borrowing was limited largely to a few larger banks. Until the 1960s other forms of borrowing, such as the issuance of negotiable, insured, and noninsured deposit claims and the issuance of longer term, non-FDIC insured nondeposit claims, were restrained by the traditionally conservative attitudes of bank management and bank regulatory institutions.

[24] In addition, the demand for credit by state and local governments and the favorable tax shelter provisions of many state and municipal securities induced banks to increase the proportion of their investments in state and local government securities from 3 percent of total loans plus investments in 1945 to 10.6 percent in 1962 to almost 13 percent in 1976.

As discussed earlier, despite the presence of interest ceilings a bank could always "attract" demand deposits by paying interest indirectly. For example, it could offer low cost or even free checking and overdraft privileges to households and it could tender a package of services such as a line of credit, payroll processing, and various advisory services to business firms. Charges for these services tend to vary directly with the market rate of interest and inversely with the size of the customer's deposit.

Two important developments in the 1960s gave the more aggressive banks newer methods to manage more closely the liability side of their balance sheets to meet loan requests and commitments (and creditor demands). First, the Federal funds market gained considerable stature as a primary source of short-term funds.[25] Buying banks came to use funds not only for covering cash flow deficits, but also for replenishing reserves and meeting increases in loan demand. Banks that were sellers of funds came to view them as a type of secondary reserve.[26] Smaller banks were able to utilize correspondent relationships with larger accommodating banks that controlled their own net funds position by adjusting their bid and offer rates. While the impact of all funds transactions still focuses on the New York banks, smaller banks have come to supply a good deal of these funds.[27] This development has enabled the banking system to mobilize reserves efficiently on a national basis.

A second development that encouraged liability management was the introduction of large-denomination negotiable certificates of deposit (CDs) in 1961. A secondary market quickly developed when United States government security dealers began trading outstanding CDs. This gave investors in CDs greater liquidity. The appearance of the large-denomination negotiable CD enabled banks to compete for funds with issuers of short-term marketable securities.

[25] The main reason for the growth in Federal funds activity was the rapid rise in interest rates during the 1960s and early 1970s. Another reason was greater knowledge among bankers of how to use the funds market. A third reason was that (in 1963) the Comptroller of the Currency exempted Federal funds transactions of national banks from the provision of the National Banking Act that forbids an unsecured loan to a single borrower in excess of 10 percent of capital and surplus.

[26] The most popular funds transaction is the unsecured sale of funds for one day. The second most popular is the secured repurchase agreement in which the selling bank receives title to United States government securities as well as a commitment from the borrower to repurchase these securities the following day at a predetermined interest rate. (Nonbanks often enter into this sort of repurchase agreement with government securities dealers in the Federal funds market.) The third most frequent funds transaction is the secured nonrepurchase agreement whereby the buying bank puts United States government securities into a custody account for the selling bank until the funds are repaid. See Parker B. Willis, *Federal Funds Market: Origin and Development,* 4th ed. (Boston: Federal Reserve Bank of Boston, 1970).

[27] Rising interest rates, increased competition for funds, the inconvenience of adjusting short-term Treasury bill positions, and a greater diffusion of knowledge and expanded communications facilities have greatly increased the participation of smaller banks (usually as sellers) in the Federal funds market in recent years. See Edward E. Veazy, "Federal Funds—Market Expansion Aids Mobilization of Funds," *Business Review,* Federal Reserve Bank of Dallas (January 1975), 1–6; and Stuart Greenbaum, "Correspondent Banking" *Monthly Review,* Federal Reserve Bank of Kansas City (March–April 1965), 9–16. Both of these articles are reprinted in Thomas M. Havrilesky and John T. Boorman, *Current Perspectives In Banking, op. cit.*

The introduction of CDs had several advantages for banks. Whenever a bank depositor purchased a marketable security, deposits were not lost to the banking system since the seller of the security would deposit the funds in his bank. This sort of transaction had no effect on the loan expansion capabilities of the banking system. However, if instead of purchasing a marketable security the depositor switched his funds from a demand deposit to a CD, which is a type of time deposit, the lower legal reserve requirement on the CD would increase the ability of the bank to acquire earning assets. In addition, if the depositors withdrew funds from nonbank institutions or from abroad in order to purchase the CD, bank loan and investment expansion would be further stimulated. Thus the development of the CD gave banks better access to money markets. It is also argued that this innovation gave savers new outlets for their investment funds. It also channeled funds from the capital markets to financial intermediaries, where they were more available to smaller borrowers at lower cost.

Once these aspects of liability management became established as standard banking practices, whenever the behavior of borrowers and creditors generated a need for additional liquidity, banks now clearly had the option of creating *additional* liabilities rather than selling alternative assets. The concept of liability management holds that banks base their loan commitments not only on anticipated changes in deposits and loan demand, but on the anticipated cost of attracting new deposit and nondeposit funds. This philosophy contributed to the decline in bank holdings of United States government securities during the 1960s. Significant stocks of these securities either were sold or were being used for pledging purposes for secured Federal funds borrowing or for borrowing advances from the Federal Reserve, discussed later in this chapter.

The major source of difficulty in CD competition was the fact that they were subject to Regulation Q, legal ceilings on interest rates payable on deposits. In 1966 and 1968 market rates of interest rose above the legal ceiling on rates payable on large-denomination CDs. As discussed above, the banking system lost "time" deposits (CDs) and gained demand deposits (from the sellers of marketable securities). As demand deposits have higher reserve requirements, the loans and investments of the banking system declined.[28]

This led large U.S. banks to develop a new type of nondeposit liability. Dollar deposits of foreigners, deposited in banks outside the United States, were borrowed by domestic banks. These Eurodollar funds were then used to finance domestic lending. Initially Eurodollar borrowing was very profitable because such borrowed funds were subject neither to interest rate ceilings nor, prior to August 1969, to legal reserve requirements. When a 10 percent legal reserve requirement was imposed, Eurodollars declined in importance and banks turned to the issuance of bank-related commercial paper.

[28] The manipulation of Regulation Q ceilings obviously also influences the distribution of reserves among banks and thrift institutions and hence affects the distribution of credit to the customers of these institutions.

Commercial paper is a short-term (less than 270 days to maturity, usually un-secured) promissary note of a nonfinancial corporation. If a bank issued a similar liability, it would be subject to the same restrictions as a deposit liability. If a bank is part of a holding company, and if a nonbank affiliate of that holding company issues commercial paper, these proceeds are subject to only a 10 percent legal re-serve requirement. A loss of confidence in commercial paper issuers during the Penn Central Crisis of 1970 brought the commercial banking industry under tre-mendous pressure. This forced the Federal Reserve first to raise, then to suspend, and by 1973 to remove the interest rate ceiling on large negotiable CDs.

By the early 1970s the commercial banking industry was thoroughly involved in liability management. Indeed, as long as there are reserve requirements on de-posits and, under Regulation Q, ceilings on interest rates payable on deposits, com-mercial banks have a definite incentive to seek new nondeposit sources of funds. As older nondeposit sources are brought under reserve requirement and other regula-tory restrictions, one can expect that ever newer sources of funds will be sought.[29]

Finally, although regulatory agencies still limit their use, banks increasingly rely on longer term uninsured debt as a source of funds. These debt issues include capital notes and CDs whose interest rates are tied to Treasury bill rates. Capital notes in denominations of over $500 with maturities of over 7 years are not considered deposits and hence are not subject to interest rate ceilings and legal reserve require-ments. Long-term capital notes and debentures have become an important source of bank capital and an impotant component of overall liability management.[30]

Current Developments in the Management of Bank Capital

The techniques of liability management have had an impact on the dependency of banks on asset liquidity. The major source of asset liquidity, securities, as a propor-tion of total assets has fallen off. Table 3.2 shows that in 1962 the ratio of invest-ments to loans plus investments was .394; by 1976 it had fallen to .333. While the spacing of loan maturities provides a cash inflow, these data suggest that bank asset portfolios may nonetheless be less liquid than they were in the early 1960s before liability management came into its own.

[29] For an interesting view of the "natural" tendency for the regulated bank to circumvent the regulations, see Edward J. Kane, "Discussion," in *Policies for a More Competitive Financial System* (Boston: Federal Reserve Bank of Boston, 1972), 190–198. Reprinted in Havrilesky and Boorman, *Currrent Perspectives in Banking, op. cit.*

[30] More recent types of bank innovations include standby letters of credit and finance bills. Both enable customers to obtain credit from third parties with the bank guaranteeing pay-ment. These transactions involve no outlay of bank funds except when the customer defaults, yet they generate a fee income for the bank.

For further discussion of liability management and other innovative techniques, see Edward J. Kane, "All for the Best: The Federal Reserve Board's 60th Annual Report," *American Economic Review* (December 1974), 842–850. Reprinted in Havrilesky and Boorman, *Current Perspectives in Banking, op. cit.*

The liquidity-generating potential of liability management must be recognized when measuring the liquidity of the entire portfolio. In this regard portfolios may be *more* liquid today than in the early 1960s. However, the evidence on *liability liquidity* is not conclusive. When cash needs arise, rather than liquidate assets banks may choose to refinance maturing liabilities or to attract new ones. If lenders are confident in the safety of the bank and if credit is not unduly tight, this could continue to be a rather low-cost source of liquidity. Nonetheless, heavy reliance on liability management could leave less safe banks unable to cope with liquidity pressures when credit is tight.[31]

Table 3.2 also reveals a change in the *composition* of bank loans. In 1962 real estate loans were 13.2 percent of total loans and investments; by 1975 this figure had risen to 16.7 percent. In the recession of 1974–1975 losses, delinquencies, and foreclosures on real estate loans led to a decrease in overall *loan quality*. In addition, banks had taken to issuing standby credit to Real Estate Investment Trusts (REITs), many of which had been organized by the same banks. When, partly because of the recession and partly because of overextension, these REITs reported enormous losses and defaulted, banks were forced to pay the creditors of these trusts. To a lesser extent the 1974–1975 recession also reduced the quality of commercial and consumer loans as the income of business firms and households fell. If a significant proportion of loans is not repaid, it could have an adverse effect on bank earnings.[32]

Not only have overall liquidity and loan quality been affected by innovations in liability management, but the financing of loan expansions by increasing liabilities without a proportional amount of equity and long-term debt financing has also resulted in a reduction in the ratio of bank net worth (or capital) to bank assets. This has, in turn, evoked considerable controversy among bank managers and regulatory agencies regarding the adequacy of bank capital. Regulators tend to rely heavily on "adequate" capital/asset, capital/deposit, and capital/risk asset ratios as elemental in determining the soundness of banks and in preventing bank failure. Should some assets "go bad," regulators prefer to see a solid excess of total assets over liabilities in order to assure that creditors will be paid in the event of liquidation. They view the failure of banks, particularly large banks, as disrupting the entire economy and reducing confidence in the banking system as a whole. Industry sources on the other hand tend to regard excessive amounts of capital as an impediment to bank earnings. While the expansion of net worth relative to assets reduces the risk of insolvency, capital financing—new equity issues, retained earnings and long-term debt issues—tends to be a more expensive source of operating funds than deposits. Bank management argues that it must aim for a level of bank

[31] For further discussion see Stuart A. Schweitzer, "Bank Liability Management: For Better or For Worse," *Business Review,* Federal Reserve Bank of Philadelphia (December 1974), 3–12. Reprinted in Havrilesky and Boorman, *Current Perspectives In Banking, op. cit.*

[32] For further discussion, see Paul Homan, *op. cit.,* and Stuart A. Schweitzer, "Bank Loan Losses: A Fresh Perspective," *Business Review,* Federal Reserve Bank of Philadelphia (September 1975), 18–28. These articles are reprinted in Havrilesky and Boorman, *Current Perspectives in Banking, op. cit.*

capital that provides the desired combination of risk and return. On the one hand, regulators tend to regard bank capital as the only defense in absorbing losses, while, on the other hand, bank management contends that adequate current earnings are the first line of defense.[33]

At one extreme, if bank capital were legally required to be sufficient to prevent all bank failure, there would be insufficient earnings incentive for banks to compete in many financial markets. Numerous financial services would therefore be more costly. At the other extreme, if bank management were free to choose its own capital cushion and responded only to the costs of risk-taking currently imposed on them by creditors, stockholders, and regulators, governmental bailing out of distressed banks could become a much more frequent occurrence and, as a consequence, considerable costs would be imposed on society. In other words, as less bank capital is required, banks are better able to offer their services to the public. As capital requirements are lowered, a greater quantity of these services are available to society at lower costs. However, as less bank capital is required, the likelihood of bank failure increases. Presumably, as capital requirements are lowered, the cost to society of bank failures rises. From this perspective it follows that there is some optimal level of bank capital.

Generally economists would contend that the optimal capital cushion for a bank exists where the (decreasing) social efficiency gains from bank competition in financial markets caused by a reduction in bank capital is just matched by the (increasing) social loss from potential bank failure. This point of view indicates that some banks should be permitted to fail. It also suggests that individuals should be better able to "signal" bank management when the risks of thin capitalization as well as other risks exceed the benefits from increased expected earnings. In short, incentives for prudent everyday banking operations ought to be built into the banking market itself, supplementing if not replacing the asset, liability, interest rate, reserve requirement, and capital regulations that lace the entire business of banking.

If the prevention of bank failure is in the public interest, bank management should continually be "signaled" by its depositors, creditors, stockholders, and insurers as it takes overall risk in the form of acquiring risky assets, engaging in costly sources of financing asset acquisition, and letting its capitalizaton decline. However, if depositors know that the regulatory authorities will insure their deposits up to $40,000 per account regardless of risks taken by bank management, and if noninsured creditors and stockholders know that the authorities always bail out larger sized distressed banks, these depositors have little or no incentive to "police" bank management. If, on the other hand, deposit insurance premia were graduated to reflect risk (as revealed by examination of asset composition, liquidity, and profit-

_____

[33] For an interesting juxtaposition of the two views, see Ronald D. Watson, "Insuring Some Progress in the Bank Capital Hassle," *Business Review,* Federal Reserve Bank of Philadelphia (July–August 1974), 3–18; Ronald D. Watson, "Banking Capital Shortage: The Malaise and the Myth," *Business Review,* Federal Reserve Bank of Philadelphia (September 1975), 3–13, and George J. Vojta, *Bank Capital Adequacy* (New York: Citicorp, 1973), 15–30. Each of these articles is reprinted in Havrilesky and Boorman, *Current Perspectives In Banking, op. cit.*

ability) taken by management, if the data and ratings from frequent bank examinations were made available to the investing public, and if some large banks were permitted to fail, then bank management would have more incentive to behave prudently.[34] Creditors, depositors, and stockholders would insist on higher returns to compensate for risk, management would fear failure and hence the risk and the cost to society of possible bank failures would be adequately priced. In case there is bank failure, the free entry and exit of banking firms into and out of the market would further encourage efficiency and vitalize the economy.

Progress toward reorganization of bank regulation to permit freer exit and entry and toward more market valuation of bank risk taking has been in the offing for some time.[35] However, it would be premature to predict at this writing, what the ultimate results will be.

The Use of Reserves in Liquidity Management

As indicated in earlier sections, a commercial bank may achieve its desired liquidity position by holding a variety of liquid assets, each with its own maturity characteristics, marketability and capital certainty, by proper design of the maturity distribution of its portfolio of earning assets and by active management of its liabilities. The exact degree of liquidity desired by a bank at any one time will be determined by the subjective weight the banker applies to each of the factors discussed in previous sections of this chapter. Those factors which influence potential cash or reserve needs include: (1) the nature, size, and stability of total bank deposit liabilities; (2) the rate of growth or decline of the bank as this affects its net "deposit flow" or clearing balances; (3) the variability of its customer loan demand; and (4) the current maturity configuration of its earning asset account.

One further important influence on the desired level of bank liquidity will be the cost of maintaining that level of liquidity. *In general, total portfolio liquidity will vary inversely with the "cost" of that liquidity.* This cost will depend primarily on two factors: (1) the alternative cost of liquid assets; and (2) the cost of covering a deficiency in reserves by borrowing reserves or by attracting new liabilities, rather than through the sale of liquid assets. The higher the return on less liquid loans and investments, or the lower the cost of borrowing or issuing new liabilities,[36] the greater the cost of maintaining the liquid asset account. Therefore, as this cost

[34] For further discussion, see Jack M. Guttentag, "Reflections on Bank Regulatory Structure," and Thomas Mayer "Preventing the Failures of Large Banks," in *Compendium of Major Issues in Bank Regulation,* Committee on Housing, Banking and Urban Affairs, U.S. Senate, 94th Congress, 2nd Session, Committee Print No. 2 (August 1975). Reprinted in Havrilesky and Boorman, *Current Perspectives in Banking, op. cit.*

[35] See, for example, "Financial Institutions in The Nation's Economy," *Discussion Principles,* Committee on Banking and Currency, U.S. House of Representatives, 94th Congress, 2nd Session (November 1975). Reprinted in Havrilesky and Boorman, *Current Perspectives in Banking, op. cit.*

[36] Total bank liquidity varies *directly* with the cost of borrowing. The greater the cost of borrowing to provide reserves, the more liquidity will be maintained.

increases, liquid asset holdings will be managed more closely and the desired level of liquidity will decrease.

In this section we shall focus on bank holdings of excess legal reserves and reserve borrowings. These are the measures that appear in the final money supply model presented in the previous chapter. It was demonstrated in the derivation of the money supply equation that the banks' demand for excess legal reserves and borrowings influence the actual money stock. We now see that these demands are closely related to the liquidity needs of the banks. This section investigates the determinants of the commercial banks' demand for both excess legal reserves and reserve borrowing.

The Determinants of Bank Holdings of Excess Reserves

A bank's demand for excess reserves must be examined within the context of its *total* liquidity needs. This was our motivation in discussing the factors that influence the *size* of the liquid asset portfolio, the priorities assigned to various asset classes, and the possibilities for liability management. Given the desired *level* of liquidity as determined by these factors, the *allocation* of bank funds to holdings of excess legal reserves may depend primarily upon (1) the alternative cost of these reserves, (2) the "penalty" rate for a required reserve deficiency, and (3) the rate of change in the level of unborrowed reserves RU supplied by the monetary authorities.

The alternative cost of holding excess legal reserves is the income foregone by not transferring these funds to income earning liquid assets. Evidence seems to indicate that banks consider short-term United States Treasury bills to be the closest interest yielding substitutes for excess reserves. Therefore, the higher the rate of return on these securities (net of transactions costs), the lower the proportion of liquid asset funds that banks may be expected to allocate to holdings of excess legal reserves.

The cost incurred by a banker in meeting a reserve deficiency depends upon his choice among several alternatives. He may liquidate securities, call in loans, or borrow reserves on a short-term basis, either through the Federal funds market or from the Federal Reserve. Each of these alternatives has a specific cost associated with it. It follows then that a banker must consider the expected penalty costs of meeting reserve deficiencies by each of these means when setting his desired level of excess legal reserves. The higher the expected cost of covering a given reserve deficiency, the greater the banker's desire to avoid that cost by holding excess reserves.

The total cost of covering a deficiency by liquidating securities or calling in loans includes the earnings foregone from the loss of the security, the possible capital loss from the sale of the instrument before maturity, and any transactions costs involved. The cost of covering the deficiency by borrowing in the Federal funds market or from the Federal Reserve is the explicit interest rate charged on borrowed funds plus any transactions costs.[37]

For the banking system as a whole only the discount mechanism (borrowing from the Federal Reserve) can add to the total of system-wide reserve balances. The other alternatives simply shift reserves among banks. Considering only this alternative, the higher the discount rate (relative to the rate on short-term securities) the less willing banks will be to risk a reserve deficiency and the higher will be desired holdings of excess legal reserves.

The rate at which the Federal Reserve changes the supply of unborrowed reserves (or reserve requirements) will influence system-wide holdings of excess legal reserves in one of two possible ways. First, if bankers do not anticipate changes in the level of unborrowed reserves, *actual* excess reserves will vary *directly* with these changes. It takes time for the commercial banks to adjust to a higher level of reserves and during that period actual excess reserves will be higher than the level desired by the banks. In this case, the change in the level of unborrowed reserves may be viewed as a short-term disturbance pushing banks away from their equilibrium positions. Second, changes in unborrowed reserves may be anticipated by banks. Anticipated changes in unborrowed reserves are generally viewed as precursors of deposit flows. In this case *desired* excess legal reserves will vary *inversely* with expected *changes* in the supply of unborrowed reserves. Thus the overall effects of this factor on excess reserves are impossible to predict on *a priori* grounds alone. Only empirical information on the behavior patterns involved can supply a unique answer to this question.

Empirical tests indicate that an inverse relationship exists between bank holdings of excess legal reserves and the United States Treasury bill rate, and that a direct relationship exists between these reserve holdings and the Federal Reserve discount rate.[38] While much less evidence has been presented on the third factor discussed above, the information available indicates that excess reserves tend to vary directly with changes in unborrowed reserves (adjusted for changes in reserve requirements).

The Determinants of Commercial Bank Borrowing

As demonstrated in the previous chapter and as emphasized above, borrowed reserves, like excess reserves, have an important influence on the supply of money. Borrowing reserves serves two primary purposes: first, it covers reserve deficiencies, as discussed immediately above; and second, it may provide liquidity for short-term

[37] There may be other implicit, nonmonetary costs involved in these actions. For an empirical study of some of the relationships discussed here, see Roger H. Hinderliter, "Market Access, Uncertainty, and the Reserve Position Adjustments of Large Commercial Banks in the 1960s," *Journal of Finance,* vol. 29, no. 1 (March 1974), 41–56. Reprinted in Havrilesky and Boorman, *Current Perspectives in Banking, op. cit.*

[38] See Leonall C. Andersen and Albert E. Burger, *op. cit.*

credit and money supply expansion. The rather high level of borrowed reserves within the banking system and the almost continuous use of this mechanism by some banks suggest that both motives for borrowing (not necessarily mutually exclusive, of course) may be relevant to this analysis. Data on bank borrowing through the discount window are presented in Table 3.3 and Figure 3.1.

Historically, each of the theories put forward to explain bank borrowing has tended to emphasize a single possible motive for bank borrowing to the exclusion of all others. The most important theories presented in this discussion fall under two basic categories, (1) the "profit" theory and (2) the "needs and reluctance" theory.

The profit theory of commercial bank borrowing holds that bankers (consistent with a profit maximizing assumption) borrow from the Federal Reserve banks whenever a profit can be made from the borrowed funds. This occurs whenever there exists a positive differential between the market loan rate and the discount rate that is sufficiently large to overcome transactions costs.

Table 3.3. Bank borrowing from the Federal Reserve*
(millions of dollars)

1954	I	194	1960	I	785	1966	I	477	1972	I	51
	II	147		II	510		II	674		II	107
	III	82		III	302		III	753		III	385
	IV	166		IV	126		IV	634		IV	743
1955	I	377	1961	I	85	1967	I	317	1973	I	1539
	II	421		II	72		II	119		II	1765
	III	714		III	52		III	89		III	2018
	IV	913		IV	106		IV	166		IV	1333
1956	I	866	1962	I	76	1968	I	423	1974	I	1194
	II	933		II	77		II	707		II	2431
	III	809		III	99		III	535		III	3315
	IV	716		IV	163		IV	587		IV	1081
1957	I	627	1963	I	142	1969	I	813	1975	I	224
	II	975		II	189		II	1268		II	156
	III	970		III	324		III	1169		III	328
	IV	775		IV	339		IV	1154		IV	163
1958	I	277	1964	I	273	1970	I	984	1976	I	71
	II	130		II	246		II	895		II	95
	III	279		III	310		III	931		III	101
	IV	490		IV	327		IV	402		IV	71
1959	I	555	1965	I	373	1971	I	339	1977	I	84
	II	788		II	501		II	310		II	88
	III	956		III	539		III	708		III	93
	IV	896		IV	465		IV	291		IV	

* Quarterly averages of monthly figures, from Federal Reserve Bulletins.

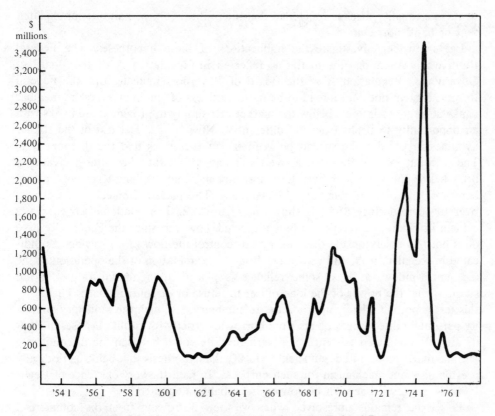

FIGURE 3.1. Member Bank Borrowing from the Federal Reserve.

When such a favorable differential exists, the profit theory postulates that banks capitalize on the potential net returns by increasing loans with borrowed funds.

The needs and reluctance theory, on the other hand, holds that bankers are averse to being in debt to the Federal Reserve and borrow funds only when unexpected cash drains compel such action. A convincing case for the needs and reluctance theory was presented by W. W. Riefler in the early 1920s.[39] He claimed that if the profit theory were indeed the true explanation of bank borrowing behavior, this would imply near equality between the discount rate and the market loan rate. If the profit motive were the overriding influence on bank borrowing decisions, whenever the market rate was above the discount rate, an increase in the supply of loans supported by borrowed reserves would lower the market rate until it approached the discount rate and eliminated the profit differential. Since his tests failed to demon-

[39] W. W. Riefler, *Money Rates and Money Markets in the United States* (New York: Harper and Bros., 1930).

strate this equality, Riefler concluded that the profit theory was an inferior explanation of bank borrowing.

Let us further investigate the implications of these hypotheses. The Federal Reserve's position on this matter is reflected in Regulation A of the Board of Governors.[40] Regulation A of the Board of Governors indicates that the Federal Reserve System does not intend to be in the business of lending reserves to member banks at a rate of interest below the market rate simply to provide these banks with an opportunity to profit from the differential. Now, as a direct test of the Riefler hypothesis, consider the spread between the market rates and the discount rate. The discount rate, while often above the Treasury bill rate, has almost invariably been below the rate on longer term instruments, such as long-term government bonds, or the rate on commercial bank loans. The pattern formed by these rates over the period since 1952 is shown in Figure 3.2. The relations between rates evident in Figure 3.2 should not be unexpected, however, since the Federal Reserve does not rely solely on the discount rate to control the flow of borrowing. As indicated in Regulation A, and as evident from an examination of the operation of the discount window, at least some reliance is placed upon administrative "moral suasion" and the power of the loan officer to refuse or discourage loans. Therefore, this test is not completely appropriate. In summary, although the monetary authority personally discourages banks from borrowing strictly for profit purposes, neither its attitude nor the persistence of a variable differential between the discount rate and the market loan rate is sufficient to falsify the hypothesis that banks periodically use the discount mechanism for such purposes. In fact, the very existence of Regulation A suggests that such borrowing is probably attempted.

This issue remains unresolved when we view borrowing from the commercial bank's side of the discount window. Many depositors, especially larger business and financial depositors, are critical of bank borrowing since, in case of insolvency, creditors' claims take precedence over the claims of depositors.[41] Thus a bank with

---

[40] For a discussion of the recent revisions in the rules governing the operation of the discount mechanism see Arnold A. Dill, "Member Bank Borrowing: Process and Experience," *Monthly Review,* Federal Reserve Bank of Atlanta (April 1973), 50–54. Reprinted in Havrilesky and Boorman, *Current Perspectives in Banking, op. cit.*

[41] This is particularly important only to depositors with deposits larger than the maximum insured by the F.D.I.C., which currently is $40,000.00. The importance of customer attitudes on certain aspects of bank management is also stressed by Donald Hodgman in his discussion of commercial bank portfolio ratios:

> No bank's management feels comfortable when its key balance sheet ratios get too far out of line with those of other banks regarded as comparable in size and character. Apart from the questions such discrepancies may raise regarding other managements' conflicting assessments of the uncertain future, there are likely to be pressures generated by the inquiries of treasurers of large corporate depositors, investment advisory services, and other individuals whose good opinion is important to the welfare of the individual bank. Bankers do not permit the judgment of such influential outsiders to substitute for their own, but they are forced to concede it some weight or risk adverse comment . . . or even adverse action such as transfer of important deposit accounts to competitors.

See Donald Hodgman, *op. cit.,* p. 8.

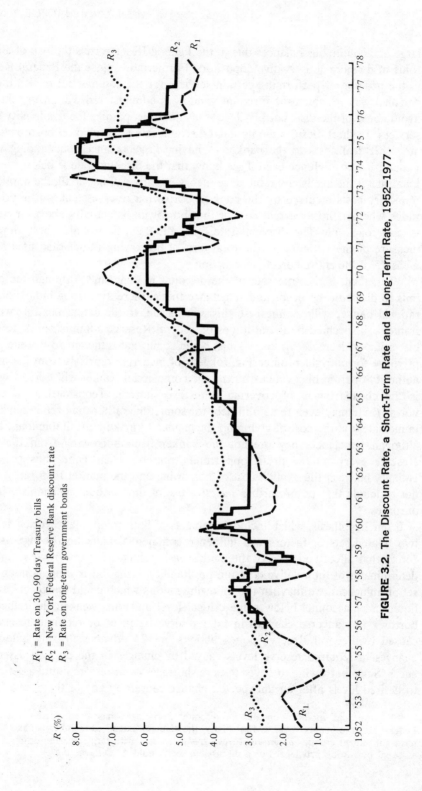

R_1 = Rate on 30–90 day Treasury bills
R_2 = New York Federal Reserve Bank discount rate
R_3 = Rate on long-term government bonds

FIGURE 3.2. The Discount Rate, a Short-Term Rate and a Long-Term Rate, 1952–1977.

large and continuous balances due to the Federal Reserve runs the risk of alienating some of its more conservative depositors. Furthermore, since the Federal Reserve is in the position of performing certain services for the commercial banks, the rather personal way in which the discount window is administered will ensure that banks avoid abuse of the discount privilege so as not to jeopardize the availability of those services. In short, besides the nominal discount rate to be paid on borrowings, there are other real costs to the banker of having large balances outstanding with the Federal Reserve. Hence even if we know that the discount rate is below the market loan rate, if the needs and reluctance theory has any validity at all, the implicit, non-monetary costs incurred by the bank in borrowing reserves makes it impossible to judge whether the *total* real cost of that borrowing is actually above or below the market loan rate. The discount rate by itself, then, is probably best viewed as a measure of the variation in the total cost of borrowing rather than as a complete measure of the entire cost of such action.

What, then, is the true role of the discount mechanism? Although the evidence fails to discredit the needs and reluctance thesis, there are strong indications that a rational banker will at times use this mechanism, to the extent possible within the framework specified by the attitudes of Federal Reserve administrators, to increase his profit or decrease his cost. Thus, while somewhat reluctant to use the discount privilege for outright profiteering, for fear of incurring reprisals from the monetary authority or from his own customers, the commercial banker will borrow when this is the cheapest way of covering a reserve shortage (considering *all* costs involved). He may even remain in debt for some time rather than repay the advances immediately at the cost of giving up the chance to make a profitable loan. In short, although reluctance may prevent the banker from borrowing from the Federal Reserve every time a profit opportunity presents itself (and thus prevent the equality between the explicit cost of borrowing and the market loan rate), we cannot conclude that he proscribes *selective* use of the discount mechanism for profit purposes.[42]

If our hypothesis, which includes elements of both traditional theories, is correct, two related sets of factors will influence commercial bank borrowing: first is the forces that affect and modify the bank's basic reluctance to borrow; second is the determinants of the relative cost and profitability of that borrowing. Among the first set of influences, we may list the following factors which could unexpectedly reduce liquid asset accounts below some critical level and thus weaken the reluctance to borrow: (1) adverse changes in total reserve balances or required reserve levels caused by Federal Reserve policy actions or (2) adverse clearing balances and changes in required reserve levels caused by changes in the public's asset preferences. Since borrowing to cover reserve shortages or to restore liquid asset positions to desired levels after an unexpected change caused by any of the above factors is

---

[42] Reform and modification of the discount "privilege" has been accomplished by the Federal Reserve in recent years. Essentially, the changes extend to member banks (1) a short-term adjustment credit, (2) an emergency means to deal with large clearing drains, and (3) a seasonal borrowing privilege. For a discussion, see Arnold A. Dill, *op. cit.*

generally considered a "legitimate" use of the discount mechanism, we would expect that commercial banks, though generally reluctant to borrow, would not hesitate to employ this means to meet such needs.

The extent to which banks will use the discount mechanism under the above circumstances will depend on the second set of factors: the cost and profit characteristics of the liquid asset alternatives open to the bank. While an unexpected shift of funds from time deposits to demand deposits, for example, would weaken the reluctance to borrow by increasing required reserves, decreasing excess reserves and possibly causing a reserve deficiency, we cannot assign any automaticity to the borrowing decision. The banks will have to consider not simply the direct (real) costs of borrowed funds but also the cost of all alternatives. The possibility of selling securities, for example, introduces the United States Treasury bill rate as an alternative cost.

In short, then, we may expect the demand for borrowed reserves by commercial banks to be determined by the following factors: the discount rate and the bill rate, or the relation between the two; Federal Reserve changes in the supply of unborrowed reserves (or reserve requirements); and the stability of the public's asset preferences.[43]

Conclusion

We have presented an analysis of commercial bank behavior, focusing on the constraints on banking operations which lead to some specific concerns in the management of bank assets and bank liabilities. Within the context of bank asset management we considered how the constraints on banking operations generate a specific set of priorities in bank portfolio management. We then examined the increasingly important and complex issues of bank liability management and the management of bank capital. Finally, we concentrated on the specific problem of the role played by excess legal reserves and borrowed reserves in bank liquidity management. The factors that determine the desired volume of excess legal reserves and borrowed reserves are doubly important because of their subsequent influence on the money supply. The way in which these factors may potentially influence the level of and changes in the level of the money supply was seen in Chapters 1 and 2.

QUESTIONS FOR CHAPTER 3

1. How would you characterize the type of businesses that rely most heavily on loans from commercial banks to finance their operations? Does a bank's specialization in this kind of loan cause any problems? Explain.

[43] Some authors have also emphasized the degree of surveillance of the Federal Reserve over the discount window as a determining factor of commercial bank borrowing. See Stephen M. Goldfeld and Edward J. Kane, "The Determinants of Member Bank Borrowing: An Econometric Study," *Journal of Finance,* vol. 21 (September 1966), 499–514.

2. If an individual bank finds itself short of reserves, it can borrow the needed reserves for a short period of time either from other banks through the Federal funds market or directly from the Federal Reserve. Historical data indicate that the rate of interest on Federal funds is generally several percentage points *above* the Federal Reserve discount rate. Yet banks often borrow in that market rather than at the discount window. Explain why this is so.

3. Relate the analysis of this chapter to the models developed in Chapters 1 and 2 by explaining the effects that increased volatility in bank demand deposits would have on the money supply.

4. In addition to "profit" and "reluctance" as important factors in the explanation of commercial bank borrowing, some writers include a third factor, the degree of surveillance of bank borrowing patterns at the discount window of the Federal Reserve. Explain how this factor would affect the volume of bank borrowing and the influence this may have on the money stock.

5. Given the premises about bank portfolio behavior outlined in this chapter, what effects do you think the Federal Reserve regulation allowing banks to count their vault cash as part of their legal reserves had upon bank excess reserve holdings and on their liquidity management in general? [See Milton Friedman, "Vault Cash and Free Reserves," *Journal of Political Economy,* vol. 69 (April 1961).]

6. Several authors have suggested abolishing the discount mechanism. Relate the bank borrowing "privilege" to the last model developed in Chapter 2 and explain why some people might feel that this mechanism weakens the monetary authority's ability to control the money supply.

7. What factors explain the shift to liability management by commercial banks in the 1960s and 1970s? Under what conditions could liability management impair bank profitability?

8. What are the differences between the views of bank management and bank regulators on the issue of capital adequacy?

BIBLIOGRAPHY FOR CHAPTER 3

ALHADEFF, DAVID A., *Monopoly and Competition in Banking* (Berkeley: University of California Press, 1954).

ANDERSEN, LEONALL C., and ALBERT E. BURGER, "Asset Management and Commercial Bank Portfolio Behavior: Theory and Practice," *Journal of Finance,* vol. 24, no. 2 (May 1969), 207–222.*

BEDFORD, MARGARET E., "Income Taxation of Commercial Banks," *Monthly Review,* Federal Reserve Bank of Kansas City (July/August, 1975), 3–11.*

Board of Governors of the Federal Reserve System, "Reappraisal of the Federal Reserve Discount Mechanism," *Federal Reserve Bulletin* (July 1968), 545–551.

BOWSHER, NORMAN M., "Excess Reserves," *Review,* Federal Reserve Bank of St. Louis vol. 45 (April 1963), 11–15.

——, "Bank Loans and Investments, 1951–1963," *Review,* Federal Reserve Bank of St. Louis vol. 45 (October 1963), 3–7.

* Reprinted in THOMAS M. HAVRILESKY and JOHN T. BOORMAN, *Current Perspectives in Banking* (Arlington Heights, IL: AHM Publishing, 1976).

BRECHLING, F. P. R., and GEORGE CLAYTON, "Commercial Bank Portfolio Behavior," *Economic Journal,* vol. 75 (June 1955), 290–316.

BROADDUS, ALFRED, "A General Model of Bank Decisions," Working Paper 74–76, Federal Reserve Bank of Richmond (April 1972).

——, "Linear Programming: A New Approach to Bank Portfolio Management," *Monthly Review,* Federal Reserve Bank of Richmond (November 1972).*

BURNS, JOSEPH E., "Compensating Balance Requirements: Integral to Bank Lending," *Business Review,* Federal Reserve Bank of Dallas (July 1972), 1–8.*

CARSON, DEANE, and IRA SCOTT, "Commercial Bank Attributes and Aversion to Risk," *Banking and Monetary Studies,* Deane Carson, ed. (Homewood, IL: Richard D. Irwin, 1963), 420–433.

COHEN, JACOB, "What Do Bank Loans Really Finance?" *Banking and Monetary Studies,* Deane Carson, ed. (Homewood, IL: Richard D. Irwin, 1963), 387–407.

COHEN, KALMAN J., "Dynamic Balance Sheet Management: A Management Science Approach," *Journal of Bank Research* (Winter 1972).*

COOPER, J. L., "Continuous Borrowing from the Federal Reserve System: Some Empirical Evidence," *Journal of Finance,* vol. 24 (March 1969), 33–48.

DE PAMPHILIS, DONALD, "A Microeconomic Econometric Analysis of the Short Term Commercial Bank Adjustment Process," Research Report 55, Federal Reserve Bank of Boston (April 1974).

DILL, ARNOLD A., "Member Bank Borrowing: Process and Experience," *Monthly Review,* Federal Reserve Bank of Atlanta (April 1973), 50–54.*

Federal Reserve Bank of Cleveland, "Sources of Commercial Bank Funds: An Example of 'Creative Response,'" *Economic Review,* Federal Reserve Bank of Cleveland (November 1965).

Financial Institutions in the Nation's Economy, "Discussion Principles," Committee on Banking and Currency, U.S. House of Representatives, 94th Congress, 2nd Session (November 1975).*

FRIEDMAN, MILTON, "Vault Cash and Free Reserves," *Journal of Political Economy,* vol. 69 (April 1961).

GOLDFELD, STEPHEN M., *Commercial Bank Behavior and Economic Activity* (Amsterdam: North Holland, 1966).

GOLDFELD, STEPHEN M., and EDWARD J. KANE, "The Determinants of Member Bank Borrowing: An Econometric Study," *Journal of Finance,* vol. 21 (September 1966), 499–514.

GREENBAUM, STUART, "Correspondent Banking," *Monthly Review,* Federal Reserve Bank of Kansas City (March–April 1965), 9–16.*

GUTTENTAG, JACK M., "Reflections on Bank Regulatory Structure," *Compendium of Major Issues in Bank Regulation,* Committee on Housing, Banking and Urban Affairs, U.S. Senate, 94th Congress, 2nd Session, Committee Print No. 2 (August 1975).*

GUTTENTAG, JACK M., and RICHARD G. DAVIS, "Compensating Balances," *Essays in Money and Credit,* Federal Reserve Bank of New York (1964).

HAVRILESKY, THOMAS M., and ROBERT SCHWEITZER, "A Model of Non-Price Competition in Banking," *Journal of Bank Research* (Summer 1975).

HESTER, DONALD D., and JAMES L. PIERCE, *Bank Management and Portfolio Behavior* (New Haven, CT: Yale University Press, 1975).

HESTER, DONALD D., and J. F. ZOELLNER, "The Relation Between Portfolios and Earnings: An Econometric Analysis," *Review of Economics and Statistics,* vol. 48 (November 1966), 372–386.

HINDERLITER, ROGER H., "Market Access, Uncertainty, and the Reserve Position Adjustments of Large Commercial Banks in the 1960s," *Journal of Finance,* vol. 29, no. 1 (March 1974), 41–56.*

HODGMAN, DONALD R., "The Deposit Relationship and Commercial Bank Investment Behavior," *Review of Economics and Statistics,* vol. 43 (August 1961), 257–268.

——, *Commercial Bank Loans and Investment Policy* (Champaign, IL: University of Illinois Bureau of Economic and Business Research, 1963).

HOMAN, PAUL, "Asset Growth—New Techniques, Diversification, Less Regulation, Poorer Quality and Less Liquidity," *Compendium of Major Issues in Bank Regulation,* Committee on Banking, Housing and Urban Affairs, U.S. Senate, 94th Congress, 1st Session (May 1975), 251–257.*

JAFFEE, DWIGHT, *Credit Rationing and the Commercial Loan Market* (New York: Wiley, 1971).

JAFFEE, DWIGHT, and FRANCO MODIGLIANI, "A Theory and Test of Credit Rationing," *American Economic Revue* (December 1969), 850–872.

JESSUP, PAUL F., ed., *Innovations in Bank Management* (New York: Holt, Rhinehart and Winston, 1969).

JONES, DAVID M., "A Review of Recent Academic Literature on the Discount Mechanism," Fundamental Reappraisal of the Discount Mechanism, Project 9, Board of Governors of the Federal Reserve System (February 1968).

KANE, EDWARD J., "All for the Best: The Federal Reserve Board's 60th Annual Report," *American Economic Review,* vol. 64, no. 6 (December 1974), 842–850.*

——, "Discussion," in *Policies for a More Competitive Financial System* (Boston: Federal Reserve Bank of Boston, 1972), 190–198.*

KLEIN, MICHAEL, "A Theory of the Banking Firm," *Journal of Money Credit and Banking* (May 1971), 205–218.

KNIGHT, ROBERT E., "The Changing Payments Mechanism: Electronic Funds Transfer," *Monthly Review,* Federal Reserve Bank of Kansas City (July–August 1974), 10–20.*

——, "Customer Profitability Analysis," *Monthly Review,* Federal Reserve Bank of Kansas City (April 1975), 11–20.*

LONGBRAKE, WILLIAM A., "Statistical Cost Analysis," *Financial Management* (Spring 1973).*

LUCKETT, DUDLEY G., "Credit Standards and Tight Money," *Journal of Money Credit and Banking* (November 1970), 420–434.

LUTTRELL, C. B., "Member Bank Borrowing, Its Origin and Function," *Quarterly Review of Economics and Business,* vol. 8 (Autumn 1968), 55–66.

MALKIEL, BURTON G., and EDWARD KANE, "Bank Portfolio Allocation, Deposit Variability and the Availability Doctrine," *Quarterly Journal of Economics,* vol. 79 (February 1965), 113–134.

MAYER, THOMAS, "Preventing the Failures of Large Banks," *Compendium of Major Issues in Bank Regulation,* Committee on Housing, Banking and Urban Affairs, U.S. Senate, 94th Congress, 2nd Session, Committee Print No. 2 (August 1975).*

MERRIS, RANDALL C., "The Prime Rate," *Business Conditions,* Federal Reserve Bank of Chicago (April 1975), 2–12.

MINGO, JOHN, and BENJAMIN WOLKOWITZ, "The Effects of Regulation on Bank Balance Sheet Decisions" (unpublished).

MOORE, BASIL J., *An Introduction to the Theory of Finance* (New York: The Free Press, 1968).

MORRISON, GEORGE R., "Liquidity Preference of Commercial Banks," Doctoral Dissertation, University of Chicago, unpublished (1963).

MORRISON, GEORGE R., and RICHARD D. SHELDEN, *Time Deposit Growth and the Employment of Bank Funds* (Chicago: Association of Reserve City Bankers, 1965).

MURPHY, NEIL B., "A Study of Wholesale Banking Behavior," Research Report 44, Federal Reserve Bank of Boston (1969).

MURPHY, NEIL, and PAUL S. ANDERSON, "Running the Bank's Money Position: A Study of Demand Deposit Fluctuation," *New England Economic Review,* Federal Reserve Bank of Boston (November 1967).*

RIEFLER, W. W., *Money Rates and Money Markets in the United States* (New York: Harper and Bros., 1930).

ROBINSON, ROLAND I., *The Management of Bank Funds* (New York: McGraw-Hill, 1962).

RUSSELL, WILLIAM R., "Commercial Bank Portfolio Adjustments," *American Economic Review, Papers and Proceedings,* vol. 54 (May 1964), 544–553.

SCHWEITZER, STUART A., "Bank Liability Management: For Better or for Worse," *Business Review,* Federal Reserve Bank of Philadelphia (December 1974), 3–12.*

——, "Bank Loan Losses: A Fresh Perspective," *Business Review,* Federal Reserve Bank of Philadelphia (September 1975), 18–28.*

SHULL, BERNARD, "Commercial Banks as Multiple-Product Price Discriminating Firms," *Banking and Monetary Studies,* Deane Carson, ed. (Homewood, IL.: Richard D. Irwin, 1964).

VEAZY, EDWARD E., "Federal Funds—Market Expansion Aids Mobilization of Funds," *Business Review,* Federal Reserve Bank of Dallas (January 1975), 1–6.*

VOJTA, GEORGE J., *Bank Capital Adequacy* (New York: Citicorp, 1973), 15–30.*

WATSON, RONALD D., "Bank Bond Management: The Maturity Dilemma," *Business Review,* Federal Reserve Bank of Philadelphia (March 1972).*

——, "Banking Capital Shortage: The Malaise and the Myth," *Business Review,* Federal Reserve Bank of Philadelphia (September 1975), 3–13.*

——, "Insuring Some Progress in the Bank Capital Hassle," *Business Review,* Federal Reserve Bank of Philadelphia (July–August 1974), 3–18.*

WILLIS, PARKER B., *Federal Funds Market: Origin and Development,* 4th ed. (Boston: Federal Reserve Bank of Boston, 1970).

WOOD, JOHN H., *Commercial Bank Loan and Investment Behavior* (New York: John Wiley and Sons, 1975).

Appendix to Chapter 3
A Model of the Profit Maximizing Bank

Introduction

Chapter 3 has shown that there are two basic aspects to bank balance sheet management. One aspect is that assets are managed with explicit recognition of the relationship between risk, rate of return, and liquidity. The other is that the type of financial intermediation carried out by a commercial bank encourages it to give considerable attention to liability management. Specifically, in order to meet customer loan demands and satisfy liquidity needs, a bank can attract funds from a wide spectrum of sources.

In this appendix we present a simple neoclassical model of banking management in which both aspects are considered. Profit maximization is assumed to be the goal of bank management,[1] with the present net worth of the bank a constraint over its "intermediate-term" planning period.[2]

We assume the following balance sheet:

$$L + V + RR = DD + TD + \overline{NW} \qquad (3A.1)$$

where L = loans, V = government securities, RR = required reserves, DD = demand deposits, TD = time deposits, and $\overline{NW}$ = net worth, which is given at the beginning of the period.

Liquidity Management

We asume that required reserves are fixed proportions ρ of demand deposits and b of time deposits:

$$RR = \rho DD + bTD, \qquad 0 < \rho, b < 1. \qquad (3A.2)$$

The legal reserve requirement is an important constraint on bank portfolio management. It requires a bank to hold a certain amount of its assets in a nonearning form.

Other important constraints on bank management, discussed in Chapter 3, have to do with the volatility of deposit shifts and currency withdrawals and the variations in customer loan demand. These random factors lead to expected cash drains that determine the bank's short-term liquidity needs. In the present model we abstract from reserve holdings motivated by deposit variability and customer loan demands.[3]

---

[1] The neoclassical approach of this appendix is only one of several possible analytical frameworks that may be used to model bank behavior. Traditionally, bank asset management was conceived as a portfolio-theoretic problem similar to the analysis presented in the Appendix to Chapter 5. This mode of analysis is still useful. See Leonall C. Andersen and Albert E. Burger, "Asset Management and Commercial Bank Portfolio Behavior: Theory and Practice," *Journal of Finance,* vol. 24, no. 2 (May 1969), 207–222. More recently linear programming models have been applied to bank asset as well as bank balance sheet management. See Alfred Broaddus, "Linear Programming: A New Approach to Bank Portfolio Management," *Monthly Review,* Federal Reserve Bank of Richmond (November 1972); and Kalman J. Cohen, "Dynamic Balance Sheet Management: A Management Science Approach," *Journal of Bank Research* (Winter 1972). All of the above are reprinted in Havrilesky and Boorman, *Current Perspectives in Banking, op. cit.*

[2] Short-term liquidity management and longer term capital management will not be considered in detail. Nevertheless, we shall outline ways in which these problems may be approached in footnotes 4 and 16, respectively.

[3] As an alternative we could assume that there exists a probability distribution of expected cash drains and that the cost associated with an expected level of cash drains rises with the

Rather, we assume that legal reserve requirements cause a bank to hold cash assets and that these holdings are simply viewed as dependent on a given level of deposits for purposes of intermediate-term planning.

Short-term liquidity management is viewed as an ongoing process that occurs *within* the context of our intermediate-term planning period. Expected cash drains that arise from expected deposit shifts and currency withdrawals and from expected variations in loan repayments and loan demand determine a bank's liquidity needs. The bank then satisfies its net short-term liquidity needs from the multiplicity of sources described in the preceding chapter: excess reserve balances, Federal funds purchases, borrowing from the Fed, offerings of short-term negotiable CDs, issues of bank-related commercial paper, Eurodollar borrowing, and the sale of short-term Treasury bills. Net liquidity needs are met from each source until the rising marginal cost of obtaining liquidity from each source is equal to the (fixed) penalty cost, including all implicit costs perceived by the borrowing bank, at which the bank borrows from the Fed.[4]

---

level of deposits and falls with the level of reserves. As discussed in the preceding chapter, there could be implicit and explicit costs to the bank that vary directly with expected cash drains. Explicit costs might include the penalty rate at which banks with reserve deficiencies can borrow reserves from the Federal Reserve. Implicit costs might include the "embarrassment" felt at borrowing from the Fed. See Michael Klein, "A Theory of the Banking Firm," *Journal of Money Credit and Banking* (May 1971), 205–218.

[4] A highly simplified model of short-term liquidity management might be sketched as follows: Assume that expected cash needs vary in direct proportion to the level of demand deposits and the level of time deposits. Let these factors of proportionality be α and β, respectively. Assume further that expected cash needs also vary proportionately with the level of loans by a factor γ. The *gross* liquidity needs of the banking firm Q_g are therefore

$$Q_g = \alpha \cdot \overline{DD} + \beta \cdot \overline{TD} + \gamma \cdot \overline{L}$$

where the bars indicate intermediate-term equilibrium values determined by the model described below.

Assume for simplicity that instead of the wide array of sources of liquidity cited above, there are only three: required reserves RR, short-term government securities V_s, and Federal funds purchases FF. Thus the *sources* of the banking firm's gross liquidity are

$$Q_g = RR + V_s + FF.$$

As required reserves are defined in Equation (3A.2), we may substitute Equation (3A.2) into the above and equate the result to the preceding equation. Rearranging allows us to equate *net* liquidity needs Q_n to the means by which these net needs may be met.

$$Q_n = \overline{DD} \cdot (\alpha - \rho) + \overline{TD} \cdot (\beta - b) + \overline{L} \cdot \gamma = V_s + FF.$$

Net liquidity needs may be met either by the bank's selling short-term securities V_s or by its borrowing in the Federal funds market FF. A short-run optimum position is obtained where the increasing marginal (interest-opportunity and transactions) costs of selling securities is equal to the given rate at which Federal funds may be borrowed. If considerable liquidity is needed for only a few days, it might be quite costly to sell (and then to repurchase) short-term securities. Conversely, if funds were needed for a longer period, repeated Federal funds borrowing might be more costly than the sale of short-term securities. See Donald DePamphilis, "A Microeconomic Econometric Analysis of the Short-Term Commercial Bank Adjustment Process," Research Report 55, Federal Reserve Bank of Boston (April 1974).

Within the intermediate-term planning period there are a number of short-term planning periods. Deposit and customer loan variability and the various interest rates will change between short-run periods. Thus, for example, the bank could be a lender of Federal funds and a purchaser of short-term securities in one short-term period and a borrower of Federal funds and a seller of short-term securities in another.[5]

To describe the pattern of short-run adjustments more specifically would require a model that is richer in detail (see footnote 4). Such a task is beyond the scope of this book. We focus rather on a model of intermediate-term planning. Over the intermediate term we shall assume for simplicity that excess or deficient reserves, holdings of short-term securities, and Federal funds purchased or sold are zero.

Loans

All loans are assumed to be negotiated directly with bank customers at the beginning of the planning period and to fall due on the last day of the period. There are no loan carryovers from the preceding period and no turnovers during the period. The public's demand curve for loans facing the bank may be viewed as the aggregate of individual demand curves of customers deemed viable by the bank. The demand curve for loan funds is shown in Figure 3A.1. It is assumed that the bank charges a uniform explicit rate to all loan customers.

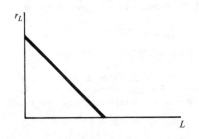

FIGURE 3A.1. Demand for loans facing the bank.

[5] The distinction between short-term and long-term planning periods is an artificial one, but it has the advantage of simplifying our discussion. In reality the bank's balance sheet undergoes a dynamic adjustment to shocks. For example, if a bank is successful at increasing its level of deposits, it may first hold excess reserves and then loan out these reserves in the Federal funds market. Next, if the new level of deposits persists, it may purchase short-term securities. Finally, if in the intermediate term it regards these deposits as secure, it may fully adjust its portfolio by increasing its loans. The process of dynamic portfolio-theoretic adjustment to exogenous forecasted changes in deposits using a variety of estimation techniques is dealt with in Donald D. Hester and James L. Pierce, *Bank Management and Portfolio Behavior* (New Haven, Yale University Press, 1975).

The assumption of a uniform loan rate is quite a simplification as it implies that the bank charges the same rate for all loans, provided the customer's qualifications exceed some minimum standard.[6] Therefore one could view this rate as representing the interest rate the bank charges for loans, net of the cost of credit investigations, processing and administering loans, and maintaining relationships with customers. In this analysis the probability of loss through customer default is built into each individual customer's loan demand curve.[7]

The linear loan demand relationship shown in Figure 3A.1 is expressed as

$$r_L = r_0 + a \cdot L \qquad (3A.3)$$

where r_0 is the intercept and a is the slope parameter; $a < 0$. The dollar level of loans is L and r_L is the loan rate. The magnitudes of the parameters, indeed the form of the relation, depend on the factors discussed above: the risk characteristics of bank customers and the production costs of the bank, as well as the competitive structure of the loan market.

As an alternative to the approach used here, we could assume that the bank is confronted by several different classes of loan customers, and that it is constrained by its legal, social, and competitive environment not to charge different profit maximizing loan rates to each loan class. Therefore, the bank may have to make credit rationing decisions—rationing credit among the customers whom it has deemed viable. In this case each individual customer's default risk and the expected profitability of other business relationships with that customer (for example, his expected deposits) are used to determine how much credit will be offered at every possible loan rate, that is, a "loan offer curve" could be drawn in (r_L, L) space.

The offer curve would be upward sloping at lower loan rates, but as default risk increases with the size of loan payments, the offer curve would change to a negative slope at higher rates. If the amount of credit demanded by a customer exceeds the amount offered at the going loan rate, then credit is rationed to that customer. Thus the rationing decision will depend on the marginal expected return on loans to the customer as well as on loan risk and the expected profitability of other relationships

[6] Because the demand curve is an aggregate of the demands of individual customers, an increase in the bank's loan standards, a decrease in the credit worthiness of loan customers (say because of a change in default risk), or a decrease in the expected deposits of loan customers could shift the loan demand curve leftward, reducing the quantity of loans at any level of the rate. The credit standards of a bank could thus become another variable controlled by bank management. In the interest of simplicity we ignore this consideration. See Dudley G. Luckett, "Credit Standards and Tight Money," *Journal of Money Credit and Banking* (November 1970), 420–434.

[7] Dealing explicitly with default would require specifying the probability of loan repayment for each customer. See Alfred Broaddus, "A General Model of Bank Decisions," Working Paper 74–76, Federal Reserve Bank of Richmond (April 1972). Thus our demand curve represents a cumulative array of customer loans ranked according to the expected rate of return, net of all loan costs including expected default costs. For a model of how such ranking might be derived, see Neil B. Murphy, "A Study of Wholesale Banking Behavior," Research Report 44, Federal Reserve Bank of Boston (1969).

with the customer; these will vary among customers.[8] It is important to note that in this sort of model the rationing of credit relates to the size of a customer's (potential) deposit balance as well as the other continuing business relationships that he or she sustains with the bank or related nonbank affiliates.[9] For customers who do not get all the credit they desire and must borrow elsewhere, rationing results in a higher cost per dollar of credit.

Long-Term Securities

The rate of return on long-term United States government securities r_V is determined in the market for government securities where the bank is only one of a great many participants. Therefore, the bank cannot influence this rate; it may acquire whatever volume of long-term government securities it desires at the going market rate $\bar{r}_V$. It is assumed that the bank does not intend to sell these long-term securities during the planning period. It is further assumed that securities transactions are costless, that securities prices and coupon yields do not change during the planning period, and that securities are held primarily for income purposes.[10]

Because the probability of default or temporary unmarketability is practically nil,[11] the rate of return on government securities is assumed always to be less than the going rate of return on loans. This reflects in a fairly simplistic fashion another fundamental constraint on bank portfolio management—a constraint imposed by the nature of the bank's earning assets.

The relationship shown in Figure 3A.2 is expressed as

$$\bar{r}_V = \bar{r}_V \qquad\qquad (3A.4)$$

[8] For a model of credit rationing see Dwight Jaffee and Franco Modigliani, "A Theory and Test of Credit Rationing," *American Economic Review* (December 1969), 850–872; and Dwight Jaffee, *Credit Rationing and the Commercial Loan Market* (New York: Wiley, 1971).

[9] The credit rationing approach makes explicit the fact that banking loan and deposit markets are not strictly independent. The availability of credit to a loan customer is "tied in" to the size of his deposit balances and other continuing relationships with the bank. See Neil B. Murphy, *op. cit.* For further discussion of the profitability of the total customer relationship, see Robert E. Knight, "Customer Profitability Analysis," *Monthly Review,* Federal Reserve Bank of Kansas City (April 1975), 11–20, reprinted in Havrilesky and Boorman, *Current Perspectives in Banking, op. cit.* For an excellent critique of the credit rationing approach as well as an alternative model of the link between loans to customers and subsequent deposits from them based on the "customer relationship," see John H. Wood, *Commercial Bank Loan and Investment Behavior* (New York: John Wiley and Sons, 1975).

[10] As discussed earlier, the traditional concentration of commercial banks on customer lending entails liquidity problems. Short-term government securities are one way of satisfying a bank's liquidity needs. However, in certain situations longer term securities are also rather liquid. In reality the distinction between holding longer term securities for income and holding them for liquidity is not clear cut.

[11] In the intermediate-term planning model we abstract from a number of risks faced regularly by bank management—the risk of reserve deficiency brought about by deposit variability, the risk of default loss on customer loans, and the financial risk of being unable to market an earning asset without extraordinary cost. The explicit introduction of risk characteristics into our model would require of the reader a knowledge of mathematical statistics. See the Appendix to Chapter 5 for a general treatment of how the problem of risk is handled in portfolio analysis.

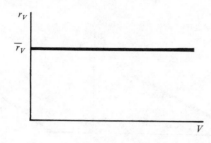

FIGURE 3A.2. Supply of government securities facing the bank.

where $\bar{r}_V$ is the money market-determined rate on long-term United States government securities. In essence, long-term securities are available in perfectly elastic supply.

Deposits

As discussed in Chapter 3, modern bank management is no longer concerned exclusively with asset management. One can no longer realistically regard the level and mix of bank liabilities as given, with all management decision making focused on the asset side. Today banks actively compete for funds in a great many markets.

Figure 3A.3 reflects this competitiveness in a fairly simplistic fashion. Two areas in which banks actively attempt to "attract" funds are depicted, the market for demand deposits and the market for time deposits. We assume that the average total cost of attracting demand deposits C_{DD} and the average total cost of attracting time deposits C_{TD} vary positively and linearly with demand and time deposit volume, respectively. We further assume that these costs are expressed as pure numbers, that is, the average number of cents expended per dollar of deposits. We do not distinguish among the various costs of attracting deposits, such as explicit interest payments on deposits, account maintenance and service costs that are not fully charged to the customer, and advertising and promotional expenditures.[12] As discussed earlier in this appendix, the variability of deposits is assumed to be so low that reserve deficiencies are ruled out by the legal reserve requirements given in Equation (3A.2). In fact, in the interest of analytical simplicity we shall assume that all

---

[12] We abstract from the problem that some costs of attracting deposits vary with the number of deposit accounts rather than the size of deposit accounts and from the fact that many costs cannot be attributed separately to either demand or time deposits, that is, the cost relations are, in reality, unlikely to be independent. See, for example, Neil Murphy and Paul S. Anderson, "Running the Bank's Money Position: A Study of Demand Deposit Fluctuations," *New England Economic Review*, Federal Reserve Bank of Boston (November 1967) and William A. Longbrake, "Statistical Cost Analysis," *Financial Management* (Spring 1973). Both are printed in Havrilesky and Boorman, *Current Perspectives in Banking, op. cit.*

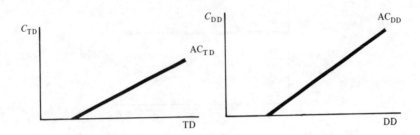

FIGURE 3A.3. Supply curves of demand and time deposits facing the bank.

deposits are zero at the outset of the planning period and are attracted by the bank and then undergo no variation during the period.[13]

The relations shown in Figure 3A.3 are expressed as follows:

$$C_{DD} = C_{DD_0} + g \cdot DD \qquad\qquad (3A.5)$$

$$C_{TD} = C_{TD_0} + m \cdot TD \qquad\qquad (3A.6)$$

where $C_{DD_0} < 0$, $C_{TD_0} < 0$, and $g > m > 0$. The parameter C_{DD_0} reflects the fact that demand deposits would be positive even if a bank expended nothing to attract them, that is, a commercial bank could attract some demand deposits even if it charged customers for all depository services and did not advertise or promote these services. This is so because entry into the business of producing depository services is limited by government. Each bank has some degree of "monopoly power" in its geographical area. The parameter C_{TD_0} reflects the notion that a commercial bank would have a small residual level of time deposits even if it paid no interest on these funds. This occurs because the bank's monopoly power in the demand deposit market will enable it to attract some time deposit funds from its demand deposit customers even if it does not pay interest on its time deposits.

Both relations have positive slopes, but the average cost of "attracting" time deposits rises less quickly than the average cost of attracting demand deposits. These graphs reflect a comparatively lower interest elasticity of demand for demand than for time deposits.[14] These differences are accounted for by the existence

[13] This analysis abstracts from time and demand deposit variability viewed either separately or as related processes and measured either as the dispersion of deposit balances about some average level during the planning period (see Alfred Broaddus, *op. cit.*) or as deposit turnover (see Neil B. Murphy and Paul S. Anderson, *op. cit.*). It does not allow us to examine how variables such as bank size and the structure of bank liabilities might affect deposit variability.

[14] This is a reasonable assertion, especially if time deposits are defined to include certificates of deposit.

of intensive price and nonprice competition for time deposit funds among commercial banks, nonbank financial intermediaries and issuers of marketable securities.[15]

As ours is an intermediate-term model, planned longer term borrowing by banks to sustain an increase in bank lending and investing activity is not considered. In the same vein, in the short run the capital or net worth position of the banking firm is assumed to be given.[16]

Profit Maximization

We assume that the objective of bank management is to maximize profit during its intermediate-term planning period. The planning period is defined to be long enough to permit the bank to control all of its decision variables. It seems reasonable to view this as a fairly short time span, perhaps three months in length. Under the assumption that all profit is retained (none is paid out as dividends) this is tantamount to assuming that the bank maximizes the increase in its net worth. In order to maximize profit, funds must be attracted in both deposit markets until the marginal cost of attracting deposit funds in both markets is equal to the marginal rate the bank can earn on the earning assets it can obtain with these funds.

We may derive the profit maximizing levels of both types of deposits. First we multiply average total cost, expressed as a pure number, an average (interest) rate, per dollar of deposits in Equations (3A.5) and (3A.6), by the level of deposits in order to obtain the total cost relation in dollars:

$$DD \cdot C_{DD} = C_{DD_0} \cdot DD + g \cdot DD^2 \tag{3A.7}$$

$$TD \cdot C_{TD} = C_{TD_0} \cdot TD + m \cdot TD^2 \tag{3A.8}$$

The marginal costs of attracting deposits, expressed as marginal (interest) rates,

[15] Because of the competitive structure of deposit markets, as yields on marketable securities rise farther above the legal ceiling on rates of interest payable on deposits, commercial banks must reduce service charges on demand deposits and increase advertising and promotional efforts in order to attract time and demand deposits. See Thomas Havrilesky and Robert Schweitzer, "A Model of Non-Price Competition in Banking," *Journal of Bank Research* (Summer 1975).

Seminal works that construct models of bank behavior that center on the competitive structure of banking credit markets and their relationship to discriminating loan pricing are David Alhadeff, *Monopoly and Competition in Banking* (Berkeley: University of California Press, 1954) and Bernard Shull, "Commercial Banks as Multiple-Product Price Discriminating Firms," *Banking and Monetary Studies,* Deane Carson, ed. (Homewood, IL.: Richard D. Irwin, 1964).

[16] In the long run bank capital can be increased either through retained earnings or through the issuance of new securities or long-term subordinated debt. Like the deposit relations, these sources of bank capital would vary positively with average cost. Banking regulation could then be introduced to this model by imposing a "bank soundness constraint" which would weigh each asset, liability, and capital category by parameters imposed by regulatory authorities. The model could then be solved subject to this additional constraint. See John Mingo and Benjamin Wolkowitz, "The Effects of Regulation on Bank Balance Sheet Decisions" (unpublished).

are the first derivatives of the quadratic total cost functions, the right-hand sides of Equations (3A.7) and (3A.8).

$$\frac{d(DD \cdot C_{DD})}{dDD} = C_{DD_0} + 2 \cdot g \cdot DD \qquad (3A.9)$$

$$\frac{d(TD \cdot C_{TD})}{dTD} = C_{TD_0} + 2 \cdot m \cdot TD \qquad (3A.10)$$

The profit maximizing bank will attract deposits until the marginal cost of each type of deposit is equal to the marginal rate at which earnings can be generated from that source of funds. There are two factors which determine the latter rate. The first is the rate of interest determined in the market for United States government securities. This interest rate is used because, while both loans and securities are earning assets, in equilibrium loans are made until the marginal loan rate is equal to the given market rate on securities. The second factor, which determines the percentage of each dollar of deposit funds that can be invested in earning assets, is the legal reserve requirement on each type of deposits. Thus one dollar of demand deposits can be invested in only $(1 - \rho)$ of a dollar of earning assets and one dollar of time deposits can be invested in $(1 - b)$ of a dollar of earning assets. Therefore the profit maximizing condition may be expressed as

$$C_{DD_0} + 2 \cdot g \cdot DD = \bar{r}_V(1 - \rho) \qquad (3A.11)$$
$$C_{TD_0} + 2 \cdot m \cdot TD = \bar{r}_V(1 - b). \qquad (3A.12)$$

The resulting expressions may be rearranged in order to solve for the profit maximizing levels of demand and time deposits, denoted as $\overline{DD}$ and $\overline{TD}$, respectively:[17]

$$\overline{DD} = \frac{\bar{r}_V(1 - \rho) - C_{DD_0}}{2 \cdot g} \qquad (3A.13)$$

$$\overline{TD} = \frac{\bar{r}_V(1 - b) - C_{TD_0}}{2 \cdot m}. \qquad (3A.14)$$

The sum of these two sources of funds plus the net worth at the beginning of the period are given on the right-hand side of Equation (3A.1). This provides the *scale* of the banking operation, the level of its total assets.

Figure 3A.4 shows graphically that the profit maximizing levels of time and demand deposits are found where the marginal cost of attracting each class of deposits is equal to the rate earned on United States government securities times one

---

[17] Formally, we are maximizing profit (the increase in net worth)

$$\pi = r_L L + r_V V - C_{DD} \cdot DD - C_{TD} \cdot TD$$

subject to $L + V - [(1 - \rho)DD + (1 - b)TD + NW] = 0$ and $V > 0$.

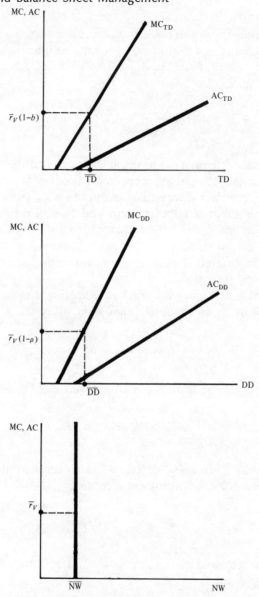

FIGURE 3A.4. Determination of the profit maximizing level of time and demand deposits.

minus the legal reserve requirement on that class of deposit. Figure 3A.4 also reflects the notion, expressed in Equation (3A.1), that these deposit sources plus net worth determine the total assets of the banking firm.

Not all deposit funds so obtained are available to be invested in earning assets. Equation (3A.2) indicates that portions of demand and time deposits must be held as required reserves. Substituting Equation (3A.2) into Equation (3A.1) and rearranging leaves the remainder

$$L + V = \overline{DD}(1 - \rho) + \overline{TD}(1 - b) + \overline{NW}$$

to be invested as earning assets.

There are two forms of earning assets in our model, and the profit maximizing bank will make a rational allocation of investable funds between them. The profit maximization (subject to risks discussed earlier in this appendix and in Chapter 3) condition requires that funds be allocated across all types of earning assets until the returns to each type of investment are equal at the margin. As the return on government securities is assumed to be given, the profit maximizing bank will invest in loans until the marginal return from loans is equal to the rate that the bank can earn on these long-term securities.

We derive the total loan revenue relation by multiplying the average rate of return on loans, Equation (3A.3), by the total dollar value of loans:

$$r_L \cdot L = r_0 \cdot L + aL^2.$$

The marginal rate of return on loans is the first derivative of this quadratic function:

$$\frac{d(r_L \cdot L)}{dL} = r_0 + 2 \cdot a \cdot L.$$

This is set equal to the given marginal rate at which earnings are generated from bank holdings of United States government securities,

$$r_0 + 2 \cdot a \cdot L = \bar{r}_V$$

and we may solve for the profit maximizing level of loans $\overline{L}$:

$$\overline{L} = \frac{\bar{r}_V - r_0}{2 \cdot a}.$$

Figure 3A.5 shows graphically how the bank's available funds are allocated among earning assets so as to maximize profits. It reflects the fact, given in Equation (3A.14), that there is a total funds constraint—only a certain amount is available to be invested in earning assets. After the profit maximizing level of loans is found, the remainder of available bank funds are allocated to long-term United States government securities.

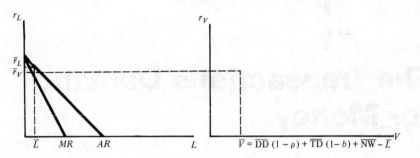

FIGURE 3A.5. Profit maximizing allocation of earning assets.

Concluding Comment

This appendix presented a very simple model of bank asset and liability management. The model centered on a planning period of intermediate length, thus abstracting from short-term liquidity needs which arise from expected deposit withdrawals and loan demands. However, it was shown that shorter run aspects of bank management, such as short-term liquidity management, could be integrated into the model. In addition, while the planning period of the model was too short to consider longer term sources of bank capital, such as equity and debt financing, it would not be difficult to include these as alternative sources of funds. Finally, while credit-rationing and other models of the link between the selling of credit and depository services are not treated in complete detail, the model provides background for further study in these areas.

The present analysis indicates how bank management decision making must focus simultaneously on assets and liabilities. It makes explicit the role of the costs of attracting deposit funds and the return on loans and investments. It also makes clear how profitability considerations impinge upon the decisions of bank management. Because of its rather general nature, this model can serve as a basis for further study of the theory of the banking firm.

4

The Transactions Demand for Money

Introduction

In previous chapters we have examined some alternative specifications of the asset-holding behavior of the public and the banks and the effects of this behavior on the supply of money. Only recently have economists done much research on the money supply relation despite the importance of the money stock in most hypotheses about aggregate economic behavior. In contrast, the *demand* for money has been more thoroughly studied, largely because the implications and predictions that follow from alternative demand-for-money hypotheses have been recognized to generate widely contrasting prescriptions for economic policy.

There are various theoretical approaches to the demand for money. The present chapter focuses on the view that money, as the generally acceptable medium of exchange, is held in the interval between the receipt and disbursement of income primarily because there is some *cost* associated with both the purchase of interest-earning assets out of income and the subsequent sale of these assets to make disbursements. This chapter begins with a review of the basic determinants of the transactions demand for money, examines William Baumol's inventory-theoretic treatment of the subject (1952), and then expands the conception of cost in examining the role of information cost in the transactions demand for money.

Chapter 5 will suggest that an individual also holds money, as one of several financial assets in his wealth portfolio, because he may thereby avoid losses from decreases in the market value of other, income-earning, assets. It describes John Maynard Keynes' original liquidity preference theory (1936) and then develops James Tobin's approach to the subject (1958). An appendix examines general portfolio theory of which the theory of the demand for money is a subset.

Chapter 6 will consider the classical demand for money together with its modern (neoclassical) reformulation.[1] The classical demand for money inspired Keynes' work and is an important antecedent of the modern neoclassical reconsideration of money demand. The latter stresses neither the role of money in facilitating transactions nor its usefulness as a hedge against the risk of loss from holding other assets, but rather treats the demand for money as part of the general theory of demand.

While, in principle, these approaches are not always incompatible with one another, they will generate different models of the demand for money and different prescriptions for economic policy.[2] In the survey of empirical tests of various demand-for-money hypotheses in Chapters 7 and 8 we shall see how well the factors suggested by each hypothesis explain variations in the demand for money.

The Transactions Motive for Holding Money

Most modern economists believe that money is demanded, like any asset, because of the flow of services it renders. With most assets the value of this flow of services is approximated by a dollar yield. With money, however, the income stream is usually not measurable by a simple nominal dollar return; by law commercial bank demand deposits, for instance, may yield no interest return yet they provide a valuable flow of services to their owners. Economists have found it useful to associate this flow of services with the functions that money performs. The functions of money are commonly said to include those of a medium of exchange, a store of value and a unit of account.[3]

As a medium of exchange, money is held between the receipt and disbursement of income because of the costs (brokerage fees, inconvenience, etc.) of converting into and out of other, earning assets which themselves are not generally acceptable as media of exchange. The amount of money demanded to finance expenditures, in principle, thus depends on these conversion *costs* as well as on the *size* of the ex-

[1] Throughout this book we use the rubrics *classical* and *neoclassical* in a manner common to many monetary economists but perhaps disconcerting to historians of economic thought. We mean by the classical–neoclassical distinction not the difference between the labor-theory-of-value and marginalist schools but rather the historical hiatus between the pre- and post-Keynesian proponents of the quantity theory of money.

[2] See, for instance, the implications that different demand-for-money functions have for monetary and fiscal policy, discussed in Chapters 11 and 14.

[3] The services associated with the store of value function of money are discussed in the next chapter. The unit of account function of money simply means that money is used commonly as a denominator or *numeraire* in which the prices of all other goods or services are reckoned. We devote no further discussion to the unit of account function of money.

penditures and how far in the future they will be made. Most economists, nevertheless, have emphasized the size of expenditures as the primary constraint affecting the demand for money as a medium of exchange. In fact, the transactions demand for money, associated with its use as a medium of exchange, is usually depicted as varying in direct proportion with the level of expenditures. Following this tradition, where

M_j/P_T = the average quantity of real transactions balances demanded by the jth individual[4]

T_j = the level of the jth individual's total real expenditures over a period of time

k_j = a proportionality factor for the jth individual with a magnitude $0 < k_j < 1$ for long periods of time, such as a month,

the individual's transactions demand function is

$$M_j/P_T = k_j T_j \qquad (4.1)$$

The order of magnitude of k_j relates the size of the average money stock needed to finance a flow of expenditures to the size of that total flow. For instance, suppose an individual is paid a monthly income of $300 on the first day of each month. Assume further that he spends this income at a uniform rate of $10 per day for 30 days until he is paid again on the first day of the next month. His average transactions balance will be $150, that is, since his holdings are $300 on the first day of the month and zero on the last day and since these balances decline uniformly over the course of the 30-day month, the average value of his transactions balances is the mean of these two figures:

$$\frac{\$300 + 0}{2} = \$150.$$

Therefore,

$$k_j = \frac{M_j/P_T}{T_j} = \frac{\$150}{\$300/\text{month}} = \frac{1}{2}\,\text{month}.$$

This individual holds an average of one-half of his monthly income *flow* in the form of a *stock* of money balances.

If we were to measure this individual's total expenditures on a yearly basis but

---

[4] The concept of real expenditures, real income, real money balances, etc., is one that abstracts from price changes and measures what the dollar totals would be if prices remained constant. Real measures may be expressed by dividing ("deflating") a nominal measure by a price index; in the present case we deflate the nominal money stock by P_T, an index of the average price level of all goods and services exchanged in the economy over a given period of time. The concept of a price index is discussed in detail in Chapter 9.

continue to assume he is paid once each month and spends his income uniformly over the course of each month,

$$k_j = \frac{\$150}{\$3600/\text{year}} = \frac{1}{24}\,\text{year} = \frac{1}{2}\,\text{month}.$$

Therefore, we may view k_j as either the average period of time over which the jth individual holds a unit of money or, more usefully, as the average proportion of his total expenditures which an individual holds in the form of transactions balances.

This example can be used to illustrate the effect of a change in the frequency of receipts (for example, a change in the length of the pay period) or the effect of a change in the frequency of cash disbursements on the average size of transactions balances. Consider first a change in the frequency of receipts. Continue to assume that this individual *earns* $300 per month and spends his income at a rate of $10 per day. However, now assume that he is *paid* every fifteen days rather than once a month. He will receive $150 on the first and sixteenth days of each month. His average transactions balance will be

$$\frac{\$150 + 0}{2} = \$75$$

and k_j will equal ¼ :

$$k_j = \frac{\$75}{\$300/\text{month}} = \frac{1}{4}\text{month}.$$

Thus an increase in the frequency of receipts reduces the average amount of money which individuals must hold as a proportion k_j of a given volume of expenditures T_j.

Now consider an example of the effect of a change in the frequency of disbursements. Assume the above individual is again being paid $300 on the first day of each month but now assume that he makes lump sum disbursements of $100 every 10 days. His transactions balances will be $300 for the first 10 days, $200 for the next 10 days, and $100 for the last 10 days of the month. His average money holdings will be

$$\frac{(\$300 \times 10\ \text{days}) + (\$200 \times 10\ \text{days}) + (\$100 \times 10\ \text{days})}{30\ \text{days}} = \$200$$

and k_j will equal ⅔:

$$k_j = \frac{\$200}{\$300/\text{month}} = \frac{2}{3}\,\text{month}.$$

In this particular case the decrease in the frequency of disbursements increases the average amount of money which individuals must hold in order to facilitate a given volume of expenditures and therefore k_j rises.

Finally, if the individual could make *all* monthly purchases on credit and make one lump sum payment on the first of the next month, his average transactions balance would be

$$\frac{29 \times \$0 + 1 \times \$300}{30} = \$10$$

and k_j will equal $\frac{1}{30}$:

$$k_j = \frac{\$10}{\$300} = \frac{1}{30} \text{ month.}$$

In this case the use of credit leads to a rather dramatic reduction in k_j.

Other aspects of individual payments and spending habits, such as different coincidences of receipts and disbursements, nonuniform rates of disbursement and the desire to maintain idle balances, influence the size of k_j. The role of individual payments and spending habits is discussed again later in this chapter and in Chapter 6. For the moment let us simply posit that k_j will always be a positive fraction of the flow of total expenditures measured over periods of time as long as a month.

Since our major concern in later chapters will be the analysis of aggregate economic behavior, we must aggregate over all individuals in the economy and show what determines the value of k for the economy as whole. The fraction that measures the individual's average transactions balance for a given flow of total expenditures over a period of time can be expressed by dividing each side of Equation (4.1) by T_j:

$$k_j = \frac{M_j/P_T}{T_j}. \tag{4.2}$$

For the economy as a whole let the average aggregate transactions balance for a given flow of aggregate total expenditures be

$$k_T = \frac{M/P_T}{T}. \tag{4.3}$$

Now to show the relationship between the individual k_j and the aggregate k_T we first sum over individual holdings of real money balances where there are n individuals in the economy:

$$\frac{M}{P_T} = \sum_{j=1}^{n} \frac{M_j}{P_T}. \tag{4.4}$$

Summing Equation (4.1) over j and substituting Equation (4.4) into the result yields

$$\frac{M}{P_T} = \sum_{j=1}^{n} k_j T_j. \tag{4.5}$$

Substituting this result into Equation (4.3) gives

$$k_T = \sum_{j=1}^{n} k_j \frac{T_j}{T}. $$

The value of k_T for the entire economy is the summation of the individual k_j, each weighted by that individual's share of aggregate total expenditures for a given period of time.

At the outset of the book we noted that theories about the demand for money are considered important because money is widely believed to affect the level of production and employment. Therefore it will be useful to reformulate the demand for transactions balances as a function of the level of output of newly produced goods and services (real income) rather than the level of total expenditures. In any economy total expenditures exceed expenditures on the aggregate output of newly produced goods and services, since total expenditures include expenditures on everything exchanged in the economy, including transactions involving financial assets (for example, stock market transactions) and second-hand physical assets, as well as intermediate transactions between business firms which do not directly add to the level of aggregate output.

Define k_o as the ratio of real aggregate transactions balances to the level of aggregate output,

$$k_o = \frac{M/P_o}{O}. \tag{4.6}$$

This can be rewritten as

$$k_o = \frac{M/P_T}{T} \cdot \frac{T}{O} \cdot \frac{P_T}{P_o}. $$

Using Equation (4.5) gives

$$k_o = \sum_{j=1}^{n} k_j \frac{T_j}{T} \cdot \frac{T}{O} \cdot \frac{P_T}{P_o}. \tag{4.7}$$

We can now see how k_o, a term which is used extensively as just k in later chapters, depends on the ratio of individuals' money holdings to their total real expenditures (as discussed above, the k_j reflect habits of payment and disbursement in the economy), the individuals' shares of aggregate total expenditures T_j/T, the ratio of aggregate total expenditures to aggregate real income T/O, and the ratio of the price index for total expenditures to the price index for newly produced goods and services P_T/P_o. Since none of these ratios is expected to change systematically as the level of aggregate real income changes, k_o is usually treated as a constant, and the demand for transactions balances is viewed as varying in direct proportion with the level of real income.[5] This relation is depicted in Figure 4.1 as a straight line through the origin with a slope of k_o.

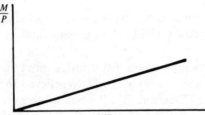

FIGURE 4.1. Aggregate transactions demand for money as a function of the level of aggregate real income, $0 < k_0 < 1$.

The Interest Rate and the Transactions Demand for Money

While many earlier economists, including Fisher and Keynes, pointed out that income was not the only variable affecting the transactions demand for money, it took some time for economists to develop rigorously a rather sophisticated hypothesis of how conversion costs might affect transactions demand. Simply conceived, as the interest rate on other financial assets rises, the *net* cost of converting into and out of money balances for a given period of time is reduced and individuals will reduce their demand for transactions balances.

Consider our earlier example. Assume a bank raises its interest rate on time

---

[5] We shall assume that the ratio of aggregate total expenditures T to aggregate income O does not change systematically with real income in the short run, even though in the long run such things as the vertical integration of business firms and increased specialization (both of which alter the level of intermediate transactions in the economy) will change this ratio. We shall also assume that, even though changes in various price indices are, in reality, seldom uniform, the ratio of the index of prices of goods and services comprising aggregate expenditures P_T to the index of prices of goods and services comprising aggregate output P_o does not change systematically with real income in the short run.

deposits from 2 percent to 6 percent per annum, payable on the 20th of each month. The individual who formerly held all $300 in transactions balances on the first day of the month, may now be induced to put $100 in the bank as a time deposit for the first 20 days of the month. He would do so because the interest income on $100 for 20 days rose from 11 cents to $33\frac{1}{3}$ cents, assumed to be enough to compensate him for the cost (inconvenience) of two monthly trips to the bank. The average transactions balance is $100 for the first 20 days and $50 for the last 10 days of the month, or $83.33\frac{1}{3}$ for the entire period.

In a similar fashion, Keynes in *The General Theory of Employment, Interest and Money* (1936),[6] Hansen in *Monetary Theory and Fiscal Policy* (1949),[7] and others rationalized that a relatively high yield on liquid nonmoney assets could effect an economization in the demand for transaction balances. Therefore we write the aggregate transactions demand for real money balances as:[8]

$$(M/P)_d = f(O,i). \qquad (4.8)$$

In this expression $(M/P)_d$ is postulated to vary *directly* with the level output O, as discussed above, and *inversely* with the market rate of interest i. It is possible that the latter relationship may hold only at "very high" interest rate levels.

---

[6] John Maynard Keynes, *The General Theory of Employment, Interest and Money* (London: Harcourt Brace and World, 1936).

[7] Alvin H. Hansen, *Monetary Theory and Fiscal Policy* (New York: McGraw-Hill, 1949).

[8] *Nominal*, as opposed to *real*, income is defined as being equal to the general price level of newly produced goods and services times the level of output, $Y \equiv P \cdot O$; the level of nominal money balances demanded as a function of the level of nominal income and the rate of interest i may be written as

$$M_d = f(Y,i).$$

While we use the demand for *real* money balances in the rest of this book, Equation (4.8) is not the original Keynesian version since Keynes was rightfully accused of having a "money illusion" in his total money demand function which added together the transactions plus precautionary demands L_1 and the speculative demand L_2. Keynes wrote the total demand for money as

$$M_d = L_1(P \cdot O) + L_2(i).$$

In the above formulation a rise in the general price level could not affect the demand for money for speculative purposes. Hence if P and M increase proportionately at a constant i, individuals have the "illusion" that they are "better off" even though their *real* money balances are unchanged.

It would be proper to include an expression for total wealth in this demand function since, as we shall see in Chapter 5, Keynesians view the speculative demand for money in terms of the proportion of total financial wealth individuals will hold in the form of money. In addition, in Chapter 8 wealth (or some measure of permanent income) is shown to explain more of the variation in money demand than current income. Moreover, in Chapters 9 and 11 we shall see that external financing of expenditures by government and business sectors has an effect on the level of wealth in the household sector. Therefore, a wealth variable will be introduced into the money demand relation in later chapters.

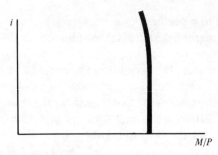

FIGURE 4.2. Aggregate transactions demand for real money balances as a
function of the yield on liquid nonmoney assets.

The relation between aggregate real transactions balances demanded and the
rate of interest is shown in Figure 4.2 where the level of aggregate real income and
other variables which could affect the transactions demand are assumed constant.
The function is drawn as it traditionally appears in money and banking and macroeconomic theory textbooks and is premised on the idea that some minimum interest
rate is necessary to cover the minimum possible transactions cost in economizing on
transactions balances.

Baumol's Approach to the Transactions Demand for Money

While the earlier work of Keynes, Hansen, and others is important, it was William
Baumol who most precisely and systematically introduced the interest rate into the
demand for transactions balances.[9] Baumol proceeds from the assumption that the
stock of real cash balances is the jth individual's inventory of the medium of exchange and that the rational individual will attempt to minimize the cost of holding
this inventory by holding the proper proportions of money and bonds. He assumes
that transactions are perfectly foreseen and occur in a steady stream over a given
time period. Real income per period is T_j dollars, and, by assumption, the individual
pays out all of his T_j dollars per period at a constant rate. Thus, as the period
progresses, he will be holding an ever-diminishing stock of assets.

In what form will these assets be held, bonds or money? If the individual holds

[9] William Baumol, "The Transactions Demand for Cash: An Inventory Theoretic Approach,"
Quarterly Journal of Economics, vol. 66 (November 1952), 545–556. For a somewhat more
difficult but equally important treatment, *see* James Tobin, "The Interest Elasticity of the
Transactions Demand for Cash," *Review of Economics and Statistics,* vol. 38 (August 1956),
241–247.

money, he will lose the interest income he could have earned on bonds. If he holds bonds, it will cost him something every time he "cashes" one in.

The jth individual is to begin the period holding all of his income in bonds. He is assumed to withdraw (disinvest) the money from bonds in lot-sized units of C_j dollars evenly spaced. For example, if an individual's T_j is $600 per month, his C_j might be $600 every 30 days, $300 every 15 days, $150 every 7½ days, or $20 per day. Whatever the value of C_j there will be T_j/C_j withdrawals made during the period. For each withdrawal he must pay a unit real transactions cost of b_j dollars. The expression $b_j \cdot T_j/C_j$ is a kind of "inventory replenishment cost" which includes not only the explicit costs (brokerage fees, transfer taxes, etc.) of selling assets to get cash but also the implicit cost (the inconvenience) of doing so.

On the assumption that his withdrawal of C_j dollars is expended at a constant rate, the individual's average cash balance is $C_j/2$, the amount of C_j dollars he holds halfway through the interval from one withdrawal to another. The cost of holding cash is equal to the return i foregone by holding part of his portfolio in the form of an asset that does not bear a monetary yield.

The expression $i \cdot C_j/2$ represents the "interest opportunity cost" from holding transactions balances in the form of cash. The total cost of holding the inventory of cash is, therefore,

$$X_j = b_j \cdot \frac{T_j}{C_j} + i \cdot \frac{C_j}{2}. \qquad (4.9)$$

The problem then becomes one of picking the value of the disinvestment lot size C_j which minimizes the total cost (transactions costs plus interest foregone) of holding the inventory of cash. At one extreme a single massive withdrawal (or disinvestment) from bonds at the outset of the period means a high interest opportunity cost; at the other extreme numerous small withdrawals mean a high inventory replenishment cost. At some point between these extremes, the *increase* in interest opportunity cost from slightly increasing C_j is just equal to the *decrease* in inventory replenishment cost from slightly increasing C_j, that is, the increment to total cost is zero. This (first-order) condition is satisfied where $dX_j/dC_j = 0$. At this point we can say that total cost is at a minimum. Solving the resulting expression for optimal C_j, that is, the value of C_j at which $dX_j/dC_j = 0$, gives[10]

$$C_j = \sqrt{(2b_jT_j)/i} \qquad (4.10)$$

[10] The derivative is $dX_j/dC_j = -\dfrac{bT_j}{C_j^2} + \dfrac{i}{2} = 0.$

This is rearranged to get Equation (4.10). The second-order condition for a minimum is likewise met:

$$d^2X_j/dC_j^2 = \frac{2b_jT_j}{C_j^3} > 0.$$

which seems to indicate that a rational individual, acting to minimize the cost of holding his transactions balances, will demand cash in proportion to the square root of the value of his transactions.

Since the optimal average balance was said to be $C_j/2$,

$$C_j/2 = (1/2)\sqrt{(2b_jT_j)/i}. \tag{4.11}$$

Now let $k_j = (1/2)\sqrt{2b_j}$ and let P_T be the general price level introduced to convert the expression into a demand for nominal balances. The above expression may be rewritten

$$M_j = k_jT_j^{1/2}i^{-1/2}P_T. \tag{4.12}$$

The result shows that (1) the jth individual's demand for transactions money balances does not generally vary in proportion to the level of total expenditures T_j, instead, there should be economies of scale in the management of cash balances,[11] (2) the quantity of transactions balances $C_j/2$ varies inversely with the interest rate i,[12] and (3) because of the transactions cost of exchanging cash for bonds ($b_j > 0$) it generally pays to hold cash, that is, in a perfectly frictionless world where purchases and sales of assets are costless, $b_j = 0$, there is *no* transactions demand for cash because it costs absolutely nothing to switch from bonds to cash when expenditures must be made.[13]

---

[11] From Equation (4.12) it can be seen that

$$\partial M_j/\partial T_j = (1/2)k_jT_j^{-1/2}i^{-1/2}P_T \neq k,$$

$$\partial^2 M_j/\partial T_j^2 = -(1/4)k_jT_j^{-3/2}i^{-1/2}P_T < 0,$$

and the elasticity, as shown in footnote 37 of Chapter 7, is 1/2.

Notice that when T_j increases the demand for money does *not* increase by the factor of proportionality, k_j. This result (falsified by empirical work reported in Chapter 8) would indicate a lack of proportionality between the demand for money and the level of income.

[12] Taking the transactions demand for money

$$M_j = k_jT_j^{1/2}i^{-1/2}P_T,$$

the inverse relationship is shown by

$$\partial M_j/\partial i = -(1/2)k_jT_j^{1/2}i^{-3/2}P_T < 0,$$

and the elasticity is $-1/2$.

[13] Keynes also postulated a demand for money to be held as a reserve against future contingencies such as personal emergencies or unforseen expenditures. Here again the existence of conversion costs explains why money is held to satisfy these needs even though it pays no dollar return. In this book, as in much of the professional literature, this precautionary demand for money is included with the transactions demand and is viewed as varying directly with the size of income and inversely with the market rate of interest.

The inventory-theoretic approach can typically be modified to incorporate an expression for the demand for precautionary balances. The only new element would be to multiply the first

Baumol's model is extremely suggestive and has implications for the macroeconomic models that are developed in Chapters 11–15. Two implications are of foremost concern. First, the demand for money can, in principle, depend upon the interest rate (as well as the level of income) without considering the speculative demand for money. The interest rate, as it affects the demand for money and therefore, is affected by changes in the supply of money, is of crucial import for policymakers who may control that supply. For instance, the model in Chapter 11 suggests that if monetary policy cannot influence the interest rate, it is less powerful.

Second, if the demand for money varies less than in proportion to the level of income, a given change in the money supply will, *ceteris paribus,* require a relatively large change in income to increase the quantity of money balances demanded and bring the money market into equilibrium. The Baumol model lends credence to the belief that monetary policy is a potent way to influence the level of income.

Given the theoretical possibility of an important role for the interest rate, is the appropriate interest rate in the money demand relation a long-term or a short-term rate? Based on the inventory-theoretic model one might reasonably assume that it would be the rate on the closest money substitutes, presumably a short-term rate. In this case changes in the supply of money would directly affect this rate, and longer term interest rates would respond only after a time lag. For example, given an increase in the supply of money, the short-term rate would decline; asset holders would then shift their portfolios out of short-term assets to higher yielding longer term ones, and this would, in turn, cause longer term interest rates to decline. In this case the process of interest rate adjustment to the initial increase in the money supply might take a considerable period of time.[14]

---

term of the total cost Equation (4.9) by some measure of statistical dispersion reflecting the probability of an unexpected cash drain. This measure of risk would therefore appear in the numerator of the square root formulas in Equations (4.10) and (4.11). An increase in the variability of cash flows would increase the demand for cash. See E. L. Whalen, "An Extension of the Baumol–Tobin Approach to the Transactions Demand for Cash," *Journal of Finance,* vol. 23 (March 1968), 113–134; and S. C. Tsiang, "The Precautionary Demand for Money: An Inventory Theoretical Analysis," *Journal of Political Economy,* vol. 77 (January–February 1969), 99–117.

[14] In a number of econometric models monetary impulses are transmitted from short-term rates to longer term rates to expenditures. See, for example, Frank de Leeuw and Edward M. Gramlich, "The Channels of Monetary Policy: A Further Report on the Federal Reserve-MIT Model," *Journal of Finance,* vol. 24, no. 2 (May 1969), 265–290.

Tests of hypotheses regarding which interest rate and which measure of income, if any, best explain variations in the demand for money are surveyed in Chapters 7 and 8.

A discussion of time lags in the effect of money on expenditures as well as an examination of why changes in money might have only small discernible effects on observed interest rates is found in Yung Chul Park, "Some Current Issues on the Transmission Process of Monetary Policy," *Staff Papers,* International Monetary Fund (March 1972), 1–45. A good survey of empirical estimation of the lags in monetary policy is Michael J. Hamburger's, "The Lag in the Effect of Monetary Policy: A Survey of Recent Literature," *Monetary Aggregates and Monetary Policy* (New York: Federal Reserve Bank, 1974), 104–111. All the studies cited in this footnote are reprinted in Havrilesky and Boorman, *Current Issues in Monetary Theory and Policy, op. cit.*

Information Costs and the Transactions
Demand for Money

In the preceding section the focus was on the *cost* of holding transactions balances. In that section the only cost explicitly avoided by an individual who held transactions balances was a brokerage cost.[15] In the real world if this were the only productive service from the holding of transactions balances, it would seem unlikely that any more than an absolute minimum quantity would be held during periods of a very high interest opportunity cost of holding money. Surely there are benefits from holding money other than the convenience of avoiding trips or calls to the "broker." Let us reconsider some of these benefits.

Earlier in this chapter we said that under the assumption that transactions costs were not zero transactions balances would be held in the *interval between receipts and expenditures*. Careful reflection will suggest that under certain circumstances a transactions balance can be avoided even if receipts and disbursements are not perfectly synchronized. For example, picture an economy where the differences in timing between receipts and expenditures are adjusted by costlessly enforced verbal promises to exchange goods later. In the interim between receipts and expenditures individuals can hold interest-earning bonds. Without further investigation of the exchange process, there would seem to be no need to hold transactions money balances at all.

An examination of the reason transactions money balances are held shall require a closer look at the process of exchange. In an hypothetical barter economy an individual is typically viewed by economists as entering the market with an initial endowment of commodities. This initial bundle of commodities may differ from the combination of commodities the individual would prefer. Once he or she learns what the relative prices of all commodities actually are, money is typically seen as making less costly the transformation of an endowed bundle to a preferred bundle.[16]

More specifically, an important way in which money is seen as reducing the cost of exchange is through its effect on saving resources that would otherwise have to be used in the search for market information. Without money the individual's search for information regarding market opportunities would be more costly. By carrying out exchange with a medium of exchange, the number of market prices to be learned is reduced because all prices can be quoted in terms of the medium of exchange; this saves on resources used to acquire, process, and store market information.[17]

In addition, without money, before an individual arrived at his or her preferred bundle, he or she would have to engage in a sequence of barter transactions. These

[15] Our emphasis on transactions in this chapter should not be interpreted to mean that only media of exchange should be included in the definition of money. The appropriate definition of money would seem rather to depend on the particular problem being addressed by the economic analyst. See Chapters 7 and 8 for further discussion of this problem.

[16] For example, see Jurg Niehans, "Money in a Static Theory of Optimal Payment Arrangements," *Journal of Money Credit and Banking*, vol. 1 (November 1969), 706–726.

[17] Karl Brunner and Allan H. Meltzer, "The Uses of Money: Money in the Theory of an Exchange Economy," *American Economic Review* (December 1971), 784–805.

exchanges too would be costly in *time* if not in income. By using a medium of exchange the individual can save resources by not having to carry out so many exchanges before he obtains his desired bundle.

It should, therefore, be clear that one of the resources saved by the holding of transactions balances is time.[18] The saving of *exchange time* through the use of transactions balances then suggests that the demand-for-money decision be viewed as a concomitant of the allocation-of-time decision. The use of money increases the amount of leisure in society. This could generate a *leisure-time valuation effect* in the demand for transactions balances.[19] Since the opportunity cost of leisure is the wage rate, this indicates that an increase in the wage rate increases the value of transactions time. This leads, in turn, to an increase in the demand for money in order to economize on that time.

This analysis suggests that an empirically observed income elasticity of unity in the demand for money need not necessarily falsify the Baumol economies-of-scale hypothesis. An observed unitary elasticity could hypothetically represent the sum of a less-than-unitary income elasticity and a less-than-unitary leisure-time valuation elasticity.[20]

The preceding analysis implies that in a world of imperfect market information the holding of inventories of transactions balances will be a means of reducing the cost of carrying out exchanges. This, in turn, implies that by bringing about lower costs of acquiring information and transacting, the "invention" of money speeded the development of the market system and freed productive resources for other uses. This suggests that a society or group within a society will never settle forever on a single monetary asset. It is, indeed, more likely that there will be a fairly continual exploration for different means of lowering transactions and information costs and that this will result in the development of new media of exchange.[21]

Finally, the preceding analysis also implies that in a world of great uncertainty

---

[18] Thomas R. Saving, "Transactions Costs and the Demand for Money," *American Economic Review,* vol. 51 (June 1971), 407–420.

[19] See Dean S. Dutton and Warren P. Gramm, "Transactions Costs, the Wage Rate and the Demand for Money," *American Economic Review,* vol. 53 (September 1973), 652–665.

[20] Assume, for example, that the level of *b,* the inventory disinvestment cost, in Equation (4.11) in the previous section varies directly and proportionately with the level of the *j*th individual's income. This simply would reflect the high correlation between an individual's income and the value of his time. Under this condition the observed income elasticity of that individual's demand for transactions balances would be unity.

[21] The pace of monetary innovation will not be constant but, like other types of innovation, will depend on the degree of uncertainty in the economic environment and also on the degree of price flexibility within the market system. For example, in a hypothetical world where exchange rates between different exchange media were flexible, in the long run a money that is stable in value would drive out an undependable one. Conversely, in the real world where exchange rates between different types of money are fixed, bad (unstable) money drives out good (stable) money. The absence of price (exchange rate) flexibility has impeded monetary innovation. Producers of unstable money (such as government) thereby have had an incentive to fixed exchange rates by having their money labeled "legal tender." See Benjamin Klein, "The Competitive Supply of Money," *Journal of Money, Credit and Banking* (November 1974), 423–454. See Chapter 15 for a discussion of the "invisible" taxation associated with the anticipated inflation arising from the issuance of government ("outside") money that is legal tender.

regarding market opportunities, the demand for money will increase because the marginal productivity of money as a means of economizing on information search costs is higher. This may help to explain the hypothetical appearance of a strong preference for liquidity (a more interest sensitive demand for money) during periods of economic instability such as a recession.[22]

Economizing on Transactions Balances

The theoretical possibility that the variables which determine the value of an individual's time, such as the wage rate and the level of income, could influence the demand for money suggests that in a high-wage, high-income economy there will be a strong demand for transactions balances. Earlier in this chapter we saw that in a high-interest-rate economy there will be considerable attempts to economize on the holding of transactions balances.

Many innovations in financial markets in recent years do, in fact, reflect attempts to economize on transactions balances. In the preceding section it was pointed out that if differences in the timing of receipts and expenditures could be adjusted by promises to pay at a later date, the demand for transactions balances would be significantly reduced. In other words, the development of credit markets is one way of economizing on transactions balances. A simple numerical example at the beginning of this chapter indicated how the use of credit could reduce the average level of transactions balances. In recent years the expanded use of credit cards, including bank credit cards, is a good example of how the development of credit markets economizes on the demand for transactions balances.[23] An additional mechanism for economizing on transactions balances is the use of trade credit. *Trade credit* is the exchange of a promise to pay the vendor later for currently received goods and services. This appears to reduce the quantity of money balances immediately necessary to finance current transactions. Some economists view unused but available trade credit as so close a substitute for transactions balances as to include it in their definition of money.[24]

The existence of a large volume of trade credit belies a serious problem of inefficiency in capital markets. If capital markets were competitively structured,

[22] See the Appendix to Chapter 14 for further discussion.

[23] With reference to the Baumol model, this could be reflected by subtracting from total transactions T_j the amount of one's purchases that are charged z_j. By replacing T_j with $T_j - z_j$ in Equation (4.12), one's average transactions balance would fall. The level of credit purchases would vary inversely with annual credit charges. As a consequence, where credit charges vary directly with the market rate of interest, the overall interest elasticity of the demand for transactions balances will fall in absolute magnitude. See A. S. Rama Sastry, "The Effect of Credit on the Transactions Demand for Cash," *Journal of Finance,* vol. 25 (September 1970), 777–782.

For some empirical estimates which do not falsify this hypothesis see Kenneth J. White, "The Effect of Bank Credit Cards on the Households Transactions Demand for Money," *Journal of Money, Credit and Banking* (February 1976), 51–61.

[24] Arthur B. Laffer, "Trade Credit and the Money Market," *Journal of Political Economy,* vol. 78 (March/April 1970), 239–267.

specialists at credit extension (financial intermediaries) would be able to satisfy such credit demands through routine means, such as short-term loans and bank credit cards. Vendors would not normally be able to compete with financial intermediaries. In addition to inefficiency in capital markets the existence of a significant volume of trade credit may also reflect an inefficiently large demand for money balances.[25]

Aside from innovations in credit markets, there have been several other developments in recent years that have reduced the transactions demand for money, where money is defined as demand deposits plus currency in circulation. A most important area of innovations has involved reductions in the cost of disinvesting in interest-earning assets, that is, reductions in the "brokerage" cost term b of Baumol's inventory theoretic model. In recent years the spread of negotiable order of withdrawal (NOW) accounts has been an important innovation in the payments mechanism. A NOW account is basically a savings deposit upon which a form of check can be written. Thereby, with such an account one need not make a trip to the savings bank or savings and loan association in order to transfer funds. This innovation has reduced the transactions cost of disinvesting in interest-earning savings accounts in order to make expenditures.

Another innovation involves the use of point-of-sale terminals. Under this system electronic terminals are placed in stores. In payment for a purchase, funds can be transferred electronically out of one's bank account into the vendor's account. This saves time in writing checks and withdrawing funds for cash purchases.[26] It also reduces the volume of outstanding checks (float) in the banking system.[27]

[25] Capital market imperfections are not unrelated to the government franchise given to commercial banks to do a checking account business. These franchises are hard to obtain. Banks, therefore, have a degree of monopoly power in both deposit and local loan markets. Because of the "customer relationship" (discussed in Chapter 3) that follows from this monopoly power and because of legal ceilings on explicit interest payments on deposits, banks may grant favorable credit terms only to big depositors. This leads to an inefficient allocation of credit because big depositors are not necessarily the most credit worthy. It also causes depositors to carry an inefficiently large quantity of demand deposit balances in order to qualify for favorable credit terms. Moreover, by making credit available to smaller depositors only at a higher cost from nonspecialists, it causes them to carry larger transactions balances than they would if credit markets were more competitively structured. The feasibility of making banking and credit markets more competitive is investigated by a number of authors in Havrilesky and Boorman, *Current Perspectives in Banking, op. cit.*

[26] With reference to the Baumol model, modified to reflect a demand for "precautionary" balances (footnote 13), there also occurs a decrease in the variability of cash flows, particularly for business firms because float is reduced and more orders are paid for immediately. This also reduces the demand for cash. See Mark J. Flannery and Dwight M. Jaffee, *The Economic Implications of an Electronic Money Transfer System* (Lexington: D. C. Heath, 1973). See also Robert E. Knight, "The Changing Payments Mechanism: Electronic Funds Transfer," *Monthly Review,* Federal Reserve Bank of Kansas City (July–August 1974), 10–20, reprinted in Havrilesky and Boorman, *Current Perspectives in Banking, op. cit.*

Flannery and Jaffee point out that lower costs of running the nation's payments mechanism might enable financial intermediaries to reduce the service charges on demand deposits, thereby reducing the interest opportunity cost of holding cash and *increasing* the quantity of transactions balances demanded.

[27] Other innovations which may be viewed as reducing the magnitude of Baumol's b include telephone transfers from savings to checking accounts, the ability to write checks on money

Concluding Comment

The incentive for financial innovations can be better appreciated if one has an understanding of the interest rate as an opportunity cost of holding total money balances, not just transactions balances. In the next chapter we explore theories regarding the demand for speculative money balances. In Chapter 6 we view the demand for money from the perspective of the neoclassical quantity theory of money. A good understanding of the demand for money will be helpful in the later study of macroeconomic models.

QUESTIONS FOR CHAPTER 4

1. "Keynes did not allow uncertainty to enter his transactions demand for money, reserving its effects entirely for his liquidity preference hypothesis." Evaluate this statement. How could uncertainty enter into the Baumol model?
2. Explain the effects which the development of an extensive credit card system would have on the transactions demand for money.
3. What are some of the ways in which a corporate treasurer could conserve on his transactions balances in order to minimize the opportunity cost of holding such balances?
4. Explain the role of the interest rate in Baumol's "inventory theoretic" hypothesis of the demand for money.
5. "As income becomes more equitably distributed in our economy, Baumol's square root rule suggests that monetary policy will be more effective." Evaluate.
6. Prove that the interest elasticity of the demand for money in the Baumol model is equal to $-\frac{1}{2}$.
7. "Trade credit reduces the demand for money." Evaluate.

BIBLIOGRAPHY FOR CHAPTER 4

BAUMOL, WILLIAM J., "The Transactions Demand for Cash: An Inventory Theoretic Approach," *Quarterly Journal of Economics,* vol. 66 (November 1952), 545–556.
BRUNNER, KARL, and ALLAN H. MELTZER, "Economies of Scale in Cash Balances Reconsidered," *Quarterly Journal of Economics,* vol. 81 (August 1967).
——, "The Uses of Money: Money in the Theory of an Exchange Economy," *American Economic Review* (December 1971), 784–805.
DE LEEUW, FRANK, and EDWARD M. GRAMLICH, "The Channels of Monetary Policy: A Further Report on the Federal Reserve–MIT Model," *Journal of Finance,* vol. 24, no. 2 (May 1969), 265–290.*

---

market mutual funds, and changes in laws allowing state and local governments to hold savings deposits. Several economists have claimed that these innovations have led in recent years to a downward shift in the demand for money. The stability of the demand-for-money function is examined in Chapters 7 and 8.

  * Reprinted in THOMAS M. HAVRILESKY and JOHN T. BOORMAN, *Current Issues in Monetary Theory and Policy* (Arlington Heights, IL: AHM Publishing, 1976).

DUTTON, DEAN S., and WARREN P. GRAMM, "Transactions Costs, the Wage Rate and the Demand for Money," *American Economic Review,* vol. 53 (September 1973), 652–665.

FLANNERY, MARK J., and DWIGHT M. JAFFEE, *The Economic Implications of an Electronic Money Transfer System* (Lexington: D. C. Heath, 1973).

HAMBURGER, MICHAEL J., "The Lag in the Effect of Monetary Policy: A Survey of Recent Literature," *Monetary Aggregates and Monetary Policy* (New York: Federal Reserve Bank, 1974), 104–111.*

HANSEN, ALVIN H., *Monetary Theory and Fiscal Policy* (New York: McGraw-Hill, 1949).

JOHNSON, HARRY G., "Notes on the Theory of the Transactions Demand for Cash," *Indian Journal of Economics,* vol. 44 (July 1963), 1–11.

——, "A Note on the Theory of Transactions Demand for Cash," *Journal of Money, Credit and Banking,* vol. 3 (August 1970), 383–384.

KEYNES, JOHN MAYNARD, *The General Theory of Employment, Interest and Money* (London: Harcourt Brace and World, 1936).

KLEIN, BENJAMIN, "The Competitive Supply of Money," *Journal of Money, Credit and Banking* (November 1974), 423–454.

KNIGHT, ROBERT E., "The Changing Payments Mechanism: Electronic Funds Transfer," *Monthly Review,* Federal Reserve Bank of Kansas City (July–August 1974) pp. 10–20.†

LAFFER, ARTHUR B., "Trade Credit and the Money Market," *Journal of Political Economy,* vol. 78 (March–April 1970), 239–267.

MILLER, H. LAWRENCE, "On Liquidity and Transactions Costs," *Southern Economic Journal,* vol. 32 (1965), 43–48.

NIEHANS, JURG, "Money in a Static Theory of Optimal Payment Arrangements," *Journal of Money, Credit and Banking,* vol. 1 (November 1969), 706–726.

PARK, YUNG CHUL, "Some Current Issues on the Transmission Process of Monetary Policy," *Staff Papers,* International Monetary Fund (March 1972), 1–45.*

SASTRY, A. S. RAMA, "The Effect of Credit on the Transactions Demand for Cash," *Journal of Finance,* vol. 25 (September 1970), 777–782.

SAVING, THOMAS R., "Transactions Costs and the Demand for Money," *American Economic Review,* vol. 51 (June 1971), 407–420.

SMITH, P. E., "Probabilistic Demand for Cash Balances and (s,S) Inventory Policies," *Weltwirtschaft. Archiv,* vol. 93 (March 1961), 72–83.

SPRENKLE, CASE, "The Usefulness of Transactions Demand Models," *Journal of Finance,* vol. 24 (December 1969).

TOBIN, JAMES, "The Interest Elasticity of Transactions Demand for Cash," *Review of Economics and Statistics,* vol. 38 (August 1956), 241–247.

TSIANG, S. C., "The Precautionary Demand for Money: An Inventory Theoretical Analysis," *Journal of Political Economy,* vol. 77 (January–February 1969), 99–117.

WHALEN, E. L., "An Extension of the Baumol–Tobin Approach to the Transactions Demand for Cash," *Journal of Finance,* vol. 23 (March 1968), 113–134.

WHITE, KENNETH J., "The Effect of Bank Credit Cards on the Households' Transactions Demand for Money," *Journal of Money, Credit and Banking* (February 1976), 51–61.

† Reprinted in THOMAS M. HAVRILESKY and JOHN T. BOORMAN, *Current Perspectives in Banking* (Arlington Heights, IL: AHM Publishing Corporation, 1976).

5

The Keynesian Speculative Demand for Money

Introduction

In the previous chapter we examined the transactions demand for money. In a world where the costs of buying and selling interest-earning assets (to be held in the interval between the receipt and disbursement of income) are not negligible, money, the generally accepted medium of exchange, will be held.

In this chapter we show that money is also held because it functions as a liquid store of wealth whose market value may be less variable than other wealth forms. (Individuals may demand money merely to hold it "idle").[1]

At first blush it seems irrational to hold financial wealth in a nonearning form. Yet, as discussed more fully in the next chapter, the earlier Cambridge economists indicated that an individual's uncertainty about future market prices of earning assets, among other things, could induce him to forego these earnings and to hold money. The market value of money may be less variable. Keynes articulated this in his liquidity preference theory, one subject of this chapter.[2]

As discussed in this chapter, Keynes asserted that the lower the market rate of

---

[1] Thus, total money demand M_d may consist of transactions (plus precautionary) balances M_1 and speculative balances M_2.

[2] What we develop here is a contemporary interpretation of the liquidity preference theory of John Maynard Keynes' *The General Theory of Employment, Interest and Money* (London: Harcourt Brace, 1936).

interest relative to an expected future rate, the greater the expected decline in the prices of earning assets. Therefore, at low rates of interest liquid money balances are a preferable hedge against the expected capital loss of holding earning assets. In a subsequent section of this chapter James Tobin's version of this hypothesis is considered. Tobin indicated that even if the expected capital loss is zero, some risk of capital loss is always present. He further stated that the lower the rate of interest, the less the individual's preference to hold earning assets and assume this risk, and the greater his preference for liquidity (money balances).

Because of these Keynesian contributions and Baumol's inventory-theoretic approach to transactions demand, economists are inclined to concede, in principle, that the total demand for money depends on the rates of interest (yields) on financial assets as well as on the level of income and/or wealth. However, the extent to which any of these variables explain variations in the demand for money is largely an empirical question. In Chapters 7 and 8 we shall present a survey of empirical work on this question.

The Relationship between Interest Rates and Bond Prices

Before we begin our analysis, it is necessary to explain the relationship between interest rates and the prices of existing debt instruments which promise to pay the holder certain periodic interest payments and to repay the principal value at maturity.

When we speak of the *yield* on debt instruments such as bonds we shall mean the "yield to maturity." One measure of the yield of an obligation may be calculated simply by dividing the dollar amount of the interest paid per year by the current market price of the instrument. However, this is not a completely satisfactory measure, for it fails to consider the capital gain or loss to be incurred if that obligation is held to maturity. For example, the *current yield* on an obligation selling for $950 and paying $50.00 per year is $50/$950 = .0526 or 5.26%. But if the face value of this bond is $1000, it will return an additional $50 above purchase price to the owner upon redemption at maturity. Thus if the bond is held to maturity the owner will realize a capital gain of $50 on his investment in addition to the yearly interest return. This capital gain must be included in the complete return when calculating the total yield to maturity on the security.

Yield to maturity may be calculated by means of a formula for computing the present value of a future stream of returns. If one wishes to calculate the present value of a single $50 payment to be made one year from today, he "discounts" that $50 according to the simple formula:

$$\text{present value} = P = \frac{50}{1 + i}$$

where i is the interest (or discount) rate. For example, the present value of $50 discounted at 2% for one year is

$$P = \frac{\$50}{1 + .02} = \frac{\$50}{1.02} = \$49.02.$$

In other words, $49.02 invested for 1 year at 2% yields $50. In general a single payment of Y dollars to be received 2 years in the future is currently valued at

$$P = \frac{Y}{(1 + i)^2}.$$

At 2%, then, the present value of this *single* $50 payment to be made 2 years from today is

$$P = \frac{\$50}{(1 + i)^2} = \frac{\$50}{(1 + .02)^2} = \frac{\$50}{(1.0404)} = \$48.06.$$

If we generalize this formula, the present value of any payment Y_n to be made n years from now is

$$P = \frac{Y_n}{(1 + i)^n}. \tag{5.1}$$

Therefore, if a debt instrument carries an obligation to pay $50 *per year* for the next 5 years and a final repayment of principal of $1000.00 at the end of the 5 year period, the present value of that stream of returns discounted at a rate of $100i\%$ per year is

$$P = \frac{Y_1}{(1 + i)} + \frac{Y_2}{(1 + i)^2} + \frac{Y_3}{(1 + i)^3} + \frac{Y_4}{(1 + i)^4} + \frac{Y_5}{(1 + i)^5} + \frac{\text{principal}}{(1 + i)^5} \tag{5.2}$$

where $Y_1 = Y_2 = Y_3 = Y_4 = Y_5 = \$50$.

For example, if the return demanded by the lender is 6 percent per year, he would be willing to pay $957.87 for a bond with these characteristics:

$$P = \frac{\$50}{(1.06)} + \frac{\$50}{(1.06)^2} + \frac{\$50}{(1.06)^3} + \frac{\$50}{(1.06)^4} + \frac{\$50}{(1.06)^5} + \frac{\$1000}{(1.06)^5}$$

$$= \$47.17 + \$44.50 + \$41.98 + \$39.60 + \$37.36 + \$747.26$$

$$= \$957.87.$$

Alternatively, knowing the current market price of the instrument, we may use the formula to calculate its yield to maturity. For example, if the obligation is currently selling for $950.00, the yield is given by the formula

$$\$950 = \frac{\$50}{(1+i)} + \frac{\$50}{(1+i)^2} + \frac{\$50}{(1+i)^3} + \frac{\$50}{(1+i)^4} + \frac{\$50}{(1+i)^5} + \frac{\$1000}{(1+i)^5}$$

$$i = .0619 \qquad 100i = 6.19\%.$$

It is clear from the formula that the higher the (interest) rate at which future expected returns are discounted (in the denominators), the lower will be the present value of that income (the market value of the obligation); conversely, the lower the rate of discount, the higher will be the present value.

It is through variations in the market price of outstanding securities (with fixed payments and a fixed face value) that the yield on those instruments is adjusted to current market conditions.

The formula suggests that when the market rate or current yield in the denominator is equal to the 5% *coupon rate* (the $50 annual interest payment divided by the $1000 principal), the bond sells in the market at "par," that is, its market price is equal to its principal value. When the market rate is greater than the coupon rate, the bond sells below par or at a discount, and when the market rate is less than the coupon rate, the bond sells above par or at a premium.

This shows how bond prices adjust, in the market where bonds are traded, to bring a bond's yield to maturity into line with the market rate of interest. It indicates that bond prices vary inversely with the market rate of interest.

Finally, the formula indicates that the market prices of longer term debt instruments will fluctuate more widely for a given change in the market rate than the prices of shorter term debt instruments, since instruments with a longer term to maturity contain larger powers of $(1+i)$ in the formula. This is important because it means longer term bonds are more subject to capital gains and losses than shorter term bonds.

In the remainder of this chapter we shall deal exclusively with *consol bonds* because the relationship between the market price of a consol bond and the market rate of interest can be reduced to a very convenient expression. A consol continues to pay interest indefinitely but does not repay principal. Therefore, the general present value formula, Equation (5.2), is written without the final term for the repayment of principal:

$$P = \frac{Y_1}{(1+i)^1} + \frac{Y_2}{(1+i)^2} + \frac{Y_3}{(1+i)^3} + \cdots + \frac{Y_n}{(1+i)^n} \qquad (5.3)$$

Now multiply both sides of this equation by $1/(1+i)$:

$$\frac{1}{1+i}P = \frac{Y_1}{(1+i)^2} + \frac{Y_2}{(1+i)^3} + + \cdots + \frac{Y_n}{(1+i)^{n+1}}. \qquad (5.4)$$

Assume that $Y_1 = Y_2 = Y_3 = \cdots = Y_n$ and subtract Equation (5.4) from Equation (5.3):

$$P\left[1 - \frac{1}{1 + i}\right] = \frac{Y}{1 + i} - \frac{Y}{(1 + i)^{n+1}}.$$

Multiply both sides by $(1 + i)$ and rearrange terms:

$$P = \frac{Y}{i}\left[1 - \frac{1}{(1 + i)^n}\right]. \qquad (5.5)$$

This is a general expression for the present value of a continuous stream of future interest payments. If we add an expression for repayment of principal, it is often a convenient way to reformulate the present value formula, Equation (5.2).

To derive the expression for the present value of a consol simply let the maturity of the bond n become infinite, so that the expression $(1 + i)^n$ becomes infinitely large and the term $1/(1 + i)^n$ becomes zero as n approaches infinity. This gives

$$P = \frac{Y}{i} \qquad (5.6)$$

which says that the present value of a consol is inversely proportional to the rate of interest.

Now we are ready to begin our analysis of the speculative demand for money. If we ignore physical assets and equities (which have roughly similar portfolio properties as physical assets),[3] an individual may hold his wealth in two forms, debt instruments and money. As discussed earlier, money has the advantage of being generally acceptable as a medium of exchange. In addition, the market value of money may be subject to less volatile swings than the market value of debt instruments. Economists traditionally have said that the confluence of these two properties make money a unique, most "liquid" financial asset.

The Early Keynesian Approach to Liquidity Preference

In *The General Theory of Employment, Interest and Money*,[4] Keynes assumes that all individuals wish to avoid losses and that the gains or losses they anticipate from holding debt instruments (bonds) depend solely on the rate of interest i_e which they are certain will occur at some uncertain date within the forthcoming time period t.[5]

[3] Both debt and money differ from physical assets and equities in that their values do not fluctuate with the price level and in that they are unattractive investments when the price level is expected to rise. In Chapters 6 and 15 the effect of price expectations on the demand for money and debt is examined as part of a discussion of the relation between nominal and real rates of interest. For the present our analysis abstracts from changes in the general price level.

[4] John Maynard Keynes, *op. cit.*

[5] The expected rate is forecasted by the individual. For analytical simplicity we overlook the behavior that generates the rate expected to occur within the forthcoming time period. We

Capital losses would be expected if the current rate of interest i were less than the expected rate i_e because, as discussed above, as bond yields rise, bond prices fall. If the current rate i were sufficiently lower than the expected rate i_e, it would be unprofitable for the individual firm or household to hold bonds now. Rather, if capital losses were greater than interest income, the individual would hold money balances until the rate i rises towards its expected level (and bond prices fall). At some point, as the interest rate rises and bond prices fall, he would buy bonds. Conversely, if the rate of capital loss were less than the current interest rate i (or if capital gains were expected), the individual would hold bonds now.[6] Thus the individual's financial wealth will consist of either all bonds or all money in Keynes' model.

Keynes proposed that the economy's speculative demand for money slopes downward because, as the current rate falls, increasingly more individuals become convinced that the rate of capital loss outweighs the interest rate, that is, as the current rate falls, more and more individuals feel that the current rate is sufficiently below their expected rate to warrant holding all of their speculative financial wealth in the form of money balances.

Mathematically the sufficient condition for the financial investor to hold all his speculative portfolio as money is

$$i + g < 0 \tag{5.7}$$

where $g < 0$. Let P_e = expected bond price and P = current bond price. The definition of the rate of capital loss is

$$g = \frac{P_e - P}{P} \tag{5.8}$$

where $P_e < P$. Substituting Equation (5.8) into (5.7),

$$i + \frac{P_e - P}{P} < 0$$

---

assume it occurs independently of the level of the current rate, that is, we assume perfectly inelastic interest rate expectations. Keynes had in mind inelastic, but not perfectly inelastic, interest rate expectations (Keynes, *op. cit.*, p. 202). They were tied to his concept of the "normal" rate. The "normal" rate of interest, according to Keynes, is the level toward which the expected rate gravitates over time. *The further the current rate diverges from normal, the more it would be expected to bounce back in the forthcoming time period.* This notion of "regressive expectations" in Keynes' theory is not confined to his money demand hypothesis. It permeates his entire theory. This is discussed in the Appendix to Chapter 14.

[6] Contrast this analysis, where the *expected value* of the capital gain or loss is nonzero and known with certainty, to Tobin's approach (pp. 123–128) where the *expected value* of the capital gain and loss in a probability distribution is zero, and yet the individual will still be wary of holding bonds because there is a "risk" of holding bonds. "Risk," in Tobin's analysis, is measured by the spread or *dispersion* of possible capital losses and gains about this zero *expected value.*

or

$$i + \frac{P_e}{P} - 1 < 0.$$

Assume for purposes of analytical convenience that all bonds are *consols* (bonds paying a fixed income in perpetuity). This makes bond prices and bond yields inversely proportional, as shown in Equation (5.6), so that the last expression may be rewritten as

$$i + \frac{i}{i_e} - 1 < 0.$$

Multiplying through by i_e, we get

$$i \cdot i_e + i - i_e < 0.$$

The condition for holding all financial wealth as money is then

$$i \cdot i_e + i < i_e \qquad \text{or} \qquad \frac{i}{1-i} > i_e.$$

As an example, assume a consol paying $50 a year is currently priced at $1000, so that $i = .05$. But it is expected to attain a market price of $950 sometime within the forthcoming period; by Equation (5.6) the expected rate i_e is .0526. At this rate it follows that $i \cdot i_e + i = i_e$ and the individual is indifferent between bonds or money. If the expected rate i_e were higher, he would hold all money; if it were lower, he would hold all bonds. The reader may calculate that where the income per year is $40 on the same bond, the current rate is .04 and the critical expected rate is .0417. A convenient (though slightly inaccurate) rule of thumb is that the expected rate which would induce an individual to hold all money must be greater than the current rate i plus its square i^2, that is, if $i + i^2 < i_e$, one would hold all money, and if $i + i^2 > i_e$, one would hold all bonds.

Now if Keynes' hypothesis is considered, the individual demand for real speculative money balances[7] M_2 may be depicted as the discontinuous function shown in Figure 5.1. When the market rate of interest i is sufficiently below the expected rate i_e as discussed, the individual holds all his speculative portfolio in the form of real money balances. Otherwise he holds all of his speculative portfolio in the form of bonds.[8]

---

[7] In future chapters we refer, as did Keynes, to transactions balances as M_1 and speculative balances as M_2. It must be pointed out now, as we do in detail in Chapter 6, that the usefulness of the concept of separable money demand components is challenged by many economists.

[8] Where future rates are not assumed to be expected with certainty, the individual may actually mix his bond–money holdings. The more the current rate departs from the "normal"

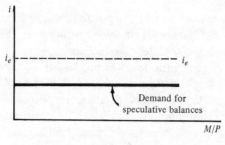

FIGURE 5.1. The individual's demand for speculative money balances.

To derive the demand curve for speculative balances for the entire economy, we simply sum across all individual demand curves. A necessary condition for the smooth downward sloping of this aggregate curve, as depicted in Figure 5.2,[9] is that as the market rate *i* falls, successively greater numbers of individuals feel that this rate is sufficiently below their expected rate to warrant holding all of their speculative portfolio in the form of real money balances.

This analysis carries several crucial implications. First, Keynes suggested that at some low interest rate practically everyone will feel the current rate is sufficiently below their expected rate to warrant holding their portfolio in the form of money balances. At this point the economy's demand-for-money function approaches an infinite interest elasticity as shown in Figure 5.2. No matter how large the increase in the money supply, only a very, very small decrease in the interest rate is sufficient

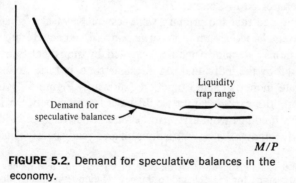

FIGURE 5.2. Demand for speculative balances in the economy.

rate, the greater the probability with which the individual expects the rate to move back to its "normal" level. In this case the greater the rise in the current rate, the greater the proportion of financial wealth held in the form of bonds and the greater the decline in the current rate, the greater the proportion held in the form of money. Unlike the Tobin approach this variation of Keynes' analysis still ties *risk* to the expected rate.

[9] Again, as in Chapter 4, to avoid Keynes' specification of money illusion, we depict the demand for *real* money balances. See footnote 8 on page 103 for a discussion of this problem.

to convince individuals to hold all of their portfolio in the form of money balances. As discussed in detail in Chapter 14, if the economy is in this "liquidity trap," it may make monetary policy completely ineffective.

Notice that Keynes did not introduce earning assets of very short maturity into his analysis. In the *real* world these assets *might* be held until bond prices fell and then would be liquidated, the funds being used for the purchase of low-priced bonds. The financial investor need not hold money which bears no explicit yield. Nevertheless Keynes' purposeful omission of such "money substitutes" does not vitiate his hypothesis that the rate of interest affects the demand for money, because, as discussed in Chapter 4, earning assets have explicit and implicit conversion costs as they are purchased and liquidated; therefore, the rational individual will generally hold some of his speculative wealth in the form of money balances.[10] Also, as Keynes assumes that the exact date of the bond price decline is not known with certainty, an individual holding even short-term assets would surely incur some (albeit a small) capital loss. Therefore, money substitutes may not be a profitable hedge against the expected loss from holding long-term bonds.

Over the years Keynes' liquidity preference hypothesis has drawn critical fire. Specifically, to the extent that the expected rate were subject to change, as Keynes suggested, the demand for money would be statistically unstable. In contrast (as reported in the survey of empirical work on the demand for money in Chapter 8), the function actually appears to be quite stable statistically. One might then attempt to preserve Keynes' hypothesis, in light of this evidence, by assuming that the expected rate is relatively constant. There has been considerable criticism of this assumption's lack of realism. In fact, in a world where all individuals have learned to expect the same or very similar "normal" rates,[11] the speculative demand schedule would have a nearly angular (convex) shape. This shape is not revealed by statistical tests reported in Chapter 7.

It has been argued that the primary weakness of Keynes' original liquidity preference hypothesis is its assumption of a *certain* expected rate.[12] In order to get the stable money demand function revealed by statistical tests, this rate must be relatively fixed by the individual. At the same time, in order to obtain the typical smooth aggregate money demand function (shown in Figure 5.2) that seems to fit the actual data,[13] the expected rate would have to differ between individuals, and each individual's holdings would have to be small relative to the total for the economy. This clearly imposes severe restrictions on an already barely tenable assumption.

---

[10] This line of reasoning suggests that the rate of interest on close money substitutes might be the most relevant one for the demand-for-money relation. For further discussion, see footnote 14 in Chapter 4 and footnote 20 in this chapter.

[11] The role of the normal rate in Keynes' analysis is discussed in footnote 5 at the beginning of this section.

[12] Axel Leijonhufvud defends this formulation of Keynes as being completely consistent with his world view. This subject is explored in the Appendix to Chapter 14. See Axel Leijonhufvud, *On Keynesian Economics and the Economics of Keynes* (New York: Oxford, 1968).

[13] As reported in the survey of empirical work in Chapter 7, most statistical tests do not indicate the presence of the liquidity trap.

The Tobin Approach to Liquidity Preference

A major advance in monetary theory was the explanation of the inverse relationship between the rate of interest and the quantity of money demanded, without the restrictive rate-forecasting assumption of Keynes. We shall now present an abbreviated, simplified version of James Tobin's hypothesis.[14]

Definitions.   Assume a two-asset economy where portfolios are comprised of money and/or consol bonds with an annual market rate of interest of i percent; also assume that each financial investor is *uncertain* about the value of the market rate in the next period. Each investor believes that the probability that the market rate will fall by x percent is equal to the probability that it will rise by x percent, and no rate is any riskier, in and of itself, than any other. (Notice how these two assumptions differ from Keynes' original necessary assumption of a *certain* expected rate that differs between individuals and results in their portfolios consisting of either bonds *or* money).

Let

A_1 = the fraction of total assets which the investor holds as money, where
$0 \leqslant A_1 \leqslant 1$

A_2 = the fraction of total assets which the investor holds as consols, where
$0 \leqslant A_2 \leqslant 1$
$A_1 + A_2 = 1$ by the assumption of a two-asset economy

E = the expected percentage increase in the value of the portfolio during a year (which by the assumption above excludes probable capital gains or losses),[15] that is,

$$E = A_2 \cdot i \tag{5.9}$$

R = the risk associated with holdings consuls, measured as a percentage, that is,

$$R = A_2 \cdot s \tag{5.10}$$

where s $(0 \leqslant s \leqslant 1)$ is a fixed coefficient measuring the risk of capital loss from holding a bond and is subjectively determined by each investor.[16]

---

[14] For all points requiring further detail, see James Tobin, "Liquidity Preference as Behavior towards Risk," *Review of Economic Studies*, vol. 25 (February 1958), 65–86.

[15] For the reader with some knowledge of elementary mathematical statistics, the individual assesses the *expected value* of probable capital gains and losses as zero and therefore the expected value of holding a bond is just its interest yield.

[16] Again, for the reader with some knowledge of mathematical statistics, the risk from holding bonds is not the *expected value* of the capital gain or loss (which is assumed to be zero) but rather the standard deviation of the probability distribution of expected future bond prices. Thus, $s = \sigma$.

Other measures of risk have been used in models of portfolio behavior. An important treatise on portfolio theory shows the Tobin model presented here to be a special case of a more general theory of asset choice. See Bernell K. Stone, *Risk, Return and Equilibrium* (Cambridge: M.I.T. Press, 1970).

Note that, unlike Keynes' original hypothesis, the capital loss from holding a bond is assumed to be independent of the *level* of the interest rate.

Utility.   Now the individual's problem is this: each bond held increases expected earnings, but it also increases the risk (possible fluctuation of value) of the portfolio. Earnings, viewed here as additions to wealth, are "good" since they add to utility; risk is "bad" since it subtracts from utility. What combination of expected earnings and risk will make the individual "happiest?" To answer this question we turn to a tool of elementary economic theory, the *indifference curve*.

Assume that every combination of expected increases in the value of the portfolio E and risk R gives the financial investor a certain amount of expected utility or "satisfaction" I. Further assume that there are numerous sets of possible combinations of E and R that give the investor *equal* amounts of expected utility, I_1, I_2, I_3, $\cdots$, I_n. In Figure 5.3 expected utility is constant along each line I.

Assume that for every level of risk R, the associated value of expected earnings E along I_2 is greater than the corresponding E along I_1. Hence I_2 represents a greater amount of expected utility than does I_1; therefore I_2 and I_1 cannot intersect in the graph. As we move from the lower right to the upper left in Figure 5.3 we go to higher and higher levels of expected total utility.

Now let us engage in an experiment. Assume that the individual in Figure 5.3 remains at a constant level of expected utility, that is, he stays on a given indifference curve. If this individual receives a small increment of risk R, in order to stay at the same level of total expected utility (to stay on the same indifference curve), he or she must be compensated with an increase in expected earnings E. This must occur because risk is "bad" and subtracts from utility, while expected earnings are "good" and add to expected utility. Therefore, the tradeoff between risk R and expected earnings E along a given indifference curve is positive, and the indifference curve slopes upward in (E,R) space, that is, dE/dR is positive.

Next consider a series of small, equal, successive increments of risk while total expected utility remains at a constant level in Figure 5.3. Consecutive *equal* increments of risk (a "bad") can preserve a constant level of total expected utility only

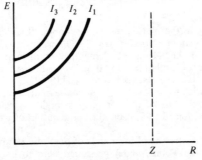

FIGURE 5.3. An indifference map in risk-expected return space.

if they are compensated for by consecutively *larger* increments of expected earnings (a "good") because of diminishing marginal expected utility of expected return. Thus the indifference curve in Figure 5.3 is convex to the origin. In Figure 5.3 it is seen that along any indifference curve as E increases, dR/dE decreases. Thus an investor whose indifference curves reflect this pattern is said to be "risk averse."[17]

Note also that total risk R has a limiting value Z, which is reached when A_2 equals unity, that is, when the entire portfolio is held as bonds. The portfolio can become no riskier.

Constraints.   We have now mapped out lines of equal expected utility, called indifference curves. The individual is indifferent between any combinations of E and R along any one curve but prefers combinations along a higher curve to those along a lower one. The problem faced by the financial investor is to maximize his expected utility by finding, among all points available to him, the combination of E and R that gives him the greatest level of expected utility. Each financial investor would like to be at the highest possible level of total expected utility. There are, however, two factors that constrain this process, the market rate of interest i and the risk coefficient s.

The market rate of interest i measures the expected percentage increase in portfolio value E that the investor can realize by increasing A_2 [that is, Equation (5.9), $E = A_2 \cdot i$]. The risk coefficient s measures the increase in risk R that is a concomitant of the increase in A_2 [that is, Equation (5.10) $R = A_2 \cdot s$] and not, as in Keynes' hypothesis, a concomitant of the level of i.

Solving Equations (5.9) and (5.10) for A_2, equating the results, and solving for E we find

$$E = \frac{i}{s} \cdot R \qquad (5.11)$$

This expression denotes what the market *allows* the investor to do. (What he would *desire* to do is shown by his indifference map.) The market allows the investor to obtain a higher (or lower) expected return E only by accepting a greater (or lesser) degree of risk R. The first derivative of Equation (5.11) with respect to R is

$$\frac{dE}{dR} = \frac{i}{s}. \qquad (5.12)$$

This shows that the successive amounts of additional E that can be obtained by accepting greater R are constant and equal to i/s.

Maximization.   The investor must reconcile his desires as expressed by the in-

---

[17] The mathematics of this analysis is given in the appendix to this chapter. Tobin mapped out the behavior of "risk lovers" and "plungers" as well. The tradeoff between risk and earnings is quite different for these individuals. However, the concept of the "risk averter" will suffice in developing the conventional speculative demand for money.

difference or equal expected utility curves, $I_1, I_2, \cdots, I_n$, to the objective limitations (constraints) imposed by the market. He must choose the desired combinations of E and R that provide maximum total expected utility subject to the known values of i and s. This may be demonstrated by plotting Equation (5.11) on the same diagram as the indifference map (Figure 5.4). As can be seen from Equation (5.11), the slope of the constraint OC is the ratio i/s. Every time the market rate i falls, the OC constraint will pivot downwards (more additional risk must be assumed for a given increment to earnings).

Tangency between a constraint and an indifference curve depicts the first-order condition for a maximization of expected utility.[18] Each indifference curve (I_1, I_2, I_3) shows how the individual *desires* to exchange E for R. Each constraint (OC_1, OC_2, OC_3) shows how the market *permits* the individual to exchange E for R. A financial investor maximizes his expected utility when the desired increase in expected return E relative to the desired increase in risk R along I is equal to the tradeoff between E and R permitted by the market OC. In short, the investor increases the proportion of consols in his portfolio by successive increments until it is no longer possible to gain more expected utility from increased expected earnings than the expected utility lost from increased risk. He moves along the given constraint OC until he reaches the highest possible level of total expected utility. This is the point where the constraint is tangent to the indifference curve.[19]

The Demand for Idle Money Balances.   As the market rate i falls and the risk coefficient of the investor s remains constant, the OC constraint pivots downward, and risk R may either rise or fall, depending on how the financial investor desires to exchange E for R. If, as shown in Figure 5.4, the preferences of the investor are

---

[18] Second-order conditions are satisfied by the convexity of the indifference curve.

[19] This may be expressed mathematically. Let the expected utility function in general notation be

$$U = U(E,R).$$

To specify movement along an indifference curve, take the total differential of this function and set it equal to zero:

$$dU = (\partial U/\partial E)dE + (\partial U/\partial R)dR = 0.$$

The "tradeoff" or marginal rate of substitution is derived by rearranging this expression to get

$$\frac{dE}{dR} = -\frac{\partial U/\partial R}{\partial U/\partial E}.$$

Set this equal to the constraint imposed by the market [Equation (5.12)] and the first-order condition for a maximum is satisfied,

$$\frac{i}{s} = -\frac{\partial U/\partial R}{\partial U/\partial E}.$$

The second-order condition is satisfied by the convexity of the indifference curve. If the expected utility function were more fully specified, the demand for money could be directly derived.

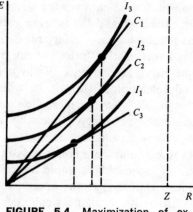

FIGURE 5.4. Maximization of expected utility.

such that the equilibrium value of R falls, from Equation (5.10) it can be seen that the equilibrium value of the fraction of the investor's wealth held as consols A_2 also falls, and hence (as $1 = A_1 + A_2$), the fraction of the investor's wealth held in the form of money balances A_1 rises. Therefore, if less risk R is acceptable at a lower market rate i, the quantity of money demanded as a proportion of total speculative wealth varies inversely with the rate of interest as shown in Figure 5.5.

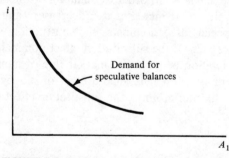

FIGURE 5.5. The risk averse individual's speculative demand for money.

Does R Fall as i Falls? In this analysis, as with the usual indifference analysis, there are an income and substitution effects associated with a shift in the constraint.

First consider the substitution effect. Given an increase in i (a fall in bond prices), risk R becomes less expensive to acquire and the investor can increase his expected earnings E by reducing A_1, his proportionate holdings of money. An increase in the rate of interest is an incentive to take more risk; in terms of the substitution effect, it reflects a substitution of earnings for safety. Conversely given a fall in i, risk R becomes more expensive and the investor can reduce R (and E) by increasing A_1. This reflects a substitution of safety for earnings—a substitution of less risk A_1 for more risk A_2 as the relative "price" of risk rises.

Now consider the income effect. As the price of any commodity falls, the individual may buy more of all commodities (that is, he will experience an "income effect") because he is "better off." Keynesian models often assume an income elasticity of the demand for money of unity. Under this assumption a rise in the interest rate raises expected earnings and, because of the income effect, the individual desires to hold more money and more bonds but to continue to hold them in the same proportion. Thus, the income effect would not counteract the substitution effect. The latter will always ensure that as the interest rate rises, the quantity of money demanded as a proportion of speculative wealth decreases.

Now relax this usual assumption and assume that risk R is an inferior good. In this case, because an individual is "better off," he will buy less of an "inferior" good as his income rises. Suppose there is a rise in i (a fall in the price of risk). Clearly, by Equation (5.9) expected earnings increase. In this case, the income effect will dictate that the individual hold less risk. Equation (5.10) shows that he can only do this by reducing A_2 and increasing A_1. If risk is an "inferior" good, the income effect will require that the investor hold proportionately fewer bonds as he is "better off."

Conversely, if there is a decrease in i (a decrease in expected earnings), the income effect will require that an individual hold more of the inferior good. In order to acquire more risk, the proportion A_2 must increase. In a sense, as i falls, the individual is increasing his proportionate bond holdings A_2 and reducing his proportionate money holdings A_1 in order to maintain his income level.

If the equilibrium value of R increases as i decreases (and vice versa), the income effect (in this special case) dominates the substitution effect. If R decreases as i decreases (and vice versa), the substitution effect dominates the income effect. To obtain an inverse relation between the market rate of interest and the fraction of the financial investor's wealth held in the form of money balances under the assumption that risk is an inferior good, the substitution effect must dominate.

Summary

Keynes asserted that the quantity of speculative balances demanded would vary inversely with the market interest rate. For the individual the lower the market rate relative to his expected rate, the greater his expected capital loss (the greater his *risk* of holding earning assets). At some level a decline in the market rate would induce the rational individual to switch from holding all of his speculative wealth in the form of bonds to holding it in the form of money balances.

Statistical findings impose two severely restrictive conditions on Keynes' hypothesis regarding the demand for money. A smooth, downward-sloping speculative demand function, as revealed by most statistical tests, requires the condition that individuals have different expected rates. Statistical tests that show the money demand function to be stable require the condition that these rates be relatively fixed.

James Tobin's more sophisticated liquidity preference hypothesis is a vast improvement because it disposes of Keynes' assumption of a certain, expected rate and the corresponding restrictions that it be fixed by the individual and differ between individuals.[20] Tobin shows that even if the expected capital loss is independent of the current interest rate an inverse relation between the interest rate and the demand for speculative balances will prevail as long as individuals are less willing to accept risk as the market rate declines.

QUESTIONS FOR CHAPTER 5

1. In a world of numerous money substitutes, individuals will never hold speculative balances. True or false?

2. Either Keynes' speculative demand is unstable or else it must be perfectly convex to the origin (L-shaped). Evaluate.

3. What shape would the speculative demand for money take if individuals felt that risk were an inferior good and if the income effect outweighed the substitution effect?

4. Relate the speculative demand for money to the bank's demand for excess reserves discussed in Chapter 3.

5. Explain why the market prices of long-term bonds are more influenced by interest rate changes than are the prices of short-term bonds.

6. "If the income elasticity of the demand for money is constrained to unity, the proportion of speculative wealth held in the form of money balances will always vary inversely with the interest rate." Evaluate.

7. Explain the relation between the market rate and the coupon rate when a bond sells "above par."

Appendix to Chapter 5
Portfolio Theory

The preceding chapters have explained a number of theories of the demand for money. All these theories focus on money as a rather unique medium in which to hold one's financial wealth. Little attempt was made to introduce other asset forms into the analyses.

[20] The Tobin analysis is important also because it is a precursor of the portfolio balance approach to monetary theory. The portfolio balance approach introduces as many financial assets and as many interest rates as there are imperfect substitutes among these assets. Statistical tests showing which are the most relevant interest rates in the money demand relation are surveyed in Chapter 7. For a review of the portfolio balance approach see Yung Chul Park, "Some Current Issues on the Transmission Process of Monetary Policy," *Staff Papers,* International Monetary Fund (March 1972), 1–45; and Roger W. Spencer, "Channels of Monetary Influence," *Review,* Federal Reserve Bank of St. Louis (January 1970), 16–21. Both are reprinted in Havrilesky and Boorman, *Current Issues In Monetary Theory and Policy, op. cit.*

Even the speculative money demand theory of Tobin considered only two assets, money, an asset paying no dollar return but having no risk of nominal loss, and bonds, an asset featuring an expected dollar return but having greater risk. Yet in reality there is a broad spectrum of financial assets available today. In addition to varying dollar yields and varying levels of risk, these assets are further differentiated by the transactions costs of acquiring and selling them, the taxability of income earned from owning them, and the nonpecuniary yields from holding them. An important characteristic of each financial asset is the combination of risk and expected return it offers. This can range from the low risk–zero expected nominal return of currency to the high risk–high expected return of a volatile common stock. In order to focus on this particular characteristic of financial assets, we shall assume in what follows that all asset characteristics other than risk and return are identical.

The purpose of the present appendix is to offer a more general, somewhat more advanced version of the portfolio theory introduced in the previous chapter.

The basic premise in all portfolio theory is that the return or yield from an asset (or liability) in a portfolio cannot be known in advance with certainty. The best one can expect is that various possible outcomes from holding specific assets can be delineated and that a likelihood or probability can be associated with each of these outcomes. This, again, is simply to say that the yield cannot be predicted with certainty. Rather the yield itself is a random variable and the outcome of the investment process can be described only in terms of probability distributions.

One can gain considerable insight into empirical and theoretical work in portfolio analysis with knowledge of only a few fundamental concepts. Basically these are the statistical properties of a distribution of random outcomes: (1) the expected return of the portfolio and its components, (2) the variability of the expected return of a portfolio—an indicator of risk, and (3) the extent to which the expected returns to the component assets of a portfolio move together. A minimum knowledge of these concepts is necessary for further work in this area. Three standard statistical measures are used extensively to reflect these concepts. These are (1) the arithmetic mean or *expected value,* (2) the *variance* or the square root of the variance, the standard deviation, and (3) the *covariance* and the *coefficient of correlation* between two series. Let us begin by defining these concepts more precisely.

When an experiment is performed in which the result, represented by a numerical quantity, will depend upon chance, the experiment may be referred to as a *random* experiment and the result a random quantity. The throwing of a six-sided die is an obvious example of such an experiment. A *random variable* may then be defined as a function which relates some numerical quantity to each possible event or outcome that could occur in a random experiment. In the case of investment in a financial asset in which the possible outcomes of the investment experiment (holding the asset for a particular period of time) are themselves numerical (percentage yields or dollar returns) the random variable may be viewed as the listing of all possible numerical outcomes of that experiment.

The random variable may by its very nature assume many different values. However, for investment purposes we often need to compare the potential results of holding different assets, each of whose yield is random. Consequently, we need some means of comparing random variables. We can do this through the associated *probability distributions*. The (probability) distribution of a random variable is simply a listing of all possible values that the random variable may assume and the associated probability of each of the outcomes which generate those values in the performance of the random experiment.[1] For example, in the die throwing experiment cited above, each of the integer values from 1 to 6 associated with the outcome of the experiment may have a probability of 1/6 associated with it.

In order to compare random variables, it is useful to be able to compare the properties of their probability distributions, most importantly, the means and variances of those distributions.

The *expected* (or *mean*) *value* of a (discrete) probability distribution is the sum of all values the random variable may assume, each weighted by its associated probability. If X is a random variable which can assume the values x_1, x_2, $\cdots$, x_n, each with an associated probability of $P(x_1)$, $P(x_2)$, $\cdots$, $P(x_n)$, then the expected value of X is

$$E(X) = \sum_{i=1}^{n} x_i \cdot P(x_i). \qquad (5A.1)$$

While the expected value is a useful measure and serves, in one sense, to locate the "center" of a probability distribution, it tells us nothing about the spread of the values which the random variable may assume around that center. For example, if the age of a person picked at random from a "group" is the random variable, the expected value of the probability distribution of that random variable may be 20 years. However, the spread of the probability distribution or the variance of the values which may occur from picking a person at random will be very much different if we are picking from a "group" comprised of the entire population of the United States or from a group comprised solely of university students. The smaller the spread of a probability distribution around its central tendency or expected value, the more confident one can be that, in the performance of a random experiment characterized by that probability distribution, the result will, in some sense, be "close to" that central tendency. In the case of financial investment, for example, if the probability distribution of the holding period yield on an asset has a relatively small dispersion, one can predict with greater confidence that the actual yield will differ from the expected yield by less than some given amount than he could in the case of an asset whose random yield had a larger dispersion. For this reason, some

---

[1] This definition is modified in the case of a continuous random variable which may theoretically assume any one of an infinite number of values. We assume here that the random variables describing the outcome of an investment "experiment" are discrete random variables, that is, random variables that may assume only a finite number of values.

measure of the spread or dispersion of the probability distribution of asset yields has been used extensively as a measure of risk.

The most commonly used measure of dispersion is the variance. The *variance* σ^2 of a probability distribution is measured as the sum of the squared deviation between each value the random variable may assume and the mean of that random variable weighted by the associated probability of that value; that is,

$$\sigma^2 = \sum_{i=1}^{n} (x_i - E(X))^2 \cdot P(x_i). \tag{5A.2}$$

An additional useful measure is the square root of the variance, referred to as the standard deviation.

Probability distributions, such as those characterizing the return on investment in specific assets, may be compared by use of the expected value and the variance. However, the relation between the outcome of two random experiments may also be of interest. For example, an expected acceleration in the rate of inflation which would cause the outcome of the holding of a particular asset, such as land, to be relatively high may also lead to a relatively high yield on some other asset, such as agricultural commodities. In such a case, repeated experiments over time may indicate that *relatively* high (above expected value) values of one random variable tend to occur at the same time as *relatively* high values of some other random variable. In this case, the random variables would be said to be positively correlated or to have a positive covariance. The *covariance* between two random variables may be defined as the sum of the products of the deviation of each possible outcome of each of the random variables from their respective means, weighted by the (joint) probability of each pair of those values occurring together; that is, where x and y are random variables:

$$\text{cov}(X,Y) = \sum_{i=1}^{n} \sum_{j=1}^{n} [x_i - (Ex)][y_j - (Ey)] \cdot P(x_i,y_j) \tag{5A.3}$$

The *coefficient of correlation* is a related measure of similarity or dissimilarity in the behavior of two random variables,

$$\rho_{xy} = \frac{\text{cov}_{xy}}{\sigma_x \sigma_y}. \tag{5A.4}$$

This measures the covariance between two random variables, not as an absolute value but relative to the product of the standard deviations of the individual variables.

These concepts can be illustrated graphically. Assume that there are two random

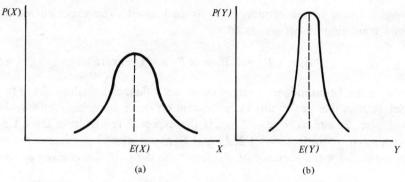

FIGURE 5A.1. Probability distributions of random variables X and Y.

variables X and Y. Their (probability) distributions are shown in Figure 5A.1.[2] When the distribution is bell-shaped, as in Figure 5A.1, it is often referred to as a *normal distribution*. This means, among other things, that the expected value and variance of the random variable are mathematically sufficient to completely specify the distribution. Assuming that X and Y are measured in the same units and that the same scale is depicted on the horizontal axes, in Figure 5A.1 the expected value of X, $E(X)$, is greater than the expected value of Y, $E(Y)$. At the same time, the variance of X is considerably greater than the variance of Y. Finally, if it happens that relatively high values of X tend to be associated with relatively high (above mean) values of Y and relatively low values of X are associated with relatively low (below mean) values of Y, they are said to be positively correlated.

If one is working with *normal distributions,* then expected return and variance are the only statistical measures one need deal with. Unfortunately, few random variables in monetary and financial economics are going to have the smooth symmetry of the curves in Figure 5A.1; today's sophisticated portfolio analysis does indeed consider abnormal distributions and their associated statistical measures.[3] However, the starting point of all work in portfolio theory confines the analysis to expected value as a measure of return and variance as a measure of risk.

The Expected Risk–Return Locus

One is generally concerned not solely with the return on any one particular asset, but rather with the return, and the variability of that return, on an entire portfolio consisting of more than one asset. The return on the portfolio will be denoted as

---

[2] These random variables are pictured as having continuous distributions for simplicity's sake.

[3] See, for example, Bernell L. Stone, *Risk, Return and Equilibrium* (Cambridge: M.I.T. Press, 1970).

the weighted sum of the returns on individual assets. The expected return on a portfolio consisting of two assets is[4]

$$E = x_1E_1 + x_2E_2 = x_1E_1 + (1 - x_1)E_2 \qquad (5A.5)$$

where x_1 is the (nonrandom) proportion of one's financial wealth held in the form of asset 1; x_2 is the (nonrandom) proportion on one's financial wealth held in the form of asset 2; and $x_1 + x_2 = 1$. E_1 is the expected return from asset 1 and E_2 is the expected return from asset 2. E_1 and E_2 are expressed as percentages.

The formula for the variance of the return on the portfolio is given as follows:[5]

$$\text{var } E = x_1{}^2 \text{ var } E_1 + 2x_1x_2 \text{ cov}(E_1,E_2) + x_2{}^2 \text{ var } E_2$$

$$\sigma^2 = x_1{}^2\sigma^2{}_1 + 2x_1x_2 \text{ cov } x_1x_2 + x_2{}^2\sigma^2{}_2$$

$$= x_1{}^2\sigma^2{}_1 + 2x_1(1 - x_1)\text{cov } x_1x_2 + (1 - x_1)^2\sigma^2{}_2 \qquad (5A.6)$$

where $\sigma^2{}_1$ is the variance of the return on asset 1 and $\sigma^2{}_2$ is the variance of the return on asset 2. The covariance must be included to reflect how variations in the return to asset 1 are offset or accentuated by variations in the return to asset 2 and vice versa.

Now in the case where the coefficient of correlation between the two returns is unity, $\rho_{12} = 1$, Equation (5A.4) can be substituted into Equation (5A.6) to yield

$$\sigma^2 = x_1{}^2\sigma^2{}_1 + 2x_1(1 - x_1)\sigma_1\sigma_2 + (1 - x_1)^2\sigma^2{}_2$$

$$= [x_1\sigma_1 + (1 - x_1)\sigma_2]^2. \qquad (5A.7)$$

The square root of Equation (5A.7) gives the standard deviation of the return on the portfolio:

$$\sigma = x_1\sigma_1 + \sigma_2 - x_1\sigma_2$$

$$= \sigma_2 + x_1(\sigma_1 - \sigma_2). \qquad (5A.8)$$

Solving Equation (5A.8) for x_1,

$$x_1 = \frac{\sigma - \sigma_2}{\sigma_1 - \sigma_2}$$

[4] This result derives from the fact that the expected value of a random variable (the return on the portfolio) defined as the sum of two or more random variables (the returns on individual assets) is equal to the sum of the expected values of those random variables.

[5] If a random variable is defined as a linear combination of two other random variables, for example, $Z = aX + bY$, where X and Y are random variables and a and b are constants, the variance of that random variable is given by the following:

$$\text{var } Z = a^2 \text{ var } X + b^2 \text{ var } Y + 2ab \text{ cov } (X,Y).$$

and substituting the result into Equation (5A.5) yields

$$E = \left(\frac{\sigma - \sigma_2}{\sigma_1 - \sigma_2}\right) E_1 + E_2 - \left(\frac{\sigma - \sigma_2}{\sigma_1 - \sigma_2}\right) E_2$$

$$= E_2 - \sigma_2 \left(\frac{E_1 - E_2}{\sigma_1 - \sigma_2}\right) + \left(\frac{E_1 - E_2}{\sigma_1 - \sigma_2}\right) \sigma, \qquad (5A.9)$$

a linear function in (E, σ) space with constant term $E_2 - \sigma_2 \left(\dfrac{E_1 - E_2}{\sigma_1 - \sigma_2}\right)$ and slope $\left(\dfrac{E_1 - E_2}{\sigma_1 - \sigma_2}\right)$.

The risk–expected return locus for this case is graphed in Figure 5A.2. In common sense terms, this line describes the tradeoff between risk and expected return when the expected returns on the two assets being considered always vary together in the same direction such that the correlation coefficient between them is positive and equal to unity. That is, whenever asset 1's return is below its average by a given number of standard deviations, the return on asset 2 is below its average by the same number of standard deviations; and whenever asset 1's return is above its average by a given number of standard deviations, the return on asset 2 is above its average by the same number of standard deviations.

If $\sigma_1 < \sigma_2$, it is seen from Equation (5A.8) that minimum risk can be established where $x_1 = 1$ at point W. At this point by Equation (5A.5) total expected return consists entirely of the expected return on asset 1, E_1, that is, if $x_1 = 1$, then $E = E_1 + E_2 - E_2 = E_1$. Total risk in Equation (5A.8) consists entirely of the variation in the return of that asset, σ_1 (that is, if $x_1 = 1$, then $\sigma = \sigma_2 + \sigma_1 - \sigma_2 = \sigma_1$). (The extreme case of the least risky asset having a zero expected return and

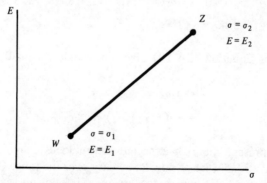

FIGURE 5A.2. Risk–return locus where two assets are perfectly correlated.

a zero risk is graphed in Figure 5.4.) As one diversifies the portfolio, that is, holds less of the less risky asset 1, the overall expected return rises because the more risky asset 2 will have a higher expected return in the market than the less risky one. At point Z the portfolio can become no riskier as it is exclusively devoted to the riskier asset 2, $x_2 = 1$.

$$E = 0 \cdot E_1 + E_2 - 0 \cdot E_1 = E_2 \quad \text{and} \quad \sigma = \sigma_2 + 0 \cdot (\sigma_1 - \sigma_2) = \sigma_2.$$

The preceding analysis may be clarified by an example of two assets with highly positively correlated returns. Two such assets might be long-term United States Treasury bonds and the long-term bonds of a typical highly rated industrial corporation. Their actual returns may move together (positively) very closely; the long-term government bond, however, has less risk, a lower variance, and, consequently, a lower expected return. If an investor confined his choice set to these two assets, a risk minimum could be realized by holding all financial wealth in long-term government bonds. A desire for higher expected return would require holding a larger proportion of riskier long-term industrial bonds.

This analysis suggests that if there existed a perfectly riskless asset that has a positive expected return (such as an FDIC insured savings account), abstracting from the various transactions and information costs discussed in Chapter 4, an investor would never hold money, narrowly defined. The risk–return locus for that asset and another risky asset with which its return was positively correlated would be a positively sloped straight line with a positive intercept. Even if the investor were completely risk averse, he could always attain zero risk and still have an expected return by holding all of his wealth in the insured savings account.

In the case where the correlation between the two returns is negative unity, $\rho_{12} = -1$, Equation (5A.4) can be substituted into Equation (5A.6) to yield

$$\sigma^2 = x_1^2 \sigma_1^2 - 2x_1(1 - x_1)\sigma_1\sigma_2 + (1 - x_1)^2 \sigma_2^2$$

$$= [x_1\sigma_1 - (1 - x_1)\sigma_2]^2. \tag{5A.10}$$

The square root of Equation (5A.10) gives the standard deviation of the portfolio

$$\sigma = x_1\sigma_1 - \sigma_2 + x_1\sigma_2$$

$$= \sigma_2(-1 + x_1) + x_1\sigma_1. \tag{5A.11}$$

In order to represent the risk–expected return locus graphically using Equations (5A.11) and (5A.5), let us now let x_1 vary over the range $0 < x_1 < 1$ to find the ordered triples (x_1, σ, E) where we assign the following values: $E_1 = 30\%$, $E_2 = 60\%$, $\sigma_1 = 10$, and $\sigma_2 = 15$. The results are given in Table 5A.1. These values will satisfy Equations (5A.11) and (5A.5) and are graphed in Figure 5A.3

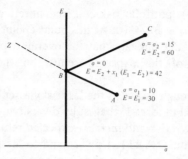

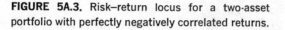

FIGURE 5A.3. Risk–return locus for a two-asset portfolio with perfectly negatively correlated returns.

as the (dashed) locus AZ. However, σ can never be negative and an absolute value restriction must be imposed on Equation (5A.11), $\sigma \geqslant 0$. This restriction yields the (solid) discontinuous locus ABC in Figure 5A.3.

Table 5A.1. Relation between the Proportion Invested in Asset 1 and the Risk and Return of the Portfolio

Proportion of Portfolio Invested in Asset 1 x_1	Risk σ	Expected Return (in percentages) E
1.0	10.0	30
.9	7.5	33
.8	5.0	36
.7	2.5	39
.6	0.0	42
.5	(−)2.5	45
.4	(−)5.0	48
.3	(−)7.5	51
.2	(−)10.0	54
.1	(−)12.5	57
0	(−)15.0	60

In common sense terms Figure 5A.3 describes the tradeoff that is possible between risk and expected return when the expected returns on the two assets always vary together in opposite directions. Whenever asset 1's return is above its average, the return on asset 2 is *below* its average by the same number of standard deviations; whenever the return on asset 1 is *below* its average, the return on asset 2 is *above* its average by the same number of standard deviations.

Table 5A.1 and Equation (5A.11) show that if the portfolio is devoted to the less risky asset ($x_1 = 1$), portfolio risk consists entirely of the risk associated with that asset, $\sigma = -\sigma_2 + \sigma_2 + \sigma_1 = 10$. At this point (point A in Figure 5A.3), Table 5A.1 and Equation (5A.5) indicate that the overall expected return for the portfolio consists entirely of the expected return on the less risky asset, $E = E_2 + E_1 - E_2 = 30$.

Nevertheless, even though asset 1 is the less risky asset, by decreasing the proportion of the portfolio held in asset 1, that is, by diversifying the portfolio, we can, up to a point, actually *reduce* risk and *increase* expected return. This may be seen from Table 5A.1 and Equation (5A.11). Upward and to the left of A, as x_1 is reduced from unity, total risk declines because the negative term $\sigma_2\,(-1 + x_1)$ increasingly offsets the positive term $x_1\sigma_1$.

Because the less risky asset has the lower expected return, as we hold less of it and more of the riskier asset with the higher return, total expected return increases. Equation (5A.11) indicates that this offsetting can proceed to the point where risk can be completely eradicated. This occurs where x_1 is set equal to $\sigma_2/(\sigma_1 + \sigma_2)$, because at that point

$$\sigma = 0 = \sigma_2(-1 + x_1) + x_1\sigma_1 = -\sigma_2 + x_1\sigma_2 + x_1\sigma_1$$

$$= -\sigma_2\left(\frac{\sigma_1 + \sigma_2}{\sigma_1 + \sigma_2}\right) + \sigma_2\left(\frac{\sigma_2}{\sigma_1 + \sigma_2}\right) + \sigma_1\left(\frac{\sigma_2}{\sigma_1 + \sigma_2}\right)$$

$$= \frac{-\sigma_2^2 - \sigma_1\sigma_2 + \sigma_1\sigma_2 + \sigma_2^2}{\sigma_1 + \sigma_2} = 0. \tag{5A.12}$$

Substituting $x_1 = \sigma_2/(\sigma_1 + \sigma_2)$ into Equation (5A.5) gives a total expected return at that point of

$$E = x_1 E_1 + (1 - x_1)E_2$$

$$= \frac{\sigma_2}{\sigma_1 + \sigma_2}E_1 + \left(1 - \frac{\sigma_2}{\sigma_1 + \sigma_2}\right)E_2$$

$$= E_2 + \left(\frac{E_1 - E_2}{\sigma_1 + \sigma_2}\right)\sigma_2$$

$$= E_2 + (E_1 - E_2)\left(\frac{\sigma_2}{\sigma_1 + \sigma_2}\right) > E_1.$$

Since $E_2 > E_1$, the second term will be negative and equal to the difference between E_1 and E_2 but weighted by $\sigma_2/(\sigma_1 + \sigma_2)$ which is less than 1. Therefore, the second term reduces total return, but not as much as the difference between E_1 and E_2. As a result, the total return at point B in Figure 5A.3 exceeds the total expected return at point A.

In summary, because of the negative correlation between returns, it is possible to reduce overall risk by holding some of the riskier asset. At the same time, because the riskier asset has a higher expected return, such *diversification* actually increases the overall expected return. Thus the rational investor would never consider a portfolio on the locus AB when he could always find a higher expected return for the same level of risk on the locus BC. Being on AB is inefficient; being on BC is efficient.

Upward from B in Figure 5A.3, as x_1 is further decreased, the negative term in Equation (5A.11), $\sigma_2(-1 + x_1)$, is increasingly less offset by the positive term, $x_1\sigma_1$. Algebraically σ becomes negative. However, because Equation (5A.11) is subject to an absolute value restriction, total portfolio risk actually increases from zero upward and to the right of B. As portfolio risk increases, total portfolio return also increases. At point C in Figure 5A.3 the entire portfolio is fully invested in asset 2, $x_2 = 1$. Here risk and expected return consist entirely of the risk and expected return associated with the riskier asset, $\sigma = -\sigma_2$ and $E = E_2$. For example, by Equation (5A.11), $\sigma = -\sigma_2 + 0 \cdot \sigma_2 + 0 \cdot \sigma_1$ subject to $\sigma > 0$, and by Equation (5A.5) $E = E_2 + 0 \cdot E_1 - 0 \cdot E_1$.

This analysis may also be illuminated by an example from the real world. Consider a portfolio consisting of two very highly, but not perfectly, negatively correlated assets. Such a situation may exist, for example, during certain stages of the business cycle. For instance, imagine a period in which the investor anticipates an acceleration of the rate of inflation. During such a period, if he were to purchase commodities to sell in the future at prices expected to prevail then, he would anticipate a higher return. During the same period, if he were to purchase long-term government bonds, he would expect a lower return. This occurs because if price inflation accelerates as he expects, as long as the acceleration had not been fully anticipated by other participants in the government bond market, the nominal yield on government bonds must rise (bond prices must fall) as other investors come to require higher yields to match the rate of inflation. The expected drop in bond prices would produce a capital loss for the bondholder.

The opposite of this pattern would occur during periods when the investor anticipates a deceleration of inflation ahead of other investors. Holding commodities would incur a lower return. Holding long-term bonds would result in a higher return because of likely capital gains to bondholders. Thus the expected returns on these two assets move in opposite directions.

Now let us assume that the rate of price inflation is never steady, it is either accelerating or decelerating. Let us further assume that commodities over the entire business or inflation cycle have higher risk but offer a higher return than long-term bonds.

If the investor confined his choice set to these two assets, he could never realize a risk minimum by holding all of his wealth in the form of bonds. Because returns always move in opposite directions, he could reduce risk *and* increase overall return by holding some proportion of his wealth in commodities.

Now in the real world expected returns are neither perfectly negatively nor perfectly positively correlated. In general the risk–return locus will fall between

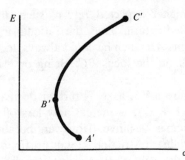

FIGURE 5A.4. Portfolio with intermediate correlation of returns.

these two extreme cases. In fact, if we solved Equation (5A.5) for x_1 and substituted the result into Equation (5A.6), the risk–return locus would be a hyperbola such as that shown in Figure 5A.4.

The riskiest portfolio, and the one with the highest expected return, is found at point C'. The least risky portfolio is found at the leftmost point, B'. However, without perfect negative correlation the locus will not reach the vertical axis; there will be no completely riskless portfolio. The closer the correlation coefficient is to $+1$, the more it will resemble the locus in Figure 5A.2; the closer the correlation coefficient is to -1, the more it will resemble the locus in Figure 5A.3.

Finally, as in the preceding analysis, we can always find a frontier of efficient combinations of risk and expected return, $B'C'$, with no rational investor choosing to stay on the inefficient locus $A'B'$.

Investor Indifference Curves

In the preceding chapter the indifference or equal-utility curves were drawn as positively sloped convex lines in risk–return space. These were said to reflect risk aversion. Our purpose now will be to present a somewhat more general formulation of investor attitudes toward risk and return. By making explicit the expected utility function, attitudes toward risk other than risk aversion can be shown. In addition, we can easily show that risk aversion reflects diminishing marginal utility of income.

Assume that an individual's total utility from income y is measurable. In a quadratic utility function

$$U = ay + by^2$$

where $a > 0$, marginal utility will be positive over a range of income beginning at zero, $dU/dy = a + 2by$. The range of b will indicate whether there is decreasing or increasing marginal utility of income; $d^2U/dy^2 = 2b < 0$ if $b < 0$, and $d^2U/dy^2 > 0$ if $b > 0$.

If we consider y a random variable, we should not talk about utility but must refer to *expected* utility. The assumption of a quadratic expected utility function is a convenient way of introducing a risk measure into the analysis. At the same time the assumption of a quadratic expected utility function has the advantage of limiting our approach to consideration of only two parameters, risk and expected return.[6]

In other words, where y is randomly, but not necessarily normally, distributed, the expected utility function

$$E(U) = E(ay) + E(by^2) \qquad (5A.13)$$

may be written

$$E(U) = aEy + b(Ey)^2 + b\sigma^2{}_y. \qquad (5A.14)$$

This follows because the expected value of a random variable times a constant is equal to the constant times the expected value of the random variable.[7] In addition, the expected value of a random variable squared is equal to the variance of that random variable plus the square of its expected value.[8]

Now in order to derive the indifference curve, we must take the total differential of Equation (5A.14) and set it equal to zero:

$$dE(U) = \frac{\partial E(U)}{\partial(Ey)} d(Ey) + \frac{\partial E(U)}{\partial \sigma_y} d\sigma_y = 0$$

$$= (a + 2bEy)dEy + (2b\sigma_y)d\sigma_y = 0. \qquad (5A.15)$$

The marginal rate of substitution,

$$\frac{dEy}{d\sigma_y} = \frac{-2b\sigma_y}{a + 2bEy} \qquad (5A.16)$$

[6] Earlier we mentioned that the assumption of a normally distributed random variable would *also* allow us to limit analysis to these two parameters.

[7] Assuming y is a discrete random variable,

$$E(ay) = \frac{1}{n} \sum_i ay_i = a \cdot \frac{1}{n} \sum_i y_i = a \cdot Ey.$$

[8] $Ey^2 = \sigma^2{}_y + (Ey)^2$
$= E(y - Ey)^2 + (Ey)^2$
$= E[(y^2 - 2y \cdot Ey + (Ey)^2] + (Ey)^2$
$= Ey^2 - 2Ey \cdot Ey + (Ey)^2 + (Ey)^2$
$= Ey^2 - 2(Ey)^2 + 2(EY)^2$
$= Ey^2$

is positive where the marginal expected utility of expected return is positive,

$$\frac{\partial E(U)}{\partial Ey} = a + 2bEy > 0 \qquad (5A.17)$$

and where $b < 0$. Where the marginal rate of substitution is positive, it can easily be shown that there will be an *increasing* marginal rate of substitution. The upward-sloping indifference curve will be *convex* to the origin if the marginal expected utility of expected return is decreasing (that is, if b in Equation 5A.16 is negative).[9] These properties generate the risk averse behavior depicted in Figure 5.3. An intuitive explanation of why the risk averter's indifference curve is upward sloping and convex to the origin is presented in the preceding chapter.

The marginal rate of substitution, Equation (5A.16), is negative where the marginal expected utility of expected return and b have the same signs. If b is positive, the marginal expected utility of expected return is positive and increasing. There will be a decreasing marginal rate of substitution and the indifference curves will be concave to the origin. This depicts "risk loving" behavior. The indifference curves for a risk lover are drawn in Figure 5A.5.

For the risk lover, risk is not a "bad." Therefore, in order to stay at the same level of expected utility as an increment to risk is acquired, there must be a decrease in expected return. Thus the risk lover's indifference curves are downward sloping. Moreover, consecutive *equal* increments to risk, a "good," can preserve a constant

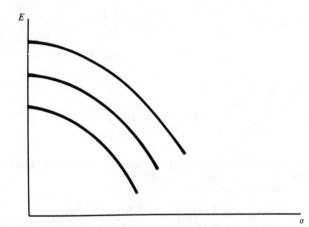

FIGURE 5A.5. Indifference curves of a risk lover.

[9]
$$\frac{d^2Ey}{d\sigma_y{}^2} = \frac{d}{d\sigma_y}\left(\frac{-2b\sigma_y}{a + 2bEy}\right) = -2b\left[\frac{a + 2bEy - \sigma_y\left(2b\dfrac{dEy}{d\sigma}\right)}{(a + 2bEy)^2}\right] 0, \qquad \text{if } b < 0.$$

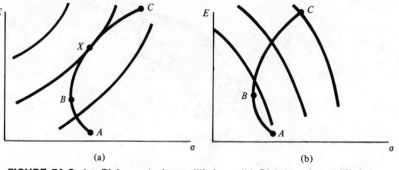

FIGURE 5A.6. (a) Risk averter's equilibrium. (b) Risk lover's equilibrium.

level of total expected utility only if they are compensated for by consecutive *increasing* reductions in expected return, because of an increasing marginal expected utility of expected return.

Risk Aversion, Risk Loving, and the Efficient Risk–Return Locus

Combining the notion of an efficient risk–return locus and two classes of behavior toward risk, we see in Figure 5A.6 contrasting modes of behavior. The risk averter chooses a point of tangency X between the risk–return locus and his indifference map. It generally pays him to diversify. An increase in the rate of expected return on an asset will result in an increase in the proportion of the portfolio devoted to that asset if that asset is a normal good. This was explained in the last part of the preceding chapter.

The optimal position for the risk lover in Figure 5A.6 will always be the upper end of the risk–return locus, C. His indifference curves can never be tangent to the efficient (upward sloping) part of the risk–return locus. The risk lover simply devotes his entire portfolio to the riskiest asset. Diversification has no advantage for the risk lover. However, in the real world even risk lovers may diversify; they may carry an inventory of a less risky asset, in order to save on transactions and information costs, as discussed in Chapter 4.

More than Two Assets

Figure 5A.7 shows the risk–return locus for a portfolio of more than two assets. In a world of three assets, there will be an additional risk–return locus in (σ, E) space representing some fixed proportion of asset 1 and asset 2 (D on the AC locus in Figure 5A.7) and a third asset. The locus DF in Figure 5A.7 represents com-

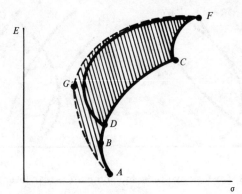

FIGURE 5A.7. Risk–return locus for the three-asset portfolio.

binations of the fixed proportion of asset 1 and asset 2 with asset 3. At point D all of the portfolio is in the fixed 2-asset combination; at point F all of the portfolio is in the third asset.

In general, every point on the AC locus represents the starting point of a three-asset portfolio. The shaded area in Figure 5A.7 represents the domain of all such loci. The external boundary AF is the relevant risk–return locus in a three-asset world. As was the case in the 2-asset world, GF represents the efficient part of this locus. One can always obtain more expected return for any given level of risk in the 3-asset world than in the 2-asset world. The efficient GF locus is everywhere upward from the BC locus. The 3-asset portfolio presents the risk averter with the ability to move to a higher level of total expected utility. There are obvious gains here to the risk averter from further diversification as long as transactions costs are ignored.

The pure risk lover will never hold more than one asset, the riskiest one. In Figure 5A.7 he, too, will be at a higher level of total expected utility at endpoint F than at C, his optimum in the 2-asset case. This analysis can easily be extended to more than three assets.[10]

[10] Obviously, in the real world of many assets an enormous number of computations would be required to identify the efficient locus because of the number of covariances involved for each pair of assets. To expedite security analysis, computational programs must be devised. The professional finance literature in this area considers a number of ways to perform the necessary calculations. See, for example, Harry Markowitz, *Portfolio Selection,* Cowles Foundation Monograph 16 (New York: Wiley, 1959). By relating return to an overall index of the performance of many assets, the burden of calculation can be reduced considerably. This line of reasoning led to the development and widespread use of the *beta* coefficient which relates the fluctuations in the price of a security to the fluctuations in the Dow-Jones Industrial Average. See William F. Sharpe, "A Simplified Model for Portfolio Analysis," *Management Science* (January 1963), 277–293.

Concluding Comment

This appendix extended the simplified analysis of the demand for money as a low-return, low-risk asset in a two-asset world to a general analysis of the risk–return locus in a world of two˙or more risky assets. The advantage of diversification and the notion of an efficient risk–return locus were important implications of this analysis.

BIBLIOGRAPHY FOR CHAPTER 5 AND APPENDIX

CHOW, GREGORY C., "On the Long-Run and Short-Run Demand for Money," *Journal of Political Economy,* vol. 74 (April 1966), 111–131.

DUESENBERRY, JAMES S., "The Portfolio Approach to the Demand for Money and Other Assets," *Review of Economics and Statistics,* vol. 45 (February 1963), supplement, pp. 9–24.

KEYNES, JOHN MAYNARD, *The General Theory of Employment, Interest and Money.* (London: Harcourt Brace and World, 1936).

KONSTAS, PANOS, and MOHMAD W. KHOUJA, "The Keynesian Demand-for-Money Function," *Journal of Money, Credit and Banking,* vol. 1 (November 1969), 765–775.

LAIDLER, D. A., "The Rate of Interest and the Demand for Money—Some Empirical Evidence," *Journal of Political Economy,* vol. 74 (December 1966), 543–555.

LATANÉ, HENRY A., "Income Velocity and Interest Rates: A Pragmatic Approach," *Review of Economics and Statistics,* vol. 42 (November 1953), 445–449.

LEE, T. H., "Alternative Interest Rates and the Demand for Money: The Empirical Evidence," *American Economic Review,* vol. 57 (December 1967), 1168–1181.

LEIJONHUFVUD, AXEL, *On Keynesian Economics and the Economics of Keynes* (New York: Oxford, 1968).

LINTNER, JOHN, "Security Prices, Risk and Maximal Gains from Diversification," *Journal of Finance* (December 1965).

MARKOWITZ, HARRY, *Portfolio Selection,* Cowles Foundation Monograph 16 (New York: Wiley, 1959).

MAYER, THOMAS, and MARTIN BRONFENBRENNER, "Liquidity Functions in the American Economy," *Econometrica,* vol. 28 (October 1960), 810–834.

MELTZER, ALLAN H., "The Demand for Money: The Evidence from the Time Series," *Journal of Political Economy,* vol. 71 (June 1963), 219–246, 768–783.

MOSSIN, JAN, "Equilibrium in a Capital Asset Market," *Econometrica* (October 1966), 768–783.

PARK, YUNG CHUL, "Some Current Issues on the Transmission Process of Monetary Policy," *Staff Papers,* International Monetary Fund (March 1972), 1–45.*

SHARPE, WILLIAM F., "A Simplified Model for Portfolio Analysis," *Management Science* (January 1963), 277–293.

——, "Capital Asset Prices: A Theory of Market Equilibrium under Conditions of Risk," *Journal of Finance* (September 1964), 425–442.

* Reprinted in THOMAS M. HAVRILESKY and JOHN T. BOORMAN, *Current Issues in Monetary Theory and Policy* (Arlington Heights, IL: AHM Publishing, 1976).

SPENCER, ROGER W., "Channels of Monetary Influence," *Review,* Federal Reserve Bank of St. Louis (January 1970), 16–21.*

STARLEAF, D. R., and R. REIMER, "The Keynesian Demand Function for Money: Some Statistical Tests," *Journal of Finance,* vol. 22 (March 1967), 71–76.

STEDREY, ANDREW C., "A Note on Interest Rates and the Demand for Money," *Review of Economics and Statistics,* vol. 41 (August 1959), 303–307.

STONE, BERNELL K., *Risk, Return and Equilibrium* (Cambridge: M.I.T. Press, 1970).

TOBIN, JAMES, "Liquidity Preference as Behavior Towards Risk," *Review of Economic Studies,* vol. 25 (February 1958), 65–86.

——, "Money, Capital, and Other Stores of Value," *American Economic Review, Papers and Proceedings,* vol. 51 (May 1961), 26–37.

——, "The Theory of Portfolio Selection," in *The Theory of Interest Rates,* F. H. Hahn and F. P. Brechling, eds. (New York: St. Martin's Press, 1965).

6

The Quantity Theory
of Money

Introduction

In Chapters 4 and 5 we examined several theories of the demand for money. Chapter 4 presented the basic analysis of the transactions demand for money, using both the traditional Keynesian approach as well as the somewhat more complex inventory-theoretic analysis of William Baumol. Two variants of the asset demand for money were described in Chapter 5: the *liquidity preference theory* of J. M. Keynes and the *risk aversion theory* of James Tobin.

In this chapter the classical view of the demand for money is surveyed. We shall present the major outlines of the theories of Irving Fisher, A. C. Pigou, Alfred Marshall, and J. M. Keynes. The analytic approach taken by these writers in the works cited is generally referred to as the *quantity theory of money*. We shall also describe the modern reformulation of the quantity theory by Milton Friedman and relate his conclusions to those implicit in the older presentations of this doctrine.

In the following chapters we shall see that the classical approach to the demand for money[1] results in a model of the aggregate economy which contrasts markedly

[1] It must be emphasized that dissimilarity in money demand functions is not the *only* distinction between the classical and the Keynesian models.

with the more familiar Keynesian model.[2] In particular, very different policy pre-scriptions are derived from these alternative forms.

Traditional Formulations of the Quantity Theory of Money

It may safely be said that the quantity theory was the theory of the value of money held by virtually all classical economists.[3] This theory is believed by many to have had its origin in the sixteenth century in the writings of Jean Bodin, an official of the French court and a philosopher as well. The impetus for his work was the great rise in prices which took place in France and in most of Western Europe during the latter part of the sixteenth century. Though Bodin recognized several possible causes for these price increases, he laid greatest stress on the rising "stocks of coin" to be found in the country as a result of the huge inflows of "precious" monetary metals from the newly settled colonies in America. His statement was far from a complete analysis of all the forces at work influencing the determination of the absolute price level (a task which has still not been completed by economists), but it did represent the first clear analysis of the relationship between *variations in the price level and changes in the stock of money.*

Though many writers, notably John Locke, David Hume, David Ricardo, and John Stuart Mill, contributed to the development of the quantity theory during the 18th and 19th centuries, it reached an acme of sophistication in the works of Irving Fisher, Alfred Marshall, A. C. Pigou, and J. M. Keynes in the early part of this century.

Irving Fisher's Equation of Exchange

Fisher's formulation of the quantity theory of money is summarized in his "equa-tion of exchange." In this equation Fisher relates the circulation of the money stock to the amount of money expended in the economy during a given period of time. If p_i is the average price of a particular commodity (the ith commodity) and q_i is the total quantity of that commodity sold, $p_i \cdot q_i$ is the total money value spent on that commodity during that time period. For all n commodities in the economy, then,

---

[2] The Keynesian model referred to in this context is the familiar textbook model that derives originally from Keynes' major theoretical work, *The General Theory of Employment, Interest and Money* (London: Harcourt Brace and World, 1936). This model is discussed in Chapter 11 and elaborated upon in Chapter 14. Keynes' earlier work, as represented in his other major works, *A Tract on Monetary Reform* (London: Harcourt Brace and World, 1923) and *A Treatise on Money* (London: Harcourt Brace and World, 1930), is more squarely in the tradi-tion of the classical quantity theory of money.

[3] By "the value of money" we mean the exchange value or the purchasing power of a unit of the monetary stock, the quantity of real goods and services commanded by one unit of "money," however defined.

$$p_1q_1 + p_2q_2 + \cdots + p_nq_n = \sum_{i=1}^{n} p_iq_i = P \cdot T$$

where P is an index of prices (a weighted average price of all goods exchanged in the economy)[4] and T is an index of the quantity of goods traded. The product $P \cdot T$ will be a measure of total monetary expenditures on all goods sold in the economy. If we divide this total level of expenditures $P \cdot T$ by the average quantity of money in the economy during the period in which those expenditures took place, the quotient, $(P \cdot T)/M$, will be the average rate of turnover of money in the exchange of those goods. Fisher terms this average rate of turnover the velocity of circulation of money V. Therefore,

$$V = (P \cdot T)/M \quad \text{or} \quad M \cdot V = P \cdot T. \tag{6.1}$$

The velocity of circulation represents the number of times an average dollar in the total money stock must change hands (during the period in which the flow of goods is measured) for that money stock to finance a given level of transactions. For example, if a money stock of 400 billion dollars serves to facilitate the transfer of 1600 billion dollars in goods and services during a given period of time such as a year, the velocity of circulation of that money stock is 4:

$$V = (P \cdot T)/M = \frac{1600 \text{ billion dollars/year}}{400 \text{ billion dollars}} = 4 \text{ times per year.}$$

Though the relation embodied in the equation of exchange must always hold true if V is viewed as a residual term defined to ensure equality between the two sides of the equation $[V = (P \cdot T)/M]$, this truism is not meaningless. Rather, the equation represents an algebraic statement of the proximate influences on the value of money ". . . through which all others (influences) whatsoever must operate."[5] (parentheses added). In addition, where V is not defined residually but is instead a variable determined by forces at work in the economy, the equation of exchange may be viewed as an equilibrium condition, summarizing the primary factors which influence the determination of the absolute price level P, that is, $P = (M \cdot V)/T$.

Within the framework provided by this equation, Fisher examined the quantity theory of money. His analysis of the factors specified within the equation led him to conclude that since an increase in the quantity of money M would generally not be expected, of itself, to change either the velocity of circulation V or the volume of transactions in the economy T, we could expect that the price level P would vary directly with the quantity of money in circulation. As he stated it, ". . . the normal effects of an increase in the quantity of money is an exactly proportional increase in

[4] See Chapter 9 for a discussion of price indexes.
[5] Irving Fisher, *The Purchasing Power of Money* (New York: Macmillan, 1911), p. 150.

the general level of prices."[6] This result, to Fisher, was the basis of the quantity theory:

> . . . we find then that, under the conditions assumed, the price level varies (1) directly as the quantity of money in circulation (M), (2) directly as the velocity of its circulation (V), (3) inversely as the volume of trade done by it. . . . The first of these three relations is worth emphasis. It constitutes the "quantity theory of money."[7]

It is clear from his own writings that Fisher did not mean to imply that V and T would never change. He viewed V, the velocity of circulation, as an institutionally determined factor influenced primarily by such things as the public's payment habits, the extent of the use of credit, the speed of transportation and communication as it influences the time required to make a payment, and other technical factors that ". . . bear no discoverable relation to the quantity of money in circulation."[8] Likewise, the volume of trade T was determined by factors other than the quantity of money, factors such as the supply of natural resources and the technical conditions of production and distribution.[9] Thus as any of these secondary influences changed, V and T could indeed change, and this could affect the general level of prices. For example, if T, the volume of trade generated in the economy, were to change significantly while the money stock M and the velocity of circulation V remained relatively constant, the price level P would have to adjust to ensure the equality embodied in the equation of exchange.

History provides us with many examples of this phenomenon. For instance, during the latter part of the 19th century in this country the secular expansion of trade T outpaced the growth of the money stock M. With T increasing faster than M and with a relatively stable V, there was a continual decline in the average price level, arrested only by the discovery of new gold deposits and the rapid expansion in the use of the checking account toward the end of the century.

But Fisher was mainly interested in the results of a particular change in the stock of money at a particular time. His conclusion on this point was that such a change would cause a proportionate change in the equilibrium price level P, *not* because V and T never change, but rather because there is no reason to believe that the equilibrium values of those variables would change *in response to* the given change in M. Thus the directly predictable result of a doubling, say, of the money stock, would be unchanged values of V and T and doubled P.

---

[6] Irving Fisher, *op. cit.*, p. 157.

[7] Irving Fisher, *op. cit.*, p. 29.

[8] Irving Fisher, *op. cit.*, p. 152. See also the discussion in the second section of Chapter 4.

[9] More specifically, the level of real income was assumed to be determined outside the system of equations represented by the equation of exchange. The body of economic theory summarized in Walrasian equations of general equilibrium is held to explain the determination of the level of output. See Milton Friedman, "A Theoretical Framework for Monetary Analysis," *Journal of Political Economy*, vol. 78, (March/April 1970), 193–238. The determination of the level of real income in a neoclassical model is featured in Chapter 13.

Although the equation of exchange, by itself, is a somewhat mechanical formulation of the factors involved in the determination of the absolute price level, in the hands of a theorist as skilled as Irving Fisher, who emphasized the myriad of secondary factors influencing the level of the variables explicitly displayed in this equation, it was a useful analytical tool. In the hands of the less skillful and more dogmatic analyst, who did not appreciate the subtleties of the complete Fisherian model, however, V and sometimes even T, degenerated into constants and the equation of exchange became a rigid tool which purported a *necessary* proportionality between M and P.

Fisher's view of the role of the equation of exchange as an analytical device was stated clearly in *The Purchasing Power of Money*.

One of the objectors to the quantity theory attempts to dispose of the equation of exchange . . . by calling it a mere truism. While the equation of exchange is, if we choose, a mere "truism," based on the equivalence, in all purchases, of the money or check expended, on the one hand, and what they buy, on the other, . . . this equation is a means of demonstrating the fact that normally the P's (price levels) vary directly as M, that is, demonstrating the quantity theory. "Truisms" should never be neglected. The greatest generalizations of physical science, such as that forces are proportional to mass and acceleration, are truisms, but, when duly supplemented by specific data, these truisms are the most fruitful sources of useful mechanical knowledge.[10]

The flexibility of Fisher's use of the equation of exchange is evidenced by two of his most important contributions to the development of the quantity theory: his discussion of the events that occur during a "transition period" which follows a monetary change[11] and his detailed statistical investigations of the determinants and behavior of the velocity of circulation. On the former point he notes

. . . that a sudden change in the quantity of money and deposits will temporarily affect their velocities of circulation and the volume of trade. . . . Therefore, the "quantity theory" will not hold true strictly and absolutely during transition periods.[12]

Thus the quantity theory conclusions refer only to the effects on the equilibrium values of the variables in the model that occur in response to a monetary change.[13] Fisher's emphasis on this point was lost on many analysts. On the latter point, the data presented in *The Purchasing Power of Money* show clearly, however, that Fisher himself was under no illusion about the variability of the velocity of circulation.

[10] Irving Fisher, *op. cit.,* p. 157.
[11] The "transition period" analysis that Fisher presents is basically a discussion of the dynamics of moving from one monetary equilibrium to another. He recognized, for example, that although a doubling of the money supply may be expected to double the price level, this result will not occur immediately or automatically. The economy will go through a transition period during which the price level increases to its new value. During that period other variables in the economy (such as the rate of interest and the level of real income) may very well be affected.
[12] Irving Fisher, *op. cit.,* p. 161.
[13] This point is discussed in greater detail in Chapters 13 and 15.

The emphasis in Fisher's model of the quantity theory of money is on the *supply of money* and on the institutional and technical factors that influence the level of production and the value of the velocity of circulation. He had little to say about the psychological factors that influence the "individual habits" that determine an individual's (and society's) velocity of money. He viewed money as a commodity that yields *no utility* to the holder and is held simply to facilitate exchange. He notes that

> The quantity theory of money rests, ultimately, upon the fundamental peculiarity which money alone of all goods possesses,—the fact that it has *no power to satisfy* human wants except a power *to purchase* things which do have such power.[14]

A. C. Pigou and the Cambridge Equation

An alternative conception of the functions performed by money was advanced by Alfred Marshall, A. C. Pigou, and other economists associated with Cambridge University in England. In this view, which is now generally accepted by most economists, *money is capable of yielding utility or satisfaction in and of itself,* since it satisfies two particular needs for the person who possesses it. The first is the provision of convenience and the second, the provision of security. As Pigou notes:

> . . . everybody is anxious to hold enough of his resources in the form of titles to legal tender (money) both to enable him to effect the ordinary transactions of life without trouble, and to secure him against unexpected demands, due to a sudden need, or to a rise in the price of something he cannot easily dispense with.[15]

The major motivation for holding money in the Cambridge version of the quantity theory remains the use it provides to the holder in facilitating transactions. If all receipts and expenditures could be perfectly synchronized as they could be in a perfectly static, timeless model, there would be no need for anyone to hold positive money balances. Even when a disparity does exist between receipts (income flows) and expenditures, in the absence of transactions costs—costs such as brokers' fees and transfer taxes incurred in switching from money to interest-yielding assets—there may still be no net demand for money balances. The absence of transactions costs would allow a person to channel his money income into interest bearing assets immediately upon receipt, and convert those assets into money only at the exact moment the money was required in exchange. In this instance, average money balances held by individuals would be zero. However, when finite transactions costs are introduced into the analysis, it becomes evident that although one could earn interest by purchasing income producing assets and divesting oneself of money balances, the cost involved in purchasing and selling these assets may well exceed the short-term return from the investment. In such a case, money balances actually yield a higher rate of

14 Irving Fisher, *op. cit.,* p. 32.
15 A. C. Pigou, "The Value of Money," *The Quarterly Journal of Economics,* vol. 32 (November 1917), 41.

return net of transactions costs than the interest yielding security. Consequently, the randomness of the timing of receipts and expenditures and the possibility of unforeseen contingencies, together with the finite transactions and information costs incurred in switching between money and earning assets, lead individuals to hold money rather than to convert all cash balances into income earning assets upon receipt of those balances.[16]

In the Cambridge formulation, the quantity of money demanded for these purposes was postulated to vary proportionately with the volume of final transactions or the level of money income, that is,

$$M_d = k \cdot Y = k \cdot P \cdot O \qquad (6.2)$$

where

M_d = the quantity of money demanded
Y = the level of money income, $= P \cdot O$
P = an index of the general price level for newly produced goods and services
O = the level of real output in the economy
k = a factor of proportionality, the Cambridge k.

Since, in equilibrium, the quantity of money demanded must equal the quantity supplied, we may equate this formula for the demand for money with the given money supply M_s, determined exogenously by the authorities. This substitution yields the famous Cambridge equation:

$$M = k \cdot Y. \qquad (6.3)$$

This formulation can be reconciled with Fisher's equation of exchange quite simply. Let O be the level of output of newly produced goods and services in the economy (real GNP) rather than a measure of *total* transactions (which include exchanges involving used goods, financial assets, etc.). This latter measure was represented by T in Fisher's model. Therefore $O < T$. Also, call V' the *income velocity of circulation of money*. Then we may write the equation of exchange to refer only to transactions in final, newly produced goods and services.[17]

$$M \cdot V' = P \cdot O. \qquad (6.4)$$

In the Cambridge version

$$M = k \cdot Y = k \cdot P \cdot O$$

[16] For a more complete discussion of the role of transactions and information costs in determining the demand for money, see Chapter 4, pp. 104–110.

[17] We assume that the prices of all goods in the economy change in the same proportion as the price index. In this way, we need not distinguish between the price index of all goods (in Fisher's equation of exchange) and the index of currently produced goods (in the Cambridge equation). For a reconciliation of these two approaches see Chapter 4, pp. 100–102.

and

$$M(1/k) = P \cdot O. \tag{6.5}$$

Therefore, the reciprocal of k, the proportionality factor, is equal to V', the income velocity of circulation or the "rate of turnover" of money in the purchase of currently produced goods and services. Thus, while Fisher was concerned with the length of time an average unit of the money stock would be held, Pigou focused on the proportion of income (or expenditures) which would, on average over that length of time, be held in the form of money. Just as V, the velocity of circulation of money, may be viewed either as a residual measure defined to ensure the equality expressed in Fisher's equation of exchange, or as a measure of the velocity of circulation of money balances *desired* by the public, that is, as a volitional measure of the public's demand for money, so too, k, the ratio of money balances to income, may be viewed either as an ". . . observed ratio so calculated as to make equation (6.3) an identity, or as the 'desired' ratio so that M is the 'desired' amount of money . . ."[18] Equilibrium in the money market then requires an equality between the desired and observed magnitudes in each of these models so as to equate the supply of and the demand for real money balances.

Pigou has commented on the relation between his own analysis and that which centers on the velocity of circulation of money. As he notes,

> . . . there is no conflict between my formula and that embodied in the quantity theory. But it does not follow that there is nothing to choose between them. . . . The claim that I make on behalf of mine is that it is a somewhat more effective engine of analysis. It focusses attention on the proportion of their resources that people choose to hold in the form of legal tender instead of focussing it on "velocity of circulation." This fact gives it, as I think, a real advantage, because it brings us at once into relation with volition—an ultimate cause of demand—instead of with something that seems at first sight accidental and arbitrary.[19]

Thus the Cambridge contribution involves much more than the renaming of variables. First of all, whereas the emphasis in the Fisherian version is on changes in the *supply of money* and on a (primarily) institutionally determined "rate of turnover" of that money stock, attention in the Cambridge version is placed equally on *money supply* and *money demand*. Second, the volitional element on the demand side of the market is more obvious in the Cambridge equation and leads one to consider the specific motivations involved in an individual's demand for money balances. Given the institutional framework outlined by Fisher, the size of k depends on the strength of the public's motivations for holding money.

This orientation led the Cambridge economists to formulate a fresh line of monetary inquiry from which emanate many of the modern developments in monetary

[18] Milton Friedman, "A Theoretical Framework . . . ," *op. cit.,* p. 200.
[19] A. C. Pigou, *op. cit.,* p. 54.

economics. By emphasizing the individual's demand for money and the utility which money balances may yield, Cambridge economists were led to examine choices facing the individual. For example, with Pigou the individual determined the size of his desired money balances by equating the marginal returns from holding those money balances with the marginal returns from the alternative use of his resources, capital investment.

The more recent manifestation of this tradition views money as simply one among many assets, both physical and financial, that an individual may hold. As a result, the determination of desired money balances involves equating the marginal returns from all these assets in the individual's portfolio. We shall return to this development later in this chapter.

Let us consider more thoroughly the determinants of k, the proportion of money income people desire to hold in the form of money balances. The historical and institutional factors that influenced Fisher's V may be viewed as characteristics of the same socio-economic framework within which the Cambridge economists studied the behavioral determinants of k.[20] These relatively objective institutional factors include (1) the length of the period between wage and salary payments, (2) the degree of sophistication of the population in the use of credit, and (3) the degree of vertical integration of business firms. The more subjective behavioral determinants of the size of k which were emphasized by the Cambridge economists include (1) the public's degree of preference for present consumption over future consumption, (2) their expectations concerning the future return from investment in "industrial activity," and (3) their expectations about price movements. On the last point, for example, Pigou notes that ". . . any expectation that general prices are going to fall increases people's desire to hold (money); and any expectation that they are going to rise has the contrary effect."[21]

In short, the Cambridge theory recognized the same institutional factors that Fisher discussed as determinants of V, but added to them a pronounced emphasis on individual psychological factors such as preferences and expectations. In the Cambridge version, $M = k \cdot Y$, just as in the Fisherian version, $M \cdot V' = P \cdot O$; if it is assumed that a change in the stock of money has no direct effect upon any of the factors except P, the price level, both versions arrive at the familiar quantity theory conclusion that the price level will vary in direct proportion to the size of the money stock. However, the emphasis on the volatile volitional determinants of k in the Cambridge formulation left no doubt that this result would be somewhat less than

[20] In Chapter 4, pp. 98–102, there is considerable discussion of the effect of these factors on the order of magnitude of k.

[21] A. C. Pigou, *op. cit.*, p. 48. Fisher also placed great emphasis on the role of price expectations in the determination of velocity, particularly in his analysis of the transition period. The Cambridge formulation of the quantity theory is better suited to the explicit inclusion of this factor into the analysis, however. For an examination of the price expectations effect and its role in the determination of the level of interest rates, see Milton Friedman, "Factors Affecting the Level of Interest Rates," *Savings and Residential Financing*, 1968 Conference Proceedings, United States Savings and Loan League (May 1968). Reprinted in Havrilesky and Boorman, *Current Issues in Monetary Theory and Policy, op. cit.*

certain, for a change in the public's preferences and expectations could easily nullify the simple quantity theory result.

Consequently, the less obvious forces in Fisher's model, which are introduced only in his discussion of "transition periods," are brought to the fore in the Cambridge theory and made an integral part of the analysis. Though the conclusions of the models often appeared identical and indeed were thought identical by their architects, it is far more obvious in the Cambridge version that the price level or the level of money income merely *tends* to follow the size of the money stock and that strict proportionality between these variables is highly unlikely.

The flexible Cambridge formulation of the quantity theory, as the foundation of much modern monetary theory, has proven more viable than the Fisherian version. However, this was not its major contribution. The most important result of the work of the Cambridge economists (and one that has not yet been completely exploited) was the fact that it provided a more promising line of inquiry than the model of Irving Fisher. It led economists to consider a utility analysis of the demand for money balances and to view money as simply one asset in a multi–asset portfolio. In this way the analysis of the demand for money came to be perceived simply as the application of the general theory of demand to a specific problem. The results of this orientation were the development of Keynes' liquidity preference theory as reviewed in Chapter 5 and the reformulation of the Fisherian model by Milton Friedman.

The Neoclassical Reformulation

Very few economists today proffer either the Cambridge or the Fisherian quantity theories in their original form. In fact, the liquidity preference theory as presented in Chapter 5 and its role in the general equilibrium macroeconomic models to be presented in Chapters 11 through 15 represents today's most widely accepted theoretical paradigm. However, the quantity theory approach is also an important analytical tool in the work of a growing number of influential theorists, most notably Milton Friedman of the University of Chicago.[22]

Friedman's quantity theory[23] is more sophisticated than the theories of Fisher and the Cambridge economists, yet it remains in their tradition. Like the earlier quantity

[22] Friedman's major works in this field include: "The Quantity Theory of Money—A Restatement," in *Studies in the Quantity Theory of Money*, Milton Friedman, ed. (Chicago: University of Chicago Press, 1956), 1–21; "The Demand for Money: Some Theoretical and Empirical Results," *Journal of Political Economy*, vol. 67 (August 1959), 327–351; and "Money and Business Cycles," with Anna J. Schwartz, *Review of Economics and Statistics*, vol. 45 (Supplement) (February 1963). These works and an essay entitled, "The Optimum Quantity of Money" are reprinted in Milton Friedman, *The Optimum Quantity of Money and Other Essays*, (Chicago: Aldine Publishing, 1969).

[23] The classification of Friedman's work as part of the "quantity theory tradition" has been challenged by Don Patinkin. See "The Chicago Tradition, the Quantity Theory, and Friedman," *Journal of Money, Credit and Banking*, vol. 1 (February 1969), 46–70.

theorists, he maintains the hypothesis that the demand for money function is the most stable macroeconomic relation economists have discovered, and he promotes it as the most reliable basis for aggregate economic analysis and policy decisions. In contrast to those who favor the familiar Keynesian analytic framework, he explicitly rejects the idea that the Keynesian consumption function (more specifically, multipliers derived from models based on the Keynesian consumption function) represents a more stable and reliable function. The theoretical money demand function which Friedman postulates appears quite different from the simple equation of exchange of Irving Fisher. Nevertheless, the final empirical form of this function, which incorporates the conclusions of his statistical analysis, supports the major conclusions of the classical quantity theory.[24]

In his analysis of the demand for money Friedman does not separate the individual's money stock into analytically distinct components, such as "active" and "idle" balances, as is a common practice in some versions of the liquidity preference theory. Rather, he views money as one kind of asset in which a wealth-owning unit may hold a part of its wealth or as a capital good that yields productive services that a business enterprise can combine with the services of other productive assets or with labor to produce an output. Money, therefore, is seen as a commodity that yields utility to its holder according to the functions it performs. As Friedman notes: ". . . the most fruitful approach is to regard money as one of a sequence of assets, on a par with bonds, equities, houses, consumer durable goods, and the like."[25]

Friedman's procedure, then, is to develop a theory of the demand for money on the basis of an examination of the services that money performs for wealth-owning units and business enterprises. He is not primarily concerned with the motives that lead people to hold money. Rather, it is taken as given that money is held by households and business firms and the principles of traditional demand theory are applied to determine the factors that may influence the size of the money balances that these groups desire. As he notes, "To the ultimate wealth-owning units in the economy, money is one kind of asset, one way of holding wealth. To the productive enterprise, money is a capital good, a source of productive services that are combined with other productive services to yield the products that the enterprise sells."[26]

Friedman's analysis of the demand for money by the ultimate wealth-owning unit is based on the theory of the demand for a consumption service. The major factors adduced by this theory as important in the determination of money demand include: the total wealth of the unit; the division of wealth between human and non-human forms; the relative returns on alternative wealth forms, including money; and

[24] For a more complete discussion of the differences between the pre-Keynesian quantity theory and its post-Keynesian reformulation, and the relationship of these theories to Keynesian liquidity preference, see David Fand, "Keynesian Monetary Theories, Stabilization Policy and the Recent Inflation," *Journal of Money, Credit and Banking,* vol. 1 (August 1969), 561–565.

[25] Milton Friedman, "The Demand for Money: Some Theoretical and Empirical Results," *op. cit.,* p. 349.

[26] Friedman, "The Quantity Theory of Money—A Restatement," *Studies on the Quantity Theory of Money, op. cit.,* p. 4.

the tastes and preferences of individuals. For the business enterprise, the theory of the demand for the services of productive resources suggests that the demand for money is determined by the cost of services yielded by money balances, that is, the cost of raising funds by borrowing or by other means, the cost of substitute productive services, and the contribution of money as a productive factor to the value of the output of the production process.

In his restatement of the quantity theory, Friedman writes the following (approximate) demand for money function:[27]

$$\frac{M_d}{P} = f\left(i_m, i_b, i_e, \frac{1}{P}\frac{dP}{dt}, W, n \right) \tag{6.6}$$

where

M_d/P = the *real* quantity of money demanded
$\quad i_m$ = the rate of return on money
$\quad i_b$ = the rate of return on bonds
$\quad i_e$ = the rate of return on equities (stocks)
$\quad P$ = an index of the general price level of newly produced goods and services

$\frac{1}{P}\frac{dP}{dt}$ = the rate of change of the price index P over time

W = wealth
$\quad n$ = the ratio of nonhuman to human wealth.

The presence of the terms i_m, i_e, i_b and $(1/P)(dP/dt)$ reflects the influence of the rates of return on alternative wealth forms in the determination of the desired level of money balances. For example, i_e measures the nominal return on equities and $(1/P)(dP/dt)$ measures (in part) the change in the real value of that return as the general price level changes. The term W is a measure of wealth and reflects the constraint imposed on an asset holder by the size of his portfolio. This variable plays a role analogous to that of the income constraint in the traditional theory of the demand for consumer goods.

The final term n is a measure of the "human wealth" component in an individual's total wealth. Since wealth is simply the discounted present value of a future stream of returns (or income) to be received from a certain stock of capital, Friedman recognizes that an individual can increase this flow of income (and his wealth) by

---

[27] A velocity function can be derived from a demand-for-money function by setting nominal money demand equal to nominal money supply, inverting the functions and multiplying by income:

$$M_s = M_d = f\left(i_m, i_b, i_e, \frac{1}{P}\frac{dP}{dt}, W, n \right)$$

$$Y/M_s = Y/f\left(i_m, i_b, i_e, \frac{1}{P}\frac{dP}{dt}, W, n \right).$$

"investing" in education or by other activities which increase the value of his labor power. To account for the human factor in the total wealth stock, Friedman includes the ratio of nonhuman to human wealth in his money demand function. We may expect that the larger the "human" component of an individual's total stock of wealth, the greater will be his demand for money, since holding a larger stock of money balances is one means of balancing the illiquidity or nonmarketability of human wealth.

The demand for money by business firms can be explained, as Friedman suggests, by the same variables that explain the demand for money by other wealth-owning units. Consequently, the demand-for-money function—or velocity function—for the entire economy will have the same form as Equation (6.6) and will include interest rate terms, wealth measures, and price factors as independent variables. Friedman indicates that the influence of both the interest rate variables and price variations on the volume of money balances demanded will be negative, while the relation between wealth and money demand is positive.

Few economists could disagree with Friedman on the general lines of his formal analysis or even his abstract formulation of the money demand (velocity) function. Nonetheless, when his theory suggests that it is some measure of *wealth* rather than *current income* that is the basic constraint on the public's desired money holdings, it contrasts with the money demand theories discussed in the previous chapters and the earlier sections of this chapter.[28] Friedman notes that "the emphasis on income as a surrogate for wealth, rather than as a measure of the 'work' to be done by money, is conceptually perhaps the basic difference between more recent work and the earlier versions of the quantity theory."[29]

Friedman's theory gives little indication of the relative importance of the variables included in the money demand function. Consequently, critical appraisal of Friedman's quantity theory of money must rest on empirical analysis of the public's money holding behavior; it is on this point (the interpretation of empirical evidence) that most of the disagreements surrounding Friedman's theories arise.

The most important questions which empirical analysis can help to answer concern:

(1) the actual importance of the various interest rates in the money demand function,

(2) the relative explanatory power of income and wealth in such a function, and

(3) the stability of the function over time.[30]

Friedman himself has presented evidence relevant to these questions.[31] However,

---

[28] However, Keynesian-type models of recent vintage do often incorporate a wealth constraint. See Chapter 12 for an example.

[29] Milton Friedman, "A Theoretical Framework . . . ," *op. cit.*, p. 203.

[30] These questions are dealt with in detail in the survey of the empirical work done in this field which appears in Chapters 7 and 8.

[31] Milton Friedman, "The Demand for Money: Some Theoretical and Empirical Results," *op. cit.*

other investigators have often disagreed both with his methods and with his conclusions. Specifically, though his reformulated quantity theory explicitly recognizes several interest rates as independent variables, Friedman concludes from his empirical studies that no statistical significance can be attached to them.[32] In other words, though *economic theory* would lead one to expect that interest rates influence the public's desired money balances, Friedman claims that the *empirical evidence* he presents shows that this influence, if present at all, is of minor importance. As he states it, he was unable ". . . to find any close connection between changes in velocity (or desired money balances) from cycle to cycle and any of a number of interest rates."[33] (parentheses added)

Of much more importance, according to Friedman's interpretation of the available evidence, is the response of the volume of real money balances demanded to changes in the level of "permanent income." Permanent income is a concept he developed in connection with a study of the consumption function.[34] It is a measure of a long-run income concept thought to be the most important factor relevant to consumer spending decisions.[35] Empirically, this figure is constructed as a weighted average of past values of "measured" income (net national product, for example).[36]

Friedman's empirical analysis leads him to conclude that a satisfactory explanation of money demand behavior can be achieved through the application of the following equation to aggregate data:

$$\frac{M_d}{NP} = \gamma \left(\frac{Y_p}{NP}\right)^{\delta}$$

where M_d and P are as defined above and N = population, Y_p = permanent income, and γ and δ are behavioral parameters.

This equation indicates that real per capita money balances demanded are an exponential function of real per capita permanent income. Thus the interest rate and the price change terms have been dropped from the empirical function as explan-

---

[32] Statistical significance means that the relationships discussed have been subjected to empirical tests and have been found "significant" or "nonsignificant" by the usual 95% interval tests applied to the coefficients in regression analysis.

[33] Milton Friedman, "The Demand for Money . . ." *op. cit.,* p. 349.

[34] Milton Friedman, *A Theory of the Consumption Function* (Princeton, NJ: Princeton University Press, 1957).

[35] The role of permanent income in the demand for money is discussed in Chapter 8, and Friedman's theory of consumption is discussed in Chapter 10.

[36] Friedman's use of this concept is partly the result of inadequate data on alternative wealth measures. As he notes,

> In practice, estimates of total wealth are seldom available. Instead, income may serve as an index of wealth. However, it should be recognized that income as measured by statisticians may be a defective index of wealth because it is subject to erratic year-to-year fluctuations, and a longer term concept, like the concept of permanent income . . . , may be useful.

Friedman, "A Theoretical Framework . . . ," *op. cit.,* p. 203.

atory variables. As Friedman notes, "In our experiments, the rate of interest had an effect in the direction to be expected from theoretical considerations but too small to be statistically significant. We have not as yet been able to isolate by correlation techniques any effect of the rate of change of prices, though a historical analysis persuades us that such an effect is present."[37] Consequently only the permanent income variable, employed as a proxy measure for the theoretically more relevant concept of wealth, remains in the final form of the equation, and it assumes a form similar to Fisher's equation of exchange.

Money Demand, the Interest Rate, and Price Expectations

Although many variables are included in his theoretical money demand function, Friedman concludes that a single measure of income (a wealth proxy) is sufficient to explain most changes in the demand for money.[38] This conclusion is disputed in much of the recent empirical literature on the demand for money.[39] Most analysts find that when the empirical money demand function includes some interest rate measure, the explanatory power and predictive capability of that equation is significantly improved. However, the presence of a statistically significant interest rate term in the money demand function is not sufficient cause, by itself, to reject the quantity theorists' formulation of the demand for money or their analysis of the aggregate economy.

Quantity theorists have long recognized that the demand for money may be influenced by interest rates. Nonetheless, in static quantity theory models of the aggregate economy, although the interest rate may enter the money demand function, adjustments in the monetary sector (changes in the supply of money, for example) do not in turn influence the equilibrium level of real interest rates.[40] They merely exert *temporary effects* on interest rates during what Fisher referred to as "transition periods." As seen in Chapter 13, the equilibrium real interest rate in static, neoclassical aggregate models is determined solely by "real" factors in the economy—productivity (investment) and thrift (saving).

Despite their independence in *static* models, in *dynamic* models there is quite an important relationship between the growth rate of the money supply, changes in the

[37] Milton Friedman, "The Demand for Money . . . ," *op. cit.*, p. 329.

[38] Some of the doubts concerning the meaning of Friedman's empirical results center on his use of the permanent income measure. His critics contend that this empirical measure ". . . combines wealth, interest rates, population, and lagged income in a single variable and thus combines their separate effects." Allan H. Meltzer, "The Demand for Money: The Evidence from the Time Series," *Journal of Political Economy* (June 1963), 221.

[39] See the survey of the empirical literature on the demand for money in Chapters 7 and 8.

[40] See Chapters 13 and 15 for a complete discussion of the assumptions which must be incorporated into the static, neoclassical model of the aggregate economy to generate these results.

average level of prices in the economy over time, and changes in the level of nominal interest rates. While the equilibrium level of real interest rates is determined by "real" phenomena in static models, in a dynamic context there are means whereby price level changes caused by monetary disturbances may influence nominal market interest rates.

Friedman's analysis begins with a discussion of the three effects that a monetary change ultimately may have on the level of interest rates. These are (1) the liquidity effect, (2) the nominal income effect, and (3) the price expectations effect. The *liquidity effect* refers to the initial short-run influence which a change in the money stock (or the rate of change of the money stock in a dynamic framework) will have on interest rates. It is recognized, for example, that an increase in the money stock, since it disturbs the equilibrium of the public's asset portfolio, will induce individuals who find themselves holding excess cash to readjust their portfolios by purchasing securities. This action will bid up security prices and temporarily decrease interest rates. This response is similar to that described in the Keynesian literature on liquidity preference. Quantity theorists emphasize, however, that this is only a transitory "first-round" effect and that the lower interest rates which may follow an increase in the money stock do not represent the final adjustment to a new equilibrium. This change is simply a manifestation of the transition period. For, generally, as interest rates fall, there will be an increase in expenditures and nominal income.[41] This, in turn, will increase the demand for loanable funds and for transactions balances, reversing the fall in interest rates and pushing them back up to their previous level. This is referred to as *the nominal income effect*.

The *price expectations effect* may actually drive interest rates beyond their previous level.[42] This reaction is suggested in the work of Irving Fisher. Fisher distinguished sharply between two components in observed (nominal) interest rates: ". . . the 'real' rate of interest, to which real saving and investment respond, and a premium based on expected changes in the price level."[43] During periods of rising prices, for example, the premium component reflects an attempt on the part of lenders to recoup through an interest return an amount equal to the loss of real purchasing power which they expect to suffer from the deterioration of the real principal value of their assets. During periods of a stable price level, when no change is anticipated in future prices, there would be no premium and the real rate and the nominal rate would be the same. However, during periods of rapidly changing prices, the nominal rate could diverge sharply from the real rate even for a long period of time.

Thus, it is this *price expectations premium* that is likely to push nominal market interest rates beyond their previous level. As the initial increase in the money supply

[41] For a more complete explanation of this mechanism see Chapter 15. Also see William E. Gibson, "Interest Rates and Monetary Policy," *Journal of Political Economy,* vol. 78 (May/June 1970), 431–455.

[42] Milton Friedman, "Factors Affecting the Level of Interest Rates," *op. cit.*

[43] William P. Yohe and Denis Karnosky, "Interest Rates and Price Level Changes, 1952–1969," *Review,* Federal Reserve Bank of St. Louis (December 1969), 18.

temporarily lowers interest rates and induces a rise in spending and nominal income, it also may induce an increase in prices. If a new rate of money supply growth persists over time, after prices have been rising for some time, individuals will eventually come to anticipate that prices will continue to rise. In these circumstances, lenders ". . . would hedge against changes in the real value of their loan principal by adding the (expected) percentage change in prices over the life of the loan to the interest charge" (parenthesis added by authors), and borrowers, ". . . expecting money income to change in proportion to prices, would readily accept the higher rate."[44]

A study by William Yohe and Denis Karnosky indicates that just such a price expectations effect may be the critical element in the explanation of the rise in nominal interest rates which occurred in the late 1960's (1952–1969). In particular, they conclude that ". . . price level changes since 1952 have evidently come to have a prompt and substantial effect on price expectations and nominal interest rates. . . . Most significant is the finding that price level changes, rather than (changes in) "real" rates, account for nearly all the variation in nominal interest rates since 1961."[45]

This discussion indicates the scope of the work currently being done by writers in the quantity theory tradition and its immediate relevance to the inflationary environment of the 1970's.[46] The quantity theory of money in its modern reformulation is not simply a static theory of the demand for money. Rather, building on the path-breaking work of Irving Fisher, the post-Keynesian quantity theory represents a theory of money income based on an analysis of money demand. It is a theory that incorporates Fisher's detailed analysis of the determinants of the velocity of circulation, the Cambridge analysis of the psychological factors influencing the public's desire for money balances, and the dynamic analysis that begins with Fisher's discussion of the "transition period."

Concluding Remarks

We have presented a review of the major theoretical formulations of the quantity theory of money as developed by Fisher, Pigou, Friedman, and others. Though seemingly diverse, each begins from the same focal point in analyzing the aggregate economy. Furthermore, they each come to similar conclusions about the role of money in the economy and the relative efficiency of monetary and fiscal policy for control of the economy. Friedman has provided the best description of what it means to be a "quantity theorist." As he states it:

[44] William P. Yohe and Denis Karnosky, *op. cit.,* p. 19.
[45] William P. Yohe and Denis Karnosky, *op. cit.,* pp. 35–36.
[46] In Chapter 15 this view of the relationship between money, inflation, and interest rates is discussed in the context of the macroeconomic model developed in later chapters. That analysis provides a useful explanation of the link between inflation, interest rates, and monetary policy over the business cycle.

The quantity theorist accepts the empirical hypothesis that the demand for money is highly stable—more stable than functions such as the consumption function that are offered as alternative key relations. . . . The quantity theorist not only regards the demand for money function as stable; he also regards it as playing a vital role in determining variables that he regards as of great importance for the analysis of the economy as a whole, such as the level of money income or of prices. . . . The quantity theorist also holds that there are important factors affecting the supply of money that do not affect the demand for money.[47]

This last point is crucial, since "a stable demand function is useful precisely in order to trace out the effects of changes in supply, which means that it is useful only if supply is affected by at least some factors other than those regarded as affecting demand."[48]

This chapter has been limited almost exclusively to an examination of the demand for money function (the equation of exchange or the velocity function, in alternative formulations) as developed in the literature on the quantity theory of money. We have not discussed at length the contributions made by the writers in this tradition to the broader aspects of macroeconomic analysis. Specifically, our brief discussion of the dynamic adjustment process incorporated in the quantity theorists' analysis of the aggregate economy is extended in Fisher's discussion of the "transition period" and in Friedman's discussion of the factors determining the level of interest rates.

In later chapters we shall incorporate the quantity theorists' contribution to the theory of the demand for money into a general equilibrium model of the aggregate economy.

QUESTIONS FOR CHAPTER 6

1. a. What is the equation of exchange? Define each variable that appears in this equation. What does it mean to say that the equation of exchange may be viewed as an "identity"?

   b. "To say that $MV = PT$ is to espouse the quantity theory." True or false? Explain.

2. What two assumptions are necessary to make the Fisher and/or Cambridge versions strict quantity theories of money?

3. a. Why does the Cambridge formulation of the quantity theory represent more than a simple renaming of the variables of the Fisherian equation of exchange?

   b. "Unmistakably Keynes' monetary theory bore the Cambridge imprint!" Do you agree or disagree?

---

[47] Milton Friedman, "The Quantity Theory of Money—A Restatement," in *Studies in the Quantity Theory of Money, op. cit.,* p. 16.

[48] Milton Friedman, "The Quantity Theory of Money—A Restatement," in *Studies in the Quantity Theory of Money, op. cit.,* pp. 16–17.

4. List the basic institutional factors which determine V, the velocity of circulation of money. What additional influences were stressed by the Cambridge economists in discussing the determinants of k, the proportionality factor in the money demand equation?

5. How does Milton Friedman's analysis of the factors affecting the demand for money differ from the Keynesian liquidity preference analysis?

6. Explain the rationale by which Friedman includes an interest rate term in his theoretical demand-for-money function. What is his empirical finding about this factor as a determinant of money demand?

7. By persistently attempting to maintain interest rates that are lower than their real equilibrium levels, the monetary authority will cause nominal interest rates to rise. Explain.

BIBLIOGRAPHY FOR CHAPTER SIX

ALLAIS, MAURICE, "A Restatement of the Quantity Theory of Money," *American Economic Review,* vol. 56 (December 1966), 1123–1157.

CHOW, GREGORY C., "On the Long-Run and Short-Run Demand for Money," *Journal of Political Economy,* vol. 74 (April 1966), 111–113.

FAND, DAVID, "Keynesian Monetary Theories, Stabilization Policy and the Recent Inflation," *Journal of Money, Credit and Banking,* vol. 1 (August 1969), 561–565.

——, "A Monetarist Model of the Monetary Process," *Journal of Finance,* vol. 25 (May 1970), 275–289.

FISHER, IRVING, *The Purchasing Power of Money* (New York: Augustus M. Kelley, Bookseller, 1963), reprint of new and revised edition, 1922.

FRIEDMAN, MILTON, "The Quantity Theory of Money—A Restatement," in *Studies in the Quantity Theory of Money,* Milton Friedman, ed. Chicago: University of Chicago Press, 1956, 1–21.

——, *A Theory of the Consumption Function* (Princeton, N.J.: Princeton University Press, 1957).

——, "The Supply of Money and Changes in Prices and Output," *The Relationship of Prices to Economic Stability and Growth: Compendium of Papers Submitted to the Joint Economic Committee,* 85th Congress, 2nd Session (March 31, 1958) (Washington: Government Printing Office, 1958).

——, "The Demand for Money: Some Theoretical and Empirical Results," *Journal of Political Economy,* vol. 67 (August 1959), 327–351.

——, "The Demand for Money," *American Philosophical Society Proceedings,* vol. 105 (June 1961), 259–264.

——, "Postwar Trends in Monetary Theory and Policy," *National Banking Review,* vol. 2 (September 1964), 1–10.

——, "Interest Rates and the Demand for Money," *Journal of Law and Economics,* vol. 9 (October 1966), 71–85.

——, "Factors Affecting the Level of Interest Rates," *Savings and Residential Financing,* 1968 Conference Proceedings, United States Savings and Loan League (May 1968).*

——, *The Optimum Quantity of Money and Other Essays* (Chicago: Aldine Publishing, 1969).

——, "A Theoretical Framework for Monetary Analysis," *Journal of Political Economy,* vol. 78 (March/April 1970), 193–238.

——, and ANNA SCHWARTZ, "Money and Business Cycles," *Review of Economics and Statistics,* vol. 45 (Supplement) (February 1963).

——, "Comment on Tobin," *Quarterly Journal of Economics,* vol. 84 (May 1970), 318–327.

GIBSON, W. E., "Interest Rates and Monetary Policy," *Journal of Political Economy,* vol. 78 (May/June 1970), 431–455.

——, "The Lag in the Effect of Monetary Policy on Income and Interest Rates," *Quarterly Journal of Economics,* vol. 84 (May 1970), 288–300.

——, "Price-Expectations Effects on Interest Rates," *Journal of Finance,* vol. 25 (March 1970), 19–34.

JOHNSON, HARRY G., "A Quantity Theorist's Monetary History of the U.S.," *Economic Journal,* vol. 75 (June 1965), 388–396.

KEYNES, JOHN MAYNARD, *The General Theory of Employment, Interest and Money* (London: Harcourt Brace and World, 1936).

——, *A Tract on Monetary Reform* (London: Harcourt Brace and World, 1923).

——, *A Treatise on Money* (London: Harcourt Brace and World, 1930).

MELTZER, ALAN H., "The Demand for Money: The Evidence from the Time Series," *Journal of Political Economy* (June 1963), 221.

——, "Irving Fisher and the Quantity Theory of Money," *Orbis* (March 1967), 32–38.

PATINKIN, DON, "The Chicago Tradition, the Quantity Theory, and Friedman," *Journal of Money, Credit and Banking,* vol. 1 (February 1969), 46–70.

PIGOU, A. C., "The Value of Money," *The Quarterly Journal of Economics,* vol. 32 (November 1917), 41.

SAMUELSON, PAUL, "What Classical and Neoclassical Monetary Theory Really Was," *Canadian Journal of Economics,* vol. 1 (February 1968).

SARGENT, THOMAS J., "Commodity Price Expectations and the Interest Rate," *Quarterly Journal of Economics,* vol. 83 (February 1969), 127–140.

TOBIN, JAMES, "Money and Income: Post Hoc Ergo Propter Hoc?" *Quarterly Journal of Economics,* vol. 84 (May 1970), 301–317.

YOHE, WILLIAM P., and DENIS S. KARNOSKY, "Interest Rates and Price Level Changes, 1952–1969," *Review,* Federal Reserve Bank of St. Louis, (December 1969), 18.

* Reprinted in Thomas M. Havrilesky and John T. Boorman, *Current Issues in Monetary Theory and Policy* (Arlington Heights, IL: AHM Publishing, 1976).

7

The Evidence on the Demand for Money: Theoretical Formulations and Empirical Results—Part I*

Introduction

Numerous theories have been proposed to explain the public's demand for money. Though the range of hypotheses implicit in these theories is extremely broad, there are certain important elements common to all of them. Most significantly, almost all of these theories can be generalized into propositions about the existence of a stable relationship between a few important economic variables and the stock of money demanded.

While diverse theories often posit similar variables to explain the demand for money, they frequently differ in the specific role assigned to each. For example, in Chapter 4 in the simplest version of the transactions theory of the demand for money, the stock of money demanded is hypothesized to be strictly proportional to a single variable—the volume of transactions to be facilitated by that money stock. In comparison, the inventory theoretic view, which recognizes the interest rate as an opportunity cost of holding money balances and introduces brokerage fees and other charges as explicit costs of switching wealth between interest bearing assets and money, denies this proportionality between money and income. In this model minimization of the total cost of managing money balances leads to a

* All the references pertaining to this chapter may be found in the bibliography that follows Chapter 8 on pp. 217–222.

solution that suggests the possibility of substantial economies of scale in the demand for money.

As another example, in Chapter 5, in the liquidity preference theories of John Maynard Keynes and James Tobin the role of money as an asset is stressed, and the motives for holding money are examined. An analysis of the costs (income foregone) and benefits (risks avoided) of holding wealth in the form of money balances suggests hypotheses in which income and the interest rate on alternative financial assets are included as the primary determinants of desired money balances. In comparison, in Chapter 6 Milton Friedman's "restatement" of the quantity theory eschews a specific focus on the "roles" of money or on the "motives" of individuals in holding money balances.[1] Instead, Friedman emphasizes the services yielded by money in individual and business portfolios. In this view money is simply one among the many assets—including physical and human assets—held by the public. This leads to the hypothesis that all the alternatives available to the wealth holder may influence his desired money balances.

These examples of alternative money demand hypotheses suggest some of the major questions that have been the focus of empirical investigation. A more complete list would include the following specific problems:

1. What empirical measure should be used to represent the theoretical concept of "money"?

2. How are empirically testable money demand functions conventionally specified? In this connection it is useful to examine some of the more common formulations that have included either a role for expectations in the determination of desired money balances or a distinction between the long-run equilibrium level and the short-run adjustment pattern by which equilibrium is approached.

3. What is the role of the interest rate in the money demand function? This issue raises several related questions.
   a. If the interest rate is statistically important in the determination of the demand for money, what is the interest elasticity of money balances?
   b. Which one of the alternative interest rate measures available is most relevant to the determination of the demand for money?
   c. Given that the interest rate is important in the money demand function, has evidence been presented that would support the existence (historical or potential) of a "liquidity trap"?

4. What is the relative significance of income, wealth, and other economic variables that have been suggested along with the interest rate as determinants of the demand for money?

[1] Milton Friedman, "The Quantity Theory of Money, A Restatement," in *Studies in the Quantity Theory of Money*, Milton Friedman, ed. (Chicago: University of Chicago Press, 1956). See Don Patinkin, "The Chicago Tradition, the Quantity Theory and Friedman," *Journal of Money, Credit and Banking*, vol. 1 (February 1969), 46–70.

5. Do money demand functions that include the essential arguments suggested by alternative theories appear to be stable over long periods of time?

These are the major issues raised in the empirical literature on the demand for money. Each of these will be considered in turn in this and the following chapter.[2]

The Empirical Definition of Money

What assets ought to be included in our measure of "the money stock"? If we focus on those theories that emphasize the transactions motive for holding money, the proper definition of the items to include in the money stock is not a profound problem. The money stock should be defined to consist only of those assets that serve as generally acceptable media of exchange. It is widely agreed that only commercial bank demand deposits and currency in circulation provide this service. However, if the public's demand for money is viewed as arising from a speculative motive, the list of assets in the definition of money may be expanded to include some assets that are stable in nominal value, that is, fixed dollar assets whose value is independent of variations in the interest rate. Finally, if the demand for money is approached as part of the general theory of demand, all assets that are close substitutes for the media of exchange (and respond to the same yields in the demand function) should be included in the definition. The latter approach clearly indicates that the proper definition of the money stock is largely an empirical question.

Allan H. Meltzer has enunciated one possible criterion for selecting the appropriate empirical definition of the money stock.

> The problem is one of defining money so that a stable demand function can be shown to have existed under differing institutional arrangements, changes in social and political environment, and changes in economic conditions, or to explain the effects of such changes on the function.[3]

This criterion focuses on the implications of the definition of the money stock for the degree of control that the monetary authority has over crucial macroeconomic variables.[4] The money stock and interest rates are thought to have a strong effect

[2] More general issues, particularly those dealing with econometric problems in the estimation of money demand functions, will be discussed—often in footnotes—at various points of the text.

[3] Allan H. Meltzer, "The Demand for Money: The Evidence from the Time Series," *Journal of Political Economy*, vol. 71 (June 1963), 222.

[4] There are, of course, additional criteria by which to define a measure of the money stock. George G. Kaufman, following Milton Friedman and David Meiselman, defines the money stock according to its correlation with income (taking into consideration the possible lead–lag relationship between money and income). In selecting the set of financial assets to be included in the money supply, he employs two criteria originally specified by Friedman and Meiselman: choose that set that (1) has the highest correlation with income and (2) has a higher correlation with income than any of the components separately. This alternative operational approach, unlike the Meltzer criterion, derives from the proposition that the equilibrium nominal money stock can be controlled by the monetary authority and suggests a rather specific theoretical model on which to base monetary policy. The Meltzer criterion is preferred here since it is

upon aggregate demand, employment, and the price level in the economy. If the demand for money is unstable (shifts unpredictably), the effect of monetary policy actions on the equilibrium money stock and interest rates will be uncertain. In short, stability of the money demand function and a capability on the part of the monetary authority to influence closely the stock of assets corresponding to the theoretical concept of money employed in that function would seem to be necessary conditions for the successful implementation of monetary policy.[5] These conditions will allow the authorities to exert a predictable influence over the equilibrium stock of money, interest rates, and other variables in the money demand equation.

Economists traditionally have defined the money stock in the "narrow" sense as the sum of demand deposit liabilities of commercial banks and currency held by the public. However, a number of analysts include time deposits at commercial banks within their measure of the money stock. Milton Friedman, for example, views time deposits as "a temporary abode of purchasing power" and includes them in the "broad" measure of money that he employs in his empirical work. A few researchers go beyond even this "broad" concept to include such things as savings and loan shares, mutual savings bank deposits, and claims against other financial intermediaries in their measure of "money." Conceptually, of course, it is possible to go even further and include still other financial assets (or even some measure of credit availability, such as unusual but available trade credit) in a measure of money.[6]

In this survey, evidence on the question of the best definition of the money stock will be judged in accord with the Meltzer criterion. David Laidler has suggested an explicit set of conditions by which to evaluate the relative stability of alternative empirical functions to implement this criterion. As he expresses it:

> A "more stable demand for money function" may be taken to be one that requires knowledge of fewer variables and their parameters in order to predict the demand

---

compatible with a more broadly defined set of money demand functions. See George G. Kaufman, "More on an Empirical Definition of Money," *American Economic Review,* vol. 59 (March 1969), 78–87. Milton Friedman and David Meiselman, "Relative Stability of Monetary Velocity and the Investment Multiplier in the United States, 1897–1957," in Commission on Money and Credit, *Stabilization Policies* (Englewood Cliffs, NJ: Prentice-Hall, 1963). Frederick C. Schadrack, in "An Empirical Approach to the Definition of Money," *Monetary Aggregates and Monetary Policy,* Federal Reserve Bank of New York (1974), 28–34 extends these empirical criteria to include goodness of fit, stability over time, and predictive accuracy in regression equations with GNP as a dependent variable and six different monetary aggregates as alternative explanatory variables.

For a methodological assault on the concept of an empirical definition of the money stock see Will E. Mason, "The Empirical Definition of Money: A Critique," *Economic Inquiry* 14 (December 1976), 525–538.

[5] See S. J. Maisel, "Controlling Monetary Aggregates," in *Controlling Monetary Aggregates,* Proceedings of the Monetary Conference of the Federal Reserve Bank of Boston (June 1969), 152–174, and Michael J. Hamburger, "The Demand for Money in 1971: Was There a Shift? A Comment," *Journal of Money, Credit and Banking,* vol. 5 (May 1973), 720–725.

[6] The rationale for including trade credit in the money stock is discussed in Chapter 4, pp. 110–111. See Arthur B. Laffer, "Trade Credit and the Money Market," *Journal of Political Economy,* vol. 78 (March/April 1970), 239–267.

for money with a given degree of accuracy or, which amounts to the same thing, one that yields parameter estimates that are less subject to variation when the same arguments are included in the function and hence enable more accurate prediction of the demand for money to be made.[7]

In an empirical study Laidler[8] contends that the most stable money demand function he has been able to isolate is one employing Friedman's broad definition of money $M2$. This contrasts with earlier results presented by Karl Brunner and Allan H. Meltzer,[9] in which they found that the narrow measure $M1$—demand deposits plus currency—yielded the most satisfactory money demand relation.

What accounts for these contrasting conclusions? First, these two studies specify different explanatory variables in their money demand equations. Second, they use data from different time periods to estimate the parameters of these relations. Finally, they employ different procedures to test their hypotheses. Since the relative performance of alternative measures of the money stock in empirical money demand functions is likely to be highly sensitive to all of these considerations, it is impossible to choose the better measure of money on the basis of these studies alone.

However, an alternative empirical approach is available. The stability of the money demand function is closely linked to the degree of substitutability that exists between money, as it is defined in that function, and other financial assets. For example, if the secular and cyclical changes in the competitive position of financial intermediaries make available substitutes for currency in circulation and demand deposits held by the nonbank public (the narrowly defined money stock), the demand for money, so defined, may shift as these substitutes appear. In such a case a demand function for some broader measure of money, one that includes these close substitutes, would be more stable, that is, would shift less over time, than a function defined on a narrow money measure.[10] Under these conditions monetary policy actions that concentrate on the narrower measure of money would be focusing on an unstable, shifting target. Policy actions that focus on broader measures of money would be more appropriate.

[7] David Laidler, "The Definition of Money: Theoretical and Empirical Problems," *The Journal of Money, Credit and Banking*, vol. 1 (August 1968), 516.

[8] David Laidler, "Some Evidence on the Demand for Money," *Journal of Political Economy*, vol. 74 (February 1966), 55–68.

[9] Karl Brunner and Allan H. Meltzer, "Predicting Velocity: Implications for Theory and Policy," *Journal of Finance*, vol. 18 (May 1963), 319–354.

[10] Gurley and Shaw, for example, emphasize the substitutability between claims on certain financial intermediaries and demand deposits at commercial banks; they argue that the money stock must be defined so as to include these substitutes. Evidence supporting this position is presented below. See John G. Gurley and Edward S. Shaw, *Money in a Theory of Finance* (Washington, DC: The Brookings Institution, 1960). This view is also embodied in the report of the Radcliffe Committee, which views "liquidity" and "the stock of liquid assets" held by the public as the relevant concept on which to focus in monetary theory and policy. In this view only policy actions that change the *total liquidity* of the public—and not simply the composition of the public's stock of liquid assets—are likely to lead to predictable results. This is so because of the high degree of substitutability that exists between the narrowly defined money stock and near-monies. See *The Radcliffe Report*, Committee on the Working of the Monetary System (London, 1959).

A substantial body of evidence has now been presented on this issue. Specifically, the question that has been addressed is the following. Are assets such as commercial bank time deposits, savings and loan shares, mutual savings bank deposits, and others that have been suggested for inclusion in a measure of "money" sufficiently close substitutes for commercial bank demand deposits to warrant treating them in a single measure?

In a study on the demand for liquid assets by the public, Edgar Feige[11] measured the cross elasticities of demand between various assets.[12] Using data on the volume of liquid assets held by households in each state of the United States for each year during the period from 1949 to 1959, Feige found that the yields on nonbank intermerdiary liabilities (savings and loan shares, etc.) did not affect the demand for money. Ownership of each of these assets was found to be highly sensitive only to its "own rate" of interest. In Feige's results there appears to be little substitutability between demand deposits, time deposits, savings and loan shares, or mutual savings bank deposits. In fact, demand deposits were found to be mildly *complementary* with savings and loan shares and mutual savings bank deposits; demand and time deposits at commercial banks were only very weak substitutes for each other. From this and other evidence Feige concludes that the narrow definition of the money stock is the preferred definition when estimating money demand functions and that analysts need not concern themselves with the effects of the activities of other intermediaries on the public's demand for money.[13]

Feige's conclusions are disputed by T. H. Lee[14] and V. K. Chetty.[15] Lee's work will be described in detail in connection with our survey of the relevance of alterna-

---

[11] Edgar Feige, *The Demand for Liquid Assets: A Temporal Cross Section Analysis* (Englewood Cliffs: Prentice-Hall, 1964).

[12] The cross elasticity of demand is the most frequently used measure of substitutability. If we consider two assets X and Y, and the returns on each, i_X and i_Y, the cross elasticity of X with respect to Y equals the percentage change in the quantity of X demanded, divided by the percentage change in the return on Y:

$$\eta_{X,Y} = \frac{\Delta X/X}{\Delta i_Y/i_Y}$$

If an increase in the return on asset $Y(\Delta i_Y$ positive) causes a switch in holdings from X to Y, ΔX will be negative and the cross elasticity will be negative. In this case the assets X and Y are said to be "substitutes." If $\eta_{X,Y}$ is positive, indicating a *direct* relationship between the return on Y and holdings of asset X, these assets are said to be "complements."

[13] Feige's methods in deriving these results are subject to several criticisms. First, there are serious questions as to whether the way in which he measures the rate of return on commercial bank demand deposits reflects the relevant return considered by asset holders in allocating their portfolios (see pp. 194–195 below). Second, his data measure the assets owned in a state by residents of all states when, in fact, the relevant measure for his purposes should have been the assets owned by the residents of each state. His data probably require the inclusion of rates on out-of-state assets in order to capture the effects of ownership that crosses state lines. These problems detract somewhat from Feige's results.

[14] T. H. Lee, "Alternative Interest Rates and the Demand for Money: The Empirical Evidence," *American Economic Review*, vol. 57 (December 1967), 1168–1181.

[15] V. K. Chetty, "On Measuring the Nearness of Near-Moneys," *American Economic Review*, vol. 59 (June 1969), 270–281.

tive interest rate measures in the money demand function. Briefly, Lee suggests that the liabilities of financial intermediaries, particularly savings and loan shares, are indeed very good *substitutes* for money. Rather than supporting Friedman's "broad" definition of the money stock, however, he claims that the definition should be extended to encompass an even broader collection of assets, including, as a minimum, shares in savings and loan associations.

Chetty makes a similar proposal. In his work a technique originally developed in production theory to measure the substitutability between capital and labor in the production process is employed to measure the substitutability among assets in the consumer's utility function.[16] Chetty assumes that consumers attempt to maximize their utility (subject to the budget constraint) by combining money (demand deposits plus currency in circulation), time deposits, and other assets to produce desired levels of liquidity at the lowest cost. By combining the conditions required for utility maximization with the budget constraint, he derives an equation that contains parameters that, when estimated, yield measures of the partial elasticities of substitution between money and other assets.

On the basis of his estimates, Chetty concludes that while savings and loan shares and mutual savings bank deposits are rather good substitutes for money, time deposits appear to be virtually perfect substitutes. This last finding supports Friedman's use of the "broad" definition of money. Nevertheless, as did Lee, Chetty suggests that an even broader measure of money may be more appropriate and shows how such a measure may be calculated. Employing weights that measure the "moneyness" of assets as implied by their substitutability with demand deposits and currency, he constructs a weighted average of demand deposits *DD* and currency *C* (with weights constrained to unity), time deposits *TD,* savings and loan shares *SL* and mutual savings bank deposits *MS*. The final form of the equation defining this average "money" stock is

$$M_s = DD + C + TD + 0.615SL + 0.88MS.$$

Note that the coefficient (unity) on the time deposit variable reflects Chetty's conclusion of perfect substitutability between these deposits and narrowly defined money.[17]

While these findings by Lee and Chetty clearly favor a broader measure of money, an important recent study by Stephen Goldfeld,[18] which provides consistent and comparable data on several of the questions addressed in this survey, contains

[16] See K. J. Arrow, H. B. Chenery, B. S. Minhas, and R. M. Solow, "Capital–Labor Substitution and Economic Efficiency," *Review of Economics and Statistics,* vol. 63 (August 1961), 225–250.

[17] This evidence also lends support to the broad measure of money used by Lydall in his empirical study of the demand for money in Britain and increases the importance of Lydall's conclusions on the issues discussed below. See Harold Lydall, "Income, Assets, and the Demand for Money," *Review of Economics and Statistics,* vol. 40 (February 1958), 1–14.

[18] Stephen M. Goldfeld, "The Demand for Money Revisited," *Brookings Papers on Economic Activity,* vol. 3 (1973), 577–638.

persuasive evidence that focusing on narrow measures of money will yield demand functions with significantly superior predictive capabilities to those that define money in some broader fashion. Goldfeld does not concentrate explicitly on the substitutability of various potential components of "money." Rather, his procedure is to confront various hypotheses with the same set of data and very closely related functional specifications. This has the advantage of limiting the number of factors that can be introduced to explain differing statistical results—the major problem in making comparative judgments on the diverse evidence presented by the authors cited above.

Goldfeld begins by noting that the inclusion of time deposits in the definition of the money stock seems questionable on theoretical grounds "since it constrains the specification . . . of $M1$ (narrow money) and time deposits to be the same" and potentially distorts the influence of interest rates on the component measures. However, he recognizes that these weaknesses could be offset if an empirically more stable demand function resulted from this formulation. His results, however, imply that this "is definitely not the case."[19]

The alternative equations Goldfeld estimated with broad money include a lagged dependent variable, income, and interest rates as arguments. His estimates are such as to make one suspicious of the use of the broad money measure as the dependent variable. First, the time deposit rate appears to have a negligible influence on holdings of broad money. This may be an empirical reflection of the offsetting effects of this rate on demand deposits and time deposits and the loss of information involved in aggregating over those components. Second, the long-run elasticity of broad money is extremely high, exceeding the elasticities estimated separately for each of the components. Both of these results suggest serious problems with a function specified on the broad money measure. Goldfeld's additional statistical tests strengthen the initial suspicion engendered by those results. While the traditional criterion statistics—R^2 and the standard error of the estimate—provide little help in choosing between the broad money or narrow money formulation, dynamic simulations and stability tests provide persuasive evidence of the superiority of the narrow money form. The broad money equation yields extremely large errors in long-run forecasting tests and is easily rejected on the basis of formal stability tests.[20]

Additional tests on the forecasting performance and stability of equations esti-

---

[19] S. M. Goldfeld, "The Demand for Money Revisited," *op. cit.*, 593.

[20] Goldfeld's primary test consists of dynamically simulating his estimated equations. This involves forecasting both within-sample and out-of-sample values for the dependent variable and evaluating the quality of those forecasts by a measure such as the root mean square error. His tests take two general forms, (1) four quarter *ex post* forecasts made by taking sequentially longer subperiods within the sample from which to derive coefficient estimates and evaluating forecasts for four quarters beyond each successive estimating period and (2) splitting the sample period in half, deriving estimates from the first half data and evaluating the long-run forecasting ability of the equation over the second half of the sample period. In both cases the broad money equation performed substantially worse than the narrow money form. These results were formally confirmed through the use of the Chow test of stability. See Stephen M. Goldfeld, *op. cit.*, 592–595.

mated for each of the components of *M2* (broad money) lead to his general conclusion that

> the simple specification used for *M1* will not work for time deposits, and . . . even given the questionable time deposit equation, the ex post forecasts of *M2* obtained from the aggregate equation are inferior to those obtained from adding together the separate component forecasts, thus suggesting that *aggregation is inflicting some positive harm* (emphasis added).[21]

In short, Goldfeld's results suggest that in model building and other work *more* rather than *less* disaggregation of the money demand equation seems to be desirable.[22]

Because of these conflicting results, many economists feel that this issue is still unresolved, and further evidence is sought. In the remainder of this survey, therefore, whenever we are reporting on empirical work, we shall cite the specific measure of money used by a particular author. In several instances, research on other issues will have direct implications for the appropriate empirical definition of the money stock. Let us now turn to an examination of the general form of the money demand functions specified in empirical work and to a review of the evidence on the role of the interest rate in determining the public's demand for money. This latter issue has critical implications for national economic policy.

Conventional Formulations of the Demand for Money Function

In most formulations of the money demand function real money balances are related to "the" interest rate on relevant substitute assets and some scale variable associated with economic activity, such as income or wealth. The equation specified is sometimes linear but more often exponential in form. These alternative forms may be specified as follows:

[21] Stephen M. Goldfeld, *op. cit.*, 595.

[22] Dickson and Starleaf suggest a similar conclusion. Their estimates of various functions that include distributed lags on all arguments suggest that "the demand functions for *M1* and *TD* (time deposits) appear to be so different as to dictate their separate, rather than combined, analysis." See Harold D. Dickson and Dennis R. Starleaf, "Polynomial Distributed Lag Structures in the Demand Function for Money," *Journal of Finance*, vol. 27 (December 1972), 1042.

A recent study of the stability of the demand for money function by Laumas and Mehra which employs the so-called "varying parameter regression approach" to determine the stability of alternative specifications of the function concludes that "Demand for money functions using *M1* or *M2* are both stable and hence a choice cannot be made on the appropriate definition of the money stock by appealing to the stability criterion . . ." This would seem to support Goldfeld's reliance on dynamic simulations and other forecasting tests as alternative and/or additional criteria for determining the "best" definition of the money stock. See Laumas, G. S., and Y. P. Mehra "The Stability of The Demand for Money Function: The Evidence from Quarterly Data" *Review of Economics and Statistics*, 58 (November 1976), 463–468.

$$\frac{M_d}{P} = m_d = a_1 + a_2 i + a_3 X \tag{7.1}$$

$$\frac{M_d}{P} = m_d = \alpha \, i^{\beta_1} X^{\beta_2}$$

where M_d/P is the stock of real money balances demanded, i is an interest rate, and X represents other variables such as wealth, permanent income, or current income.[23] When Equation (7.2) is employed, a logarithmic transformation is made so that the equation is *linear* in the logarithms of the variables and, more importantly, linear in the parameters to be estimated. Taking natural logs of both sides of the equation,

$$\ln \frac{M_d}{P} = \ln m_d = \ln \alpha + \beta_1 \ln i + \beta_2 \ln X. \text{[24]} \tag{7.3}$$

---

[23] Money demand functions are generally cast in real terms on the assumption that the price elasticity of nominal money balances is unity. The implication of this assumption is that price-level changes alone will cause no change in the demand for *real* money balances or, alternatively, that the demand for nominal balances is proportional to the price level. This assumption implies that the public is free of money illusion in its demand for real money balances. Let us examine this assumption further. Let X in Equation (7.2) be a measure of real wealth W. Then,

$$\frac{M_d}{P} = \alpha \cdot i^{\beta_1} \cdot W^{\beta_2}.$$

If *nominal* money balances were specified as a function of *nominal* wealth, this equation would be

$$M_d = \alpha \cdot i^{\beta_1} \cdot (P \cdot W)^{\beta'_2}.$$

But these two equations are quite different. The first equation implies that the price level elasticity is unity—the exponent of P equals 1—and β_2 is the wealth elasticity of *real* money balances. But in the latter form β_2' is some *average* of the price level and wealth elasticities of nominal money balances. Consequently, if the price level elasticity is really unity, but the true wealth elasticity is not equal to one, β_2' will be *biased* toward that value and will not be a good estimate of the true wealth elasticity. To avoid that bias, investigators have generally chosen to work with functions cast in real terms.

The validity of this procedure is supported by evidence presented by Allan H. Meltzer, "The Demand for Money: The Evidence . . . ," *op. cit.* His work indicates that when the price variable is included as a separate argument in a log–linear equation, its coefficient is very close to unity. Furthermore, if nominal wealth is employed in an equation with nominal balances specified as the dependent variable, the wealth elasticity is closer to unity than if these measures are cast in real terms. The work of Goldfeld, *op. cit.*, supports Meltzer's conclusion with regard to the price variable.

Additional evidence on this point has been presented by Harold D. Dickson and Dennis R. Starleaf, *op. cit.* Employing an equation similar in form to Equation (7.3) but with distributed lag functions defined on the independent variables, including GNP, they found that the estimated price elasticity of the narrowly defined money stock $M1$ was not significantly different from unity. On this evidence they concluded that the demand for real money balances is homogenous of degree zero in the price level; therefore the demand for money is free of money illusion. On this and other evidence the assumed proportionality of nominal money balances to the price level discussed in Chapter 4 would appear to have a firm basis in empirical analysis.

[24] In this form the coefficients β_1 and β_2 can be directly estimated by linear regression techniques, and those coefficients will be elasticities. This may be shown as follows. Let $\eta_{m \cdot i}$ denote

These simple linear (in the coefficients) models may be fitted to empirical observations of variables if and only if two additional assumptions are made. First, we must assume that the money market is always in equilibrium so that desired money balances M_d equal the actual money stock reported in the statistical series M.[25] Second, we must assume that there exist exact empirical counterparts to the theoretical variables specified; for example, the average of daily rates quoted by the New York Federal Reserve bank on United States Treasury bills may be chosen as the empirical measure of "the" interest rate. With data on each of the variables specified in the equation, multiple-regression methods may be employed to derive estimates of the coefficients in these single-equation models.[26]

---

the interest elasticity of money demand (let m in this instance represent real money balances demanded). Then,

$$\eta_{m \cdot i} = \frac{\partial m/m}{\partial i/i} = \frac{\partial m}{\partial i} \cdot \frac{i}{m}.$$

But from Equation (7.2),

$$\partial m/\partial i = \beta_1 (\alpha X^{\beta_2}) \cdot i^{(\beta_1 - 1)}.$$

Therefore,

$$\eta_{m \cdot i} = \beta_1 (\alpha X^{\beta_2}) \cdot i^{(\beta_1 - 1)} \quad \frac{i}{\alpha X^{\beta_2} \cdot i^{\beta_1}} = \frac{\beta_1 \cdot i^{\beta_1}}{i^{\beta_1}} = \beta_1.$$

Consequently, elasticities may be estimated directly by employing the log–linear form of Equation (7.2) in the regression procedure.

Paul Zarembka, using a likelihood ratio test, found that the log–linear form was more appropriate than the linear form where the short-term interest rate and current income were explanatory variables. He found, however, that the appropriate form was sensitive to the choice of the dependent variable. P. Zarembka, "Functional Form of the Demand for Money." *Journal of the American Statistical Association,* vol. 63 (June 1968), 502–511.

[25] Artis and Lewis in their study "The Demand for Money in the United Kingdom: 1963–1973," *Manchester School of Economics and Social Studies* vol. 44 (June 1976), 147–181, address the problem that money demand functions ". . . capable of explaining the 1960's failed to make sense of the additional observations afforded by the inclusion of the very limited data now available for the 1970's." Rather than accepting this result as evidence of instability in the demand for money, the authors question the way in which the measurement of the demand for money has been approached and they propose instead that stability has persisted but that ". . . the money market does *not* clear within (a) quarter." They suggest that the apparent instability in recent estimates results from the fact that the amount of money actually observed is not always equal to the amount demanded because of substantial exogenous changes in the money supply. Thus, challenging the assumption that money is demand determined, they formulate a model which allows for partial (or over-) adjustment of income and interest rates to injections of money. This model seems to perform well in explaining the apparent "instability" of money demand as resulting in part from very substantial short run changes in the money supply and suggests further need for continued development of simultaneous equation models which integrate explicitly the supply and demand process. The issue of stability is discussed further on pp. 212–216 of the next chapter.

[26] Least squares regression analysis may be defined as a procedure whereby an hypothesized relationship may be confronted with actual data in order to derive numerical estimates of the parameters specified in that relationship. Under specified conditions concerning the nature of the hypothesized relationship and the characteristics of the data employed, these techniques will yield estimates with certain desirable statistical properties. In the models above, for example,

Several modifications can be made to this basic equation to introduce significant additional flexibility into the hypotheses. One of the most important of these is the introduction of the concept of "desired," as opposed to "actual," money balances together with a "partial adjustment" mechanism whereby actual holdings adjust to desired levels.

For example, desired real money balances m_T^* may be postulated to depend upon the same variables included in Equation (7.3):

$$\ln m_T^* = \ln \alpha + \beta_1 \ln i_T + \beta_2 \ln X_T \qquad (7.4)$$

and the adjustment process of actual to desired levels of money demand may be expressed as follows:

$$(\ln m_T - \ln m_{T-1}) = \lambda(\ln m_T^* - \ln m_{T-1}). \qquad (7.5)$$

In this form λ, the adjustment coefficient, measures the rate at which adjustments are made to bring *actual* money holdings in line with the current *desired* level. Generally λ is specified to be between 0 and 1, indicating that any such process of adjustment is only partially successful during one period. The magnitude of λ will often be explained in empirical literature as reflecting the cost of adjusting portfolios relative to the cost of not adjusting them.

While m_T^*, the current desired level of real money holdings, is not directly observable or measurable, the above adjustment process allows derivation of an estimating equation with solely observable quantities. Substituting Equation (7.4) into the adjustment Equation (7.5) and rearranging, yields

$$\ln m_T = \lambda \ln \alpha + \lambda\beta_1 \ln i_T + \lambda\beta_2 \ln X_T + (1 - \lambda) \ln m_{T-1}. \qquad (7.6)$$

In this form λ can be calculated from the coefficient estimate of the lagged dependent variable m_{T-1} and α, β_1, and β_2 can be deduced from this value and the coefficients estimated for the other terms. If, for example, a coefficient of .60 is estimated on the lagged term, then $\lambda = (1 - .60) = .40$, suggesting that in each period 40 percent of the gap between actual and desired money balances will be closed by the public's actions.[27]

---

data on the size of the money stock, the value of the interest rate, and, say, national wealth may be employed in regression analysis to derive estimates of β_1, the interest elasticity of money demand, and β_2, the wealth elasticity of money demand. For a discussion of the mechanics of least squares regression and the properties of least squares estimators, see S. Hymans, *Probability Theory* (Prentice-Hall, Englewood Cliffs, NJ, 1966), ch. 8, and J. Kmenta, *Elements of Econometrics* (Macmillan, New York, 1971), chs. 7 and 10.

[27] In this formulation, the long-run interest and income (or wealth) elasticities are β_1 and β_2, respectively. The short-run elasticities are given by $\lambda\beta_1$ and $\lambda\beta_2$, the estimated coefficients in the regression equation. For example, in steady-state equilibrium, $m_T = m_{T-1} = m_{T-2} \cdots$ Then, from Equation (7.6),

While this form has proved useful in many applications, it has the unfortunate characteristic of restricting the adjustment pattern in the dependent variable to be the same regardless of the source of the initial disturbance. Whether an interest rate change or an income (or wealth) change perturbs the initial (long-run) equilibrium, the adjustment path to a new equilibrium must be identical. There are several cogent theoretical reasons why this is not likely to be the case. In addition, empirical results often suggest implausibly long lags for the adjustment process. Such long lags are difficult to explain on the basis of the magnitude of costs that are likely to be involved in adjusting financial portfolios.

An alternative, and perhaps superior, rationale for the presence of a significant lagged term in the money demand function derives from the "adaptive expectations" model. In this formulation it is assumed that the public is actually holding its desired level of money balances, but that level itself is assumed to depend upon expected values of one or more of the independent variables rather than on current actual values. Thus,

$$\ln m_T = \ln \alpha + \beta_1 \ln i_T + \beta_2 \ln X^e_T \qquad (7.7)$$

where X^e_T is the value of X expected to prevail in period t. Since X^e_T is not observable, some hypothesis must be specified on how expectations are formulated. It may be posited, for example, that current expectations are formed by modifying previous expectations in the light of current experience. For example;

$$\ln X^e_T - \ln X^e_{T-1} = (1 - \lambda)(\ln X_T - \ln X^e_{T-1}) \qquad (7.8)$$

or equivalently,

$$\ln X^e_T = (1 - \lambda)\ln X_T + \lambda \ln X^e_{T-1}, \qquad 0 \le \lambda < 1.$$

This formulation depends upon knowledge of X_T in period t. An alternative formulation, which avoids this implicit assumption that X_T be known in advance of formulating the expectation, makes the revision of expectations dependent upon the most recent error in expectations, assuming data on current period values are not available; that is,

$$\ln X^e_T - \ln X^e_{T-1} = (1 - \lambda)(\ln X_{T-1} - \ln X^e_{T-1}). \qquad (7.9)$$

$$\ln m_T - (1 - \lambda)\ln m_{T-1} = \lambda \ln \alpha + \lambda \beta_1 \ln i_T + \lambda \beta_2 \ln X_T$$

$$\ln m_T[1 - 1 + \lambda] = \lambda \ln \alpha + \lambda \beta_1 \ln i_T + \lambda \beta_2 \ln X_T$$

$$\ln m_T = \ln \alpha + \beta_1 \ln i_T + \beta_2 \ln X_T$$

as in Equation (7.4). Because of the assumed constraint on λ, short-run elasticities will be smaller (in absolute terms) than longer run elasticities.

In this form expectations are revised by some fraction of the discrepancy between last period's expectations and the actual value of X_{T-1}.

Either of these forms can be employed to derive an estimating equation specified solely in terms of observable values. For example, substituting the first of the adaptive expectations models specified (7.8) into the basic demand relation (7.7) and applying a Koyck transformation, yields[28]

$$\ln m_T = (1 - \lambda) \ln \alpha + (1 - \lambda) \beta_1 \ln i_T + (1 - \lambda) \beta_2 \ln X_T +$$
$$\lambda \ln m_{T-1}. \quad (7.10)$$

In this formulation the adaptive expectations model is formally the same as the partial adjustment model, although the interpretation of the estimated coefficient on the lagged dependent variable and other variables is very different in the two equations. The adaptive expectations model, however, is the starting point for a whole family of models that allow the introduction of a great many alternative hypotheses into the basic structure. In particular, different expectational patterns may be specified for each of the independent variables in the equation, or expectations on one or more of the variables may be allowed to adjust in different proportions to two or more of the previous expectations (forecasting) errors.[29] For example,

$$\ln X^e_T - \ln X^e_{T-1} = (1 - \lambda_1)(\ln X_T - \ln X^e_T) + (1 - \lambda_2)(\ln X_{T-1} -$$
$$\ln X^e_{T-1}) \quad (7.11)$$

where λ_1 is not restricted to equal λ_2. In addition, the adaptive expectations model may be combined with the partial adjustment model to capture the potential lagged effects generated by each. An example of this will be seen below.

Unfortunately, the capacity to incorporate new and richer lag structures rather quickly surpasses econometric capability to derive useful statistical estimates of the included parameters.[30] Because of this limitation, a far more general lag model has gained wide popularity. The Almon distributed lag technique allows estimation of a rather general lag pattern that can be rationalized in any number of ways. Only the length of the lag and the degree of the polynominal along which the weights lie must be specified in advance.[31] Perhaps the major advantage of this form over the models developed above is the elimination of the somewhat restrictive assumption that the weights describing the assumed adjustment process lie along a simple monotonically declining geometric lag path. On the other hand, the Almon method

---

[28] See J. Kmenta, *op. cit.*, 474 ff.

[29] See Stephen M. Goldfeld, "The Demand for Money Revisited," *op. cit.*, 600.

[30] See Zri Griliches, "Distributed Lags: A Survey," *Econometrica*, vol. 35 (January 1967), 16–49.

[31] See Shirley Almon, "The Distributed Lag between Capital Appropriations and Expenditures," *Econometrica*, vol. 33 (January 1965).

requires less care in the formulation of detailed hypotheses to rationalize the introduction of any lag structure.

Some form of one of the basic models discussed above underlies most of the empirical research on the money demand function. We shall now turn to an examination of the results of that research for one of the most important issues in this area—the importance of the interest rate in determining the public's money demand.

The Role of the Interest Rate in the Money Demand Function

Single-Equation Estimates

The stimulus for much of the econometric work on the demand for money and for the primary focus of that work on the importance of the interest rate as an argument in the money demand function derives from Keynes' presentation of the liquidity preference theory in *The General Theory of Employment, Interest, and Money* (1936).[32] Keynes' theory is examined in Chapter 5. Although Pigou as early as 1917 had suggested that the interest rate was a potentially important factor in determining the public's money holding behavior, it was Keynes' full explication of the "speculative" motive for holding "idle" money balances that provided the major impetus for testing this hypothesis. Research has been further encouraged by the work of Milton Friedman.[33] Contrary to the findings of most other investigators, he finds little basis for assigning a significant role to the interest rate in determining the demand for money.

One of the earliest studies to address this issue was done by Henry A. Latané.[34] Latané specified and tested three alternative models of the demand for money. In his first test he proposed a constant ratio of total money balances to nominal national income, $M/Y = k$. This hypothesis represented a crude form of the quantity theory. By showing graphically that this ratio was highly variable, fluctuating between a low of .26 to a high of .50 in the period from 1919 to 1952, Latané rejected this hypothesis.

In his second test Latané proposed a Keynesian-type money demand function, in which the total demand for money balances expressed as the sum of a transactions component dependent on the level of income and an asset or speculative component dependent on the rate of interest:

$$M = a\left(\frac{1}{i}\right) + bY + c. \qquad (7.12)$$

[32] John Maynard Keynes, *The General Theory of Employment, Interest, and Money* (London: Harcourt, Brace and Co., 1936).

[33] Milton Friedman, "The Demand for Money—Some Theoretical and Empirical Results," *Journal of Political Economy,* vol. 67 (June 1959), 327–351.

[34] Henry A. Latané, "Cash Balances and the Interest Rate—A Pragmatic Approach," *Review of Economics and Statistics,* vol. 36 (November 1954), 456–460.

Latané showed that this form implies a continually declining ratio of money balances to income as income increases (and the interest rate remains constant).[35] Since empirical evidence indicated that this was not the case, Latané also rejected this form.

Latané's last model proposed that the ratio of nominal money balances to (nominal) aggregate income was dependent upon the rate of interest:

$$\frac{M}{Y} = f(i). \tag{7.13}$$

In testing this model, he specified a simple linear form, and derived the following regression estimates:

$$\frac{M}{Y} = .0074 \left(\frac{1}{i} \right) + .1088.$$

This equation was then used to predict values of the dependent variable for dates not included in the original data. The success of these predictions prompted Latané to conclude that he had identified a stable behavioral relation between cash balances, income, and the long-term rate of interest. Specifically, "In the past thirty years, each 1.0 percent change in $1/i$ has tended to be associated with a change of 0.8 percent in gross national product held as currency and demand deposits."[36]

One characteristic of Latané's last model, shared by the money demand functions tested by several other authors, should be mentioned. The equation form chosen by Latané to test the interest sensitivity of the cash balance ratio constrains the income elasticity of the demand for money to equal unity.[37] The effects of this

---

[35] This may be seen by dividing both sides of Equation (7.12) by Y:

$$\frac{M}{Y} = \frac{a}{i \cdot Y} + b + \frac{c}{Y}.$$

If Y increases, a/Y and c/Y will decline. Thus with the interest rate constant, the proportion of income held in the form of money balances would decline as income increased.

[36] H. A. Latané, op. cit., 460.

[37] This may be shown as follows. Let $\eta_{M \cdot Y}$ denote the income elasticity of money balances. Then,

$$\eta_{M \cdot Y} = \frac{\Delta M / M}{\Delta Y / Y} = \frac{\Delta M}{\Delta Y} \cdot \frac{Y}{M}.$$

But from Latané's basic model (7.13) we may write $\Delta M = f(i) \cdot \Delta Y$. Therefore,

$$\eta_{M \cdot Y} = f(i) \cdot \frac{Y}{M} = \frac{f(i) \cdot Y}{f(i) \cdot Y} = 1.$$

One alternative but equally restrictive approach to the demand for transactions balances is represented by the inventory theoretic model of the Baumol–Tobin type, discussed in Chapter 4, pages 105–107. In this model the demand for money is shown to conform to the familiar "square root law" of inventory analysis, that is,

arbitrary restriction on the value of the income elasticity of money balances can only be judged by comparing the results of this model with those derived from models that are not so constrained.

Several investigators, in testing the liquidity preference theory, have attempted to isolate the "asset" or "idle" balance component of the public's total money holdings from money balances held strictly for transactions purposes and to estimate the influence of the interest rate on the former component alone. James Tobin[38] in an early study, and Martin Bronfenbrenner and Thomas Mayer[39] in subsequent work, employed this approach.

In calculating the idle balance component of total money balances, Tobin (like Latané) assumed that desired *transactions* balances are proportional to the level of income. To determine the exact factor of proportionality between transaction balances and income, Tobin further assumed that during periods of very high interest rates and high economic activity, when the ratio of total money holdings to income is at its lowest level, idle balances are zero and the total money stock is held solely for transactions purposes. The minimum value for this ratio was found to occur in 1929. Therefore, Tobin asserted that this 1929 ratio actually measures the constant factor of proportionality between transactions balances and income. This may be seen symbolically. Let

$$M_d = \frac{1}{2}\sqrt{\frac{2bT}{i}} = \frac{1}{2} \cdot \sqrt{2b} \cdot T^{1/2} \cdot i^{-1/2}$$

where T is the volume of expenditures financed in a given period, b is the cost of switching between income earning assets and money, and i is the interest rate. In this case

$$\eta_{M \cdot T} = \frac{\partial M}{\partial T} \cdot \frac{T}{M} = \frac{\frac{1}{2} \cdot \frac{1}{2} \cdot \sqrt{2b} \cdot T^{-1/2} i^{-1/2}}{1} \cdot \frac{T}{\frac{1}{2} \cdot \sqrt{2b} \cdot T^{1/2} \cdot i^{-1/2}} = \frac{1}{2}$$

that is, the transactions (or income) elasticity of the demand for money balances is one half. In this framework one would expect to find substantial economies of scale in the holding of money balances. These are ruled out in Latané's formulation as they are in the crude form of the quantity theory. See W. Baumol, "The Transactions Demand for Cash: An Inventory Theoretic Approach," *Quarterly Journal of Economics,* vol. 66 (November 1952), 545–556.

It should be noted here that the lack of data on brokerage costs and other transactions costs of adjusting money balances, such as the 'b' term in the Baumol model, has resulted in their omission from most empirical studies. This could bias many of the interest and income elasticities reported in the literature. See, Jared Enzler, Lewis Johnson and John Paulus "Some Problems of Money Demand" *Brookings Papers on Economic Activity,* vol. 9 (1976), 261–280. In Chapter 4, pages 108–109, it was indicated that the wage rate could serve as a proxy for these brokerage and transactions costs because it reflects the opportunity cost of time used in adjusting money balances. Two studies have reported estimates that show a statistically significant effect of the wage rate on the demand for money: Donald S. Dutton and Warren P. Gramm, "Transactions Costs, the Wage Rate and the Demand for Money," *American Economic Review,* vol. 63 (September 1973), 652–665; Edi Karni, "The Value of Time and the Demand for Money: An Empirical Study," *Journal of Money, Credit and Banking,* vol. 6 (February 1974), 45–64.

[38] James Tobin, "The Interest Elasticity of Transaction Demand for Cash," *Review of Economics and Statistics,* vol. 38 (August 1956), 241–247.

[39] Martin Bronfenbrenner and Thomas Mayer, "Liquidity Functions in the American Economy," *Econometrica,* vol. 28 (October 1960), 810–834.

$$M_{\text{total}} = M_{\text{idle}} + M_{\text{trans}} = f(i) + kY$$

where

$$M_{\text{idle}} = f(i) \qquad \text{and} \qquad M_{\text{trans}} = kY.$$

If $M_{\text{idle}} = f(i) = 0$, as Tobin asserts for 1929, then in that year

$$M_{\text{total}} = kY \qquad \text{and} \qquad \frac{M_{\text{total}}}{Y} = k.$$

Since k (the reciprocal of the transactions velocity of circulation of money, V) was assumed to be a constant, this allowed a calculation of idle balances for other years as

$$(M_{\text{idle}})_t = (M_{\text{total}})_t - (M_{\text{trans}})_t = (M_{\text{total}})_t - k_{1929}(Y_t).$$

Tobin plotted idle balances calculated in this manner for each year against interest rates. For the period ending in 1945 he obtained excellent representations of what appeared to be Keynesian liquidity preference functions—the roughly hyperbolic functions depicted in the discussion of Keynesian theory in Chapter 4. Although the scatter diagrams did not appear to yield such well-behaved relations for subsequent years, it did appear that Tobin had isolated a statistical liquidity preference function.

In their work Bronfenbrenner and Mayer[40] estimated regression coefficients in equations that contained a wealth measure and lagged money balances as explanatory variables, in addition to the interest rate. As the dependent variable, they alternately used total money balances and a measure of idle balances, similar to the one originally defined by Tobin. The equation they estimated in log-linear form was

$$\log (M/P)_t = \alpha_1 + \alpha_2 \log i + \alpha_3 \log W + \alpha_4 \log (M/P)_{t-1}. \qquad (7.14)$$

This is virtually identical to the basic form derived in the previous section. In the equations employing idle balances as well as in those specifying total money balances as the dependent variable, the coefficient of the interest rate had a negative sign attached to it and was statistically significantly different from zero at the 1 percent level.[41]

---

[40] Martin Bronfenbrenner and Thomas Mayer, *op. cit.*

[41] To say that a coefficient is "statistically significantly different from zero" at the 1 percent level is to imply that there is less than one chance in a hundred that the estimated coefficient differs from zero solely because of random (chance) factors affecting the data from which the estimate was derived. If we cannot judge a coefficient to be significantly different from zero at

In further tests based on equations similar to Equation (7.14) Bronfenbrenner and Mayer concluded that the liquidity preference hypothesis did a better job of predicting the movement of money balances from year to year than did a "naive" model that assumed that there would be no relation (or a random relation) between movements in the interest rate and money balances. This again appeared as evidence favorable to the liquidity preference hypothesis.

Virtually all research presented since the Bronfenbrenner and Mayer study has wisely avoided the arbitrary classification of money balances into active and idle components. Even earlier authors, such as Latané, felt that such a distinction did not allow for the possible effect of the interest rate on "active balances."[42] Many economists believe that such a dichotomy is unreasonable since total money balances are simply one of many assets held for the services they provide and cannot be separated into unique components.[43]

Among studies specifying total money balances as the dependent variable are those by Allan H. Meltzer,[44] Karl Brunner and Allan H. Meltzer,[45] David Laidler,[46] H. R. Heller,[47] Gregory Chow,[48] and Stephen M. Goldfeld.[49] These works use different time periods to test their basic hypotheses; they include variables other than the interest rate in the money demand equation; and often they differ in the empirical measure chosen to represent "the" interest rate, some incorporating the rate on United States Treasury bills or short-term commercial paper, while others employ the rate on long-term government bonds or corporate securities. Yet, in spite of these many differences, these studies, like the ones above, show that the interest rate measure is an important factor in explaining variations in the demand for money. Some of the more important characteristics of this research are summarized in Table 7.1

In addition to the unanimous conclusion that the interest rate is an important determinant of the demand for money, these studies demonstrate a strong consis-

---

the 1 percent level or 5 percent level of significance, we generally have little confidence in the hypothesized relation which that coefficient represents.

[42] Latané, *op. cit.*, 456–457. See Chapter 4 for a discussion of the potential effect of the interest rate on "active" balances.

[43] Milton Friedman, "The Demand for Money—Some Theoretical and Empirical Results," *op. cit.*

[44] Allan H. Meltzer, "The Demand for Money: The Evidence from the Time Series," *op. cit.*

[45] Karl Brunner and Allan H. Meltzer, "Predicting Velocity . . . ," *op. cit.*, and "Some Further Evidence on Supply and Demand Functions for Money," *Journal of Finance*, vol. 19 (May 1964), 240–283.

[46] David Laidler, "Some Evidence . . . ," *op. cit.*; and "The Rate of Interest and the Demand for Money—Some Empirical Evidence," *Journal of Political Economy*, vol. 74 (December 1976), 545–555.

[47] H. R. Heller, "The Demand for Money—The Evidence from the Short-Run Data," *Quarterly Journal of Economics*, vol. 79 (June 1965), 291–303.

[48] Gregory Chow, "On the Short-Run and Long-Run Demand for Money," *Journal of Political Economy*, vol. 74 (April 1966), 111–131.

[49] Stephen M. Goldfeld, "The Demand for Money . . . ," *op. cit.*

Table 7.1. The Demand for Money in Some Representative Single-Equation Studies

Study	Interest Rate Elasticity of M	Interest Rate Measure Employed	Other Variables in M_D Function	Data and Time Period
1. Latané (1954)	$-.7$ (M1)	R_B	GNP	1919–1952 (A)
2. Bronfenbrenner and Mayer (1960)	(a) $-.3$–$-.5$ (M_{idle})	R_{4-6}	GNP, wealth	1919–1956 (A)
	(b) approx. $-.1$ (M1)	R_{4-6}	GNP, wealth	1919–1956 (A)
3. Meltzer (June 1963)	(a) $-.7$–$-.9$ (M1)	$R_{20\,yr}$	Net nonhuman wealth	1900–1958 (A)
	(b) $-.5$–$-.6$ (M2)	$R_{20\,yr}$	Net nonhuman wealth	1900–1958 (A)
	(c) $-.4$ (M3)	$R_{20\,yr}$	Net nonhuman wealth	1900–1949 (A)
4. Heller (1965)	(a) $-.1$ (M1)	R_{60-80}	GNP	1947–1958 (Q)
	(b) $-.1$ (M2)	R_{60-80}	Private nonhuman wealth	1947–1958 (Q)
5. Laidler (Feb. 1966)	(a) not available (M1)	R_{4-6}	Permanent income	1920–1960 (A)
	(b) not available (M2)	R_{4-6}	Permanent income	1892–1960 (A)
6. Laidler (Dec. 1966)	(a) $-.18$–$-.20$ (M1)	R_{4-6}	Permanent income	1919–1960 and sub-periods (A)
	(b) $-.5$–$-.8$ (M1)	$R_{20\,yr}$	Permanent income	1919–1960 and sub-periods (A)
	(c) approx. $-.15$ (M2)	R_{4-6}	Permanent income	1892–1960 and sub-periods (A)
	(d) $-.3$–$-.5$ (M2)	$R_{20\,yr}$	Permanent income	1892–1960 and sub-periods (A)
7. Chow (1966)	(a) approx. $-.75$ (M1)	$R_{20\,yr}$	Permanent income	1897–1958 (excl. war years) (A)
	(b) approx. $-.79$ (M1)	$R_{20\,yr}$	Current income and lagged money stock	1897–1958 (excl. war years) (A)
8. Goldfeld (1973)	(a) $-.07$ (M1)	R_{4-6}	GNP	1952–1972 (Q)
	$-.16$	R_{TD}		
	$-.07$ (M1)	R_{4-6}		
	(b) $-.15$	R_{TD}	GNP	1952–1972 (Q)
			(Almon lags)	

$M1 = DD + C$; $M2 = M1 + TD$; $M3 = M2 +$ deposits at mutual savings banks and the postal savings system; $R_B =$ interest rate on high-grade corporate bonds; $R_{20\,yr} =$ rate on 20-year corporate bonds; $R_{4-6} =$ rate on 4–6 month prime commercial paper; $R_{60-80} =$ rate on 60–80 days commercial paper; $R_{TD} =$ commercial bank time deposit rate; $A =$ annual; $Q =$ quarterly.

tency in their estimates of the interest elasticity of money balances. (As discussed below, such consistency over different periods of time suggests a rather stable demand for money function.) Those researchers employing a long-term rate of interest report elasticities in the range of −.4 to −.9. However, the estimates in the lower half of this range occur only when money is defined in a "broad" sense (inclusive of commercial bank time deposits). Considering only those studies that use the narrow measure of money we find that the range of elasticity estimates narrows to −.7 to −.9.[50]

When the short-term rate of interest is employed, the estimated elasticities range from −.07 to −.50. However, the estimates in the upper part of this range derive from those works that specify "idle" balances as the dependent variable. If we exclude these results and consider only *total* money balances as the dependent variable, the elasticity of money balances with respect to the short-term interest rate lies in the range from −.07 to −.20. This result holds whether the money stock is defined in the "narrow" or "broad" sense. The difference between the long-rate and the short-rate elasticities may be an indication of the different rates of adjustment by the public to what they consider to be temporary versus long-term movements in financial variables. Statistically, it also reflects the fact that the long-term rate fluctuates far less than the short-term rate. We shall consider this point again below.

Simultaneous-Equation Models

All of the studies reported in Table 7.1 have one basic characteristic in common: the estimates of interest elasticities are derived from single-equation models. Elementary statistics teaches that in order for estimated coefficients derived by least squares regression methods to have certain desirable characteristics (unbiasedness, efficiency, etc.), there must be a one-way causation from the independent to the dependent variable with no direct feedback. Thus in the single-equation models specified above, the interest rate and other explanatory variables must be assumed to influence the stock of money, the dependent variable, but the stock of money must not, in turn, influence these variables.

In contrast, if the conventional aggregate economic model is considered, it is obvious that the causation between interest rates, real factors, and the money stock is not unidirectional. There are simultaneous interrelations between both the supply of and demand for money as well as between monetary and real factors. This leads to what is commonly referred to as an "identification" problem.[51]

[50] For a thorough survey of time-dated demand deposit and narrow money supply elasticities with respect to various short-term rates and income, see Edgar L. Feige and Douglas K. Pearce, "The Substitutability of Money and Near-Monies: A Survey of the Time-Series Evidence," *Journal of Economic Literature,* vol. 15 (June 1977), 439–469.

[51] The source and nature of "simultaneous-equation bias" may be illustrated as follows. Consider the usual supply–demand relationship as drawn in Figure F51(a).

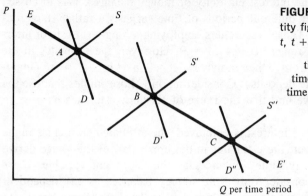

FIGURE 51(a). Observed price-quantity figures are A, B, and C at times, t, t + 1, and t + 2, respectively.

time t: supply S, demand D
time t + 1: supply S', demand D'
time t + 2: supply S'', demand D''

An attempt to fit a statistical demand or supply curve to empirical observations will not, in fact, yield the desired relationship except in very special circumstances. The usual time series observations of price P and quantity Q do not correspond to either any one demand curve or any one supply curve. Rather, they are intersection points of various supply and demand curves that are almost continuously shifting either randomly or systematically due to the influence of outside factors.

Attempts to derive single-equation estimates of these curves on the basis of observed data will result in a statistical construct that is neither a supply curve nor a demand curve. For example, the least squares regression line that could be fit to the data in Figure 51(a) would be EE'. This line would have a negative slope in the situation drawn here only because of the tendency for the supply curve to shift relatively more than the demand curve. Yet a statistical study of the data involved could easily be misunderstood by the unwary to represent the true demand relation. This would lead one to accept a meaningless estimate of the slope and, thus, of the elasticity of the demand curve.

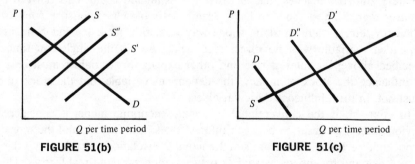

FIGURE 51(b)   FIGURE 51(c)

The only way in which such time series data could readily yield true structural estimates of the parameters of either the supply curve or the demand curve from single equation estimates would be in the very special circumstances where one of the curves is stable and the shifting of the other curve traces out points along the desired curve. This is pictured in Figures 51(b) and (c). To get around this problem, the true interaction of supply–demand relations in determining price–quantity figures must be considered. This may be done by specifying a simultaneous-equation model including both a supply equation and a demand equation and by taking care to observe well defined rules for "identification." See G. Tintner, *Econometrics,* (New York: John Wiley & Sons, 1962), ch. 6.

Fortunately, a substantial body of empirical work does assume simultaneity either between money supply and money demand or, more generally, between the monetary and the (real) expenditure sectors of the economy. These studies employ statistical techniques designed to correct for the interaction among "dependent" and "independent" variables specified within a single equation and to derive estimates which have certain desirable statistical properties. In this research the money demand function is estimated as one element in a multi-equation model. Some examples of the results are presented in Table 7.2[52]

The results derived from simultaneous-equation models generally confirm the single-equation results reported above. Those studies employing a short-term market rate of interest in the money or demand deposit demand equation report elasticities in the range of −.08 to −.18. This compares with the −.7 to −.2 range reported in the single-equation studies in Table 7.1. The elasticity estimates with respect to the rate on commercial bank time deposits is generally −.17 or −.18.[53] The elasticity measures based on long-term rates are again substantially higher than the short-term rate elasticities. They range from −.35 in de Leeuw's work to −.75 in Brunner and Meltzer's model. Since de Leeuw's measure is a weighted average of rates on private securities of different maturities, and not a long-term rate comparable to the corporate bond yields used in the other studies, these results are not inconsistent with the evidence presented in Table 7.1

Most of the equations reported in Table 7.2 are estimated within an explicit structural model either of the monetary sector or of the monetary and expenditures sectors combined.[54] Several authors, interested primarily in the money demand relation outside the framework of a fully specified multi-equation model but cognizant of the potential estimation problems implicit in the single-equation approach, have employed the method of instrumental variables in deriving their estimates of the parameters in the money demand equation. Essentially this method allows one to act as if he were operating within a fully specified structural model by postulating the exogenous variables that would appear in the model were it to be fully defined. In this way those exogenous variables can be employed as "instruments" in the first stage of a two-stage least squares estimation process with the predicted values of the "endogenous" or jointly dependent variables from this first-stage estimation being used in the money demand function in the second stage.

One interesting example of this approach is contained in a recent paper by

[52] All of the studies reported in Table 7.2 employ two-stage least squares in the estimating process. For a discussion of the mechanics of this technique and the characteristics of the estimates derived from it, see J. Johnston, *Econometric Methods* (New York: McGraw-Hill, 1963), ch. 9, or J. Kmenta, *op. cit.*, ch. 13.

[53] This is virtually identical to the result obtained by Goldfeld in his single-equation study. See Table 7.1.

[54] It should be pointed out that none of the studies surveyed here impose a balance sheet constraint as discussed in Chapter 12. A publication that does is: Edward M. Gramlich and John H. Kalchbrenner, *A Constrained Estimation Approach to the Demand for Liquid Assets*, Special Studies Paper No. 3 (Washington: Federal Reserve Board, 1970).

Table 7.2. Money and Deposit Demand in Some Representative Simultaneous-Equation Models

Study	Representative Equation (seasonal dummies omitted where appropriate)	Interest Elasticity	Interest Rate Measure	Data
1. Brunner and Meltzer (1963)	$M1 = -18.994\,r^* + .201\,W/Pa - 54.72\,Y/Y_p + .0347 P_y$ W/Pa = real public wealth, P_y = price index, Y/Y_p = ratio of current to permanent income $M2 = -16.806\,r^* + .340\,W/Pa - 44.81\,Y/Y_p + .290 P_y$	$-.75$ $-.42$	r = bond yield r = bond yield	1930–1959 (A) 1930–1959 (A)
2. Teigen (1966)	$\Delta D = 3.101 + .0719 Y^* - .0018 r_b^* Y^* - .0066 r_p Y^* - .1895\,D_{T-1}$ D = demand deposits adjusted at commercial banks, Y = gross national product	$-.10$ $-.43$	r_b = Treasury bill rate r_p = rate on bank time deposits	1953–1964 (Q)
3. de Leeuw (1965)	$\dfrac{\Delta D}{W} = .0067 - .158 \left(\dfrac{D}{W}\right)_{T-1} - .00355 r_s^*$ $\quad -.0451 r_p^* - .140 \dfrac{\text{Inv}}{W_{T-1}} + \text{other terms}$ W = wealth measure, Inv = business investment	$-.35$ $-.17$	r_s = yield on private securities r_p = rate on bank time deposits	1948–1962 (Q)
4. Goldfeld (1973)	$\Delta D = -.270 - .127 D_{T-1} + .140 Y^* - .0066 r_b^* Y^* - .012 r_p Y^*$ Y = gross national product	$-.11$ $-.18$	r_b = Treasury bill rate r_p = rate on bank time deposits	1950–1962 (Q)
5. Dickson and Starleaf (1972)	$M1 = \ln a_0 + .660 \ln Y^a - .077 \ln R^a_{4-6} - .182 \ln R^a_{TD} + 1.037 \ln P^a$	$-.08$ $-.18$	R_{4-6} = commercial paper rate R_{TD} = commercial bank time deposit rate	1952–1969 (Q)

Where ^{a} indicates weighted average of current and past values; estimated using Almon distributed lags.

* An asterisk is used to denote an independent variable used in the money or demand deposits demand function, which is treated as endogenously determined within the multiequation model as a whole. A = annual; Q = quarterly.

Harold D. Dickson and Dennis R. Starleaf.[55] Their work is all the more interesting because it applies this technique to an equation that contains Almon-estimated distributed lag terms on each of the independent variables—income, the interest rate, and the price level. Their results, reported in Table 7.2, are broadly consistent both with the results of simultaneous-equation models and with the single-equation results presented by Goldfeld, which employ a similar equation form. Using quarterly data for 1952–I through 1969–IV, they obtain estimated interest elasticities of −.077 and −.182 for the 4–6 month commercial paper rate and the rate on commercial bank time deposit, respectively.

In summary, it should be emphasized that both those studies based on single-equation models as well as those that apply multi-equation estimation techniques appear to support the hypothesis that the interest rate is an important determinant of the demand for money. Furthermore, since the multi-equation estimates are less likely to be biased because they take explicit consideration of the simultaneous nature of the relations involved, the similarity of results from those studies with those in single-equation work lends strong support to the single-equation estimates and indicates that, in this case, the identification problem may not be particularly serious.

Alternative Interest Rate Measures in the Money Demand Function

The studies cited in the previous section contain virtually overwhelming evidence that some interest rate should appear in the demand for money function. However, there is still disagreement as to which empirical measure should be used to represent the theoretical argument. It should be recognized that some interest rate data, such as yearly time series observations or quarterly series on the interest paid on savings and loan shares, may be of limited reliability.[56] Also, much of the available evidence that attempts to determine which rate best explains the demand for money is inconsistent. Furthermore, tests by different analysts often employ data from different time periods, specify different dependent variables, and include dissimilar constraints within the function, making comparisons among these empirical studies rather tenuous.

The problem may stem partly from the fact that theory provides little guidance on this issue. Some writers, like Brunner and Meltzer, argue that the demand for money should be treated within the broad theory of portfolio selection discussed in the Appendix to Chapter 5 and suggest that this demand depends on the yield on equities as well as that on bonds. Others, like Bronfenbrenner and Mayer, Laidler, and Heller, argue that some short-term interest rate is the more relevant argument since it measures the opportunity cost of holding money as the rate of return on

---

[55] Harold D. Dickson and Dennis R. Starleaf, *op. cit.*
[56] Harvey Galper, "Alternative Interest Rates and the Demand for Money: Comment," *American Economic Review* 59 (June 1969), 401–407.

what they consider to be money's closest substitutes. Still others, including Gurley and Shaw,[57] emphasize the liquidity of money and the minimal risks associated with changes in its nominal value. They argue that the closest substitutes for money are assets with similar characteristics, such as the liabilities of financial intermediaries (for example, savings and loan associations), and that it is the rates on these assets that are most relevant to the money demand function.[58]

One attempt to present direct evidence on this issue was made by Heller in 1965. In alternative money demand equations Heller compared the performance of the long-term rate of interest as measured by the rate on U.S. government bonds with that of a short-term rate, measured as the yield on 60–90-day commercial paper. Regression coefficients were estimated for equations in log–linear form using quarterly observations for the period of 1947–1958. Both $M1$ and $M2$ were tried as dependent variables with the interest rate and current income or nonhuman wealth specified as alternative constraints. In these regressions the long-term rate of interest *never* appeared as a statistically important explanatory variable,[59] while the short-term rate was important in all equations but one. Consequently, Heller concluded,

> The short-term rate is of greater importance (than the long-term rate) in the money function. The closest substitute for money available, a 60–90-day commercial paper, is most influential in deciding whether to hold assets in the form of money or not. Long-term interest rates do not influence the quantity of money demanded. . . .[60]

Results presented by Laidler generally support Heller's conclusions. Laidler examines evidence derived from equations fit to annual data for the period 1892–1960 and for subperiods therein. He bases his analysis on the following proposition:

> Given that the interest rate is an important variable in the demand for money, and that movements of various interest rates are related to one another, one would expect almost any rate chosen at random to show some relationship to cash balances . . . however, though all interest rates are interrelated, there is no reason to suppose that the nature of their interrelationship remains unchanged for all time. Thus if the demand function for money is stable, one would expect the "right" interest rate to show the same relationship to the demand for money in different time periods while the "wrong" one need not.[61]

Laidler uses the rate on 4–6 month commercial paper and the yield on 20-year bonds as his alternative interest rate measures. His equations are in log–linear form and include only permanent income as an additional explanatory variable. When his dependent variable is $M2$, he claims that "there is little question of the superior

---

[57] John G. Gurley and Edward S. Shaw, *op. cit.*

[58] See the first section of this chapter for some implications of this view.

[59] The long-term rate was never significant at the 5 percent level, and in some of the equations it appeared with the wrong sign.

[60] H. R. Heller, *op. cit.*, 297.

[61] David Laidler, "The Rate of Interest . . . ," *op. cit.*, 547.

explanatory power of the shorter interest rate."[62] When the dependent variable is *M*1, his results are somewhat contradictory. When he uses levels of the logarithms of the variables, the long-term rate explains more of the variation in *M*1 for most periods than does the short rate. Nonetheless, he maintains his original conclusion that a short-term rate is the relevant rate measure in the money demand function arguing that "the contradictory conclusions obtained with the narrower definition reflect only the fact that that definition is an unsatisfactory one."[63] The basis for his conclusion on this matter is to be found in our comments on his previous paper,[64] reported in the second section of this chapter.

The conclusions derived from this work by Heller and Laidler are challenged by Michael Hamburger. In his study of the demand for money by households Michael J. Hamburger[65] concludes that long-term interest rates are the relevant determinants of the demand for money. Employing a model that includes distributed lags to measure the rate of adjustment of households to changed market conditions, he finds that in the household demand for money function "for short-run analysis . . . , it is useful to include two yields—one on debts and one equities—and that the elasticities of the demand for money are approximately the same with respect to both of these rates."[66] His findings show that government bills (short-term securities) may be poorer substitutes for money for the household sector than longer term securities. Commenting on previous work, Hamburger claims that Heller's conclusions depend on his choice of time period. During the peroid of 1947–1951 the Federal Reserve pegged interest rates thereby distorting more normal market relationships. When Hamburger reruns Heller's regressions excluding these years, he discovers that the long-tem rate and the short-term rate appear equally important.

Additional evidence has been reported by T. H. Lee.[67] Lee criticizes the previous work done by the cited authors because they restrict their comparisons to only two alternative rate measures. Furthermore, he argues that the *differentials* between interest rates and the yield on money, rather than simply interest rate *levels,* are the relevant measures that should appear in money demand functions.

Like Laidler, Lee specifies a Friedman-type permanent income money demand model as the basic framework for his tests. He tries both *M*1 and *M*2 as dependent variables and, in addition to his alternative interest rate measures, either permanent income or permanent income and lagged money balances as explanatory variables. His regression estimates show that "the yield on nonbank intermediary liabilities is

[62] David Laidler, "The Rate of Interest . . . ," *op. cit.,* 547. Work by Laumas and Mehra, *op. cit.,* p. 467 supports this conclusion. They note "For all specifications (that is, demand functions specifying either *M*1 or *M*2 as the dependent variable) only the short- and intermediate-term interest rates yield stable demand-for-money functions."

[63] David Laidler, "The Rate of Interest . . . ," *op. cit.,* 553.

[64] David Laidler, "Some Evidence . . . ," *op. cit.*

[65] Michael J. Hamburger, "The Demand for Money by Households, Money Substitutes, and Monetary Policy," *Journal of Political Economy,* vol. 74 (December 1966), 600–623.

[66] The rates Hamburger used were Moody's Aaa rate on long-term corporate bonds and Moody's dividend yield. M. J. Hamburger, *op. cit.,* 608.

[67] T. H. Lee, *op. cit.*

the most significant interest rate variable in affirming the demand for money."
Specifically, "the yield on savings and loan shares performs the best in terms of R^2
among respective regressions of static or dynamic formulations."[68]

With the exception of Lee's work, the interest rate measure included in the
money demand functions cited was the absolute level of the rate on some asset
alternative to money.[69] One implication of this formulation is that the (marginal)
rate of return on money is assumed to be zero. Like Lee, Robert J. Barro and
Anthony M. Santomero have argued that "at least one component of (narrowly
defined) money, demand deposits, bears a form of interest that should be taken into
account in determining the opportunity cost of holding money."[70] Their argument
rests on the assumption that the provision of services or the remission of charges by
banks in accordance with the size of a customer's deposit balance represents an
effective interest return on those deposits. The scope and nature of these services is
covered in Chapter 3 and its Appendix.

To test this proposition, Barro and Santomero surveyed the largest one hundred
commercial banks in the United States to determine "the rates at which they have
remitted service charges as a function of demand deposit balances."[71] From the
survey results an annual series measuring the imputed marginal rate of return on
demand deposits was constructed for 1950–1968. This measure was then employed
within the framework of a Baumol-Tobin inventory theoretic model of the demand
for money by households.[72] Relating real per capita money balances M/PN, real
per capita consumption expenditure Y/PN, and the differential between the rate on

[68] T. H. Lee, *op. cit.*, 1171. In addition to Lee's study, the work of Goldfeld, *op. cit.*, the
survey of time series evidence by Feige and Pearce, *op. cit.*, and the research of Cagan and
Schwartz also show that rates of return on money substitutes exert a systematic influence on
the demand for demand deposits and time deposits at commercial banks. Phillip Cagan and
Anna J. Schwartz. "Has the Growth of Money Substitutes Hindered Monetary Policy?" *Journal
of Monetary Credit and Banking* (May, 1975), 137–160.

[69] Hamburger later criticized Lee's evidence because his "findings depend critically on the use
of interest rate differentials. Once this procedure is abandoned and the yield on money is
introduced as a separate variable, there is little evidence that savings and loan shares are closer
substitutes for money (narrowly defined) than other assets. In addition, the demand for money
appears to adjust more slowly to changes in yields on savings and loan shares than to changes
in other rates." Hamburger, "Alternative Interest Rates . . . ," *op. cit.*, 407.

[70] Robert J. Barro and Anthony M. Santomero, "Household Money Holdings and the Demand Deposit Rate," *Journal of Money, Credit and Banking*, vol. 4 (May 1972), 397.

[71] Robert J. Barro and Anthony M. Santomero, *op. cit.*, 399.

[72] This contradicts the conventional view that inventory models are necessarily associated
with economies of scale as shown in Chapter 4, pages 106–107. As Barro and Santomero
argue: "The key element which is typically neglected is transactions costs. As transaction
volume increases, economies of scale are realized only to the extent that transactions costs rise
less than transactions volume. Since transactions costs depend largely on value of time, and
since value of time may increase even faster than transactions volume, diseconomies of scale
(money being a "luxury") is quite compatible with the inventory approach." Robert J. Barro
and Anthony M. Santomero, *op. cit.*, 408. This issue is further explored in Chapter 4, pages
108–109. Empirical studies of this problem are reported in footnote 37 of this chapter.

an alternative asset—the dividend rate on savings and loan shares—and the imputed demand deposit rate, the following estimates are derived:

$$\log \left(\frac{M}{PN}\right)_T = -3.96 + 1.044 \log \left(\frac{Y}{PN}\right)_T - .549 \log \left(r_S - r_D\right)_T.$$

These results support the basic hypothesis: There is a substantial interest elasticity of household money demand with respect to the rate differential $(r_S - r_D)$.

It is important to note that the estimated interest elasticity applies solely to the rate differential. Since that differential (as measured by Barro and Santomero) has been fairly constant over the postwar period, the elasticity with respect to the level of rates may be quite small. On a separate issue, the coefficient of real per capita expenditures in these results indicates that the expenditures elasticity of money demand is close to unity, suggesting an absence of economies of scale in household demand for money.

The highly tentative nature of all these results should now be evident. While Heller and Laidler insist that the short-term rate is the relevant measure in the money demand function, this conclusion is challenged by both Hamburger and Lee. Lee's results further indicate that it may be the differential between the yield on money and the yield on the liabilities of some financial intermediary rather than a market interest rate that is the most appropriate constraint on desired money balances. But this contention is disputed by Hamburger. Barro and Santomero's results favor the addition of some measure of the return on demand deposits to the equation.[73] Additional investigation in which a serious attempt is made to make new results comparable to those of previous investigators will be required before any firm conclusions are possible on this critical empirical issue.

Interest Elasticity and the Liquidity Trap

The evidence reviewed above clearly supports the Keynesian notion of an interest sensitive demand for money or liquidity preference function.[74] However, Keynes

[73] Subsequent attempts to improve the measurement the return on demand deposits are reported in articles by Benjamin Klein, "Competitive Interest Payments on Bank Deposits and the Long-Run Demand for Money," *American Economic Review*, vol. 64 (December 1974), 931–949; and John H. Boyd, "Household Demand for Checking Account Money," *Journal of Monetary Economics*, vol. 1 (January 1976), 81–98. Rather than try to calculate it directly from survey data, Klein argued that competition compels banks to pay implicitly a return on deposits equal to that earned on assets net of required reserves. He entered this return separately in his regressions and, in finding that its coefficient was opposite in sign but similar in magnitude to the coefficient on the yield of a marketable security, corroborated the appropriateness of using the interest differential as a variable.

[74] All the studies cited above employ data from the United States. The evidence employing data from the United Kingdom is somewhat less conclusive on this matter. See, for example, Alan A. Walters, "The Radcliffe Report—Ten Years After: A Survey of Empirical Evidence," in *Money in Britain 1959–1969*. O. R. Croome and H. G. Johnson, eds. (Oxford: 1969). David

went further than merely to posit the interest rate as a determinant of the public's demand for money. In *The General Theory of Employment, Interest, and Money* he also speculated briefly about the shape of the liquidity preference function. Specifically, he noted,

> There is the possibility . . . that, after the rate of interest has fallen to a certain level, liquidity preference may become virtually absolute in the sense that almost everyone prefers cash to holding a debt which yields so low a rate of interest. In this event the monetary authority would have lost effective control over the rate of interest. But while this limiting case might become practically important in the future, I know of no example of it hitherto.[75]

In spite of Keynes' disclaimer, his suggestion that the liquidity preference curve *may* become perfectly interest elastic at some low level of the interest rate attracted much attention and stimulated a substantial amount of "searching" for this phenomenon. His suggestion is responsible for the shape given the liquidity preference curve in most texts (as shown in Figure 7.1).

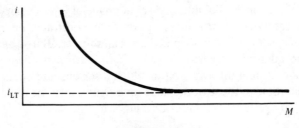

FIGURE 7.1.

The implication of this hypothesis is that the interest elasticity of the liquidity preference function should increase as the interest rate declines. This proposition has been tested by Martin Bronfenbrenner and Thomas Mayer,[76] Allan H. Meltzer,[77] David Laidler,[78] Panos Konstas and Mohamad W. Khouja,[79] and others.

Laidler and J. Michael Parkin, "The Demand for Money in the United Kingdom, 1956–1967: Preliminary Estimates," *Manchester School*, vol. 38 (September 1970), 741–809 and M. R. Gray, R. J. Ward, and G. Zis, "World Demand for Money" in Parkin and Zis (eds.), *Inflation in the World Economy* (Manchester: University of Manchester Press, 1976).

[75] John Maynard Keynes, *op. cit.*, 207.

[76] Martin Bronfenbrenner and Thomas Mayer, *op. cit.*

[77] Allan H. Meltzer, "The Demand for Money: The Evidence . . . ," *op. cit.*

[78] David Laidler, "The Rate of Interest . . . ," *op. cit.*

[79] Panos Konstas and Mohamad W. Khouja, "The Keynesian Demand-for-Money Function: Another Look and Some Additional Evidence," *Journal of Money, Credit and Banking*, vol. 1 (November 1969), 765–777.

Bronfenbrenner and Mayer, after examining the relation between the short-term interest rate and the Cambridge *k, M/Y,* tested to see if the elasticity of their estimated liquidity functions increased as the interest rate fell. Specifically, they calculated the "rank" correlation coefficient between elasticities and the level of interest rates. This involves ordering the level of interest rates from highest to lowest and comparing the ordering of the elasticities associated with those rates. If the highest rate were associated with the lowest elasticity, the lowest rate with the highest elasticity, and so on for all rates in between, there would be perfect negative rank correlation between these two measures. However, Bronfenbrenner and Mayer calculated a rank correlation coefficient of +0.16, which not only is not statistically significant, but is of the wrong sign. They concluded that "the absence of a negative correlation in a period when interest rates were at times quite low, casts doubt on, if not the truth, then at least the relevance of the liquidity trap proposition. . . ."[80]

Other investigators have supported these conclusions. In 1963 Allan H. Meltzer fit velocity functions for the six decades from 1900 to 1958. As he interprets his results, "The data deny that the interest elasticity of the demand for money or velocity became exceptionally large during that decade (the 1930s). Indeed, the interest elasticity of V_1 was slightly below the average for the (entire) fifty-nine years."[81] This evidence of a lower than average interest elasticity during periods of low interest rates is consistent with Bronfenbrenner and Mayer's positive rank-correlation coefficient.

Meltzer's research with Karl Brunner adds additional support to this position. Using estimates derived from data for the 1930s, they were able to predict the velocity of circulation for the 1950s with sufficiently small mean errors to conclude that the velocity function remained highly stable over these periods of differing interest rate levels. They conclude that "the liquidity trap proposition is denied by the evidence."[82]

David Laidler has submitted evidence from a test somewhat similar to Bronfenbrenner and Mayer's. Employing both the narrow *M*1 and the broad *M*2 definitions of money and testing both the long rate and the short rate of interest in separate regressions, Laidler divided the observations for the period of 1892–1960 into two subsets: those years in which the relevant interest rate was above the mean and those in which it was below the mean. The general equation tested was

$$\ln M = a + b_1 \ln Y_p + b_2 \ln i$$

where Y_p is permanent income. Laidler's results, using both logarithms and first differences of logarithms of the variables defined above, demonstrated very little

---

[80] Martin Bronfenbrenner and Thomas Mayer, *op. cit.,* 831.

[81] For the purpose of these tests, Meltzer defines income as the return on wealth, that is, the interest rate or rate of return *r* times the wealth stock *W.* The wealth measure used to calculate income in this formula is net nonhuman wealth of the public—the same variable employed in his money demand functions. The measure of money he employs is narrow money *(DD + C).* Allan H. Meltzer, *op. cit.,* 243.

[82] Karl Brunner and Allan H. Meltzer, "Predicting Velocity . . . ," *op. cit.,* 350.

tendency for the interest elasticity b_2 to be higher (in absolute value) for the low interest rate observations than it was in the equations fitted to the high interest rate observations. As he notes, "the elasticity with respect to the short rate seems to fall a little at low rates of interest, though the elasticity with respect to the long rate rises slightly at low interest rates. . . . Thus, the hypothesis of the liquidity trap, as it is usually presented, appears to be refuted."[83]

Konstas and Khouja also report statistical tests relevant to this problem. In their study the authors attempt to specify a functional form for the demand for money relation which accurately portrays the characteristics originally suggested by Keynes. In their model, "In regard to the speculative part of the demand for money. . . . the function which is consistent with Keynesian requirements must be stated in the following manner:

$$M_2 = \frac{\beta}{r - \alpha}; \qquad \beta > 0, \qquad \alpha > 0."[84]$$

This formulation quite accurately reflects the properties of the function shown in Figure 7.1. It allows for a minimum interest rate level α and for increasing interest elasticity of money balances as interest rates decline toward α. The authors estimate the parameters of this model using annual observations for the period of 1919–1965. In general, the data seem to fit this relationship rather closely.

Konstas and Khouja use their estimated relation to examine the claim that the United States economy was in a liquidity trap in the 1930s. Specifically, they calculate an estimate of the speculative component of total money balances by subtracting estimated transactions balances from (actual) total money balances for each of the years of 1919–1965. The pattern indicated in the relation between the long-term interest rate and calculated idle balances fails to confirm the belief that monetary policy was impotent in the 1930s because of the very high interest elasticity of the demand for money. They conclude that their test "does not seem to offer much evidence in support of this claim."[85] These results add to the weight of the evidence reported above.

Most of the individual tests cited in this section approach the question of the liquidity trap indirectly. Nevertheless, the majority of this work together with tests premised on liquidity preference relations more akin to the normal rate hypothesis

---

[83] David Laidler, "The Rate of Interest . . . ," *op. cit.,* 550.

[84] Panos Konstas and Mohamad W. Khouja, "The Keynesian Demand for Money Function: Another Look and Some Additional Evidence," *Journal of Money, Credit and Banking,* vol. 1 (November 1969) 767.

[85] Panos Konstas and Mohamad W. Khouja, *op. cit.,* 744. Research by Pifer, using a method similar to Konstas and Khouja's, found no evidence of a positive-valued floor to the interest rate. H. W. Pifer, "A Nonlinear, Maximum Likelihood Estimate of the Liquidity Trap," *Econometrica,* vol. 37 (April, 1969), 324–332. However, subsequent reworking of Pifer's tests in separate articles by Eisner and Spitzer has uncovered some evidence of a minimum value for the long-term interest rate. Robert Eisner, "Nonlinear Estimates of the Liquidity Trap," *Econometrica* (September, 1971), 861–864 and John J. Spitzer "The Demand for Money, the Liquidity Trap and Functional Forms," *International Economic Review,* vol. 17 (February, 1976), 220–227.

originally used by Keynes,[86] do not support the liquidity trap hypothesis. Only the results of some of Laidler's tests with the long-term rate of interest together with Eisner's and Spitzer's tests tend to support the existence of the low-level trap. However, these results all use a long-term interest rate. There is no evidence of a trap when short-term rates are used. Moreover, much of the data for the liquidity trap tests comes from the 1940s when monetary policy attempted to keep long-term rates low and stable, which suggests that money *supply* rather than money *demand* behavior explains the observed phenomenon. Therefore, the weight of all studies taken together seems sufficient to allow a tentative judgment against the historical existence of the liquidity trap. In addition, work by Brunner and Meltzer has shown that the necessary and sufficient conditions for the occurrence of a liquidity trap in the demand function for money are extremely restrictive.[87] Consequently, a judgment favoring the absence of a liquidity trap would seem, at this time, to be warranted by the lack of substantive falsifying evidence.

Concluding Comment

In this Chapter we have defined the major issues upon which empirical studies of the demand for money have focused and have examined in detail the evidence on three of those issues: the appropriate definition of money, the form and specification of empirically testable money demand functions, and the role of the interest rate in explaining variations in the demand for money. While uncertainty still surrounds each of these matters, we have tried to indicate the areas of agreement which have been found by analysts working on these problems as well as to define areas of continuing contention.

In the next Chapter, Professor Friedman's work on the role of permanent income and the interest rate in explaining variations in the velocity of circulation of money will be reviewed as will the voluminous counter-evidence to his analysis. This will require an examination of the evidence on the appropriate scale variable to be included in money demand functions—income, wealth or some other measure of fluctuations in earnings and/or asset balances—and the critical issue for policy makers, the stability over time of estimated money demand relations.

[86] Other studies that claim to formulate and test Keynes' original liquidity preference hypothesis more accurately than is done in some of the literature cited above, see Dennis R. Starleaf and Richard Reimer, "The Keynesian Demand Function for Money: Some Statistical Tests," *Journal of Finance,* vol. 22 (March 1967), 71–76. Their work relates primarily to the Keynesian proposition that it is not necessarily the absolute level of the rate of interest that is important in determining the demand for money but the relationship of that current rate to a conceptual "normal" rate as indicated in footnote 5 on pages 118–119 of Chapter 5. Starleaf and Reimer found no evidence to suggest that the normal rate, as they calculated it, was an important variable in the demand for money. In contrast, Courchene and Kelley found for Canada evidence that a normal rate affected asset demand functions but not to the extent of causing a liquidity trap. Thomas J. Courchene and S. K. Kelly, "Money Supply and Money Demand: An Econometric Analysis for Canada," *Journal of Money, Credit and Banking,* vol. 3 (May, 1971), 368–371.

[87] Karl Brunner and Allan H. Meltzer, "Liquidity Traps for Money, Bank Credit, and Interest Rates," *Journal of Political Economy,* vol. 76 (February 1968), 1–37.

BIBLIOGRAPHY FOR CHAPTER 7

The bibliography to this chapter is found at the end of Chapter 8.

QUESTIONS FOR CHAPTER 7

1. In empirical money demand relations why are money balances usually expressed in *real* rather than nominal terms?

2. Describe the difference between the interpretation of the estimated coefficient of the lagged dependent variable in a partial adjustment model and an adaptive expectations model.

3. What is simultaneous-equation bias? Do the estimated interest elasticities in the money demand functions of simultaneous-equation models conform to the elasticities estimated from single-equation models?

4. Enumerate the issues involved in specifying the appropriate measure of the interest rate in an empirical demand for money function.

5. Does the empirical evidence support the existence of a liquidity trap?

6. Monetary *theory* clearly indicates the definition of the money stock; the empirical debate over how to define the stock of money is a controversy in monetary *policy*. Evaluate.

The Evidence on the
Demand for Money:
Theoretical Formulations
and Empirical Results—Part II

One implication of the work surveyed in the previous chapter is that cyclical variations in interest rates are important determinants of the evident cyclical variations in the demand for money and the velocity of circulation of money. This view has been disputed by at least one important analyst, Milton Friedman. Although in his "restatement" of the quantity theory of money Friedman develops a theoretical money demand function that includes several interest rate terms as explanatory variables, his statistical research leads him to question the empirical significance of the interest rate in determining actual money holdings.

An Alternative View: Interest Rates, Permanent Income, and Variations in Velocity

Friedman's empirical work begins with an observation on the behavior of the income velocity of money. He notes that from 1870 to 1954, over long periods of time, the income velocity of circulation Y/M moved in a direction opposite to that of real income, but over shorter periods of time, during business cycles, these variables moved in the same direction.[1] He attempts to reconcile these observations by explaining the public's behavior regarding the demand for real money balances.

Friedman argues that the *nominal* stock of money in the economy is determined in the first instance on the supply side of the market by the monetary authority and that "holders of money cannot alter this amount directly." In contrast, however, the holders of money "can make the *real* amount of money anything in the aggregate they want to."[2] For if individuals find themselves holding too large a stock of nominal money balances, their attempt to decrease these balances by increasing expenditures will reduce the real quantity of money to the desired level by raising money income and prices. Conversely, lowering expenditures to increase money holdings will lower money income and prices, thereby raising the real quantity of money to the desired equilibrium level.

This analysis suggests that since the *nominal* stock of money is predetermined by the monetary authority, an explanation of the observed behavior of the *real* volume of money balances and the income velocity of money requires an examination of the demand for money.[3] It may be possible to explain the patterns exhibited by velocity through an analysis of the historical behavior of the explanatory variables that enter a stable demand for money function. However, Friedman's attempt to find variables in addition to income that enter the money demand function and that "exert an influence opposite to that of income . . . sufficiently potent to dominate the [cyclical] movement of velocity" is unsuccessful. As he reports, ". . . the other variables that come first to mind are interest rates, and these display cyclical patterns that seem most unlikely to account for the sizable, highly consistent, and roughly synchronous cyclical pattern in velocity."[4] As an alternative approach, suggested by his work on the consumption function which we review in Chapter 10, Friedman employs the concept of permanent income in the money demand function to reconcile the cyclical and secular behavior of velocity. This attempt starts by viewing "the statistical magnitude called 'real income' as corresponding to a different theoretical construct in the cyclical than in the secular analysis." This reconciliation depends on the relation between measured and permanent income. If permanent income rises less than measured income during

---

[1] The inverse long-term relation between income and velocity implies more than simply a direct relation between income and money. It implies that as income increases, money demanded increases more than proportionately, so that money may be viewed as a "luxury" good. This long-term relationship has not prevailed in the postwar period, however, as velocity has trended upward rather strongly.

[2] Milton Friedman, "The Demand for Money—Some Theoretical and Empirical Results," *Journal of Political Economy,* vol. 67 (June 1959), 330.

[3] Following Fisher in employing the equation of exchange, Friedman often couches his analytical discussion in terms of the velocity of circulation of money rather than the demand function for money balances. But since $V = Y/M$, an increase in the demand for nominal balances relative to nominal income will be reflected in a decrease in the income velocity of circulation of money and, conversely, a decrease in the demand for money will be reflected as an increase in velocity.

[4] Milton Friedman, "The Demand for Money . . . ," *op. cit.,* 332.

cyclical expansions and falls less than measured income in contractions, and if money balances are adapted to permanent income, "they might rise and fall more than in proportion to permanent income, as is required by our secular results, yet less than in proportion to measured income, as is required by our cyclical results."[5]

On the basis of this theoretical reconciliation of the conflicting behavior of observed velocity, Friedman turns to an empirical examination of this phenomenon. As he notes, "An interpretation in terms of interest rates can also rationalize the qualitative results; [but] we reject it because it appears likely to be contradicted on a more detailed quantitative level."[6]

In his empirical tests Friedman measures both money balances and permanent income in real (that is, deflated) per capita form and specifies the following exponential money demand function:

$$\frac{M}{NP} = \alpha \left(\frac{Y_p}{NP} \right)^{\delta}$$

or, in logarithmic form,

$$\ln \frac{M}{NP} = \ln \alpha + \delta \ln \left(\frac{Y_p}{NP} \right) \tag{8.1}$$

where P is an index of (permanent) prices, N is population, and Y_p is permanent income.[7]

Friedman fits this function to cycle-average data for the period of 1869–1957. His estimate of δ, the permanent income elasticity of real money balances, is 1.8. Using this relationship, he calculates annual within-cycle projections of the velocity of circulation of money and finds that his formulation predicts actual velocity figures fairly well. Most importantly, however, he also discovers that the *errors that are evident in these predictions are almost completely unrelated to the level of interest rats*. Thus he concludes that there is little role for the interest rate, in addition to permanent income, in explaining variations in the velocity of circulation of money or the variation in money balances.[8]

Friedman achieves these results by using some statistical techniques not generally

---

[5] Milton Friedman, "The Demand for Money . . . ," *op. cit.,* 334.

[6] Milton Friedman, "The Demand for Money . . . ," *op. cit.,* 535.

[7] Friedman originally derived his permanent income concept in connection with his studies on the consumption function. As discussed in Chapter 10, permanent income is calculated as a weighted average of past income levels with the weights attached to the income levels of past periods declining geometrically. See Milton Friedman, *A Theory of the Consumption Function* (Princeton, NJ: Princeton University Press, 1957), 142–147.

[8] Friedman's conclusion would seem to be supported for the postwar period in evidence presented by Sam Peltzman. Challenging the conventional conclusion, Peltzman argues that his "results do imply strongly that interest rate movements cannot explain the postwar rise in velocity" (p. 134). In Peltzman's work this increase is associated with a secular trend in (unspecified) factors other than income and interest rates. See Sam Peltzman, "The Structure of the Money–Expenditure Relationship," *American Economic Review,* vol. 59 (March 1969),

applied by other investigators. His use of cycle-average data,[9] for example, contrasts with the more common practice of employing chronologically determined, annual or quarterly data in regression studies. Also, his use of the broad definition of money is claimed by many to bias his results against finding any role for the interest rate in the determination of money demand.[10] This latter contention may be explained as follows. If demand deposit balances are negatively related to interest rates, but time deposits are positively related to the rate paid on such deposits, a general increase in interest rates will decrease the demand for demand deposits and increase the demand for time deposits. If these two assets are added together in a single measure, these movements will tend to cancel out and the sum, $DD + TD$, may appear to be completely interest insensitive.

In addition, David Laidler[11] has pointed out that over the period covered by Friedman's study there was a slight downward trend in interest rates and that by omitting an interest rate term from his regression equation some of the (trend) influence of the interest rate on money balances was attributed to the trend in the permanent income variable. Since the decline in rates over this period would be expected to cause a relative increase in money balances, the absence of an interest rate term in the equation may help to explain the rather high (1.8) income elasticity estimated in Friedman's tests.

Friedman's results have been even more seriously challenged in the work of other analysts. Several of the studies reported in Table 7.1 include interest rates along with Friedman's measure of permanent income in log–linear money demand functions. For example, Allan H. Meltzer[12] showed that the long-term rate of interest generally appears as a highly significant variable in his regressions. He suggests that Friedman's use of the permanent income measure combines the influence of income, wealth, and interest rates into a single measure and obscures the separate impact

129–137. For a critique of Peltzman's methodology, see Dwight M. Jaffee, "The Structure of the Money Expenditure–Relationship: Comment," *American Economic Review,* vol. 60 (March 1970), 216–219. In light of the serious econometric problems that arise in interpreting Peltzman's use of second differences and Jaffee's use of first differences, the uncertainty surrounding Peltzman's assumption about the public's behavior as regards the formulation of expectations about changes in the money stock, and the fact that Jaffee found some role for the interest rate in Peltzman's "reformulated" model, the overwhelming evidence on this issue from other sources would seem to stand.

[9] An annual time series of observations on a given variable X represents a list of values for that variable for each year over a specified period of time. Cycle-average data on the other hand rely not on calendar years to generate observations, but rather on the cyclical swings in economic activity as defined by the National Bureau of Economic Research. Those who use cycle-average data argue that such a choice of values is economically more meaningful than the arbitrary designation of the calendar (or fiscal) year as the standard measure of time used to generate statistical data.

[10] See the discussion of this problem in connection with some results reported by Stephen M. Goldfeld, "The Demand for Money Revisited," *Brookings Papers on Economic Activity,* vol. 3 (1973), 577–638.

[11] David Laidler, "The Role of Interest and the Demand for Money—Some Empirical Evidence," *Journal of Political Economy,* vol. 74 (December 1966), 545–555.

[12] Allan H. Meltzer, "The Demand for Money: The Evidence from the Time Series," *Journal of Political Economy,* vol. 71 (June 1963), 219–246.

of each on money demand. In addition to demonstrating the significant role of the interest rate when explicitly included in the function, Meltzer derives an estimate of the (permanent) income elasticity that is closer to unity than to Friedman's estimate of 1.8. This would appear to confirm Laidler's contention mentioned above.

Other investigations by Karl Brunner and Allan H. Meltzer[13] and Gregory Chow[14] confirm the important role of the interest rate in alternative money demand or velocity functions. However, one important point with respect to these studies must be mentioned in defense of Friedman. These studies employ annual time series data, and these data are not strictly comparable to Friedman's (perhaps more subtle) cycle-average data. Consequently, their results do not represent a satisfactory refutation of his findings. However, Laidler,[15] employing cycle-average data for the period of 1891–1957, refitted Friedman's original equation and compared the results with those obtained when an interest rate term was included in the equation. His results are as follows:

$$\log \frac{M}{NP} = -2.017 + 1.618 \log\left(\frac{Y_p}{NP}\right)$$

$$\log \frac{M}{NP} = -1.403 + 1.430 \log\left(\frac{Y_p}{NP}\right) - .158 \log i_e$$

where i_e is the rate on 4–6-month commercial paper.

Laidler used these estimates to predict annual levels of per capita real money balances—a procedure very similar to Friedman's use of his equation to predict annual within-cycle values for the velocity of circulation of money. The mean error of prediction[16] for the equation that includes the interest rate is less than half that for the equation that contains only permanent income. Since the interest rate equation explains the data significantly better than Friedman's original equation, Laidler concludes that "the difference in the intercept and coefficient of the logarithm of permanent income that results from the omission of the interest rate is sufficient to produce misleading results (about the relation between prediction errors and the level of the rate of interest)." It appears that there was indeed "some secular (long-term) correlation between permanent income and [the] interest rate which caused permanent income to pick up part of the effect of interest rates in the regression from which the latter variable was omitted." As Laidler points out, then, the evidence coming from so many different sources is so persuasive that "it is probably safe to conclude that the rate of interest must be included in the demand function for

[13] Karl Brunner and Allan H. Meltzer, "Predicting Velocity: Implications for Theory and Policy," *Journal of Finance,* vol. 18 (May 1963), 319–354.

[14] Gregory Chow, "On the Short-Run and Long-Run Demand for Money," *Journal of Political Economy,* vol. 74 (April 1966), 111–131.

[15] David Laidler, "The Rate of Interest . . . ," *op. cit.*

[16] The mean error of prediction is the arithmetic average of the absolute value of the difference between the actual and predicted values of a given variable for all points for which a prediction is obtained.

money."[17] Friedman's results may be attributed in large part to his rather special statistical techniques.

The Scale Factor in Money Demand Functions: Current Income, Permanent Income, or Wealth

The results surveyed above suggest that the performance of any given interest rate measure in an empirical money demand function depends both on the manner in which the dependent variable is defined and on the choice of other explanatory variables included in the equation. As already indicated, the other factors most commonly specified as determinants of the demand for money are income and wealth. The use of income—or some other measure of the volume of transactions—as a constraint on the level of money demand is generally related to the role of money as a medium of exchange. This is stated explicitly in the Keynesian demand function, $M_d = L_1(Y) + L_2(i)$, in the Cambridge equation, $M = k \cdot Y$, and in the inventory theoretic model of money demand, $M_d = (\frac{1}{2}) \sqrt{2bT/i} \cdot P$, where Y is the level of nominal income and T is a measure of the real volume of total transactions and P is price index (see chapters 4 and 6).

On the other hand, when the role of money as a productive asset or a durable consumer good is stressed, a wealth measure is generally proposed as the relevant explanatory variable in the demand for money function. Attention centers on "the equilibrium of the balance sheet, the allocation of assets, and the services that money provides." In this view "effecting a volume of transactions is but one of these services."[18]

In statistical work three measures have most frequently been employed as empirical counterparts to these theoretical constraints: current income, proposed as a proxy for the volume of transactions to be effected by the money stock; non-human wealth, measured as consolidated net worth in the balance sheet of the public; and Friedman's "permanent income," proposed as a proxy for a wealth concept that includes the present value of future labor income as well as the present value of real physical assets. This last measure includes the value of both human and non-human wealth.[19]

Meltzer[20] tests all three of these variables in log-linear equations that specify both $M1$ and $M2$ as dependent variables and which include the yield on corporate bonds as the measure of the interest rate. Meltzer's basic model proposes nonhu-

[17] David Laidler, "The Rate of Interest . . . ," op. cit., 546.

[18] Allan H. Meltzer, "The Demand for Money: The Evidence . . . ," op. cit., 232.

[19] Permanent income may be interpreted as "reflecting the effect of those factors that the unit regards as determining its capital value or wealth: the nonhuman wealth it owns; the personal attributes of the earners in the unit, such as their training, ability, personality; the attributes of the economic activity of the earners, such as the occupation followed, the location of the economic activity, and so on. It is analogous to the "expected" value of a probability distribution." Milton Friedman, A Theory of the Consumption Function, op. cit., 21.

[20] Allan H. Meltzer, "The Demand for Money: The Evidence of . . . ," op. cit.

man wealth W as the relevant constraint on money demand. He finds the elasticity of "narrow" money $M1$ with respect to this measure of wealth to be close to unity. This contrasts with Friedman's finding (reported above) of an elasticity of "broad" money balances with respect to permanent income (a proxy for "total" wealth) of 1.8.

Meltzer attempts to reconcile these results. His findings, which are confirmed by those of Laidler, suggest that Friedman's use of "broad" money as the dependent variable in his equation and the absence of an interest rate term from that equation are responsible for his very high estimate of this parameter. Meltzer contends that it is time deposits which are highly elastic with respect to wealth and that by including these deposits in his measure of "money" Friedman has overstated the wealth elasticity of money defined as $DD + C$. More importantly, Meltzer claims that his measure of nonhuman wealth produces an empirical money demand function which explains a slightly higher proportion of the variance of money balances defined either as $M1$ or $M2$ than does Friedman's permanent income measure.[21]

Meltzer also discovers that his wealth measure is "superior" to current income in the empirical demand for money function; for when both wealth and income are included in the equation, the income variable appears to play no significant role in explaining the variation in money balances, whereas the wealth variable maintains approximately the same size coefficient (and significance) in all tests. Thus Meltzer concludes that a nonhuman wealth measure is slightly superior to Friedman's permanent income variable and far more important than current, measured income in explaining variations in the demand for money.

These results are supported in further tests carried out by Karl Brunner and Allan H. Meltzer. Their experiments involved comparisons of the predictions of measured velocity made from various formulations of the money demand function. In their words,

> . . . the tests sharply discriminate between the effects of income and wealth on the demand for money. . . . income appears to play a much smaller role than wealth as a determinant of desired money balances. The evidence from a number of Keynesian-type equations that take income as a constraint and ignore the effect of wealth suggests that, in general, such equations will not predict velocity or desired money balances as well as a "naive" model.[22]

Their tests on human versus nonhuman wealth measures as explanatory variables in the money demand function yield less certain results. They conclude that

---

[21] Meltzer's basic "wealth" definition is the "total wealth" estimated by Goldsmith, adjusted to exclude government securities, inventories, public land, and the monetary gold and silver stock and to include the monetary and nonmonetary debt of state, local, and federal governments. R. W. Goldsmith, *A Study of Savings in the United States* (Princeton, NJ: Princeton University Press, 1956).

[22] Karl Brunner and Allan H. Meltzer, *op. cit.*, 350. The "naive" model referred to by the authors is a model that assumes that velocity in any one year will be the same as actual velocity in the previous period.

the relative importance of these two measures remains an "open question" in their work.

Further evidence has been put forward by H. R. Heller,[23] David Laidler,[24] Gregory Chow,[25] Stephen M. Goldfeld and others.[26] Employing quarterly data for the postwar period, Heller calculates regression coefficients for six alternative relations. Both $M1$ and $M2$ are specified as dependent variables in equations that include income and the short-term rate of interest, wealth and the short-term rate, or both income and wealth and the short-term rate as explanatory variables. The coefficients of both GNP and wealth are statistically significant in all equations in which only one of these variables appears with the short-term interest rate. However, when both of these constraints are included in the same equation, only one of them retains its significance: GNP in the $M1$ equation and wealth in the $M2$ equation.

Heller attributes this result to the fact that time deposits (included with the $M2$ measure) are related positively to wealth and negatively to income. A negative income coefficient results when time deposits are regressed against both income and wealth in a single equation. This indicates a substitution effect between time deposits and demand deposits, that is, with wealth constant an increase in GNP will cause a fall in the volume of time deposits and a rise in the quantity of currency and demand deposits. Heller interprets this evidence as showing that time deposits and demand deposits are demanded for different reasons: "the transactions motives for cash and demand deposits and the speculative or precautionary motive for time deposits."[27]

The results of tests such as those conducted by Heller appear to be quite sensitive to the quarterly time frame in which the data are measured. Sharply contrasting results are derived from annual data. For example, Laidler set out to compare the explanatory power of four alternative money demand hypotheses. These include (1) the conventional textbook equation with current income and an interest rate as constraints, (2) a Friedman-type permanent income formulation, (3) a model that includes permanent income as a proxy for the volume of transactions and a measure of accumulated transitory income and negative transitory consumption to account for the allocation of funds from these sources to money balances, and (4) a model that includes the last factor above and a nonhuman wealth measure defined as accumulated savings out of permanent income.

Implicit in Laidler's tests of these hypotheses is a comparison of the explanatory power of current income, permanent income, and his indirect measure of nonhuman wealth (accumulated savings out of Y_p) as explanatory variables in the money demand function. From his regressions, which employ first differences of

[23] H. R. Heller, "The Demand for Money—The Evidence from the Short-Run Data," *Quarterly Journal of Economics,* vol. 79 (June 1965), 291–303.

[24] David Laidler, "Some Evidence on the Demand for Money," *Journal of Political Economy,* vol. 74 (February 1966), 55–68.

[25] Gregory Chow, *op. cit.*

[26] Stephen M. Goldfeld, "The Demand for Money Revisited," *op. cit.*

[27] H. R. Heller, *op. cit.,* 300.

annual observations, Laidler finds that "though the results are not absolutely decisive, they strongly suggest that permanent income provides a better theory of the demand for money than does either nonhuman wealth or any other set of variables tested."[28]

Laidler's third hypothesis, which includes a measure of transitory income in the money demand equation, performs the least satisfactorily over the period covered by his data. Although both the nonhuman wealth (4) and the permanent income (2) hypotheses explain the variation in the dependent variable quite satisfactorily, Laidler judges the results with permanent income to be marginally superior. More importantly, both wealth and permanent income explain more of the variation in the dependent variable than does the current income (1) hypothesis. Furthermore, this last finding obtains regardless of the definition of money employed. Thus, using annual data rather than quarterly figures, Laidler challenges Heller's assertion that current income is the relevant constraint on narrow money balances.

An interesting set of experiments performed by Gregory Chow may shed some light on the apparent inconsistencies in these results. Chow attempts to isolate two different sets of factors influencing money holdings: those that determine the long-run equilibrium demand for money and those that influence the rate at which people will make short-run adjustments to restore equilibrium. These adjustments take place when a discrepancy exists between the long-run desired level of money balances and actual money holdings.

Chow reasons that money may be treated as a consumer durable good. He applies to the analysis of the demand for money a model originally developed to explain the demand for automobiles. In this model the long-run demand for money is posited to depend on some measure of the individual's total assets (a wealth measure) and the opportunity cost of holding those balances, the interest rate. The short-run demand for money, however, will depend on the rate at which individuals try to adjust their actual money balances to this long-run desired level. This speed of adjustment in turn depends on the actual size of any discrepancy between actual and desired balances and the rate of change of the individual's total assets (or the rate of savings)—the source from which money balances may be accumulated. Chow summarizes these factors as follows:

> Three sets of factors govern the demand for money. The first set is derived from considering the demand for services from holding money in the long-run. The second is due to time lags in the adjustment of demand to equilibrium. The third is from treating the change in the money stock as a part of saving.[29]

This model reflects both the expectational factors and the partial adjustment mechanism described in the second section of the previous chapter.

[28] David Laidler, "Some Evidence . . . ," *op. cit.,* 63.
[29] Gregory Chow, *op. cit.,* 115.

Like Laidler, Chow tests his hypothesis on annual data. The period covered is 1897–1958. In the long-run equilibrium demand function, permanent income always performs far better than current income but, as in Laidler's work, only marginally better than a wealth measure.[30] However, in the short-run functions that attempt to measure the speed of adjustment to equilibrium current income is preferable to either wealth or permanent income.

A word of caution is in order in interpreting these estimates. The use of permanent income as the constraint variable determining the long-run desired level of money balances muddies the results. Permanent income is an expected magnitude which is calculated as a weighted average of lagged levels of measured income. Consequently, the long-run demand for money function that employs this variable may be written as follows (ignoring interest rates):

$$\left(\frac{M_d}{P}\right)_T = f(Y_p) = b(Y_p)_T = b[\beta_0 \, Y_T + \beta_1 \, Y_{T-1} + \cdots + \beta_n \, Y_{T-n}].$$

Assuming the weights β_i exhibit a geometrically declining lag function (following Friedman), we may write

$$\left(\frac{M_d}{P}\right)_T = b[\beta_0 \, Y_T + \beta_0(1 - \beta_0) \, Y_{T-1} + \beta_0(1 - \beta_0)^2 \, Y_{T-2} + \cdots + \beta_0(1 - \beta_0)^n \, Y_{T-n}].$$

But if $(1 - \beta_0)^j \to 0$ as $j \to n$, by a Koyck transformation,[31] this can be shown equivalent to

$$\left(\frac{M_d}{P}\right)_T = (1 - \beta_0)\left(\frac{M_d}{P}\right)_{T-1} + b\beta_0 Y_T. \qquad (8.2)$$

On the other hand, if the public only partially adjusts its current money holdings to the long-run desired level and this desired level depends on *current measured income, Y,* the following may be specified to describe this behavior:

$$\left(\frac{M}{P}\right)_T - \left(\frac{M}{P}\right)_{T-1} = \lambda\left[\left(\frac{M}{P}\right)_T^* - \left(\frac{M}{P}\right)_{T-1}\right]$$

where $(M/P)_T^*$ is the desired level of money balances and $(M/P)_T^* = a \, Y_T$. Substituting,

---

[30] Chow uses the same measure of net nonhuman wealth as was employed by Meltzer.

[31] See also R. J. Wonnacott and T. H. Wonnacott, *Econometrics* (New York: John Wiley & Sons, 1970), 145–146, and J. Kmenta, *Elements of Econometrics* (New York: Macmillan, 1971), pp. 474 ff.

$$\left(\frac{M}{P}\right)_T - \left(\frac{M}{P}\right)_{T-1} = \lambda \left[a\, Y_T - \left(\frac{M}{P}\right)_{T-1} \right]$$

$$\left(\frac{M}{P}\right)_T = (1 - \lambda) \left(\frac{M}{P}\right)_{T-1} + \lambda a\, Y_T. \qquad (8.3)$$

Thus Equation (8.3) is derived from a partial adjustment model which postulates that desired money balances depend on current measured income and reflect the lagged adjustment of actual to desired balances. It is indistinguishable from Equation (8.2), which postulates that the demand for money depends on permanent income and reflects the lagged impact of experience on expectations.

These relationships make unique interpretation of Chow's findings impossible. They suggest that in his short-run adjustment relation, from which he concludes that current income is the appropriate explanatory variable in the demand for money function, he may simply have been measuring an equilibrium relation between desired money balances and permanent income. In short, this result is not sufficient to distinguish between the hypothesis that the demand for money balances depends on permanent income which does not immediately respond to measured income and the hypothesis that the demand for money balances depends on current measured income but that the public does not immediately adjust actual money balances to long-run desired levels; it does not discriminate between partial adjustment lags and expectation lags.[32]

However, Chow's results do suggest a possible reconciliation of the conflict between those obtained by Heller using quarterly data and those presented by Laidler based on annual data. Heller's method may have picked up the influence of short-run adjustment factors which dominate the quarterly figures, but are less important in the longer run annual observations.

Additional evidence using quarterly data is presented by Stephen M. Goldfeld. Within the framework of his basic log–linear model—which includes a lagged dependent variable (derived from a partial adjustment hypothesis) and both the commercial paper rate and the rate on bank time deposits—he compares the relative power of income, net worth, and changes in net worth in explaining holdings of narrow money. His results show that the absence of an income variable reduces the estimated speed of adjustment to an unreasonably low figure. When income and wealth are both included, the latter is insignificant while the former remains im-

---

[32] A paper by Edgar Feige which admits the *a priori* possibility of either partial adjustment lags (Equation 8.3) or expectation lags (Equation 8.2), using annual data and a narrow definition of money, estimates extremely short adjustment lags and thus resolves the choice in favor of the permanent income formulation (Equation 8.2); a study by Paul Meyer and J. Neri begins from a similar premise and, using annual data and a broad definition of money, presents estimates that also tend to favor the permanent income formulation. Edgar Feige, "Expectations and Adjustments in the Monetary Sector," *American Economic Review,* vol. 57 (May 1967), 462–473; Paul A. Meyer and J. A. Neri, "A Keynes-Friedman Money Demand Function," *American Economic Review,* vol. 65 (September 1975), 610–623.

portant. When the change in wealth is added as a third constraint, "the level effect of net worth is obliterated."[33]

The comparative predictive ability of Goldfeld's wealth equation in dynamic simulations is far inferior to that of his original income-only equation. In addition, though the inclusion of the change in the net worth variable "improves the explanatory power of the equation, [it] slightly worsens its predictive ability."[34]

In summary, the bulk of the evidence available from studies employing annual data indicates rather clearly that some measure of wealth rather than measured income is the most relevant constraint on the equilibrium level of the long run demand for money balances. Whether this constraint is best represented by a permanent income measure that purports to include a human wealth component or by a nonhuman wealth measure, such as those employed by Chow or Meltzer, is somewhat less apparent. At the same time, other evidence certainly suggests that current income may be related to the demand for money through short-run adjustments made to bring *actual* money balances in line with *desired* money holdings. (Unfortunately, measurement difficulties make the results of tests employing quarterly nonhuman wealth data difficult to interpret.) For pragmatic policy purposes one may wish to choose that variable that performs best when the criteria are predictive and forecasting accuracy. On these grounds, measured income, as suggested by Goldfeld's results, is probably the most useful scale factor to employ in short-run money demand functions. Since current and lagged values of measured income are more closely related to permanent income than they are to nonhuman wealth and since Goldfeld's results are not inconsistent with a permanent income hypothesis, permanent income is probably a preferable scale variable in the long run demand-for-money function.

The Stability of the Money Demand Function

Harry G. Johnson, in his 1962 survey of monetary theory, listed three unsettled issues related to the demand for money. These issues included the appropriate empirical definition of the money stock, the choice of arguments to be included in the money demand function, and the stability of the empirical relationship between those arguments and the monetary aggregate.[35] These are not, of course, separable issues. The stability of any empirical function will depend upon the variables included in that function. Likewise, the criterion for choosing the appropriate measure of money has most often been enunciated in terms of the stability of the demand function for that monetary measure. However, for heuristic purposes we have

[33] Stephen M. Goldfeld, "The Demand for Money Revisited," *op. cit.,* 614.

[34] Stephen M. Goldfeld, "The Demand for Money Revisited," *op. cit.,* 615.

[35] Harry G. Johnson, "Monetary Theory and Policy," *American Economic Review,* vol. 52 (June 1962), 335–384.

The importance of the stability of the money demand function to Milton Friedman's policy proposals is understood in the Appendix to Chap. 11.

attempted to separate these issues in the empirical literature. By this point in the survey the major areas of agreement and of continuing contention on the first two issues noted by Johnson have become evident.

It should be clear, however, that an underlying assumption throughout this discussion has been the assumption that we were in fact dealing with stable relationships. While the diversity of functional forms and data periods employed by various researchers has made more difficult the task of reconciling divergent results, the similarity of elasticity estimates over these wide ranging studies would seem to support the essential validity of this assumption. It is worthwhile, however, briefly to consider the stability issue more explicitly.

One serious attack on the apparent stability of postwar money demand functions was presented by William Poole. Employing a log–linear money demand function similar to Equation (7.3), Poole estimated interest elasticities of real money balances by constraining the values of the income elasticities within a range of 0.5–3.0. Employing quarterly data for 1947–1969, his results demonstrate a *direct* relation between the constrained income elasticity and the estimated interest elasticity. More importantly, he finds that "the goodness of fit is practically unchanged over an extremely wide range of income elasticities," implying that there is insufficient information in the statistics to permit a choice among these results. On this evidence he makes the very strong assertion that "using postwar data alone, it is impossible to obtain a satisfactory estimate of the demand for money function."[36]

Stephen M. Goldfeld has taken up this issue and persuasively countered Poole's critique. Employing an equation similar to the one specified by Poole but including a lagged dependent variable, he finds that "the interest elasticities display a clear tendency to increase with [the constrained income elasticity] but the rise is not nearly as pronounced as Poole found."[37] While Goldfeld also finds uniformly high R^2 for the various forms of the equations, he claims that this is misleading and convincingly demonstrates it by additional testing.

Though the R^2 are uniformly high for all equations, they tend to rise slightly with the constrained value of the income elasticity. However, this statistic is not strictly

[36] William Poole, "Whither Money Demand?" *Brookings Papers on Economic Activity,* vol. 3 (1970), 489. Poole's final conclusion is not that we must give up on money demand functions, but rather that since postwar data are unreliable, additional weight must be given to long-run estimates.

[37] Goldfeld, "The Demand for Money Revisited," *op. cit.,* 585. Strong support for Goldfeld's results is to be found in G. S. Laumas and Y. P. Mehra, "The Stability of the Demand for Money Function: The Evidence from Quarterly Data," *Review of Economics and Statistics,* 58 (November 1976), 463–468. Using the varying parameter regression approach developed by Cooley and Prescott to test the stability of postwar money demand functions in the United States, the authors conclude that "money demand equations that do not assume that all the adjustment of actual cash balances to desired cash balances occurs within a given quarter are stable money demand functions. On the other hand, all the specifications of money demand equations that assume complete adjustment within a quarter and hence *omit one lagged value of the* dependent variable are unstable. . . . Those specifications of money demand equations that constrain the lagged dependent variable coefficient to zero are subject to specification error and fail the stability test" (p. 467). Poole's equations differ from Goldfeld's primarily in that they do in fact omit a lagged dependent variable.

comparable across equations and cannot be used alone as a selection criterion. Gold-feld demonstrates this by constraining the income elasticity to the value first derived in an unconstrained form of the same equation. The constrained form reproduces the results of the unconstrained form except for the R^2, indicating the noncompara-bility of the R^2 resulting from the use of different dependent variables.[38]

However, there may still be a statistical means by which to choose among these equations. Goldfeld first examines the standard error of the regression and finds it lowest, as it must be, for the value derived from the unconstrained form. He then evaluates the equations by examining the root-mean-square error derived from two different types of dynamic simulations on the estimated equations. As he notes, this is a more stringent test of the estimation results and is likely to be more relevant from a forecasting point of view. His results show clearly that the root-mean-square errors deteriorate even more rapidly than the standard error of the regression as elasticity values diverge further from the value estimated in the unconstrained equa-tion. He concludes, then, that Poole's rejection of estimates derived from postwar data is unwarranted and that the "income elasticity can be pinned down within a reasonable range of accuracy."[39] The estimate that he derives is .68, significantly less than unity and consistent with the proposition that there are economics of scale in holding money balances.

Additional dynamic simulations of his basic equation convince Goldfeld that the relationship underlying his empirical estimates has remained rather stable in the postwar period. Both short-term (out of sample) forecasts four quarters ahead of various defined subsamples of the data period and longer term simulations over a later part of the sample period based on estimates for an earlier subperiod suggest reasonable stability. A formal Chow test of stability, carried out by splitting the data sample into two subperiods suggested by the major institutional change brought about by the introduction of certificates of deposits (CDs) in 1961, also fails to deliver evidence upon which to reject the hypothesis of stability.[40]

The evidence on the postwar stability of the money demand relation generally conforms to the results of work that has examined the issue over longer periods with annual data. The work by Karl Brunner and Allan H. Meltzer,[41] Allan H. Meltzer,[42] David Laidler,[43] and other authors cited directly supports this long-run stability. Recent work by Moshin S. Khan, using a new and more flexible technique to deter-

[38] The dependent variable is $(\ln M_T - e \ln Y_T)$, where e is the constrained income elasticity. This variable will differ, of course, for each assumed value of the elasticity constraint.

[39] Stephen M. Goldfeld, "The Demand for Money Revisited," op. cit., 589.

[40] For an alternative view of the effect of the creation of the CD market, see M. B. Slovin and M. E. Sushka, "A Financial Market Approach to the Demand for Money and the Implica-tions for Monetary Policy," Board of Governors of the Federal Reserve System (1972).

[41] Karl Brunner and Allan H. Meltzer, "Comment on the Long-Run and Short-Run Demand for Money," Journal of Political Economy, vol. 76 (November/December 1968), 1234–1239.

[42] Allan H. Meltzer, "The Demand for Money: The Evidence . . . ," op. cit.

[43] David Laidler, "A Survey of Some Current Problems," in Monetary Theory and Monetary Policy in the 1970s, C. Clayton, J. C. Gilbert, and R. Sidgewick, eds. (New York: Oxford University Press, 1971).

mine whether a regression estimate is stable over a full sample period, adds to the weight of evidence in favor of this conclusion. Using either current income or permanent income along with a long-term rate of interest, his tests fail to offer any support for the hypothesis that there were significant structural shifts in the money demand relations over the 1901–1965 period.[44]

One final piece of evidence is worth citing on this issue. In 1971, both within and outside of the Federal Reserve, it was fairly widely held that, regardless of the historical stability of the money demand function, a substantial shift had occurred in the early part of that year. Even the Council of Economic Advisers in the "Economic Report to the President" in 1972 expressed this view: "In the first half of 1971, the public apparently wanted to hold more money balances at the prevailing level of interest rates and income than past relations among income, interest rates, and money balances suggested."[45]

Michael J. Hamburger has examined this view in the light of more recent evidence. Fortunately for the conclusions reached in the studies cited above, but unfortunately for those monetary economists and policy makers who thought they had recognized a short-run shift in money demand, recent evidence fails to confirm instability during the second quarter of 1971; in the face of an increase in interest rates and a decline in the rate of growth of income, and contrary to what highly simplified theory would predict, there was a sharp *increase* in the stock of narrow money balances demanded. But there is a certain weakness in conventional theory in its simplest form in that it fails to consider delayed reactions ("adjustments") to *previous* income and interest rate changes. Hamburger suggests that within the framework of the FRB-MIT-PENN model, once allowance is made for such lagged adjustments, even "the evidence that was available in 1971 provided only marginal support for the hypothesis that there was an upward shift in the demand for money" at that time.[46] On the basis of results obtained with more recent versions of the model that incorporate the influence of inflation on money demand, even that marginal support disappears. Perhaps more disturbing, equations developed since that time to explain month-to-month changes in $M1$ have no difficulty "explaining the rapid growth of $M1$ during the second quarter of 1971 *with relationships derived from earlier periods*" (emphasis added).[47]

This episode is reviewed here to point out a continuing dilemma facing policy makers. While it can be shown that the existence of a stable demand for money function is necessary for the conduct of effective monetary policy, and while it is

---

[44] Kahn's tests with the short-term rate suggest some instability in the relationship around 1948. This instability appears whether money is defined narrowly or broadly. In this respect, Kahn's results conflict with Laidler's conclusion that the most stable demand function is one that includes the short-term rate as an explanatory variable. See Moshin S. Khan, "The Stability of the Demand for Money Function in the United States, 1901–1965," *Journal of Political Economy,* vol. 82 (November/December 1974), 1205–1219.

[45] Council of Economic Advisers, "Economic Report to the President" (January 1972), 58.

[46] Michael J. Hamburger, "The Demand for Money in 1971 . . . ," *op. cit.,* 721.

[47] Michael J. Hamburger, "The Demand for Money in 1971 . . . ," *op. cit.,* 723.

widely accepted, on the basis of the evidence surveyed here, that this condition has been met over a long period in the United States, it is difficult for policy makers and their advisers "to make reasonably accurate on-the-spot judgments as to whether changes in the demand for money are occurring at particular points in time."[48] At this point the science of the economist becomes partner to the artistry of the policy maker.

Concluding Comment

The first and most important result of the survey of the empirical literature on the demand for money presented in these two chapters is that the evidence supporting the existence of a reasonably stable demand for money function would seem to be overwhelming. This is true both of long-term evidence covering the last seventy years or so and of the evidence from the postwar period.

Second, and perhaps next in importance for the conduct of monetary policy, the vast majority of this same evidence supports the hypothesis that the interest rate plays a significant role in the determination of the public's desired money holdings. Furthermore, the range of estimates for the interest elasticity of money balances has been fairly narrowly circumscribed, with the best results suggesting an elasticity of about $-.2$ for the short rate and approximately $-.7$ for the long rate. Unfortunately it is not yet possible to state confidently which particular interest rate measure yields the most stable money demand relationship. Moreover, this question is so intimately connected with the problem of the appropriate definition of the money stock that judgment must be suspended on this issue pending additional work, including work on the term structure of interest rates.

Third, there appears to be little support for the liquidity-trap hypothesis.

Finally, the best evidence to date suggests that, in addition to an interest rate measure, some measure of wealth—either a direct balance sheet measure or a proxy variable such as permanent income—would seem to be most relevant to the public's long-run decision to hold money balances. However, as there is a growing body of evidence that short-run movements in money balances, determined by the speed at which people adjust their actual money holdings to a long-run equilibrium level, may be dependent upon the flow of income in the current period and in the recent past. As current and past income levels determine the level of permanent income, the latter is probably the most appropriate scale variable to include in the long-run demand-for-money function.

These conclusions rest primarily on the evidence cited in this study. Other important works, many of which are included in the Bibliography, could also have been used to support some of these conclusions. The studies were selected because of their historical importance in the debate on the issues to which we have directed our

---

[48] Michael J. Hamburger, "The Demand for Money in 1971 . . . ," *op. cit.,* 724.

attention or because they represent the best starting point for students of these problems. In short, despite the fact that the Bibliography contains over one hundred items, no claim is made that this survey represents an exhaustive review of all the literature in this field.

QUESTIONS FOR CHAPTER 8

1. Milton Friedman's empirical work on the demand for money uses a broad definition of money, omits an interest rate variable and yields a rather high estimated elasticity of permanent income. What are some of the criticisms of this work?

2. Under what conditions is a measure of wealth the most relevant constraint on the equilibrium level of money balances? Under what conditions is it a measure of current income?

3. How is the stability of the demand for money function related to the successful conduct of monetary policy?

4. "Despite the enormous quantity of empirical work done, there is still little precise knowledge of the true demand for money relation."
Do you agree or disagree?

BIBLIOGRAPHY FOR CHAPTERS 7 AND 8

ALMON, S., "The Distributed Lag between Capital Appropriations and Expenditures," *Econometrica,* vol. 33 (January 1965), 147–181.

ARROW, K. J., H. B. CHENERY, B. S. MINHAS, and R. M. SOLOW, "Capital–Labor Substitution and Economic Efficiency," *Review of Economics and Statistics,* vol. 63 (August 1961), 225–250.

ARTIS, M. J. and LEWIS, M. K., "The Demand for Money in the United Kingdom: 1963–1973," *Manchester School of Economic and Social Studies,* vol. 44 (June 1976).

BARRO, ROBERT J., "Inflation, the Payments Period, and the Demand for Money," *Journal of Political Economy,* vol. 78 (November/December 1970), 1228–1263.

——, and ANTHONY M. SANTOMERO, "Household Money Holdings and the Demand Deposit Rate," *Journal of Money, Credit and Banking,* vol. 4 (May 1972), 397–413.

BAUMOL, W., "The Transactions Demand for Cash: An Inventory Theoretic Approach," *Quarterly Journal of Economics,* vol. 66 (November 1952), 545–556.

BOYD, JOHN H., "Household Demand for Checking Account Money," *Journal of Monetary Economics,* vol. 1 (January 1976), 81–98.

BRONFENBRENNER, MARTIN, and THOMAS MAYER, "Liquidity Functions in the American Economy," *Econometrica,* vol. 28 (October 1960), 810–834.

BRUNNER, KARL, and ALLAN H. MELTZER, "Predicting Velocity: Implications for Theory and Policy," *Journal of Finance,* vol. 18 (May 1963), 319–354.

——, "Some Further Evidence on Supply and Demand Functions for Money," *Journal of Finance,* vol. 19 (May 1964), 240–283.

——, "Economies of Scale in Cash Balances Reconsidered," *Quarterly Journal of Economics,* vol. 81 (August 1967), 422–436.

——, "Liquidity Traps for Money, Bank Credit, and Interest Rates," *Journal of Political Economy,* vol. 76 (February 1968), 1–37.

——, "Comment on the Long-Run and Short-Run Demand for Money," *Journal of Political Economy,* vol. 76 (November/December 1968), 1234–1239.

CAGAN, PHILLIP and ANNA J. SCHWARTZ, "Has Growth of Money Substitutes Hindered Monetary Policy?" *Journal of Money, Credit and Banking* (May 1975), 137–160.

CHETTY, V. K., "On Measuring the Nearness of Near-Moneys," *American Economic Review,* vol. 59 (June 1969), 270–281.

CHOW, GREGORY, "On the Short-Run and Long-Run Demand for Money," *Journal of Political Economy,* vol. 74 (April 1966), 111–131.

——, "Long-Run and Short-Run Demand for Money: Reply and Further Notes," *Journal of Political Economy,* vol. 76 (November/December 1968), 1240–1243.

COUNCIL OF ECONOMIC ADVISERS, "Economic Report to the President" (January 1972).

COURCHENE, THOMAS J. and A. K. KELLY, "Money Supply and Money Demand: An Econometric Analysis for Canada," *Journal of Money, Credit and Banking,* vol. 3 (May 1971), 368–371.

DICKSON, HAROLD D., and DENNIS R. STARLEAF, "Polynomial Distributed Lag Structures in the Demand Function for Money," *Journal of Finance,* vol. 27 (December 1972), 1035–1043.

DUTTON, DONALD S., and WARREN P. GRAMM, "Transactions Costs, the Wage Rate and the Demand for Money," *American Economic Review,* vol. 63 (September 1973), 652–665.

EDWARDS, FRANKLIN P., "More on the Substitutability Between Money and Near Monies," *Journal of Money, Credit and Banking,* vol. 4 (August 1972), 551–572.

EISNER, ROBERT, "Another Look at Liquidity Preference," *Econometrica,* vol. 31 (July 1963), 531–538.

EISNER, ROBERT, "Nonlinear Estimates of the Liquidity Trap," *Econometrica,* vol. 39 (September 1971), 861–864.

ENZLER, LEWIS JOHNSON and JOHN HAUDUS, "Some Problems of Money Demand," *Brookings Papers on Economic Activity,* vol. 9 (1976), 261–280.

FEIGE, EDGAR, *The Demand for Liquid Assets: A Temporal Cross Section Analysis.* (Englewood Cliffs Company: Prentice-Hall, 1964).

——, "Expectations and Adjustments in the Monetary Sector," *American Economic Review,* vol. 57 (May 1967), 462–473.

FEIGE, EDGAR L., and DOUGLAS K. PEARCE, "The Substitutability of Money and Near-Monies: A Survey of the Time-Series Evidence," *Journal of Economic Literature,* vol. 15 (June 1977), 439–469.

FRIEDMAN, MILTON, *A Theory of the Consumption Function* (Princeton, NJ: Princeton University Press, 1957).

——, "The Quantity Theory of Money, A Restatement," in *Studies in the Quantity Theory of Money,* Milton Friedman, ed. (Chicago: University of Chicago Press, 1956).

——, "The Demand for Money—Some Theoretical and Empirical Results," *Journal of Political Economy,* vol. 67 (June 1959), 327–351.

——, and ANNA J. SCHWARTZ, *A Monetary History of the United States, 1867–1960.* (Princeton, NJ: National Bureau of Economic Research, 1963).

——, and DAVID MEISELMAN, "Relative Stability of Monetary Velocity and the Investment Multiplier in the United States 1897–1957," in *Stabilization Policies,* Commission on Money and Credit (Englewood Cliffs, NJ: Prentice-Hall, 1963).

GALPER, HARVEY, "Alternative Interest Rates and the Demand for Money: Comment," *American Economic Review,* vol. 59 (June 1969), 401–407.

GOLDFELD, STEPHEN M., *Commercial Bank Behavior and Economic Activity* (Amsterdam: North-Holland, 1966).

——, "The Demand for Money Revisited," *Brookings Papers on Economic Activity,* vol. 3 (1973), 577–638.

GOLDSMITH, R. W., *A Study of Savings in the United States* (Princeton, NJ: Princeton University Press, 1956).

GRAMLICH, EDWARD M., and JOHN H. KALCHBRENNER, *A Constrained Estimation Approach to the Demand for Liquid Assets,* Board of Governors of the Federal Reserve System, Special Studies Paper No. 3.

GRAY, M. R., R. J. WOOD, and G. ZIS, "World Demand for Money," in M. Parkin and G. Zis (eds.), *Inflation in the World Economy* (Manchester: Manchester University Press, 1976).

GRILICHES, Z., "Distributed Lags: A Survey," *Econometrica,* vol. 35 (January 1967), 16–49.

GURLEY, JOHN G., and EDWARD S. SHAW, *Money in a Theory of Finance* (Washington, DC: The Brookings Institution, 1960).

HAMBURGER, MICHAEL J., "The Demand for Money by Households, Money Substitutes, and Monetary Policy," *Journal of Political Economy,* vol. 74 (December 1966), 600–623.

——, "Alternative Interest Rates and the Demand for Money: Comment," *American Economic Review,* vol. 59 (June 1969), 407–412.

——, "The Demand for Money in 1971: Was There a Shift? A Comment," *Journal of Money, Credit and Banking,* vol. 5 (May 1973), 720–725.

HELLER, H. R., "The Demand for Money—The Evidence from the Short-Run Data," *Quarterly Journal of Economics,* vol. 79 (June 1965), 291–303.

HYMANS, S., *Probability Theory* (Englewood Cliffs, NJ: Prentice Hall, 1966), ch. 8.

JAFFEE, DWIGHT M., "The Structure of the Money–Expenditure Relationship: Comment," *American Economic Review,* vol. 60 (March 1970), 216–219.

JOHNSON, HARRY G., "Monetary Theory and Policy," *American Economic Review,* vol. 52 (June 1962), 335–384.

JOHNSTON, J., *Econometric Methods* (New York: McGraw Hill, 1963), ch. 9.

JONES, DAVID, "The Demand for Money: A Review of the Empirical Literature," Staff Economic Studies of the Federal Reserve System, paper presented to the Federal Reserve System Committee on Financial Analysis in St. Louis (October 1965).

KAMINOW, I. P., "The Household Demand for Money: An Empirical Study," *Journal of Finance,* vol. 24 (September 1969), 679–696.

KARNI, EDI, "The Value of Time and the Demand for Money," *Journal of Money, Credit and Banking,* vol. 6 (February 1974), 45–64.

KAUFMAN, GEORGE G., "More on an Empirical Definition of Money," *American Economic Review,* vol. 59 (March 1969), 78–87.

KEYNES, JOHN MAYNARD, *The General Theory of Employment, Interest, and Money* (London: Harcourt, Brace and Co., 1936).

KHAN, MOSHIN S., "The Stability of the Demand of Money in the United States, 1901–1965," *Journal of Political Economy,* vol. 82 (Nov./Dec., 1974), 1205–1219.

KLEIN, BENJAMIN, "Competitive Interest Payments on Bank Deposits and the Long-Run Demand for Money," *American Economic Review,* vol. 64 (December 1974), 931–949.

KMENTA, J., *Elements of Econometrics* (New York: Macmillan, 1971), chs. 7 and 10.

KONSTAS, PANOS, and MOHAMAD W. KHOUJA, "The Keynesian Demand-for-Money Function: Another Look and Some Additional Evidence," *Journal of Money, Credit and Banking,* vol. 1 (November 1969), 765–777.

LAFFER, ARTHUR B., "Trade Credit and the Money Market," *Journal of Political Economy,* vol. 78 (March/April 1970), 239–267.

LAIDLER, DAVID, "Some Evidence on the Demand for Money," *Journal of Political Economy,* vol. 74 (February 1966), 55–68.

——, "The Rate of Interest and the Demand for Money—Some Empirical Evidence," *Journal of Political Economy,* vol. 74 (December 1966), 545–555.

——, *The Demand for Money: Theories and Evidence* (New York: Dun-Donnelley, 1977), 2nd edition.

——, "The Definition of Money: Theoretical and Empirical Problems," *Journal of Money, Credit and Banking,* vol. 1 (August 1969), 509–525.

——, "A Survey of Some Current Problems," in *Monetary Theory and Monetary Policy in the 1970s,* G. Clayton, J. C. Gilbert, and R. Sidgewick, eds. (New York: Oxford University Press, 1971).

LAIDLER, DAVID, and J. MICHAEL PARKIN, "The Demand for Money in the United Kingdom, 1956–1967: Preliminary Estimates," *Manchester School,* vol. 38 (September 1970), 741–809.

LATANÉ, HENRY A., "Cash Balances and the Interest Rate—A Pragmatic Approach," *Review of Economics and Statistics,* vol. 36 (November 1954), 456–460.

LAUMAS, G. S., and Y. P. MEHRA, "The Stability of The Demand for Money Function: The Evidence from Quarterly Data," *Review of Economics and Statistics,* vol. 58 (November 1976), 463–468.

LEE, T. H., "Alternative Interest Rates and the Demand for Money: The Empirical Evidence," *American Economic Review,* vol. 57 (December 1967), 1168–1181.

DE LEEUW, FRANK, "A Model of Financial Behavior," in *The Brookings Quarterly Econometric Model of the United States,* James Duesenberry, Gary Fromm, Lawrence Klein, and Edwin Kuh, eds. (Chicago: Rand McNally and Company, 1965), 464–530.

LYDALL, HAROLD, "Income, Assets, and the Demand for Money," *Review of Economics and Statistics,* vol. 40 (February 1958), 1–14.

MAISEL, S. J., "Controlling Monetary Aggregates," in *Controlling Monetary Aggregates,* Proceedings of the Monetary Conference of the Federal Reserve Bank of Boston (June 1969), 152–174.

MASON, WILL E., "The Empirical Definition of Money: A Critique," *Economic Inquiry,* vol. 14 (December 1976), 525–538.

MELTZER, ALLAN H., "The Demand for Money: The Evidence from the Time Series," *Journal of Political Economy,* vol. 71 (June 1963), 219–246.

——, "The Demand for Money: A Cross Section Study of Business Firms," *Quarterly Journal of Economics,* vol. 77 (August 1963), 405–422.

MEYER, PAUL A., and J. A. NERI, "A Keynes-Friedman Money Demand Function," *American Economic Review,* vol. 65 (September 1975), 610–623.

OCHS, J., "The Transaction Demand for Money and Choices Involving Risk," *Journal of Political Economy,* vol. 76 (March/April 1968), 289–291.

PATINKIN, DON, "The Chicago Tradition, the Quantity Theory and Friedman," *Journal of Money, Credit and Banking,* vol. 1 (February 1969), 46–70.

PELTZMAN, SAM, "The Structure of the Money–Expenditure Relationship," *American Economic Review,* vol. 59 (March 1969), 129–137.

PIFER, H. W., "A Nonlinear Maximum Likelihood Estimate of the Liquidity Trap," *Econometrica,* vol. 37 (April 1969), 324–332.

POOLE, WILLIAM, "Whither Money Demand?" *Brookings Papers on Economic Activity,* vol. 3 (1970), 485–500.

SANTOMERO, ANTHONY M., "A Model of the Demand for Money by Households," *Journal of Finance,* vol. 29 (March 1974), 89–102.

SCHADRACK, FREDERICK C., "An Empirical Approach to the Definition of Money," *Monetary Aggregates and Monetary Policy,* Federal Reserve Bank of New York (1974), 28–34.

SHAPIRO, A. A., "Inflation, Lags, and the Demand for Money," *International Economic Review,* vol. 16 (February 1975), 81–96.

SHAPIRO, HAROLD, "Distributed Lags, Interest Rate Expectations and the Impact of Monetary Policy: An Econometric Analysis of a Canadian Experience," *American Economic Review,* vol. 57 (May 1967), 444–461.

SLOVIN, M. B., and M. E. SUSHKA, "A Financial Market Approach to the Demand for Money and the Implications for Monetary Policy," Board of Governors of the Federal Reserve (1972).

STARLEAF, DENNIS R., and RICHARD REIMER, "The Keynesian Demand Function for Money: Some Statistical Tests," *Journal of Finance,* vol. 22 (March 1967), 71–76.

TAYLOR, L. D., and J. P. NEWHOUSE, "On the Long-Run and Short-Run Demand for Money: A Comment," *Journal of Political Economy,* vol. 77 (September/October 1969), 851–856.

TEIGEN, RONALD, "Demand and Supply Functions for Money in the United States. Some Structural Estimates," *Econometrica,* vol. 32 (October 1964), 477–509.

——, "An Aggregated Quarterly Model of the U.S. Monetary Sector, 1953–1964," presented to the Conference on Targets and Indicators of Monetary Policy, University of California, Los Angeles (April 1966).

TINTNER, G., *Econometrics* (New York: John Wiley & Sons, 1962), ch. 6.

TOBIN, JAMES, "Liquidity Preference and Monetary Policy," *Review of Economics and Statistics,* vol. 29 (May 1947), 124–131.

——, "The Interest Elasticity of Transaction Demand for Cash," *Review of Economics and Statistics,* vol. 38 (August 1956), 241–247.

——, "Liquidity Preference as Behavior Towards Risk," *Review of Economic Studies,* vol. 25 (February 1958), 65–86.

TSIANG, S. C., "The Precautionary Demand for Money: An Inventory Theoretical Analysis," *Journal of Political Economy,* vol. 77 (January/February 1969), 99–117.

TURNOVSKY, STEPHEN J., "The Demand for Money and the Determination of the Rate of Interest under Uncertainty," *Journal of Money, Credit and Banking,* vol. 3 (May 1971), 183–204.

WALTERS, ALAN A., "The Demand for Money—The Dynamic Properties of the Multiplier," *Journal of Political Economy,* vol. 75 (June 1967), 293–298.

——, "The Radcliffe Report—Ten Years After: A Survey of Empirical Evidence," in *Money in Britain 1959–1969,* O. R. Croome and H. G. Johnson, eds. (Oxford: Oxford University Press, 1969).

WHALEN, EDWARD L., "A Cross-Section Study of Business Demand for Cash," *Journal of Finance,* vol. 20 (September 1965), 423–443.

WONNACOTT, R. J., and T. H. WONNACOTT, *Econometrics* (New York: John Wiley & Sons, 1970), 145–146.

ZAREMBKA, P., "Functional Form in the Demand for Money," *Journal of the American Statistical Association,* vol. 63 (June 1968), 502–511.

Income and Expenditures: Basic Concepts

How Economists View the Macroeconomy

The Conceptual Framework

Theories help reduce the complications of the real world to manageable dimensions. In order to generate useful theories about economic behavior, economists have developed a highly simplified conception of the economy. They view the economy as consisting of three sectors of behavioral units: households, business firms, and government.[1] Economists see ours as basically a market economy consisting of two fundamental types of markets, product markets in which households and government buy quantities of goods and services at market prices from business firms, and factor markets in which households sell quantities of the factors of production at market prices to business firms. In the markets for goods and services, the quantities of goods and services exchanged times the prices at which they are exchanged generate a dollar magnitude called *expenditures*. In the markets for factors of production, quantities exchanged times the prices at which they exchange generate a dollar magnitude called *income*.

In this abstract view of the economy, economists assume that households own all

[1] Actually, there is a fourth sector, the foreign sector, but as no material in this text considers transactions with foreigners, this sector is ignored. For a text that treats the foreign sector see, for instance, William Branson, *Macroeconomic Theory and Policy* (New York: Harper and Row, 1972).

the factors of production (labor, capital, land, and entrepreneurial talent) and earn all the income (wages, interest, rent, and profit) generated by selling these factors. This does no violence to reality as households in fact actually do own all business firms directly through single proprietorships or partnerships or indirectly through ownership of the equity claims (common and preferred stock) issued by corporations. Thus households are conceived by economists as making both the decision to sell their factors of production and the decision to consume now or in the future the income earned thereby. Business firms, on the other hand, are seen as making the decision to produce goods and services, to sell them, and to hire factors of production necessary to carry out these activities. Government is envisioned as making the decisions to tax and to spend.

Economists generally focus on economic activity during a particular interval of time. All aggregate income and aggregate expenditures are measured as dollars per time period because they are *flows* rather than *stocks*. Flows can only be measured between two points in time. For example, a flow phenomenon in nature that can only be measured between two points in time is the volume of water passing over a waterfall. In economics some examples of flow phenomena are the volume of personal income tax receipts and the volume of investment expenditures. Stocks, in contrast, are measured at a point in time. An example of a stock phenomenon in nature is the volume of a lake. In economics some examples of stock phenomena are the supply of money, the stock of physical capital and other forms of wealth in the economy.

Figure 9.1 presents a simplified version of how economists conceptualize the flow of aggregate income and expenditures. On the right-hand side of Figure 9.1 different "levels" signify the markets in which certain types of transactions take place. At level I are the factor markets. At this level the services of the productive factors, labor, capital, land, and entrepreneurial talent, are exchanged for the corresponding factor earnings: wages, interest, rent, and profit. Services of the productive factors are employed in production of goods and services. The earnings generated thereby are shown at level I to flow entirely to the household sector. That is, in the present simplified version the business sector retains no earnings. Later in this chapter retained earnings are introduced. Moreover, in the present representation of how economists view the macroeconomy, the government sector receives no earnings. This also is modified later in the chapter.

Transfer payments are defined as one-way, nonmarket flows—grants for which no directly related exchange or reciprocating flow is normally expected. In Figure 9.1 at level II, the only transfer payment is the payment of personal income taxes by households to government. Economists assume that households do not individually believe that their income tax payments generate a reciprocal flow of government services. There is not a direct exchange of part of household income for a related flow of governmental services. Therefore at level II in Figure 9.1, in return for the payment of income taxes shown going from households to government, there is no flow of government services shown going in the opposite direction. For the sake

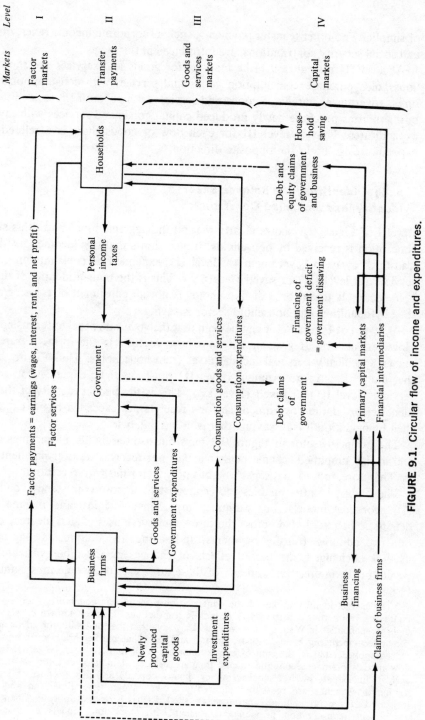

FIGURE 9.1. Circular flow of income and expenditures.

of simplicity no other transfer payments, such as corporate income taxes, dividends, and social security contributions, are introduced at this stage.

At level III in Figure 9.1 the markets for goods and services are shown. Here households purchase consumption goods and services with consumption expenditures, government purchases goods and services with government expenditures, and business firms purchase newly produced capital goods and services with investment expenditures. Thus at level III for each flow of goods there is a related flow of expenditures going in the opposite direction.

Budget Identities, the Balance Sheet Identity, and Financing Constraints

Level I of Figure 9.1 shows clearly that all the aggregate income in this simplified conception is received by households. It also shows that this income must be either transfered away to government (at level II), expended on consumption goods and services (at level III) or saved (level IV). This is the budget identity of the household sector. If the income of households is not all consumed or transferred away, then by definition, the household sector is saving.

At level I of Figure 9.1 it can be seen that the government sector earns no income. However, at level II government does have receipts in the form of transfer payments, specifically personal income taxes from households. Thus Figure 9.1 shows that the receipts of government (level II) must either be expended on goods and services (level III) or saved (level IV). This is the budget identity of the government sector. If the government sector's receipts are exceeded by its expenditures, then by definition it is dissaving, that is, it has a deficit.

The business sector in Figure 9.1 pays out to households all earnings at level I and in this simplified scheme neither makes nor receives transfer payments at level II. Therefore, in a formal sense, the business sector has zero receipts.

The budget identity enables the economist to impose consistency conditions on his theoretical models. For example, any change in household income must, by definition, be distributed across the three alternative uses of that income: consumption expenditures, transfer payments, and saving. In addition, as long as income itself is unchanged, the partial effects of changes in any other variable, such as wealth or the interest rate, on any of these three uses of income must sum to zero.[2]

---

[2] The budget identity is one of the conservation principles in economics. Conservation principles ensure internal consistency in economic transactions. The best known conservation principle in economics is Walras' Law. Walras' Law says that the total value of goods and services demanded (including bonds, money, capital, and labor) at market prices must equal the total value supplied (that is, the sum of excess demands in all markets must be zero). In the stock-flow models of macroeconomic theory that are developed in later chapters, Walras' Law, as such, is inadequate because stocks (money, bonds, capital) and flows (consumption, taxation, saving, investment) are measured differently; flows have a time dimension and stocks are measured at a point in time. Therefore we shall discuss here and apply in Chapters 10 and 12 *separate* conservation principles consistent with stock-flow models of macroeconomic theory: the *budget identity* (referring to flows), the *balance sheet identity* (referring to stocks), and the *financing constraint* (which relates flows to stocks).

Level IV of Figure 9.1 indicates what happens to the flow of aggregate income that is saved by households. This saving goes into capital markets where it is obtained at market prices (rates of interest) by business firms and government. At level III of Figure 9.1 business firms then use these funds to acquire new capital goods from other business firms that produce them. Thus business firms are viewed by economists as making the decision to carry out investment expenditures.

This process may also be viewed in terms of the budget identity of the business sector. At level I of Figure 9.1 business firms are assumed to pay out all earnings to households; they retain no earnings. At level II firms are assumed neither to receive nor to make transfer payments; there are no corporate income taxes or dividend payments. Therefore business firms can carry out investment expenditures (level III) only by tapping the flow of household saving in capital (credit) markets (level IV).[3] As discussed later, in exchange for their saving, however, households receive evidences of debt and ownership, that is, they receive bonds and equities issued by business firms. These evidences of debt and ownership are claims on the future earnings of business firms. In short, the business sector is *constrained* to *finance* its investment expenditures by issuing claims to households in capital (credit) markets.[4]

As discussed earlier, the government sector also has a budget identity. In Figure 9.1 at level III government purchases goods and services. (Economists usually assume that these goods and services are then used to produce "free" government services such as police and fire protection.) If the government sector's expenditures at level III do not equal its tax receipts at level II, it will have a surplus or deficit. Like the business sector, when government decides to expend more on goods and services than it gets in receipts, it must finance the difference by entering capital markets (level IV). Government is *constrained* to *finance* its deficit by tapping the flow of household saving entering capital markets. In exchange for their saving, households receive evidences of government debt. Like the evidences of debt and ownership issued by business firms, these financial claims are usually acquired at market prices—they earn a rate of interest.

Therefore, for both business and government sectors we have seen that expenditures in excess of receipts require financing, that is, the business sector and the government sector are *constrained* to *finance* expenditures in excess of receipts by issuing claims against themselves. The *financing constraint* requires that a sector's expenditures not paid for with receipts (or decreases in that sector's asset holdings) be financed by borrowing in capital markets. The financing constraint enables economists to relate flows of expenditures and receipts to changes in the stock of financial claims. This constraint will be used extensively in later chapters.

[3] We abstract from expenditures that are financed by reducing holdings of other assets.

[4] Capital markets is a phase usually reserved for the locus of long-term debt borrowing by business firms. We refer here to the broad spectrum of financial markets. In this expansive perspective capital market transactions include equity issuance by the business sector as well as long- and short-term debt issuance by government and business sectors; the latter covers direct borrowing as well as indirect borrowing through financial intermediaries. (An alternative description would be "credit" markets.) Household financing of consumer durable expenditures is excluded from the present highly aggregative perspective because the household sector is, on balance, not a net borrower, but rather a net lender.

Acquisition of the financial claims of business firms and government entities by a household is viewed as increasing its wealth. Economists call these claims financial assets. The reason that financial assets in the form of debt and equity claims issued by business firms increase the wealth of an individual household is because they represent claims on future income. The household saving for which these claims were exchanged has gone to finance the acquisition of newly produced capital goods by business firms. Capital goods are productive; if used efficiently, they increase the level of future production in the economy. In fact, economists sometimes define capital as "the produced means of production." As the financial assets held by an individual household are claims against the future revenues of business firms, they are considered part of that household's wealth.

Debt claims issued by government and held by an individual household are often considered part of its wealth. This is sometimes rationalized in terms of government's ability to pay the interest earned on these claims and to retire them simply by taxing the future earnings of households and business firms. In this sense, these financial assets, like the debt and equity issues of the business sector, are claims on future earnings.[5]

The total wealth of an individual household in the mind's eye of the economist consists of evidences of debt and evidences of ownership of the capital stock issued by firms, evidences of debt issued by government, its stock of consumer durables and the present market value of all the other factors of production that it owns directly. The financial assets in this definition of wealth are accumulated largely as a result of the financing activities of the business and government sectors.

Evidences of debt and ownership may include deposit claims against business firms called financial intermediaries, such as commercial banks. Financial intermediaries get their name because they can profitably "intermediate" in the financing process that takes place in capital markets (level IV of Figure 9.1) by acquiring

[5] However, here the parallel may end; while the debt and equity issues of the business sector are envisioned as giving rise to private capital formation, the debt issues of government do not (necessarily) give rise to the formation of "public" or social capital. (Some government entities are permitted to go into debt simply to meet current expenses.) Moreover, as we shall see later, in national income accounting, government is not viewed as a repository of capital goods. This leads to considerable confusion when government debt in private hands is labeled "wealth."

The private sector's liability for future taxation would suggest that government expenditures, no matter how they are financed, would tend primarily to displace private consumption because of a decrease in disposable permanent income and that government debt is therefore not part of private wealth. The only way out of this conundrum is to assume that government goes into debt to acquire "social" capital goods and that these enhance future production above and beyond the value of such interest payments. Debt-financed government expenditures would then be viewed as increasing private wealth. As seen in Chapter 10 an increase in the government debt outstanding, therefore, would tend to reduce private saving and, to an extent that remains to be investigated in Chapter 12, to displace or crowd out private investment as well as private consumption, because of a resulting rise in market rates of interest. For a survey of the literature on the effect of tax-and-debt financing of government expenditures that agrees, in general, with our observations, see George M. von Furstenberg, and Burton G. Malkiel, "The Government and Capital Formation: A Survey of Recent Issues," *Journal of Economic Literature,* vol. 15 (September), 835–878.

the debt claims of business firms (as their earning assets) and issuing specialized debt claims against themselves. In this way they may more efficiently mobilize the flow of saving. Thus at level IV in Figure 9.1 business firms may either issue debt or equity claims directly to households in primary capital markets or issue debt claims to financial intermediaries. Financial intermediaries then issue specialized debt claims against themselves to households. Government is pictured at level IV of Figure 9.1 as issuing debt claims in primary capital markets and not using financial intermediaries to help finance its debt.

Some of the specialized debt claims of financial intermediaries are interest bearing (savings deposits) and some are noninterest bearing (demand deposits). The latter (demand deposits) together with privately held noninterest bearing claims against government (currency in circulation) are usually counted as part of the nation's money supply. As these claims are traded in capital markets and as the interest rates that are established therein have an effect on the economy, the proportions in which individuals decide to hold financial claims will have a significant influence on the economy. Therefore, theories concerning the supply of and demand for financial claims (that is, bonds, equities and money) are of considerable importance in monetary economics.[6]

Heretofore we have considered the wealth of the *individual* household; now we examine all households taken as a whole. If for the sake of simplicity we ignore the stock of consumer durables, the wealth of the household sector consists of debt claims against business firms and government, claims of ownership in business firms, and human wealth, the present value of all human resources.[7] When we aggregate across all individual households, all privately issued debt claims cancel out. The debt claims issued by a private business firm are assets of the households that hold them but liabilities of the households that hold ownership claims in that business firm. Therefore, the nonhuman wealth of the private sector is thus defined as being identically equal to equity claims (the market value of the physical capital of the private sector) plus interest bearing (bonds) and noninterest bearing (money) debt claims against government.

The *balance sheet identity* of the private sector enables the economist to impose consistency conditions on his theoretical models. For instance, as long as income is

---

[6] Theories of how the quantity of one particular form of specialized debt (money) is determined are the subject of Chapters 1 and 2. Theories of the demand for money and other financial assets are discussed in Chapters 4–6.
assets are discussed in Chapters 4–6.

[7] Consumer durable goods generate a flow of future consumption services and as such rightfully belong in the definition of wealth. The exclusion of consumer durables is, nevertheless, consistent with the simplistic view that the only goods that generate future services are physical capital goods which, by definition, are possessed by business firms and are represented in the definition of wealth by the ownership claims held by households.
Future income expected from the sale of one's time in the market for labor has a present value. Often it is useful for economists to distinguish between human wealth (the present value of expected future labor income) and nonhuman wealth (the present value of expected future property income). For example, this distinction is made in theoretical and empirical work on the demand for money discussed in Chapters 6–8.

unchanged, any change in private wealth must be distributed across these assets. In addition, as long as wealth is unchanged, the partial effects of a change in the interest rate or the level of income on each asset must sum to zero.

We have shown that the sectoral and aggregate *budget identities,* the aggregate *balance sheet identity,* and the sectoral *financing constraints* are important considerations in macroeconomic reasoning. Indeed, as we shall see in later chapters, attempts to model the economy may run afoul when these basic principles are too lightly regarded. We return to these concepts later in this chapter, in the next chapter, and in Chapter 12.

Equilibrium

Figure 9.1 indicates that the flow of aggregate income Y at level I is defined as being either consumed C at level III, saved S at level IV, or transferred away T at level II. Therefore we may write the following aggregate budget identity defining the disposition of income:

$$Y \equiv C + S + T. \tag{9.1}$$

The flow of aggregate expenditures at level III of Figure 9.1 is defined as either consumption expenditures C, investment expenditures I, or government expenditures G,

$$\text{expenditures} \equiv C + I + G. \tag{9.2}$$

One of the traditional problems of macroeconomics is concerned with whether the flow of *planned* aggregate expenditures at level III of the circular flow diagram will be sufficient to absorb the flow of aggregate output *planned* to be produced by business firms. In other words, "will the income generated by the planned production of goods and services all be spent on these goods and services?" If the dollar flow of aggregate income generated by the planned production of goods and services is intended to be expended on these goods and services, then business firms will experience no shortages or excesses of production. They will have no incentive to change their production plans or their prices and rates of remuneration. The dollar flows of aggregate income and aggregate expenditures will not change over time. The absence of any tendency for a system to change is called *equilibrium.*

In contrast, if quantities produced are either excessive or deficient relative to demand, then firms will have an incentive to change their production and/or prices. The dollar flows in Figure 9.1 will change over time and there will be *disequilibrium* in the economy.

Equilibrium in the circular flow that depicts the income–expenditures sector of the economy may be represented by the following equations:

$$\text{income} = \text{expenditures}$$

$$Y = C + I + G. \tag{9.3}$$

If the dollar flow of aggregate income (based on the production *plans* of business firms) at level I of Figure 9.1 and in Equation (9.3) is matched by the dollar flow of aggregate expenditures (based on the independent expenditures *plans* of households, business, and government) at level III of Figure 9.1 and in Equation (9.3), then the income–expenditures sector of the economy is said to be in equilibrium.

An alternative statement of the equilibrium condition is developed by substituting Equation (9.1) into the left-hand side of Equation (9.3):

$$C + S + T = C + I + G$$
$$S + T = I + \cdot G. \tag{9.4}$$

In terms of level IV of Figure 9.1 this says that when aggregate "leakages" from the income stream (planned saving and taxation) are matched by aggregate "injections" into the spending stream (planned investment and government spending), the income–expenditures sector of the economy will be in a state of equilibrium. When the saving and taxation decisions *planned* by households and government, respectively, are matched by investment and government spending decisions *planned* by business firms and government, respectively, the income–expenditures sector will be in equilibrium.

As one can see, the equilibrium condition is satisfied only when the independent plans of millions of households, hundreds of thousands of business firms, and tens of thousands of governmental units balance in a special way. In order to understand the processes which sustain equilibrium and the behavior that generates a new equilibrium, we must examine closely the consumption behavior of households and the investment behavior of business firms. That will be the main purpose of the next chapter. However, before we can do this it will be useful to gain some insight into how aggregate income and aggregate expenditures are measured.

The Measurement of Aggregate Income

Value Added

Progress was made in macroeconomic theory and policy when the flows represented in Figure 9.1 were successfully measured. As all production decisions and factor payments are assumed to be made by firms, a logical place to begin the measurement process is the accounting statements of the business firm. The basic building block of economic measurement is the statement of operations of the business firm.

Table 9.1 represents a very simplified statement of operations (profit and loss statement).

A conceptual problem for the economist is to measure the contribution of a particular firm to the flow of aggregate income during the current year. We call this the "value added" by the firm. All contributions to aggregate income made by other firms but reflected in a particular firm's statement of operations will have to be deducted from each side of that firm's statement to derive its value added. If this were not done, intermediate sales from one business firm to another would be counted in measuring aggregate income. This would result in a great deal of "double counting" as goods are often processed and sold many times among business firms in the chain of production and distribution before they are sold to the final purchaser. In the statement of operations of the Friendly Corporation are the expense categories: purchases of materials, advertising, and heat, light, and power. These expenses represent payments made to other firms and income generated for factors of

Table 9.1. Friendly Corporation
Statement of Operations
Year Ending 12/31/78

			Sales	$1000
* Purchases of materials		$ 300		
Beginning inventory	200			
Less ending inventory	100			
Change in inventory		100		
Indirect business taxes				
(sales, property, and				
excise taxes)		25		
Wages and salaries		175		
Rent		50		
Interest		60		
* Advertising		15		
* Heat, light and power		150		
Depreciation		25		
Profit		100		
		$1000		$1000

Items marked with an asterisk represent purchases of goods or services from other business firms.

production employed by other firms. These expense categories are marked by asterisks; to obtain the *value added* by Friendly Corporation they must be subtracted from each side of its statement of operations. When this is done, these items disappear from the left hand side; when subtracted from sales on the right hand side, the remainder is called, in Table 9.2, *final sales*.

The only other step necessary to derive the value added to the aggregate flow of income and production by the Friendly Corporation is to adjust for the goods it sold this year but produced in a previous year. This dollar amount is reflected in Friendly Corporation's decrease in inventory. The difference between beginning inventory and ending inventory is an expense to the Corporation as its assets were reduced by this amount. Items sold out of inventory are also reflected in sales during the current year. However, as these goods were on hand at the beginning of the current year, they represent value added by production during a previous year and in measuring value added for the current year, they must be subtracted from each side of the statement of operations. The decrease in inventory thereby is canceled out on the left-hand side and is subtracted from sales on the right-hand side. In contrast, an *increase* in inventory would represent goods produced this year (hence value added this year) but not sold during the year. Therefore we would *add* them to either side, thereby canceling out the increase in inventory (beginning minus ending inventory) on the left-hand side and *adding* it to the right-hand side.

These two steps will yield the statement of value added for Friendly Corporation for 1978 shown in Table 9.2.

Even though Friendly Corporation had sales of $1,000, it only added value of $435 by its own production during 1978. This is because it purchased $465 worth of goods and services from other firms. As mentioned above, this amount will be recorded in the statements of value added of other firms and must be deducted here

Table 9.2.   Friendly Corporation
Statement of Value Added
Year Ending 12/31/78

Sales and property taxes	$ 25	Sales	$1,000
Wages and salaries	175	Less payments to other firms	465
Rent	50	Final sales	535
Interest	60	Plus increase (less decrease)	
Depreciation	25	in inventory	(100)
Profit	100		
		Value added	$ 435
Value added	$435		

to avoid double counting. In addition, Friendly Corporation sold $100 worth of goods out of its inventory. These goods were produced in earlier years; therefore they represent value added by this firm and by other firms in earlier years and have to be deducted from sales this year to arrive at value added this year.

Aggregate Income

In order to derive a statement of aggregate income for the economy as a whole we first simply sum across the statements of value added for all firms. This is reflected in Table 9.3. For each firm in the economy we subtract its payments to other firms and add the increase or subtract the decrease in inventory. Therefore on the left-hand side of the statement of aggregate income no payments to other firms or changes in inventory will appear.

Table 9.3. Statement of Aggregate Income for Year Ending 12/31/78

Indirect business taxes	Sales
Wages and salaries	Less payments to other firms equals
Rent	
Interest	Final Sales which equals
Depreciation	Consumption expenditures C
Profit	(final sales to households
	on current account) plus
Aggregate income	
(Gross National Product)	Investment expenditures I
	(final sales to business firms
	on capital account) plus
	Government expenditures G
	(final sales to government on
	current and capital account)
	Increase in inventories I
	(less decrease in inventories)
	Aggregate income
	(Gross National Product)

All that remains are factor payments (wages, interest, rent, profit), depreciation, and indirect business taxes. Indirect business taxes are not factor payments; they are taxes such as sales taxes, excise taxes, and property taxes; the revenue from these taxes goes directly to government and their cost is directly passed on to the customer. Therefore indirect business taxes like any expense enter the market price of the product.

Depreciation is a cost of production; an expense, not paid out by the firm, but retained ostensibly in order to finance replacement of its existing capital stock. Depreciation is discussed at greater length later in this chapter.

On the right-hand side of the statement of aggregate income, sales less payments to other firms represent *final sales* of goods and services to their final purchaser. Final sales consist of final sales of noncapital goods, either to households C or to government G, plus final sales of newly produced capital goods to other business firms I or to government G.[8] All noncapital goods sales to business firms were canceled out by the subtraction of "payments to other firms" in deriving value added, because these, by definition, are "intermediate" (nonfinal) transactions. Increases or decreases in inventories are not part of final sales but, as explained above, must nevertheless be included; they are measured as part of investment expenditures on the right hand side of the statement.

Our initial assumption that all production (value added) comes from business firms is not quite realistic. In fact, imputations must be made for value added by

[8] Net sales to foreigners are usually included, but as subsequent discussions in this book do not include a foreign sector, they are excluded here.

government (government's processing the goods and services it purchases before it distributes them) and value added by certain kinds of household activity; after these imputations we will have gross national product on both sides of the statement. Value added by government is measured as the wages and salaries paid by government. This amount is added to wages and salaries on the left-hand side and to government expenditures on the right-hand side of the statement of aggregate income. No imputation is made for the contribution to production of the capital and natural resources owned by government.[9]

All value added by household production is ignored (largely because of difficulties in estimation) except for the services associated with home ownership and the consumption by farmers of their own production. When a household purchases a home it is measured as investment. Throughout the useful life of the structure rent and depreciation are imputed on the left-hand side and an equivalent value for consumption is imputed on the right-hand side of the statement of aggregate income.[10]

After imputations each side of the statement of aggregate income is equal to gross national product. Because the left-hand side is equal to the right-hand side, one should not infer that the economy is always in equilibrium. As discussed earlier, equilibrium refers to the equality between *planned* magnitudes, not measured or *actual* ones.

In the statement of aggregate income all dollar magnitudes are *actual* ones. This means, for example, that if *planned* dollar expenditures were $C(\$700$ billion$) + I(\$100$ billion$) + G(\$200$ billion$) = \$1000$ billion and planned output (at market prices) Y were $\$1100$ billion, the economy would not be in equilibrium. Nevertheless, *actual* expenditures always equal *actual* income. This occurs in several ways. For example, at unchanged prices a deficient level of dollar expenditures means that inventories would have to accumulate in the amount of $\$100$ billion. As this (unplanned) change in inventory enters the right-hand side of the statement, the identity of *actual* income and *actual* expenditures would be maintained.

Earnings, Receipts, and Expenditures by Sector

It is instructive to break down the statement of aggregate income (GNP) by sector. This helps one to understand each sector's income and expenditures patterns. It also clarifies the financing of investment expenditures and government deficits and their relation to private nonhuman wealth. This is done in Table 9.4.

Assume that all business firms are corporations and initially retain all profits and

[9] This treatment flies in the face of reality. It is the result of practical difficulty in measuring government's capital stock as well as the conceptual reluctance of economists to treat government as a locus of the decision to produce. This treatment makes it difficult for some economists to perceive privately held government debt as a form of wealth. (See footnote 5 above.)

[10] Estimates of farm households' consumption of their own production generate imputed factor payments on the left-hand side and imputed consumption on the right-hand side of the statement of aggregate income.

Table 9.4. Income and Expenditures by Sector

Row	Item	Households	Business	Government	Total
1	Earnings	Wages and salaries, Rent, Interest $(w + i + r)$	Net corporate profits, Depreciation $(\pi + d)$	Indirect business taxes T_i	GNP Y
	minus				
2	Transfer Payments	+ Government transfers, + Dividends, − Personal income taxes, − Social security contributions $-T_h$	− Dividends, − Corporate income taxes $-T_b$	− Government transfers, + Personal and corporate income taxes, + Social security contributions $+(T_h + T_b)$	0
	equals				
3	Final Receipts	Personal disposable income Y_d	Retained earnings (business saving) S_b	Net government receipts T_n	GNP Y
	equals				
4	Current Expenditures	Consumption C_h	0	Government expenditures G	$C + G$
	plus				
5	Saving	Personal saving S_h	Business saving S_b	Government saving (+ surplus or − deficit) S_g	S
6	Capital Expenditures	0	Gross investment expenditures I_g	0	I_g
7	Budget Identities	$w + i + r \equiv C_h + S_h + T_h$	$\pi + d \equiv T_b + S_b$	$T_i \equiv G - T_h - T_b + S_g$	$Y \equiv C_h + S_h + S_b + T_n$
8	Financing Constraints	$S_b + S_h = \Delta K + \Delta M_g + \Delta V$	$\Delta K = I_g = S_b + \left(\begin{smallmatrix}\text{external}\\\text{financing}\end{smallmatrix}\right)$	$S_g = T_n - G = -(\Delta M_g + \Delta V)$	—
9	Private Balance Sheet Identity	$W \equiv M_g + V + K$			

depreciation as "earnings" instead of automatically paying them out to households as in Figure 9.1. Let us further assume that the "earnings" of the government sector consist of indirect business taxes net of subsidies. These are not factor payments, yet they are reflected in the market prices at which goods and services exchange, so they are included as "earnings." The sector totals in row 1 of Table 9.4 will sum to GNP as they do on the left-hand side of the statement of aggregate income (Table 9.3). (Each "earnings" item in row 1 has a counterpart in level I of Figure 9.2 on page 238.)

Row 2 reflects some basic transfer payments between sectors. As defined above, transfer payments represent unilateral nonmarket flows—grants for which no immediate reciprocal flow or exchange is expected and which reflect no current contribution to the production process. The transfer payments listed in Table 9.4 are self-explanatory except for the catch-all "government transfers." This category includes government interest payments, unemployment compensation, social security benefits, etc. Dividends and corporate income taxes are treated as transfer payments because the levels of both are established by custom or by law and are only remotely related in the short-run to market exchanges; that is, they are not direct factor payments and do not directly influence market prices. (Each transfer payment has a counterpart in level II of Figure 9.2.) Table 9.4 shows that transfer payments sum to zero. Models of real income determination in the income–expenditures sector often contain relations that model these transfers as functions of real income.

Row 3 identifies final receipts by sector; these sum once again to GNP. Each item of final receipts is the sum of earnings (in level I of Figure 9.2) plus or minus transfer payments (in level II of Figure 9.2).

After *current* (that is, noncapital expenditures are deducted in row 4, the residual in row 5 represents (positive or negative) saving by sector. Row 6 represents the capital expenditures of the business sector. As a matter of convention all government expenditures are treated as current expenditures. As our measure of income is *gross* national product, the consistent measure of investment is *gross* investment expenditures. (Net measures are introduced later in this chapter.) The sum of current expenditures and capital expenditures, rows 4 and 6, is equal to GNP viewed from the right-hand side of the statement of aggregate income (Table 9.3). (Each expenditures item in row 4 and row 6 is shown in level III of Figure 9.2.)

The budget identities for the three sectors are given in row 7. Earnings items from row 1 appear on the left-hand sides; transfer payments (row 2), saving (row 5) and current expenditures (row 4) appear on the right-hand sides.

The household sector's budget identity is similar to the one discussed earlier, except that gross corporate profits (net corporate profits plus depreciation) are not part of household earnings on the left-hand side, and that several classes of transfer payments are included on the right-hand side. As shown in row 3, household earnings plus or minus these transfer payments is called personal disposable income.

The business sector's budget identity now consists of earnings (net corporate

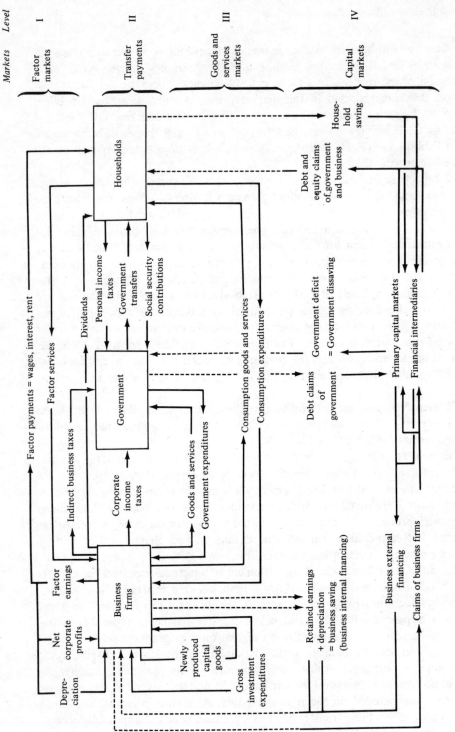

FIGURE 9.2. Circular flow of income and expenditures.

profits plus depreciation). Dividends and corporate income taxes are the relevant transfer payments. The final receipts of the business sector, earnings minus transfer payments, is called retained earnings in row 3.

As discussed, the government sector has one source of "earnings": indirect business taxes. These, plus or minus the various transfer payments, generate net government receipts in row 3. When government expenditures are subtracted from this figure in row 4, the remainder is called government saving (government surplus or deficit) as shown in row 5.

The terms on the left-hand sides of the sectoral budget identities displayed in row 7 appear on the left-hand side of the statement of aggregate income (Table 9.3) and sum to GNP in row 1 of Table 9.4 and in level I of Figure 9.2. The sum of the terms on the right-hand sides of the sectoral budget identities displayed in row 7 are, in turn, equal to the sum of rows 4 and 6 which corresponds to the right-hand side of the statement of aggregate income (Table 9.3); they appear in level III of Figure 9.2.

Row 9 defines private nonhuman wealth as the private capital stock K plus debt claims of government held in interest-earning V and noninterest-earning (M_g) forms. Row 8 shows how increases in the wealth of the private sector ($\Delta K + \Delta M_g + \Delta V$) may occur. Increases in the outstanding debt of government ($\Delta M_g + \Delta V$) occur because of government deficits ($G > T_n$). Increases in the private capital stock ΔK occur because of investment expenditures I_g.[11] Investment expenditures are financed, in part, internally out of business saving S_b and, in part, externally out of personal saving S_h. Both types of saving add to private wealth because both increase the value of equities held by the household sector. The remainder of private saving finances the deficit of government. Internal and external financing are shown in level IV of Figure 9.2.

Figure 9.2 depicts the flows of income and expenditures given in Table 9.4. It is similar to Figure 9.1 except that in the factor markets (level I) net corporate profits (plus depreciation) are not included in the earnings flow to households. Instead they are channeled directly to the business sector where, after dividend (transfer) payments to households (level II), they contribute to the (internal) financing (level IV) of gross investment expenditures (level III).

Another difference between Figure 9.1 and Figure 9.2 is the introduction of indirect business taxes. In Table 9.4 indirect business taxes are treated as "earnings" of government. Therefore in Figure 9.2 they are included in factor markets (level I).

Consistent with Table 9.4 there is a much more extensive network of transfer payments shown in Figure 9.2. In level II we now include not only personal income taxes but corporate income taxes, dividends, social security contributions, and government transfers (to households) of all kinds.

The imputations for value added by government measured as government wages

---

[11] Strictly speaking, the capital stock increases only when there are positive investment expenditures, net of replacement investment expenditures. This is discussed in the next section.

and salaries and the imputations for value added by owner-occupied dwellings and farmers' consumption of their own production could be added to Figure 9.2. However, their inclusion would excessively complicate the diagram.

Net Aggregate Income

Economists have long defined net income as the amount of resources that can be consumed without depleting the capital stock.[12] In the economy as a whole, every year capital goods are typically replaced as they wear out. Ideally, this replacement investment in the economy should match depreciation. Depreciation is a cost of production representing the writing off as an expense of the historical cost of the firm's stock of physical capital over its useful life. The use of historical cost rather than replacement cost to calculate depreciation is an accounting convention. Unlike all other expenses, depreciation is an expense that is *not* paid out by the firm. Therefore, accountants, economists, and others often view it as part of a firm's "cash (in) flow."

Depreciation, the part of GNP that represents the cash flow retained by business firms to replace their capital stock as it wears out, should, according to the above definition of income, be deducted from both sides of the statement of aggregate income. If depreciation is subtracted from either side of the statement, on the left-hand side it disappears (only net profit remains as earnings of the business sector), and on the right-hand side it is subtracted from gross investment to yield net investment. Aggregate income measured in this way is called net national product.

Net investment and net national product (NNP) are often considered to be superior measures to gross investment and gross national product (GNP) because they avoid a type of double accounting. When a capital good is produced, it is recorded as net investment on the right-hand side of the statement of aggregate income and as factor payment by the firm that produced it on the left-hand side of the statement. If gross investment and GNP are used in each year of the capital good's useful life, it is counted again in GNP as this capital good becomes embodied in final consumption (that is, gets "used up"). It is recorded on the right-hand side of the statement of aggregate income as the replacement portion of gross investment, and on the left-hand side as depreciation. Clearly the use of NNP and net investment entails a depreciation deduction equal to the value of capital that is embodied in currently produced goods and thereby avoids counting each unit of capital twice in aggregate income.

An even more "net" measure of aggregate income is found by deducting indirect business taxes from both sides of the statement of aggregate income (NNP). This generates a measure called national income. It measures aggregate income at factor cost by excluding the taxes that are not factor payments but are added to the prices of products.[13]

[12] See John Hicks, *Value and Capital* (Oxford: Clarendon Press, 1946). For an interesting alternative see Irving Fisher, *The Nature of Income and Capital* (New York: Macmillan, 1930).

[13] Even more "net" measures of aggregate income are possible. Consider the classical defini-

The Measurement of the Price Level

In this chapter we have shown how economists conceptualize and measure the flow of aggregate income and expenditures. We indicated at the beginning of the chapter that income and expenditures are measured in dollars. They were said to be the products of quantities exchanged and the market prices at which the exchanges occurred.

Therefore, any change in income or expenditures so measured over time could be the result of a change in quantities exchanged, a change in market prices, or both. It will be useful to distinguish between the two. For example, people want to know whether any given rise in GNP over time is the result of an increase in the price level or an increase in output. As another example, in the economic theories developed in later chapters, magnitudes are conceived in "real" or "purchasing power" terms (just as the demand for money in Chapters 4–8 was viewed in "real" terms). When something is converted into "real" terms it means it is measured in terms of what the dollar totals would be if prices remained constant over time. A "real" magnitude may be expressed by dividing (deflating) a dollar or nominal magnitude by the price level. As a consequence, the price level must be conceived and measured as a separate variable.

Unfortunately there is no such thing as *the* price level; there are only price indices. Price indices are averages of many prices of individual commodities weighted by the quantities purchased of those commodities. There is no unique way of calculating a price index.

Assume, for instance, that GNP consists of only two commodities, food and clothing. Assume further that the actual prices and quantities consumed of these commodities in two separate years are given in Table 9.5.

Table 9.5

	Base Year (o)		Present Year (t)	
	Price	Quantity	Price	Quantity
Food	$10.00	100	$15.00	200
Clothing	$20.00	50	$25.00	150

GNP in current prices is $2000 in the base year and $4500 in the present year. In order to assess the increase in the real or purchasing power value of GNP (that

---

tion of net income together with a broad definition of capital to include human capital. A good deal of what we measure as net income above consists of expenditures necessary to keep the *human* capital stock intact. If these social subsistence consumption expenditures were deducted from either side, aggregate income would shrink considerably.

is, the value of the goods and services produced at unchanged prices) between the two years, it is necessary to determine how much the price level rose.

One way to solve this problem is to calculate a price index which is a weighted average of the two prices, using the quantity of each commodity produced in the base year as a weight. The formula for the price index using the base year quantities as weights is:

$$P = \frac{\sum_{i=1}^{n} p_i^t q_i^0}{\sum_{i=1}^{n} p_i^0 q_i^0} \times 100.$$

The term 100 transforms the index into a dimension in which the price level can easily be expressed as a percentage. In this example;

$$P = \frac{(15 \times 100) + (25 \times 50)}{(10 \times 100) + (20 \times 50)} \times 100 = 137.5.$$

This indicates that it would cost $37\frac{1}{2}$ percent more in the current year to purchase the goods actually purchased in the base year. Basically, this is the technique used in calculating the consumer price index (CPI).

As an alternative, one could use the quantities consumed in the present year as weights. The formula for the price index using the present year quantities as weights is

$$P = \frac{\sum_{i=1}^{n} p_i^t q_i^t}{\sum_{i=1}^{n} p_i^0 q_i^t} \times 100.$$

Using Table 9.5 yields

$$P = \frac{(15 \times 200) + (25 \times 150)}{(10 \times 200) + (20 \times 150)} \times 100 = 135.0.$$

This indicates that it would cost approximately 35 percent more to purchase the quantities in the present year than it would have cost if they had been purchased in the base year. This is basically the technique used in calculating the implicit GNP price deflator.

Both techniques have two deficiencies. First, both have an upward bias because the quality of products, and hence their prices, are likely to have increased over time. Even more troublesome are technological improvements which raise quality and, at the same time, lower price. Second, in periods of rising prices each technique either over- or understates the inflation rate. The base year weight index has an upward bias because it ignores substitution of commodities whose prices increase very little for commodities whose prices increase a good deal. It ignores what the market basket actually is in the present year after consumers have made the substitutions induced by the changes in relative prices. The present year weight index tends to *under*estimate the rise in living costs because it ignores what the market basket would have been in the base year, and therefore overestimates the cost of living in the base year.

Throughout this text, nominal income Y will mean the product of real income Y/P and the price index P. The index used will be the implicit price deflator because it is based on all the goods and services counted in GNP.

Concluding Comment

A clear picture of how economists view the processes that generate income, expenditures, and wealth is important before the study of macroeconomic and monetary theories of the determination of income and expenditures can proceed. Without an understanding of the basic conception of the economy, its building blocks and the aggregation procedure, the study of macroeconomic and monetary theories can easily degenerate into an uncritical, mechanical exercise in curve shifting.

Improving the theoretical description of the economist's vision of the macroeconomy, however, is not the only purpose of this study. Understanding of the measurement of the variables being described and the constraints on their expected magnitudes is useful to those who empirically estimate macroeconomic relationships. Those who develop and use monetary and macroeconomic models for purposes of predicting the economic future may avoid costly errors of misapplication and misinterpretation if the conceptual framework that these models purport to describe is well understood. In addition, those in government and private industry who use economic models will have a better perception of their limitations and applicability if they understand how data with which they work are measured.

In later chapters we will have the occasion to refer back to the conceptual framework outlined in this chapter. The relationships between earnings, transfers, receipts, expenditures, financing, and wealth constitute the foundation of aggregate monetary analysis.

QUESTIONS FOR CHAPTER 9

1. What is the budget identity of the household sector? What is the business sector's balance sheet identity?

2. Assume that some households dissave and that some governmental units have surpluses. Show how this would modify Figure 9.2.

3. Indicate whether the following items are measured in GNP. Then see if you can tell *how* they are measured on the *right*-hand side of the statement of aggregate income.

    a. Earnings of government employees

    b. Services of a lawyer hired by a corporation

    c. An automobile purchased by a business firm

    d. An automobile purchased by a household

    e. A share of stock purchased by a household

    f. Some land purchased by a household

    g. Property taxes paid by a business firm

    h. Federal personal income taxes

4. I. M. Flush buys a diamond ring for his wife from the Gem Sales Corporation sales-room. It is sold out of inventory where it is recorded at $5,000. The markup is 20%. The sales person's commission is 10 percent and the sales tax is 5 percent. There is a 50 percent personal income tax and a 25 percent corporate profits tax. Fill in the following table:

	Households	Business Firms	Government	Total
Earnings				
Transfers				
Receipts				
Current expenditures				
Saving				
Capital Expenditures				

5. Why might the consumer price index overstate inflation?

6. "True aggregate net income consists only of economic rents." Evaluate.

7. As the debt issued by business firms to finance capital expenditures is *not* included in private wealth, how will the stock of capital goods acquired thereby be reflected in the private wealth of households?

8. Why should government debt be included in private wealth when households are fully cognizant of their liability for future interest payments on that debt?

BIBLIOGRAPHY FOR CHAPTER 9

BRANSON, WILLIAM, *Macroeconomic Theory and Policy* (New York: Harper and Row, 1972).

FISHER, IRVING, *The Nature of Income and Capital* (New York: Macmillian, 1930).

HICKS, JOHN, *Value and Capital,* 2nd ed. (Oxford: Clarendon Press, 1946).

KENDRICK, JOHN W., *Economic Accounts and Their Uses* (New York: McGraw-Hill, 1972).

POWELSON, JOHN P., *National Income and Flow of Funds Analysis* (New York: McGraw-Hill, 1960).

RUGGLES, RICHARD, and NANCY D., *National Income Accounts and Income Analysis* (New York: McGraw-Hill, 1956).

——, *The Design of Economic Accounts* (New York: National Bureau of Economic Research, 1970).

VON FURSTENBERG, GEORGE M., and BURTON MAKIEL, "The Government and Capital Formation: A Survey of Recent Issues," *Journal of Economic Literature* (September 1977), 835–878.

10
Some Fundamentals of Macroeconomic Theory

The purpose of this chapter is to begin to use the concepts developed in the previous chapter in theoretical explanations of economic behavior. This chapter concentrates on the income and expenditures concepts. Later chapters integrate the wealth and financing concepts into the analysis, complementing the development with the theories of money supply and money demand presented in previous chapters.

In the very basic model of income and expenditures determination with which we begin, several very strong and unrealistic assumptions are made about the economy. For example, the price level is assumed constant at all levels of income and expenditures. This implies that whenever a dollar magnitude, such as consumption expenditures, investment expenditures, government expenditures, income, or wealth, is mentioned, that measure is viewed in real or purchasing power terms. It means that all behavioral entities are concerned only with the real values of the variables influencing their decisions to consume, invest, and produce.

Together with the assumption of given prices, the level of nominal wages is also assumed given. This implies that we shall postpone until later chapters a detailed analysis of the decisions of firms to hire labor, produce output, and adjust the price of that output, and the decisions of laborers to sell their services or engage in leisure activities. In this chapter we shall not inquire as to the effect of changes in production on employment, nominal wages, and the price level.

Finally, in addition to assuming that nominal wages and price levels are constant, we also assume that the market rate of interest is given and is not affected by any of the activities described in this chapter. Thus when aggregate expenditures change in our model, there is no pressure on interest rates, and hence, no "feedback" from interest rates to aggregate expenditures. Later in the chapter when the interest rate (and wealth) are explicitly introduced as determinants of consumption, saving, and investment behavior, we shall simply assume that the rate is given by forces outside our model.

These are very unrealistic assumptions. They are made in order to allow one to get an uncluttered grasp of key expenditures decisions. The implications derived from models in which these assumptions are maintained should probably be regarded with great caution. In subsequent chapters, as these assumptions are gradually relaxed, we may gain a more realistic view of the economy.

Consumption: The Keynesian Theory

Consumption was defined in the previous chapter as total current expenditures of households on newly produced goods and services. Keynes' "fundamental psychological law," promulgated in his *General Theory of Employment, Interest and Money,* is that consumption expenditures depend positively on current income and that an increase in current income will result in an induced increase in consumption expenditures which is somewhat smaller than the increase in income. Thus the "marginal propensity to consume," in a linear relation the *slope* of the consumption function, is greater than zero but less than unity, $0 < \Delta C/\Delta Y < 1$.

Keynes further stated that at all levels of income the marginal propensity to consume, the change in consumption with respect to the change in income $\Delta C/\Delta Y$, is less than the average propensity to consume, the ratio of the level of total consumption to the level of total income C/Y. Therefore Keynes' theory may be represented by the following equation:

$$C = a + bY \tag{10.1}$$

where $a > 0$, $0 < b < 1$ and

C = consumption expenditures
Y = current income
a = *autonomous* consumption expenditures (that level of consumption which is autonomous of, that is, "independent" of, the level of income)[1]
b = the marginal propensity to consume, $\Delta C/\Delta Y$

and where bY is *induced* consumption expenditures (that level of consumption expenditures which depends on the level of income). Equation (10.1) is graphed

---

[1] Whether or not a and b are constants or are proxies for other variables is examined later in this chapter.

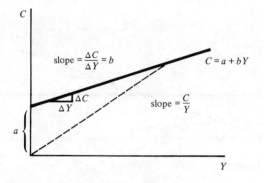

FIGURE 10.1. Short-run Keynesian consumption function.

in Figure 10.1. The intercept term represents autonomous consumption expenditures *a*. The slope term is the marginal propensity to consume *b*.

Equation (10.1) embodies Keynes' notion that the average propensity to consume, the ratio of consumption to income, will always be greater than the marginal propensity to consume. Dividing Equation (10.1) by Y yields

$$\frac{C}{Y} = \frac{a}{Y} + b \qquad (10.2)$$

since $a/Y > 0$, $a/Y + b > b$; this is reflected graphically in Figure 10.1. The slope of any ray from the origin to any point on the function, reflecting the ratio C/Y, will always exceed the magnitude of the slope of the function *b*.

Consider now the aggregate budget identity which indicates that all income must be consumed (C), saved (S), or transferred away as taxation (T).

$$Y \equiv C + S + T. \qquad (10.3)$$

Substituting Equation (10.1) into (10.3) and assuming initially that taxation T is zero, yields the saving function

$$S = -a + (1 - b)Y = -a + sY. \qquad (10.4)$$

Here

S = saving
$-a$ = autonomous (dis)saving (the negative of autonomous consumption)
s = the marginal propensity to save

where $a > 0$ and $0 < s = (1 - b) < 1$.

Substituting Equations (10.1) and (10.4) back into (10.3) gives

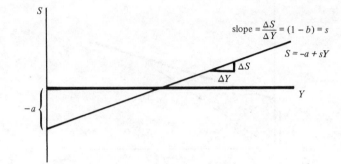

FIGURE 10.2. Keynesian saving function.

$$Y \equiv a + bY - a + sY \equiv (b + s)Y$$

indicating that $b + s \equiv 1$, that is, the marginal propensity to save plus the marginal propensity to consume equal unity. In other words, if taxation is zero, all income must either be consumed or saved.

In Figure 10.2 Equation (10.4) is graphed. The intercept term represents autonomous dissaving $-a$. The slope term is the marginal propensity to save s.

Where taxation is included, more sophisticated and realistic versions of the saving or consumption relations are sometimes specified as follows:

$$C = a + bY_d \tag{10.5}$$

and

$$S = -a + sY_d \tag{10.6}$$

where

$$Y_d \equiv Y - T \tag{10.7}$$

is the definition of disposable income from Table 9.4. Here both saving and consumption vary positively with disposable income Y_d, defined as aggregate income Y less the taxation, net of transfer payments, paid to government T.[2]

A traditional problem in macroeconomic theory centers on the determination of the equilibrium level of aggregate income. In Chapter 9 the condition for equilib-

---

[2] Using the budget identity and defining T as a constant T_a, we can still demonstrate that the marginal propensity to save plus the marginal propensity to consume out of disposable income equals unity. Substituting Equation (10.7) into (10.5) and (10.6), and the results into (10.3),

$$Y \equiv a + bY - bT_a - a + sY - sT_a + T_a$$

$$\equiv (b + s)Y - (b + s)T_a + T_a.$$

Therefore, $Y - T_a \equiv Y_d \equiv (b + s)Y_d$ and $b + s = 1$. This shows the importance of the budget identity introduced in Chapter 9 in developing income–expenditures models.

rium in the income-expenditures sector of the economy was said to be the equality of aggregate income to aggregate demand,

$$Y = C + I + G \tag{10.8}$$

Using the budget identity (10.3), and substituting into (10.8), the equilibrium condition can also be expressed as

$$S + T = I + G, \tag{10.9}$$

which says that "leakages" from the spending stream $(S + T)$ are equal to "injections" into the spending stream $(I + G)$.

Assuming that investment, taxation and government expenditures are autonomous (i.e., independent of any other variable in the model) we may write:

$$I = I_a \tag{10.10}$$
$$T = T_a \tag{10.11}$$
$$G = G_a \tag{10.12}$$

Having written relations for all the components of aggregate demand, we may now develop a simple model of income determination.

Substituting autonomous taxation (10.11) into the definition of disposable income (10.7) and the result into the consumption function (10.5) yields

$$C = a + bY - bT_a. \tag{10.13}$$

Substituting this result together with autonomous government expenditures, Equation (10.12), and autonomous investment, Equation (10.10), into the expression for total aggregate demand yields

$$C + I + G = a - bT_a + I_a + G_a + bY. \tag{10.14}$$

Substituting this relation into the equilibrium condition (10.8) and rearranging terms provides the solution for the equilibrium level of income,[3]

$$Y_e = \frac{a + I_a + G_a - bT_a}{1 - b}. \tag{10.15}$$

The model can be graphed to show this same result.

In Figure 10.3 the consumption function, Equation (10.13), is graphed to show

---

[3] Alternatively, use the saving function (10.6) instead of the consumption function (10.5). Then use the leakages = injections definition of equilibrium (10.9) instead of the aggregate demand = aggregate income definition (10.8). This approach yields the same solution as Equation (10.15).

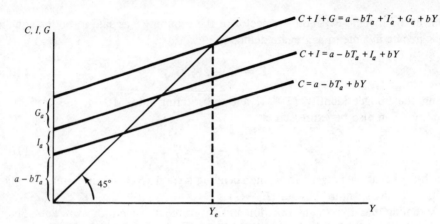

FIGURE 10.3. Solution for the equilibrium level of aggregate income.

an intercept consisting of autonomous consumption a less autonomous taxation times the marginal propensity to consume $-bT_a$. Each subsequent line adds to total consumption at every level of income a constant level of autonomous expenditures by an additional sector. The top line represents the sum of autonomous aggregate demand $(a - bT_a + I_a + G_a)$ and induced aggregate demand bY. The equilibrium condition is graphed as a 45° line from the origin. At any point along this line directed distances measured horizontally equal directed distances measured vertically. Therefore, at every point along this line aggregate income and aggregate expenditures are equal. The intersection of the aggregate demand function and the 45° line yields the equilibrium level of aggregate income [Equation (10.15)].

One of the most politically relevant implications of all monetary and macroeconomic theory is the Keynesian autonomous expenditures multiplier. In the present model the Keynesian autonomous expenditures multiplier is simply $1/(1 - b)$. Any change in the equilibrium level of aggregate income is the product of a change in any element of autonomous aggregate demand and the multiplier. This may easily be seen algebraically. The original equilibrium level of income was

$$Y_e = \frac{a + I_a + G_a - bT_a}{1 - b}. \qquad (10.15)$$

After allowing one of the components of autonomous aggregate demand to change (ΔG_a), we get a new equilibrium level of income:

$$Y_e' = \frac{a + I_a + G_a - bT_a + \Delta G_a}{1 - b}. \qquad (10.16)$$

The change in income is the difference between Equation (10.16) and (10.15):

$$\Delta Y = Y_e' - Y_e = \frac{a + I_a + G_a - bT + \Delta G_a}{1 - b} - \frac{a + I_a + G_a - bT_a}{1 - b}$$

$$= \left(\frac{1}{1 - b}\right)\Delta G_a. \tag{10.17}$$

Therefore the autonomous expenditures multiplier in this model is

$$\frac{\Delta Y}{\Delta G} = \left(\frac{1}{1 - b}\right). \tag{10.18}$$

The same multiplier would obtain for changes either in autonomous consumption a or in autonomous investment expenditures I_a.

There are a number of alternative perspectives on the autonomous expenditures multiplier. One is to use the alternative way of expressing income–expenditures equilibrium,

$$S + T = I + G. \tag{10.9}$$

Assuming that taxation T is constant, any change in government expenditures G with investment expenditures I unchanged must be matched by an equal change in saving S. Similarly, any change in investment expenditures I with government expenditures G unchanged must also be matched by an equal change in saving S. Otherwise the equilibrium condition would not be satisfied. According to the saving relation (10.4), saving will change if and only if income Y changes in the same direction.

Therefore, assuming a change in autonomous investment expenditures ΔI, with taxation T and government expenditures G unchanged, in order to sustain equilibrium in income and expenditures,

$$\Delta S = \Delta I. \tag{10.19}$$

Since by Equation (10.4)

$$\Delta S = s\Delta Y, \tag{10.20}$$

substitution of Equation (10.20) into (10.19) and rearranging yields

$$\frac{\Delta Y}{\Delta I} = \frac{1}{s} = \frac{1}{1 - b} \tag{10.21}$$

which is the autonomous expenditures multiplier. The greater the value of the marginal propensity to consume b, the smaller the value of the marginal propensity to save s, and the larger the change in income ΔY that is necessary to generate the

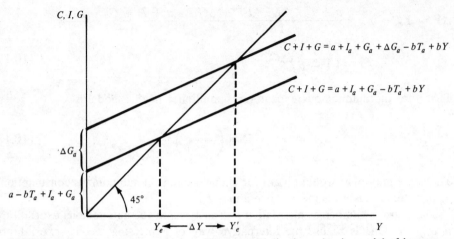

FIGURE 10.4. The autonomous expenditures multiplier in a simple model of income determination.

necessary change in saving ΔS to match the initial change in autonomous investment expenditures ΔI.

The autonomous expenditures multiplier process may also be shown graphically. In Figure 10.4 the change in aggregate income is a "multiple" of the change in autonomous aggregate demand. It can be seen that given any change in autonomous expenditures, the greater the slope of the aggregate demand relation (the greater the marginal propensity to consume), the greater the change in income from one equilibrium position to the other. This can be seen in Figure 10.5. Here two alterna-

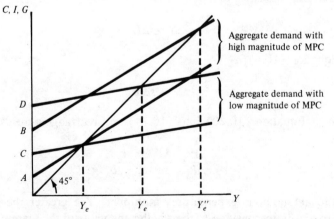

FIGURE 10.5. Demonstration of the relationship between the size of the multiplier and the magnitude of the MPC.

tive aggregate demand functions are drawn to produce the same equilibrium level of income at Y_e. Then both aggregate demand relations shift upward by the same amount ($AB = CD$) as a result of an increase in autonomous aggregate demand. For the aggregate demand function with the smaller slope or the lower marginal propensity to consume (MPC), the new equilibrium level of income is Y_e'. For the aggregate demand function with the larger slope or the greater marginal propensity to consume, the new equilibrium level of income is Y_e''. This demonstrates graphically that the magnitude of the autonomous expenditures multiplier varies directly with the magnitude of the marginal propensity to consume. It explains that the degree to which an initial increase in the level of income generates further increases in income is the core of the multiplier principle.

The multiplier process can also be explained intuitively. We have seen that, in equilibrium aggregate income equals aggregate expenditures. Any shock to equilibrium in the way of an increase in autonomous expenditures creates a situation of disequilibrium. Equilibrium can only be restored if aggregate income rises once again to equal aggregate demand. If the MPC is quite small (positive but near zero in magnitude), a relatively small rise in aggregate income can restore equilibrium. In fact, where b is very small, income need rise only by an amount equal to the increase in autonomous aggregate demand [by Equation (10.18) as $b \rightarrow 0$, $1/(1 - b) \rightarrow 1$]. If, on the other hand, the MPC is quite large, only a relatively large increase in aggregate income can restore equilibrium. This obtains because as income rises with a relatively large MPC, more aggregate (consumption) expenditures are induced by the rise in income. In fact, where b is large but still less than unity, the size of the autonomous expenditures multiplier approaches infinity [by Equation (10.18) as $b \rightarrow 1$, $1/(1 - b) \rightarrow \infty$].

This simple model can also be manipulated to yield multipliers premised on changes in the other components of autonomous aggregate demand. For example, changing autonomous taxation T_a in Equation (10.15) and working through an algebraic process similar to Equations (10.16) and (10.17) yields an autonomous taxation multiplier:

$$\frac{\Delta Y}{\Delta T_a} = \frac{-b}{1 - b}. \tag{10.22}$$

The autonomous taxation multiplier is negative and smaller in absolute magnitude than the autonomous expenditures multiplier. This occurs because any change in autonomous taxation affects autonomous aggregate demand through its effect on autonomous consumption.

For example, a lump sum tax increase of ΔT_a does not reduce autonomous aggregate demand by ΔT_a, but rather through the consumption function,

$$C = a + bY_d - bT_a \tag{10.13}$$

it reduces autonomous aggregate demand by $-b$ times the tax increase or

$(-b)(\Delta T_a)$. Thus, the effect on aggregate income is the decrease in aggregate demand induced by the tax increase times the autonomous expenditures multiplier or

$$\Delta Y = (-b)(\Delta T_a) \cdot \frac{1}{1-b}$$

which after rearranging yields

$$\frac{\Delta Y}{\Delta T_a} = \frac{-b}{1-b}, \tag{10.22}$$

the autonomous taxation multiplier.

A particularly celebrated concept is the balanced budget multiplier. The balanced budget multiplier specifies the change in income that will result from any change in autonomous government expenditures that is matched by an equal change in autonomous taxation so that there is no change in the deficit or a surplus that is run in the government budget. Thus, the condition for an incrementally balanced budget is

$$\Delta G_a = \Delta T_a. \tag{10.23}$$

Assume that our initial equilibrium is described by

$$Y_e = \frac{a + I_a + G_a - bT_a}{1-b} \tag{10.15}$$

and that the increase in autonomous government expenditures alone would cause income to rise to

$$Y_e' = \frac{a + I_a + G_a - bT_a + \Delta G_a}{1-b} \tag{10.16}$$

as described above. However, under condition (10.23) the increase in autonomous government expenditures is matched by an equal increase in autonomous taxation. Therefore the new equilibrium level of income will be

$$Y_e'' = \frac{a + I_a + G_a - bT_a + \Delta G_a - b\Delta T_a}{1-b} \tag{10.24}$$

and the change in income is the difference between Equations (10.24) and (10.15):

$$\Delta Y = Y_e'' - Y_e = \frac{a + I_a + G_a - bT_a + \Delta G_a - b\Delta T_a}{1-b} -$$

$$\frac{a + I_a + G_a - bT_a}{1-b}. \tag{10.25}$$

Substituting Equation (10.23) into (10.25) and simplifying yields

$$\Delta Y = \left(\frac{1-b}{1-b}\right)\Delta G$$

Therefore, the balanced budget multiplier in the present model is unity:

$$\frac{\Delta Y}{\Delta G} = \left(\frac{1-b}{1-b}\right) = 1. \tag{10.26}$$

This can be seen in Figure 10.6. Here the increase in income, resulting solely from the increase in autonomous government expenditures which is not subject to the incrementally balanced budget condition (10.23), would have been identical to the increase shown in Figure 10.5,

$$Y_e' - Y_e = \Delta G_a\left(\frac{1}{1-b}\right).$$

However, because the budget must be incrementally balanced, the aggregate demand function has a "net" upward shift of only $\Delta G_a - b\Delta T_a$, or the net result of shifting upwards by ΔG_a (the effect of the increase in autonomous government expenditures) *and* shifting downwards by $-b\Delta T$ (the effect of the increase in lump sum taxation on autonomous consumption). Since $\Delta G = \Delta T$ by the assumption of an incrementally balanced budget (10.23), this "net" increase in autonomous aggregate demand is $\Delta G(1-b)$, as shown in Figure 10.6. As expressed earlier, the increase in income is equal to the autonomous expenditures multiplier times this "net" change in autonomous expenditures, or

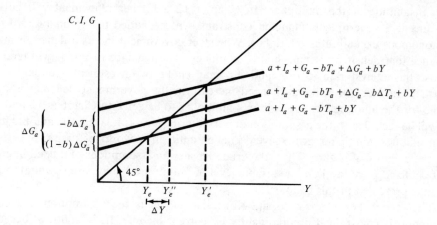

FIGURE 10.6. Balanced budget multiplier.

$$\Delta Y = \Delta G(1 - b)\left(\frac{1}{1 - b}\right).$$

Collecting terms gives the balanced budget multiplier

$$\frac{\Delta Y}{\Delta G} = \left(\frac{1 - b}{1 - b}\right) = 1. \tag{10.26}$$

The foregoing analysis adds a few complications to the simple model of income determination. A number of textbooks add even more. However, because the model is predicated on several extremely unrealistic assumptions, it is more important to modify these assumptions than to continue to manipulate the model and its multipliers.

The preceding analysis has made it clear that the magnitude of the various multipliers varies directly with the magnitude of the marginal propensity to consume b and inversely with the magnitude of the marginal propensity to save $(1 - b)$. We have shown that Keynes' "fundamental psychological law," his consumption relation, is indeed fundamental to his "multiplier principle." Nevertheless, lying behind the multiplier principle are two salient aspects of a crude Keynesian view of the economy which should be made explicit.

The first is that when aggregate demand changes, prices do not change but only quantities produced do. Thus in the very basic Keynesian model the price level and the interest rate are assumed constant. These assumptions are retained throughout the present chapter. In the next chapter the assumption of a fixed interest rate will be relaxed and it will be shown, in a more sophisticated model, that a much smaller autonomous expenditures multiplier may result. Under this more realistic assumption it will be seen that as the level of income increases, there may occur a rise in the rate of interest which serves to choke off investment expenditures and reduce the magnitude of the multiplier. In Chapter 12 a further refinement will be introduced; a government financing constraint will be added to the analysis of the autonomous expenditures multiplier. Whenever government incurs a deficit, it must finance that deficit by issuing bonds or money. The issuance of bonds will tend to cause the interest rate to rise, and this may choke off investment spending even further. In fact, for a bond-financed increase in the government deficit it is possible for the autonomous expenditures multiplier to be zero. In Chapters 13 and 14 it will be seen that as the assumption of a fixed price level is relaxed, the autonomous expenditures multiplier grows even smaller until, in a world of assumed perfect price flexibility, it is zero. Thus, the crude Keynesian assumptions of a fixed interest rate, a fixed price level and a variable level of output production are essential to the results presented in this chapter.

The second key element to the Keynesian model is the assumption that consumption is constrained predominantly by current income. If, in contrast, because of borrowing, current consumption can be carried out even if current cash income is low, then consumption depends only weakly on current income and the multiplier loses some theoretical power. Consequently, an examination of alternative theories of consumption is of theoretical importance for the development of improved theories of aggregate economic activity.[4]

Consumption: The Neoclassical Theory

We begin the analysis with a household that has a two-period planning horizon. Assume that the household begins and ends each period with the same stocks of assets (there is no running down of assets), and that the household expects with certainty an income of Y_1 in period 1 and an income of Y_2 in period 2. Assume further that the rate of interest paid by borrowers is the same as the rate earned by lenders.

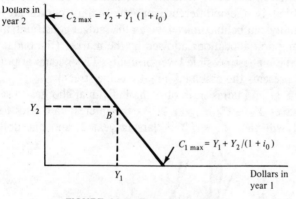

FIGURE 10.7. Budget constraint.

The household begins at point B in Figure 10.7. In Figure 10.7 the maximum amount of consumption in year one can be realized by consuming *all* of year 1's income ($\$Y_1$) and consuming nothing in year 2, thereby borrowing against *all* of year two's income $\$Y_2$. At a market rate of i_0, this borrowing would yield additional resources of $\$Y_2/(1 + i_0)$ in year one. Therefore, the maximum consumption in year 1 is $C_{1\,max} = Y_1 + Y_2/(1 + i_0)$. In contrast, in year 2 maximum consumption is obtained by consuming all of year 2's income in that year and by spending nothing in year 1 (saving) and lending it at the market rate until year 2. This would yield maximum consumption of $C_{2\,max} = Y_2 + Y_1(1 + i_0)$.

By saving the amount $(Y_1 - C_1)$ in year 1 and lending it at a rate of interest i_0 the household can increase consumption in year 2 by $(1 + i_0)\,(Y_1 - C_1)$. Con-

---

[4] In the Appendix to Chapter 14, we explain why modern theorists claim that Keynes' price rigidity and the form of his consumption function, as well as other "Keynesian" features, are consistent parts of a well integrated world view.

versely, in order to dissave the amount $(C_2 - Y_2)$ in year 2, the household must decrease consumption by $(C_2 - Y_2)/(1 + i_0)$ in year 1. In short, the market allows the household to consume anywhere along (or below) a locus connecting maximum consumption in year 1 with maximum consumption in year 2. This locus, the budget line, has a slope of $-(1 + i_0)$.

The amounts the household will actually choose to consume and save will depend on its utility from consumption in each year. Assume that there exists a family of intertemporal indifference or equal-utility curves (in Figure 10.8, I_0, I_1, and I_2). Because total utility is the same at all points along each equal-utility curve, and because consumption in each year generates positive utility (that is, consumption in each year is "good"), as consumption in one year is increased, consumption in the other year must decrease (that is, the indifference or equal-utility curves must have a negative slope). Moreover, if we assume diminishing marginal utility of consumption in each year, as consumption in one year is increased in consecutive units of one dollar, consumption in the other year must decrease by consecutively smaller absolute amounts (that is, the indifference or equal-utility curves are convex to the origin). Total utility can be maximized, given the budget constraint, at a point where the set of consumption allocations allowed by the market (the budget line) reaches (is tangent to) the highest possible level of utility. This occurs at point A in Figure 10.8; point B represents the assumed initial income stream.

In Figure 10.8 at an interest rate of i_0 the individual chooses to save $Y_1 - C_1$ in year 1 and dissaves $Y_2 - C_2$ in year 2. As the interest rate rises to i_1, one dollar saved in year 1 will yield $(1 + i_1)$ dollars in year 2, and one dollar dissaved in

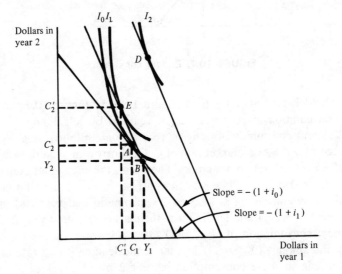

FIGURE 10.8. Indifference curves and changes in the budget constraint.

year 2 will require sacrifice of $[1/(1 + i_1)]$ dollars of consumption in year one. The budget line becomes steeper but as initial income is unchanged it must still go through point B. In other words, one dollar saved in year 1 will yield a larger return in year 2 when the interest rate is i_1 than when it is i_0. As the rate rises to i_1, and the reward to saving increases, the household depicted in Figure 10.8 maximizes its utility at point E; it chooses to increase its saving in year 1 from $(Y_1 - C_1)$ to $(Y_1 - C_1')$. This allows the household to increase its consumption in year 2 by $(C_2' - C_2)$.

At work here are both a substitution effect and an income effect. As the interest rate rises, the "price" of present consumption relative to future consumption rises, that is, it costs a household more to consume in the present year because for each dollar of goods consumed presently more future goods are being sacrificed. A rational household would substitute the cheaper good, future consumption, for the more expensive one, present consumption, under these circumstances. The substitution effect applies unambiguously to all households—lenders (present savers who will save more at higher rates) such as the one pictured in Figure 10.8, as well as borrowers (present dissavers who will borrow less at higher rates).

An income effect is also at work. As the interest rate rises for lenders (savers in year 1), such as the household in Figure 10.8, the level of real income from dollars saved in the present year rises. Therefore, if consumption goods in each year are not "inferior goods," lenders will increase consumption in both years. For borrowers (dissavers in year 1) as the interest rate rises, the level of their real income in the present year declines. Therefore if consumption goods are not inferior, borrowers will reduce consumption in both years.

For the household depicted in Figure 10.8 (a lender) the substitution effect of an increase in the rate of interest in reducing present consumption outweighs the income effect of an increase in the interest rate in increasing present consumption. The combined (substitution plus income) effect of an increase in the interest rate on consumption is negative; present consumption declines. (For other individual lenders it would, of course, be possible for the income effect to outweigh the substitution effect.)

For the economy as a whole an increase in the interest rate will generate a substitution effect which will cause both present savers (lenders) and present dissavers (borrowers) to consume less. For the economy as a whole an increase in the interest rate will have an income effect that will cause present savers to consume more and present dissavers to consume less. If, for the economy as a whole, a change in the market rate of interest cannot create any new resources, then it cannot raise the level of real income. There will then be no more resources available after the interest rate change than there were before the change. Under this condition, for the economy as a whole there can only be a substitution effect. A rise in the rate of interest has a positive income effect on the consumption of present savers (lenders), but this is assumed to be exactly offset by its negative income effect on the consumption of present dissavers (borrowers). Since the substitution effect is unambiguous for lenders and borrowers, we may specify that current aggregate consumption varies inversely with the market rate of interest

$$C = f(i), \qquad f_i < 0. \tag{10.27}$$

Using the household budget identity,

$$Y \equiv C + S + T, \tag{10.3}$$

where current income is unchanged, assuming transfer payments are not affected by interest rates, the effect of an interest rate change on consumption must be exactly offset by an equal and opposite effect on saving. Therefore, for the economy as a whole saving varies positively with the market rate of interest.[5]

$$S = g(i), \qquad g_i > 0. \tag{10.28}$$

Let us return once more to the individual household. If a household's income should increase in year 2, the present (year 1) value of its income stream will increase. Likewise, if year 1 income should increase, the future (year 2) value of its income will increase; this is evident from Figure 10.7. At point B the budget line has coordinates Y_1, Y_2. If either Y_1 or Y_2 rises, point B would move horizontally or vertically. Thus an increase in income in any year would move the budget line out without changing its slope. This will allow the household to reach a new higher level of utility. If consumption in any period is not an inferior good, an increase in one year's income should increase consumption expenditures in both years. This is the case in Figure 10.8. When the budget line shifts out, consumption expenditures are seen to increase in both years to point D.

The relation between the present value of an income stream PV and current consumption expenditures can be generalized by looking at income beyond two periods:

$$C = k(PV) = k \sum_{t=0}^{n} \left[\frac{Y_t}{(1 + i)^t} \right], \qquad 0 < k \leqslant 1 \tag{10.29}$$

where t is the number of years in the future in which a particular household's income is received. This says that a household's consumption in time t varies positively with the present time t value of all future income.[6]

---

[5] This represents further use of one of the three conservation principles developed in the previous chapter, the budget identity, the balance sheet identity, and the financing constraint. The partial effects of a change in the interest rate or any variable on consumption, saving, and transfers must sum to zero as long as income is unchanged. For a survey of recent research on the interest sensitivity of saving, see George M. von Furstenberg and Burton G. Malkiel, "The Government and Capital Formation: A Survey of Recent Issues," *Journal of Economic Literature*, vol. 15 (September 1977), 840–842.

[6] The condition $k \leqslant 1$ follows from the constraint that the present value of future consump-

The right-hand side of Equation (10.29) is the present discounted value of an income stream. The income stream includes current income as well as all future income. For the time being, let us define wealth as the present discounted value of all future income *excluding current income*. (This dichotomy is related to the Modigliani–Ando treatment below.) Therefore, the present value of an income stream is, under this definition of wealth, the sum of current income and wealth;

$$Y_0 + \sum_{t=1}^{n} \frac{Y_t}{(1+i)^t} = \sum_{t=0}^{n} \frac{Y_t}{(1+i)^t}. \tag{10.30}$$

Equation (10.29) can be written out to show the effect of current income and the present value of all future income, that is, wealth, on current consumption:

$$C = k \left(Y_0 + \frac{Y_1}{(1+i)} + \frac{Y_2}{(1+i)^2} + \cdots + \frac{Y_n}{(1+i)^n} \right). \tag{10.31}$$

The parameter k, being positive but less than unity, indicates that current consumption varies directly with the level of current income as well as with the level of wealth.

The effect of current income and wealth on current saving can now be derived by using the budget identity

$$Y \equiv C + S + T. \tag{10.3}$$

For analytical simplicity we shall assume that T (current taxation) is constant. Substituting Equation (10.31) into (10.3) and rearranging yields

$$S = Y_0 - kY_0 - k\frac{Y_1}{(1+i)} - k\frac{Y_2}{(1+i)^2} - \cdots - k\frac{Y_n}{(1+i)^n} - T$$

$$= (1-k)Y_0 - k \sum_{1}^{n} \frac{Y_t}{(1+i)^t} - T. \tag{10.32}$$

Thus current saving varies positively with current income but inversely with the level of wealth as defined above. This indicates that, as long as current income is unchanged, when wealth, so defined, increases current saving will decline.[7]

---

tion is equal to the present value of future income. Therefore, one can currently consume no more than the present value of one's future income. Negative consumption in any period is ruled out as being unreasonable.

[7] Once again, the budget identity allows us to show that the partial effects of a change in wealth on consumption, saving, and transfer payments must sum to zero as long as current income is unchanged.

Equation (10.29) also indicates that the longer the planning horizon of the household, the smaller the effect of a change in any one year's income (including the current year) on current consumption. Thus the effect of current income on current consumption in the neoclassical theory could be quite small. Focusing on current income as but one component of the present value of an income stream could considerably reduce the theoretical magnitude of the marginal propensity to consume. As a consequence, neoclassical theories of the relationship between current consumption and current income, wealth, and the rate of interest, will generally modify in a downward direction the expected magnitude of the autonomous expenditures multiplier.

A Reconciliation of Keynesian and Neoclassical Theories of Consumption: Albert Ando and Franco Modigliani

The foregoing should not suggest that the consumption theory of Keynes is inconsistent with neoclassical consumption theories. To the contrary, Albert Ando and Franco Modigliani have reconciled the Keynesian and neoclassical theories by breaking up the income stream into labor income (Y_{Lt}) and property income (Y_{Pt}) components. Property income has a present market value and is referred to as a household's net nonhuman wealth a. Wealth is therefore defined to include both human and nonhuman wealth. As in Equation (10.29), Ando and Modigliani begin with the relation between current consumption and the present value of an income stream,

$$C = k(PV) = k \sum_{t=0}^{n} \left[\frac{Y_t}{(1 + i)^t} \right], \qquad 0 < k \leqslant 1 \qquad (10.29)$$

where present value now is broken up into human and nonhuman components:

$$(PV) = Y_{L_0} + \sum_{1}^{n} \frac{Y_{L_t}}{(1 + i)^t} + a. \qquad (10.33)$$

The first two terms measure the human component. The last term, the nonhuman component, may be defined as

$$a = \sum_{0}^{m} \frac{Y_{P_t}}{(1 + i)^t}. \qquad (10.34)$$

On the assumption that current labor income is a multiple of the present value of future labor income,

$$\lambda Y_{L_0} = \sum_1^n \frac{Y_{L_t}}{(1 + i)^t} \tag{10.35}$$

present value is expressed as

$$PV = Y_{L_0} + \lambda Y_{L_0} + a. \tag{10.36}$$

By substituting Equation (10.36) into (10.29), Ando and Modigliani derive a consumption function that looks remarkably Keynesian:

$$C = k(1 + \lambda)Y_{L_0} + k \cdot a \tag{10.37}$$

where $k(1 + \lambda)$ is the marginal propensity to consume out of current labor income (estimated to be .7) and k is the marginal propensity to consume out of nonhuman wealth (estimated to be .06).[8]

A Reconciliation of Keynesian and Neo-classical Theories of Consumption: Milton Friedman

Milton Friedman's theory of consumption behavior also uses a wealth approach. However, rather than separating current income from wealth, Friedman works entirely within the concept of wealth, defined to include current as well as future income from human and nonhuman sources.

Because wealth is not easily measured, Friedman develops a new concept called permanent income,[9] which theoretically is the product of wealth and a rate of interest. Friedman contends that a household forms expectations about its permanent income, and hence its wealth, from past experience:

[8] See Albert Ando and Franco Modigliani, "The 'Life Cycle' Hypothesis of Saving: Aggregate Implications and Tests," *American Economic Review* (March 1963). Where the assets comprising the nonhuman wealth term *a* are defined to include bonds and equities, monetary policy that lowers interest rates effects capital gains for households. The money–equities link has proven important in several econometric studies. See, for example, Frank de Leeuw and Edward M. Gramlich, "The Channels of Monetary Policy," *Federal Reserve Bulletin*, no. 55 (1969). For a survey of possible wealth effects on aggregate demand, see Roger W. Spencer, "Channels of Monetary Influence: A Survey," *Review*, Federal Reserve Bank of St. Louis (November 1974). Both of the last two studies are included in Havrilesky and Boorman, *Current Issues in Monetary Theory and Policy.*

[9] Milton Friedman, *A Theory of the Consumption Function* (Princeton, NJ: Princeton University Press, 1957).

$$Y_{p_t} = \beta Y_t + \beta(1 - \beta)Y_{t-1} + \beta(1 - \beta)^2 Y_{t-2} + \cdots +$$
$$\beta(1 - \beta)^n Y_{t-n} \quad (10.38)$$

where Y_{p_t} is permanent income in period t, β is the factor which determines the weights attached to prior years' incomes, and Y_{t-j} is income as measured j years earlier. The term β is assumed to have a range between zero and unity, $0 < \beta < 1$, so that the further back one looks, the smaller the weight attached to that year's income. That is, if β is .5, the weights on the right-hand side of Equation (10.38) decline in a geometric pattern as follows: .5, .25, .125, etc.

The equation for last year's permanent income is

$$Y_{pt-1} = \beta Y_{t-1} + \beta(1 - \beta)Y_{t-2} + \cdots + \beta(1 - \beta)^{n-1}Y_{t-n} +$$
$$\beta(1 - \beta)^n Y_{t-(n+1)}. \quad (10.39)$$

Rewriting in this fashion allows substantial simplification as every term in Equation (10.38) after βY_t is equal to $(1 - \beta)$ times every term in Equation (10.39) except the last term. Because that last term is very small, it follows approximately that

$$Y_{pt} \cong \beta Y_t + (1 - \beta)Y_{pt-1} \quad (10.40)$$

which says that permanent income is a weighted average of current income and the previous period's permanent income. If current income is equal to last period's permanent income, then $Y_{pt} = Y_t$. If current income is different from last period's permanent income, this period's permanent income will change, but by less than the difference.

The permanent income hypothesis is that current consumption is proportional to permanent income:

$$C_t = \alpha Y_{pt} \quad (10.41)$$

where $0 < \alpha < 1$. Substituting Equation (10.40) into (10.41) yields

$$C_t = \alpha \beta Y_t + \alpha(1 - \beta)Y_{pt-1}. \quad (10.42)$$

If $\alpha(1 - \beta)Y_{pt-1}$ is treated as a constant, this equation may be regarded as an individual household's short-run consumption function with intercept $\alpha(1 - \beta)Y_{pt-1}$ and slope $\alpha\beta$. This function is graphed in Figure 10.9.

Where current income OZ equals permanent income, the household is on both its permanent and its short-run consumption functions. If current income increases from Z to X, consumption rises from C_1 to C_2. Equation (10.40) indicates that permanent income will then rise by a fraction (β) of ZX or by ZD. Thus it *appears* that the increase in consumption was caused by the rise in current income ZX, when

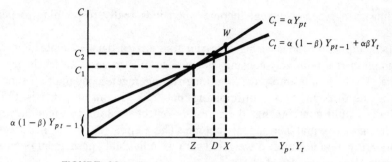

FIGURE 10.9. The permanent income hypothesis.

in fact it was caused by the rise in *permanent* income ZD. If current income remains at X, Equation (10.39) indicates that eventually current income will equal last year's permanent income Y_{pt-1}, and the intercept of Equation (10.42) in Figure 10.9 would increase until both functions intersect above X at W.

Empirical Studies of Consumption Behavior

Many empirical studies of short-run consumption behavior have estimated a relationship between the current consumption of different households and their current income.[10] These cross section estimates tend to show that households spend a declining percentage of current income on consumption goods and services as current income increases. A number of economists have argued that if C/Y declines as an individual household's income rises, then C/Y should decline as the aggregate of all households' incomes rises. Additional empirical estimates using short-run (quarterly) time series data on aggregate current income and aggregate current consumption show that C/Y does indeed decline as aggregate income rises. Thus the cross section and short-run time series empirical estimates seem to be consistent with the aggregate short-run Keynesian consumption relations, given in Equations (10.1) and (10.2) at the beginning of this chapter. They would also appear to be consistent with the Ando-Modigliani consumption function [Equation (10.37)].

Friedman would argue that the empirical studies which use cross section data are merely reflecting the illusion discussed above. Individual household consumption *appears* to respond to current income when it really is responding to permanent income. The short-run time series estimates may be similarly interpreted. Aggregate consumption, reflecting the behavior of individual households, *appears* to be re-

[10] Empirical studies of the consumption function are surveyed in most macroeconomics texts. See for example, William Branson, *Macroeconomic Theory and Policy* (New York: Harper and Row, 1972); Michael K. Evans, *Macroeconomic Activity, Theory, Forecasting and Control* (New York: Harper and Row, 1967); and David J. Ott, Attiat F. Ott, and Jang H. Yoo, *Macroeconomic Theory* (New York: McGraw-Hill, 1975).

sponding to aggregate current income when it is really responding to permanent income.

Other empirical studies using long-run time series data estimate that aggregate consumption is a relatively constant percentage of income at all levels of aggregate income. These results imply that the long-run aggregate consumption function is a straight line through the origin implying that C/Y is constant, that is, $C = \gamma \cdot Y$. Friedman would contend that these results reflect the long-run tendency of measured income to equal permanent income. The estimated long-run aggregate consumption function is simply a weighted sum of individual (permanent) consumption functions [Equation (10.41)].

Numerous hypotheses have proposed that Keynes' short-run consumption function is the empirically "true" relationship. These hypotheses suggest that the long-run data simply represent points on different short-run consumption functions and that variables other than income have induced shifts in the short-run consumption function over time. Many alternative dependent variables have been added to try to explain these shifts in order to improve the fit of the short-run Keynesian relation with longer run time series data. (For example, in the Ando–Modigliani estimate (10.37) if nonhuman wealth a increases, the function shifts upward.) Among the variables empirically tested have been various measures of household assets, the composition of the population, the size of the household and its composition, and prices.

Income has been measured in a multitude of ways; for example, lagged income, per capita income, income relative to a prior peak level of income (relative income), money income, and net income. As a consequence, these approaches and comparisons between them tend to be cumbersome. They result in macroeconomic models that contain a large number of variables and that do not perform much better than simpler models at predicting the level of income.

In contrast, Friedman's consumption theory does not add new variables.[11] It reconciles the short-run empirical estimates of the consumption function with the long-run estimates by showing that the observed short-run relationship does indeed shift upward over time. However, it carries out this reconciliation as well as the reconciliation between neoclassical and Keynesian theories of consumption within a traditional neoclassical apparatus.

While empirical studies of consumption behavior are interesting and important, what most interests us is Friedman's and Ando and Modigliani's explicit emphasis on the role of wealth and the interest rate in the theory of consumption. These treatments have their antecedents in neoclassical (Austrian) capital theory of Boehm–Bawerk, as amplified by Irving Fisher and others. They constitute a body of theo-

---

[11] Friedman's permanent income is a proxy for wealth. Claims that wealth does not have a strong or even statistically significant empirical effect on current consumption are sometimes made. Nevertheless, many of the variables that are usually statistically significant in estimates of the consumption function are in fact proxies for wealth such as lagged income and equities.

retical and empirical evidence which suggests that consumption and saving behavior cannot be explained in a satisfying and empirically relevant way without reference to wealth and interest rate variables. They explain the observed data as well as, if not better than, theories of consumption that simply add variables, and yet they have the weight of decades of intellectual labor on their side. Therefore, in the macroeconomic models of later chapters both wealth and the interest rate (as well as the level of current income) will explicitly influence aggregate consumption (saving) behavior. Thus a more sophisticated consumption function in linear form can be written:

$$C = a + bY_d + vW + ei$$

where $a > 0, 0 < b, 0 < v < 1,$ and $e < 0$.

Using the budget identity $Y_d \equiv C + S$, this may be written as the saving relation:

$$S = -a + sY_d - vW - ei$$

where $s \equiv (1 - b)$.[12] In later chapters we shall employ these basic relations extensively.

Investment Expenditures

In the elementary model of income–expenditures determination developed earlier in this chapter, investment expenditures were assumed given and autonomous of any other variable in that model. In more realistic models this assumption is not retained. Investment expenditures may realistically be viewed as depending on a number of variables. Perhaps the most important of these is the interest rate. In what follows we shall present the theory that investment expenditures vary inversely with the market rate of interest.

Aggregate net investment expenditures are defined as the change in the capital stock of the economy. Capital is an input into the firm's production process. Therefore, in order to develop the theory of investment, one must start with the theory of production of the firm.

We assume that for a profit maximizing firm units of some factor X are a variable productive input and that other inputs Z are conceptually held constant. The model may be specified as follows:

---

[12] These equations satisfy the conditions that, where transfer payments are assumed constant, the partial effects of a change in disposable income on saving s and consumption b must sum to unity, the partial effects of a change in the interest rate on saving $-e$ and consumption e must sum to zero, and the partial effects of a change in wealth on saving $-v$ and consumption v must sum to zero.

$$\pi \equiv R - C \qquad \text{definition of profit} \qquad (10.43)$$

$$R \equiv PQ \qquad \text{definition of revenue} \qquad (10.44)$$

$$C \equiv P_x X + c \qquad \text{definition of cost} \qquad (10.45)$$

$$\pi \equiv PQ - P_x X - c \qquad\qquad (10.46)$$

$$Q \equiv f(X, Z) \qquad \text{production function} \qquad (10.47)$$

where

π = profit
R = revenue
C = cost
P = the price of output
Q = the quantity of output
P_x = the price of a unit of X
X = the quantity of X
Z = other inputs
c = the total cost of inputs other than X.

Equation (10.43) is the definition of profit as revenue less cost. Equation (10.44) is the definition of revenue as a product of the price of output and the quantity of output. Equation (10.45) is the definition of total cost as the product of the price and quantity of the variable input X plus the assumed fixed cost of other inputs. Equation (10.46) is the definition of profit after Equations (10.44) and (10.45) are substituted into (10.43). Equation (10.47) is the production function which is the behavioral relation between output Q and the variable input X and the fixed input Z.

To maximize profit units of X should be hired until the increment to profit is zero, that is, until the marginal cost of an additional unit is equal to the marginal revenue generated by employment of that unit. (We shall assume without examination that second-order conditions are satisfied.) Hiring a unit of X directly affects output through Equation (10.47):

$$\frac{\partial Q}{\partial X} = \frac{\partial (f(X, \bar{Z}))}{\partial X}$$

where $\partial Q / \partial X$ is the marginal product of the input X which is assumed to be positive. It also affects cost in Equation (10.45):

$$\frac{dC}{dX} = \frac{d(P_x X)}{dX} = \frac{dP_x}{dX} X + P_x \frac{dX}{dX}$$

where dC/dX is the marginal factor cost of the input X. The increase in output directly affects revenue through Equation (10.43):

$$\frac{dR}{dQ} = \frac{d(PQ)}{dQ} = \frac{dP}{dQ} Q + \frac{dQ}{dQ} P$$

where dR/dQ is marginal revenue.

The effect on profit of hiring one unit of X is therefore

$$\frac{\partial \pi}{\partial X} = \frac{\partial R}{\partial X} - \frac{\partial C}{\partial X}$$

$$= \frac{dR}{dQ} \frac{\partial Q}{\partial X} - \frac{\partial C}{\partial X}$$

$$= \frac{\partial Q}{\partial X} \frac{dP}{dQ} Q + \frac{dQ}{\partial X} \frac{\partial Q}{dQ} P - \frac{dP_x}{dX} X - \frac{dX}{dX} P_x. \qquad (10.48)$$

Setting this derivative equal to zero (the first-order condition) and collecting terms, we get

$$\frac{\partial Q}{\partial X}\left(\frac{dP}{dQ} Q + \frac{dQ}{dQ} P \right) = \left(\frac{dP_x}{dX} X + \frac{dX}{dX} P_x \right)$$

$$\frac{\partial Q}{\partial X}\left(P + \frac{dP}{dQ} Q \right) = \left(P_x + \frac{dP_x}{dX} X \right)$$

$$\frac{\partial Q}{\partial X}\left[P\left(1 + \frac{1}{\varepsilon_d}\right)\right] = P_x \left(1 + \frac{1}{\varepsilon_s}\right),^{13} \qquad (10.49)$$

where $\varepsilon_d = PdQ/QdP$, the elasticity of demand, the percentage change in quantity of output divided by the percentage change in price of output; and $\varepsilon_s = P_x dX/XdP_x$, the elasticity of factor supply, the percentage change in quantity of input divided by the percentage change in the input's price. This (first-order) condition for a profit maximum says that the marginal physical product ($\partial Q/\partial X$) times marginal revenue $P(1 + 1/\varepsilon_d)$ equals the marginal factor cost, $P_x(1 + 1/\varepsilon_s)$. Under circumstances of pure competition in product and factor markets, both elasticities approach infinity and the profit maximizing condition is

$$\frac{\partial Q}{\partial X} \cdot P = P_x. \qquad (10.50)$$

This indicates that X is hired until its marginal physical product times the price at which output is sold is equal to the price of a unit of X.

[13] This gives the familiar relationship between marginal revenue and marginal factor cost and their respective elasticities. Where demand is perfectly elastic ($\varepsilon_d \rightarrow -\infty$), marginal revenue, the term within the square bracket on the left-hand side, is equal to the price of output because $(1/\varepsilon_d) \rightarrow 0$. Where factor supply is infinitely elastic ($\varepsilon_s \rightarrow \infty$), marginal factor cost, the term on the right-hand side, is equal to the price of the factor input because $(1/\varepsilon_s) \rightarrow 0$.

Now if X is units of *capital*, this profit maximizing condition will determine how much capital the firm will hire, only if it is recognized that capital, by definition, has a useful life that goes beyond the current period n years into the future. Therefore, the left-hand side of Equation (10.49) must be written as a discounted present value:[14]

$$PV = \sum_{j=1}^{n} \frac{\left(\frac{\partial Q}{\partial X}\right)_j \left[P_j\left(1 + \frac{1}{\varepsilon_d}\right)\right]}{\left(1 + i\right)^j} = P_x\left(1 + \frac{1}{\varepsilon_s}\right). \qquad (10.51)$$

where the interest rate is assumed fixed. Under circumstances of pure competition in both markets Equation (10.51) is written as

$$PV = \sum_{j=1}^{n} \frac{\left(\frac{\partial Q}{\partial X}\right)_j P_j}{(1 + i)^j} = P_x. \qquad (10.52)$$

Let $(\partial Q/\partial X)_j P_j$, representing the expected marginal revenue product of capital in the jth year, be expressed as Y_j. Because of the assumption of diminishing marginal productivity of capital, Y_j is positive but decreases as additional units of capital are employed. Equation (10.52) simplifies to

$$PV = \sum_{j=1}^{n} \frac{Y_j}{(1 + i)^j} = P_x. \qquad (10.53)$$

The market rate of interest i at which the expected income stream Y_j is discounted represents the "cost" of capital funds at which the firm must borrow. If it is financing its projects externally, this is the rate at which the firm must borrow in capital markets. If the firm is financing internally, it is the rate at which its funds could earn if invested in financial assets of comparable risk and durability. The profit maximizing condition generates the following decision rule for the firm: *hire units of capital until the present value of the last unit hired is just equal to its dollar cost.* This indicates that, as long as the actual capital stock is less than the desired capital stock given by this decision rule, the firm will add to its physical capital stock until $PV = P_x$. This is reflected in Figure 10.10. The firm's net investment I is the change in its capital stock.

Each locus in Figure 10.10 slopes downward and to the right because, given any

---

[14] The notion of present value was discussed earlier in the theory of consumption; a more detailed discussion appears in Chapter 5.

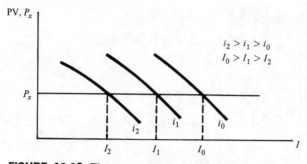

FIGURE 10.10. The present value criterion for the investment decision.

market rate of interest, as the quantity of capital goods hired increases, the marginal physical product of capital $(\partial Q/\partial X)_j$ declines over the expected life of the unit of capital. This means that the marginal revenue product of capital $(\partial Q/\partial X)_j P_j$ also declines. Therefore at a given market rate of interest the present value PV declines as shown.

If we relax the assumption of pure competition in the output market, each locus in Figure 10.10 would decline more rapidly, because as the quantity of capital goods hired increases, the quantity of output would rise. This increase in output would reduce marginal revenue [the term within the square brackets on the left-hand side of Equation (10.51)] because of a decrease in price in the product market associated with higher output. This would cause the marginal revenue product of capital, the numerator on the left-hand side of Equation (10.51), to decline for two reasons, diminishing marginal product and decreasing marginal revenue.

If we relax the assumption of pure competition in the market for capital goods, any purchase of capital goods would tend to put upward pressure on the price of these goods. Therefore, the P_x locus would be replaced by an upward sloping marginal factor cost line representing the right-hand side of Equation (10.51). In this case, units of capital would be hired until this upward sloping marginal factor cost locus intersected the present value locus in Figure 10.10. In both cases it can readily be seen that there would be less investment and less production if markets were not competitive in structure.

The example in Table 10.1 will elucidate the relationships described above. Assume that there is pure competition in product and factor markets so that Equations (10.52) and (10.53) apply. Column 4 shows that all output can be sold at the going market price of $100. Column 8 shows that all capital units can be purchased at the going market price of $7,000. Columns 2 and 3 depict the diminishing marginal physical product of capital. Column 5 shows the decreasing marginal revenue product of capital. If we assume for simplicity that this marginal revenue stream is constant for each unit of capital, and that each unit is infinitely lived, then in Equation (10.53) present value reduces to the simple perpetuity form discussed in Chapter 5:

Table 10.1. Present Value and the Marginal Expected Internal Rate of Return

1 Units of Capital	2 Output Q	3 Marginal Physical Product of Capital $\partial Q/\partial X$	4 Price of Output P	5 Marginal Revenue Product of Capital $(\partial Q/\partial X)P$	6 Market Rate of Interest i	7 Present Value PV	8 Price of a Unit of Capital P_x	9 Marginal Expected Internal Rate of Return
0	10	—	$100	$ 0				
1	20	10	$100	$1000	10%	$10,000	$7,000	14.3%
2	29	9	$100	$ 900	10%	$ 9,000	$7,000	12.6%
3	37	8	$100	$ 800	10%	$ 8,000	$7,000	11.4%
4	44	7	$100	$ 700	10%	$ 7,000	$7,000	10.0%
5	50	6	$100	$ 600	10%	$ 6,000	$7,000	8.6%
6	55	5	$100	$ 500	10%	$ 5,000	$7,000	7.1%

$$PV = \frac{Y_j}{i} = P_x. \tag{10.54}$$

Using the given market rate of interest in column 6, we may thereby derive the present value of each unit of capital in column 7. In order to maximize profit, capital is hired until this present value equals the price of a unit of capital. This occurs when four units are hired.

Table 10.1 and Equation (10.54) can be used to show an alternative to the present value decision rule. Rather than solve for the present value, let us ignore the market rate of interest and, dividing the expected income stream Y_j by the price of a unit of capital P_x, solve for the marginal expected internal rate of return, or marginal efficiency of capital. The marginal efficiency of capital is the rate of return that sets the present value, the left-hand side of Equation (10.54), equal to the price of capital, the right-hand side. Each unit of capital in Table 10.1 will then have a unique expected internal rate of return or marginal efficiency starting with $1,000/ $7,000 = 14.3% on the first unit, $900/$7,000 = 12.6% on the second, 11.4% on the third, and so on. Profit is maximized where this rate, given in column 9, is just equal to the market rate of interest of 10%, or at four units of capital.[15]

For the economy as a whole net investment is defined as the change in the capital stock. Given the desired capital stock as derived above, if the actual capital stock of the economy is less than its desired level, the level of net investment expenditures in the economy is positive. As the interest rate increases, the desired capital stock, and hence the level of investment, decreases. This is evident in Figure 10.10; the relationship between the interest rate and aggregate investment is shown in Figure 10.11.

There is, of course, a good deal more to the analysis of the theory of investment.[16]

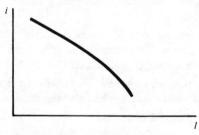

FIGURE 10.11. The aggregate investment relation.

---

[15] These two criteria will not always generate the same decisions. The present value criterion would have the firm use the market rate of interest in ordering or ranking investment projects. The marginal efficiency criterion does not use this information in ranking investment projects. Thus it could generate incorrect decisions in some cases. For example, a project with a higher internal rate of return than another project might actually have a smaller present value if its returns were relatively great in the distant future and the market rate at which future returns are discounted were quite high. In other cases the internal rate of return decision rule may be impracticable because Equation (10.53) may not yield a unique solution for i.

[16] See Robert Solow, *Capital Theory and the Rate of Return* (Chicago: Rand McNally,

Nevertheless, for our purposes it is sufficient to note that for the firm as well as the economy as a whole, there will be an inverse relationship between the market rate of interest and the level of investment. In the macroeconomic models that follow we express the relation between the market rate of interest and the level of investment expenditures in linear, slope-intercept form:

$$I = a' + hi$$

where $h < 0$, $a' > 0$.

Concluding Comments

This chapter has developed a basic overview of elementary macroeconomic theory. We began with the basic Keynesian theory of consumption and the related model of income determination. This theory is far from a satisfactory explanation of real-world behavior, and alternative, more realistic versions of its basic behavioral relations, the consumption and investment relations, were explored. Generally these more sophisticated functions entailed the introduction of an interest rate variable and (in the case of the consumption relation) a wealth variable. With these relations we may now proceed to the development of more realistic models of income (and interest rate) determination.

QUESTIONS FOR CHAPTER 10

1. Explain the autonomous expenditures multiplier principle in words. Why is Keynes' MPC so important?

2. What would be the effect on consumption of a once-and-for-all reduction in autonomous taxation according to the permanent income theory of consumption as compared to the Keynesian theory of consumption?

3. Show that a businessman who chooses investment projects according to their expected internal rate of return may not be behaving rationally.

4. Consider the following model of the income-expenditure sector:

$$C = 100 + .8Y_d$$
$$I = 200$$
$$G = 360$$
$$T = 200$$
$$C + I + G = Y$$
$$Y_d \equiv Y - T$$

1964); John Meyer and Edward Kuh, *The Investment Decision* (Cambridge: Harvard University Press, 1957); Jack Hirschliefer, *Investment, Interest and Capital* (Englewood Cliffs, NJ: Prentice-Hall, 1970), ch. 2–4; and Dale W. Jorgenson, "The Theory of Investment Behavior," in *Determinants of Investment Behavior*, Robert Ferber, ed. (New York: Columbia, 1967).

What is autonomous consumption? What is the marginal propensity to consume? The marginal propensity to save? What is the government deficit? What is the average propensity to consume at the equilibrium level of income? What is the value of the autonomous expenditures multiplier?

5. Based on the above solution, fill in the following table:

	Households	Business Firms	Government	Total
Earnings				
Transfers				
Receipts				
Current expenditures				
Saving				
Capital expenditures				

6. Explain in words why an individual's saving varies positively with the market rate of interest.

7. Explain in words why an individual's saving varies negatively with his wealth.

BIBLIOGRAPHY FOR CHAPTER 10

ANDO, ALBERT, and FRANCO MODIGLIANI, "The 'Life Cycle' Hypothesis of Saving: Aggregate Implications and Tests," *American Economic Review* (March 1963).

BAILEY, M., "Formal Criteria for Investment Decisions," *Journal of Political Economy,* vol. 62 (October 1959), 476–488.

BOEHM-BAWERK, EUGEN VON, *Positive Theory of Capital* (New York: Stechert, 1923).

BRANSON, WILLIAM H., *Macroeconomic Theory and Policy* (New York: Harper and Row, 1972), ch. 11.

DE LEEUW, FRANK, and EDWARD M. GRAMLICH, "The Channels of Monetary Policy," *Federal Reserve Bulletin,* no. 55 (1969).*

DUSENBERRY, JAMES, *Income, Saving and the Theory on Consumer Behavior* (Cambridge: Harvard University Press, 1949).

EVANS, MICHAEL K., *Macroeconomic Activity: Theory, Forecasting and Control* (New York: Harper and Row, 1967).

FISHER, IRVING, *The Theory of Interest* (New York: Macmillan, 1930).

FRIEDMAN, MILTON, *A Theory of the Consumption Function* (Princeton, NJ: Princeton University Press, 1957).

HIRSCHLIEFER, J., *Investment, Interest and Capital* (Englewood Cliffs, NJ: Prentice-Hall, 1970), chs. 2–4.

JORGENSON, D. W., "The Theory of Investment Behavior," in *Determinants of Investment Behavior,* R. Ferber, ed. (New York: Columbia, 1967).

LERNER, A. P., *The Economics of Control* (New York: Macmillan, 1944).

MEYER, JOHN, and EDWARD KUH, *The Investment Decision* (Cambridge: Harvard University Press), 1957.

* Reprinted in THOMAS H. HAVRILESKY and JOHN T. BOORMAN, *Current Issues in Monetary Theory and Policy* (Arlington Heights, IL.: AHM Publishing Corporation, 1976).

OTT, DAVID J., ATTIAT F. OTT, and JANG H. YOO, *Macroeconomic Theory* (New York: McGraw-Hill, 1975).

SOLOW, ROBERT, *Capital Theory and the Rate of Return* (Chicago: Rand McNally, 1964).

SPENCER, ROGER W., "Channels of Monetary Influence: A Survey," *Review,* Federal Reserve Bank of St. Louis (November 1974).*

VON FURSTENBERG, GEORGE M., and BURTON G. MALKIEL, "The Government and Capital Formation: A Survey of Recent Issues," *Journal of Economic Literature,* vol. 15 (September 1977), 835–878.

* Reprinted in THOMAS H. HAVRILESKY and JOHN T. BOORMAN, *Current Issues in Monetary Theory and Policy* (Arlington Heights, IL.: AHM Publishing Corporation, 1976).

11

Aggregate Demand

Introduction

In the previous chapter a simplistic model of the income–expenditures sector of the economy was developed. Earlier chapters examined money demand and money supply relations in some detail. The present chapter is our first attempt to integrate the income–expenditures and monetary sectors of the economy. We will develop a model which simultaneously determines equilibrium in the flow of income and expenditures as well as in the stock of money supplied and demanded.[1] Unlike previous chapters, the rate of interest will not be assumed given outside the model. Instead the interest rate—more specifically the long-term rate—is treated as a variable whose equilibrium value is determined simultaneously with that of the level of income.[2]

Despite this improvement, several aspects of the model developed in this chapter remain rather unrealistic. It is assumed that nominal wage and price levels are constant, so that all quantities are expressed in dollars of constant purchasing power. Government expenditures, taxation, and transfers are assumed to be zero. Relation-

[1] The ideas capsuled here originate in Alvin H. Hansen's *A Guide to Keynes* (New York: McGraw-Hill, 1953) and in Sir John R. Hicks' "Mr. Keynes and the 'Classics,' A Suggested Interpretation," *Econometrica*, vol. 5 (1937), 147–159. Among the early mathematical treatments is Lawrence Klein's *The Keynesian Revolution* (New York: Macmillan, 1947). As a teaching device, this piece draws inspiration from Edward C. Budd's "Note on Money, Interest, and Income" (unpublished).

[2] As indicated in the early chapters of this book, there are many interest rates in the real world which are closely interrelated. For simplicity we focus only on the long-term rate as it may be most relevant for the investment decision.

ships between expenditures, financing, and wealth will not be considered in detail. Later chapters will handle these elements in a more realistic manner.

The IS (Income–Expenditures Equilibrium) Curve

In the preceding chapter we saw that planned saving and planned consumption vary directly with the level of income, and that the level of planned investment varies inversely with the market rate of interest. We defined saving as current income not allocated to the purchase of consumption goods and services. These propositions, together with the familiar condition that planned saving must equal planned investment in equilibrium, suggest equilibrium combinations of the four variables (income, saving or consumption, investment, and interest rate).

The set of equilibrium relationships between the interest rate and the level of spending (consumption and investment expenditures) is called the *IS* curve. The *IS* curve shows, for a given interest rate, the level of income that will generate planned saving equal to planned investment. Some economists call this relationship the income–expenditures equilibrium curve, since for any level of production (or income), it shows the interest rate required to generate total aggregate expenditures (investment expenditures plus consumption expenditures) sufficient to absorb this output (or real income). In other words, with *given* commodity prices, there are unique combinations of interest rates and income levels which would clear the relevant markets without excess demand or supply, and hence without unplanned inventory change or unplanned saving.

The *IS* curve is derived from the investment and consumption functions and the condition that the economy must be in equilibrium. Figure 11.1 demonstrates the derivation of this relationship (where *positive* quantities are measured along all axes).

Saving is an increasing function of the level of income (quadrant 4 of Figure 11.1). For purposes of construction, the saving function replaces the consumption function (it will be recalled from the budget identity of the previous chapter that they can be used interchangeably). The saving function is assumed to be linear in Figure 11.1 and may be represented as follows:

$$S = -a + sY \tag{11.1}$$

where s is the marginal propensity to save, $0 < s < 1$, and $-a$ is the level of dissaving or negative saving that occurs autonomously of the level of income; this negative autonomous saving is constant at all levels of income, $a > 0$. Consumption expenditures—equivalent to the volume of income that is not saved—are measured as the directed distance between the 45° line and the saving function. For the present we overlook the influence of the interest rate and the level of wealth on saving. These variables will be introduced into the saving function in later chapters.

On the assumptions of profit maximizing behavior by business firms and diminishing returns in production, investment expenditures are a decreasing function of the rate of interest (quadrant 2 of Figure 11.1) as expressed in Equation (11.2). This is consistent with the theory discussed in the previous chapter. The principle of diminishing returns means that as a business firm acquires more units of a newly produced capital good, *ceteris paribus,* the discounted expected present value of successive units of that good declines.[3] In order to maximize profits, a business firm will invest in desired units of capital until the discounted expected present value of the last capital good acquired is equal to the incremental cost of that capital good. Since the present value varies inversely with the rate at which expected future income is discounted (the market rate of interest), the lower the market rate, the greater the desired stock of newly produced capital goods.[4]

The investment function can, therefore, be expressed in general notation as

$$I = I(i). \tag{11.2}$$

In Figure 11.1 the investment demand curve is drawn with a negative slope (the level of investment expenditures varies inversely with the market rate of interest) and concave to the origin. (Remember all axes measure positive quantities.) We present the equation more simply in our model by writing this function as the linear relationship:

$$I = a' + hi \tag{11.2'}$$

where h and a' are parameters and $h < 0$ and $a' > 0$.

The condition for equilibrium in the income–expenditures (flow) sector of the economy is that planned (or intended) saving equals planned (or intended) investment (quadrant 3 of Figure 11.1):

$$S = I. \tag{11.3}$$

To determine a point on the *IS* curve, assume an arbitrary level of income (say Y_1) and from Equation (11.1) derive the amount of planned saving S_1 concomitant

[3] At the margin of production, each newly produced capital good in the economy will have a successively smaller expected future income stream. Thus as the flow of future income to the marginal investment good declines, its present value declines. The relationship between the future income stream from a capital good and its present value is discussed in the final section of Chapter 10.

[4] It should be pointed out that investment expenditures will be positive provided the stock of capital goods that is desired at the going market rate of interest exceeds the actual capital stock. Otherwise net investment will be negative and equal to depreciation (capital consumption allowances) until the actual capital stock falls below the desired capital stock, *ceteris paribus.*

It should also be noted that in the present chapter we ignore the fact that the *financing* of investment expenditures by the business sector must increase the *wealth* of the private sector, and that increases in private wealth will have effects on both consumption expenditures (as seen in Chapter 10) and the demand for money (as discussed in Chapters 4 and 6). These matters will be taken up in Chapter 12, where *financing constraints* and *the balance sheet identity* are explicitly considered.

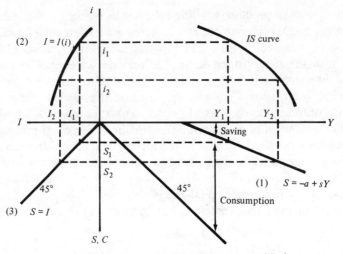

FIGURE 11.1. Income–expenditures equilibria.

with that income level. From Equation (11.3) determine the amount of planned investment I_1 that necessarily must equal planned saving S_1 in order to maintain income–expenditures equilibrium. The line drawn in Figure 11.1 to represent Equation (11.2) discloses that this amount of investment will result only if the rate of interest is i_1. Hence i_1 and Y_1 represent a point of income–expenditures equilibrium which must lie on the *IS* curve and is therefore consistent with all three equations. Other points, such as i_2 and Y_2, are similarly derived.

The *IS* curve depicts a crucial macroeconomic relationship between the interest rate and the level of income in the income–expenditures sector of the economy. As the interest rate declines, planned investment spending increases [Equation (11.2)]. As investment spending increases, the level of income will rise; the rise in the level of income will generate sufficient planned saving [Equation (11.1)] such that the flow of planned saving will equal the flow of planned investment and the income–expenditures sector of the economy will be in equilibrium [Equation (11.3)].[5] The *IS* curve is not a demand or a supply curve but an income–expenditures equilibrium curve.

Substituting Equations (11.1) and (11.2′) into Equation (11.3), we may solve for the level of income Y in terms of all parameters and the rate of interest i. Because Equation (11.2′) indicates that the level of investment I is a linear function of the market rate of interest i, the income–expenditures equilibrium curve will be linear; its slope being constant and equal to h/s:

$$Y = \frac{a + a'}{s} + \frac{h}{s} \cdot i. \tag{11.4}$$

[5] As elementary macroeconomic theory teaches, the presence of equilibrium in a Keynesian model does not necessarily indicate a *full-employment* equilibrium.

The LM (Money Market Equilibrium) Curve

In the previous section we used three linear equations to develop the income–expenditures equilibrium curve for the economy. Yet within this system there are four unknowns: investment I, saving S, the interest rate i, and the level of income Y. Clearly, unless one of the variables is given in a fourth equation (say the interest rate, $i = i_0$), one cannot find the equilibrium level of income, saving, or investment for the economy. We must add n equations in $n - 1$ unknowns in order to make a formal solution for this model possible.

Nevertheless, it would be unrealistic in the extreme to assume that the interest rate is given by dictate of the monetary authority. In the more general case, let us assume that the monetary authority attempts to control the nominal supply of money in existence.[6] Indeed, the interest rate, instead of being dictated, is the "price" which equates the stock of money supplied (so determined) to the stock of money demanded. The demand for money is, in turn, an increasing function of the level of income as well as a decreasing function of the interest rate.

In short, three additional behavioral equations (money supply, money demand, and the money market equilibrium condition) may be specified for the monetary sector of the economy. It is then possible to derive an equilibrium curve that combines these three equations and relates, for any given level of income, the rate of interest necessary to equate the demand for, and supply of, money. This curve, the "money market equilibrium curve," is denoted by LM and, in conjunction with the IS curve, expresses a complete general equilibrium model of aggregate demand in six equations and six unknowns. The LM curve as shown in Figure 11.2 is derived from these three basic monetary relations.

The total demand for money is considered to be a function of the level of income and the interest rate. The demand-for-money function used in this model derives from the analysis presented in Chapters 4 and 5. It is treated as consisting of two separate components. The first component of the demand for money is a function of the level of income and is drawn in quadrant 4 of Figure 11.2. This demand for "active" money balances is identified with the transactions motive for holding money. A high interest rate has been shown to bring about an economization of transactions balances. Accordingly, as discussed in Chapter 4, it is reasonable to indicate that the transactions demand will vary inversely with the interest rate and will vary less than in proportion to Y. Nevertheless, for the time being and in the interest of analytical simplicity the interest rate variable will be ignored in this portion of the total demand function for money, and the quantity of transactions balances demanded will be represented as varying in direct proportion to the level of current income:

---

[6] It is important to keep in mind that we assume that the general price level is constant in this model so that the monetary authority appears to be able to control the *real* stock of money. This is, of course, quite unrealistic. In fact, the Federal Reserve can control only the *nominal* stock of money. This restriction will be made explicit in subsequent chapters.

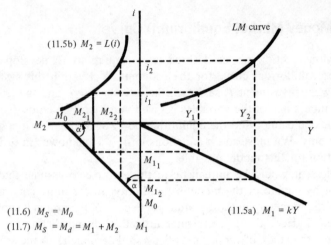

FIGURE 11.2. Money market equilibria.

$$M_1 = kY \qquad (11.5a)$$

where k is a parameter and the reciprocal of the income velocity of "active" money balances. As the price level is assumed constant, this represents a demand for real money balances. (In this discussion the precautionary motive for holding money is not explicitly related to any variable but, as mentioned in Chapter 4, may be assumed in all cases to be related to the same variables as the transactions motive.)

The second component of the demand for money M_2 is a function of the interest rate and is shown in quadrant 2 of Figure 11.2, where again all axes measure positive quantities. This portion of the total demand is identified with the speculative motive for holding money (or the "asset" demand for money). It is sometimes called the demand for "idle" balances and, as discussed in Chapter 5, is inversely related to the rate of interest. The liquidity preference function representing this relationship is shown in quadrant 2 of Figure 11.2. The function is negatively sloped and is convex to the origin. For simplicity's sake the equation of the liquidity preference curve can be expressed in general notation as

$$M_2 = L(i). \qquad (11.5b)$$

The reasons for the negative slope of the liquidity preference curve, as drawn in Figure 11.2 and described above, were examined in Chapter 5. In Tobin's analysis, for example, a larger percentage of financial wealth is held in the form of money as the interest rate declines, because a lower interest rate makes less attractive the risk of holding bonds. Later in this discussion it will be useful to write this portion of the total demand for money M_2 as the linear function

$$M_2 = m + ui \qquad (11.5b')$$

where u and m are, respectively, slope and intercept parameters, and where $u < 0$ and $m > 0$.

The nominal quantity of money supplied M is assumed to be determined by the monetary authority as M_0. In the present analysis we shall assume that this consists entirely of the noninterest bearing debt of government.[7]

$$M_s = M_0. \tag{11.6}$$

In quadrant 3 of Figure 11.2 the quantity of money supplied is measured as both the directed distance M_0 on the M_1 (vertical) axis and the directed distance M_0 on the M_2 (horizontal) axis. By geometry it may be seen that where the angle α equals the angle α' in the third quadrant, that portion of the money supply *not* held as transactions balances on the M_1 axis must be held as speculative balances on the M_2 axis. For instance, the directed distance on the M_1 axis, $M_{1_1}M_0$, is equal to the directed distance on the M_2 axis, OM_{2_1}, and the directed distance on the M_1 axis, $M_{1_2}M_0$, is equal to the directed distance on the M_2 axis, OM_{2_2}. Thus the third quadrant of Figure 11.2 depicts the condition that the supply of money M_0 must equal the quantity of money demanded $(M_1 + M_2)$:

$$M_s = M_1 + M_2 = M_d. \tag{11.7}$$

To determine a point on the LM curve, assume an arbitrary level of income (say Y_1) and derive from Equation (11.5a) the amount of M_1 (that is, M_{1_1}) concomitant with that level of income; the quantity that is necessary to satisfy the transactions demand for money or to "finance" the level of income Y_1. If M_{1_1} is desired as transactions balances and M_0 is the fixed money supply, by geometry it may be seen that only the amount M_{2_1} is available to satisfy the speculative demand for money. Given the liquidity preference function (11.5b), the interest rate i_1 is required to ration the supply of idle balances M_{2_1} among asset holders. Therefore i_1 is necessary to equate the demand for money $(M_{1_1} + M_{2_1})$ and the supply of money M_0 at the assumed income level of Y_1. The point i_1, Y_1 represents a point of money market equilibrium which must lie on the LM curve and is therefore consistent with all three equations. Other points, for example, i_2, Y_2, are similarly derived.

The LM curve then is a set of equilibrium points for the monetary sector of the economy. Each point is consistent with the demand for money [Equations (11.5a) and (11.5b)], the supply of money [Equation (11.6)] and money market equilibrium [Equation (11.7)].

The LM curve depicts a crucial macroeconomic relationship between the interest rate and the level of income in the monetary sector of the economy. As the level of

---

[7] The interest bearing debt of government and all other forms of wealth, indeed the balance sheet identity, are not considered in the present chapter. Therefore, we overlook the influence of wealth on the demand for money and consumption, even though in previous chapters these variables played important roles. In the next chapter wealth and its relation to the financing of government expenditures and investment expenditures are introduced.

income Y rises, the quantity of transactions balances desired M_1 rises [Equation (11.5a)]. Given a fixed money supply M_0 [Equation (11.6)], individuals who desire more transactions balances must acquire them from those who hold idle balances M_2, that is, they must sell "bonds" to holders of idle balances. Holders of idle balances will only relinquish these money holdings for bonds when "bribed" by a higher interest rate, that is, a lower bond price [Equation (11.5b)]. Therefore, as the level of income rises, the interest rate must rise in order to maintain equilibrium between the supply of, and the demand for, money [Equation (11.7)], and the monetary sector of the economy will be in equilibrium. The *LM* curve is not a supply or demand curve but rather it is a money market equilibrium curve.

Substituting Equations (11.5a), (11.5b'), and (11.6) into Equation (11.7), we may solve for the level of income Y in terms of all parameters and the market rate of interest i. Because Equation (11.5b') shows the quantity of speculative balances demanded M_2 as a linear function of the market rate of interest i, the money market equilibrium curve will be linear, and its slope will be constant and equal to $-u/k$:

$$Y = \frac{M_0 - m}{k} - \frac{u}{k} \cdot i. \tag{11.8}$$

The unique equilibrium level of income and the equilibrium rate of interest can be determined by the intersection of the *IS* and the *LM* curves when both are plotted on the same graph in Figure 11.3. At this point both the monetary and the income–expenditures sectors of the economy are in equilibrium. Every point on *LM* represents a position of money market equilibrium; every point on *IS* represents a position of income–expenditures equilibrium. Where the two curves intersect, both sectors, and hence the entire model of aggregate demand, are in equilibrium.

Where Equations (11.2) and (11.5b) are linear, as Equations (11.2') and (11.5b'), the solution for the equilibrium level of income is derived from six equations in six unknowns (Y,i,M_d,M_s,S,I) by rearranging both Equations (11.4) and (11.8) with the interest rate on the left-hand side:

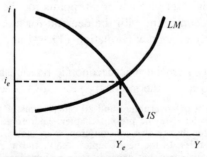

FIGURE 11.3. Aggregate equilibrium: the *LM* and *IS* curves.

$$i = \frac{M_0 - m}{u} - \frac{k}{u} Y \tag{11.8'}$$

$$i = \frac{-(a + a')}{h} + \frac{s}{h} Y. \tag{11.4'}$$

Setting the above expressions for the interest rate equal to each other and rearranging terms,

$$Y \left(\frac{s}{h} + \frac{k}{u} \right) = \frac{M_0 - m}{u} + \frac{a + a'}{h}.$$

Solving for the equilibrium level of income,

$$Y_e = \frac{\dfrac{M_0 - m}{u} + \dfrac{a + a'}{h}}{\dfrac{s}{h} + \dfrac{k}{u}}$$

$$= \left(\frac{M_0 - m}{u} + \frac{a + a'}{h} \right) \frac{hu}{su + hk}$$

$$= \frac{u(a + a') + h(M_0 - m)}{su + hk} \tag{11.9}$$

How Autonomous Expenditures Influence the IS Curve

As in the elementary macroeconomic theory presented in Chapter 10, autonomous expenditures may be treated as autonomous aggregate demand, the sum of autonomous investment expenditures and autonomous consumption expenditures.[8] Hence, an increase in autonomous expenditures can be reflected in Figure 11.1 either by moving the investment schedule horizontally to the left, or by shifting the saving schedule upward (an increase in autonomous consumption is identical to a decrease in autonomous saving). Thus at each point along the old *IS* curve there will be an excess aggregate demand for newly produced goods and services. In fact, in Figure 11.4 the entire region to the left of the new curve *IS'* is a region of excess aggregate demand for goods and services. From any point in this region, a specific rise in the level of income (or a specific rise in the interest rate) is necessary to increase output (or reduce aggregate demand) sufficiently to keep the income–expenditures sector in equilibrium.

---

[8] A government sector, which includes autonomous government expenditures and their financing by taxation or the issuance of debt and therefore involves fiscal policy, is introduced in the next chapter.

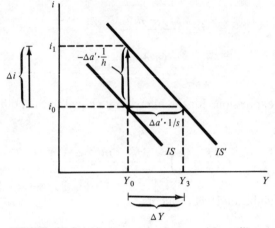

FIGURE 11.4. A change in income–expenditures equilibrium.

In terms of saving and investment, at any point to the left of *IS'* in Figure 11.4 saving is less than investment. Either the level of income must rise (stimulating saving) or the rate of interest must rise (reducing investment) to bring the income–expenditures sector into equilibrium. At any point to the right of *IS'*, saving exceeds investment. Either the level of income must fall (reducing saving) or the rate of interest must fall (stimulating investment) in order to bring the income–expenditures sector into equilibrium.

Therefore, starting from an initial position of equilibrium at any point on *IS* in Figure 11.4, an increase in autonomous expenditures will shift the curve to the right to *IS'*. Measured horizontally the *IS* curve shifts by the amount of the increase in autonomous aggregate demand times $1/s$. The rationale for this is quite clear. Take any level of income on the initial *IS* curve,

$$Y_0 = \frac{a + a'}{s} + \frac{h}{s} \cdot i_0. \tag{11.4}$$

Now change autonomous expenditures and observe the new level of income Y_1 which keeps the income–expenditures sector in equilibrium when the interest rate is held constant at i_0:

$$Y_1 = Y_0 + \Delta Y = \frac{a + a' + \Delta a'}{s} + \frac{h}{s} \cdot i_0.$$

Only if income increases by ΔY,

$$\Delta Y = Y_1 - Y_0 = \Delta a' \frac{1}{s}$$

at a fixed interest rate will sufficient saving ΔS be generated to equal the increase in autonomous investment $\Delta a'$ (or the decrease in autonomous saving),

$$\Delta a' = \Delta S = \Delta Y \cdot s$$

thus keeping the income–expenditures sector in equilibrium on the new curve *IS'* and satisfying Equation (11.3).

$$S + \Delta S = I + \Delta a'.$$

Similarly, measured vertically in Figure 11.4 the shift in the *IS* curve is $\Delta a'(1/h)$. This may be readily seen. Rewrite Equation (11.4) with the interest rate on the left-hand side and take any interest rate on the initial *IS* curve:

$$i_0 = \frac{-(a + a')}{h} + \frac{s}{h} \cdot Y_0. \tag{11.4'}$$

Now change autonomous expenditures and observe the new level of the interest rate i_1 which keeps the income–expenditures sector in equilibrium if the level of income is held constant at Y_0:

$$i_1 = i_0 + \Delta i = \frac{-(a + a' + \Delta a')}{h} + \frac{s}{h} \cdot Y_0.$$

Only when the interest rate rises by Δi,

$$\Delta i = i_1 - i_0 = -\Delta a'\frac{1}{h}$$

at a fixed income level will investment spending be *reduced* sufficiently,

$$\Delta i \cdot h = -\Delta I$$

to offset the initial increase in autonomous investment $\Delta a'$ (or decrease in autonomous saving), thus keeping the income–expenditures sector in equilibrium and satisfying Equation (11.3) on the new curve *IS'*,

$$S = I + \Delta a' - \Delta I.$$

So far we have only discussed the effect of a change in autonomous aggregate demand upon the entire income–expenditures equilibrium curve. The effect on the unique level of income and interest rate which keep *both* the income–expenditures and monetary sectors in equilibrium is discussed later in this chapter. Only when we consider the effect of changes in autonomous aggregate demand on both sectors can we develop a more sophisticated version of the autonomous expenditures multiplier principle of elementary macroeconomic theory.

How Money Influences the LM Curve

Because money is a stock and not part of the flow of spending and income and because in the present model it does not enter the saving and investment relations directly, monetary policy does not affect the *IS* curve. Rather it influences the *LM* curve. An increase in the quantity of money supplied will be shown as an increase in the length of the legs of the triangle in quadrant 3 of Figure 11.2. Thus at each point along the old *LM* curve there will be an excess supply of money (which will be used by individuals to acquire bonds).[9] In fact, the entire region to the left of *LM'* is a region of an excess supply of money. From any point in that region a specific rise in the level of income or specific decline in the interest rate is necessary to stimulate the demand for money sufficiently to keep the money market in equilibrium. Any point to the right of *LM'* is one of an excess demand for money. A specific fall in the level of income or a specific rise in the interest rate is necessary to reduce the demand for money sufficiently to keep the money market in equilibrium. Thus, given an increase in the money supply only a specific lowering of the interest rate and/or a specific raising of the level of income will cause the increased money supply to be absorbed into transactions balances M_1 and/or speculative balances M_2 and keep the money market in equilibrium.

An increase in the money supply will, therefore, shift the *LM* curve to the right to *LM'* in Figure 11.5 by the amount of the increase in the money supply ΔM_s times $1/k$. This may be seen as follows. Take any level of income on the initial *LM* curve, Y_0,

$$Y_0 = \frac{M_0 - m}{k} - \frac{u}{k} \cdot i. \tag{11.8}$$

Now increase the money supply ΔM_s and observe the effect on the level of income which keeps the money market in equilibrium where the interest rate is held constant at i_0:

$$Y_1 = Y_0 + \Delta Y = \frac{M_0 - m + \Delta M_s}{k} - \frac{u}{k} \cdot i_0.$$

We see that only if income increases by ΔY,

[9] Because money is a stock and the consumption of goods and services is a flow, there can never be a situation where money is used to acquire consumer goods and services directly; only bonds or capital goods (defined to include consumer *durables*) can be acquired. By the balance sheet identity of Chapter 9, where the capital stock is assumed to be zero and where the supplies of money and bonds are assumed to be given, an excess supply of money is synono-

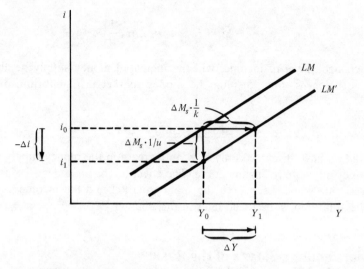

FIGURE 11.5. A change in money market equilibrium.

$$\Delta Y = Y_1 - Y_0 = \Delta M_s \frac{1}{k}$$

at an unchanged interest rate will the increased money supply be absorbed into transactions balances, thus keeping the money market in equilibrium on the new curve LM',

$$\Delta Y \cdot k = \Delta M_d = \Delta M_s.$$

Similarly, we may measure vertically the shift from LM to LM' in Figure 11.5 by $\Delta M_s (1/u)$. Rewrite Equation (11.8) with the interest rate on the left-hand side and take any interest rate on the LM curve, i_0,

$$i_0 = \frac{M_0 - m}{u} - \frac{k}{u} \cdot Y_0. \qquad (11.8')$$

Now increase the money supply ΔM_s and observe the new interest rate i_1 which keeps the money market in equilibrium if the level of income is held constant at Y_0:

$$i_1 = i_0 - \Delta i = \frac{M_0 - m + \Delta M_s}{u} - \frac{k}{u} \cdot Y_0.$$

Only if the interest rate falls by $-\Delta i$,

mous with an excess demand for bonds. The relationship between money, bonds, and capital goods is examined in greater detail in the next chapter.

$$-\Delta i = i_1 - i_0 = \Delta M_s \frac{1}{u}$$

at an unchanged level of income, will the increased money supply be absorbed in speculative balances, thus keeping the money market in equilibrium on the new curve LM',

$$-\Delta i \cdot u = \Delta M_d = \Delta M_s.$$

Thus far we have discussed only how an increase in the money supply affects the entire money market equilibrium curve. The effect on the *unique* level of income and the interest rate which keep *both* the money market and the income expenditures sector in equilibrium is discussed later in this chapter.[10]

Multipliers and the Slopes of the Basic Functions: An Increase in Autonomous Expenditures

The two previous sections examined how changes in the autonomous expenditures and money supply parameters of our model disturbed the equilibrium in the money and income–expenditures sectors *separately* and shifted the *IS* or *LM* curves. Now let us examine how they affect overall, aggregate demand equilibrium. In Chapters 7 and 8 we saw that a good deal of theoretical and empirical controversy centered around hypotheses about the manner in which the interest rate and a measure of income affect the demand for money. Now we shall see the crucial influence of these hypotheses on the strength of the multipliers in this macroeconomic model. We shall assume in all cases that sufficient time passes in order for the multipliers to reach their (comparative static) equilibrium values.[11]

[10] Because money is assumed to consist entirely of the debt of government (outside money), money created by banks (inside money) is not considered. Thus this analysis overlooks the process by which total reserves (and/or the monetary base) are increased and results in a variable money supply expansion depending on the portfolio behavior of the banks and the public. (The reader may want to study Chapters 1 and 2 which elaborate on these factors in the money supply expansion process.) In short, for the immediate purposes of this analysis, the effects in the monetary sector of a simple, discrete expansion of the money supply are illustrated in Figure 11.5. Money created by a private banking system is introduced in Chapter 15.

[11] In Chapter 8 it was pointed out that permanent income explained more of the variation in the demand for money than current income. It was shown in Chapters 8 and 10 that the use of permanent income, as a weighted average of past and present levels of measured income, does not remove current income from the money demand and consumption functions, but rather adds a *lagged* value of income as a new explanatory variable in these relations. This modification of the basic model of this chapter simply means that while changes in the money supply or autonomous expenditures still affect income in the same direction, they would not *immediately* work their full multiplier effect. Instead, since past changes in income would also affect current income, any monetary or expenditures stimulus would take *time* to develop the full multiplier effect on income.

The inclusion of money market behavior and the rate of interest in this model modifies the form of the autonomous expenditures multiplier of elementary macroeconomic theory. The solution for income in the linear model was

$$Y_e = \frac{u(a + a') + h(M_0 - m)}{su + hk}. \tag{11.9}$$

The autonomous expenditures multiplier shows the change in income caused by a change in "autonomous" expenditures *a,* which shifts the *IS* curve. In Figure 11.6 the new equilibrium level of income Y'_e will be

$$Y'_e = Y_e + \Delta Y = \frac{u(a + a' + \Delta a) + h(M_0 - m)}{su + hk}.$$

Therefore, the change in income is

$$\Delta Y = \frac{u(\Delta a)}{su + hk}$$

and the autonomous expenditures multiplier is a function of the slopes of the basic functions,

$$\frac{\Delta Y}{\Delta a} = \frac{u}{su + hk}. \tag{11.10}$$

In the previous chapter the model, which considered only the income–expenditures sector and assumed a constant interest rate, had an autonomous expenditures multiplier of $1/s$. This is considerably larger than the present autonomous expenditures multiplier, a multiplier that is derived from a more general equilibrium model which contains a money market as well as an income–expenditures sector and does not assume a constant interest rate.[12]

The effect of monetary phenomena on the autonomous expenditures multiplier is illustrated in Figure 11.6. The *IS* curve is drawn on the assumption that $a = 0$ and $0 < s < 1$. The marginal efficiency of investment schedule is located in the same quadrant as is the *IS* curve. The initial equilibrium position is at *A,* where equilibrium income Y_e is equal to *OF;* investment *OD;* consumption *DF;* and the rate of interest *OK.* If the investment schedule shifts to the right by an amount ΔI ($=CE$) and if the rate of interest were fixed at *OK,* the equilibrium level of income would rise by $FH = (1/s\,CE)$ to *OH.* However, the increase in aggregate

---

[12] Those contemporary economists who believe that the effectiveness of fiscal policy has been overrated sometimes contend that the proponents of fiscal policy overlook this salient point. See, for example, David Fand, "Some Issues in Monetary Economics: Fiscal Policy Assumptions and Related Multipliers," *Review,* Federal Reserve Bank of St. Louis (January 1970), 23–27.

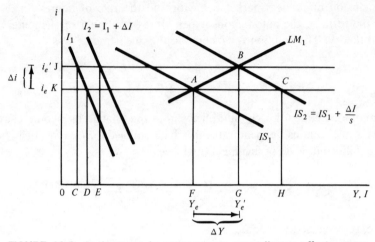

FIGURE 11.6. An increase in autonomous expenditures affects aggregate general equilibrium.

income will induce an increase in the transactions demand for money and force the rate of interest up to OJ. The new equilibrium level of income Y'_e will be OG, and the increase in the level of income ΔY will only be FG rather than FH. The increase in the rate of interest has reduced the level of induced investment spending by CD and hence the level of income by $GH = (1/s\ CD)$. This occurs because, as the level of income increases, the demand for transactions balances M_1 increases and can only be satisfied, given a fixed money supply M_0, if speculative balances M_2 are relinquished. Speculative balances will only be relinquished and bonds accepted if the rate of interest rises. Because of the rise in the rate of interest, the level of investment spending falls by CD and the level of income will only rise to G.

Clearly, the rise in the interest rate reduces the size of the autonomous expenditures multiplier. The size of the multiplier depends upon the slopes of the basic functions from which it is derived. The slope of the saving schedule (11.1) is s and reflects the increase in saving, given a unit increase in the level of income. The slope of the investment schedule in linear form (11.2′) is h and reflects the amount by which investment must fall, given a unit increase in the interest rate, that is, $h = dI/di$.

The slope of the transactions demand for money schedule (11.5a) is k and reflects the increase in transactions balances demanded, given a unit increase in the level of income. The slope of the liquidity preference curve in linear form (11.5b′) is u and reflects the amount by which the quantity of speculative balances demanded must decrease, given a unit increase in the rate of interest, that is, $u = dM_2/di$. Hence the effect of the interest rate and the level of income on the demand for money greatly influences the results brought about by a change in autonomous expenditures.

In reality, these slopes may not be constant for all points in the schedules (the functions may not be linear), although we assumed they are linear for purposes of deriving, most simply, the solution for the level of income. As explained for the more general case in Equations (11.2) and (11.5b), the absolute value of h falls as we move down along the investment schedule, and the absolute value of u rises as we move down along the liquidity preference schedule.[13] As discussed in Chapter 4, where the transactions demand is less than proportional, for example, under Baumol's square root rule, the interest rate will not be "bid up" much as income increases (the LM curve will be flatter), and, as can be seen in Equation (11.10), the autonomous expenditures multiplier will be greater in magnitude.

Within the more convenient linear framework the slope of the IS curve is equal to h/s and the slope of the LM curve is then equal to $-u/k$. This may be verified by examining the mathematical expressions for the IS and LM curves, Equations (11.4) and (11.8). (Remember $u, h < 0$ and $1 > k, s > 0$.)

In order to compare the new LM–IS autonomous expenditures multiplier to the simple autonomous expenditures multiplier of the elementary model of the previous chapter, $1/s$, it is instructive to rewrite it as

$$\frac{\Delta Y}{\Delta a} = \frac{1}{s + \dfrac{hk}{u}}. \tag{11.10}$$

If $dM_2/di = u = -\infty$ (a perfectly interest elastic liquidity preference schedule and hence *a horizontal LM curve*), or if $dI/di = h = 0$ (a completely interest inelastic investment schedule, and hence *a vertical IS curve*), then Equation (11.10) reduces to the simple autonomous expenditures multiplier. Aggregate demand would not be "choked off" by a rise in interest rates as income rose, either because the interest rate would not be bid upward ($u = -\infty$), or because the rise in the rate would not affect spending ($h = 0$).

On the other hand, if $dM_2/di = u = 0$ (a completely interest inelastic speculative demand schedule, and hence *a vertical LM curve*), or if $dI/di = h = -\infty$ (a completely interest elastic investment schedule and *hence a horizontal IS curve*), any increase in autonomous expenditures would *not* affect the level of income because the rise in the interest rate would "choke off" all the increased aggregate demand, that is, the autonomous expenditures multiplier would be zero, either because

---

[13] To the extent that low interest rates are associated with massive unemployment, this model suggests that fiscal policy is a more reasonable stabilization tool during periods of unemployment (and monetary policy is more reasonable during periods of nearly full employment). See Phillip Cagan, "Current Issues in the Theory of Monetary Policy," in *Patterns of Market Behavior: Essays in Honor of Philip Taft,* Michael J. Brennan, ed. (Providence, RI: Brown University Press, 1965), 135–154.

the rise in the interest rate would be immense as idle balances were sought to "finance" increased expenditures ($u = 0$), or because any rise in the rate would completely "choke off" spending ($h = -\infty$). In this case only an increase in the quantity of money, effecting a horizontal shift in the LM curve, could cause the level of income to rise.

The existence of a very interest inelastic demand curve for money ($u \to 0$) or a very interest elastic investment demand schedule ($h \to -\infty$) makes the change in the level of income following from a change in autonomous expenditure insignificant. This may be seen from Equation (11.10). Therefore, when the liquidity preference schedule is relatively interest inelastic or when investment spending is very interest sensitive, government policies to affect autonomous expenditures are considered to have a relatively less powerful effect on income.

Conversely, when the speculative demand for money schedule is very interest elastic ($u \to -\infty$) or when investment demand is very interest inelastic ($h \to 0$) as can be seen in Equation (11.10), the change in the level of income following from a change in autonomous expenditures approaches the value of the simple multiplier $1/s$ of elementary models without a monetary sector. Therefore, when investment spending is very interest insensitive or when the liquidity preference schedule is relatively interest elastic, government policies to affect autonomous expenditures are considered to have a relatively more powerful effect on income.

Thus, we see that the order of magnitude of the autonomous expenditures multiplier is related to the orders of magnitude of the four slope parameters of our model, h, u, s, and k. The greater the absolute value of u, reflecting greater sensitivity of the public's holdings of speculative money balances to changes in the interest rate, the greater the magnitude of the autonomous expenditures multiplier in Equation (11.10). This is illustrated in Figure 11.7 which compares the orders of magnitude of the increases in income which follow from an increase in autonomous expenditures (shown as a shift in the IS curve from IS_1 to IS'_1) given two alternative LM curves. The steeper LM curve (LM_1) reflects a lesser absolute value of u, a less interest sensitive demand for money function; the less steep LM curve (LM_0) represents a more interest sensitive demand for money function. The curve with a greater absolute value of u (LM_0) will give a larger change in the equilibrium level of income ΔY_0.

The less the absolute value of h, reflecting less sensitivity of investors to fluctuations in the interest rate, the greater the size of the autonomous expenditures multiplier in Equation (11.10). This is illustrated in Figure 11.8, which compares the orders of magnitude of the increases in income which follow from an increase in autonomous expenditures shown alternatively as a shift in the IS curve either from IS_0 to IS'_0 or from IS_1 to IS'_1 with a given LM curve. The steeper pair of IS curves (IS_1, IS'_1) reflect a lesser absolute value of h, a less interest sensitive investment spending function; the less steep pair of IS curves (IS_0, IS'_0) represents a more interest sensitive investment function. The steeper IS curves, the ones with a lesser absolute value of h, will give a larger change in the equilibrium level of income ΔY_1.

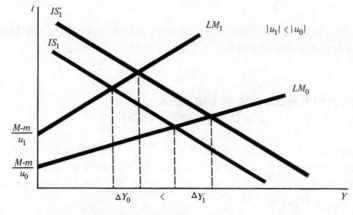

FIGURE 11.7. The greater the interest sensitivity of the demand for money, the greater the autonomous expenditures multiplier.

Note that Figure 11.7 is constructed so as to hold all parameters constant except for u and autonomous expenditures a; Figure 11.8 is constructed so as to hold all parameters constant except for h and autonomous expenditures a. As seen in Figure 11.8, the magnitude of the horizontal shift in the IS curve is identical for IS_0, IS'_0 and for IS_1, IS'_1. Note also that; as in the case of the autonomous expenditures multiplier of elementary macroeconomics, the smaller the marginal propensity to save s, the larger is the multiplier in Equation (11.10).[14] Finally the smaller the

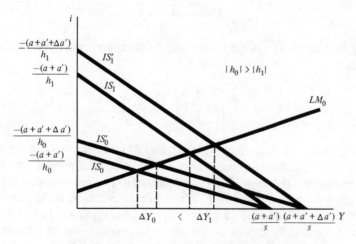

FIGURE 11.8. The less the interest sensitivity of the investment demand, the greater the autonomous expenditures multiplier.

[14] In more complex models additional leakages such as induced taxation, induced business saving (retained earnings), and induced imports may further reduce the magnitude of the multiplier.

proportionality factor in the transactions demand for money k, the larger is the autonomous expenditures multiplier in Equation (11.10).[15]

Multipliers and the Slopes of the Basic Functions: An Increase in the Money Supply

The multiplier concept applies also to a shift in the LM curve caused by a change in the quantity of money supplied or a shift in the money demand function. In Figure 11.9 the new equilibrium level of income Y'', caused by a change in the quantity of money supplied ΔM is,

$$Y''_e = Y_e + \Delta Y = \frac{u(a + a') + h(M_0 - m + \Delta M)}{su + hk}.$$

Therefore the change in income is

$$\Delta Y = \frac{h\Delta M}{su + hk}$$

and the multiplier is a function of the slopes of the basic functions, or

$$\frac{\Delta Y}{\Delta M} = \frac{h}{su + hk}$$

which may be written in a form which can be compared with previous multiplier expressions,

$$\frac{\Delta Y}{\Delta M} = \frac{h}{u}\left(\frac{1}{s + hk/u}\right). \tag{11.11}$$

The difference between Equations (11.10) and (11.11) lies only in the term h/u. An increase in autonomous expenditures as depicted by Equation (11.10) raises aggregate income by the multiple $[1/(s + hk/u)]$. The autonomous expenditures multiplier portion of Equation (11.11), the term in brackets, is the same as Equation (11.10). But an increase in M, as depicted by Equation (11.11), increases the level of income only insofar as it reduces the market rate of interest i and increases the level of investment spending I. The reduction in the market rate depends on the size of u (the fall in i with respect to an increase in M_s). The rise

---

[15] A decrease in the order of magnitude of either s or k increases *both* multipliers.

in investment spending depends on the size of h (the rise in I with respect to a fall in i). By calculus

$$\frac{dY}{dM} = \frac{di}{dM} \cdot \frac{dI}{di} \cdot \frac{dY}{dI}.$$

The existence of a very interest inelastic investment demand schedule ($h \to 0$) makes the change in the level of income following from a change in the quantity of money supplied ΔM insignificant. This can be seen from Equation (11.11). Even though a change in the money supply affects the interest rate, the rate has little effect on investment. Therefore if investment is interest insensitive, as it may well be in many sectors of the economy, policies that affect the money supply are relatively less powerful.[16]

Also, the existence of a very interest elastic speculative demand schedule ($u \to -\infty$) makes the change in the level of income following from a change in the quantity of money supplied ΔM insignificant. This can be seen from Equation (11.11). Even if investment is interest sensitive, under these circumstances the money supply may be increased without much effect on the rate of interest, as individuals can be "induced" to hold additional speculative money balances without much decline in the interest rate. Therefore, when the speculative demand schedule is relatively interest elastic, policies that affect the money supply are less powerful.[17]

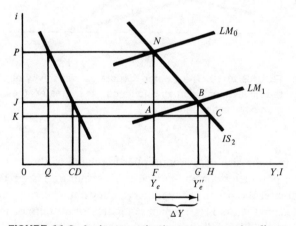

FIGURE 11.9. An increase in the money supply affects aggregate general equilibrium.

[16] See, for example, Phillip Cagan, *op. cit.*

[17] Estimated interest elasticities of the demand for money are reported in Tables 7.1 and 7.2 of the survey of empirical tests of the money demand function.

The effect of change in the money supply on the level of income, as shown in Equation (11.11), is illustrated in Figure 11.9. The initial equilibrium at N is disturbed by an increase in the quantity of money supplied ΔM. As discussed earlier, the LM curve shifts horizontally to the right by an amount equal to $\Delta M/k$. At the initial equilibrium level of income OF, the rate of interest will fall by $PK(=(1/u)\Delta M)$, that is, as excess money balances are used to acquire "bonds," the price of bonds rises and the market interest rate falls. At the lower interest rate, investment is stimulated by $QD(=(h/u)\Delta M)$. If the interest rate were fixed at OK, the simple multiplier process would move the economy to C, and the level of income would rise by FH. However, as discussed earlier in this section and illustrated in Figure 11.6, an increase in the level of income will force the interest rate back up to OJ as transactions balances must be obtained at the expense of speculative balances. The increase in the level of income will be limited to FG and the increase in the level of investment will be limited to QC.

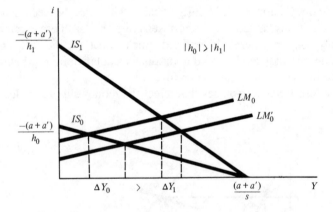

FIGURE 11.10. The greater the interest sensitivity of the investment demand function, the greater the monetary policy multiplier.

Thus we see that the size of this multiplier is related to the orders of magnitude of the four slope parameters of our model, h, u, s, and k. The greater the absolute value of h, the greater the size of the monetary policy multiplier in Equation (11.11). This is illustrated in Figure 11.10 which compares the orders of magnitude of the increases in income which follow from an increase in the money supply (shown as a shift in the LM curve from LM_0 to LM'_0) given two alternative IS curves. The steeper IS curve (IS_1) reflects a lesser absolute value of h, a less interest sensitive investment demand function; the less steep IS curve (IS_0) represents a more interest sensitive investment function. The IS curve with a greater absolute value of h (IS_0) will give a larger change in the equilibrium level of income ΔY_0.

The less the absolute value of u, the greater the size of the monetary policy

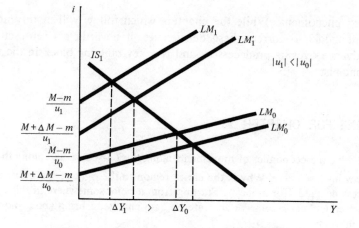

FIGURE 11.11. The less the interest sensitivity of the demand for money, the greater the monetary policy multiplier.

multiplier in Equation (11.11). This is illustrated in Figure 11.11 which compares the orders of magnitude of the increases in income which follow from an increase in the money supply, shown alternatively as a shift in the LM curve either from LM_0 to LM'_0 or from LM_1 to LM'_1 with a given IS curve. The steeper pair of LM curves (LM_1, LM'_1) reflect a lesser absolute value of u, a less interest sensitive demand for money function; the less steep pair of LM curves (LM_0, LM'_0) represent a more interest sensitive demand for money function. The steeper LM curves, the ones with a lesser absolute value of u, will give a larger change in the equilibrium level of income ΔY_1.

Figure 11.10 is constructed so as to hold all parameters constant except for h and the supply of money; Figure 11.11 is constructed so as to hold all parameters constant except for u and the supply of money. The magnitude of the horizontal shift in the LM curves is identical for LM_0, LM'_0 and LM_1, LM'_1.

Summary

This chapter has developed a framework within which the level of aggregate income and the rate of interest are simultaneously determined as part of a general equilibrium model of aggregate demand. Economists often analyze real-world problems with this paradigm in mind. However, the theory has its limitations. Government cannot be introduced into this model in any realistic way because it pays insufficient attention to the relationship between the flow of expenditures, the stock of wealth, and financing. Moreover, nominal wage and price levels were assumed given in the present model. This makes it an inadequate tool for analyzing inflation and related phenomena. While the chapters which follow will modify and extend the present model to correct these deficiencies, it nevertheless represents an important advance over its predecessors and is a key building block in the repertoire of the economist.

QUESTIONS FOR CHAPTER 11

1. Describe the economics of movements along the *LM* curve and along the *IS* curve.

2. Draw an *LM* curve. Why is the entire region to the right of the curve a region of excess demand (for money)? Starting from a point somewhere in this region, how must either real income or the interest rate change to bring about money market equilibrium?

3. Draw an *IS* curve. Why is the entire region to the left of the curve a region of excess aggregate demand? Starting from a point somewhere in this region, how must either the level of income or interest rate change to bring about equilibrium in the income–expenditures sector? Explain the assumed behavior which will bring about these changes.

4. Assume the Council of Economic Advisors (CEA) announces that the marginal propensity to save has fallen. Using the *LM–IS* model of this chapter, what would be the effect on the multipliers discussed in this chapter.

5. Assume the CEA announces that the amount of transactions balances held as a porportion of income has risen. What would be the effect on the multipliers discussed in this chapter?

6. Assume the CEA announces that the interest elasticity of investment demand has increased. Again, what would be the effect on the multipliers?

7. Explain completely (without the aid of graphs) why the size of the autonomous expenditures multiplier depends upon the interest sensitivity of the demand for money function.

8. Explain (without the aid of graphs) why a change in autonomous expenditures may be totally ineffective in changing the level of income in the economy if the demand for money function is interest insensitive.

9. Suppose all expenditures demand functions in the economy were completely unresponsive to changes in the rate of interest. What would the basic *LM–IS* graphical portrayal of this model look like? What would be the relative efficacy of monetary policy in such an economy? Explain.

10. Explain why the autonomous expenditures multiplier derived from the model of the income-expenditures sector which assumes a constant interest rate is generally larger than the autonomous expenditures multiplier derived from a more general equilibrium model which contains a money market and does not assume a constant interest rate.

11. Construct a graph similar to Figure 11.7 in this chapter, which shows the effect of a change in autonomous expectations where all parameters except *k*, the

proportionality factor in the transactions demand for money, are held constant. Then construct a graph similar to Figure 11.8, which shows the effect of a change in autonomous expenditures where all parameters except *s,* the marginal propensity to save, are held constant.

Appendix to Chapter 11
Alternative Formulations of Money Demand in the Model of Aggregate Demand

In Chapter 6 we examined several formulations of the quantity theory of money. At that time we quoted Milton Friedman to the effect that a "quantity theorist" could be distinguished by his emphasis on the stability of the demand for money function, the independence of the factors affecting the supply of and the demand for money, and the crucial role of the money demand function in the determination of the equilibrium values of several important aggregate economic variables. In this appendix we shall assume a money demand function of the form presented by some quantity theorists and examine the implications in *LM–IS* analysis of using this functional form in place of the familiar Keynesian liquidity preference function.[1]

We begin by repeating the Fisherian equation of exchange (11A.1), the Cambridge equation (11A.2), and the final empirical money demand equation presented by Friedman (11A.3):

$$M \cdot V' = P \cdot O' = Y \qquad (11A.1)$$

$$M = kY \qquad (11A.2)$$

$$M_d/(N \cdot P) = \gamma[Y_p/(N \cdot P)]^\delta . \qquad (11A.3)$$

A distinguishing characteristic of these equations is that each one contains some measure of income as the primary variable explaining the quantity of money balances demanded and excludes the interest rate as an explanatory variable. In the quantity theory tradition, then, the demand for money is viewed as a function of the level of income. In liquidity preference theory, on the other hand, the rate of interest is included as a significant determinant of desired money balances. An obvious point of dispute among some, but not all, advocates of these theories then centers on the empirical significance of the interest rate in the money demand function.[2]

---

[1] We must emphasize that this analysis never goes beyond the realm of statics and thus leaves out much of the richness of the quantity theorists' approach, as represented in Fisher's analysis of transition periods and Friedman's discussion of the monetary transmission mechanism. Furthermore, the assumption of perfect interest inelasticity of the money demand function is made for convenience of exposition and, as shown in Chapter 13, is not absolutely necessary to arrive at the general conclusions presented here.

[2] This issue is considered in detail in Chapters 7 and 8.

The role of the liquidity preference theory in the determination of aggregate income was demonstrated in Chapter 11 through the use of the *LM–IS* curves. That analysis affirmed the feasibility of influencing the level of aggregate income through policies which affect both the money supply and the level of autonomous expenditures. Let us reexamine this model after substituting a quantity theory money demand function for the Keynesian one. In terms of the basic static model, this simply eliminates the interest rate term from the money demand function. Here, as in Chapter 11, we assume that the price level remains constant. Therefore quantities are expressed in dollars of constant purchasing power, and nominal and real values may be assumed to be the same.[3]

The essentials of the analysis of Chapter 11 are reviewed in Figure 11A.1 and in the linear Equations (11A.4) to (11A.9);

the income–expenditures equations:

$$S = S(Y) = -a + sY \qquad (11A.4)$$

$$I = I(i) = a' + hi \qquad (11A.5)$$

$$S = I \qquad (11A.6)$$

the monetary sector equations:

$$M_d = M_1 + M_2 = kY + m + ui \qquad (11A.7)$$

$$M_s = M_0 \qquad (11A.8)$$

$$M_d = M_s. \qquad (11A.9)$$

The necessity for the simultaneous solution of the equilibrium level of income Y_e and the equilibrium rate of interest i_e results from the fact that in both the income–expenditures sector [Equations (11A.4)–(11A.6)] and the monetary sector [Equations (11A.7)–(11A.9)] there are only three equations and four unknowns. In general there must be as many equations as there are unknowns to be able to solve a set of simultaneous linear equations.[4] Since *two* of the four unknowns in each of the markets are the same, however, we may combine the models of each market to derive a complete six equation model in exactly six unknowns (S, I, Y, i, M_d, and M_s). The global model of aggregate demand may be solved for these unknowns. This is demonstrated graphically in Figure 11A.1.

In the present formulation the income–expenditures sector may be represented exactly as above. Therefore, we retain Equations (11A.4)–(11A.6) and we employ the same *IS* curve as in Figure 11A.1. Yet the income–expenditures sector is still

---

[3] Neoclassical models frequently assume, as shown in chapters 13 and 15, that *real* income is constrained to a full employment level, that *real* money balances are demanded, and that *nominal* money balances are supplied and determine the level of *nominal* income. Therefore, the present analysis is firmly Keynesian except for the money demand function.

[4] More specifically, unique solutions for n unknowns can be derived from a system of n linear equations if these equations are consistent, independent, and nonhomogeneous.

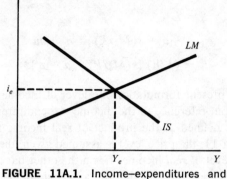

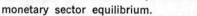

FIGURE 11A.1. Income–expenditures and monetary sector equilibrium.

indeterminate by itself. Equations (11A.4)–(11A.6) can only yield various combinations of Y and i which establish equilibrium in this sector; the equations cannot yield unique solutions for these variables.

Eliminating the liquidity preference equation and substituting a quantity theory relation (specifically, the Cambridge equation) into the monetary sector provides the following set of equations:

$$M_d = k \cdot Y \qquad (11A.7')$$

$$M_s = M_0 \qquad (11A.8)$$

$$M_s = M_d. \qquad (11A.9)$$

With this specification the money market is no longer indeterminate by itself. It is, instead, a separable (segmentable) subsystem. There are now only three unknowns (M_d, M_s, and Y) in these three linear equations, since the interest rate no longer appears in the money demand function. Therefore, rather than deriving an LM curve that relates various possible combinations of Y and i which will establish equilibrium in the money market, we may solve Equations (11A.7'), (11A.8) and (11A.9) directly for a unique level of income:

$$M_s = M_d$$

$$M_0 = k \cdot Y$$

$$Y = M_0/k. \qquad (11A.10)$$

Adding this solution as a fourth equation in the income–expenditures sector [Equations (11A.4)–(11A.6)], we may derive solutions for the remaining unknowns (i, S, and I):

$$S = -a + sY = -a + s(M_0/k)$$

$$S = I$$

$$-a + s(M_0/k) = a' + hi$$

$$i_e = (1/h) [s(M_0/k) - a - a'].[5] \tag{11A.11}$$

Consequently, in the present formulation the level of income is determined by the monetary sector without reference to the income–expenditures sector.

Nominal income is defined as the product of real income and the general price level. If, as in Chapter 11, the price level is assumed given, the solution in Equation (11A.10) is for the level of *real* income. If, on the other hand, the quantity of output is assumed to be determined outside the aggregate demand system, say by the workings of the labor market—aggregate supply sector, the solution for income really represents a solution for the general price level. This situation is examined in detail in Chapter 13.[6] In either case simultaneous methods employing the models of both income–expenditures and monetary sectors are no longer necessary to derive an equilibrium solution for the level of nominal income. Rather, a unique solution for the nominal income variable can be derived from the monetary sector alone. This equilibrium level of nominal income can then be assumed given in the expenditures equations which then yield solution values for the remaining variables ($S, I,$ and i). In this fashion the system of aggregate demand equations is solved *recursively*—one separable subsystem at a time—yielding solutions which then determine equilibrium values in other subsystems.

In the current framework the interest rate serves only to assure equilibrium between saving and investment in the income–expenditures sector. This may be demonstrated graphically (Figure 11A.2).

Figure 11A.2(a) shows that the intersection of the money supply curve (fixed at M_0 by the monetary authority) and the money demand curve determine a unique equilibrium level of income Y_e; that is, given the constant k in the money demand

[5] Equations (11A.10) and (11A.11) are reduced-form equations derived from the structural equations of our model. Each of these equations yields a solution for one of the endogenous variables—variables whose equilibrium values are determined within the model—in terms of parameters and exogenous variables—variables whose value is assumed to be known from outside our model such as the money stock.

[6] In Chapter 13 we shall see that when complete price–wage flexibility is assumed in a neoclassical model, equilibrium in the economy will occur only at full employment. The nominal income level determined in the monetary sector in the model, Y_e, will represent the product of a full-employment level of output O_f, given by the equilibrium level of full employment determined in the labor market, and the equilibrium price level P_e, that is, $Y_e = O_f \cdot P_e$. In effect, then, the monetary sector of the model would serve to determine only the equilibrium price level. However, with the price level assumed constant—as it is in the traditional *LM–IS* analysis—the equilibrium nominal income level Y_e may not represent full employment. In this case the money market serves to determine more than simply the absolute price level. This distinction has important implications for the issue of the neutrality of money discussed in Chapter 15. See Milton Friedman, "A Theoretical Framework for Monetary Analysis," *Journal of Political Economy,* vol. 78 (March/April 1970).

function (or V, the velocity of circulation in Fisher's formulation), there is only one income level, Y_e, which will assure that the public will desire to hold the entire money stock supplied by the monetary authorities. In Figure 11A.2(b) the vertical *LM* curve drawn at the equilibrium level of income determined in part (a) reflects the fact that the level of income is the only variable that can affect conditions in the monetary sector. The interest rate has no influence in that market. The intersection of the *LM–IS* curves serves only to determine the equilibrium interest rate. The level of income is predetermined by the position of the *LM* curve as determined in part (a). Thus the interest rate serves only to induce a level of investment spending sufficient to offset the level of saving that will be forthcoming at the level of income predetermined in the monetary sector.

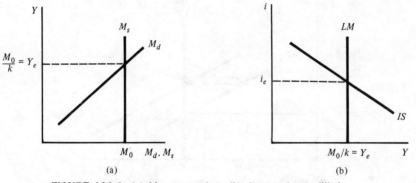

FIGURE 11A.2. (a) Money market. (b) Aggregate equilibrium.

The importance of these conclusions can be seen as follows. Suppose that a change in government taxation or expenditures (fiscal policy) is reflected as a shift in the saving function or the investment demand schedule. This will cause a shift in the *IS* curve.[7] As Figure 11A.3 demonstrates, a shift in the *IS* curve in the present model will affect only the interest rate and not the level of income.

This can also be demonstrated by use of the reduced form equations for the equilibrium interest rate (11A.11) and the equilibrium level of income (11A.10) presented above. Note that since none of the parameters in the expenditures equations (a, a', s, or h) enter the reduced form equation for the equilibrium level of income, no change in these parameters can affect that income level. From Equation (11A.11), however, it is clear that such changes will affect the equilibrium interest rate. Furthermore, as Equation (11A.10) clearly indicates, only changes in the

[7] Government expenditures and taxation do not explicitly appear in the income–expenditures equations (11.4–11.6). A shift in the *IS* curve simply *approximates* the effect of changes in these magnitudes. We shall see in the next chapter that the effect of government expenditures cannot realistically be confined to the *IS* curve.

money supply M_0 or the parameter of the money demand function k can bring about a change in the equilibrium level of income. Consequently, within the present framework autonomous expenditures are powerless to influence the level of aggregate income. Government spending and taxation can only influence the allocation of resources between the government and the private community. Therefore, higher government outlays would not mean greater aggregate income but only less private consumption and investment expenditures. Only a change in money market conditions, such as a change in the supply of money or a change in the parameter k (or V, the velocity of circulation) which would shift the LM curve, can bring about a change in the level of income. In short, only monetary policy instruments can be used effectively to manage the level of aggregate income.

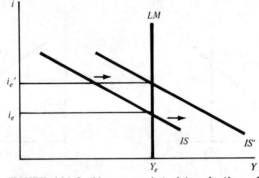

FIGURE 11A.3. Money market determination of the level of income.

For many years Milton Friedman proposed that policymakers deemphasize fiscal policy and concentrate primarily on monetary policy. Nevertheless, he did not approve of monetary policy as it had been conducted. He felt and continues to feel that our knowledge of the time lags involved in monetary processes and of the "transmission mechanism" through which monetary changes affect the economy is much too limited for us to manage the economy on a day-to-day or even month-to-month basis.[8] He is convinced that the acceleration or deceleration of the rate of

[8] *See* Milton Friedman and Anna Schwartz, "Money and Business Cycles," Conference on the State of Monetary Economics, *Review of Economics and Statistics,* Supplement (February 1963); and Milton Friedman, "The Lag Effect in Monetary Policy," *Journal of Political Economy* (October 1961), 447–466; and "The Role of Monetary Policy," *American Economic Review,* vol. 58 (March 1968), 1–17. For a survey of lag effects see Michael J. Hamburger, "The Lag Effect in Monetary Policy: A Survey of the Recent Literature," *Monetary Aggregates and Monetary Policy,* Federal Reserve Bank of New York (1974). The role of acceleration and deceleration of money supply growth as a causal factor in economic fluctuations is discussed

growth of the money supply, rather than other factors such as shifts in the demand for money, is a key cause of economic instability. Hence he proposes that we simply establish a fixed rule for the monetary authority to follow: increase the money supply at a steady, predetermined rate; he suggests 3–5% per year—the approximate long term growth rate of real income—as an appropriate range. He would hope by this technique to induce a steady increase in the level of aggregate income with minimum disturbance caused by fluctuating federal taxation and expenditures levels. In recent years Federal Reserve policy has paid increasing attention to the need for stable money supply growth.

This discussion indicates the importance of the dispute over the role of interest rates in the public's money demand behavior. A great deal of empirical work has been carried out to provide information on this question. Most of the studies have taken the form of regression analysis, in which money balances are the dependent variables and various interest rates, measures of income, and measures of wealth are independent variables. Though Friedman's work supports the neoclassical quantity theory tradition, many investigators do not agree with his interpretation of his results. As revealed in Chapter 7, most empirical studies indicate that the interest rate is an important argument in the money demand function and that variations in the quantity of money balances demanded can be more completely explained by assigning a critical role to the interest rate. More importantly, other empirical results indicate that *both* monetary and fiscal measures have some role to play in the array of policy tools with which the government can manage the aggregate economy.[9]

---

in Chapter 15. Controversy over the statistical stability of the demand for money is discussed on pages 212–216 of Chapter 8.

[9] For the results of some interesting tests carried out to measure the relative effectiveness of monetary and fiscal actions in stabilization policies, see Frank de Leeuw and Edward M. Gramlich, "The Channels of Monetary Policy: A Further Report on the Federal Reserve MIT Model," *Journal of Finance,* vol. 24, no. 2 (May 1966), 265–290; Leonall C. Andersen and Keith M. Carlson, "St. Louis Model Revisited," *International Economic Review,* vol. 15, no. 2 (June 1974), 305–327; Dan M. Bechter, "Money and Inflation," Federal Reserve Bank of Kansas City, *Monthly Review* (July/August 1973), 3–6; David Fand, "Some Issues in Monetary Economics: Fiscal Policy Assumptions and Related Multipliers," *Review,* Federal Reserve Bank of St. Louis (January 1970), 23–27; Raymond E. Lombra and Raymond G. Torto, "Measuring the Impact of Monetary and Fiscal Actions: A New Look at the Specification Problem," *Review of Economics and Statistics,* vol. 56, no. 1 (February 1974), 104–107.

For a survey of opinions concerning the importance of the monetary authority's attempts to keep money supply growth rates within certain preannounced ranges, see Thomas Mayer, "A Money Stock Target," *Monetary Policy Oversight,* Hearings before the Committee on Banking, Housing, and Urban Affairs, U.S. Senate, 94th Congress, 1st Session (1975), 179–186 and Milton Friedman "Statement on the Conduct of Monetary Policy," and Paul A. Samuelson, "Statement on the Conduct of Monetary Policy," both in *Second Meeting on the Conduct of Monetary Policy,* Hearings before the Committee on Banking, Housing, and Urban Affairs, U.S. Senate, 94th Congress, 1st Session (1975), 42–55.

All of the articles cited above are reprinted in Havrilesky and Boorman, *op. cit.* A survey of empirical tests of the demand for money function appears in Chapters 7 and 8.

BIBLIOGRAPHY FOR CHAPTER 11

ANDERSEN, LEONALL C., and KEITH M. CARLSON, "St. Louis Model Revisited," *International Economic Review,* vol. 15, no. 2 (June 1974), 305–327.*

ANDO, A., and STEPHEN GOLDFELD, "An Econometric Model for Evaluating Stabilization Policies," *Studies in Economic Stabilization,* Albert Ando, Edgar C. Brown, and Ann Friedlander, eds. (Washington, DC: The Brookings Institution, 1968), 215–287.

BECHTER, DAN M., "Money and Inflation," Federal Reserve Bank of Kansas City, *Monthly Review* (July/August 1973), 3–6.*

BRUNNER, KARL, "The Role of Money and Monetary Policy," *Review,* Federal Reserve Bank of St. Louis, vol. 50 (July 1968), 9–24.

BUDD, EDWARD C., "Note on Money, Interest, and Income" (unpublished).

CAGEN, PHILLIP, "Current Issues in the Theory of Monetary Policy," in *Patterns of Market Behavior: Essays in Honor of Philip Taft,* Michael J. Brennan, ed. (Providence, RI: Brown University Press, 1965), 135–154.

CHOW, GREGORY, "Multiplier, Accelerator and Liquidity Preference in the Determination of the National Income of the United States," *Review of Economics and Statistics* (February 1967), 1–15.

DE LEEUW, FRANK, and EDWARD M. GRAMLICH, "The Channels of Monetary Policy: A Further Report on the Federal Reserve MIT Model," *Journal of Finance,* vol. 24, no. 2 (May 1966), 265–290.*

FAND, DAVID, "Some Issues in Monetary Economics: Fiscal Policy Assumptions and Related Multipliers," *Review,* Federal Reserve Bank of St. Louis (January 1970), 23–27.*

FRIEDMAN, MILTON, "The Lag Effect in Monetary Policy," *Journal of Political Economy* (October 1961), 447–466.

———, "The Role of Monetary Policy," *American Economic Review,* vol. 58 (March 1968), 1–17.

———, "Statement on the Conduct of Monetary Policy," *Second Meeting on the Conduct of Monetary Policy,* Hearings before the Committee on Banking, Housing, and Urban Affairs, U.S. Senate, 94th Congress, 1st Session (1975), 42–55.*

———, "A Theoretical Framework for Monetary Analysis," *Journal of Political Economy,* vol. 78 (March/April 1970).

FRIEDMAN, MILTON, and ANNA SCHWARTZ, "Money and Business Cycles," Conference on the State of Monetary Economics, *Review of Economics and Statistics,* Supplement (February 1963).

HAMBURGER, MICHAEL J., "The Lag Effect in Monetary Policy: A Survey of the Recent Literature," *Monetary Aggregates and Monetary Policy,* Federal Reserve Bank of New York (1974).*

HANSEN, ALVIN H., *A Guide to Keynes* (New York: McGraw-Hill, 1953).

HICKS, JOHN R., "Mr. Keynes and the 'Classics,' A Suggested Interpretation," *Econometrica,* vol. 5 (1937), 147–159.

* Reprinted in THOMAS H. HAVRILESKY and JOHN T. BOORMAN, *Current Issues in Monetary Theory and Policy* (Arlington Heights, IL.: AHM Publishing Corporation, 1976).

KLEIN, LAWRENCE, *The Keynesian Revolution* (New York: Macmillan, 1947).

LEIJONHUFVUD, AXEL, *On Keynesian Economics and the Economics of Keynes* (New York: Oxford University Press, 1968).

LOMBRA, RAYMOND E., and RAYMOND G. TORTO, "Measuring the Impact of Monetary and Fiscal Actions: A New Look at the Specific Problem," *Review of Economics and Statistics,* vol. 56, no. 1 (February 1974), 104–107.*

MAYER, THOMAS, "A Money Stock Target," *Monetary Policy Oversight,* Hearings before the Committee on Banking, Housing and Urban Affairs, U.S. Senate, 94th Congress, 1st Session (1975), 179–186.*

RITTER, LAWRENCE, "The Role of Money in Keynesian Theory," in *Banking and Monetary Studies,* Deane Carson, ed. (Homewood, IL: Richard D. Irwin, 1963), 134–150.

SAMUELSON, PAUL A., "Statement on the Conduct of Monetary Policy," *Second Meeting on the Conduct of Monetary Policy,* Hearings before the Committee on Banking, Housing, and Urban Affairs, U.S. Senate, 94th Congress, 1st Session (1975), 42–55.*

SCOTT, ROBERT H., "Estimates of Hicksian *IS* and *LM* Curves for the United States," *Journal of Finance,* vol. 21 (September 1966), 479–487.

* Reprinted in THOMAS H. HAVRILESKY and JOHN T. BOORMAN, *Current Issues in Monetary Theory and Policy* (Arlington Heights, IL.: AHM Publishing Corporation, 1976).

The Government Sector in Macroeconomic Models: The Financing Constraint, The Balance Sheet Identity, and Crowding Out

Introduction

In the preceding chapter the concepts of an income–expenditures sector equilibrium *IS* curve and a monetary sector equilibrium *LM* curve were developed. The effects of changes in autonomous expenditures and the supply of nominal money on the equilibrium level of real income were explored. Nevertheless, that model cannot be considered an accurate representation of reality for at least two fundamental reasons. First, it completely ignored the relationships between stocks and flows, the financing constraint, developed in Chapter 9. Second, it assumed that the price level, also discussed in Chapter 9, was constant. In the present chapter the financing constraint is introduced into the *LM–IS* model. In following chapters the assumption of constant price and nominal wage levels will be relaxed.

In most macroeconomics textbooks government expenditures are depicted as having an effect only on the *IS* curve. Nevertheless, our examination of the flow of income and expenditures in Chapter 9 indicates that this practice is misleading. In any sector of the economy the difference between that sector's income and its expenditures is constrained to be financed by its changing its net claims on other sectors. For example, the financing of the government sector's deficit may be viewed as leading to an increase in government debt claims held by the private sector.[1] If we assume that private individuals view these claims as increasing their wealth, then the financing of government deficits could have effects on private consumption expenditures and the private demand for money. Through this mechanism the financing of government expenditures can affect the monetary sector as well as the income–expenditures sector.

Let us elaborate. Government expenditures must be financed either by an increase in taxation or by issuance of government interest bearing or noninterest bearing debt. As discussed in Chapter 9, national income accounting relations show that an increase in taxation will initially reduce private disposable income. In Chapter 10 a reduction in disposable income was seen to reduce private consumption expenditures. In the present chapter an increase in autonomous taxation matched by a rise in autonomous government expenditures will therefore have two effects on the *IS* curve. First, the increase in autonomous taxation will cause the *IS* curve to shift leftward reflecting the decrease in consumption expenditures. This partially offsets the second effect—the increase in autonomous government expenditures which will cause the *IS* curve to shift to the right.

A hike in government spending financed by the government increasing its outstanding stock of interest bearing debt rather than by increasing taxation will also have two effects on the *IS* curve. First, as in the case of tax-financed expenditures, the increase in autonomous government expenditures will make the *IS* curve shift to the right. Second, the increase in government debt is assumed to raise the nonhuman wealth of the private sector.[2] An increase in private nonhuman wealth, as discussed in Chapter 10, will have a stimulative effect on the level of private consumption expenditures. This, too, will shift the *IS* curve to the right.

However, debt-financed government spending could also affect the *LM* curve. On the one hand, an increase in privately held government debt could increase the demand for money, as individuals seek to maintain a desired proportion of bonds to money in their portfolios. This would cause the *LM* curve to shift leftward. On the other hand, if the government sector finances its deficit by issuing noninterest bearing debt (money), the supply of money would increase and the *LM* curve would shift rightward. With *LM* and *IS* curves both shifting, determining the magnitude of the multiplier effect is not as simple a matter as it appeared to be in Chapter 11 and closer inspection is required.

Recognition of a *government financing constraint* in our model is the first order

[1] A deficit can also be financed by a reduction in the deficit sector's asset holdings; a surplus can be disposed of by reducing its outstanding debt claims or by increasing its assets.

[2] The basis of this postulate is discussed in footnote 5 of Chapter 9 and page 315 of this chapter (including footnotes).

of business.[3] Because any change in the size of government debt in private hands affects private wealth, the *balance sheet identity* of the private sector must also be made explicit.[4] In this fashion a fairly realistic comprehension of the effect of government spending will be gained. In particular, an attempt will be made to understand the extent to which government spending "crowds out" private expenditures in the Keynesian model.[5]

A Stock-Flow Model of Aggregate Demand

We shall assume, as in the previous chapter, that the nominal wage and general price levels are constant. Therefore, the only adjustments to changes in aggregate demand are *quantity* (of output) rather than *price level* adjustments. We shall further assume, as in the previous chapter, a less than fully employed economy in which sufficient time elapses between equilibria in order for the multipliers to attain their full, short-run (comparative static) equilibrium values.

In order to facilitate analysis let us modify the basic model of aggregate demand to reflect explicitly the interrelated existence of government expenditures, government taxation and government indebtedness together with the effect of wealth on consumption (and saving) and on the demand for money (and bonds).

The revised model of aggregate demand may be presented as follows:

$$S = -a + sY_d + vW \tag{12.1'}$$

$$I = a' + hi \tag{12.2}$$

$$S + T = I + G \tag{12.3'}$$

$$M_d = kY + m + ui + zW \tag{12.4'}$$

$$M_s = M_0 \tag{12.5}$$

$$M_s = M_d \tag{12.6}$$

---

[3] This derives from Carl Christ, "A Simple Macroeconomic Model with a Government Budget Constraint," *Journal of Political Economy* (January 1968). It was explained earlier in Richard Musgrave's *The Theory of Public Finance* (McGraw-Hill, 1956).

[4] This concept is nicely expressed in William Brainard and James Tobin, "Pitfalls in Financial Model Building," *American Economic Review, Proceedings* (May 1968).

[5] Two articles with significant impact in this area are William Silber, "Fiscal Policy in *IS–LM* Analysis: A Correction," *Journal of Money, Credit and Banking* (November 1970), and Laurence H. Meyer, "The Balance Sheet Identity, the Government Financing Constraint and the Crowding Out Effect," *Journal of Monetary Economics* (January 1975). The original discussion seems to have been Abba Lerner's, "The Burden of the Public Debt," in *Income, Employment and Public Policy* (New York: W. W. Norton, 1948). Increased crowding out is said to occur when increases in wealth brought about by a bond-financed government deficit cause the demand for money to rise, inducing an increase in the market rate of interest. This, in turn, causes private investment to decrease. A useful survey of the crowding out literature is contained in Roger W. Spencer and Keith Carlson, "Crowding Out and Its Critics," *Review*, Federal Reserve Bank of St. Louis (December 1975), reprinted in Thomas Havrilesky and John Boorman, *Current Issues in Monetary Theory and Policy, op. cit.*

$$W \equiv M + V \tag{12.7}$$
$$(G - T) = \Delta V + \Delta M \tag{12.8}$$
$$Y_d \equiv Y - T \tag{12.9}$$
$$T = \bar{T} \tag{12.10}$$
$$G = \bar{G} \tag{12.11}$$

where a, a', $\bar{G}$, $\bar{T}$, m, $M_0 > 0$; h, $u < 0$; $-1 < v < 0$ and $0 < z$, k, $s < 1$. (A prime on an equation number signifies that it is a modified version of a similar equation used in Chapter 11.) A bar over a variable indicates that the value assumed by that variable is taken to be determined outside the model (that is, exogenously determined). The new variables are

W = the nonhuman wealth of the private sector[6]
T = the level of taxation
G = government spending
V = the outstanding stock of government interest bearing debt.

Equation (12.1'), the saving relation, is modified to express saving as an increasing linear function of disposable income ($Y_d \equiv Y - T$) and a decreasing linear function of nonhuman wealth W. For simplicity the effect of the market rate of interest is suppressed.

Let us examine the relationship between saving and wealth more closely. The aggregate budget identity, discussed in Chapter 9, requires that saving plus consumption be identically equal to disposable personal income. (The budget identity makes one of the two behavioral relations, either the saving function or the consumption function, redundant.) In Chapter 10 we saw that consumption expenditures vary positively with wealth. If current disposable income is defined not to vary with nonhuman wealth,[7] then as consumption increases, saving must decrease (that is, the parameter v is negative). Moreover, this parameter, reflecting the relationship between the level of wealth and the level of saving, is also constrained to be greater than minus unity (that is, an *increase* in wealth will induce a decrease in current saving but that decrease will not be larger in absolute terms than the causative change in wealth). As shown in Chapter 10, individuals will never increase their consumption expenditures in a single period (decrease their saving) by more than the increase in their stock of wealth during that period.

Equation (12.2), the investment expenditures relation, is unchanged from the previous chapter. Equation (12.3'), the income–expenditures equilibrium condition,

[6] An individual's nonhuman wealth is the discounted present value of the future income stream to be received from his stock of physical and financial assets. Although individuals may also invest in themselves, human capital investments are not considered in the present model; only nonhuman wealth is included. The use of an expanded definition of wealth would increase the importance of the wealth argument in our saving function. See Chapter 10 for further discussion.

[7] Many theories of consumption exclude current income from the definition of nonhuman wealth. See, for example, the Modigliani and Ando treatment in Chapter 10.

is modified to recognize the existence of an additional type of "injection," government spending G, into the spending stream and an additional "leakage," government taxation T, from the spending stream.[8]

Equation (12.4') is the money demand relation, modified to reflect the positive effect of wealth W on the quantity of money balances demanded. The relevance of wealth in the money demand relation was pointed out in Chapters 4 and 8. The greater one's wealth, the greater are one's desired holdings of money balances. The parameter z is less than unity because an individual is assumed never to increase his money balances by more than the increase in his wealth.[9] Equation (12.5), the money supply relation, and Equation (12.6), the money market equilibrium condition, are unchanged from the previous chapter.

Equations (12.7) through (12.11) are new to the analysis. Equation (12.7) is the definition of net nonhuman wealth held by the private sector. The first term in this definition is the stock of money issued by government and held by the public (outside money). It does not include deposits issued by banks (inside money) on the assumption that, while these deposits are assets of depositors, they represent liabilities of bank stockholders and, therefore, cancel out in the definition of private wealth.[10]

The second term V in the definition of wealth is the value of the interest bearing debt of government. Bonds issued by and held in the private sector are not part of aggregate wealth because the private bond *issuer's* liability is canceled out by the private bond *holder's* asset. To simplify the analysis we assume that the government bonds included in this measure have a fixed nominal price of $1 and a variable coupon. This permits us to ignore the interest-induced changes in the market value of wealth that are associated with fixed coupon–variable price bonds.[11]

---

[8] As discussed in Chapters 9 and 10, another way of expressing the equilibrium condition is $C + I + G = Y$. Where aggregate income is, by definition, either consumed or saved or taxed away, $Y \equiv C + S + T$, this condition becomes $C + I + G = C + S + T$, which is rewritten as Equation (12.3)', $I + G = S + T$.

[9] This is discussed at greater length below. In a world of more than two assets it is not strictly necessary that the demand for money vary positively with wealth; the portfolio decision could result in money demand reactions to increases in wealth that cause the *LM* curve to shift rightward instead of leftward as shown below. For example, if the third asset is short-term bonds and if these are very close substitutes for money, an increase in the supply of short-term bonds, *ceteris paribus*, may *reduce* the demand for money. See James Tobin, "An Essay in the Principles of Debt Management," *Fiscal and Debt Management Policies*, Commission on Money and Credit (Englewood Cliffs, NJ: Prentice-Hall, 1963) and Yung Chul Park, "Some Current Issues in the Transmission Process of Monetary Policy," *Staff Papers*, International Monetary Fund (March 1972). The latter is reprinted in Havrilesky and Boorman, *op. cit.*

[10] This question is examined in greater detail in Chapter 15.

[11] If we assume, for simplicity, that this type of bond is a perpetuity bond or consol, the formula for its price (taken from Chapter 5) is $PV = Y(1/i)$, where Y is the nominal interest return paid on the bond. We assume all bonds are fixed price–variable coupon bonds. If the market rate of interest i changes, the dollar value of coupon payments Y changes in the same proportion such that the nominal price of the bond PV is fixed. For fixed coupon bonds the nominal price would vary inversely with the market rate of interest and every time the market rate of interest changes, the nominal market value of the bond changes. The latter type

Crucial to this analysis is the assumption that government debt is part of the non-human wealth of the private sector. In this view the purposes of public expenditures are seen by the public as being related to the way those expenditures are financed. This suggests that tax financing and debt financing of government expenditures have different *ex ante* effects on consumption. Tax financing of expenditures displaces private consumption because it reduces disposable income but debt financing of government expenditures stimulates consumption because it increases private wealth. This is implicit in the formulation of the behavioral relations of the model presented above.[12]

There is no reason to assume that in an underemployed economy debt-financed government spending will displace or crowd out private investment, *ex ante.* However, it may do so *ex post,* and this is what the present model shall determine.[13] Nevertheless, regardless of what the *ex post* equilibrium effects are, in the initial equilibrium we assume that the public views an increase in government debt as an addition to its nonhuman wealth.[14]

The *balance sheet identity* tells us that an increase in wealth must be held as either bonds or money. (The value of the private capital stock is not included in the

---

of bond would unnecessarily complicate our analysis. An example of a fixed price–variable coupon "bond" in the private sector is a savings account.

[12] If taxes increase, disposable income declines, inducing a decrease in *both* saving and consumption; if wealth increases because of deficit financing by the government, saving declines, but consumption increases.

[13] The ability of debt financed government spending to stimulate aggregate demand and thereby to increase income is irrelevant to the public's view that government debt is wealth. In fact, later in this chapter we expand the definition of wealth to include the private capital stock. There we shall see that while debt financed government expenditures stimulate the level of income, they nevertheless reduce the private capital stock.

Our model will ignore both the government's own factor demands and the private consumption benefits of government purchases of goods and services. A complete analysis of the crowding out phenomenon would require attention to these effects. A number of papers have explored these issues and are surveyed in George M. von Furstenberg and Burton G. Malkiel, "The Government and Capital Formation: A Survey of Recent Issues," *Journal of Economic Literature*, vol. 15 (September 1977), 835–878.

[14] One view has been that if individuals anticipate increased future tax liabilities to pay the interest and transactions costs of funding and refunding the debt, this debt will, on balance, have no value in terms of aggregate private wealth, that is, the discounted present value of future interest payments is more than offset by the discounted present value of future tax payments. A somewhat more moderate assertion has been that government-issued financial assets represent net private wealth only to the extent that future costs are discounted at a higher rate than the future benefits. See Don Patinkin, *Money, Interest and Prices,* 2nd ed. (New York: Harper and Row, 1965), ch. 12. Robert Barro has argued that unless government debt generates unique efficiencies in the economy, future benefits in excess of cost will not be perceived. Robert Barro, "Are Government Bonds Wealth," *Journal of Political Economy,* vol. 82 (November/December 1974).

Analogous to debt financed private capital formation, if the present value of the expected increase in future income exceeds the present value of expected future liabilities, the private sector perceives the debt financed activity as generating wealth. The view in the present chapter is that individuals see debt financed government expenditures as generating future benefits for the economy in excess of future interest and transactions costs. This issue is also discussed in footnote 5, page 228 and footnote 29, page 329.

definition of wealth until later in the chapter.) Any change in the demand for money brought about by a change in the level of income or the rate of interest with total wealth unchanged must be exactly offset by a change in the demand for bonds of equal size but in the opposite direction. These "adding up" conditions indicate that the bond and money markets are not independent. When equilibrium exists in one market, by definition the other must also be in equilibrium. Therefore, in developing models of the financial sector we do not have to write equations for both markets. The *balance sheet constraint* makes one of the asset markets redundant.[15]

Equation (12.8) indicates that any government deficit $(G - T)$ must be matched by either an increase in interest bearing debt ΔV or an increase in noninterest bearing debt, outside money, ΔM. This *financing constraint* for the government sector requires that government expenditures be financed by some combination of tax receipts and issuance of government liabilities. A financing constraint for the private sector is included later in the chapter. The government financing constraint translates the change in the *flow* of government expenditures less taxation over a time interval into the change in the *stock* of wealth that occurs over the same interval.

We shall assume that we are starting from a long-run balanced budget equilibrium. In initial long-run equilibrium no additions are being made to wealth. This reflects the exclusion of the capital stock (and changes in that capital stock through net investment) from wealth in the present model. Given a change in government (deficit) expenditures and a related change in wealth, the economy will no longer be in long-run equilibrium. The new equilibrium will be a short-run one in which both the income–expenditures sector and the monetary sector of the aggregate

---

[15] This can easily be proven. Assume a demand for bonds $V_d = V_d(Y, i, W)$ and a demand for money $M_d = M_d(Y, i, W)$. Since by the balance sheet identity private wealth is defined as bonds plus money, it must be held in either of these two forms. Substituting these demand functions into the private balance sheet identity, Equation (12.7), yields

$$M + V = V_d + M_d$$

and rearranging yields

$$M - M_d = V_d - V$$

which shows that the two asset markets are not independent; an excess supply (demand) for money must be identically equal to an excess demand (supply) of bonds. If any of the three variables, i, Y or W, change, these asset demands will change. However, the above balance sheet identity tells us that any change in the demand for money caused by a change in the level of income or the interest rate, *ceteris paribus*, must be offset by an equal but opposite change in the demand for bonds ($\partial M_d/\partial i = -\partial V_d/\partial i$ and $\partial M_d/\partial Y = -\partial V_d/\partial Y$) because neither a change in the interest rate nor a change in the level of income will change the supplies of either asset as the current model is formulated.

The balance sheet constraint also requires that, for a given level of income and a given interest rate, any change in the demand for money caused by a change in wealth *plus* any change in the demand for bonds caused by a change in wealth must equal the change in wealth (that is, $\partial V_d/\partial W + \partial M_d/\partial W = 1$).

One can deduce from these "adding up" conditions that in Y, i space a bond market equilibrium curve must be identical to the money market equilibrium curve. When other interest-, income-, or wealth-sensitive assets are introduced into the definition of wealth, such as equities and consumer durables, the two curves will not generally be identical. See Don Patinkin, *op. cit.*

demand *LM–IS* model attain new, mutually consistent positions. We shall not go beyond a one-period time interval to consider the long-run effects of continued financing of the government's deficit at the new short-run equilibrium level of income.[16]

Equation (12.9) is the definition of disposable personal income Y_d as aggregate income Y less net taxation by government T. We do not explicitly include the interest payments of government on its outstanding debt in the definition of disposable income.

In Chapter 9 the budget identity of the government sector was defined as government spending plus government transfer payments minus government taxation equal government deficit or surplus. In the present model we shall assume that government transfer payments to households consist only of interest payments on the government debt and that lump-sum tax revenues are always varied to cover these payments such that autonomous taxation minus government interest payments is constant. Thereby variations in the interest rate affect neither disposable income nor the size of the government's deficit. Equations (12.10) and (12.11) indicate that we assume that both government spending and taxation are given.[17]

To derive the *IS* curve substitute Equation (12.10) into (12.9) and the result into Equation (12.1′). Then take this result and substitute it with Equations (12.2) and (12.11) into (12.3′):

$$Y = \frac{a + a' - vW - (1 - s)\bar{T} + \bar{G}}{s} + \frac{h}{s} i. \tag{12.12}$$

Compared to the *IS* curve [Equation (11.4)] in Chapter 11, there are a few new terms in the intercept of this *IS* curve. Government expenditures G are treated simply as another component of total autonomous expenditures. Government taxation may be viewed as negative autonomous expenditures; the effect of autonomous taxation is to *reduce* autonomous consumption by $(1 - s)$ times the level of that taxation.

[16] Only in long-run equilibrium will the government's budget be balanced. Unless additional taxation is induced by the rise in income, there is no reason to believe that the deficit will disappear as income rises. Therefore, in models without induced taxation the long-run equilibrium effect of a change in government expenditures is zero. In models with induced taxation, income must rise sufficiently to induce added tax receipts to match the increase in government expenditures. See Carl Christ, *op. cit.;* and Robert M. Solow and Allan S. Blinder, "Does Fiscal Policy Matter?" *Journal of Public Economics,* vol. 2 (1973), 319–337, reprinted in Havrilesky and Boorman, *op. cit.*

[17] In slightly more complicated models of the income–expenditures sector the level of taxation may be more realistically viewed as an increasing function of the level of income. These and other more complicated leakages from the spending stream such as induced business saving (retained earnings) are omitted in order to focus on the financial sector of the present model. The introduction of induced leakages would have an effect on the short-run multipliers of the present model similar to that of an increase in the marginal propensity to save s. The presence of induced leakages, such as induced taxation and induced business saving (retained earnings), can readily be seen to reduce the magnitude of the short-run fiscal and monetary policy multipliers.

Another new variable in this equation for the *IS* curve is the level of private wealth. As discussed in Chapter 9 and earlier in this chapter, an increase in wealth raises the level of consumption and, assuming current income remains unchanged as that increase in wealth occurs, reduces the level of saving.

The *IS* relation indicates that an increase in private wealth, *ceteris paribus,* will shift the *IS* curve to the *right* by $\Delta W(-v/s)$. An increase in autonomous taxation, *ceteris paribus,* will shift the *IS* curve to the *left* by $\Delta T(-(1-s)/s)$ and an increase in government spending, *ceteris paribus,* will shift the *IS* curve to the *right* by $\Delta G(1/s)$. The directions of these shifts follow from the magnitude of the parameters, $0 < s < 1$, $-1 < v < 0$. The economic reasoning behind any shift in the *IS* curve was discussed in the previous chapter.

By substituting Equations (12.4') and (12.5) into (12.6) and rearranging terms, we derive the *LM* curve:

$$Y = \frac{M_0 - m - zW}{k} - \frac{u}{k}\ i. \tag{12.13}$$

Compared to the previous chapter the only new variable here is the level of private wealth. An increase in the level of private wealth at an unchanged rate of interest will shift the *LM* curve to the *left* by $\Delta W(-z/k)$. The direction of this shift follows from the magnitude of the parameters, $0 < k,z < 1$. The economic reasoning behind a shift in the *LM* curve and all of the other properties of the *LM* and *IS* curves were discussed in the previous chapter.[18]

The solution for the equilibrium level of aggregate income is

$$Y = \frac{u(a + a' - vW - (1-s)\bar{T} + \bar{G}) + h(M_0 - m - zW)}{su + hk} \tag{12.14}$$

subject to

$$(G - T) = \Delta V + \Delta M, \tag{12.8}$$

the government financing constraint.

Fiscal Policy I: Financing Increases in Government Expenditures by Raising Taxes

An increase in autonomous government spending matched by an increase in autonomous taxation (an incrementally "balanced budget") will have the following effect:

[18] If we were to assume that government bonds are fixed coupon-variable price bonds (instead of fixed price–variable coupon bonds), any change on the market rate of interest would change the *intercepts and slopes* of the *LM* and *IS* curves. This would occur because any change in the interest rate would also change the market value of the outstanding government debt and this would, in turn, change the market value of wealth in the private sector. The result would be nonlinear relations that would greatly complicate our model. Therefore in the present chapter we abstract from these "interest-induced" wealth effects.

$$\Delta Y = \left(\frac{u}{su + hk}\right)\Delta \bar{G} - \left(\frac{(1-s)u}{su + hk}\right)\Delta \bar{T}. \qquad (12.15)$$

The first product on the right-hand side measures the positive effect of an increase in government expenditures on aggregate income. The second product measures the negative effect of an increase in autonomous taxation on consumption expenditures and, hence, on aggregate income. Since $\Delta \bar{G} = \Delta \bar{T}$ by the assumption of an incrementally balanced budget, we rearrange Equation (12.15) to get

$$\frac{\Delta Y}{\Delta G} = \left(\frac{su}{su + hk}\right). \qquad (12.16)$$

The net effect on income is positive but rather small compared to the size of the autonomous expenditures multiplier discussed in Chapter 11. Because $0 < s < 1$, the autonomous expenditures multiplier for a balanced budget, while positive, is less than the simple autonomous expenditures multiplier discussed in Chapter 11, $u/(su + hk)$.

Moreover, it can be seen that the multiplier in Equation (12.16) is less than unity. In Chapter 10 it was demonstrated that the autonomous expenditures multiplier, where the interest rate was assumed constant, was $1/s$; the autonomous taxation multiplier was $-(1-s)/s$; and the balanced budget multiplier was $s/s = 1$. In Chapter 11, where the interest rate could vary, the autonomous expenditures multiplier was $u/(su + hk) = 1/(s + (hk)/u)$, which is less than $1/s$ since $hk/u > 0$. But since

$$\frac{1}{s + hk/u} < \frac{1}{s}$$

it is clear that

$$\frac{s}{s + hk/u} < \frac{s}{s} = 1.$$

Therefore,

$$\frac{su}{su + hk} < 1.$$

This results from the fact that the increase in taxation crowds out private consumption expenditures, and the rise in the interest rate brought about by the increase in aggregate income generates even further crowding out of private investment expenditures. Consequently, the overall rise in income is less than the increase in government expenditures. This is shown in Figure 12.1.

Here the increase in government expenditures is reflected in the shift from *IS* to

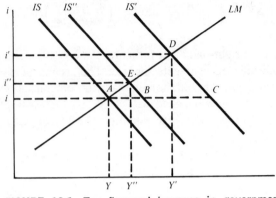

FIGURE 12.1. Tax financed increase in government expenditures.

IS'. With the interest rate unchanged at i, this would result in a move from A to C; the multiplier would be $1/s$. A rise in taxation in the same amount is reflected in the shift from IS' to IS''. With the interest rate constant this would result in a move from C to B; the multiplier would be $-(1-s)/s$. The balanced budget rise in government expenditures with no change in the interest rate is reflected in the shift from IS to IS''. This would result in a "net" move from A to B; the balanced budget multiplier would be $(1/s) - [(1-s)/s] = s/s = 1$.[19]

In the LM–IS model, however, the interest rate is not constant. Therefore, when IS shifts to IS', equilibrium is at D and income rises only from Y to Y'. The simple autonomous expenditures multiplier is $u/(su + hk)$. Moreover, in the LM–IS model when IS' shifts to IS'', equilibrium is at E and income falls from Y' to Y''; the autonomous taxation multiplier is $-(1-s)u/(su+hk)$. The "net" shift from IS to IS'', therefore, generates an increase in income from Y to Y''; the balanced budget multiplier is $su/(su+hk)$.

Fiscal Policy II: Financing Increases in Government Expenditures by Increasing Government's Interest Bearing Debt

An increase in autonomous government expenditures financed entirely by an increase in the level of government interest bearing debt outstanding V will increase G as well as W.[20] The effect on real income occurs because government issues bonds

---

[19] The balanced budget multiplier was examined in detail in Chapter 10, pages 254–256.

[20] Deficit financing by the government absorbs private saving and increases private wealth. Whether this consequently crowds out private investment expenditures *ex post* is problematic. David and Scadding take the view that crowding out occurs *ex ante* because the

to the private sector and spends the proceeds of the bond sale on goods and services in the, assumed underemployed, economy. The total effect on income from Equation 12.14 is

$$\Delta Y = \Delta G \left(\frac{u}{su + hk} \right) + \Delta W \left(\frac{-vu}{su + hk} \right) + \Delta W \left(\frac{-hz}{su + hk} \right) \quad (12.17)$$

The first product on the right-hand side measures the positive effect of an increase in government expenditures on income. The second term in this product is identical to the autonomous expenditures multiplier of the previous chapter. The second product measures the positive wealth–expenditures effect of an increase in wealth on income. (The rise in wealth causes an increase in consumption expenditures which stimulates a rise in the level of income.) The third product on the right-hand side of Equation (12.17) captures the negative monetary effect of an increase in wealth on income. (The rise in wealth engenders an increase in the demand for money, which causes the interest rate to rise, the level of investment to fall and the level of income to decline.)

Since $\Delta G = \Delta W$ we can collect terms:

$$\frac{\Delta Y}{\Delta G} = \frac{u(1 - v)}{su + hk} - \frac{hz}{su + hk}. \quad (12.18)$$

The bond financed government expenditures multiplier[21] has two components. The first term is the total expenditures effect, combining the autonomous expenditures effect and the wealth (induced consumption) expenditures effect. The second term is the monetary effect.

In the previous chapter it was shown that both the autonomous expenditures and monetary multipliers are positive,

$$\frac{u}{su + hk} \text{ and } \frac{h}{su + hk} > 0.$$

Now since wealth has a positive effect on consumption (a negative effect on saving), that is, $-1 < v < 0$, the total expenditures effect is even greater in magnitude than the autonomous expenditures multiplier of the previous chapter:

---

public anticipates a reduction in private investment. See Paul A. David and John L. Scadding, "Private Savings: Ultrarationality, Aggregation and 'Denison's Law'," *Journal of Political Economy*, vol. 82, (March/April 1974). The David and Scadding perspective, as well as other views on crowding out, are surveyed in Spencer and Carlson, *op. cit.*

[21] The comparative static multipliers of this chapter all assume that the government begins from a balanced budget equilibrium and the economy fully adjusts to that initial change in G and the associated first-period financing, all in the first period. The multipliers so derived do not represent the full multiperiod effect, since the economy cannot be in full equilibrium unless all budgets are balanced.

$$\frac{u(1 - v)}{su + hk} > \frac{u}{su + hk}$$

since $1 - v > 1$. In short, a debt financed increase in government expenditures shifts the *IS* curve further to the right than in models which disregard the effect of an increase in private holdings of government debt on consumption expenditures.

In the present model a rise in nonhuman wealth increases the demand for money. This means that the monetary effect of an increase in wealth on income will be negative,

$$\frac{-hz}{su + hk} < 0,$$

since $0 < z < 1$. The increase in government debt will cause the demand for money to increase, resulting in a leftward shift in the *LM* curve.

Whether the overall (expenditures plus monetary) effect on the equilibrium level of income is negative or positive will depend jointly on the orders of magnitude of the terms u, h, v and z. This may be seen by collecting the terms in the multiplier expression (12.18):

$$\frac{\Delta Y}{\Delta G} = \frac{u(1 - v) - hz}{su + hk}$$

where $u, h < 0$, $-1 < v < 0$ and $1 > z > 0$.

If $|u(1 - v)| > |hz|$, the bond financed government expenditures multiplier will be positive. The bond financed government expenditures multiplier varies directly with the interest sensitivity of the demand for money in absolute terms $|u|$ and the effect of nonhuman wealth on consumption expenditures v; it varies inversely with the interest sensitivity of investment expenditures in absolute terms $|h|$ and the effect of nonhuman wealth on the demand for money z.

An alternative way of looking at this process may provide added insight. The bond financed government expenditures multiplier may be viewed as having three impacts, a *fiscal impact* of an increase in government spending, $\Delta G[u/(su + hk)]$, a *wealth impact* associated with the increase in wealth on consumption, $\Delta G[-uv/(su + hk)]$ and a *portfolio impact* associated with the effect of wealth on the demand for money, $\Delta G[-hz/(su + hk)]$.[22]

Figure 12.2 indicates that without the shift in *LM*, equilibrium would occur where *IS'* intersects *LM;* the increase in income would be

$$Y'' - Y = \Delta G \left[\frac{u(1 - v)}{su + hk} \right].$$

---

[22] In reality these impacts do not occur separately. However, they are quite useful in helping one to understand the processes involved here. These labels and the inspiration for many of the simplifying assumptions used in the following presentation come from Laurence H. Meyer's excellent paper, "The Balance Sheet Identity, the Government Financing Constraint and the Crowding Out Effect," *Journal of Monetary Economics* (January 1975).

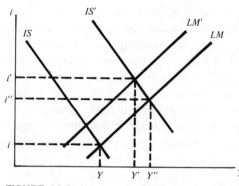

FIGURE 12.2. Increase in government expenditures financed by an increase in interest bearing government debt.

This depicts the combined *fiscal impact* and *wealth impact* of a bond financed increase in government expenditures. However, with a shift in the *LM* curve to *LM'*,
the increase in income is reduced because of the *portfolio impact* of a bond financed
increase in government expenditures. The total overall effect is therefore

$$\Delta Y = \Delta G \left[\frac{u(1 - v) - hz}{su + hk} \right].[23]$$

In the present model there is a sizable effect of a bond financed government
deficit on the market rate of interest. As discussed in Chapter 11, to the extent
that interest rates are bid up, private investment expenditures are choked off. (We
exclude any impact of interest on consumption or saving in the present model but
in more sophisticated models consumption expenditures could also be affected.) This
is represented in the movement upward along the *IS* curve as *i* increases to *i'*; it
reflects the crowding out of private spending by government spending. Crowding

[23] Without the portfolio impact the bond financed government expenditures multiplier is
unambiguously positive unless the parameters of the model take on extreme values (such as,
$u = 0$ and $h = -\infty$). In the present model because the *portfolio impact* shifts the *LM* curve
to the left, the net effect of bond financed fiscal policy is ambiguous. A zero multiplier (reflecting complete crowding out of private investment expenditures by government expenditures) or
a negative multiplier (reflecting more than complete crowding out) can occur without parameters taking on extreme values.

In more sophisticated models, discussed in the next footnote, a negative multiplier and a
decrease in income could lead to a reduction in the tax receipts of government. This, in
turn, would increase the necessary size of the deficit, increase the size of the government debt
and shift *LM* further left, which would reduce income even more, requiring an even greater
deficit, and shift *LM* even further left. The situation is unstable because income never stops
falling. See Robert M. Solow and Allan S. Blinder, "Does Fiscal Policy Matter?" *Journal of
Public Economics,* vol. 2 (1973), pp. 319–337, reprinted in Thomas Havrilesky and John
Boorman, *Current Issues in Monetary Theory and Policy, op. cit.* See also, William M. Scarth,
"A Note on the 'Crowding Out' of Private Expenditures by Bond–Financed Increases in Public
Spending," *Journal of Public Economics,* vol. 5 (April–May 1976), 385–387.

out is caused by the bidding upward of the market rate of interest from i to i'' because of the stimulus to aggregate demand wrought by the increase in debt-financed government spending. Additional crowding out is caused by the bidding upward of the market rate of interest from i'' to i' because the increase in private wealth affects the demand for money. There is, in short, an increased quantity of government securities being marketed with no decrease in the stock of outstanding private securities and no increase in the money supply to offset or absorb it.

Without a financing constraint, a balance sheet identity and related wealth effects, there would still be some crowding out of private investment expenditures in a less than fully employed economy as long as there were a *fiscal impact* on the interest rate. However, crowding out is increased by the presence of a *wealth impact* and a *portfolio impact* brought about by introducing the above constraints. An increase in wealth boosts consumption expenditures. This *wealth impact* accentuates the rightward shift in the *IS* curve and the rise in the interest rate. In addition, an increase in wealth increases the demand for money. This *portfolio impact* shifts the *LM* curve leftward and further accentuates the rise in the interest rate.[24]

Fiscal Policy III: Financing Increases in Government Expenditures by Increasing Government's Noninterest Bearing Debt, The Outside Money Supply

An increase in government expenditures financed by an increase in the supply of outside money will increase G, W and M:

$$\Delta Y = \Delta G\left(\frac{u}{su + hk}\right) + \Delta W\left(\frac{-vu}{su + hk}\right) + \Delta W\left(\frac{-hz}{su + hk}\right) +$$
$$\Delta M\left(\frac{h}{su + hk}\right) \quad (12.19)$$

---

[24] The rise in the market rate of interest could have effects not treated in this analysis. If government bonds were of the fixed coupon–variable price type–a change in the market rate of interest would change the market value of the government debt (see footnote 11). (If the private capital stock were included in our definition of private wealth, a rise in the market rate would also decrease the market value of the capital stock.) This *interest-induced wealth effect* would result in smaller absolute *wealth* and *portfolio* impacts and a smaller rightward shift of the *IS* curve and a smaller leftward shift of the *LM* curve.

We have heretofore assumed that changes in the interest rate are always matched by changes in autonomous taxation such that disposable income and the government's deficit are not affected by a change in the interest rate. If we instead assumed that tax receipts did not vary with government interest payments as the market rate of interest rose, disposable income would rise and the government's deficit would increase. The increase in consumption expenditures out of disposable income would raise the *fiscal impact* and the greater debt would increase the absolute values of the *wealth impact* and the *portfolio impact*. This would result in larger rightward shifts in the *IS* curve and larger leftward shifts in the *LM* curve.

The first three products are the same as the terms on the righthand side of Equation (12.17), which measures the effect on income of an increase in government expenditures financed by issuing interest bearing debt. The fourth product reflects the effect of an increase in the supply of money. An increase in the money stock is expansionary because, unlike the bond financed deficit, it raises the liquidity of portfolios in the private sector; that is, the proportion of money to bonds in private portfolios rises.

The effect of an increase in government expenditures on the income–expenditures *IS* sector of the model is the sum of the first two products of Equation (12.19). The first effect is the direct *fiscal impact;* the second is the (positive) *wealth impact* of the deficit. Abstracting from the money market effects of the financing (the *portfolio impact* and *liquidity impact*), the increase in income would be

$$Y_2 - Y_0 = \Delta G\left(\frac{u(1-v)}{su+hk}\right).$$

This is shown in Figure 12.3 at the intersection of the old *LM* curve, *LM,* and the new *IS* curve, *IS'*. This total expenditures effect is positive, as discussed earlier in this chapter.

The effect of the increase in the supply of money on the monetary *LM* sector of the model is measured by the sum of the third and fourth products of Equation (12.19). Abstracting from income–expenditures sector effects of the increase in government expenditures and their financing (the *fiscal impact* and the *wealth impact*), the increase in income would be

$$Y_4 - Y_2 = Y_1 - Y_0 = \Delta M\left(\frac{h}{su+hk}\right) + \Delta W\left(\frac{-hz}{su+hk}\right).$$

The first term reflects the *liquidity impact* of the increase in the money stock. This increase in liquidity causes the interest rate to decline and the level of income to increase, as discussed in Chapter 11. In Figure 12.3 it is depicted as a rightward shift of *LM* to *LM'*. This effect alone would cause the interest rate to fall from i_0 to i_3 and income to increase from Y_0 to Y_3. The second term above reflects the

---

We have also assumed, heretofore, that taxation does not vary with the level of income. If we were to assume instead that as aggregate income rose, taxation and disposable income rose by lesser amounts, then, at an unchanged rate of interest, the *fiscal impact* would be smaller. In addition, because the deficit would be smaller, at an unchanged rate of interest, the absolute value of the *wealth* and *portfolio impacts* would also be smaller.

What would be the overall effect of these more realistic additions to our model? In the real world the effect of variations in income tax receipts on government's deficit and private disposable income far outweigh the effect of government interest payments on the same magnitudes. In addition, interest induced wealth effects are quite sizable in some econometric models. Therefore, overall, in a more realistic model the *wealth* and *portfolio* impacts would probably be smaller in absolute terms. The negative multiplier and more than complete crowding out, mentioned in the previous footnote, would be less likely.

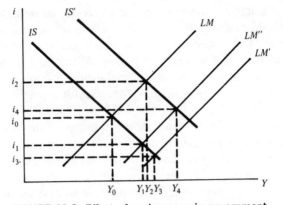

FIGURE 12.3. Effect of an increase in government spending financed by an increase in the money supply.

effect of the *portfolio impact* of the increase in wealth. This causes an increase in the demand for money and has a negative effect on income, as discussed in the previous section. It is depicted in Figure 12.3 as a leftward shift from LM' to LM''.

Since $\Delta W = \Delta M$, the total monetary effect on income is

$$Y_1 - Y_0 = \Delta M \left(\frac{h(1-z)}{su+hk} \right). \tag{12.20}$$

Where $0 < z < 1$, the monetary multiplier inclusive of the portfolio impact must be positive. The total monetary effect is shown in Figure 12.3 at the intersection of the old IS curve, IS, and the new LM curve, LM''. The rightward shift of the LM curve represents the net effect of the positive liquidity impact which accounts for the rightward shift from LM to LM' and the negative portfolio impact which accounts for the leftward shift from LM' to LM''.

Since $\Delta G = \Delta W = \Delta M$, the total expenditures and total monetary effects may be combined:

$$Y_4 - Y_0 = \Delta Y = \Delta G \left(\frac{u(1-v) + h(1-z)}{su+hk} \right). \tag{12.21}$$

In this case we have a "supermultiplier" combining the positive *fiscal, wealth* and *liquidity* impacts and the negative *portfolio* impact of an increase in government expenditures financed by an increase in the money supply. The new equilibrium level of income in Figure 12.3 (Y_4) is found at the intersection of the new LM and IS curves (LM'' and IS').

This analysis also demonstrates that unless parameters take on extreme values ($u = 0$, $h = -\infty$), a zero change in income can never occur when the fiscal deficit is financed by an increase in the money supply. Even if the entire increase in wealth is initially held in the form of money balances ($z = 1$) such that the total monetary effect is zero,

$$\frac{h(1 - z)}{su + hk} = 0$$

there will still be a positive total expenditures multiplier,

$$\frac{u(1 - v)}{su + hk} > 0.$$

It can also be seen from Figure 12.3 that in this Keynesian model there will be little crowding out of private investment expenditures if government expenditures are financed through money supply expansion because there will be little rise in the market rate of interest. Unlike the case of a bond financed deficit, the increased quantity of government debt can be absorbed into private portfolios without a sizable increase in the rate of interest because this debt was issued in a very liquid form—money.

Monetary Policy: Open Market Operations

The effect of a government open market operation in which outside money M is given to the private sector in exchange for bonds V would be represented simply by a *liquidity impact*. This is reflected in the final term of Equation (12.19). In Figure 12.3 it is depicted as a rightward shift of the LM curve from LM to LM'. The effect on real income is shown as the movement from Y_0 to Y_3. The liquidity impact is similar to the monetary policy multiplier discussed in Chapter 11. The magnitude of this multiplier is $h/(su + hk)$.

An open market operation in the present model involves neither a portfolio impact nor a wealth impact. Open market purchases (or sales) simply represent the exchange of one wealth form, money, for another, bonds. Total private wealth is unchanged.

As portfolio or wealth impacts do not arise in the present model, the analysis of the liquidity impact is identical to the analysis of the monetary policy multiplier in Chapter 11. At an initial LM–IS equilibrium private holdings of money increase (relative to private holdings of bonds). There exists an excess supply of money and an excess demand for bonds (see footnote 15). Private portfolios can only come into balance if the interest rate declines or the level of income rises. Thus portfolio adjustments stimulate investment expenditures and consumption expenditures. The subsequent increase in the equilibrium level of income by a multiple of the initial open market operation is referred to as the *liquidity impact* or monetary policy multiplier.[25]

[25] The overall monetary policy multiplier need not be synonomous with the liquidity impact. Let us consider the effect of more realistic treatment of wealth and taxation on the effect of

The processes examined here are, of course, rather unrealistic as they are predicated on the assumption that the general price level is given. If the price level is treated as a variable, as it is in Chapters 13–15, at least part of the increase in aggregate demand caused by increased government expenditures or government open market operations will be reflected not in an increase in real income but rather in an increase in the general price level.[26]

A Private Sector Financing Constraint

Heretofore a financing constraint was imposed on the government sector but not on the private sector. Wealth was identified as the value of private holdings of government interest bearing and noninterest bearing debt but did not include the value of the private capital stock.

Our model of aggregate demand is now modified to include household ownership of (claims on) the physical capital stock of business firms, net of business indebtedness. Thus privately issued and held bonds still cancel out in the private sector's balance sheet identity but equity ownership of the business firms by households (an elementary postulate of macroeconomic theory) is finally explicitly recognized. Private nonhuman wealth is defined as the sum of the values of outside money, government interest bearing bonds and the capital stock:[27]

---

open market operations. These embellishments of our basic model parallel those introduced in the previous footnote. If an interest induced wealth effect were introduced, an open market purchase would cause (the interest rate to fall and) private wealth to increase. This would not affect the basic liquidity impact (the monetary policy multiplier of Chapter 11). However, it would generate a positive wealth impact and a negative portfolio impact. The *IS* curve would shift rightward and the *LM* curve would not shift as far rightward.

If the effect of government interest payments on disposable income were introduced, an open market operation would cause government interest payments and disposable income to decline, *ceteris paribus*. Lower disposable income would reduce the magnitude of the liquidity impact because even though investment expenditures rose as the interest rate fell, this would be offset by reduced consumption expenditures. The reduction in the government's deficit would also generate a positive portfolio impact and a negative wealth impact.

Finally, if, as aggregate income changed, taxation and disposable income changed by lesser absolute amounts, the *liquidity impact* would be smaller than in our basic model because as aggregate income rose, there would not be as great an increase in consumption expenditures. In addition, because government's deficit would decline, there would be a positive portfolio impact and a negative wealth impact.

The overall effect of these embellishments on the *IS* and *LM* curves remains ambiguous unless the model is specified in more detail.

[26] In Chapter 15 increases in the general price level reduce the real value of nonhuman wealth and cause private expenditures to decrease. In Chapters 13 and 14 increases in the general price level reduce the real value of the money stock and cause the interest rate to rise, thereby causing private expenditures to decrease. Therefore, depending on the extent to which the increase in government expenditures causes the price level and the interest rate to rise, private expenditures will be further crowded out by the increase in government spending.

[27] This definition of wealth is consistent with the conceptual view of the economy developed in Chapter 9. We shall continue to abstract from interest induced wealth effects. In many

$$W \equiv M + V + K. \tag{12.21'}$$

We assume for simplicity that privately held government bonds V and private equity claims K are both fixed in price, have variable coupon rates and are close substitutes.[28] We use just one market equilibrium curve (the LM curve) to represent financial sector equilibrium. The assumption of close substitutability between bonds and equities helps to assure us that an increase in nonmonetary wealth will shift this curve leftward. Our model of aggregate demand is now also modified to reflect the wealth effect of private capital formation. As shown in Chapter 9, in the real world investment is either financed internally through retained earnings or externally through the sale of debt claims or equity claims to households. Whether financing proceeds internally or externally, the wealth of the private sector must still reflect a normal return to the owners of (the equity of) the enterprise.[29] In the present model we shall, therefore, assume that positive net investment expenditures are fully reflected in increases in the value of the equity holdings of the private sector regardless of how they are financed.

Therefore, the flow of net investment increases the stock of capital:

$$\Delta K = I = a' + hi. \tag{12.22}$$

The model now fully accounts for the interrelationship between *flows* ($G - T$, S and I) and changes in *stocks* ($\Delta M,\ \Delta V,\ \Delta K$). As discussed in Chapter 9, the flow of saving must result in the acquisition of stocks of assets:

---

econometric models the effect of interest rate changes on wealth is rather important. For a survey of these effects see Roger W. Spencer, "Channels of Monetary Influence: A Survey," *Review,* Federal Reserve Bank of St. Louis (November 1974).

[28] This assumption also rules out any ambiguity for the portfolio impact of a bond financed government deficit that would obtain in a world of three or more assets [that is, the condition $0 < z < 1$ in Equation (12.4') still holds]. For example, if bonds were very close substitutes for money, the demand for money might *decrease* as these money substitutes became available. This would create a positive portfolio impact and make a bond financed deficit more expansionary. Similarly, if bonds and money were close substitutes, changes in the money supply would affect bond yields but might have only very remote effects on equity yields. If equity yields were the relevant market rate of interest in the investment expenditures relation and if interest induced wealth effects were ignored, the liquidity impact (that is, monetary policy) might be viewed as rather weak. This is sometimes characterized as a *nonmonetarist* view. For excellent survey articles on this subject see Roger W. Spencer, *op. cit.*; and Yung Chul Park, "Some Current Issues on the Transmission Process of Monetary Policy," Staff Papers, International Monetary Fund (March 1972), reprinted in Havrilesky and Boorman, *Current Issues in Monetary Theory and Policy.*

In general, a great number of ambiguities arise when our assumption of perfect bond–equity substitutability is relaxed. See, for example, Arthur Benavie, "Equities in the Keynesian Model," *Eastern Economic Journal* vol. 1 (January 1975), 10–22.

[29] As long as investment is profitable, the present discounted value of a future income stream associated with a unit of capital will always exceed or equal the present value of the future interest costs of financing it (see footnote 14). Viewed another way, the expected marginal internal rate of return for a unit of capital will always exceed or equal the market rate of interest. If this were not the case, investment would not occur.

$$S = I + (G - T) = \Delta W = \Delta M + \Delta V + \Delta K.$$

Once again flows are measured over intervals of time and are assumed to be fully reflected in changes in stocks over the same period.[30]

Substituting the new definition of wealth into the saving relation (12.1') yields

$$S = -a + sY_d + vM_0 + vV + vK. \tag{12.1''}$$

As net investment in any initial equilibrium is zero, the presence of nonzero net investment expenditures will, as shown in Equation (12.22), always increase the level of wealth by adding to the capital stock:

$$K = K_0 + \Delta K. \tag{12.23}$$

Substitute (12.22) into Equation (12.23) and then substitute the result, together with the definition of disposable income, $Y_d = Y - T$, into Equation (12.1''). Taking that result together with (12.22) and substituting it into the equilibrium condition, $S + T = I + G$, yields the *IS* curve:

$$Y = \frac{a + a'(1-v) - vM_0 - vV - vK_0 + \bar{G} - (1-s)\bar{T}}{s} + \frac{h(1-v)}{s}i. \tag{12.24}$$

A nonzero level of investment expenditures will affect the *slope* and *intercept* terms of the *IS* curve.

The slope of the *IS* curve is "flatter" in *Y,i* space

$$\left| \frac{dY}{di} \right| = \left| \frac{h(1-v)}{s} \right| > \left| \frac{h}{s} \right|$$

since $0 > v > -1$. This occurs because consumption expenditures are now interest sensitive. A change in the interest rate now affects the size of the capital stock and the level of wealth. A change in the level of wealth affects consumption and saving. This effect is reflected in the numerator by the product $-hv$.

Substituting the same definition of wealth into the demand for money yields

$$M_d = kY + ui + m + zM + zV + zK. \tag{12.4''}$$

Substitute (12.22) into Equation (12.23) and the result into Equation (12.4''). Then using this result together with the supply of money, $M_s = M_0$, in the equilibrium condition, $M_s = M_d$, yields the *LM* curve:

---

[30] As in the previous section we consider here only short-run, single-period effects. If there is no population growth or technological change the model can only be at full long-run equilibrium if all budgets are balanced. That is, $S = I + (G - T) = 0$ only if there is no net capital formation.

$$Y = \frac{M_0(1 - z) - zV - zK_0 - za' - m}{k} - \frac{(u + zh)}{k} i. \quad (12.25)$$

A nonzero level of investment expenditures will affect the slope and intercept of the *LM* curve. The *LM* curve is "flatter" in *Y,i* space.

$$\frac{dY}{di} = \frac{-(u + zh)}{k} > \frac{-u}{k}.$$

This occurs because the demand for money is now more interest sensitive. A change in the interest rate now affects the size of the capital stock and the level of wealth. A change in the level of wealth affects the demand for money. This is reflected in the numerator by the product *zh*.

Given nonzero investment expenditures, the one period equilibrium solution for the level of aggregate demand is

$$Y = \frac{(u + zh)[a + a'(1 - v) - vM_0 - vV - vK_0 + \bar{G} - (1 - s)\bar{T}]}{su + szh + hk - hvk} +$$

$$\frac{(h - hv)[M_0(1 - z) - m - za' - zV - zK_0]}{su + szh + hk - hvk}. \quad (12.26)$$

The multiplier for a bond financed increase in government expenditures is now

$$\frac{\Delta Y}{\Delta G} = \frac{(u + zh)(1 - v) + (h - hv)(-z)}{su + szh + hk - hvk} = \frac{u - uv}{su + szh + hk - hvk} =$$

$$\frac{u(1 - v)}{s(u + zh) + hk(1 - v)} \quad (12.27)$$

where $u,h,v < 0$ and $z > 0$.

The numerator in this multiplier has a greater absolute order of magnitude than the numerator of the multiplier without a private financing constraint, Equation (12.18):

$$|u - uv| > |u - uv - hz|, \quad |u(1 - v)| > |u(1 - v) - hz|.$$

Even though the fiscal impact and wealth impact (the rightward shift in *IS*) are the same in both models, the portfolio impact (the leftward shift in the *LM* curve) is zero in the present model. This is because as the demand for money increases, as a result of the increase in bond wealth, the rise in the interest rate chokes off investment spending and, consequently, capital formation and household wealth then decline by an equal amount. The portfolio impact (the increase in the demand for money because of the increase in outstanding government bonds) disappears.

The *LM* curve does not shift to the left as additional government bonds are issued, because the rise in the interest rate reduces investment spending and hence the size of the capital stock by an equal amount.[31]

The denominator in this multiplier is greater in absolute value than the denominator of the multiplier without a private financing constraint, Equation (12.18).[32] Therefore, the multiplier in Equation (12.27) could be larger or smaller in absolute magnitude than the multiplier in Equation (12.18).

However, the denominator is unambiguously negative, as all terms in it are negative. Therefore, as both the numerator and the denominator are negative, the multiplier in Equation (12.27) is unambiguously nonnegative.

This implies that the effect of a bond financed government deficit on income can never be negative—there cannot be more than complete crowding out, *ex post*. Because the *LM* curve cannot shift leftward, the interest rate can never be bid upward sufficiently to create a negative multiplier.

Summary

Elementary models of government fiscal and monetary policy can be misleading because the *stock* effects of government deficits are not integrated into the models. In this chapter we first defined the effect that a government deficit would have on wealth and the effect that changes in wealth would have on expenditures and the demand for money. This enabled us to derive fiscal and monetary policy multipliers within the context of the *LM–IS* model. The main feature of these exercises was that debt financed government expenditures had not only the positive fiscal impact on income associated with the autonomous expenditures multiplier of the previous chapter but they also had a positive wealth impact and a negative portfolio impact on income. These latter two impacts could make the bond financed government expenditures multiplier larger or smaller than autonomous expenditures multipliers in models where stock effects are not specified. In fact, the autonomous expenditures multiplier could even be negative in magnitude.

When the government deficit is financed by an expansion of the money stock, the multiplier is unambiguously positive because the *liquidity impact* of additional money balances offsets the *portfolio impact* which increases the demand for money.

[31] This rather unrealistic implication directly follows from the assumption of an initial balanced budget equilibrium with no capital formation. Reductions in the capital stock, balanced budgets, etc., all take *time* to accomplish. To pursue thoroughly the questions that have surfaced in this chapter requires the use of *dynamics,* the study of movement in a system over time. Unfortunately, dynamic models require the use of a type of mathematics that is beyond the scope of this text. For a dynamic model which is addressed to some of the issues raised in this chapter, see Edmund S. Phelps, and Karl Shell, "Public Debt, Taxation and Capital Intensiveness," *Journal of Economic Theory,* vol. 1 (October 1969), 330–346.

[32] In other words $|su + szh + hk - hvk| > |su + hk|$, because $|h(sz + k - kv)| > |hk|$ as $|sz + k - kv| > k$ and $|sz + k(1 - v)| > k$, which follows from the specification $v < 0$.

Finally, when a private financing constraint is introduced to the model, the bond financed government expenditures multiplier is again unambiguously positive, and the crowding out effect is reduced.

QUESTIONS FOR CHAPTER 12

1. Why is the long-run balanced budget multiplier so different from the short-run bond financed government expenditures multiplier?

2. Why is there little disagreement that money financed government deficits stimulate the economy more than bond financed ones? What does this suggest about the power of "fiscal policy" to stimulate output?

3. Explain how an increase in government spending crowds out private spending in the short run when these expenditures are financed by raising the level of taxation.

4. What is the importance of the assumption in the *LM–IS* model that bonds and capital goods are perfect substitutes?

5. Derive a *bond* market equilibrium curve in *i,Y* space. Under what conditions will it be different from the *money* market equilibrium (*LM*) curve.

6. Can an open market purchase by the monetary authority ever create wealth rather than simply make portfolios more liquid?

7. Do interest induced wealth effects on balance tend to increase or reduce the magnitude of the bond financed government expenditures multiplier?

8. Compare the effects of a bond-financed government deficit in the present model with the effects in a price-flexible neoclassical model, such as the ones presented in Chapters 13 and 15.

BIBLIOGRAPHY FOR CHAPTER 12

BARRO, ROBERT, "Are Government Bonds Wealth?" *Journal of Political Economy,* vol. 82 (November/December 1974).

BENAVIE, ARTHUR, "Equities in the Keynesian Model," *Eastern Economic Journal,* vol. 1 (January 1975), 10–22.

BRAINARD, WILLIAM, and JAMES TOBIN, "Pitfalls in Financial Model Building," *American Economic Review, Proceedings* (May 1968).

CHRIST, CARL, "A Simple Macroeconomic Model with a Government Budget Constraint," *Journal of Political Economy* (January 1968).

DAVID, PAUL A., and JOHN L. SCADDING, "Private Savings: Ultrarationality, Aggregation and 'Denison's Law', *Journal of Political Economy,* vol. 82 (March/April 1974).

HANSEN, ALVIN H., *A Guide to Keynes* (New York: McGraw-Hill, 1953).

LERNER, ABBA, "The Burden of the Public Debt," in *Income, Employment and Public Policy* (New York: W. W. Norton, 1948).

MEYER, LAURENCE H., "The Balance Sheet Identity, the Government Financing Constraint and the Crowding Out Effect," *Journal of Monetary Economics* (January 1975).

MUSGRAVE, RICHARD, *The Theory of Public Finance* (New York: McGraw-Hill, 1956).

PARK, YUNG CHUL, "Some Current Issues on the Transmission Process of Monetary Policy," Staff Papers, International Monetary Fund (March 1972).*

PATINKIN, DON, *Money, Interest and Prices,* 2nd ed. (New York: Harper and Row, 1965), ch. 12.

PHELPS, EDMUND S., and KARL SHELL, "Public Debt, Taxation and Capital Intensiveness," *Journal of Economic Theory,* vol. 1 (October 1969), 330–346.

SILBER, WILLIAM, "Fiscal Policy in *IS–LM* Analysis: A Correction," *Journal of Money, Credit and Banking* (November 1970).

SOLOW, ROBERT M., and ALLAN S. BLINDER, "Does Fiscal Policy Matter!" *Journal of Public Economics,* vol. 2, (1973), 319–337.*

SCARTH, WILLIAM, "A Note on the 'Crowding-Out' of Private Expenditures by Bond-Financed Increases in Public Spending," *Journal of Public Economics,* vol. 5 (April–May 1976), 385–387.

SPENCER, ROGER W., "Channels of Monetary Influence: A Survey," *Review,* Federal Reserve Bank of St. Louis (November 1974).*

SPENCER, ROGER W., and KEITH CARLSON, "Crowding Out and Its Critics" *Review,* Federal Reserve Bank of St. Louis (December 1975).*

SPENCER, ROGER W., and WILLIAM P. YOHE, "The Crowding Out of Private Expenditures by Fiscal Policy," *Review,* Federal Reserve Bank of St. Louis (October 1970), 12–24.

TOBIN, JAMES, "An Essay in the Principles of Debt Management," *Fiscal and Debt Management Policies,* Commission on Money and Credit (Englewood Cliffs, NJ: Prentice-Hall, 1963).

TOBIN, JAMES, and WILLIAM BUITER, "Long Run Effects of Fiscal and Monetary Policy on Aggregate Demand," *Monetarism,* Jerome Stein, ed. (Amsterdam: North Holland, 1976).

VON FURSTENBERG, GEORGE M. and BURTON G. MALKIEL, "The Government and Capital Formation: A Survey of Recent Issues," *Journal of Economic Literature,* vol. 15 (September 1977), 835–878.

* Reprinted in THOMAS M. HAVRILESKY and JOHN T. BOORMAN, *Current Issues in Monetary Theory and Policy* (Arlington Heights, IL.: AHM Publishing Corporation, 1976).

13

Aggregate Supply and Aggregate Demand: Price and Wage Flexibility

Introduction

In Chapter 11 we introduced a basic *LM–IS* analysis of the Keynesian model of aggregate demand. In that model the income–expenditures sector was represented by three linear equations, a saving function, an investment function and an equilibrium condition. Three linear equations also served to describe the monetary sector: a money demand function, a money supply equation and a market equilibrium condition. The aggregate economy was said to be in equilibrium when these six equations were solved simultaneously for the values of all of the variables, including income and the interest rate, which would satisfy the equilibrium conditions in both sectors.

Two crucial assumptions were made in the development of that model. First, the price level was assumed to be constant, so that changes in nominal values were also changes in real values. Second, equilibrium in aggregate demand (that is, in the income–expenditures sector and the monetary sector simultaneously) was referred to as equilibrium for the aggregate economy as a whole. No explicit reference was made to the supply (production and labor market) sector of the economy.

In this chapter we expand that analysis of the aggregate economy. To accomplish this four major modifications are made in the traditional *LM–IS* model presented in Chapter 11. First, the money supply is made an endogenous variable, as suggested in Chapters 1 and 2; second, the influence of the interest rate on saving, first discussed in Chapter 10, is included; third, the price level and the level of nominal wages are introduced as explicit variables in the analysis; and fourth, a supply (labor market) sector is added.

In the next three chapters the order of presentation is based on the historical development of the theories attempting to explain the operation of the aggregate economy. We begin in the present chapter with a neoclassical model from which the quantity theory conclusions are derived. Keynesian factors such as wage rigidity, the liquidity trap and interest insensitive investment demand will be introduced in Chapter 14. Unlike Chapter 12, financing constraints, wealth and the government sector are ignored in these two chapters. However, in Chapter 15 we will reintroduce these considerations and examine their workings in a neoclassical model.

Aggregate Demand[1]

The Income–Expenditures Sector

All behavioral relations in the income–expenditures sector of our model are specified to be relations between *real variables,* that is, neither households nor business firms suffer from money illusion. Money illusion refers to the notion that an equiproportionate change in both the nominal money stock and the prices of all commodities, even though it leaves all relative prices, real wealth and the real value of money balances M/P unchanged, will nonetheless cause a change in some *real* aspect of an individual's economic behavior. As Don Patinkin notes ". . . if the initial paper-money endowment of an *illusion-free* individual were suddenly increased and he were simultaneously confronted in the market by new money prices, all of which had increased in the same proportion, he would once again have *no reason* for changing the amount demanded of any commodity."[2] (Italics added.) An individual whose demand for or supply of some commodity *would change* in these circumstances would be said to be suffering from money illusion.

We assume that the investment decision depends on the interest rate and that the saving decision depends on the level of income and the interest rate. (The effect of wealth on consumption is ignored and for the time being government spending

---

[1] The development of this model relates to the following works: Martin Bailey, *National Income and the Price Level* (New York: McGraw-Hill, 1962), chs. 2 and 3; Boris Pesek and Thomas Saving, *Money, Wealth, and Economic Theory* (New York: Macmillan, 1967), chs. 1 and 2; Robert Rasche, "A Comparative Static Analysis of Some Monetarist Propositions," *Review,* Federal Reserve Bank of St. Louis (December 1973), 15–23; Warren Smith, "A Graphical Exposition of the Complete Keynesian System," *The Southern Economic Journal,* vol. 23, no. 3 (October 1956), 115–125. The latter two articles are reprinted in Thomas Havrilesky and John Boorman, *Current Issues in Monetary Theory and Policy, op. cit.*

[2] Don Patinkin, *Money, Interest and Prices,* 2nd ed. (New York: Harper and Row, 1965), 22.

and taxation are also ignored.) The absence of money illusion implies that at given levels of real income and the interest rate, individuals will have the same amount of real saving and real investment regardless of the prevailing price level.[3] The relations embodying these assumptions may be written as follows:[4]

$$\frac{S}{P} = S\left(\frac{Y}{P}, i\right) = -\frac{a}{P} + s \cdot \frac{Y}{P} + \frac{e}{P} \cdot i \tag{13.1}$$

where $0 < s < 1$ and $a, e > 0$ and

$$\frac{I}{P} = I(i) = \frac{a'}{P} + \frac{h}{P} \cdot i \tag{13.2}$$

where $h < 0$ and $a' > 0$. These relations were derived from first principles in Chapter 10.

All variables other than the price level P and the interest rate i and all parameters other than the marginal propensity to save s are stated in nominal dollar terms, but are deflated by the index of the average price level to yield real values. Thus the terms a/P, a'/P, Y/P, etc., represent real values as implied by the assumed absence of any money illusion. This assumption further implies that if the price level should double, a, a', Y and the other nominal values would have to double in order to maintain a/P, a'/P, Y/P and the other real variables at constant real levels. This

---

[3] This is most easily rationalized if we assume unitary elasticity of price expectations. This implies that people expect the current price level to prevail in the future; but if prices change (unexpectedly), the public will then expect the new price level to prevail, that is, they would expect neither a return to the old price level nor a continuation of the rate of price change in its current direction. This concept was introduced by J. R. Hicks, in *Value and Capital* (Oxford: Clarendon Press, 1939), 205. As he states: "If the elasticity of expectations is unity, a change in current prices will change expected prices in the same direction and in the same proportion; if prices were previously expected to be constant at the old level, they are now expected to be constant at the new level; changes in prices are expected to be permanent."

[4] The following symbols are employed in this chapter:

P an index of the average price level in the economy
S aggregate saving in nominal dollars
Y aggregate income (national income) in nominal dollars
i an index of relevant interest rates in the economy
I aggregate investment expenditures in nominal dollars
M_s the money supply
M_d the demand for money
N_s the supply of labor
N_d the demand for labor
w the nominal wage rate
O the volume of real output (or measure of production)
K the capital stock
DD aggregate demand
SS aggregate supply

makes the linear saving and investment demand equations homogeneous of degree zero in nominal values and prices.[5]

By expressing the behavioral relations in this form and by assuming unitary elasticity of price expectations the average price level P is eliminated as a separate variable in these equations for the income–expenditures sector. Regardless of changes in the price level, real decisions remain unchanged. Consequently, the unknowns in these equations are specified as S/P, I/P, Y/P and i.

When these two behavioral relations are combined with the equilibrium condition for the income expenditures sector (for a closed economy where government expenditures and taxation are both assumed to be zero),

$$\frac{S}{P} = \frac{I}{P} \tag{13.3}$$

we derive a three-equation model in *four* unknowns. This linear system cannot be solved for equilibrium values of all four variables but it can, through substitution, be reduced to one equation in two unknowns.

Substituting Equations (13.1) and (13.2) into (13.3) yields

$$-\frac{a}{P} + s \cdot \frac{Y}{P} + \frac{e}{P} \cdot i = \frac{a'}{P} + \frac{h}{P} \cdot i$$

$$\frac{Y}{P} = \frac{a/P + a'/P}{s} + \frac{-e/P + h/P}{s} \cdot i. \tag{13.4}$$

This linear form is very similar to the *IS* curve developed earlier, Equation (11.4). The intercept term is $(a/P + a'/P)/s$ which is identical to that of the *IS* curve of Chapter 11. The slope of the present *IS* curve is somewhat larger in absolute value (more interest sensitive) than that of the earlier *IS* curve:

$$\left| \frac{-e/P + h/P}{s} \right| > \left| \frac{h/P}{s} \right|$$

because of the inclusion in the numerator of $-e$, the (negative of the) slope of the saving function with respect to the interest rate. The marginal propensity to save out of real income is positive but less than unity; h/P is negative; while e/P can be expected to be positive; therefore, $(-e/P + h/P) < 0$. As a result, the slope of this equation, which represents all combinations of real income Y/P and the interest rate i which bring equilibrium to the income–expenditures sector (that is, combinations which equate planned saving and planned investment), will be negative. This equation is graphed in Figure 13.1.

---

[5] We shall not consider certain distributional effects of a changing price level in this discussion. Instead, we assume that when the average price level P changes, the prices of all goods and services in the economy change in the same proportion.

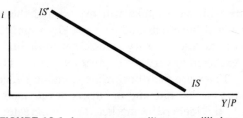

FIGURE 13.1. Income–expenditures equilibrium curve *IS*.

Recalling the assumption about the absence of money illusion, examination of Equation (13.4) indicates that the *position of this curve is independent of the price level.* If the price level should increase, all nominal values would increase in the same proportion and the slope and intercept terms in Equation (13.4) would remain unchanged.

The Monetary Sector

The analysis of the monetary sector begins with the assumption that the *nominal stock of money supplied to the economy is an increasing function of the interest rate.* As already seen in Chapters 1, 2 and 3 institutional and legal conditions establish the framework within which the public, commercial banks and the monetary authority interact to determine the actual nominal money supply. For example the monetary authority sets the reserve requirements which determine the volume of legal reserves that member banks must hold against their demand and time deposit liabilities. Also, the monetary authority has the power to control the size of the monetary base. The public, on the other hand, determines its preferred asset ratios, which influence the allocation of the monetary base among its alternative uses either as reserves against demand deposits, reserves against time deposits or as currency holdings of the public (see Chapters 1 and 2).

Given these factors, commercial bank behavior generates the final volume of money that will be created. Bank borrowing from the central bank can increase reserve holdings and expand the deposit creating capabilities of the banks. Holding reserve balances in excess of requirements tends to absorb legal reserves and to decrease the money creating abilities of banks. In this way the money stock depends on the behavior of banks relating to their desired holdings of excess and borrowed reserves.

As discussed in the last section of Chapter 2, one of the important factors affecting this aspect of bank behavior is the market interest rate. If the market rate is relatively high, banks will be induced to hold a relatively small volume of reserves in excess of legal requirements, since the interest rate represents the alternative cost of holding those reserves. But the lower the volume of desired excess legal reserves, the greater the volume of loans banks will extend and the larger the volume of deposit liabilities they will have outstanding for a given monetary base. Therefore, as holdings of excess legal reserves vary inversely with the market interest rate, the money stock can be expected to vary directly with variations in that rate.[6]

Similarly, banks will increase their borrowing from the Federal Reserve when the differential between the market rate and the discount rate increases. As a result, for a given discount rate, the higher the market rate, the greater the volume of bank borrowing and the larger the stock of liabilities created by the commercial banks.

Therefore, given the monetary base, the required reserve ratios set by the authorities and the preferred asset ratios of the public, the nominal money supply can be expected to vary directly with the rate of interest, that is, ,

$$M_s = \gamma(i), \qquad \frac{\partial M_s}{\partial i} > 0. \tag{13.5}$$

This relationship is shown in Figure 13.2. The position of this curve is assumed to depend on all the factors listed above. For example, if the monetary authority increases the monetary base, the curve will shift from M_s to M_s'. The slope of the curve will depend on the marginal responses of desired excess and borrowed reserve levels of commercial bankers to changes in the interest rate.

On the demand side of the money market we assume that the desire for money balances on the part of the public stems from two sources: first, a desire for real

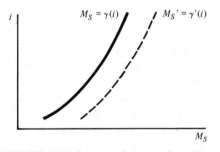

FIGURE 13.2. Supply of money function.

[6] A money supply model that incorporates this relation in a structural equation is presented in Chapter 2. Note that having the money supply depend on the (endogenous) interest rate causes the money stock *to be affected* by economic activity as well as *to affect* that activity. It is this point that lies at the center of much of the so-called "reverse causation" controversy over the econometric models which purport that the money supply is a statistically exogenous variable. Compare, for example, David I. Fand, "Some Issues in Monetary Economics: Fiscal Policy Assumptions and Related Multipliers," *Review,* Federal Reserve Bank of St. Louis (January 1970), 23–27, and Raymond Lombra and Raymond Torto, "Measuring the Impact of Monetary and Fiscal Actions: A New Look at the Specification Problem," *Review of Economics and Statistics,* vol. 56, no. 1 (February 1974), 104–107. Both of these are reprinted in Havrilesky and Boorman, *op. cit.*

transactions balances to facilitate a real volume of output and second, a desire to maintain some proportion of real financial wealth in the form of real money balances.[7] In other words, the public demands a stock of *real* money balances, both to facilitate transactions and to hold as speculative (asset) balances. Following the discussion in Chapters 4–6 we express the transactions demand for real money balances as an increasing function of the level of real income Y/P and the speculative demand for real money balances as a decreasing function of the market rate of interest i; the public's behavior is again assumed free of money illusion. The effect of the level of wealth on the demand for money is ignored.

$$(M/P)_d = L(Y/P, i),^8 \qquad \frac{\partial(M/P)_d}{\partial(Y/P)} > 0, \quad \frac{\partial(M/P)_d}{\partial i} < 0. \qquad (13.6)$$

Equilibrium in the money market requires that the *real* volume of money in circulation be just sufficient to satisfy the public's demand for real money balances:

$$\frac{M_s}{P} = \left(\frac{M}{P}\right)_d. \qquad (13.7)$$

To make Equation (13.5) consistent with the equilibrium condition, we divide both sides of that equation by the price level P. Substitution of Equations (13.5) and (13.6) into (13.7) then yields the money market equilibrium equation:

$$\frac{1}{P} \cdot \gamma(i) = L(Y/P, i). \qquad (13.8)$$

In order to solve this system of equations for equilibrium solutions in terms of the exogenous variables and the parameters of the model, let us assume linear functional forms to represent the relations between the nominal stock of money supplied and the interest rate and between the stock of real money balances demanded and real income and the interest rate. Thus,

$$M_s = \gamma(i) = j + d \cdot i,^9 \qquad (13.9)$$

[7] See Alfred Marshall, *Money, Credit and Commerce* (London: Macmillan, 1923).
[8] Differing demand for money hypotheses lead to the same *general* functional form for the money demand relation. Our structural analysis is completely compatible with these alternative formulations. It is the *a priori* restrictions placed on the partial derivatives of these forms and the empirical specification of these equations that we would expect to differ under varying formulations of the theory of money demand. See Chapters 4–8 for a detailed analysis of the alternative hypotheses that yield these specifications.
[9] Compare this formulation to the linear functional forms [Equations (2.10) and (2.22) of Chapter 2]. Here the monetary base may be assumed to be incorporated in the intercept term *j*. This explains how the monetary base could appear as an exogenous variable in reduced form equations such as Equation (13.11).

and

$$\left(\frac{M}{P}\right)_d = L(Y/P, i) = \frac{m}{P} + k\frac{Y}{P} + \frac{u}{P}i. \tag{13.10}$$

Then, in equilibrium,

$$\frac{1}{P} \cdot M_s = \left(\frac{M}{P}\right)_d$$

$$\frac{1}{P} \cdot (j + di) = \frac{m}{P} + k\frac{Y}{P} + \frac{u}{P}i$$

$$\frac{Y}{P} = \frac{1}{k}\left[\left(\frac{1}{P} \cdot j - \frac{m}{P}\right) + \left(\frac{1}{P} \cdot d - \frac{u}{P}\right)i\right]. \tag{13.11}$$

It is extremely important to note that the parameters j and d from the (nominal) money supply equation *do not* react to price changes in the same way as the parameters m and u from the (real) money demand relation. The assumption of no money illusion on the part of individuals who demand real money balances implies that when the price level P changes, the nominal values m and u change by the same proportion, leaving the ratios m/P and u/P unchanged. The supply of money, however, is specified in nominal terms. It follows then that there is no reason for the parameters j and d to change when the price level changes. Consequently, in the money market equilibrium equation (13.11) there are three unknowns, real income Y/P, the interest rate i and the price level P. The presence of the price level as a distinct variable in this equation reflects our assumption that the behavior of the public, the banks and the monetary authority determines the *nominal* money stock.

The equilibrium condition in this market can be depicted as a family of market equilibrium curves. The graphical derivation of these *LM* curves is shown in Figure 13.3.

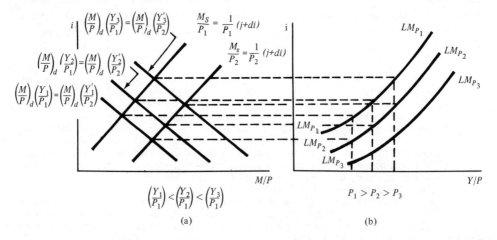

FIGURE 13.3. Monetary sector equilibrium curves *LM*.

In Figure 3(a) real money balances M/P are measured along the horizontal axis. Since the demand for money depends upon both the level of real income and the interest rate, a family of money demand curves appears in the real money balances–interest rate plane. Each curve shows the volume of real money balances demanded at every level of the interest rate for a given level of real income. For example, $(M/P)_d Y_1/P_1$ shows how the demand for real money balances varies with the interest rate when real income is assumed to be Y_1/P_1. For any given level of the interest rate, real money balances demanded will be greater the greater the level of real income. As a result $(M/P)_d Y_2/P_1$, representing the demand for real money balances at income level, $Y_2/P_1 > Y_1/P_1$, lies to the right of $(M/P)_d Y_1/P_1$.

A given real income level Y_1/P_1 represents any one of an infinite number of nominal income–price level combinations. For example, if nominal income is Y_1 and the price level is P_1, real income will be Y_1/P_1. But this same real income level would also result from a nominal income level of $2Y_1$ and a price level of $2P_1$, that is, $2Y_1/2P_1 = Y_1/P_1$.

Let us assume an initial price level of P_1. If $Y_1 < Y_2 < Y_3$, then $Y_1/P_1 < Y_2/P_1 < Y_3/P_1$. Three curves showing how the demand for real money balances varies with the interest rate at these real income levels are drawn in Figure 13.3(a).

Since the money supply relation is expressed in nominal terms, it must be modified to depict the real values reflected in our diagram. This is done simply by dividing the nominal money supply function by the average price level. Thus for an assumed initial price level P_1 the money supply relation $M_s/P_1 = (1/P_1)(j + di)$ is shown in Figure 13.3(a) as an upward sloping line.

Given the price level, the intersection point of the single money supply curve with the family of money demand curves yields combinations of the interest rate and the level of real income which equate the supply of and demand for real money balances. These points may be used to locate the money market equilibrium curve LM_{P_1} in Figure 13.3(b).

As shown by Equation (13.11) for a given price level, the LM curve has an intercept of $(j/P - m/P)/k$ and a slope of $(d/P - u/P)/k$. This makes it quite similar to the LM curve of Equation (11.8). The slope of the present LM curve is somewhat flatter (more interest sensitive) than that of the earlier LM curve, $(d/P - u/P)/k > (-u/P)/k$, because of the inclusion of d/P, the slope of the money supply relation in the numerator.

What happens to the money demand curve if the price level should change? Suppose, for example, that the price level falls to $P_2 < P_1$. There is some nominal income level $Y_1' < Y_1$ such that $Y_1'/P_2 = Y_1/P_1$. Therefore, the money demand curve $(M/P)_d(Y_1'/P_2)$ coincides with $(M/P)_d(Y_1/P_1)$, both curves showing the relation between real money balances demanded and the interest rate at a given level of real income. But what happens to the money supply curve if the price level should change? Since the money supply function is specified in nominal terms, when the price level falls, the same volume of nominal balances supplied by the monetary system will represent a greater real volume of money balances. Therefore, at each interest rate $M_s/P_2 = 1/P_2(j + di)$ lies to the right of $M_s/P_1 = 1/P_1(j + di)$.

The new money supply curve together with the family of money demand curves generate a new money market equilibrium curve LM_{P_2}. The new curve lies to the right of LM_{P_1}, indicating that in money market equilibrium at the lower price level P_2 each interest rate level will now be associated with a higher level of real income and each real income level will now be associated with a lower interest rate. Along the new money market equilibrium curve LM_{P_2}, nominal money balances supplied to the economy at each interest rate represent a larger real stock of balances at the lower price level. Therefore, at unchanged interest rate levels only a higher level of real income can cause the nonbank public to demand these additional real money balances (for transactions purposes), thereby bringing the money market into equilibrium. As a consequence, at each interest rate level the new money market equilibrium curve LM_{P_2} lies *to the right* of the old money market equilibrium curve LM_{P_1}.

As another way of looking at this, at unchanged real income levels only a lower interest rate can cause the nonbank public to demand the additional real money balances (for speculative purposes), thereby bringing the money market into equilibrium. As a consequence, at each real income level the new money market equilibrium curve LM_{P_2} lies *below* the old money market equilibrium curve LM_{P_1}. (The simple analytics of a shift in the *LM* curve are discussed in more detail in Chapter 11.)

Proceeding in this manner, we can derive a family of money market equilibrium curves, one for each possible price level. For example, in Figure 13.3(b) the curve LM_{P_3} represents money market equilibrium for a still lower level of prices than the curve LM_{P_2}.

Aggregate Demand Equilibrium

Now consider the equilibrium curve for the monetary sector [Equation (13.11)] together with the equilibrium curve for the income–expenditures sector [Equation (13.4)]. If, as in Chapters 11 and 12, we assume that the price level is constant we are restricted to just one of the family of money market equilibrium curves. In Figure 13.4, where the two curves intersect, there is equilibrium in both the income–expenditures sector and the monetary sector.

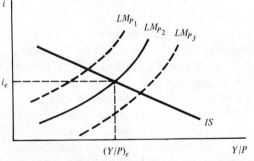

FIGURE 13.4. Expenditures and money market equilibrium at fixed prices.

Analytically this is equivalent to solving Equations (13.4) and (13.11) simultaneously for the level of income and the interest rate at an assumed (constant) level of prices. This solution is presented below for an assumed price level P_2:

$$\frac{Y}{P_2} = \frac{a/P_2 + a'/P_2}{s} + \frac{-e/P_2 + h/P_2}{s} \cdot i \qquad (13.4)$$

$$\frac{Y}{P_2} = \frac{1}{k}\left[\left(\frac{1}{P_2} \cdot j - \frac{m}{P_2}\right) + \left(\frac{1}{P_2} \cdot d - \frac{u}{P_2}\right) \cdot i\right]. \qquad (13.11)$$

Solving each of these equations for the interest rate i yields

$$i = \frac{s}{-e/P_2 + h/P_2} \cdot \frac{Y}{P_2} - \frac{a/P_2 + a'/P_2}{-e/P_2 + h/P_2} \qquad (13.4')$$

and

$$i = \frac{-k}{[(-1/P_2) \cdot d + u/P_2]} \cdot \frac{Y}{P_2} + \frac{[(1/P_2) \cdot j - m/P_2]}{[(-1/P_2) \cdot d + u/P_2]} \qquad (13.11')$$

Substitution then yields the solution (in terms of the parameters of the model) for the equilibrium level of income:

$$\frac{Y}{P_2}\left(\frac{s}{-e/P_2 + h/P_2} + \frac{k}{[(-1/P_2) \cdot d + u/P_2]}\right) =$$

$$\frac{a/P_2 + a'/P_2}{-e/P_2 + h/P_2} + \frac{[(1/P_2) \cdot j - m/P_2]}{[(-1/P_2) \cdot d + u/P_2]}$$

$$\frac{Y}{P_2} = \frac{\left[\dfrac{a/P_2 + a'/P_2}{-e/P_2 + h/P_2} + \dfrac{[(1/P_2) \cdot j - m/P_2]}{[(-1/P_2) \cdot d + u/P_2]}\right]}{\left[\dfrac{s}{-e/P_2 + h/P_2} + \dfrac{k}{[(-1/P_2) \cdot d + u/P_2]}\right]}.$$

Collecting terms,

$$\frac{Y}{P_2} =$$

$$\frac{(a/P_2 + a'/P_2)[(-1/P_2) \cdot d + u/P_2] + [(1/P_2) \cdot j - m/P_2](-e/P_2 + h/P_2)}{s[(-1/P_2) \cdot d + u/P_2] + k(-e/P_2 + h/P_2)}$$

This equation is directly comparable to Equation (11.9). It differs only in its explicit inclusion of price level P_2 and in the inclusion of the new behavioral parameter e from the saving function.[10] The solution processes are identical.

---

[10] The effects of a change in some component of autonomous expenditures may be seen in this equation. For example, assume that the volume of autonomous investment spending, a'/P, increases and shifts the *IS* curve:

Implicit in the analysis so far has been the assumption that the response of aggregate supply to changes in the level of aggregate demand consists exclusively of a quantity (real output) adjustment. This is implied by our earlier assumption of a constant, exogenously determined, general price level. In contrast, if we assume instead that the response of aggregate supply to changes in aggregate demand is not constrained to a pure quantity adjustment, then the general price level becomes a variable endogenous to our model.

With a variable price level, no single *LM* curve can be isolated to represent the locus of money market equilibrium values for the level of real income and the level of the interest rate and no unique solution for these variables can be found in the *LM–IS* quadrant. This is illustrated in Figure 13.4. In other words, the aggregate demand sector *LM* and *IS* curves are not sufficient by themselves to provide a determinate solution for our model because we will have added to our aggregate demand sector a new variable, the general price level, but no new equations. Therefore, in order to be able to discuss the determination of the general price level jointly with the determination of the level of real income, the interest rate and all the other variables of the model, we now add a set of behavioral relations describing the aggregate supply (production and labor market) sector of the economy.

Aggregate Supply

We first explicitly introduce the labor market and aggregate production function into this model and examine its comparative-static characteristics under the neoclassical assumptions of perfect flexibility of the price level and the nominal wage level and no money illusion on either side of the labor market. Pure competition is assumed in all markets; the quantity of labor N is measured as a number of homogeneous man-hours.

$$\frac{\partial(Y/P_2)}{\partial(a'/P_2)} = \frac{(-1/P_2) \cdot d + u/P_2}{s[(-1/P_2) \cdot d + u/P_2] + k(-e/P_2 + h/P_2)}$$

$$= \frac{1}{s + \dfrac{k(-e/P_2 + h/P_2)}{(-1/P_2) \cdot d + u/P_2}}$$

This derivative indicates the order of magnitude of the change in real income caused by an increase in autonomous investment expenditures. It may be employed in a strictly qualitative way to determine the direction of the effect of an increase in autonomous investment expenditures on the level of income. Since $1 > s > 0$, $1 > k > 0$, $(-e/P_2 + h/P_2) < 0$, $u/P_2 < 0$, and $1/P_2 \cdot d > 0$, the last term in the denominator

$$\frac{k(-e/P_2 + h/P_2)}{(-1/P_2) \cdot d + u/P_2}$$

will be positive. As a result, the derivative is seen to be *positive* and an *increase* in autonomous investment expenditures will *increase* the level of income. This result is directly comparable to Equation (11.10).

The Supply of Labor. Assume that individuals attempt to balance the marginal disutility of labor against the marginal utility of income. Since the utility to be derived from money income depends on its real value or purchasing power, the quantity of labor supplied will depend primarily on the real return from offering labor services—the real wage rate w/P. Under the joint assumptions of diminishing marginal utility of consumption (out of earned income) and increasing marginal disutility of work, the labor supply function will have a positive slope indicating that laborers will only supply more labor at higher real wage rates. We may express this as follows:

$$N_s = N_s(w/P), \qquad \frac{\partial N_s}{\partial (w/P)} > 0. \qquad (13.12)$$

The Demand for Labor. On the demand side of the market, the profit maximizing condition indicates that under conditions of pure competition in all markets firms hire workers up to the point where the real wage they must pay is equal to the marginal productivity of labor.[11] Assume a simple aggregate production function,

$$O = Y/P = l(N, K) \qquad (13.13)$$

where O is the real volume of output from production and K is the capital stock used in the production process. Then

$$\frac{w}{P} = \frac{\partial O}{\partial N} = l'(N, K) \qquad (13.14)$$

where $l'(N, K)$ is the first derivative of the aggregate production function with respect to labor input. Diminishing marginal productivity of labor (derived from the aggregate production function under the assumption that the stock of capital K

---

[11] For the individual firm, given its production function, the demand curve for its product, and the labor supply curve it faces, profit may be defined as $\pi = P \cdot O - w \cdot N - c$, where c represents constant capital costs. The first-order condition for profit maximization requires

$$\frac{\partial \pi}{\partial N} = \left[\frac{dP}{dO} \cdot O + P \right] \frac{\partial O}{\partial N} - \left[\frac{\partial w}{\partial N} \cdot N + w \right] = 0$$

which simplifies to the general proposition that the profit maximizing firm will hire labor until its marginal revenue product equals its marginal factor cost,

$$\frac{\partial O}{\partial N} \left[P \left(1 + \frac{O}{P} \cdot \frac{dP}{dO} \right) \right] = w \left(1 + \frac{N}{w} \cdot \frac{\partial w}{\partial N} \right).$$

The reciprocals of the product terms in the brackets on either side of the equation represent the price elasticity of product demand and the wage elasticity of labor supply, respectively. In pure competition, these terms are equal to zero and the expression simplifies to the condition that the profit maximizing firm will hire labor until its marginal physical product is equal to the real wage, $\partial O / \partial N = w/P$. For further elaboration on the theory of the input decision of the profit maximizing firm see the last section of Chapter 10.

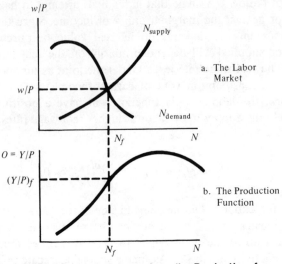

FIGURE 13.5. (a) Labor market. (b) Production function.

and the level of technology are held constant and that the function increases monotonically over the relevant domain) implies a downward sloping demand for labor curve. These relations are represented graphically in Figure 13.5.

If we assume perfect flexibility of the nominal wage and price levels and perfectly competitive conditions in the labor market, the nominal wage rate will be bid to a level which, together with the current price level, will establish a real wage that equates the supply of and demand for labor. This is the position of intersection shown in Figure 13.5(a). Since everyone who is willing to offer his labor services at this wage rate will be employed, this position is defined as full employment. When this level of employment is substituted into the production function [in Figure 13.5(b)], the full employment level of real output $(Y/P)_f$ is determined.[12]

This may be shown symbolically. We may represent the aggregate supply sector

---

[12] The reader will note that we have associated full employment with the equilibrium solution in the labor market. Likewise, in the present model, which presents labor supply and labor demand as functions of the real wage, involuntary unemployment will be associated with disequilibrium or with points off the supply curve of labor. In discussing these definitions Don Patinkin notes: "The norm of reference to be used in defining involuntary unemployment is the supply curve of labor, for this curve shows the amount of employment which the workers of the economy want to obtain in the light of the money wage, price level, and budget restraints with which they are confronted. Hence as long as workers are "on their supply curve"—that is, as long as they succeed in selling all the labor they want to at the prevailing real wage rate—a state of full employment will be said to exist in the economy. . . . Thus, by definition, the extent of involuntary unemployment is identical with the extent of the excess supply of labor which exists at the prevailing wage rate." Don Patinkin, *Money, Interest and Prices*, 314–315.

as a system of four equations—labor supply, labor demand, the equilibrium condition and the production function—in four unknowns—N_s, N_d, Y/P and w/P. These relations are

$$N_s = N_s(w/P) \tag{13.12}$$

$$N_d = N_d(w/P) \tag{13.14'}$$

$$N_s = N_d \tag{13.15}$$

$$Y/P = l(N, K) \tag{13.13}$$

where K, the capital stock, is assumed fixed. By substitution we can solve Equations (13.12), (13.14') and (13.15) for the level of employment N:

$$N_f = N(w/P).$$

Then from the production function [Equation (13.13)] we may solve for the full employment volume of output (Y/P):

$$(Y/P)_f = l(N(w/P), K) = \phi(w/P). \tag{13.16}$$

The Equilibrium Solution for All Three Markets

The solution for the equilibrium values of all the variables in our model may be viewed as follows. The labor market represents a fully determinate (that is, separable) subset of the global model. There are four equations, (labor demand, labor supply, the equilibrium condition and the production function) and four unknowns (N_s, N_d, w/P and Y/P). This subset is sufficient to determine the level of employment, the volume of real output and the real wage rate (as shown in Figure 13.5). The substitution of this solution for the volume of real output into the income–expenditures equilibrium equation [Equation (13.4)] determines the rate of interest (that rate which will equate real planned saving S/P and real planned investment I/P at the full employment level of output.

The subsequent substitution of these solution values for Y/P and i into the monetary sector equilibrium equation [Equation (13.11)] determines the price level. Prices will be at that level sufficient to equate the *real* value of the *nominal* supply of money balances provided through the monetary system with the volume of real money balances demanded at the levels of Y/P and i determined in the labor market and the income–expenditures sector, respectively. Finally, the nominal wage rate w will be set at that level which, together with the absolute price level determined in the

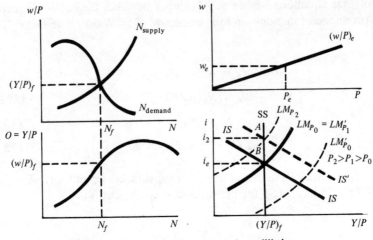

FIGURE 13.6. Aggregate general equilibrium.

monetary sector, will equal the real wage w/P determined in the labor market. This model is presented graphically in Figure 13.6.[13]

Let us examine some of the characteristics of this model.

(1) The levels of employment N, real output Y/P and the real wage rate w/P are determined in the labor market (in conjunction with the production function).

(2) The interest rate i is a "real" phenomenon determined in the income–expenditures sector by the intersection of the IS curve (IS) with the vertical line SS constructed over the full employment level of output $(Y/P)_f$ in Figure 13.6. It is that rate which is just sufficient to equate the real supply of saving with the real volume of investment demand at full employment.

(3) The absolute price level is determined in the monetary sector. Prices will adjust to that level necessary to make the real value of the quantity of nominal money balances supplied equal to the quantity of real money balances demanded at the level of real income and interest rate determined in the labor market and the income–expenditures sector, respectively. Graphically the

---

[13] This model is said to be solved *recursively*. One subset of the model, the labor market, is isolated and solved for the equilibrium values of the variables that enter the equations of that subset. One of these variables, real income Y/P, may then be treated as predetermined or "known" in another subset of the global model, the income–expenditures sector. Solution values for the remaining variables in the equations of that subset may now be determined. Again, one of the variables from that subset, the interest rate i, together with the level of real income may be treated as predetermined or "known" in the money market equations and those equations may be solved for the equilibrium values of the remaining variables—the price level, the real quantity of money demanded and the real value of the stock of nominal money balances supplied.

determination of the absolute price level isolates LM_{P_0} from the entire family of monetary sector equilibrium curves [as shown in Figure 13.6].

(4) The nominal wage rate w will adjust to that level which together with the absolute price level P determines the equilibrium real wage rate W/P.

These conclusions reflect the neoclassical tenets that the interest rate is a real variable determined by *productivity* (investment) and *thrift* (saving) and that the quantity theory of money is a theory of the value of money (the absolute price level) rather than a theory of income determination or employment (see Chapter 6). In this neoclassical model the monetary variables (the absolute price level, the nominal wage rate and the money stock) are determined solely by the monetary relations in the model. Thus the equilibrium values of the real variables are independent of both the supply of and the demand for money.[14] In this way the neoclassical economists indicated that monetary forces determined not the value of real variables in the economy but rather only the absolute price level, that is, the value of money.[15]

Let us demonstrate these quantity theory results by examining the effects of an increase in the money supply. For example, assume the initial equilibrium exists at B in Figure 13.6. Suppose there is an exogenous increase in the monetary base which causes a shift in the money supply curve from $M_s = \gamma(i)$ to $M_s' = \gamma_2(i)$.

Now assume further that at each interest rate the nominal stock of money which would be supplied by the banking system is exactly twice as large as before. At each and every interest rate–real income level combination along the old money market equilibrium curve there exists an excess supply of money. The family of money market equilibrium curves shifts to the right since some combination of a higher level of real income or a lower interest rate is necessary to generate an increase in the demand for money to absorb the increase in supply, thereby maintaining money market equilibrium. As a result, in Figure 13.6, LM_{P_0} shifts out to LM'_{P_0}.

In terms of economic behavior, the increased monetary base at existing price and interest rate levels will provide banks with undesired excess reserves. As banks expand loans and increase their deposit liabilities, the nonbank public finds itself with excess real money balances. As mentioned above, the excess supply of money can

[14] This may be seen from the recursive nature of our equation system. Since the equilibrium values of all real variables are in a sense "predetermined" in the production and expenditures sectors, if we change either the supply of or demand for money, *only* those variables determined in the monetary subset (P and w) will be affected. All variables predetermined in the production and expenditures subsets remain unchanged (in equilibrium).

[15] The equilibrium solution of this neoclassical model may be contrasted to that of a crude neoclassical model. In the crude neoclassical model the equations are the same as above except that the level of real income does not enter the saving-investment equations and the interest rate does not enter the money market equations. This results in the labor market determining the real wage, employment and real income as above; the saving-investment sector determining real saving, real investment and the interest rate; and the monetary sector (given the level of real income determined in the labor market) determining the equilibrium money stock and the general price level.

only be absorbed if there occurs some combination of an increase in real income or a decline in the interest rate.

However, in the present model real income cannot increase because the economy is at a full employment capacity level. Therefore, as individuals use their excess real money balances either (1) to purchase investment and consumer durable goods or (2) to purchase financial assets, only the general price level can rise. If the excess supply of money is spent directly on investment and consumer durable goods, there will be an immediate excess demand for these goods. If the excess supply of money is spent on financial assets, there will be a temporary increase in the price of those assets and a decrease in the market rate of interest, which also stimulates an increase in the demand for investment goods and consumer durables. Either way, there then occurs an excess demand for all goods and services which will exert upward pressure on the general price level. This will cease only when the price level has *exactly doubled* so as to restore real money balances to their previous equilibrium level. Finally, with real money balances restored to their former level, the *LM* curve in Figure 13.6 *LM'*$_{P_1}$ is back at its original position but with prices and all nominal values exactly doubled. At the new equilibrium point *B* all real variables will have the same values they had prior to the increase in the money supply. The levels of employment, output, the interest rate and the real wage are unchanged. They will have been "neutral" to this increase in the money stock.[16]

With the interest rate at its original level i_0, the nominal money stock will be exactly twice as high as before ($M_s' = \gamma_2(i)$). Therefore, if prices exactly double, real money balances will be the same as in the initial equilibrium,

$$\frac{2M_s}{2P} = \frac{M_s}{P}.$$

The economy adjusts to a higher nominal money stock simply by reducing the value of that money stock to the equilibrium real value M/P. This adjustment requires a change in the price level but no change in any real variables.

We should note explicitly that the interest rate (and other real variables) may diverge from its equilibrium value during the period of changing prices, while the economy is adjusting to the new higher stock of money. Although the equilibrium rate of interest is determined by real factors (productivity and thrift), during transition periods[17] (the period during which the economy is adjusting to a new monetary equilibrium) the interest rate may be influenced by monetary forces. In the final equilibrium in this static model, however, the interest rate will have returned to its previous value.

Let us now relax the assumption that there is no government sector and consider the effect on an increase in government deficit spending. We shall treat the increase

---

[16] "Monetary neutrality" defines a situation in which the equilibrium values of the real variables are independent of changes in the money supply. In Chapter 15 we shall examine this question more completely.

[17] See Irving Fisher, *The Purchasing Power of Money* (New York: Augustus M. Kelly, Bookseller, Reprints of Economic Classics, 1963), ch. 4. Transition periods and dynamics were discussed in Chapter 6 and will be discussed again in Chapter 15.

as being analogous to an increase in autonomous expenditures. Of course, as discussed in Chapter 12, this is not a completely accurate analogy because it overlooks the fact that government deficits must be financed. Nevertheless, we shall temporarily ignore the financing of the government's deficit.

Consider the equilibrium at point *B* of Figure 13.6. Under these assumptions an increased government deficit is depicted as a rightward shift in the *IS* curve from *IS* to *IS'*. Since we ignore the financing of this deficit, there is no further effect on *IS* and no effect on *LM*. The new *IS* curve intersects the old *LM* curve LM_P to the right of the full employment level of income. As real income is constrained to the full employment level, to the right of $(Y/P)_f$ there is excess aggregate demand.

Since real income is unchanged, the excess of expenditures requires a reallocation of saving and investment such that total expenditures remain unchanged. This can only occur if the market rate of interest rises to i_2 (as pointed out earlier, the rate of interest is a real phenomenon determined by the intersection of the *IS* curve and the *SS* curve).

With real income unchanged at a higher real market rate of interest, there exists an excess supply of money. As described above, an excess supply of money causes the price level to rise. As the price level increases, the money market equilibrium curve shifts leftward to LM_{P_2}. A new position of aggregate demand equilibrium is established at *A*. Thus the new higher price level is caused by the excess supply of money–the quantity theory of money holds.

Thus the increase in government deficit spending causes the real market rate of interest to rise. It has no effect on any other real variables. Employment, output, and the real wage are unchanged as shown in Figure 13.6. (The real wage is unchanged because the nominal wage and price levels change equiproportionately.) The autonomous expenditures multiplier is zero in this neoclassical model.

At *A* on the *IS* curve in the income–expenditures sector the level of real income is equal to the level of real expenditures. Compared to the previous equilibrium position *B* government expenditures have increased. Since real income has not increased, this implies that private expenditures must have fallen in an amount equal to the rise in government expenditures. In essence, greater government expenditures result in lower private expenditures. The government deficit causes the real interest rate to increase and this makes private consumption and private investment expenditures decline. Thus under these assumptions there is a *complete crowding out* of private expenditures by government expenditures.[18]

Aggregate Supply and Aggregate Demand: An Alternative Approach

We have seen that in this model with perfect price–wage flexibility the economy tends toward full employment through the competitive bidding for labor and jobs

---

[18] This should be contrasted to the model of Chapter 12 in which under a regime of rigid nominal wages and prices complete crowding out took place only under rather extreme assumptions.

in the labor market; the interest rate is a real phenomenon determined by productivity and thrift; and the absolute price level P will be proportional to the nominal money stock (the quantity theory obtains).

This analysis may be presented by means of an alternative technique— a technique that makes the determination of the equilibrium price level more explicit. Let us consider first the aggregate demand subset (the income–expenditures sector and the monetary sector) of our global model.

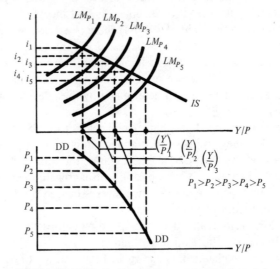

FIGURE 13.7. Derivation of the aggregate demand curve.

For the aggregate demand subset [Equations (13.1)–(13.4), and (13.9)–(13.11)], Figure 13.7 shows how the family of *LM* curves (reproduced from Figure 13.3) may be combined with the *IS* curve to yield a single aggregate demand curve *DD* in the *P, Y/P* plane. This curve shows the level of aggregate demand for real output at various price levels. For example, for the nominal money stock which would be supplied at interest rate i_1 to be sufficient to induce a level of aggregate demand equal to $(Y/P)_1$, the price level would have to be P_1. At any *lower* price level fewer *nominal* transactions balances would be required and more real money balances would be available for asset holding purposes by the public, leading to a lower interest rate, higher investment demand and a higher level of real aggregate demand. Thus, the *DD* curve slopes downward to the right.[19]

Let us derive the equation for this aggregate demand curve in the *P, Y/P* plane.

[19] The *DD* curve is drawn concave to the origin to maintain consistency with the graphs presented later when nonlinearities are introduced into the basic relationships. This does not influence our essential conclusions in any way.

For analytical simplicity assume that the nominal money stock is fixed by the monetary authority: $M_s = M_0$. Continue to assume a linear demand for money function:

$$\left(\frac{M}{P}\right)_d = \frac{m}{P} + k \cdot \frac{Y}{P} + \frac{u}{P} \cdot i.$$

In equilibrium,

$$\frac{1}{P} \cdot M_s = \left(\frac{M}{P}\right)_d$$

Substituting

$$\frac{1}{P} \cdot M_0 = \frac{m}{P} + k\frac{Y}{P} + \frac{u}{P} \cdot i$$

$$\frac{Y}{P} = \frac{1}{k}\left[\frac{1}{P} \cdot M_0 - \frac{m}{P} - \frac{u}{P} \cdot i.\right]. \tag{13.17}$$

Solving Equation (13.4), the equilibrium equation for the income–expenditures sector, for the interest rate yields

$$i = \frac{s}{-e/P + h/P} \cdot \frac{Y}{P} - \frac{a/P + a'/P}{-e/P + h/P}. \tag{13.4'}$$

Substitution of this result into Equation (13.17) yields

$$\frac{Y}{P} = \frac{1}{k}\left(\frac{1}{P} \cdot M_0 - \frac{m}{P}\right) - \frac{1}{k} \cdot \frac{u}{P}\left[\frac{s}{-e/P + h/P} \cdot \frac{Y}{P} - \frac{a/P + a'/P}{-e/P + h/P}\right]$$

$$\frac{Y}{P}\left[k + \frac{u}{P}\left(\frac{s}{-e/P + h/P}\right)\right] = \left(\frac{1}{P} \cdot M_0 - \frac{m}{P}\right) + \frac{u}{P}\left(\frac{a/P + a'/P}{-e/P + h/P}\right)$$

$$\frac{Y}{P} = \frac{(-e/P + h/P)[(1/P)M_0 - m/P] + u/P(a/P + a'/P)}{s(u/P) + k(-e/P + h/P)}. \tag{13.18}$$

This equation is represented by the *DD* curve in Figure 13.7. It is similar to the solution for aggregate demand derived earlier in this chapter and only slightly more complicated than Equation (11.9).

In accord with our initial assumptions, when the price level P changes, all the nominal values, a, a', m, etc., change in equal proportion, leaving the *real* values a/P, a'/P, m/P, etc., unchanged. However, M_0 is determined by the monetary authority. Therefore, when P increases (decreases), M_0/P will decrease (increase) causing a decrease (increase) in Y/P; in other words in Equation (13.18):

$$\frac{\partial(Y/P)}{\partial P} = \frac{-M_0(1/P^2)(-e/P + h/P)}{s(u/P) + k(-e/P + h/P)} < 0.$$

There are two unknowns, Y/P and P, in Equation 13.18. We may solve for equilibrium values of these variables by reintroducing the aggregate supply sector.

First, we shall rewrite the labor market and production relations. The basic differences with the earlier development will be to treat the price level as a separate variable in the labor market and to write the labor demand and supply relations with the nominal wage as the dependent variable. The supply function is

$$w_s = f(N, P) \tag{13.12'}$$

where

$$\partial w_s/\partial N > 0 \text{ and } \partial w_s/\partial P > 0;$$

the demand function is

$$w_d = g(N, P) \tag{13.14'}$$

where

$$\partial w_d/\partial N < 0 \text{ and } \partial w_d/\partial P > 0.$$

Equation (13.12') indicates that the nominal supply price of labor (the nominal wage asked by labor) varies directly with the quantity of labor supplied and directly with the general price level. This means that at a given price level labor suppliers will require an ever higher nominal wage as the quantity of labor hours they supply increases. It implies that, at a given level of employment, as the price level increases, labor suppliers shall ask for a higher nominal wage. If *money illusion* is completely absent, as the price level increases workers shall ask for a *proportionately* higher nominal wage. In this case Equation (13.12') is the equivalent of Equation (13.12) introduced earlier.[20]

Equation (13.14') indicates that the nominal demand price of labor, the nominal wage bid by employers, varies inversely with the quantity of labor demanded and directly with the general price level. This means that at a given price level labor demanders will be willing to pay an ever lower nominal wage as the quantity of labor demanded increases. It means that at a given level of employment employers will pay a higher nominal wage as the price level increases. If *money illusion* is completely absent, employers shall pay a *proportionately* higher money wage and Equation (13.14') will be the equivalent of Equation (13.14) introduced earlier.

[20] There are *income* and *substitution* effects here. The real wage is the opportunity cost of leisure. As the real wage rises, leisure is more expensive, so the labor supplier substitutes labor for leisure, and the quantity of labor hours supplied increases. Conversely, as the real wage rises, real income rises, and more of all goods are "purchased," including leisure, and the quantity of labor hours supplied decreases. We shall assume that the substitution effect dominates the income effect and that there is an unambiguous positive relationship between the real wage and the quantity of labor hours supplied.

The equilibrium condition is expressed as an equality between the nominal supply price and the nominal demand price of labor,

$$w_s = w_d. \qquad (13.15')$$

This relation is simply another way of viewing labor market equilibrium. If the market is in equilibrium, quantity demanded equals quantity supplied [Equation (13.15)] *and* supply price equals demand price [Equation (13.15')].

The aggregate production function is unchanged from the earlier analysis

$$Y/P = l(n, K). \qquad (13.13)$$

The present model is essentially very similar to the previous analysis of the labor market. It merely allows us to break out the general price level and the nominal wage as separate variables in the labor market.

The preceding four equations are represented graphically in Figure 13.8 on the next page.

Now consider the effect of an increase in the general price level from P_1 to P_2. Under the assumption that $\partial w_s/\partial P = \partial w_d/\partial P$, the increase in the price level shifts the labor supply curve to the left by the same amount that it shifts the labor demand curve to the right. If neither labor suppliers nor employers have *money illusion,* that is, if both are equally aware that an increase in the price level decreases the real wage, the magnitude of the shifts will be equal. As a result the nominal wage will rise in the same proportion that the price level increased and the equilibrium quantity of labor hours will be unchanged. As labor input is unchanged, the level of output in Equation (13.13) is unchanged. The aggregate supply curve is the vertical line in Figure 13.8.

As discussed in the previous section, in the aggregate supply subset [Equations (13.12')–(13.15')], if prices and nominal wages are *perfectly flexible* and if there is no *money illusion,* the nominal wage rate will always adjust to assure full employment, regardless of the absolute price level. Therefore, regardless of the price level, the full employment volume of output $(Y/P)_f$ will be supplied and the aggregate supply curve will appear as *SS* in Figure 13.9. Thus aggregate supply *SS* and aggregate demand *DD* together determine the equilibrium price level. More correctly, conditions in the money market determine the price level *given* the interest rate and the volume of output supplied. Equilibrium occurs at point *A* in Figure 13.9. This represents the solution value obtained by substituting the full employment level of output determined in Equation (13.16),

$$(Y/P)_f = \phi(w/P)$$

into Equation (13.18) and solving for the price level *P.* The four characteristics of the equilibrium solution discussed in the previous section continue to apply for this alternative formulation.

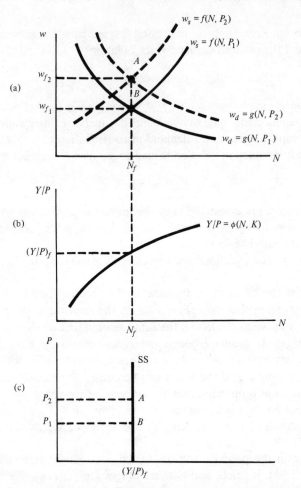

(a)

(b)

(c)

FIGURE 13.8. Labor market and production sector with nominal wage and price level as separate variables.

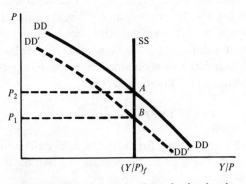

FIGURE 13.9. Determination of price level.

Consider a decrease in aggregate demand caused by a drop in autonomous investment expenditures. In the neoclassical model this causes the interest rate to decline sufficiently to restore aggregate demand to its full employment level. This in turn causes the price level to decline. The fall in the price level causes the nominal wage level to decrease in the same proportion such that the real wage and the level of employment are unchanged.

We employ Figures 13.6, 13.8 and 13.9 to describe these effects. In Figure 13.9 a decrease in aggregate demand causes a downward shift in the *DD* curve to *DD'*. Full employment equilibrium would be restored at P_1. In Figure 13.6 on page 350 the aggregate demand sector is in equilibrium at *A* with *IS'* and LM_{P_2}, the relevant curves. A decrease in autonomous expenditures causes a shift from *IS'* to *IS,* which causes the market rate of interest to decline to i_0. With real income unchanged the lower interest rate creates an excess demand for money and an excess aggregate supply of output at the initial price level P_2. As described earlier, this condition creates downward pressure on the general price level. The decline in the price level to P_1 increases the real value of mony balances such that money market equilibrium is restored at *B* in Figure 13.6.

As the price level declines from P_2 to P_1 in the labor market, depicted in Figure 13.8 on the previous page, demand shifts leftward and supply shifts rightward by the same amount. This causes the nominal wage to decline from w_{f_2} to w_{f_1} which is proportionate to the decrease in the price level. Therefore the real wage is unchanged, $w_2/P_2 = w_1/P_1$, at the full employment level.

In this situation there are no restraints on the nominal wage, the price level or the interest rate. As a result, given any decrease in aggregate demand, all three can adjust sufficiently to induce a volume of aggregate demand necessary to equal the full employment volume of aggregate supply. For example, if for some reason the market rate of interest did not immediately adjust when autonomous expenditures decreased, excess aggregate supply at P_2 in Figure 13.9 would cause the general price level to decline and real balances to increase. This would, in turn, lead to a decrease in the interest rate and stimulate induced investment spending so as to restore aggregate demand at the full employment level.

Summary

In this chapter the general price level was no longer assumed constant. The rational and informed behavior of labor suppliers and labor demanders was shown to make nominal wages perfectly flexible at a full employment level of production. As a consequence, only the general price level and not, as in previous chapters, the level of output responded to changes in the supply of money and the level of autonomous expenditures.

In Chapter 15 these and other implications of the neoclassical model will be examined more closely. Before that can be done, however, it is instructive to take a closer look at behavior in the labor market as well as other sectors of the model.

Our purpose in the next chapter will be to probe more precisely the interface between the degree of nominal wage flexibility and the corresponding extent to which the price level rather than the level of output responds to changes in aggregate demand.

QUESTIONS FOR CHAPTER 13

1. What is the effect of an increase in government deficit spending in the neoclassical model? Does this effect differ for a "crude" neoclassical model (see footnote 15)?

2. a. Derive the *LM* curve for the "crude" neoclassical model (footnote 15).
   b. Derive the *IS* curve for the "crude" neoclassical model.
   c. What is the effect of introducing liquidity preference into 2(a)?
   d. What is the effect of introducing a Keynesian consumption function into 2(b)?

3. Prove that the aggregate demand relation slopes downward in $Y/P,P$ space. Prove that for a crude neoclassical model this relation has an elasticity of -1.

4. Derive the neoclassical aggregate supply curve.

5. Incorporate a neoclassical aggregate supply sector with a Keynesian aggregate demand sector. Are the implications Keynesian or neoclassical?

6. Assume that in the long run the structure of the economy assumes neoclassical properties. What are the long run implications for private expenditures in a world of escalating government expenditures?

BIBLIOGRAPHY FOR CHAPTER 13

ANDERSEN, LEONALL C., and KEITH M. CARLSON, "St. Louis Model Revisited," *International Economic Review,* vol. 15, no. 2 (June 1974), 305–327.*

BAILEY, MARTIN, *National Income and the Price Level* (New York: McGraw-Hill, 1971), chs. 2 and 3.

BRANSON, WILLIAM, *Macroeconomic Theory and Policy* (New York: Harper and Row, 1972).

FAND, DAVID I., "Some Issues in Monetary Economics: Fiscal Policy Assumptions and Related Multipliers," *Review,* Federal Reserve Bank of St. Louis (January 1970), 23–27.*

FISHER, IRVING, *The Purchasing Power of Money* (New York: Augustus M. Kelly, Bookseller, Reprints of Economic Classics, 1963).

HICKS, J. R., in *Value and Capital* (Oxford: Clarendon Press, 1939), 205.

——, "Mr. Keynes and the Classics: A Suggested Interpretation," in American Economic Association, *Readings in the Theory of Income Distribution* (New York: McGraw-Hill-Blakiston, 1946), 461–472.

  * Reprinted in THOMAS M. HAVRILESKY and JOHN T. BOORMAN, *Current Issues in Monetary Theory and Policy* (Arlington Heights, IL.: AHM Publishing Corporation, 1976).

JOHNSON, HARRY G., Monetary Theory and Keynesian Economics, *Pakistan Economic Journal,* vol. 8 (June 1958), 56–70. Reprinted in Warren Smith and Ronald Teigen, *Readings in Money, National Income, and Stabilization Policy* (Homewood, IL: Richard D. Irwin, 1965), 32–43.

KEYNES, J. M., *The General Theory of Employment, Interest and Money* (London: Macmillan, 1936).

LOMBRA, RAYMOND, and RAYMOND TORTO, "Measuring the Impact of Monetary and Fiscal Actions: A New Look at the Specification Problem," *Review of Economics and Statistics,* vol. 56, no. 1 (February 1974), 104–107.*

MARSHALL, ALFRED, *Money, Credit and Commerce* (London: Macmillan, 1923).

METZLER, LLOYD A., "Wealth, Saving and the Rate of Interest," *Journal of Political Economy,* vol. 59 (April 1951), 93–116.

PATINKIN, DON, "Price Flexibility and Full Employment," *American Economic Review,* vol. 38 (September 1948), 543–564.

——, *Money, Interest and Prices,* 2nd ed. (New York: Harper and Row, 1965).

PESEK, BORIS, and THOMAS SAVING, *Money, Wealth, and Economic Theory* (New York: Macmillan, 1967), chs. 1–3.

RASCHE, ROBERT, "A Comparative Static Analysis of Some Monetarist Propositions," *Review,* Federal Reserve Bank of St. Louis (December 1973), 15–22.*

SMITH, WARREN, "A Graphical Exposition of the Complete Keynesian System," *Southern Economic Journal,* vol. 23, no. 3 (October 1956), 115–125.*

TUCKER, DONALD P., "Macroeconomic Models and the Demand for Money under Market Disequilibrium," *Journal of Money, Credit and Banking,* vol. 3 (February 1971), 57–83.

* Reprinted in THOMAS M. HAVRILESKY and JOHN T. BOORMAN, *Current Issues in Monetary Theory and Policy* (Arlington Heights, IL.: AHM Publishing Corporation, 1976).

14

Aggregate Supply and Aggregate Demand: Price and Wage Inflexibility

Introduction

In Chapters 11 and 12 under the assumption of nominal wage and price rigidity the level of output responded to changes in the money supply and autonomous expenditures. While the exact magnitudes of the multipliers were shown to be sensitive to the specification of the behavioral parameters, under reasonable conditions it was seen that the level of output could be affected by appropriate government policies. Then in Chapter 13, with the assumption of perfect nominal wage and price flexibility, the diametric opposite occurred—output was constant at a full employment level and the general price level responded to changes in the supply of money and autonomous expenditures. In what follows we shall examine in detail the interface between the degree of nominal wage flexibility and the extent to which the price level rather than the level of output responds to changes in aggregate demand.

A General, Aggregate Supply-Aggregate Demand Model

We begin by modifying the assumption of perfect nominal wage flexibility of the previous chapter. Rather we shall assume that the nominal wage is imperfectly flexible. This may occur for two reasons. One reason is that laborers may suffer from a degree of money illusion in the labor market; that is, they may determine the volume of labor they are going to supply on the basis of the *nominal* wage rate rather than the *real* wage rate. Alternatively, because of the contract structure in the labor market or because of imperfect information regarding available job openings and prevailing rates,[1] nominal wages may be rigid. In either case the assumption of imperfect flexibility of the nominal wage rate will modify the conclusions of our model.

To demonstrate this we return to the basic model represented in the previous chapter and impose special conditions on the labor supply equation:

$$w_s = f(N, P) \qquad (13.12')$$

where $\partial w_s/\partial N \to 0$ and $\partial w_s/\partial P \to 0$,

$$w_d = g(N, P) \qquad (13.14')$$

where $\partial w_d/\partial N < 0$ and $\partial w_d/\partial P > 0$, and

$$w_s = w_d \qquad (13.15')$$

$$Y/P = l(N, K). \qquad (13.13)$$

In this case, not only is there money illusion on the supply side of the labor market but there is also rigidity of the nominal wage rate. The supply price of labor in the short run not only fails to respond to price level changes ($\partial w_s/\partial P \to 0$) but it is also invariant with respect to the quantity of labor supplied ($\partial w_s/\partial N \to 0$). This is depicted by the labor supply and aggregate supply curves in Figure 14.1. Assume that the price level decreases from P_f to P_1. Labor demanders, employers, decrease their demand for labor because they will now sell their output at lower prices, that is, the marginal revenue product of labor has decreased. Employers have no money illusion.

In contrast, labor suppliers not only do not offer to work for lower nominal wages as the price level falls (they have money illusion, $\partial w_s/\partial P \to 0$), but also they do not offer lower nominal wages as employment decreases. Workers not only fail to realize that as the price level falls their real wage is rising and they can afford to reduce their nominal wage but they also fail to learn that they can obtain more employment by cutting their nominal wage offer.

Therefore in Figure 14.1, as the equilibrium quantity of labor hours decreases

[1] This is the basis of cases I and II in the model which follows. For further reading in this area, see Edmund S. Phelps, *Microeconomic Foundations of Employment and Inflation Theory* (New York: Norton, 1970). Another exposition of this approach is Robert Rasche "A Comparative Static Analysis of Some Monetarist Propositions," *Review*, Federal Reserve Bank of St. Louis (December 1973), 15–22. This is reprinted in Havrilesky and Boorman, *Current Issues in Monetary Theory and Policy* (Arlington Heights, IL.: AHM Publishing Corporation, 1976).

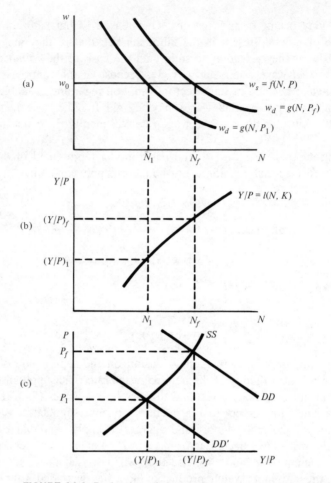

FIGURE 14.1. Derivation of the aggregate supply curve with nominal wage rigidity and money illusion on the supply side of the labor market.

from N_f to N_1, output falls from $(Y/P)_f$ to $(Y/P)_1$; the decrease in the price level from P_f to P_1 is consistent with the decrease in output from $(Y/P)_f$ to $(Y/P)_1$.[2] Figure 14.1 shows that with a less than perfectly vertical aggregate supply

[2] The slope of the aggregate supply curve depends on the slope of the production function and, implicitly, on the slope of the demand for labor curve. Assuming the money wage rate fixed at w_0, Equation (13.16) becomes

$$(Y/P) = \phi(w_0/P)$$

where $\partial(Y/P)/\partial P > 0$.

This can be simply proven. Assume $w = w_0$. Profit maximization by employers, under conditions of pure competition, yields the condition that the real wage equals the marginal physical product of labor,

curve decreases in aggregate demand from *DD* to *DD'* will cause decreases in both the general price level and the level of output.

It is now possible to demonstrate the proposition that a key difference between Keynesian and neoclassical models is the wage and price sensitivity of the labor supply relation. In Figure 14.2(a) there are three kinds of labor supply curves.

Case   *I* is the Keynesian case in which the nominal supply price of labor w_s is perfectly insensitive to the quantity of labor hours supplied, $\partial w_s/\partial N \to 0$ and perfectly insensitive to the general price level, $\partial w_s/\partial P \to 0$; that is, the nominal wage is fixed.

Case   *II* is the "intermediate" case in which the supply price of labor responds positively to changes in the quantity of labor hours supplied, $\partial w_s/\partial N > 0$ but does *not* respond to the general price level, $\partial w_s/\partial P \to 0$.

Case   *III* is the neoclassical case in which the supply price of labor responds positively to changes in quantity supplied, $\partial w_s/\partial N > 0$ and responds positively to changes in the general price level, $\partial w_s/\partial P > 0$. As in the

$$w_0/P = l'(N,\bar{K}).$$

Rearranging terms and recalling that pure competition in the goods market means that price equals marginal cost,

$$P = MC = w_0/l'(N,\bar{K}).$$

Then the slope of the aggregate supply curve *SS* is

$$\frac{\partial P}{\partial (Y/P)} = \frac{\partial P}{\partial l'(N,K)} \cdot \frac{\partial l'(N,K)}{\partial N} \cdot \frac{\partial N}{\partial Y/P}.$$

Since a decline in the marginal physical product causes an increase in marginal cost and hence the price of output,

$$\frac{\partial P}{\partial l'(N,K)} < 0$$

since an increase in labor input causes a decrease in its marginal physical product,

$$\frac{\partial l'(N,K)}{\partial N} < 0$$

and since output varies directly with labor input,

$$\frac{\partial N}{\partial (Y/P)} > 0.$$

Therefore,

$$\frac{\partial P}{\partial (Y/P)} > 0.$$

Here, as assumed in the discussion of aggregate supply in the previous chapter, the production function increases monotonically over the relevant domain.

The presence of a fixed nominal wage implies that the labor market is not automatically at full employment equilibrium and that the above relation $Y/P = \phi(w_0/P)$ will not always represent a full employment solution.

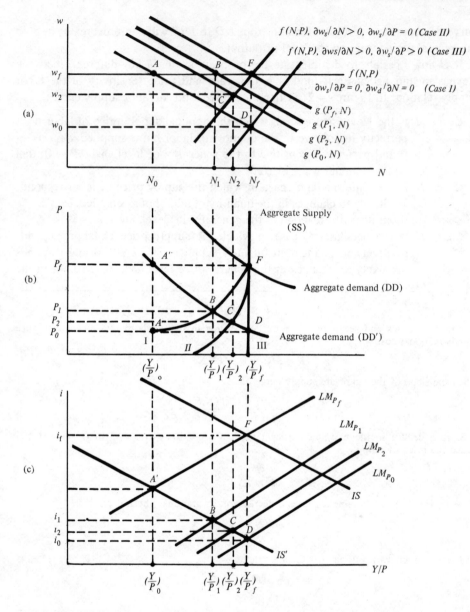

FIGURE 14.2. Global aggregate model under Keynesian, "intermediate," and neo-classical conditions on the supply side of the labor market.

previous chapter, we shall assume that the latter response is of the same magnitude as the response of the labor demand curve to the general price level, $\partial w_s/\partial P = \partial w_d/\partial P$.

In Figure 14.2(b) there are three aggregate supply curves, one for each of the Cases discussed above. Figure 14.2(c) shows the source of the movements in aggregate demand in Figure 14.2(b). The *shift* in the aggregate demand curve in Figure 14.2(b) is caused by the shift in the *IS* curve in Figure 14.2(c). The movements *along* the aggregate demand curve in Figure 14.2(b) are caused by shifts in the *LM* curves (induced by changes in the general price level, P_j) in Figure 14.2(c).

Starting out from an assumed full employment equilibrium at *F,* all markets on the aggregate supply side clear, all markets on the aggregate demand side clear and there is no involuntary unemployment or excess capacity. Now assume a decrease in real autonomous expenditures $\Delta a/P$. This causes a shift in the *IS* curve in Figure 14.2(c). The change in Y/P which will keep the income–expenditures sector in equilibrium is a multiple of the change in autonomous expenditures. There is an autonomous expenditures multiplier effect at work that causes real output to fall by the directed distance $(Y/P)_f - (Y/P)_0$ as shown in Figures 14.2(b) and 14.2(c). With the price level unchanged at P_f the aggregate demand sector goes to points labeled A' in these graphs. At A' the aggregate demand sector is in equilibrium. However, the economy is only partially in equilibrium; the aggregate supply sector is not in equilibrium at A'.[3]

The excess supply of output, $(Y/P)_f - (Y/P)_0$, causes the general price level to decline. The decrease in the general price level from P_f to P_0 causes the demand for labor to shift to the left to $g(P_0, N)$. At the higher real wage w_f/P_0 less labor is demanded. Assuming Case I is applicable, the supply price of labor is not responsive to changes in P or to the reduction in employment. The aggregate supply sector is in equilibrium at points A in Figures 14.2(a) and 14.2(b) but the aggregate demand sector is not.

The decrease in the price level affects real aggregate demand by causing the stock of real money balances to increase, thereby causing the *LM* curve to shift rightward. In Figure 14.2(c) this is reflected as a movement downward along the *IS'* curve; in Figure 14.2(b) it is reflected as a movement downward along the aggregate demand curve. As real aggregate demand increases, real output increases.

Now switching to the aggregate supply sector, as output rises from $(Y/P)_0$ to $(Y/P)_1$ in Figure 14.2(b) the price level rises from P_0 to P_1. The rise in the price level causes the demand for labor to increase to $g(P_1, N)$ in Figure 14.2(a). The upward movement along the aggregate supply curve in Figure 14.2(b) is a concomitant of the upward shift in the demand curve for labor in Figure 14.2(a) because

---

[3] Points A' represent aggregate demand equilibrium; the labor market nevertheless is not in equilibrium. As the price level (as well as the nominal wage) is assumed unchanged, at points A' we are off the labor demand and aggregate supply curves; there is *involuntary unemployment* in the labor market.

the rise in the price level from P_0 to P_1, at a fixed nominal wage w_f, lowers the real wage to w_f/P_1. The lower real wage, in equilibrium, is consistent with the decrease in the marginal productivity of labor caused by the rise in output.

Switching back to the aggregate demand sector, at price level P_1 the relevant LM curve is LM_{P_1}, which gives a level of real aggregate demand of $(Y/P)_1$ in Figures 14.2(b) and 14.2(c). Points B in all three graphs are positions of full quasi–equilibrium—"full" because aggregate demand and aggregate supply sectors are in equilibrium (that is, all markets clear) and "quasi" because there is still involuntary unemployment and excess capacity in the economy.[4]

Now assume that labor suppliers respond to the reduced level of demand for labor by lowering their nominal wage requests. The nominal wage is no longer perfectly rigid, $\partial w_s/\partial N > 0$. This means that Case II is applicable in Figure 14.2(a) and 14.2(b). The aggregate supply curve in Figure 14.2(b) now reflects a greater sensitivity of the price level to changes in output. Compared to Case I the decline in nominal wage offers causes costs and, hence, supply prices to decline at all levels of output. As above, in the aggregate demand sector the decline in the general price level shifts the LM curve to the right. The new position of full quasi–equilibrium occurs with a lower general price level P_2, a lower nominal wage w_2 and a higher level of real income Y/P_2. The lower price level shifts the demand for labor leftward to $g(P_2, N)$. Points C in all three figures are positions of full quasi–equilibrium.

Now assume that labor suppliers also respond positively to the lower price level (they realize that with a lower price level *real* wages are higher). This means that Case III is applicable in Figure 14.2 (a) and 14.2(b). At a lower price level the supply curve of labor shifts rightward in Figure 14.2(a) to $f(N,P)$ where $\partial w_s/\partial P > 0$. As the price level declines in Figure 14.2(b) and 14.2(c), aggregate demand is stimulated. The increase in aggregate demand associated with a lower price level in Figure 14.2(b) and 14.2(c) causes output to rise. The increase in output lowers the marginal productivity of labor and therefore the real wage.

Points D represent a position of full equilibrium in the macroeconomy. Compared to points C output has increased from $(Y/P)_2$ to $(Y/P)_f$, and the price level has fallen from P_2 to P_0. However the nominal wage level has fallen from w_2 to w_0 such

---

[4] At this point a traditional policy prescription was to promote once and for all nominal wage cuts which would shift the cost and supply curves of business firms (and hence SS in Figure 14.2(b)) downward. Whether the concomitant reduction in the price level would stimulate aggregate demand is a moot point. In the case of DD in Figure 14.2(b), a downward shift of SS would stimulate aggregate demand along DD. Real output and employment would rise. Consistent with the increase in output and employment and decrease in the marginal product of labor, the real wage rate would fall. With the increase in output there is therefore some upward pressure on marginal costs and prices and therefore the decrease in nominal wages exceeds the decrease in prices. For reasons developed in the final section of this chapter aggregate demand may not be price sensitive; in fact it may be perfectly price inelastic. In this case if nominal wages fall, output does not increase, prices fall proportionately and the system remains unchanged in real terms. Such an aggregate demand function in the P, Y/P plane would be a vertical line through B.

that the real wage has fallen from w_2/P_2 to w_0/P_0. The new lower price level causes the demand for labor to shift leftward to $g(P_0, N)$.

Notice that if we had assumed a Case III (neoclassical) world at the outset, given the decrease in real aggregate demand, prices, nominal wages and the interest rate would have adjusted downward to maintain full employment output $(Y/P)_f$ at an unchanged real wage, $w_0/P_0 = w_f/P_f$. All four neoclassical implications discussed on pages 350–351 in the previous chapter would obtain.

It should be noted that for Cases I and II final equilibrium values of the real variables in the model ($N, Y/P, I/P, S/P,$ etc.) are no longer independent of the absolute level of money wages and prices as they are in Case III, which assumed perfect price and wage flexibility. In contrast to the neoclassical model there are, in the solution of the Keynesian system, no separable subsets of the global model which may be solved recursively. All (labor market, income-expenditures and monetary sector) equations are solved simultaneously.

The influence of monetary conditions on the final Keynesian equilibrium can also be seen in Figure 14.2(b). Since a change in the nominal money supply causes a shift in the family of *LM* curves and thereby a shift in the aggregate demand curve *DD'*, this purely monetary change will affect the intersection of *DD'* and *SS* and, thereby, change the equilibrium values of real income and employment in Cases I and II. In short, money is no longer neutral. Modigliani stated this nicely:

> Systems with rigid wages share the common property that the equilibrium value of the "real" variables is determined essentially by monetary conditions rather than by "real" factors. . . . The monetary conditions are sufficient to determine money income and, under fixed (money) wages and given technical conditions, to each money income there corresponds a definite equilibrium level of employment. This equilibrium level does not tend to coincide with full employment except by mere chance.[5]

The preceding analysis demonstrates the importance of nominal wage rigidity and money illusion in the labor market for the implications of the global model. The greater the nominal wage rigidity and the greater the degree of money illusion on the supply side of the labor market, the less steep is the aggregate supply curve and the greater the extent of quantity adjustments (changes in output and employment) rather than price level adjustments to change in aggregate demand.

The policy implications of this analysis are quite interesting. If labor suppliers and labor demanders respond quickly to price and wage information there is a good deal less likelihood that changes in aggregate demand can have serious impact on output and employment. Most of the effect of changes in demand will be felt on the price and nominal wage levels. This, in turn, suggests that less credence be placed in the notion that inflation-causing increases in aggregate demand can reduce unemployment other than temporarily, the idea of the Phillips curve.[6]

[5] Franco Modigliani, "Liquidity Preference and the Theory of Interest and Money," *Econometrica* (January 1944). Reprinted in *Readings in Monetary Theory,* Friedrich A. Lutz and Lloyd W. Mints, eds. (Homewood, IL: Richard D. Irwin, 1951), 211.

[6] In footnote 2 the tradeoff between the increase in the price level and employment is captured in the slope of the aggregate supply curve. If there is no money illusion among labor suppliers, the aggregate supply curve is vertical.

This can be succinctly seen by substituting Equations (13.12′) and (13.14′) into (13.15) and taking the total differential:

$$\frac{\partial w_s}{\partial N} dN + \frac{\partial w_s}{\partial P} dP = \frac{\partial w_d}{\partial N} dN + \frac{\partial w_d}{\partial P} dP.$$

Rearranging and multiplying by $\partial(Y/P)/\partial N$ (the marginal product of labor), the slope of the aggregate supply curve is

$$\frac{d(Y/P)}{dP} = \frac{\partial(Y/P)}{\partial N} \quad \frac{dN}{dP} = \frac{\partial(Y/P)}{\partial N} \left(\frac{\partial w_d/\partial P - \partial w_s/\partial P}{\partial w_s/\partial N - \partial w_d/\partial N} \right).$$

The above expression shows that the greater the degree of nominal wage rigidity, the smaller is $\partial w_s/\partial N$ and, as $-\partial w_d/\partial N$ is positive, the greater is $\partial(Y/P)/\partial P$ and the flatter is the "slope" of the aggregate supply curve. It also indicates that the more prevalent is money illusion among labor suppliers, the flatter is the aggregate supply curve; that is, as $\partial w_s/\partial P$ decreases, $\partial(Y/P)/\partial P$ increases. In the neoclassical case where money illusion is absent, $\partial w_s/\partial P = \partial w_d/\partial P$, there is no wage rigidity and the aggregate supply curve is vertical, $\partial(Y/P)/\partial P = 0$.

One may view Keynesian and neoclassical models as lying on a spectrum in terms of the magnitude of quantity adjustments to changes in aggregate demand, that is, the magnitude of the basic autonomous expenditures multiplier. At the Keynesian extreme of this spectrum, in models without interest rate variations and with constant price and nominal wage levels, the autonomous expenditures multiplier is quite sizable; this essentially was the autonomous expenditures multiplier of Chapter 10. When money is introduced, changes in autonomous expenditures generate increases in the rate of interest, thereby choking off some expenditures—but the price and nominal wage levels are still held constant and the autonomous expenditures multiplier is somewhat smaller in magnitude; this basically was the multiplier of Chapter 11. When the interest rate *and* the price level are allowed to vary, but the nominal wage is still held constant (Case I in Figure 14.2), quantity adjustments to changes in aggregate demand are even smaller. When the interest rate, the price level and the nominal wage level are all variable, quantity adjustments to changes in aggregate demand become very small, depending on the degree of money illusion on the supply side of the labor market. This is reflected in Case II in Figure 14.2. Finally in a model of complete interest, wage and price flexibility and no money illusion, quantity adjustments are zero and the neoclassical implications prevail.

The processes discussed above can be viewed in a dynamic context. In the short run the price level and the nominal wage are rigid; in the long run they are perfectly flexible. In Figure 14.2 the economy may traverse over time a path from F to A' to B to C to D. Given a decrease in aggregate demand, the economy first responds in a Keynesian fashion, points A', and then works its way to a neoclassical position, points D.[7] Of course, the analysis can serve equally well in the other direction. The movement to points F *from* points D in Figure 14.2 because of an *increase* in aggregate demand can also be regarded as a dynamic process.

In the next section we illustrate this process. For simplicity we shall confine the analysis to the labor market. Keep in mind that now we will be talking about an *increase* in aggregate demand, not a decrease as in Figure 14.2.

Phillips Curve Analysis and the Rational Expectations Hypothesis

A slight modification will allow the effect of money illusion in the labor market to be expressed in terms of a Phillips curve. Assume no nominal wage rigidity. We have already seen that an increase in the price level will normally stimulate employment if there is more money illusion among labor suppliers than among labor demanders. Now assume that whatever change occurs in the flow of real aggregate expenditures, so as to cause the general price level to increase, this rate of increase will persist over time. This means that the resulting increase in the price level will itself persist over time and may, therefore, be expressed as a *rate* of inflation $\dot{P}$.[8] If this rate of price inflation is *not* fully anticipated by labor suppliers and *is* fully anticipated by labor demanders, the level of employment will temporarily rise and the rate of change of the nominal wage $\dot{w}$ will rise at a rate less than the rate of inflation.

This effect, seen in Figure 14.3, is a dynamic analog of the preceding static treatment of the labor market with money illusion on the supply side. At the initial level of full employment D, labor suppliers and labor demanders both perfectly anticipate the prevailing rate of price increase $\dot{P}_0$. This is reflected in a rate of nominal wage increase $\dot{w}_0$ that equals the rate of increase in the price level. Then because of a (persistent) increase in aggregate demand (associated, for example, with a persistent increase in the rate of money supply growth), the rate of price inflation rises from $\dot{P}_0$ to $\dot{P}_f$. As in the previous static analysis, if we assume that labor demanders have less money illusion than labor suppliers, employers will (more completely)

---

[7] Actually, in the most extreme Keynesian case, the quantity adjustment that occurs in a world of complete nominal wage, price level *and* interest rate rigidity, the world of the simple minded 1/1-MPC autonomous expenditures multiplier, is not even shown in Figure 14.2. It is measured as the horizontal displacement of the *IS* curve at an unchanged interest rate in Figure 14.2(c). That quasi–equilibrium would occur where the new *IS* curve *IS'* intersects the horizontal dotted line $i_f - F$ in Figure 14.2(c). Given a decrease in aggregate demand, with *all* prices including interest rates rigid, the economy might first tend to respond in this extreme Keynesian fashion. As interest rates begin to adjust downward, the movement would be to points A' in Figure 14.2; then, as the price level begins to adjust, the movement would be to points B; increasing the degree of nominal wage flexibility would subsequently carry the economy to points C and D.

[8] The rate of inflation is the derivative of the price level with respect to time, expressed as a percentage $(dP/dt)/P = \dot{P}$.

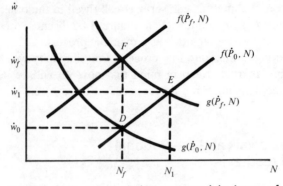

FIGURE 14.3. Labor market expressed in terms of
rates of nominal wage and price level changes.

anticipate the rise in the rate of inflation and the demand for labor will rise. Employers anticipate that their marginal revenue product will rise because they expect to sell their output at higher prices. The rate of increase of the nominal wage rises from $\dot{w}_0$ to $\dot{w}_1$.

This increase in demand raises the level of employment from N_f to N_1 (point E in Figure 14.3). Individuals who were previously searching for new jobs now accept employment more readily. They choose to reduce the amount of time they would normally spend unemployed because they perceive a higher opportunity cost of being unemployed. They perceive a new higher rate of increase of the nominal wage without perceiving the new higher rate of price inflation, that is, they mistakenly believe that the real wage is increasing.

The response of labor suppliers to a perceived higher real wage may be viewed in terms of income and substitution effects. The substitution effect is the substitution of labor for leisure as the opportunity cost of leisure, the *perceived* real wage, increases. The income effect is the "purchase" of more noninferior goods, including leisure time, as the real wage rises. On the assumption that the substitution effect dominates the income effect, the quantity of labor hours supplied will vary positively with a perceived increase in the real wage.

After a lag, labor suppliers will learn about the new rate of price inflation $\dot{P}_f$ and ask for a proportionately higher rate of increase in their nominal wage $\dot{w}_f$. In Figure 14.3 the supply curve shifts leftward and employment falls back to N_f. The market clears at point F. Individuals who are in the process of searching for new jobs are now aware that the real wage is not increasing, and they spend as much time searching for jobs as they did before the rate of inflation accelerated. The fiscal and monetary authorities can now increase employment (reduce unemployment among those searching for jobs) only by accelerating the rate of price inflation even further.

All of this can be translated into Phillips curve analysis. Assuming a fixed labor force, the level of unemployment U is defined as the difference between the labor force L and the level of employment N. In Figure 14.4 at point D there is an initial full employment level of output; the number of workers temporarily between jobs is $L - N_f = U_f$. This represents a "natural" level of unemployment; at this level of unemployment the rate of price inflation $\dot{P}_0$ is equal to the rate of increase of the nominal wage $\dot{w}_0$. The real wage is not changing. It may be said that all unemployment here is "frictional employment."

Assuming a persistent increase in the level of real aggregate demand, the rate of price inflation rises from $\dot{P}_0$ to $\dot{P}_1$, and as employment rises to N_1 in Figure 14.3, the level of unemployment initially falls to $U_1 (= L - N_1)$ in Figure 14.4. In Figure 14.3 when the rate of increase of nominal wages rises from $\dot{w}_0$ to $\dot{w}_1$, labor suppliers believe that the real wage is rising because they do not yet perceive the rise in the rate of inflation. Consequently, those in the process of searching for new jobs will expedite the searching process as they now believe it more costly to remain unemployed. The relevant point is E in Figure 14.4.

This decline in unemployment is only temporary as workers' wage requests come to reflect the new anticipated rate of price inflation. The Phillips curve shifts rightward from S_f to S_1 as this new rate of price inflation $\dot{P}_f$ becomes fully anticipated. Those workers that are temporarily searching for jobs will no longer be induced to hasten the process because of the (false) perception of a higher real wage (the opportunity cost of being unemployed). We go to point F in Figure 14.4. Except for improvements in the job search process in the labor market, the only way in which unemployment can be reduced would be for government once again to accelerate the rate of price inflation such that it is unanticipated by labor suppliers, thereby inducing temporary movements along the short-run Phillips curve S_1.

The vertical line above U_f represents the long-run Phillips curve. The economy can be at a full employment equilibrium at any fully anticipated rate of price inflation. Only unexpected acceleration and deceleration of the rate of inflation can induce (temporary) changes in employment and production. The vertical, long-run Phillips curve is a dynamic analog of the vertical aggregate supply curve in Figure 14.2b.

On the one hand a sizable number of economists accept this view of the short-run Phillips curve but insist that some money illusion remains among labor suppliers in

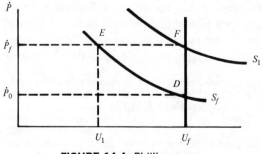

FIGURE 14.4. Phillips curve.

the long run because price expectations are based on past experience and are adjusted with a lag (the *adaptive expectations hypothesis*). Under this hypothesis, with a steadily rising inflation labor suppliers always expect inflation to be less than it actually is. This will produce a downward sloping (nonvertical) *long-run* Phillips curve. This implies that labor suppliers will tend to accept (some) reductions in real wages if they are accomplished by inflation.[9]

On the other hand many economists contend that it is unrealistic to believe that price expectations adapt only with a lag to historical price data. They argue that expectations are likely formed from all sorts of contemporaneous information. If individuals develop expectations rationally, they should be able to anticipate price inflation by getting information about its cause, the rate of increase of aggregate demand. Thus in a world of *rational expectations* changes in monetary and fiscal policy can affect output and employment only to the extent that such changes are unanticipated. According to the *rational expectations hypothesis* monetary and fiscal policy actions can successfully affect output and unemployment only to the extent that they are unpredictable.[10]

Other Sources of Inconsistency in the Aggregate Model

The likelihood of a rigid nominal wage structure or money illusion in modern industrialized economies was not the only problem posed by Keynes in his criticism of the market economy for its failure to maintain full employment. In fact, even under a regime of perfect price–wage flexibility, certain conditions may preclude the economy from automatically attaining a full employment level of output. Consequently, although the assumption of imperfect flexibility in the nominal wage rate may be realistic when analyzing the short-run behavior of the aggregate economy, let us restore our original assumption of perfect price–wage flexibility and examine some of the problems that may arise even under these circumstances.

Keynes suggested two possible features that could lead to unemployment within the framework of our static model, even though wages and prices were perfectly flexible. One of these is the liquidity trap and the other is a special case of interest insensitive aggregate demand. Each of these possibilities involves a situation in which the full employment level of saving is greater than the level of investment which could be induced at *any attainable* interest rate. In short, aggregate demand at full employment is less than aggregate supply at all attainable interest rates.

---

[9] For further discussion of the Phillips curve controversy, see Thomas M. Humphrey, "Changing Views of the Phillips Curve," *Monthly Review,* Federal Reserve Bank of Richmond (July 1973), 2–13; reprinted in Havrilesky and Boorman, *op. cit.*

[10] See Thomas J. Sargent and Neil Wallace, "Rational Expectations and the Theory of Economic Policy," *Journal of Monetary Economics* (April 1976). This has suggested to some analysts that incumbent politicians have an incentive to stimulate the economy in order to produce temporarily lower unemployment rates prior to elections and then to switch to recession-causing, ani-inflationary policy after elections. William D. Nordhaus, "The Political Business Cycle," *Review of Economic Study,* vol. 42 (April, 1975): 169–189.

In the case of the liquidity trap money demand becomes perfectly elastic at some positive interest rate. For example, when conditions are such that virtually everyone expects bond prices to fall, people will prefer money to bonds. They will absorb any increase in the money stock into asset balances without requiring a reduction in the interest rate (see Chapter 5). Therefore, regardless of how large the supply of money may be, the market rate cannot fall below the level determined by money demand. Hence, even if sufficient investment could be induced to offset full employment saving at some low rate of interest, the actual market rate can never attain that low level and investment will remain insufficient at the attainable rate.

In the case of interest insensitive aggregate demand (with no liquidity trap) investment and consumption expenditures may be so unresponsive to changes in the interest rate that even at a near zero rate of interest sufficient investment cannot be generated to match full employment saving.

Graphically, we may present these two cases in terms of our original *LM–IS* curves. Note that in the case of the liquidity trap full employment equilibrium could be attained if the money market equilibrium curve could be shifted down so as to intersect the income-expenditures and full employment curves at point *B* [Figure 14.5(a)]. However, because of the liquidity trap, there is a floor in the level of the interest rate at i_1 and hence sufficient investment spending is not forthcoming at that rate to match full employment saving. Thus at point *A* aggregate demand is below aggregate supply and prices will continually fall. Though decreasing prices shift the upward-sloping portion of the monetary sector equilibrium curve out to the right (as shown by the dashed *LM* curves), they leave the horizontal section of the curve around point *A* unaffected. Hence, as the model is constructed, falling prices are not sufficient to restore equilibrium in a liquidity trap situation.

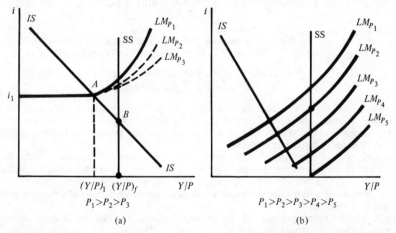

FIGURE 14.5. Inconsistent aggregate models with flexible prices. (a) Liquidity trap. (b) Inelastic demand.

In the case of interest inelastic aggregate demand [Figure 14.5(b)], the interest rate can be reduced as prices fall. Price deflation shifts the money market curve so that it intersects the income–expenditures curve at consecutively lower interest rates. Nevertheless, even if the interest rate is reduced to near zero, investment will be insufficient to match full employment saving. Again we have a situation in which prices will fall continually and yet are not capable of reducing the interest rate to the level necessary to restore full employment.

These two cases are demonstrated in terms of aggregate supply and demand relations in Figure 14.6. Since we are assuming complete price–wage flexibility, the aggregate supply curve is again a vertical line at the full employment level of income. However, at some price level the aggregate demand curve becomes vertical at a level of aggregate demand for real output which is short of the full employment level. Because of the liquidity trap and interest inelastic expenditures, aggregate demand does not respond to price changes; it is relatively price inelastic over some range.[11] In our original model a fall in prices was always sufficient to free some money balances from use in transactions and make them available for asset-holding (speculative) purposes. Price level reductions were always sufficient to lower the interest rate and thereby stimulate additional investment expenditures and consumption expenditures and increase aggregate demand. As a result the aggregate demand curve DD sloped downward to the right over its entire range. In the present models, however, there is some price level [P_1 in the liquidity trap case, Figure 14.5(a) and P_5 in the interest insensitive expenditures case, Figure 14.5(b)] below which further price declines have no effect on the interest rate and, therefore, cannot induce additional spending in order to increase aggregate demand. Consequently, in Figure 14.6 the DD curve would become vertical at those price levels.[12]

The policy implications of these cases are very important. Since monetary policy (changes in the stock of money) works through shifts in the monetary sector equilibrium curve, monetary policy is no longer effective in restoring full employment. (This was previously demonstrated.) Therefore, only a policy that can bring about a

---

[11] This may be seen in terms of Equation (13.18). That equation represents the aggregate demand relation depicted by the DD curve in Figure 14.6. As in Equation (13.18),

$$\frac{\partial(Y/P)}{\partial P} = \frac{-(-e/P + h/P)M_0 \ (1/P^2)}{k(-e/P + h/P) + s(u/P)}.$$

In the case of the liquidity trap, the interest rate coefficient in the money demand relation u/P becomes infinite (the public demonstrates an unlimited preference for liquidity). Consequently, as $u/P \to \infty$, $\partial(Y/P)/\partial P \to 0$ and changes in the price level become ineffective as a force for changes in aggregate demand.

In the case of perfectly interest insensitive expenditure demand functions, h/P, the interest rate coefficient in the investment demand equation, goes to zero. If saving is also perfectly interest inelastic, $e/P = 0$, and $\partial(Y/P)/\partial P = 0$. Again, price level changes cannot induce an increase in aggregate demand. Under these conditions the DD curve becomes vertical over some range as depicted in Figure 14.6.

[12] The survey of empirical tests of the money demand function in Chapter 7 shows little evidence of the liquidity trap.

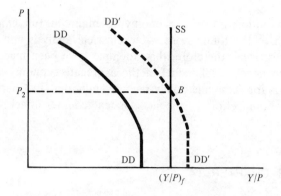

FIGURE 14.6. Liquidity trap and interest insensitive investment demand in terms of aggregate
supply and demand curves.

positive shift in the income–expenditures sector curve (and, thus, the aggregate demand curve *DD*) can restore full employment. Since government expenditures are a part of aggregate demand and government taxation policy can affect aggregate demand indirectly through its influence on private expenditures decisions, government fiscal policy alone may be sufficient to stimulate the volume of expenditures necessary to generate full employment. In the case above, for example (Figure 14.6), an increase in aggregate demand brought about by fiscal policy would shift *DD* to *DD'* and would restore full employment at price level P_2 (point *B*).[13]

Therefore, even with complete nominal wage–price flexibility certain cases may arise which prevent the economy from automatically reaching full employment equilibrium. Furthermore, in these cases it is possible to restore full employment *only* by the positive intervention of the government through fiscal policy.

The destruction of the assumed automaticity of the market economy (even under the assumption of price–wage flexibility) together with the summoning of govern-

---

[13] We may again employ the aggregate demand relation of Chapter 13 to demonstrate this point. Government fiscal policy (an increase in government expenditures, for example) affects our model through its impact on the autonomous expenditures parameters a/P and a'/P. As in Equation (13.18),

$$\frac{\partial(Y/P)}{\partial(a/P)} = \frac{\partial(Y/P)}{\partial(a'/P)} = \frac{u/P}{k(-e/P + h/P) + s(u/P)} > 0.$$

Thus an increase in autonomous expenditures will increase aggregate demand. The relative response in aggregate demand to a given change in autonomous expenditures will be determined by the parameters in the preceding equation. Most importantly, the numerically larger is u/P, the interest rate coefficient in the money demand function and a determinant of the interest elasticity of the demand for money balances, the greater will be the change in aggregate demand. Likewise, the smaller the sum of the interest coefficients in the expenditures demand equations $(-e/P + h/P)$, the less will induced expenditure be cut back as the interest rate rises in response to the increase in autonomous demand and the greater will be the net increase in aggregate demand in the economy. These principles were discussed in Chapter 11.

mental fiscal intervention into the economy to maintain full employment were serious blows both to the foundations of neoclassical analysis and to free market ideals. It is not surprising, therefore, that attempts have been made to restore the automaticity of the neoclassical model of the aggregate economy as an engine of analysis and a basis for economic policy recommendations. In Chapter 15 we shall examine an outstanding effort in the neoclassical counter-attack, the Pigou real balance effect.

QUESTIONS FOR CHAPTER 14

1. Evaluate: Given a position of unemployment, a once and for all cut in nominal wages will increase real output and employment because lower prices will
   a. Lower directly the real interest rate.
   b. Increase real income and hence real consumption.
   c. Increase real money balances and hence lower the interest rate.
   d. Lower real wages and hence the quantity of labor supplied will decrease.
   e. Cause anticipations of further price declines.

2. Rank the following Keynesian propositions in the order of their importance to the result of underemployment equilibrium.
   a. A high interest elasticity of the speculative demand for money.
   b. The absence of an international sector in many models.
   c. Rigid nominal wages.
   d. The concept of income induced consumption spending.
   e. A low interest elasticity of investment demand.
   f. Rigid prices.

3. Why does the following reduce the magnitude of the autonomous expenditures multiplier?
   a. A variable interest rate.
   b. A flexible price level with a rigid nominal wage.
   c. Flexible price and nominal wage levels with money illusion on the part of labor suppliers.

4. Can a little (acceleration in) inflation be a good thing?

5. Using the Phillips curve model show that an "inflationary recession" is not a theoretical economic enigma.

6. What is meant when it is said that neoclassical economics has a flow theory of interest while Keynesian economics has a stock theory of interest?

7. "Monetary and fiscal policy can affect output and employment only to the extent that policy changes are unpredicted." Evaluate.

8. Reconcile the definition of involuntary unemployment in this chapter (footnote 3) with Patinkin's definition in Chapter 13 (footnote 12). Compare these notions of involuntary unemployment with the (expectations augmented) Phillips Curve precept that all unemployment is frictional, as implied by the discussion in the third section of this chapter pp. 370–374.

Appendix to Chapter 14
A Modern Synthesis of the Economics of
Keynes and Neoclassical Economics

The previous three chapters have attempted to draw a fairly clear distinction between neoclassical and Keynesian economics. Chapters 13 and 14 presented the fundamental view that the Keynesian system of underemployment (quasi) equilibrium and quantity adjustment rests on two possible, special and unrelated, modifications of the neoclassical model. One could assume nominal wage rigidity and money illusion on the supply side of the labor market or, in models with flexible nominal wages and no money illusion, one could assume a liquidity trap and/or an extremely interest inelastic aggregate demand function. The next chapter will examine the hypothesis that the real balance effect could compensate for the effects of the latter phenomena and restore full employment equilibrium in a world of flexible wages and no money illusion.

This has been the received conventional wisdom of standard macroeconomic theory for some time. In recent years certain scholars of the works of Keynes have argued that the elements of the Keynesian system (nominal wage rigidity or money illusion in the labor supply equation and the liquidity trap or interest inelastic expenditures on the aggregate demand side) should not be viewed as unrelated, special cases of the presumably more general neoclassical model.

Rather, these authors contend that Keynes (and his modern, unreconstructed followers)[1] had a theory that was conceptually much different from that of the neoclassical model. They say Keynes' work was premised on a very different image of the market exchange process. They hold that Keynes' theory is not consistent with the neoclassical view of the market system in which supplies are fixed, prices are flexible and market information is perfect and immediately available—a system in which trades occur only after an equilibrium set of prices is established. On the contrary, they argue that Keynes' economics presupposes a different kind of market system. They say that in Keynes' view of the market, supplies were flexible, prices were fixed in the short run and information about "equilibrium" prices was poor or unavailable. In this sort of market economic exchanges must still go on. Within this context, nominal wage rigidity or money illusion, the liquidity trap and interest inelastic aggregate demand are *not* seen as unrelated, special cases, as in the neoclassical model, but rather as integral features of a consistent world view. Let us elaborate.

In the neoclassical vision of the market process the fixed supply assumption is based on the short-run "market period" of Marshall in which supply cannot be

---

[1] See, for example, Robert W. Clower, "A Reconsideration of Microfoundations of Monetary Theory," *Western Economic Journal,* vol. 6 (1967); Axel Leijonhufvud, *Keynesian Economics and the Economics of Keynes* (New York: Oxford University Press, 1968). For an excellent survey, see A. G. Hines, *On the Reappraisal of the Economics of Keynes* (London: Martin Robertson, 1971). The latter is reprinted in Havrilesky and Boorman, *op. cit.*

increased as it is at full capacity. As demand changes, suppliers react by changing their prices. Demanders then react to new equilibrium price levels by adjusting quantities demanded.

The means whereby demanders discover the new set of equilibrium prices is called *tatonnement*. Assume some shock is imposed on a system of markets in equilibrium; in the tatonnement model no actual trading takes place; rather, price information and bids are exchanged until prices are set at levels at which all markets would clear in equilibrium. Only then does actual trading occur. Thus the transition from one equilibrium to another takes place in an immediate, once and for all, quantum leap.

The parallel between the two processes and the neoclassical macroeconomic model is clear. In the neoclassical model the assumption of fixed quantities supplied is reflected in the full employment level of output. Once aggregate supply is given, the price level and interest rate instantaneously adjust in the aggregate demand sector to bring about equilibrium.

Now consider an alternative picture of the market process. Production and employment plans, as well as future price expectations, are formulated by firms and workers for the *current* period based on market data for the *previous* period. During this short-run planning period prices and nominal wages are essentially fixed.

Under these conditions changes in demand are met, where possible, by adjustments in inventories. After inventories change prices may adjust as soon as plans for the next period are made. All this takes time, and individuals continue to carry out transactions even if prices are not in equilibrium and there is some excess demand (or supply) in the system.

The parallels between the above disequilibrium process and the Keynesian model of earlier chapters are clear. Assume an exogenous disturbance in the labor market stemming from a decrease in some autonomous expenditures component of aggregate demand such that, at the prevailing nominal wage, supply exceeds demand. Disequilibrium may not disappear ("involuntary unemployment" may persist) because labor suppliers have formulated their plans in terms of a given nominal wage. At first they expect that the unemployment resulting from the decrease in aggregate demand is local and transitory. They will continue to make offers to work at that wage because they expect it to persist into the near future. (They have inelastic expectations, that is, if the nominal wage were to change, they assume it would soon return to its present level.) The information that would enable them to make rational alternative offers is not costlessly obtained.[2]

This reduction in aggregate demand simultaneously hits business firms; rather than immediately cut prices they will let inventories accumulate. Like labor suppliers, business firms, too, are quantity adjusters in the short run. As inventories build up, some pressure for price cuts develops. Therefore two possibilities present

---

[2] In the longer run they will search for employment at the expected wage, balancing the cost of search against the probability of a better offer. The latter would be a decreasing function of the length of the search period. See Armen Alchian, "Information Costs, Pricing and Resource Unemployment," *Western Economic Journal* (June 1969).

themselves to producers: either to cut prices and attempt to pay a proportionately lower nominal wage (leaving employment and production unchanged) or to cut prices and, in the face of an unchanging nominal wage (a rising real wage), to reduce employment and production. In view of nominal wage inflexibility only the latter option is feasible.

Under this condition labor suppliers are unable to convert their excess supply of labor at the given nominal wage into cash income. They cannot "liquidate" their "endowment" of available labor time. Therefore they cannot absorb the (full employment) level of output produced by business firms without borrowing against future income. Producers continue, therefore, to find inventories accumulating. They too cannot liquidate.[3]

The desire of labor suppliers and producers to become liquid leads to attempts to sell off financial assets. This helps arrest any decline in the interest rate that would otherwise have occurred as real income decreased. Moreover, expected future interest rates are formed in the same fashion as expected nominal wage rates—on the basis of recent market experience. Interest expectations are therefore inelastic, just like wage and price expectations. Therefore any present decline in the interest rate will be expected to be followed by a rise of nearly equal magnitude. This bearish prospect further heightens the preference for liquidity and further helps arrest any decline in the interest rate. This explains why Keynes' liquidity trap is consistent with "wage stickiness" in the labor market.[4]

With the interest rate "trapped" at "too high" a level by the preference for liquidity, aggregate expenditures cannot be stimulated by declining interest rates. In addition, with the interest rate trapped at too high a level, individuals are less inclined to borrow against future income in order to sustain recent levels of consumption expenditures. They are also less likely to be able to borrow because lenders view any present decline in the interest rate as likely to be followed by a nearly equal rise. This would lead to a capital loss from holding debt. Lenders, therefore, also want to be liquid.

Consumption expenditures thus tend to be constrained to depend heavily on current cash income.[5] This explains why consumption (and saving) are not sensitive to the interest rate. It also accounts for interest inelastic aggregate expenditures.

The fact that consumption expenditures are tied so inextricably to current income

---

[3] Clower characterizes this as a "dual decision hypothesis." Under this hypothesis each transactor may make two decisions, (1) to maximize his utility subject to notional income, and (2) if *notional income* is less than *actual income* to maximize utility subject to *actual* income. *Notional income* is associated with the transformation of labor time of workers and goods of producers into purchasing power. Actual income is the income actually obtained from the sale of one's endowment of labor time or goods. If actual is less than notional, it is the second decision that provides the relevant market signals. See Robert W. Clower "The Keynesian Counterrevolution: A Theoretical Appraisal," in *The Theory of Interest Rates,* F. H. Hahn and F. Brechling, eds. (New York: Macmillan, 1965).

[4] Keynes' inelastic or regressive expectations view of the demand for speculative balances was discussed in Chapter 5.

[5] This rationalizes the high marginal propensity to consume and the absence of wealth and interest rate arguments in Keynes' consumption function discussed in Chapter 10.

implies that the initial decline in autonomous aggregate demand will generate an even more sizable decline in aggregate real income. Thus Keynes' consumption function and related autonomous expenditures multiplier are illiquidity phenomena.

This simplistic sketch conveys the notion that the heralded features of Keynes' theory (his "sticky" nominal wage labor supply function, liquidity trap, interest inelastic expenditures relation and consumption function) are not separate special cases of a more general neoclassical model but rather are integral parts of a rather different world view.

The unique feature of Keynes' world view is the difficulty with which individuals can get and respond to accurate information about future equilibrium prices. If that information is unavailable, there will be considerable uncertainty about future market-clearing prices and prices will be the outcome of a *nontatonnement* search process.[6] Uncertainty leads to wage–price stickiness, inelastic price expectations, absolute liquidity preference, interest inelastic aggregate expenditures and the Keynesian consumption function and multiplier principle. Reduce the degree of uncertainty and these conditions are ameliorated as the economy becomes more neoclassical in terms of the properties of its structural equations. In short, the degree of uncertainty in the economy may help explain where behavior will fall in the spectrum between the Keynesian and neoclassical paradigms.

Is the degree of price uncertainty given or can it be reduced by appropriate governmental policies? Many economists would opt for the latter. For example, they would contend that policies which help disseminate market information, for instance in the labor market, would militate against the socially costly variations in output and employment that mark the Keynesian theory. As another example, many economists would argue that a stable monetary environment, featuring a stable rate of money supply growth, would promote less uncertainty regarding future prices. This, for instance, could reduce the degree of money illusion on the part of labor suppliers that was seen in Chapter 14 to generate quantity rather than price adjustments to changes in aggregate demand. According to the *rational expectations hypothesis* discussed earlier in this chapter, a stable policy regime would also reduce the number of unanticipated and hence quantity adjustment-creating shocks imposed on the economy by policymakers.

This thesis suggests that Keynesian and neoclassical theories are not irreconcilable.[7] Rather, it indicates that in a less stable macroeconomic policy environment

---

[6] A nontatonnement process thus arises from uncertainty about the future. The speculative, liquidity preference aspects of this process were mentioned earlier. See Robert W. Clower, "The Keynesian Counterrevolution . . . ," *op. cit.* Finding the suitable microeconomic foundations for these macroeconomic adjustment processes is a major open question in economic theory. Recent analysis is concerned with information costs, search behavior and imperfect adjustment. For example, see Robert Barro and Herschel Grossman, *Money, Employment and Inflation* (New York: Cambridge University Press, 1976).

[7] John Wood, "Money and Output: Keynes and Friedman in Historical Perspective," *Business Review,* Federal Reserve Bank of Philadelphia (September 1972), 13–21. Reprinted in Havrilesky and Boorman, *op. cit.*

the economy will tend to sustain a Keynesian structure (the Keynesian short run will persist for a longer period); in an economy marked by a more stable money supply growth (and minimal fiscal shocks) the structure will tend to be more neoclassical (the Keynesian short run will be shorter lived). Thus, there would seem to be a remarkable complementarity between the behavior of the policy maker and the structure of the economy.[8] Having considered some of the adverse effects of monetary instability, in the final section of the next chapter we shall consider some of the sources of monetary policy instability.

BIBLIOGRAPHY FOR CHAPTER 14

ALCHIAN, ARMEN, "Information Costs, Pricing and Resource Unemployment," *Western Economic Journal* (June 1969).

BARRO, ROBERT, and HERSCHEL GROSSMAN, *Money, Employment and Inflation* (New York: Cambridge University Press, 1976).

BRANSON, WILLIAM, *Macroeconomic Theory and Policy* (New York: Harper and Row, 1972).

CLOWER, ROBERT W., "A Reconsideration of Microfoundations of Monetary Theory," *Western Economic Journal,* vol. 6 (1967).

——, "The Keynesian Counterrevolution: A Theoretical Appraisal" in *The Theory of Interest Rates,* F. H. Hahn and F. Brechling, eds. (New York: Macmillan, 1965).

HINES, A. G., *On the Reappraisal of the Economics of Keynes* (London: Martin Robertson, 1971).*

HUMPHREY, THOMAS M., "Changing Views of the Phillips Curve," *Monthly Review,* Federal Reserve Bank of Richmond (July 1973), 2–13.*

KEYNES, J. M., *The General Theory of Employment, Interest and Money* (London: Macmillan, 1936).

LEIJONHUFVUD, AXEL, *Keynesian Economics and the Economics of Keynes* (New York: Oxford University Press, 1968).

LEONTIEF, WASSILY, "Postulates: Keynes' General Theory and the Classicists," in *The New Economics,* Seymour E. Harris, ed. (New York: Alfred A. Knopf, 1947), 232–242.

MODIGLIANI, FRANCO, "Liquidity Preference and the Theory of Interest and Money" in American Economic Association, *Readings in Monetary Theory* (New York: McGraw-Hill Blakiston, 1951), ch. 11.

——, "The Monetary Mechanism and Its Interaction with Real Phenomena," *Review of Economics and Statistics,* vol. 45 (February 1963), 79–107.

---

[8] Complementarity between the behavior of the policy maker and the structure of the economy further implies that many of the *micro*economic policies of government, such as manpower policies and incomes policies, while based on observed structural relations, such as wage–price insensitive labor supply curves, are ultimately conditioned by the degree of stability of the government's *macro*economic policy.

* Reprinted in THOMAS M. HAVRILESKY and JOHN T. BOORMAN, *Current Issues in Monetary Theory and Policy, op. cit.*

NORDHAUS, WILLIAM D. "The Political Business Cycle," *Review of Economic Studies,* vol. 42 (April, 1975), 169–189.

PHELPS, EDMUND S., *Microeconomic Foundations of Employment and Inflation Theory* (New York: Norton, 1970).

RASCHE, ROBERT, "A Comparative Static Analysis of Some Monetarist Propositions," *Review,* Federal Reserve Bank of St. Louis (December 1973), 15–22.*

SARGENT, THOMAS J., and NEIL WALLACE, "Rational Expectations and the Theory of Economic Policy," *Journal of Monetary Economics* (April 1976).

TOBIN, JAMES, "Money Wage Rates and Employment," in *The New Economics,* Seymour E. Harris, ed. (New York: Alfred A. Knopf, 1947), 572–587.

WOOD, JOHN H., "Money and Output: Keynes and Friedman in Historical Perspective," *Business Review,* Federal Reserve Bank of Philadelphia (September 1972).*

15

The Price-Flexible Model: The Analysis Extended

Introduction

In Chapter 13 we expanded the basic *LM–IS* model of Chapter 11 to include flexible nominal wage and price levels, an endogenous money supply, the influence of the market rate of interest on saving and a very simple production (labor market) supply sector. In this chapter we will continue the modification and expansion of that model. In particular we introduce private wealth into our analysis and examine its effect on the conclusions derived in previous chapters. We begin with an examination of the *Pigou* or real-balance effect. Then we apply the aggregate demand–aggregate supply model with perfectly flexible nominal wages and prices to the analysis of a number of real-world problems.

The Real Balance Effect

The introduction of the Pigou effect into the price-flexible model of Chapter 13 requires a reformulation of the saving function to include the *net real value of financial wealth* or "real balances" as an independent variable. The Pigou or real balance effect refers to the hypothesis that saving varies inversely (and therefore consumption varies directly) with the current net real value of financial wealth held by individuals.

In Chapter 10 the relationship between consumption, saving and wealth was explored. There wealth was defined to consist of human and nonhuman wealth. In the present chapter, as in Chapter 12, we shall not include human wealth in the definition. Wealth is defined to consist solely of the net debt and equity (financial) claims held in the private sector.

Assume for the moment that there are only two financial assets in the economy, bonds issued and purchased solely in the private sector and fiat money spent into circulation by the government.[1] In this economy the *net* value of holdings of privately issued bonds is zero since the holdings of debtors and creditors within the private sector of the economy cancel out. Under these assumptions the total value of net financial wealth held by the public is equal to the value of government fiat money in circulation. The nominal value of this money stock is designated by the symbol M_g. Thus M_g/P = real money balances = net real financial wealth of the public.

Assume that the household sector is influenced by the level of private nonhuman wealth when making its consumption (and saving) decisions. As we are (temporarily) defining wealth to consist only of the real value of money issued by government, the linear saving function of the previous chapter is modified to include this new variable:

$$\frac{S}{P} = S\left(\frac{Y}{P}, i, \frac{M_g}{P}\right) = \frac{-a}{P} + s \cdot \frac{Y}{P} + \frac{e}{P} \cdot i + v \cdot \frac{M_g}{P} \qquad (15.1)$$

where $a, e > 0, 0 < s < 1$ and $v < 0$.

The specific hypothesis implied by the real-balance effect is that there is an inverse relationship between the value of net real financial wealth held by the public M_g/P and the level of real saving. For any given level of real income and the interest rate, the greater the value of an individual's current real money balances, the less his desire to save and add to his wealth and therefore the greater his consumption expenditures.

Let us examine the effects that this new variable has on our previous conclusions. Substitution of the modified saving function together with the investment demand function into the equilibrium condition yields the following income–expenditures sector equilibrium (*IS*) equation:

$$\frac{-a}{P} + s \cdot \frac{Y}{P} + \frac{e}{P} \cdot i + v \cdot \frac{M_g}{P} = \frac{a'}{P} + \frac{h}{P} \cdot i \qquad (15.2)$$

$$\frac{Y}{P} = \frac{1}{s}\left[\frac{a}{P} + \frac{a'}{P} + \left(\frac{-e}{P} + \frac{h}{P}\right) \cdot i - v \cdot \frac{M_g}{P}\right]. \qquad (15.3)$$

---

[1] The money stock in this model will consist solely of government fiat money spent into circulation for the purchase of goods and services by the government. By assumption, then, there are no demand deposit liabilities issued by the commercial banking system and the net financial wealth of the public consists solely of monetary claims against the government. The rationale for these assumptions will become clear in the following discussion. We relax these restrictions in the third section of this chapter.

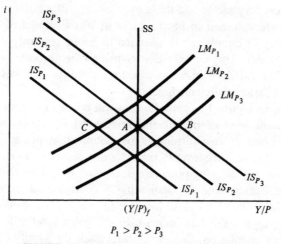

$P_1 > P_2 > P_3$

FIGURE 15.1. Aggregate general equilibrium.

In the models of previous chapters, the income–expenditures equilibrium equation was linear in two unknowns, Y/P and i. Therefore we were able to represent it graphically as a straight line in the real income (Y/P)–interest rate (i) quadrant, as in Figure 15.1. The equation was assumed to be homogeneous of degree zero in all nominal values $(Y, a, a', etc.)$ and prices. Since we assumed no money illusion, the price level appeared only as a deflator of nominal values (which varied proportionately with prices) and not as an independent argument in the equation. Consequently, a change in the price level, *by itself,* could not change the form of the income–expenditures equilibrium equation.

This will no longer be true. The *nominal* money stock M_g is assumed to be controlled by the authorities and to remain unchanged when the price level changes. Under these circumstances, M_g/P, the *real* value of net financial wealth held by the public, will be diminished by a rise in the price level. As a result an increase (decrease) in P will tend to raise (lower) the level of saving.

In the new income–expenditures equilibrium equation (15.3) P is now a separate variable. We now have a single equation in three unknowns. This relation can no longer be represented as a single curve in two dimensions. Instead, we must represent this relation as a family of curves similar to the family of monetary sector equilibrium curves presented in Chapter 13. There will be one income–expenditures equilibrium curve in the $Y/P, i$ quadrant for each different level of prices.

Since saving varies inversely with real financial wealth M_g/P and since real financial wealth is inversely related to the price level, aggregate expenditures vary inversely with the general price level. The income–expenditures equilibrium curve will shift to the right when the price level decreases. This is shown graphically in Figure 15.1.

Let us combine this new analysis of the income–expenditures sector with an analysis of the monetary sector and the supply sector. All relations except the money supply equation are assumed to be the same as in the model of Chapter 13. The stock of fiat money in circulation is assumed to be exogenously determined by the government, $M_s = M_g$. This modification changes (the absolute value of) the slope and elasticity of the family of monetary sector equilibrium curves but leaves all its other significant characteristics unchanged.

As can be seen in Figure 15.1, equilibrium will occur in this model at point A, at the full employment level of output and price level P_2. In order to see that this point truly is a point of equilibrium let us assume that prices are at some level other than P_2, say P_3. At price level P_3 the monetary sector and income–expenditures equilibrium curves intersect at point B. But point B lies to the *right* of the full employment real income line SS, indicating a condition of excess aggregate demand. This condition will lead to an increase in prices (as the economy is assumed to be at full employment). The increase in the price level will decrease the real stock of money in circulation, thereby shifting back the family of monetary sector equilibrium curves (LM_{P_j}) to the left (just as in the original model). But this price movement will also increase saving because of the reduction it causes in the real value of money balances M_g/P. As a result there will also be a leftward movement of the family of income–expenditures sector equilibrium curves IS_{P_j}. These shifts will continue until the price level has increased to P_2. At this higher price level P_2, real money balances will have shrunk sufficiently to decrease aggregate demand enough to eliminate the condition of excess aggregate demand in the economy.

Similarly, if the price level were P_1 (point C), excess aggregate supply would lead to a decrease in the price level, an increase in real money balances and an increase in aggregate demand. Again, prices will fall to the level P_2 where expenditures are sufficient to eliminate excess aggregate supply and restore the economy to full employment.

A Comparative Static Analysis of the Real Balance Model

Let us examine the comparative static characteristics of the equilibrium solution of the real balance model. Assume that the initial equilibrium at point A in Figure 15.1 is disturbed by an increase, say a doubling, of the nominal quantity of money. The effects of this change are demonstrated in Figure 15.2. The increase in the money stock will cause a rightward shift of the entire family of monetary sector equilibrium curves. The curve relevant to equilibrium at point A, LM_{P_2} will shift out to LM'_{P_2}.

In addition, because of the influence of real money balances on saving, the increase in nominal money balances M_g will increase the net real wealth of the public and cause a rightward shift in the family of income–expenditures sector equilibrium curves. The curve relevant to equilibrium at A, IS_{P_2} will shift out to IS'_{P_2}. The immediate effect of the increase in the nominal money stock will be to increase aggregate demand (point B in Figure 15.2). Since the economy is already at full employment, the result will be price rise. As prices rise, the real money stock M_g/P will decrease and both the relevant money market equilibrium curve LM'_{P_2} and the relevant income–expenditures equilibrium curve IS'_{P_2} will shift back to the left. Equilibrium will be restored only when the price level has exactly doubled to a new equilibrium level, $2P_2 = P_e$, the real money stock has been reduced to its initial level, $2M_g/2P_2 = M_g/P_2$, and both the money market equilibrium curve and the income–expenditures equilibrium curve have moved back to their initial positions.[2] In the real balance model then, just as in our original neoclassical model with flexible nominal wage and price levels, an increase in the nominal money stock causes a proportionate increase in the price level, restoring real money balances to the level at which they stood prior to the monetary disturbance.

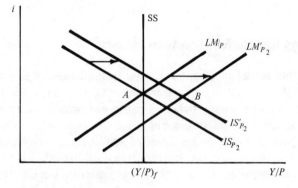

FIGURE 15.2. Initial effect of an increase in the nominal stock of money.

[2] The logical necessity of this result may be demonstrated as follows. If the price level increases by a smaller proportion than the nominal money stock in the assumed new "equilibrium," real money balances $2M_g/P'_e$ will be *greater* than they were before the increase in the money stock (M_g/P_e in Figure 15.2). This net increase in real wealth will induce additional consumption expenditures. Consequently, for this to represent a new equilibrium the interest rate would have to be *higher* than before to discourage an amount of investment spending equal to the increase in consumption spending (that is, to decrease I/P by an amount equivalent to the decrease in full employment S/P). At the same time, the larger stock of money balances will be absorbed into the public's portfolio (as indicated in the money demand function) only at a *lower* interest rate. Thus there is a logical contradiction between the conditions required for equilibrium in the income–expenditures sector and those required for a new equilibrium in the money market. As a result this cannot be a general equilibrium solution. In a similar fashion, if prices increased by a greater proportion than the money stock, real money balances $2M_g/P'_e$ would be less than in the initial equilibrium. To generate a new equilibrium in the income–expenditures sector under these conditions, interest rates would have to *fall* to induce investment expenditures to offset the decrease in consumption caused by the decrease in the value of net real wealth. But the public will willingly hold fewer real money balances only at an increased interest rate. Therefore, in the money market the interest rate would have to *rise*. Consequently, if prices can change by neither a greater nor a lesser proportion than the money stock, they must change by an equal proportionate amount.

Although A. C. Pigou and Gottfried Haberler were among the first to point out the role of real money balances in affecting expenditures, it was Don Patinkin in his *Money, Interest and Prices* who incorporated and refined their suggestions in a complete analytical framework and fully examined the properties and implications of this model. Specifically, he demonstrated that through the introduction of real money balances as a determinant of aggregate demand in a regime of complete price–wage flexibility: (1) the quantity theory conclusions (that the price level varies directly and proportionately with the nominal money stock and that equilibrium values of the real variables are independent of the size of that money stock) could be maintained, and (2) the full employment solution was the only equilibrium solution within a static framework. We shall return to this latter point subsequently. Now let us carefully examine the first point made above: the question of the neutrality of money and the conditions under which that neutrality will hold.

The Conditions for the Neutrality of Money

In the price-flexible model of Chapter 13 and in the model of this chapter, which takes account of the real balance effect, money is neutral. This means that changes in the supply of nominal money balances cause equiproportionate changes in the price level and in all nominal values but leave the equilibrium values of all real variables in the model (such as the level of real income, employment, real consumption, real investment and the interest rate) unaffected. This result depends on six important assumptions. Four of these were discussed in Chapter 13:

(1) There is complete flexibility of the nominal wage and price levels in all markets.

(2) There is no money illusion in the expenditures or money demand relations in these models.

(3) There are no distributional effects caused by changes in the price level.

(4) The elasticity of price expectations is unity.[3]

Two additional assumptions necessary to demonstrate the neutrality of money in a real balance model were introduced in this chapter:

(5) All money is "outside" money.

(6) There is no interest bearing government debt outstanding.

---

[3] While the present model is essentially static in nature, attention should also be paid to the policy implications of anticipated and unanticipated rates of price change (induced by acceleration and deceleration of the growth rate of the money supply). See Milton Friedman, "The Role of Monetary Policy," *American Economic Review,* vol. 58. (March 1968), 1–17. We examine the implications of accelerating and decelerating rates of money supply growth in the preceding chapter as well as later in this chapter.

Outside Money

Assume that all money is outside money. Outside money may be defined as a monetary claim against an agent external to (outside) the private sector in our model (the government). This is in contrast to "inside" money which consists of claims against an institution or an individual internal to the private sector (that is, the commercial banks of the private sector). The essence of this distinction lies in the response of holders and issuers of monetary claims to changes in the real value of these claims.

In the case of outside money the government, the issuer of outside money, is assumed to be unaffected by a change in the real value of its monetary debt. In making its fiscal decisions the government does not consider the burden of its outstanding liabilities; that is, the government, in its spending and taxing decisions, ignores the existence of this money as a claim against itself.[4] The public, on the other hand, is sensitive to the net real value of its financial wealth. As a result, changes in the price level which affect the real value of its monetary claims against the government will influence private expenditure decisions. A price rise, for example, will decrease the real value of the public's claims against the government thereby decreasing private expenditures; the government's spending is assumed not to react to the change in the real value of its liabilities. Consequently, a change in prices will induce a net change in *total* real expenditures in the economy.

If there is no interest bearing government debt outstanding, all bonds in the system are issued and held only by individuals in the private sector. Under this assumption the bonds of the private sector cancel out when the individual balance sheets of that sector are consolidated. Consequently, these assets do not contribute to private net wealth.

Given these assumptions, "private net financial wealth" consists solely of the monetary claims against the government held by the public. We designated the real value of this stock M_g/P as a determinant of private saving. As demonstrated in the second section of this chapter, an increase, say a doubling to $2M_g$, in this stock of nominal outside money in the economy leads to an equiproportionate rise in the average price level P. Initially the increase in nominal money balances increases

---

[4] If this assumption is relaxed and government is affected by the real value of its debt, then it has no incentive not to expand its nominal debt without constraint. This would lead to inflation. If the issuance of a quantity of government debt in exchange for real goods and services (deficit financing) results in unanticipated inflation and a lower real value of that quantity of debt, government will have effected a tax on the private sector. The public will have transferred to government a quantity of goods and services worth more than the ultimate real value of the debt claims it holds. This is, in essence, the tax from *unanticipated inflation.* In addition, even if the public fully and correctly anticipates the subsequent inflation, taxation will still occur. This tax, the tax from *anticipated inflation,* is examined later in this chapter. In the real world there are some constraints on government deficits and resulting increases in government indebtedness. Nevertheless, the fact that inflation can transfer real resources to government plus the likelihood, discussed in the previous chapter, that unanticipated inflation can (temporarily) increase employment and output in the economy would seem to provide government with some incentive to expand the nominal stock of its indebtedness.

real private financial wealth. This, in turn, increases aggregate demand. However, since the economy is already at full employment, excess aggregate demand leads to an increase in the price level. Prices continue to rise until the real value of the stock of nominal balances is reduced to its initial level. In this case $2M_g/2P_e = M_g/P_e$. With a proportional change in the price level the equilibrium values of all real variables in the model are restored to their original levels, that is, money is neutral.

Outside Bonds

If any of these assumptions are relaxed, money may not be neutral in the system. For example, let us relax the assumption that only private debt is issued and held in the economy and introduce interest bearing government debt, outside bonds, into the analysis. In this instance "net private financial wealth" W_f/P will equal the real value of (outside) money issued by the government (as in our previous model) *plus* the real market value of bonds issued by the government and held by the public:

$$\frac{W_f}{P} = \frac{M_g}{P} + \frac{V}{P}$$

where V is the nominal market value of government debt outstanding and is equal to H/i, H being the number of government bonds outstanding (multiplied by one dollar), i is the market rate of interest, and, under the simplifying assumption that bonds are perpetuities, $1/i$ is the price of the bond. The saving function of our real-balance model must now be specified to include this additional component of private net wealth:

$$\frac{S}{P} = \frac{-a}{P} + s\frac{Y}{P} + \frac{e}{P}\,i + v \cdot \left(\frac{M_g}{P} + \frac{V}{P}\right).^5 \qquad (15.4)$$

The effect of this modification on our model has been succinctly stated by Patinkin:

> . . . since the net financial assets of the private sector no longer coincide with its real money holdings, the wealth effect of a change in the price level no longer coincides with the "real-balance" effect. Correspondingly, the impact of such a change on the demands for various goods should no longer be analyzed in terms of this latter effect but in terms of an analogous "net-real-financial-asset effect."[6]

[5] Implicit in this statement is often the assumption that the public does not fully discount the value of its future tax liabilities, that is, the tax liabilities that will arise due to the necessity of paying interest on the public debt. If the full value of these future tax liabilities were considered by the public, the *net* value of its bond holdings might be zero and they might not represent net wealth. Although we proceed in our analysis as if the public does not recognize *any* burden to the future taxes which will be levied to finance interest payments on the public debt, the essence of our conclusions requires only that the public not discount the burden of future tax liabilities *completely*. In Chapter 12, p. 315, we argue that even if future tax liability were completely discounted to the present, government debt should still count as part of private wealth.

[6] Don Patinkin, *Money, Interest and Prices*, 2nd ed. (New York: Harper and Row, 1965), 290.

Let us examine the effects of a change in the nominal money stock in this system. When nominal money balances are increased (by deficit financing, for example), net real financial wealth increases. This will stimulate an increase in aggregate demand above its initial full employment level and prices will begin to rise. However, an exactly proportionate increase in the price level will not restore equilibrium.

This may be demonstrated as follows. Suppose that the nominal stock of outside money is doubled to $2M_g$. Since the real (and nominal) stock of money balances is now greater than initially, the equilibrium of the private sector is disturbed. The public finds itself with excess money balances. This disequilibrium in the relative proportions of bonds and money held by the public will be marked by an excess demand for bonds (that is, at the initial price and interest rate levels the public will try to restore the original balance between its holdings of bonds and money) and an excess demand for consumer durables and capital goods. In either case, as discussed in Chapter 13, the increase in expenditures will create excess aggregate demand and the price level will rise.

A rise in the price level proportional to the initial increase in the nominal money supply will not restore equilibrium. Assuming a doubling of both the stock of outside money and the general price level, at an unchanged rate of interest the nominal market value of outside bonds held by the public, $V = H/i$, will not have increased and its real market value will have decreased, $V/2P < V/P$.[7] Therefore the net real financial wealth held by the public, $2M_g/2P + V/2P$, will have decreased from its initial equilibrium level. Consequently, in the absence of other changes a doubling of the general price level alone will not restore equilibrium.

The decline in net real financial wealth at the doubled price level will have two repercussions. First it will create a decrease in real aggregate demand (an excess supply of goods and services). This decline in real aggregate demand will take the form of a reduction in real consumption expenditures as individuals try to save more in an attempt to restore their initial net real wealth position. Second, the decrease in the proportion of outside bonds in net financial wealth means that an excess demand for bonds will persist.

Equilibrium will be restored when the excess supply of goods and services and the excess demand for bonds are eliminated. The excess supply of goods and services will cause the general price level to fall and the excess demand for bonds will cause the interest rate to fall. A fall in the price level and a decline in the market rate of interest will cause net financial wealth to rise and will thereby stimulate consumption expenditures.[8] The decline in the interest rate will also stimulate investment expenditures and reduce the demand for bonds.

---

[7] If the increase in the money stock took place via an open market operation in which outside money was exchanged for outside bonds, H would have fallen in the amount that M increased and the nonneutrality effects discussed below would be more pronounced. The effects of an open market operation in a price inflexible world are discussed in detail in Chapter 12.

[8] Bonds are defined as the fixed interest–variable price type. This means that a change in the market rate of interest will affect the level of private wealth. There will be interest-induced wealth effects which we will ignore as a matter of convenience. As discussed in Chapter 12, this creates nonlinearities in the model.

Comparing the new final equilibrium to the initial equilibrium, the interest rate will have fallen and investment expenditures will have risen. The decline in net real financial wealth will have caused real consumption expenditures to have fallen by the amount that real investment expenditures rose so as to keep real aggregate demand and hence real output unchanged at their full employment levels. A desired proportion between real outside money and real outside bonds will have been restored (at a higher ratio of real outside money to real outside bonds, consistent with the lower rate of interest and lower equilibrium value of the stock of outside bonds). The price level will have increased by some proportion smaller than the increase in the nominal money stock. Therefore, in a system which contains outside bonds and outside money, money is not neutral.

Inside Money

As a final example, consider the effects of introducing "inside" money into the analysis. Inside money consists of monetary claims issued by individuals in the private sector. It may be thought to consist primarily of demand deposit liabilities of commercial banks. In this case total money balances in the system will equal the sum of the public's monetary claims against the government (outside money M_g) and the public's monetary claims against the banks (inside money M_b), that is, $M/P = M_g/P + M_b/P$. However, under certain conditions we can assume that the market value of the debt of the nonbank public to the banking system (in the form of loans and securities issued by the public and held by the banks) cancels out against the demand deposit liabilities of the banks in the consolidated private balance sheet identity. If the canceling out assumption is made, the *net* real financial wealth of the public will consist solely of its claims against the government; in this case, since we once again assume government interest–bearing debt (outside bonds) is zero, financial wealth consists only of the public's monetary claims against government. Therefore, $W_f/P = M_g/P$.

A canceling out would only occur if inside money were costlessly produced and if the market values of claims, including inside money, held by the nonbank public and produced by the banking system were equal to the market value of claims held by the banking system and issued by the nonbank public. The latter condition would result if the markets in which banks sold the claims they issue against themselves as well as market(s) in which banks acquired claims were purely competitive.[9]

---

[9] Because inside money in such a costless and purely competitive banking system would not add to the measured wealth of society, it should not be inferred that the existence of money does not add to society's well-being or welfare. Any good or service which has "utility" adds to social welfare even though it may be costlessly produced and, in purely competitive markets, evaluated at a zero market price. See Harry G. Johnson, "Inside Money, Outside Money, Income, Wealth and Welfare in Monetary Theory," *Journal of Money, Credit and Banking,* 1969, 30–45. For further review of the issue of inside money as wealth, see Yung Chul Park, "Some Current Issues in the Transmission Process of Monetary Policy," *Staff Papers,* International Monetary Fund (March 1972), 1–45, reprinted in Havrilesky and Boorman, *op. cit.*

If, however, in these markets a bank had some monopoly power, it would produce claims against itself only to the point where the marginal cost of producing such claims was equal to the marginal revenue from claims it acquired. Elementary economics indicates that in this case excess profits or quasi–rents would be realized by the banking system. The present value of future expected quasi–rents would add to the value of a banking franchise and be reflected, together with the market value of its capital assets (in the case where production is not costless), in the market value of its equity issues. Thus the present value of future quasi–rents which arise from the ability of a nonpurely competitive banking system to issue inside money would not enter the definition of wealth as part of the money stock but would rather appear as part of the market value of banking enterprises.[10]

Regardless of the definition of wealth, money will not be neutral since an increase in one of the types of money in the system will not lead to a proportionate increase in the price level. This may be indicated as follows. If outside money M_g is increased to $2M_g$ and the price level doubles, net real financial wealth will be restored to its initial equilibrium level:

$$\frac{W_f}{P} = \frac{M_g}{P} = \frac{2M_g}{2P} \tag{15.5}$$

but the real value of total money balances will have decreased:

$$\frac{2M_g}{2P} + \frac{M_b}{2P} < \frac{M_g}{P} + \frac{M_b}{P}.^{11} \tag{15.6}$$

This reduction in real money balances, with all other variables assumed to be at their initial equilibrium levels, will create an excess demand for money. Thus equilibrium will be restored only when this excess demand is eliminated. Restoration of equilibrium will involve an increase in the interest rate and a subsequent decline in investment expenditures. The decline in investment spending will reduce aggregate demand and the rise in prices will be reversed. As prices begin to fall, net real financial wealth will increase, inducing a rise in consumption.

In the final equilibrium, then, interest rates will have increased (decreasing investment by an amount equal to the increase in consumption), net real financial wealth and consumption will have increased and the price level will have risen less than in proportion to the initial increase in the nominal stock of money. Again, since the equilibrium values of real variables change in response to a change in the

[10] The private capital stock is included in the definition of wealth in the next section.

[11] There is one important exception to this analysis, the case in which the institutional framework and the behavior of the banking system are such that a fixed proportionate relationship is maintained between the stock of outside money (bank reserves, for example) and the volume of inside money created by the banking system. For a discussion of this point, see Don Patinkin, *Money, Interest and Prices*, 298–302.

nominal stock of money, in a model which contains inside money, money is not neutral.[12]

Equity Effects

The expansion of the definition of real wealth to include the present value of the real capital stock, assumed to be reflected in the real market value of equities (evidences of ownership of the economy's capital stock) tends to increase the nonneutrality of money. In this case, net private wealth consists of outside money, outside bonds and equities:

$$\frac{W_f}{P} = \frac{M_g}{P} + \frac{H}{iP} + \frac{P_k K}{P}$$

where P_k is the market value of a unit of capital and K is the number of units of capital. Even if P_k fully and instantaneously reflects changes in the general price level P, a doubling of the outside money stock and a doubling of the price level will not represent an equilibrium position (an excess demand for bonds *and* equities together with an excess supply of goods and services will exist) and money will be nonneutral. The analysis is similar to the discussion of the previous section.

There are many other special cases we could examine to determine those conditions under which money is neutral. The most exhaustive analysis of this issue is contained in Don Patinkin's *Money, Interest and Prices* and we refer the interested reader to his volume, especially to Chapter 12.

Full Employment Equilibrium in the Real Balance Model

In order to demonstrate that the full employment solution is the only equilibrium solution in a real balance model that assumes price level and nominal wage flexibility, we must reexamine the two situations discussed in Chapter 14 which could lead to less than full employment solutions in our model of the aggregate economy. We must show that even under the conditions described by the liquidity trap and interest insensitive investment demand, the real balance model yields a consistent solution only at full employment.[13]

As the reader will recall from the previous chapter, those situations led to equilibrium at less than full employment because price adjustments could in no way

---

[12] The general framework developed in this example may be employed to demonstrate the results of other assumptions. For example, in a "pure outside money" economy $M_b = 0$. Therefore $M/P = M_g/P$ and $W_f/P = M_g/P$, and our model reduces to that developed in the first part of this chapter. At the other extreme, if all money is of the inside variety, $M_g = 0$. In this case $M/P = M_b/P$ and $W_f/P = 0$, and our model reduces to that discussed in the early sections of Chapter 13, that is, there will be no real-balance effect. In both of these instances, where the money stock consists solely of inside money or solely of outside money, the neutrality of money is easily established as long as the first four assumptions cited on page 390 hold.

[13] In the rest of this discussion we shall assume an economy in which private wealth consists entirely of outside money.

induce a full employment level of aggregate demand. A change in the general price level shifted the monetary sector equilibrium curve but such movements could not induce sufficient investment through interest rate reductions to offset the full employment level of saving. In the case of the absolute liquidity trap, additional real money balances created by the falling general price level were simply absorbed by the public at the current interest rate and no rate reduction was forthcoming. In the case of interest insensitive investment demand, although a decline in the price level could decrease the interest rate, this lowered rate was insufficient to generate a level of investment capable of offsetting the full employment volume of saving.

In the present model, however, since a reduction in the price level increases the value of real money balances, it increases consumption and decreases saving at every level of income. This is represented by the rightward shift of the IS_{Pj} curves in Figure 15.3. In this way continual deflation reduces the full employment level of saving to any level necessary to match the volume of investment forthcoming at some attainable positive rate of interest. [This solution occurrs at price level P_3 and interest rate i_e in Figure 15.3(a) and P_3 and i_0 in Figure 15.3(b).] Therefore the Pigou real balance effect would seem to counter the Keynesian attack on the ability of the market economy automatically to produce full employment under conditions of complete nominal wage–price flexibility.[14] Neither the liquidity trap

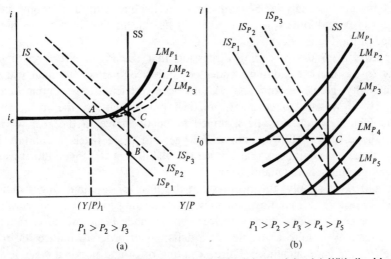

FIGURE 15.3. Real-balance effect in price-flexible models. (a) With liquidity trap. (b) With interest insensitive investment demand.

[14] The Pigou effect may be viewed as increasing the price sensitivity of real aggregate demand in such a way that a full employment equilibrium is always possible in the P, Y/P plane of Figure 14.6, p. 377. However, we must recall at this point our previous assumptions about the elasticity of price expectations as well as other necessary factors given on page 390.

nor interest inelastic investment demand would seem to be sufficient to bring about a static equilibrium at less than full employment.

Therefore, on the basis of this analysis we state the following proposition: if the Pigou effect is operative, there will exist (even in the case of a liquidity trap or insufficient investment demand) some price level which is sufficient to induce the proper level of aggregate demand to assure full employment. Most importantly, the introduction of the real balance effect appears to restore the automatic self-stabilizing character of the market economy under the assumption of wage–price flexibility. Within a static analysis, then, the Keynesian case of a less than full employment equilibrium rests squarely and completely on his assumption of imperfect flexibility of the nominal wage rate. This conclusion is maintained in a real balance model. If the nominal wage is rigid, the *modus operandi* of the Pigou effect, a falling price level, has been impeded. Aggregate demand cannot be greatly stimulated through increases in the real value of the public's net financial wealth brought about by a falling price level. This is the only case, however, in which a less than full employment static equilibrium can be generated in the model. Underemployment static equilibrium, therefore, depends on the assumption of imperfect flexibility of the nominal wage.

The Real Balance Effect in the Real World

These conclusions raise two very important questions. First, what are the policy implications of this analysis? Second, if we are dealing with an economy in which nominal wages and prices are not perfectly flexible in the short run, what is the relevance of the Pigou effect?

It appears from the preceding discussion that the Pigou effect restores automaticity to the market economy under conditions of perfect nominal wage–price level flexibility. However, our analysis has been restricted to a comparative static framework. If we are to consider practical policy matters, the introduction of dynamic factors which may be assumed to be operative in the real world may weaken the case for allowing nominal wage and price levels to adjust. Let us examine three considerations that reduce the viability of the Pigou effect as a basis for economic policy in a dynamic world.

First and most simply, the decrease in the level of nominal wages and prices required to restore full employment may take too long to be politically acceptable to public officials. Second, even if prices can be made to adjust fairly rapidly, the Pigou effect may require a sizable price deflation in order to induce the required increase in aggregate demand.[15] Third, a falling price and nominal wage level may set up adverse anticipations in the short run which lead to decreases rather than

[15] The argument that wealth effects are weak, however, overlooks the fact that *interest induced* wealth effects and lagged income (as a proxy for wealth) are often empirically estimated to have significant impact on the level of consumption spending. See Yung Chul Park, *op. cit.*; and Roger W. Spencer, "Channels of Monetary Influence," *Review*, Federal Reserve Bank of St. Louis (January 1970), 16–21. Both are reprinted in Havrilesky and Boorman, *op. cit.*

increases in aggregate demand. For example, as prices fall, though real money balances are increasing, consumers may postpone expenditures in the hope of buying the desired items at a later time at lower prices. Likewise, investors may postpone investment projects in the hope of further price declines. Construction, for example, may be postponed in the hope that wages of construction workers will decline further and decrease the cost of the investment project. Falling prices may also discourage investment because of the uncertainty of the future selling price of newly produced goods. Building factories at today's high prices for the sale of goods at tomorrow's low prices is not a prospect likely to stimulate businessmen's confidence in their profit margins.[16] Any one of these arguments represents an attack on the potential usefulness that price flexibility has as a basis for policy making.[17]

What is the relevance of the Pigou effect if it is impractical to wait for it to work or if wages and prices are inflexible downwards in the short run? There are four main points to be made in this connection. First, the Pigou effect, if significant, remains an important analytical tool in the analysis of inflationary economies. *Upward* price flexibility involves a Pigou effect through the decrease in real money balances effected by rising prices. This may be significant for the stability of economies in times of rapidly rising prices.

Second, though it may be impossible to decrease the price level because of rigidities in the economy, real money balances can still be increased by changing M. Thus monetary policy is effective in our model as long as a significant Pigou effect can be demonstrated.

Third, under certain conditions imposed on the models of the previous chapter, monetary policy was shown to be ineffective as a means of increasing aggregate demand. Under the circumstances assumed in those models, monetary policy was ineffective because the liquidity impact of increases in the money stock could not decrease interest rates and stimulate investment. With the insertion of the Pigou effect, defined more broadly to represent a net financial wealth effect, into these models, this conclusion no longer holds. Under these same circumstances the insertion of the Pigou effect allows monetary policy to become effective through the influence of net financial wealth on saving and consumption.

Finally, attempts by policymakers to "fine tune" the economy through variations in the money supply and government deficits may be a greater source of macroeconomic instability than a policy of simply waiting for the adjustments in real balances to restore full employment equilibrium. In general, when we apply the price-flexible model to some real-world problems in the following sections, it will be seen that monetary policy actions to compensate for shocks to the economy, in the form of excessive union wage demands or increases in aggregate expenditures caused by inflationary price expectations or increased government deficits, may

[16] See Don Patinkin, "Price Flexibility and Full Employment," *American Economic Review,* vol. 38 (September 1948), 543–564.

[17] Pigou himself writes ". . . The puzzles we have been considering . . . are academic exercises, of some slight use perhaps for clarifying thought, but with very little chance of ever being posed on the chequerboard of actual life." "Economic Progress in a Stable Environment," *Economica,* vol. 14 (1947), 188.

be a source of considerable inflationary distress. This suggests that a passive monetary policy of maintaining a stable level or growth rate of the money supply may promote more stability than one of varying the money supply in the name of correcting for various perceived imbalances.

Some Applications of the Neoclassical Model

Cost Push Inflation and the Real Balance Model

It is often contended that individual money prices are determined by costs and that exogenous cost increases can raise the general price level. In its extreme form, this view leads to the belief that unions and oligopolists unilaterally cause inflation. If so, it often is alleged that price inflation can be curbed exclusively by some form of wage and price controls, guidelines, or "jawboning."

This outlook is inconsistent with the fact that in the history of the western world there has never been a period of sustained price inflation that has not been preceded by and directly associated with a sustained increase in the growth of the money supply. If unions in some sector of the economy ask for higher nominal wages and/or if oligopolists unilaterally raise their prices, elementary microeconomic theory indicates that costs and prices in that sector will indeed rise, thus exerting upward pressure on the price level in general, especially where wages and prices in other industries are not perfectly flexible downward. However, as the price level rises, the value of real money balance declines. The real balance model developed earlier indicates that the pressure of excess capacity and unemployed resources generated by the decline in aggregate demand will eventually reverse the price level increase and cause full employment equilibrium to be restored.

In Figure 15.4 the economy is in full employment equilibrium at point D at a price level of P_0. If unions raise the nominal wage in excess of productivity gains,

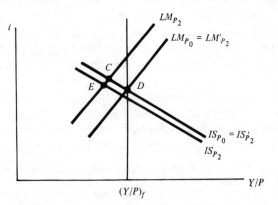

FIGURE 15.4. Cost push inflation and the real-balance model.

prices are "pushed" up.[18] This causes the *LM* curve in Figure 15.4 to shift from LM_{P_0} to LM_{P_2}. The shift in *LM* occurs because of the reduction in the stock of real money balances as the nominal wage and hence the price level increase. If a real balance effect were not operative, aggregate equilibrium would occur at point *C*; if a real-balance effect were operative, aggregate equilibrium would be at *E* because the *IS* curve would shift to IS_{P_2}, reflecting the decrease in consumption expenditures induced by the rise in the price level. At either *C* or *E,* however, there is excess capacity and unemployment in the economy. The price level must return to P_0 in order to restore equilibrium.

Monetary and fiscal authorities may believe, as discussed in the previous section, that as a matter of political convenience the process of deflation would take too long to restore full employment. Such a belief might lead the Federal Reserve to increase the money supply, causing the *LM* curve to shift to LM'_{P_2} so that full employment is sustained at the new higher price level P_2. If the real balance effect were operative, *IS* would shift back to IS'_{P_2} as real balances are restored to their original level. In this fashion the Federal Reserve would ratify or validate the wage–price spiral.[19]

Anticipated Inflation in the Real Balance Model

Throughout Chapters 11–14 we did not distinguish between nominal and real rates of interest. And yet in Chapter 6 we saw that changes in the price level affect the return on financial assets. For example, if a lender is to receive a $100 interest income on a $1000 loan, the nominal rate of interest *i* is 10 percent. Nevertheless, if by the date of maturity of the loan, the price level has risen by 7 percent, the real rate of interest on the loan *r* is approximately 3 percent. This relationship may be approximated, *ex post,* as

$$i = r + \frac{\Delta P}{P} \qquad (15.7)$$

where $\Delta P/P$ stands for the percentage rate of change of the price level. More precisely, $\Delta P/P$ is the discrete equivalent of $(dP/dt)/\dot{P}$, or *P* for short, the derivative

---

[18] This process can be seen in detail in Figure 14.2, page 366. Suppose the economy were at a full employment equilibrium such as *D*. A rise in the nominal wage requests of a union is reflected as an upward shift in the labor supply curve. This establishes a position of temporary underemployment equilibrium at *C*. The move from LM_{P_0} to LM_{P_2} in Figure 15.4 is consistent with the movement *along DD'* in Figure 14.2b from *D* to *C*; the move from LM_{P_2} to LM'_{P_2} in Figure 15.4 would be consistent with a *shift* in *DD'* in Figure 14.2b such that it intersects *SS* at P_2.

[19] A similar analysis applies to price level increases seemingly caused by an increase in the price of strategic imported raw materials such as petroleum. Where the demand for these goods is inelastic, a rise in their prices should shift purchasing power away from other goods and services whose prices should fall. Where these other prices are rigid downward, the price index will rise and real balances will decline as in the preceding analysis. Once again, the pressure on the monetary authority to validate the price spiral is significant.

of the general price level with respect to time, expressed as a percentage. If there are uniform price expectations on the part of debtors and creditors regarding an increase in the future rate of inflation, then the current *nominal* rate of interest will rise. In Chapter 6 this was called the price expectations effect.[20] The impact of price expectations on the nominal interest rate may be expressed, *ex ante,* as

$$i = r + \dot{P}_e. \tag{15.8}$$

where $\dot{P}_e$ is the expected rate of price inflation.

Let us examine the effect of inflationary expectations on our flexible price model. Initially we will assume that there is no real balance effect at work on expenditures. The real rate of interest and the general price level are at equilibrium levels and real income is at the full employment level. At this initial equilibrium the actual rate of price inflation is zero and individuals expect a zero rate of inflation.

Now, for a reason that we shall soon make explicit, assume that everyone suddenly expects the price level to rise in the future by a certain percentage rate each year. Given this expectation, we shall see how the nominal rate of interest rises by the amount of the expected rate of inflation as indicated by Equation (15.8). The nominal rate of interest will exceed the real rate of interest by an amount equal to the expected rate of inflation.

If an increase is expected in the rate of inflation from $\dot{P}_{e_0}$ to $\dot{P}_{e_1}$ in Figure 15.5 investment expenditures will increase as business firms accelerate their capital spending plans at the old nominal interest rate i_0. This is reflected in the shift in the *IS* curve from IS_0 to IS_1. As discussed in Chapter 10, the decision to invest in newly produced capital goods depends on the market rate of interest. When the nominal value of future returns rises because the flow of future output is expected to be sold at higher prices, the present value of this future income stream rises and the demand for capital goods increases at the unchanged market rate of interest which is used to discount this future income stream. Business firms also may realize that if the price of capital goods is expected to rise by, say, 5 percent during the forthcoming period, in order to obtain the same quantity of capital goods by the end of the period, they presently have to increase their nominal investment expenditures by 5 percent. As a result of this increase in investment demand, the nominal interest rate then rises in approximate proportion to expected future price inflation. Assuming an equiproportionate increase in all individual prices, this leaves real investment expenditures unchanged; it also leaves the real expected internal rate of return on investment

---

[20] If we can assume that historical rates of inflation are predictors of future rates of inflation, a series for P_e can be constructed and the real rate of interest can be derived from the observed nominal rate. There are several studies of the effect of price expectations on interest rates. For example, William P. Yohe and Denis Karnosky, "Interest Rates and Price Level Changes, 1952–1969," *Review,* Federal Reserve Bank of St. Louis (December 1969), 18–38; William E. Gibson, "Interest Rates and Inflationary Expectations," *American Economic Review* (December 1972), 854–865; and Thomas Sargent, "Anticipated Inflation and the Nominal Rate of Interest," *Quarterly Journal of Economics* (May 1972), 212–225.

funds unchanged at r. In Figure 15.5 the level of real investment expenditures is the same at B as it is at A.[21]

Now consider the effect of a rise in the nominal rate of interest on the demand for money. As discussed in Chapter 6, the demand for real money balances varies inversely with the *nominal* rate of interest because the nominal rate is the opportunity cost of tying up financial wealth in a noninterest earning form. With real income unchanged the increase in investment expenditures can only drive up the nominal rate of interest to i_1. At this higher equilibrium interest rate at an unchanged level of real income, there will be an excess supply of money. In Figure 15.5 IS_1 and LM_{P_0} intersect at $(Y/P)_2 > (Y/P)_f$. As discussed earlier the fact that real income cannot rise above $(Y/P)_f$ ensures that the excess supply of money will cause the general price level to rise.

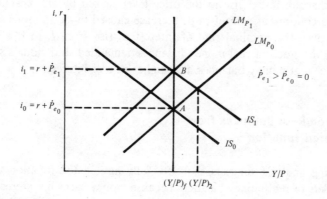

FIGURE 15.5. Price expectations in the price-flexible LM–IS model.

As the general price level rises from P_0 to P_1, the real stock of money declines and the LM curve shifts leftward to LM_{P_1}. (If a real balance effect were at work on the expenditures side of the model, the IS curve would also shift leftward.) The new equilibrium level of the nominal rate of interest is $i_1 = r + \dot{P}_{e_1}$.

Thus the expectation of inflation causes an increase in the price level and the expectation is self-fulfilling. If expected inflation persists at $\dot{P}_{e_1}$, but the money supply is not increased, no further price level increases can occur. When individuals

[21] In reality, observed nominal rates of interest may not rise in proportion with anticipated inflation (that is, *real* rates of interest may fall). This may occur because real investment expenditures (private capital formation) may actually decline in response to the uncertainty (of future returns) that businessmen associate with high levels of inflation. There may also be modest increases in real saving as inflation erodes real financial wealth and creates consumer pessimism. This too would cause real rates of interest to decline.

realize that the price level has stopped increasing, the expected rate of inflation will return to zero. The *IS* curve will shift leftward to IS_0 as business firms no longer desire to maintain the same flow of investment expenditures at the nominal rate of interest i_1. A reduced expected rate of inflation will cause investors to reevaluate downward the expected future income stream associated with investment projects. Decreases in the market rate of interest and the general price level will take place.

Now the leftward shift in the *IS* curve may cause a temporary decline in the level of output and employment. Realizing this and (as discussed in the preceeding section) not desiring to wait for the market economy to correct itself, monetary policymakers may choose to increase the growth rate of the money supply. In fact, the only way $\dot{P}_{e_1}$ can be sustained in equilibrium in Figure 15.5 is for the Federal Reserve to continuously increase the nominal supply of (outside) money at the rate equal to the expected rate of inflation $\dot{P}_{e_1}$, *ceteris paribus*. Only then will expectations be continuously realized. The *price expectations effect* will be validated. Taken together, an initial rise in the price level caused by an expectation of inflation *plus* the continuous rate of price increase caused by continuous money supply expansion cause the nominal rate of interest to rise from i_0 to i_1 and result in a reduction in the stock of real money balances demanded. Individuals simply choose to hold fewer real money balances at a higher rate of interest.

The Tax on Real Balances from Anticipated Inflation[22]

The foregoing analysis suggests that any fully anticipated inflation will impose a loss on holders of real money balances because money earns no interest. A principal gainer from inflation will be issuer of money—government. Let us examine this process more carefully.

Figure 15.6 shows the aggregate demand curve for real money balances as a decreasing function of the nominal rate of interest. Because real money balances earn no interest, the nominal rate of interest represents the number of cents an individual must give up per time period for every dollar of real money balances held. If the fully anticipated rate of inflation is $\dot{P}_e$, individuals are anticipating that government will, in the future, be increasing the nominal supply of money at a rate that will produce an inflation rate of $\dot{P}_e$. This generates the nominal rate i_M in Figure 15.6. Assuming that output is constant, the quantity of real money balances demanded at an interest rate i_M is $(M/P)_M$. In this situation, in order to *maintain* real money balances at $(M/P)_M$ individuals must sacrifice consumption, be forced to save, in order to add to their nominal money balances at a rate $\dot{M}$ equal to the anticipated rate of inflation $\dot{P}_e$. Thus $\dot{P}_e$ is tantamount to a "tax" (rate), a tax on real money

---

[22] This analysis does not discuss the tax from *unanticipated* inflation that was mentioned in footnote 4 earlier in this chapter.

balances. In short, individuals must give up consumption every period to acquire additional *nominal* money balances from government at a rate equal to the anticipated rate of inflation. Only in this fashion can they keep their *real* money balances at the desired level $(M/P)_M$.

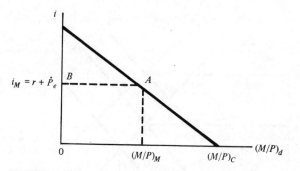

FIGURE 15.6. Tax from a fully anticipated rate of inflation.

If we assume for simplicity a zero real rate of interest, then the expected growth rate of money itself determines the nominal rate of interest because it determines the anticipated rate of inflation. Under this assumption, in Figure 15.6 the inflation tax rate is OB and the tax proceeds to government from inflation is the area $O–B–A–(M/P)_M$. If government would choose not to tax by inflation, then the (optimal) quantity of real money balances demanded would be $(M/P)_c$. There would be a (welfare) gain to the private sector from a zero-inflation policy of area $(M/P)_M–A–(M/P)_c$ in Figure 15.6.[23]

The Effect of an Increase in the Nominal Money Supply on the Nominal Interest Rate

Now let us examine once more the effects of an increase in the money supply on the nominal interest rate. If in our price–flexible *LM–IS* model we were to hold both the price level and the level of real income constant and if price inflation were not anticipated, then the initial effect of an increase in the nominal supply of money would be to reduce the nominal rate of interest. In Chapter 6 this was called the *liquidity effect.*

[23] It can be seen that the government revenue maximizing rate of inflation is where the rectangle under the curve is largest. Another name for the proceeds to government from its right to issue money is *seigniorage*. For further discussion, see Martin J. Bailey, "The Welfare Costs of Inflationary Finance," *Journal of Political Economy* (June 1956).

We begin from a position of static full employment equilibrium at point *A* in Figure 15.7. Assume that the rate of money supply growth and the rate of inflation here are zero. Now assume a once and for all increase in the supply of money. As *LM* shifts to LM'_{P_0} the *liquidity effect* drives the interest rate down from i_0 to i_1 (from *A* to *B*) in Figure 15.7.

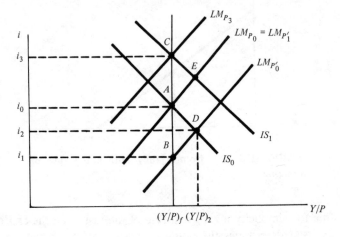

FIGURE 15.7. Liquidity, income and price expectations effects of an increase in the money supply.

In Chapters 11–14 we saw that in an economy where the price (and nominal wage) level is assumed fixed an increase in the money supply will cause real income to rise. If real income *could* rise from $(Y/P)_f$ to $(Y/P)_2$, there would be upward pressure on the interest rate; it would rise from i_1 to i_2 (at point *D* in Figure 15.7). This is the *income effect* of money on interest discussed in Chapter 6.[24] The combined *liquidity and income effects* of an increase in the money supply would cause a net decline in the market rate of interest from i_0 to i_2 as long as there is a fixed nominal wage and price level. The decrease in the market rate is, of course, consistent with the rise in real income of the Keynesian models discussed in Chapters 11, 12 and 14.

In the flexible-price model of Chapter 13 as well as in the present chapter real income is constrained not to rise above the full employment level. Excess aggregate demand (an excess of actual over desired real money balances) causes the general

[24] In Chapter 12 the combined liquidity effect and income effect of an increase in money on real income was called the "liquidity *impact*" multiplier. Here we refer to the liquidity *effect* of money on the interest rate. The two labels should not be confused.

price level to rise from P_0 to P_1.[25] After the initial rightward shift to LM'_{P_0} caused by the initial increase in the money stock, the *LM* curve shifts leftward back to LM'_{P_1} and full-employment equilibrium is restored at a price level and a level of nominal income that have risen proportionately with the increase in the nominal stock of money. In this case after an initial decline from the liquidity effect the market rate of interest returns to its original level i_0 at point *A* in Figure 15.7. The *nominal income effect* just offsets the *liquidity effect* and the equilibrium interest rate does not change.

As discussed earlier the expectation of future increases in prices may cause an increase in expenditures. This is reflected as a shift in the *IS* curve to IS_1 in Figure 15.7.[26] As the price level is driven upward by this increase in aggregate demand, the *LM* curve shifts leftward to LM_{P_3}. Thus the *price expectations effect* on the nominal rate of interest is $i_3 - i_0$.[27] The new point of equilibrium is *C* in Figure 15.7. The new higher price level and interest rate will be sustained only if the money supply, which was initially assumed not to be growing, now increases at a rate equal to the expected rate of price inflation. If it does not, the rate of price inflation must decline and the nominal rate of interest will return to i_0.

We have not yet shown how price expectations effects develop. We have simply assumed a sudden appearance of inflationary expectations. However, it is reasonable to assume that such expectations are formed either on the basis of recent inflationary experiences (adaptive expectations) or other experiences, including the pattern of recent monetary and fiscal policy actions. Essentially, if the price *level* has recently been rising in a fairly consistent manner, individuals may come to expect it to continue to rise. Thus a fairly constant *rate* of price inflation may be anticipated.[28] Moreover, since a sustained rise in the price level can result only from a con-

---

[25] The only way in which any additional output can be generated, to the right of Y/P_f at *D* in Figure 15.7 and *B* in Figure 15.8, is through money illusion in the labor market, whereby labor demanders anticipate an increase in the price *level* and labor suppliers do not. This static phenomenon was examined in Chapter 14, pages 363–379.

[26] Once again, the only way in which additional output can be generated, to the right of $(Y/P)_f$ at *E* in Figure 15.7 and *D* in Figure 15.8, is through money illusion in the labor market, whereby labor demanders anticipate an increase in the *rate* of price inflation and labor suppliers do not. This dynamic (short-run Phillips curve) phenomenon was discussed in Chapter 14, pages 371–374.

[27] For further discussion of nominal versus real rates in a dynamic context see the survey article by Yung Chul Park, *op. cit.,* as well as Milton Friedman, "Factors Affecting the Level of Interest Rates," *1968 Conference Proceedings, Savings and Residential Financing* (Chicago: U.S. Savings and Loan League, 1969), 10–27. Both are reprinted in Havrilesky and Boorman, *op. cit.*

[28] As discussed in Chapter 14 there are two main theories of the formation of anticipations, *adaptive expectations* and *rational expectations.* Both, however, may use data from the past to predict the future. For further detail, see G. E. D. Box and G. M. Jenkins, *Time Series Analysis: Forecasting and Control* (San Francisco: Holden-Day, 1970); J. F. Muth, "Rational Expectations and the Theory of Price Movements," *Econometrica* (July 1961); and Thomas J. Sargent and Neil Wallace, "Rational Expectations and the Dynamics of Hyperinflation," *International Economic Review* (June 1973).

tinual increase in the supply of money, inflationary expectations may arise from individual's learning about the way in which the money supply is handled by the monetary authority.

For instance, the monetary authority may be attempting to control the nominal rate of interest. It can be seen from our model that if the Federal Reserve attempts to set the nominal rate of interest at any level other than the one which is equal to the equilibrium real rate of interest, it must result in either inflation or deflation.

Consider a case where the Federal Reserve is trying to keep the interest rate lower than the equilibrium real rate, perhaps because of concern in certain sectors of the economy with an interest rate that is "too high" or because of the belief that a lower interest rate can permanently stimulate real income and employment.

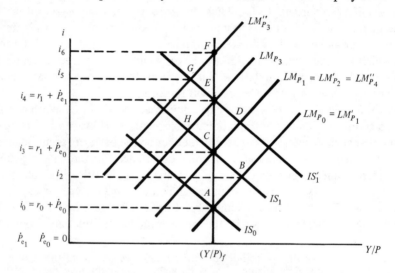

FIGURE 15.8. Effect of the monetary authority's attempt to control the interest rate.

For example, assume that the economy is initially in equilibrium at point A of Figure 15.8. Assume further that at this point the rate of inflation and the rate of money supply growth are both zero. Now consider an increase in the government deficit. (For simplicity we ignore the financing of the deficit.) This is represented by the shift in the IS curve from IS_0 to IS_1. This drives the real rate of interest up so that the nominal rate rises to i_3. At nominal interest rate i_3 the excess supply of money exerts upward pressure on the price level which causes LM to shift to LM_{P_1} such that the new equilibrium is at point C. If i_3 is popularly considered "too high" an interest rate, pressure may be brought on the monetary authority to "do something" about the high interest rate and it may therefore increase the supply of money.

This will cause the LM curve to shift rightward to LM'_{P_1}. As we have seen, an initial liquidity effect may succeed temporarily in keeping the rate of interest down to i_0. Nevertheless, A is no longer an equilibrium position and the rise in the price level from P_1 to P_2 will cause LM to shift to LM'_{P_2}. The nominal income effect will drive the interest rate back to i_3.

If whenever the interest rate rises above i_0 the money supply increases, the *rate* of money supply growth will eventually increase and the price level will begin to rise, period after period, so that a positive *rate* of inflation is established. As this rate of inflation comes to be expected $\dot{P}_{e_1}$, expenditures will increase in anticipation of inflation, and, as described earlier, the IS curve will shift to IS'_1. The price expectations effect will then drive the nominal rate of interest even higher to i_4. If the money supply continues to grow at the rate that established this expectation, the equilibrium stock of real money balances must fall to a level that is consistent with the now higher opportunity cost of holding real money, i_4. This is depicted as a leftward shift of LM to LM_{P_3}. A new equilibrium position consistent with the new positive rate of money supply growth and fully anticipated rate of inflation is established at E in Figure 15.8.[29]

Now assume that the public grows weary of inflation. The Federal Reserve reduces the rate of money supply growth back to zero. In short–run, single period, analysis a constant nominal money stock combined with an increase in the price level, created by continued inflation, causes the LM curve to shift leftward to LM''_{P_3} in Figure 15.8. This initial liquidity effect causes a rise in the interest rate from i_4 to i_6 at point F. The graph simplistically shows that with a positive rate of inflation a cut back in money supply growth will result in a shortage of liquidity. Under conditions of subsequent wage–price stickiness or money illusion in the labor market this liquidity shortage could bring about a temporary reduction in real income and the economy will gravitate toward point G and the interest rate will decline to i_5.[30]

In a regime of flexible wages and prices the rate of price inflation declines rather quickly toward zero, consistent with the zero growth rate of the money supply. As this occurs, the liquidity shortage will be less severe. The LM curve may be depicted as shifting less further leftward than LM''_{P_3} in short-run, single period, analysis. If the price inflation goes immediately to zero, the income effect of zero inflation completely offsets the liquidity effect of zero money supply growth and the LM curve may be depicted as not shifting beyond LM_{P_3}.

As the new lower rate of money supply growth persists, the demise of inflationary expectations will shift the IS curve leftward to IS_1. The price expectations effect generates a decline in the nominal rate of interest. With an unchanged nominal

---

[29] Therefore the curve LM_{P_3} reflects an equilibrium stock of real money balances that has been determined by an equilibrium *rate* of price inflation that is consistent with the positive growth *rate* of the nominal money supply that established the expectation of that inflation. The term P_3 in LM_{P_3} does not refer to a price *level*.

[30] Because of money illusion in the labor market, there may be a temporary decline in output and employment at point G in Figure 15.8. This can be depicted as a movement to the right of the natural rate of unemployment along a short-run Phillips curve.

money supply the resulting increased demand for real money balances can only be satisfied if the price level declines. The decrease in the price level causes the *LM* curve to shift to LM''_{P_4}. Equilibrium is restored at point *C* in Figure 15.8 with the market rate of interest being i_3.

Thus despite the machinations of the monetary authority, the nominal rate of interest returns (whence it began) to equality with the real long-run equilibrium rate of interest, *ceteris paribus*. By attempting to keep the interest rate below this level, the monetary authority accelerated the money supply growth rate which, to the extent that it generated unanticipated inflation, caused real income, output and employment to exceed *temporarily* their full employment levels such as at points *B* and *D* in Figure 15.8. This phenomenon was discussed in Chapter 14. As a result of inflation the nominal rate of interest rose. Public concern over inflation then induced the monetary authority to restrict the growth of the money supply and the market interest rate reached an even higher level. This caused real income and output to fall temporarily below their full employment levels at points *G* and *H* in Figure 15.8. In the long run given the initial increased government deficit, a no inflation, full employment equilibrium is attainable only at *C*.

This model suggests that in an otherwise stable economy, a process of boom and bust, inflation and recession, can result from the destabilizing policies of a monetary authority. In this particular case unstable patterns of money supply behavior arose from attempts to maintain a low interest rate in the face of an increased government deficit. Other stimuli for an unstable monetary environment might include a systematic pattern of "excessive" union wage settlements (discussed earlier in this chapter), increases in the prices of important raw material imports and periodic crop failures. In these instances, as discussed on pages 400–401, the monetary authority might increase the growth rate of the money supply, thereby "validating" these price increases, in order to forestall any temporary recessionary effects. In addition, it has been argued that even political considerations such as upcoming elections provide elected officials with an incentive to stimulate the economy in order to produce temporarily lower levels of unemployment.[31] Because variations in government deficits and these other factors will cause the *IS* and *LM* curves to shift, a policy of trying to compensate for the effect of these shifts on the market rate of interest and real income may be more destabilizing than a policy of sustaining stable money supply growth. For example, when the *IS* curve shifted from IS_0 to IS_1 in Figure 15.7, there would have been a good deal less instability had the monetary authority not responded and simply let the system gravitate toward *C*.

It can further be argued that the unstable monetary environment discussed in the

---

[31] The political business cycle was discussed briefly on page 374, footnote 10.

A satisfactory theory of monetary instability would have to explain why the monetary authority is wont to validate inflationary pressures, monetize deficits, and purposely stimulate the economy at some times but not at others. See Thomas Havrilesky, "A Theory of Monetary Instability," Lombra, Kaufman and Dooley (eds.), *The Political Economy of Policymaking* (New York: Sage Publications, 1979).

preceding paragraphs can generate inelastic price, wage and interest rate expectations and that these in turn generate even *more* instability, inefficiency and unemployment in the economy than described above.[32] These are all important problems which cannot be explored further here. They are a proper subject for an entire book in the theory and practice of monetary policy.

In a regime where the monetary authority systematically attempts to keep money supply growth rates in line with prearranged *target* rates of growth, market participants will respond to deviations of actual money growth from target growth. A positive deviation may be viewed as a precursor of slower money supply growth and temporarily higher interest rates in the future. A negative deviation may be seen as a harbinger of faster money supply growth and temporarily lower interest rates in the future. In this sort of a policy environment the immediate liquidity and income effects described above may disappear and price expectations effects will primarily be associated with target money supply growth rates. Short run interest rate movements are likely to be less volatile than under the less stable monetary policy regime portrayed in the preceding paragraphs and, aside from temporary "monetary policy anticipation effects," may more closely reflect movements in the underlying real rate of interest caused by shifts in saving, investment and government deficits.

QUESTIONS FOR CHAPTER 15

1. a. What is the Pigou effect?
   b. How does the insertion of a variable into a model of the aggregate economy to account for the Pigou effect modify the structural form of that model (that is, which behavioral equations are affected and in what specific ways)?

2. The liquidity trap and the interest insensitive investment demand function are often presented as specific cases that make possible a "Keynesian" underemployment equilibrium. Yet Harry Johnson notes: "In my opinion . . . the Pigou effect finally disposes of the Keynesian contention that underemployment equilibrium does not depend on the assumption of wage rigidity. *It does.*"
   a. How does the Pigou effect guarantee full employment equilibrium in an economy with complete price–wage flexibility? Consider, for example, the case of an economy at less than full employment and in a situation in which full employment saving is greater than investment at all positive interest rates. Demonstrate this situation graphically. Explain and show how the real balance mechanism is supposed to restore the economy to full employment.
   b. Granting Johnson's statement is true, demonstrate graphically how rigid money wages within the framework of a real balance model could lead to a situation of less than full employment (equilibrium).

[32] See the Appendix to Chapter 14, page 382.

3. Again, granting the truth of Johnson's statement above, on the basis of the analysis of the real balance effect, should we press for the restoration of complete price–wage flexibility to restore "the self-regulating and self-correcting mechanism" of the market economy (that is, is downward price–wage flexibility likely to be an acceptable and successful policy for the restoration of full employment from a below full employment position)? Why or why not?

4. Has the real balance effect any significance or importance in the analysis of an economy in which there is no downward flexibility in wage and price levels?

5. Assume government calculates that its real indebtedness increases when prices fall. Further assume that government raises taxes or reduces spending accordingly. What effect will this have on the real balance effect?

6. Analyze the effect of an increase in the price of imported oil in terms of the *LM–IS* real balances model. Now do the same with the complete aggregate demand–aggregate supply model of Chapter 13.

7. Would the ability of government to tax by inflation be modified if interest were paid on all money balances?

8. How are the price expectations discussed in this chapter formed? Is it true that the price level must rise if it is *expected* to rise? Does this falsify the quantity theory of money?

9. Can the rate of interest or the real stock of money be determined by the monetary authority? Why or why not?

10. The unstable behavior of the money supply arises from dissatisfaction within the economy and between economies over the distribution of income. This generates pressures for large and growing government deficits and pressures for rapid increases in nominal wages; the Federal Reserve must yield to these pressures. Thus, the degree of monetary instability is related to the extent of discord in the economy. Evaluate.

11. Consider chronic bond-financed government deficits. Assume a politically grounded Federal Reserve sensitivity to "high" interest rates. Develop the consequences.

12. When money supply growth accelerates above its long-run trend, nominal interest rates may fall for a short time (the liquidity effect), then they will begin to rise (the income effect). If acceleration continues, expectations of higher inflation will be formed (the price expectations effect). If a new money growth trend is established, interest rates will surely rise and bond and stock prices will fall, as the Federal Reserve validates the price expectations effect.

Conversely, when money growth rates decelerate below trend, interest rates will temporarily rise (the liquidity effect). When the economy cools off they will begin to fall (the income effect). If deceleration continues, expectations of lower price inflation will be formed (the price expectations effect). If a new trend line is established, they will shortly decline as the Federal Reserve validates the price expectations effect.

Using the present value formula of Chapter 5, describe how you would use this theory to develop a strategy for speculation in the stock and bond markets.

BIBLIOGRAPHY FOR CHAPTER 15

BAILEY, MARTIN J., "The Welfare Costs of Inflationary Finance," *Journal of Political Economy* (June 1956).

BOX, G. E. D., and G. M. JENKINS, *Time Series Analysis: Forecasting and Control* (San Francisco: Holden-Day, 1970).

FRIEDMAN, MILTON, "Factors Affecting the Level of Interest Rates," *1968 Conference Proceedings, Savings and Residential Financing* (Chicago: U.S. Savings and Loan League, 1969), 10–27.*

——, "The Role of Monetary Policy," *American Economic Review,* vol. 58 (March 1968), 1–17.

FRIEDMAN, MILTON, and ANNA J. SCHWARTZ, "The Definition of Money," *Journal of Money, Credit and Banking,* vol. 1 (February 1969), 1–14.

GIBSON, WILLIAM E., "Interest Rates and Inflationary Expectations," *American Economic Review* (December 1972), 854–865.

HABERLER, GOTTFRIED, *Prosperity and Depression,* 3rd ed. (Geneva: The League of Nations, 1941), 491–503.

HAVRILESKY, THOMAS M. "A Theory of Monetary Instability," *The Political Economy of Policymaking,* Lombra, Kaufman and Dooley, eds. (New York: Sage Publications, 1979).

JOHNSON, HARRY G., "Monetary Theory and Keynesian Economics," *Pakistan Economic Journal,* vol. 8 (June 1958).

——, "Inside Money, Outside Money, Income, Wealth and Welfare in Monetary Theory," *Journal of Money, Credit and Banking,* vol. 1 (February 1969), 30–45.

LANGE, OSCAR, "Say's Law: Restatement and Criticism," in *Studies in Mathematical Economics and Econometrics* (Chicago: University of Chicago Press, 1942).

MARTY, ALVIN, "Inside Money, Outside Money, and the Wealth Effect: A Review Essay," *Journal of Money, Credit and Banking,* vol. 1 (February 1969), 101–111.

MAYER, THOMAS, "The Empirical Significance of the Real Balance Effect," *Quarterly Journal of Economics,* vol. 73 (May 1959), 275–291.

MUTH, J. F., "Rational Expectations and the Theory of Price Movements," *Econometrica* (July 1961).

PARK, YUNG CHUL, "Some Current Issues in the Transmission Process of Monetary Policy," *Staff Papers, International Monetary Fund* (March 1972), 1–45.*

PATINKIN, DON, "Price Flexibility and Full Employment," *American Economic Review,* vol. 38 (September 1948), 543–564.

——, "Money and Wealth: A Review Article," *Journal of Economic Literature,* vol. 7 (December 1969), 1140–1160.

——, *Money, Interest and Prices,* 2nd ed. (New York: Harper and Row, 1965).

PESEK, BORIS, and THOMAS SAVING, *Money, Wealth and Economic Theory* (New York: Macmillan, 1967), chs. 2 and 3.

PIGOU, A. C., "The Classical Stationary State," *Economic Journal,* vol. 53 (1943), 343–351.

——, "Economic Progress in a Stable Environment," *Econometrica,* vol. 14 (1947), 180–190.

* Reprinted in THOMAS M. HAVRILESKY, and JOHN T. BOORMAN, *Current Issues in Monetary Theory and Policy* (Arlington Heights, IL.: AHM Publishing Corporation, 1976).

SAMUELSON, PAUL, "Money, Interest Rates and Economic Activity," *Proceedings of a Symposium of Money, Interest Rates and Economic Activity* (New York: American Bankers Association, 1967), 45–57.

SARGENT, THOMAS, "Anticipated Inflation and the Nominal Rate of Interest," *Quarterly Journal of Economics* (May 1972), 212–225.

SARGENT, T. J., and N. WALLACE, "Rational Expectations and the Dynamics of Hyperinflation," *International Economic Review* (June 1973).

SCHOTTA, CHARLES R., "The Real Balance Effect in the United States, 1947–1963," *Journal of Finance,* vol. 19 (December 1964), 619–630.

SMITH, WARREN L., "A Graphical Exposition of the Complete Keynesian System," *The Southern Economic Journal,* vol. 23 (October 1956), 115–125.*

——, "A Neo-Keynesian View of Monetary Policy," *Proceedings of a Monetary Conference of the Federal Reserve Bank of Boston* (June 1969), 105–126.

SPENCER, ROGER W., "Channels of Monetary Influence," *Review,* Federal Reserve Bank of St. Louis (January 1973), 16–21.*

TIMBERLAKE, RICHARD HENRY, "Patinkin and the Pigou Effect: A Comment," *Review of Economics and Statistics,* vol. 39 (August 1957), 346–348.

TYDALL, H. F., "Savings and Wealth," *Australian Economic Papers,* vol. 2 (December 1963), 228–250.

YOHE, WILLIAM P., and DENIS KARNOSKY, "Interest Rates and Price Level Changes, 1952–1969," *Review,* Federal Reserve Bank of St. Louis (December 1969), 18–38.

* Reprinted in THOMAS M. HAVRILESKY, and JOHN T. BOORMAN, *Current Issues in Monetary Theory and Policy* (Arlington Heights, IL.: AHM Publishing Corporation, 1976).

Author Index

Subject Index